MW00630168

# PRISON CONVERSATIONS

# PRISON CONVERSATIONS

## Prisoners at the Washington State Reformatory Discuss Life, Freedom, Crime and Punishment

### By Craig Gabriel

**TERIBOOKS**
Arroyo Grande, California

FIRST EDITION

PRINTED AND BOUND IN THE UNITED STATES OF AMERICA

ISBN 0-9755354-0-4

LIBRARY OF CONGRESS CONTROL NUMBER 2004095811

For Teri Donaldson.

On The Infrequent Occasions I Actually Accomplish Something In Which I Can Take Pride, It Is Always With You In Mind.

I Love You.

# Contents

# INTRODUCTION

Typical session of the "Prison Awareness" class. This one is from 1999. (Photo courtesy of Linda Coleman.)

I n January 1997, I signed up for an adult education class entitled "Prison: A View From the Inside," put on by a group called the "Prison Awareness Project" (PAP). It consisted of seven two-hour Tuesday evening sessions, and it was held in an actual prison, specifically the Washington State Reformatory (WSR). WSR is in Monroe, Washington, about an hour's drive northeast of Seattle, where I was living at the time.

The class had to be held inside the prison, it turned out, because the instructors themselves were prisoners.

The class—known more informally as the "Prison Awareness" class—was offered on an irregular basis several times a year, most often as a series of Tuesday evening meetings like the one I took, and occasionally as an all-day, one-session class on a Saturday. Class size was typically in the mid to high single digits. There were six students in my particular class.

PAP is one of many volunteer programs at WSR whose membership consists of both prisoners and volunteers from the community. (The term "programs" is preferred over their other informal name—"clubs"—for historical reasons. "Clubs" was the term used for the forerunners of today's programs during the time when some of them were little more than internal prison gangs, and many of their volunteer members simply outside accomplices. The '70s especially are remembered as a time of comparative prison anarchy in Washington, where the prisoners had considerable autonomy to run their own affairs, and misused that autonomy more often than not. The clubs were a common vehicle for their nefarious doings.)

Most of the programs fall into one of two categories. Some are racial, ethnic, or religious groups. Others, such as Alcoholics Anonymous, Alternatives to Violence, Toastmasters, etc., have a specific self-help or educational mission.

PAP fits neatly into neither category. It has no racial, ethnic, nor religious basis, and its mission is decidedly vague. To the extent that it has a describable purpose at all, it is a social one. Once a week, on Wednesday evenings, the members get together in a large meeting room inside the prison and mostly just hang out together in an unstructured, casual manner.

The theory behind PAP is that if law-abiding members of the community regularly interact with prisoners, the prisoners will gradually absorb some of the values and social skills of the outside members, and the outside members (and those with whom they in turn discuss their experiences) will come away with a greater understanding of prisoners and of what goes on inside these increasingly ubiquitous facilities that are still so mysterious to many of us.

The class began with an orientation session, held on the prison grounds but not inside the walls, and for that reason conducted by a prison administrator and a non-prisoner volunteer member of PAP, rather than by prisoners.

This session was a hodgepodge of mixed signals. We were given a considerable amount of printed material, including such nuggets as instructions on what to do when taken hostage by prisoners. (Cooperate with them; be a good, empathic listener; don't be hostile; don't try to be a hero; don't call attention to yourself by becoming hysterical or losing control of your bodily functions.) We were shown an old, amateur prison volunteer video clearly made by and for some Christian group, which, among other things, warned us not to touch the prisoners. A simple businesslike handshake was acceptable, but anything beyond that, the video warned us, would be apt to be interpreted in a sexual way by a prisoner. (This admonition was accompanied by a dramatization of a young, white, female volunteer and an African American male prisoner maintaining a respectful distance after their handshake.)

The administrator also assured us, though, that we were not putting ourselves in any danger by entering the prison. The prisoners very much want volunteers and students there; they aren't going to do anything to harm us or drive us away. The administrator told us he had worked with some of these prisoners for twenty years and more, and had complete confidence that he could trust many of them with his life.

In several decades of these programs, only one volunteer had ever been harmed in the prison, he said. Back in the late '70s, a volunteer had been sexually assaulted by a prisoner in the chapel. By the time correctional officers arrived on the scene, the other prisoners were well into the process of tearing the assailant limb from limb.

Of course, once is still one time too many for something like that, but it does indicate that prison volunteers are victimized in prison at a considerably lower rate of frequency than if they spent the same amount of time at home, on the job, on a college campus, walking down a public street, etc.

WSR is, we were informed, a medium security facility, mostly holding long-term prisoners who had more or less behaved themselves and thus were considered not to need the even tighter control of a higher custody level prison. (Shortly thereafter it was gradually converted to a close custody facility, which is basically the equivalent of maximum security.* The state of Washington had too many prisoners requiring a

---

*Prisons in Washington differ according to custody level, with maximum being the highest, then close, medium, and four levels of minimum. Maximum facilities are just close custody facilities with a death row.

higher custody level, and not enough facilities outfitted to take them.)

For the next six Tuesday evenings, we entered the prison proper for the class itself. There was always at least one PAP outside volunteer, and usually several, to accompany us into the facility.

The journey into this forbidding world goes something like this.[*]

First you drive up to a guard tower, stop, identify yourself into a speaker on the driver's side of the vehicle, and wait for permission to proceed, which the correctional officer in the tower gives you, usually immediately.

After parking, you then enter a reception and administration building where the students and PAP volunteers gather so you can all go in at once. An officer has you sign in, checks your ID against a list, and gives you an opportunity to put any personal belongings into a locker.

There's very little a volunteer or student is permitted to bring into the prison. They allow an unopened pack of cigarettes and matches, a pen and blank paper, and written or printed matter that could be construed as teaching material for the program in question, and that's about it. (That last can be fudged considerably—they tend not to look for reasons to disallow written notes, copied magazine articles, and such.) But no wallets, money, keys, food, gum, etc.

The next step is to go through a metal detector, like at the airport only much more sensitive. Watches, pens, belts, etc. can set it off. Most types of shoes set it off. Underwire bras consistently set it off.

If you try to go through the metal detector several times unsuccessfully, you must sign a waiver and have an officer of your gender take you into a side room and pat you down. (It happened to me once, and the pat down was perfunctory.)

Your hand is stamped and you are given a red identification tag to wear on your chest.

The correctional officers at the prison, at least the ones with whom the volunteers are most likely to interact, are, with rare exceptions, polite and professional. A substantial number are female. For the most part they are not ogres looking for excuses to abuse you or the prisoners. Many of them are quite friendly, and virtually all of them are at least civil.

You then pass through a series of doors that are opened and closed remotely, one at a time, into an adjoining building. You are now in the main, secure area of the prison, where the prisoners themselves live.

---

[*]Certain details changed later. This is how it was when I first entered the prison in 1997.

As you walk down the first floor corridor of this building, among other things you pass the laundry, the chow hall, and a side corridor that leads to the "hole." The second floor and above contain the bulk of the cells themselves, as well as the clinic and the visiting room.

Emerging back outside at the opposite end of this building, you come to a gate, and the guard tower that controls it. An officer will normally buzz you through immediately. This gate separates the cell blocks from the rest of the grounds of the prison, and prisoners are only allowed through it during specified "movement" times. If they miss a movement, they're stuck on whatever side of the gate they're on until the next one.

After passing through that gate, to your left is a gymnasium, with an outdoor area where the prisoners work out with weights. To the right is the "yard," a large open area with an oval track and a ball field. Both are fenced off from where you are walking. Farther off in the distance you can see the chapel, and another gate that leads to the building that houses most of the industries run by private employers that use prison labor.

There are no trees on the inside, but you do pass areas of greenery, including some impressive prisoner-tended gardens.

Your destination is the "Prison Activities Building," a large one-story building that houses the library, the music room, several large meeting rooms for the programs (e.g., PAP), and several small rooms that function as prisoner offices for these programs. There are typically a few prisoner members of PAP loitering outside the building waiting for you, and a few more already in the meeting room when you get there. The rest gradually drift in within a few minutes.

The prisoners wear ordinary street clothes, not any kind of institutional clothing, and certainly not the striped outfits of the Halloween costume convict.

What comes as a surprise to many newcomers is that you are right there amongst the prisoners themselves for almost the whole time you are inside the prison. You rub shoulders with dozens of these men in the open areas on your way to the Prison Activities Building.

To the extent that they acknowledge outside people at all, it is generally with a wave or a polite hello as they pass. They do not stop and try to talk to you beyond that, and there is no threatening or harassing behavior. The women volunteers might draw a few appreciative looks, but there are no whistles or catcalls, and indeed the behavior toward them is generally more respectful than what women endure walking down the average public street.

Another surprise to some is the lack of visible staff within the prison. From the cell blocks to the Prison Activities Building, as you pass through all these prisoners, you will encounter few if any officers, other than the one overhead in the guard tower. In the Prison Activities Building itself, there is an officer near the door to check you in, but I don't know that I've ever seen more than two or three officers in the whole building at one time (not including inside the library, where I assume there is at least one staff member). This in spite of the fact that this building routinely contains several dozen prisoners spread out over numerous rooms.

There are no officers in the meeting rooms themselves, and only infrequently does one pass by in the hallway and look in the window.

And the officers are not armed (other than the ones in the towers), because they don't want prisoners to be able to obtain a gun simply by overpowering an officer.

Make no mistake, there are quite a number of officers on the premises, just not out visibly patrolling. But if there is a fight or any sign of trouble, a large number of officers will come trotting out en masse from the cell blocks to deal with it.

Still, the staff is not in the kind of direct and obvious control of the institution that I would have expected. The few officers that you see are there to be unarmed eyes and ears rather than enforcers. There's nothing or no one really stopping one or a group of prisoners from attacking each other or you, except the deterrent that it'll likely be witnessed, and they will face some sort of punishment after the fact.

Had I been aware of this going in, I might have been more concerned. Instead I approached my first trip inside a prison with an attitude (shared by all those who've died sky diving or in roller coaster accidents) of "Well, they wouldn't let us do it if it were dangerous," and an assumption that surely there were countless armed guards all over the place whose job it was to protect us from any harm by the prisoners.

What you come to find out the more time you spend in the prison is that this is the prisoners' world, not the state's, not the staff's, not any outsiders'. If the prisoners engage in certain behavior or refrain from certain behavior, it's by their choice, and as a result of subtle incentives and disincentives, not due to direct coercion by staff. Sure, the officers are there, and that means the prisoners' behavior will bring consequences, but the prisoners are the ones with whom you are in direct contact, and they could certainly harm you if they chose.

Luckily, you simultaneously come to understand that they have no particular reason to do so, and plenty of reason not to, hence the one attack in several decades of these programs. As we were told in the orientation, the prisoners want us there. They appreciate us being there. We are their guests. And even if there were some who felt otherwise and would want to harm us, the others would intervene on our behalf much more quickly and forcefully than would the officers.

The room used for the classes and for the PAP meetings contains a blackboard, four or five long tables—two up front by the blackboard and the others pushed against the side walls, upon one of which is an urn full of hot water and a tray of cups, plastic spoons, instant coffee, tea bags, and sometimes sugar (all supplied and paid for by the prisoners themselves, by the way)—and several dozen folding chairs. For our class, the chairs were arranged in a large circle.

For each class session, there were present in this meeting room several non-prisoner, outside volunteer PAP members, and perhaps twenty-five prisoners (and no staff). Volunteers and prisoners varied from session to session, though there were many regulars who attended every class.

The prisoners ranged in age from teenagers to senior citizens. The average age was probably a little higher than that of the general prison population, but all age groups were well represented.

I'd estimate 60%-70% of the PAP prisoner members were white, 10%-15% African American, and 5%-10% each Hispanic, Native American, and Asian. This is not representative of the nationwide prison population, as whites constitute a distinct minority at many prisons, but—true to PAP's nature as a multi-ethnic, multi-racial program—it was reasonably close to the statewide breakdown in Washington prisons.[*]

The prisoners seated themselves so as to strategically leave empty chairs spaced evenly around the circle for us, which had the effect of preventing the students from huddling together with each other or the volunteers for safety. Instead we were spread out, with each of us having a prisoner on one or both sides.

There were a few minutes of unstructured socializing at the beginning and sometimes at the end of our two-hour sessions, as well as a break at the midway point. I recall these being my least favorite times, as I was self-conscious that my usual discomfort and social awkwardness in a room full of strangers would be misinterpreted as fear of or hostility toward the prisoners.

For the more formal portion of the sessions, one prisoner functioned as "class coordinator" for the entire multi-week class, which meant he made some opening comments for each session, introduced the main topics, introduced the other prisoner(s), etc. In addition, each individual session had a different prisoner "facilitator" who would stand in the center of the circle and speak to us, then call upon other prisoners to join him or to speak from their seats to share their experiences and relate them to the topic at hand.

Early in the first session, the class coordinator had everyone—prisoners, volunteers, and students—take a moment to introduce themselves. The students were asked to

---

[*]According to the Washington Department of Corrections (DOC) website, the statistics for Washington prisoners are: White: 71.3%, African American: 21.6%, Hispanic: 11.8%, Native American: 3.7%, Asian: 2.7%, All Others: 0.7%. (Clearly there is some overlap in how these groups are counted.)

state why we had chosen to take this class. The prisoners mostly just stated their first names and, if they chose, the crime for which they were serving time. Some also stated how long they had been in and/or how much longer they had to serve. (One of the rules at PAP is that the guys are free to talk as much or as little as they want about their crime. It is strictly optional for them to reveal this information. It is understood, however, that the PAP prisoners will not allow into this group anyone serving time for a sex-related offense, or any other crime that puts a prisoner at the bottom of the prison "pecking order.")[*]

This led to one of the bigger surprises. As we went around the circle, about 80% of the prisoners identified their crime as murder, with maybe 10% stating some other crime, and 10% declining to say. This was certainly not representative of the general prison population.[†]

During a break, I asked a prisoner whom I took to be one of the leaders about this overabundance of murderers. "Whatever happened to knocking over a liquor store?" I said, "Judging from this group, it seems like everybody in prison is here for murder." He explained that a prisoner typically has to have served at least five years elsewhere and stayed out of trouble in order to come to WSR. Furthermore, prisoners who know they have a lot more time to do are more likely to commit to programs like this; the short-timers with one foot out the door tend to have a different focus. Put those two things together—long time in and long time remaining—and almost all PAP prisoners are serving ten-year or greater terms. Given that sex offenders are excluded, most of the prisoners doing that kind of serious time are murderers.

I was in a prison, for the first time in my life. I was surrounded by felons—the majority murderers in fact—with no guards present.

Yet, in all honesty, it was really not a frightening or uncomfortable situation. I think one of the things the prisoners were particularly good at was anticipating and defusing any such intimidation or fear. They know what "squares" like us have likely absorbed from the media about prisons and prisoners. They know many of us will be predisposed to expect the worst. And so they are unfailingly polite and friendly, they are solicitous of questions from us, and they incorporate a certain amount of good-natured and self-deprecating humor into the class. They are as earnest as Frankenstein's monster trying not to frighten a child, and decidedly more successful.

---

[*]Not that they're infallible in determining this. Years later there was a mini scandal when one of our members—after he had left PAP and indeed after he had finished his sentence and left prison entirely—was discovered to have been convicted of a violent sex offense decades earlier. Had his crime been widely known in the group, he would never have been allowed to be a member.

[†]According to the Washington DOC website, fewer than 15% of prisoners statewide are doing time for murder.

I found out later that one of their pet peeves is when a journalist or other visitor writes about the experience "inside" as though being amongst the prisoners had taken great courage. I'm sure there are a small number of people who sincerely feel that way, but by far the more common reaction is the pleasant surprise that the prisoners are "regular guys," and pretty enjoyable to spend time with.*

Though the atmosphere in our classroom was not as ominous as expected, the proceedings themselves were pretty intense. Week after week the prisoners opened up to us about their experiences, and gave us their take on the criminal justice system. They ordered the topics roughly chronologically, taking us on what they called the "journey" from arrest, to jail, to trial, to prison, and to re-entry into society.

Many things they shared with us stick with me to this day. Among them:

•Upon arrest and initial incarceration, they said, almost everyone shuts down mentally and physically; the exhaustion overcomes everything else they're feeling and causes them to crave sleep more than anything.

•They almost all had a preference for prison over jail. (Jail, they explained, is where you go before you're convicted and sentenced, and for sentences of less than a year. Prison is where you go after receiving a sentence of longer than a year.) Most jails are overcrowded, disorganized mad houses where they are stuck with a bunch of unpredictable newbies and short-termers, whereas prison at least has a certain stability to it.

•They strongly derided mainstream media representations of prison, dismissing them as self-evidently inaccurate, sensationalist, and designed to appeal to the basest fears and prejudices of the public.

•Their take on plea bargaining was distinctly different from the commonly held perception. I had always assumed a plea bargain was where the prosecution let one

*The prisoners later told me of a woman who runs one of the self-help programs at WSR, and who had written an account of her experiences for a local newspaper. She was allegedly quite self-congratulatory in her portrayal of herself as some sort of plucky heroine taking her life in her hands to work amongst such dangerous characters. It was the kind of sensationalism that causes most of the prisoners to roll their eyes, shake their heads, or just laugh, and certainly to respect her honesty a lot less.

plead guilty to something less than what one had actually done, in exchange for relieving them of the bother and expense of a trial (as well as the risk of a loss). The prisoners, though, insisted that the prosecution was apt to threaten to charge them with far more than what they had done, and since they could never know what a jury could be convinced of, they often would relinquish their rights to a trial and plead guilty to a charge that, though bargained down, was still more than what they had done.

•They told the story of a long time practice at another Washington prison. There, the staff subjected arriving prisoners to digital probes. They would stick a greased finger up the prisoner's rectum and wipe it on his leg, then send him on to his cell without an opportunity to wash. The proceedings were videotaped, and it was discovered later that some members of the staff were taking tapes home and gathering together to play them for laughs. The prisoners also noted that while the alleged purpose of the digital probes was to look for contraband stuck up there, a) they never found any, and b) the videotapes reveal that they didn't even bother to search the pockets of the clothes the prisoners were wearing.

•In perhaps the single most riveting moment, an older, dignified, very soft-spoken prisoner who had been incarcerated for thirty-two years for first degree murder, detailed for us his experiences and emotions on death row before his sentence was commuted. (He had come as close as twenty-five hours to his scheduled execution.) At times his voice would drop to just above a whisper, or he would have to pause for several seconds to remain in control of his emotions. This was especially true when he told us of his meeting with the mother of his victim. Ultimately they established a surprising but positive bond.

I found this trip into the prison world to be a fascinating experience. I didn't want it to end, which is exactly how they like it. The classes, I quickly inferred, are not offered solely for the purpose of educating the public, but also as recruitment for PAP volunteers.

Finding volunteers for many of these programs is a real struggle. Some go through periods where they have only one or two regulars. It's very difficult to get the word out to people who might consider volunteering that these programs even exist.

That's where PAP has a huge edge. These classes are constantly bringing new people in and exposing them to PAP. The vast majority of PAP volunteers first took the Prison Awareness class.

I immediately signed on as a volunteer when the class ended.

PAP has a cap of fifty prisoner members, and is always full with a waiting list. Of those fifty members, anywhere from five to thirty-five come to a typical meeting. The size of the outside volunteer roster varies, but on average there are about twenty-five PAP volunteers approved for entry into the prison, and on a normal Wednesday evening, five to ten show up.

I was a PAP volunteer from March 1997 to September 2000. During this time, I made the drive out to the prison for about 90% of the weekly Wednesday evening meetings. I also was present fairly often when they offered the Prison Awareness class on Tuesday evenings or all day Saturday. In addition, I was there for occasional PAP-related special events or projects on other days.

All told, I'm sure I averaged entering the prison as a volunteer at least once a week over the course of that three and a half years. PAP became a significant part of my life.

In some respects, I must say the class was something of a high point, and the time I spent in the PAP program itself disappointing by comparison.

What I was most drawn to about the class was the way the prisoners opened up and talked about themselves and their lives, the way they encouraged questions and dialogue from outsiders, the way collectively we could dig into a lot of important and emotionally powerful subjects. I also appreciated how the prisoners bent over backwards to be friendly and polite toward us, almost to a deferential degree.

I had assumed PAP would simply be a continuation of the class, where we could get deeper into these issues without the artificial six or seven week time limit.

But that isn't PAP. PAP is a social group. The only part of the class it resembled was the beginning and end of the class sessions where people broke up into smaller groups and made small talk.

The class had a certain formality to it, and the prisoners were on their best behavior. At PAP, some of them seemed relieved to not have to be "on" like that. They could just relax and hang out.

The class had been more consistently illuminating and engaging; PAP itself had terrific moments like that, but they would come sporadically and unpredictably. There were enough of them, though, to keep me there for three and a half years.

The vast majority of the PAP volunteers are white. Virtually all of the regulars are middle-aged or older. Some volunteers are under 35, but almost all of these are either non-regulars, or they are people who spend only a few weeks or months in the program before moving on. The older people are the ones who settle in for the long term.

75% – 80% of the volunteers are female.

I had wondered about that, because many years earlier I had had a long conversation with a woman who, in her early 20s, worked briefly as a correctional officer in a juvenile facility for teen males. She told me that during their orientation, they had been told flat out that it was imperative they not fall for the inmates, that indeed one of the things they were hoping to teach the youths was that—contrary to what many of the boys had figured out was a great perk of the criminal lifestyle—the "bad boy" routine wasn't going to automatically attract all women to them.

Their efforts, she told me, were a complete and total failure. Virtually every female who entered the facility, including herself, found that she had zero ability to resist the inmates. Putting a female in an environment with violent, abusive, ill-mannered, crude, don't-take-no-for-an-answer, trample-on-the-rights-of-others, won't-play-by-society's-rules toughs, was comparable to dropping a male into an all-girl party at the Playboy Mansion and expecting him to keep his mind on—well, on anything other than what guys' minds are always on anyway.

Would these prison programs be anything like the way she had described her experiences, I wondered?

Thankfully, mostly not. Perhaps it is because they are older, but PAP female volunteers aren't looking for the cheap thrills of rubbing shoulders with "bad boys."

Which is not to say that there is zero sexual tension, or zero flirting, or that prisoners and volunteers never develop a non-platonic interest in each other. Sometimes a volunteer finds herself gradually drifting into a one-to-one relationship with a prisoner rather than interacting with the group as a whole, and sometimes she then leaves the program to get on his individual visiting list. (The rule is, you cannot be in a volunteer program and also be a visitor for one of the prisoners. In fact, to even be eligible to visit an individual prisoner, you have to wait at least six months after resigning from any volunteer program.)

Still, I would say there is a clear advantage in being female. Some prisoners are in the program for the sole purpose of enticing a female volunteer onto their visiting list. For them, male volunteers like myself are invisible. Other prisoners aren't quite as extreme as that, but they appreciate the novelty of having (non-staff) females in the prison to interact with, and while they don't ignore the male volunteers entirely, all else being equal, they certainly tend to gravitate to the women.

I think a lot of them have a little more trouble trusting a male volunteer, or fathoming why he'd be there. Infrequently, we have a male volunteer who behaves in a stereotypically "gay" manner, and it is especially difficult for them. There is no open hostility from the prisoners toward them, but the vast majority give such volunteers the cold shoulder. They do not reach out to them, do not welcome them, do not make them feel appreciated for volunteering. As a result, such volunteers never last long.

For the other male volunteers it isn't nearly that bad, but you still have to "prove yourself" more than the women, to be patient and wait a little longer for the prisoners to warm up to you, and open up to you.

Spiritual motives for volunteering are common, but by no means pervasive. PAP includes a fair number of conventional Christians motivated by their faith, a few offbeat folks who are eager to share the latest New Age inanities with the prisoners, and the occasional volunteer with some other religious or spiritual purpose, but the group does not have a predominantly religious feel to it. In large part, this is because there are so many other outlets for volunteers of faith.

PAP volunteers, as a rule, are not as politically motivated as I might have expected. A few are of an activist bent, but not the majority.

To the extent that they are political at all, the volunteers are, not surprisingly, nearly always liberal on prison issues. That is true of the students who sign up for the periodic Prison Awareness classes too, which I always found a little disappointing. I'd like to see more people from the community who hold more mainstream or conservative views take the class so they could be exposed to "the other side." But that is close to unheard of. People are attracted to the class because they are already sympathetic to prisoners, so unfortunately PAP tends to "preach to the converted."

I do chuckle a bit when the prisoners cite us as examples of "typical members of the community," or "squares," or "people with conventional, mainstream values." That's how most of them see those who don't pursue a criminal lifestyle—as vaguely bland, suburban, stable folks who conform to all societal expectations and never make trouble.

But the PAP volunteers are mostly quirky non-conformist social misfits, just not specifically non-conformist in the sense of being prone to commit crimes. The volunteers include many artists, students, lesbians, New Agers, writers, and so on, but only a comparatively small number of 1950s sit com-style responsible adults who work 9 to 5 and raise conventional families.

On the whole, the volunteers are a good group of people; well-motivated folks just wanting to interact in a positive way with people who are mostly despised by the general public.

The prisoners, too, are mostly good guys. I was disappointed about certain things about some of them the longer I was in PAP, but in all those years I never experienced a general disillusionment. I liked them more than not based on my first impressions, and I liked them more than not when I left three and a half years later.

One has to be very careful generalizing from the PAP prisoners to all prisoners. They are, in many respects, more evolved than the typical prisoner. Not in terms of their crimes being milder. Remember, this is a group where the clear majority have been convicted of murder. But in other ways.

Though WSR was a medium security prison when I became a volunteer, and later was changed to a close custody (maximum security) facility, it is still something of a reward for a prisoner to be there. They must have behaved themselves reasonably well at other institutions, and once at WSR they must continue to be on their best behavior. They must actively "program" (meaning work full time, take part in the minimal schooling that is still available, or participate in the cultural, self-help, social, religious, or other programs like PAP.) So a prisoner's mere presence in this institution is already evidence that he is someone above the norm.

Furthermore, PAP itself is something of an elite group within this elite group. Members are carefully screened (by the prisoner leaders of PAP, not by the prison staff) to ensure that they have something positive to contribute to the group and will not in any way be dangerous. In short, they are the most "presentable" prisoners.

And you can take it even one step beyond that and say that within PAP, the prisoners who attend regularly, who participate most actively, who are in the leadership positions—basically, the ones with whom we volunteers are most likely to interact and to get to know as individuals—are in turn above the norm of PAP prisoners. They tend to be the most mature, intelligent, articulate; the most socially comfortable with people like us from the "straight" world.

On the other hand, let's not overstate it. Their being the best of the best of the best of the prisoners does not mean they are somehow free of all dishonesty, laziness, unreliability, pettiness, and so on. They aren't going to cut your throat, and they aren't going to fulfill whatever ugly stereotypes people might have of prisoners, but they're still human.

Just like with the same size group of people in the office building where you work, or the Starbucks where you socialize, you will find all levels of quality of interaction. You will have intelligent conversations and engage in inane small talk. There will be people available for a genuine human connection and people playing games or pursuing their own little agendas. There will be warm people, people you can laugh with, and people who are positively annoying.

Once your preconceptions fall away, you come to understand that they're just people. They aren't uniquely noble, and they aren't inscrutably evil. They're just guys, and mostly pretty cool.

Then again, there are tendencies, cultural differences if you will, that are prevalent amongst the prisoners that you will not find in most groups on the outside. Theirs is a different world. A large part of why I spent those years in PAP, and why I worked with the guys for as long as I did on this book project, was my desire to better understand it.

Above all else there is the "convict code." This code of behavior shapes the prisoners' interactions with each other, with the prison staff, and with outside people. Indeed for most of the prisoners it has a crucial influence on their sense of self-worth. A prisoner judges himself and those around him according to how well they adhere to his interpretation of the code.

At the root of the code is the division into enemy camps of the prisoners themselves and the prison staff, or at times the prisoners themselves and the rest of the world. The single most important behavioral imperative that flows from this is that a prisoner is never to share information or otherwise cooperate with the staff in a way that adversely affects any other prisoner.

No matter what the circumstances, no matter whether you are acting offensively or defensively, no matter how justified you are in your conflict with another prisoner, you simply must not ally yourself with the "Man" in your pursuit of your ends.

Say for instance you have been disrespected in some fairly minor way by another prisoner. If you retaliate by sneaking up on him and stabbing him and taking his life, you have not violated the code. There's nothing in the code forbidding the use of excessive force in defense of yourself and your good name, nor is there anything about fighting "fair."

However, if you tell a correctional officer what the prisoner did to you, and as a result he gets some minimal time in the hole as punishment for it, you have flagrantly violated the code and are unfit to associate with any prisoner with any self-respect. You are labeled and ostracized for life, and are prone to being retaliated upon with no limits by the prisoner you ratted on, or really by any true believer prisoner who is disgusted by what you did.

Everything else in the code is secondary to this principle of non-cooperation with authority.

Much of the rest of the code is not opposed to "mainstream" values. You rise in the estimation of your fellow prisoners through such means as keeping your word, displaying physical bravery, exercising kindness and generosity toward other prisoners, being willing to sacrifice or put yourself at risk for other prisoners, and so on. Basically, the prisoners want to know, "Can we rely on you? Can we rely on you when the going gets tough and weaker people wouldn't hold up?"

On the victimization of prisoners by other prisoners, the code is ambiguous. Prisoners have mixed reactions to instances where a prisoner cheats another prisoner, or assaults him, or even rapes him. On the one hand, there is the sense that turning on each other rather than focusing on the true enemy is not consistent with the ideals of the code. On the other hand, there seems to be a grudging kind of macho respect for the perpetrators of such acts, or at least an attitude that it's the victim's fault for not being man enough to take care of himself.

Certainly there is not the kind of clarity on this point that there is concerning informants. A rat is regarded as totally and unambiguously in the wrong, and unfit to live. As for these other things, well, it depends on whom you ask, precisely how you frame the hypothetical, the context, the history between the people, and on and on.

Related to the code is the informal hierarchy amongst the criminals, based in part on your crime, and in part on your behavior thus far in prison (again, mostly whether you have cooperated with staff against your fellow prisoners). On top are the prisoners with the "honorable" crimes, which would include most murders. On the bottom are those whose crimes had any kind of sexual component, and those who in some way victimized children (or, to a lesser extent, those who in some way victimized some other segment of the population that the prisoners implicitly treat as pseudo-children in their helplessness and need for protection, namely women and the elderly), and of course rats. Everyone else is somewhere in the middle.

The convict code is akin to a dogmatic religion. To some extent the prisoners I worked with for the book were willing to talk about it, but in general, it is almost a taboo subject. It is not to be questioned, it is not to be doubted. It just is, and always will be.

The reality is that the code, the way different prisoners interpret it, and the way different prisoners apply it, is at best ambiguous and at worst contradictory. There are conflicts between the code and the common sense moral principles of fairness and integrity and such that the prisoners claim to accept. Yet almost invariably when I raise this with the prisoners, they react with visible discomfort and avoid being drawn into thinking or talking about the code in any deep or critical way.

Though they might not articulate it quite like this, I read their reaction as telling me that my whole approach is misguided. The code is not something that they believe in because they have painstakingly thought it through and found it to be defensible in every last one of its particulars; it is a way of life to which they have made an emotional commitment. It might well be that there are prima facie flaws or inconsistencies in the code, they seem to say, but this is our life, this is our culture, this is the basis of our self-respect and the respect we exchange with others.

The most vociferous defenders of the code are generally the youngest prisoners. The middle aged and older prisoners occasionally adopt a more casual attitude toward the code, and even express doubts about certain aspects of it. But the younger prisoners have to make sure, as loudly as possible, that everyone knows they are rock solid for the code.

Of course, words and behavior are quite different. So while just about all the prisoners feel an obligation to pay lip service to the code, it is understood that it is frequently violated. A "no tolerance" policy is the rule in theory, but in practice the prisoners know that there are very few of their peers that they can fully trust, and that, for instance, the administration could find out pretty much everything that goes on in PAP and the other programs, because you can always assume there's at least one rat in any decent size group of prisoners.

Also, WSR is such a unique prison for rehabilitative programs and for somewhat respectful interactions between prisoners and correctional officers, that a lot goes on there that would violate the code or at least be viewed very suspiciously at other prisons. Contrary to a simplistic reading of the code, the prisoners cannot perceive the officers at WSR as the enemy. Not every form of communication or cooperation with an officer is seen as evidence that the fraternizer is a rat.

Conventional wisdom states that one must never show fear in prison. There's something to that, but from my experience in PAP, I have a little different understanding.

It's really all about what you do because of that fear.

Take the case of a new prisoner who is threatened by one or more prisoner bullies. It could be obvious that he's scared to death. He could be visibly shaking as they approach. His only defense could be a futile flailing away at them as he bawls his eyes out. But if he's standing up for himself, however ineffectually, and if he keeps his mouth shut when an officer comes around and asks what the commotion is about, then he's doing what the situation calls for and he'll win a certain respect.

On the other hand, imagine a prisoner who talks tough, whose stone face never betrays the slightest fear, and who is by all appearances the coolest customer around. If he conveniently makes himself scarce when his partners are under threat and need him, he can expect only scorn from his fellow prisoners.

It is not unacceptable to experience fear. It is not unacceptable to display fear. What is unacceptable is to succumb to that fear and to break weak and prove yourself unreliable.

PAP prisoners tend on average to more readily talk about their emotions, show vulnerability, and get "touchy-feely" than the typical person—at least the typical male—I meet in everyday life outside of prison. In some of the Prison Awareness classes especially, prisoners share stories that put them in anything but a tough guy, in control, macho light. They talk about the times they've felt most alone and scared and vulnerable. And the other prisoners are generally supportive. Whatever ribbing ensues is typically good-natured, and offered with an air of "Hey, we've all been there."

But there are exceptions.

On three occasions during my tenure in PAP, the prisoners staged role-playing demonstrations. A few prisoners would take on the role of staff, and a few of us students or volunteers would be cast as prisoners, with everyone else just part of the audience.

Through make-believe, we experienced what it's like to step up awkwardly onto the prison bus while chained together at the ankle. We were greeted at prison by drill sergeant-type correctional officers, faced with attempts at intimidation and extortion by veteran prisoners, tempted by the administration to turn informant, and so on.

Though usually well-behaved, PAP prisoners were noticeably unruly as an audience for the role-playing. Their responses ranged from mild teasing and taunting to hooting and catcalling.

At the time, I just found it rude and irritating. Later, though, it occurred to me that what was going on in the audience was as revealing as what the role-players were attempting to demonstrate. The prisoners could talk about these matters in the abstract, could even, some of them, talk about their own experiences as new arrivals in prison. But when confronted with a re-creation of those early days, many of them couldn't handle it.

They shifted anxiously in their seats. They masked their discomfort with bravado. They distracted themselves from memories of their own victimization by heckling the role-players and each other. See? We're not afraid. This isn't bothering us. Would we be laughing like this and having such an obvious good time if this were bothering us?

If they could react this way to such small scale reenactments, I thought, they must truly make life miserable for real life newcomers to prison. It was easy to see how a hazing subculture is self-perpetuated.

At PAP, the prisoners and the outside volunteers interact as equals. The prisoners are not poor misunderstood waifs needing only advice and guidance from noble, kind-hearted upstanding citizens like ourselves. Conversely, the prisoners are not sinister masters of evil manipulating and exploiting those they have enticed into their world.

In theory, the socialization provided by PAP humanizes the prisoners. Its benefits are subtle and gradual, but over time, you do see prisoners displaying leadership qualities, improving their communication and social skills, manifesting greater self-confidence, and being willing to ask for help or show some vulnerability. You see a softening of their harsher, more violent or macho attitudes. Maybe some of this would be happening anyway just as people mature, so it's impossible to pinpoint exactly what is and what is not an effect of PAP, but I believe the improvements are at least partly attributable to PAP and the other programs available at WSR.

And the benefits are not uni-directional. The prisoners often ask us why we participate in the program. To them it is self-evident that our being there is good for them, but they have trouble seeing how it could be good for us.

Well, we're not a bunch of inexplicably altruistic people. We get a lot out of PAP, and only some of it is the satisfaction of thinking we might have made a positive difference for others.

The benefits we derive are the benefits of friendship. These aren't friends we call when we need a lift to the airport, or friends we go clubbing with. They don't come over to our place for dinner, and we don't car pool with them. Our relationships with them are severely limited by circumstance, but they are friends nonetheless.

We laugh with them. We discuss serious and not so serious matters with them. We learn about lives that are often vastly different from ours. We come to care very much what happens to them, and vice versa.

Genuine friendships develop. And genuine friendships are beneficial to all parties involved. Simple as that.

I was fortunate enough to make several friends like that. Spending time with them gave me the idea of pursuing a project that would enable them to tell their stories to a broader audience than just those who visit the prison.

The Prison Awareness class, and PAP itself, are about prison and crime, but they are not just abstract bloodless discussions. We learn about these things by getting to know a small number of actual prisoners as individuals. They let us into their lives so that we can better understand them and the world they inhabit.

Getting to know these prisoners as individuals can take one a step closer to a better understanding of broader issues of prison and crime. Such insight into individuals does not replace abstract theorizing, empirical statistical studies, or other valuable forms of knowledge, but it can be one part of the package.

In the summer of 1997, I approached eight to ten prisoners to ask them if they would be interested in participating in an oral history format book. As I became better acquainted with other prisoners, over the course of roughly the next year I asked another eight to ten. In addition, six or seven prisoners I had not asked heard about the project and volunteered.

Some of the prisoners declined, and others accepted but then dropped out as soon as they saw some of the questions I intended to ask. In some cases, I assume it was because they hadn't realized I'd be challenging them in sensitive areas. Even amongst those who approached me and volunteered, over half later backed out.

In the end, nine prisoners remained as interview subjects for this book. Some were very cooperative, and others participated only on a much smaller scale. But I did manage to interview all participants a minimum of twice.

I decided to be aboveboard with the prison administration about this project, and so sought their formal permission to interview certain prisoners and ultimately publish the results. It took several months to get that permission. I don't think they were hostile to the project; it seemed to be more just a case of bureaucratic lethargy. But I was not able to commence interviewing the prisoners until early 1998.

These interviews continued off and on through 1998, 1999, and part of 2000.

Initially my plan had been to use written correspondence for the interviews. I preferred this to taping interviews, because I thought the immediacy of tape would have more the feeling that I was ambushing the subjects, that they were being tested on how fast they could think on their feet. I figured if we did it in writing, they would always have ample opportunity to answer thoughtfully and at their own pace, and in their own style.

I had to modify this plan as I went along. Some participants never did respond to my written questions, and many of the others dragged their feet. Almost all of them, though, were much more cooperative about letting me tape conversations with them. So I switched to mostly taped interviews. The final book contains transcripts of both, with more tapes than written correspondence.

Often the interviews were completely spontaneous and I just let the conversation develop naturally. Less frequently I brought with me a list of questions, or at least some notes, but even on those occasions we ended up playing it by ear to a large extent.

My style with the prisoners was not to feign some kind of neutrality or detachment, ask the briefest possible questions, and then try to stay completely in the background. These are conversations, and they are mostly conversations with people I know and like. We didn't lapse into more formal personae when the tape recorder was running; we spoke familiarly, needled each other, laughed, occasionally argued.

I tried to give them every opportunity to speak their minds and to tell their stories, but I also challenged them and I dropped in my own points and gave them a chance to respond.

I did not systematically ask every prisoner the same questions, but there are common themes running throughout the interviews. These include:

•The story behind the crime for which they are currently incarcerated.

•Some background on them individually—age, criminal history, childhood, etc.

•The convict code and the prison pecking order.

•What day-to-day life is like in prison.

•How someone who is not from a criminal background, such as myself or the typical "square," would fare in prison.

•Comparisons of prison life at different institutions or at different times.

•Their take on private industry employers using prison labor, as happens at WSR.

•Their take on the kind of rehabilitation programs available at WSR.

•How they intend to stay out of prison if and when they are released.

This list is by no means exhaustive; there are countless other topics I discussed with one or more of the prisoners.

The transcripts are presented chronologically, with connective material before and/or after each one providing some information on what was happening with that prisoner, with WSR, or with the book project itself.

I edited the transcripts for clarity, not for content. No changes have been made in order to sensationalize, sugarcoat, or otherwise alter the substance of what was said.

Much of the editing is just a reflection of the fact that spoken English differs from written English far more than most people realize. A verbatim, raw transcript of a spoken conversation includes a great deal of repetition and stuttering, sentence fragments, and filler phrases such as "you know," "like," "I mean," etc. I cleaned up the majority of these things, though I did leave some in for the sake of realism. My goal was to make the transcripts readable, not to transform the speech of myself and the prisoners to something more formal or sophisticated.

Less often I rearranged some material, or deleted some redundant material. For instance, if a prisoner told me a story in January but in too abbreviated a form for me to be confident it would make sense to readers, the next time I conversed with him on tape in March I might have asked him to give me that story again. In the book, though, I include the story just once, with the wording being a composite of the two versions he told to me.

I also changed the names of third parties, other than public figures.

I did considerably less editing of the written correspondence. I cleaned up obvious typos and such, but in general the transcripts of the prisoners' written responses included here are very close to the originals.

I would like to thank the administration and staff of WSR, and the many PAP volunteers and students for their role in my PAP experiences and in this book project.

My thanks also to freelance editor Susan Stewart, who offered many helpful suggestions on the non-interview transcript portions of this book.

Most of all I want to thank the prisoners themselves, especially but not only the nine individuals who ended up being the primary subjects of this book. Without them, this book would not exist. I am deeply grateful to them.

In the end, I want you to feel like you know these men—how they think, how they feel, why they do what they do. You don't have to like them, you don't have to agree with them, you don't have to sympathize with their gripes. You don't have to listen uncritically to what they say. By all means, listen critically. But listen.

# JIMI—January 1998

*"I have always allowed myself the freedoms of 'natural selection,' if you will, whenever I've been on the run. My boundaries expand far beyond those accepted and expected in society. I prey upon those who present an opportunity for fast cash, which is why I've generally resorted to armed robbery."*

Jimi in 1997.

J imi* was the first good friend I made at the prison. From early on, there were several prisoners with whom I established at least some small amount of rapport, and with whom I enjoyed conversing, but Jimi was different. I felt I made a more significant connection with him.

When I was still a newbie and had not yet gotten to know many of the guys very well, one of my pet peeves about the PAP meetings was that too many of them were unstructured and quickly degenerated into something akin to a boring cocktail party. People would collect in little circles and make small talk, and I—being the sort of person who decidedly does not excel in such situations—would stand around feeling socially awkward and wondering why I had bothered to come.

But when Jimi was there, I always felt welcome and comfortable. I always had someone to hang out with. He'd greet me with that big grin on his face, and soon we'd fall to talking like the oldest of friends. He was interested in what I had to say, and I was interested in what he had to say. We'd talk about prison, yes, but about much more besides. Our connection quickly transcended the roles of prisoner and volunteer; we were friends.

With some of the prisoners, I quickly picked up on the fact that they were there primarily to talk to the women, and so I tried not to monopolize their time and keep them from that. With Jimi, though, I never felt like he was just spending time with me to be polite.

Though well past 30, Jimi is, in the best and worst of ways, a big kid. He has a friendly, open, extroverted personality, an eagerness and excitability that borders on the charmingly goofy. His criminal history is characterized more by impulsiveness and irresponsibility than by malevolence.

Jimi has been in and out of prison for much of his adult life, and spent time in juvenile facilities before that. A big reason he's lived so much of his life behind bars is simple: Drugs.

It's a common story, of course. Drugs are, directly or indirectly, a large part of the explanation for why a great number of criminals commit the crimes they do.

For some, drug trafficking is simply a moneymaking opportunity. The drugs themselves are of little or no importance to them; drive the price of something else up by criminalizing it, and they'd sell that instead. Close off all such illegal opportunities and they'd hustle used cars or anything else that gave them the chance to exploit others for money. They are capitalists first, not drug abusers, and tend to be averse to getting heavily into drug use themselves, as this would impair their moneymaking.

On the other hand, there are the Jimis of the world. They might sell some of the drugs that come their way, but they are users primarily. They are not businessmen, but junkies.

*Jimi has chosen to be identified by his first name only.

On the streets, Jimi liked to party. He didn't have the attention span, the discipline, the maturity to sustain a "straight" job and lifestyle for any significant length of time. It was all too much of a burden. Better to lose himself in Harleys, fast cars, women, booze, and drugs.

Jimi's crimes were crimes of economic necessity. He needed money for drugs, and he discovered that the easiest way for him to get that money was to steal it.

And so, when he was desperate for money, as he often was, he would get a gun and hold people up.

Jimi was never a cold, calculating, criminal mastermind, premeditating brilliant and complex heists. His crimes came in panicky sprees. Having fucked up whatever job, relationship, etc. he had established at a given point in his life, he'd hit the road, losing himself in a manic spiral of ever-increasing drug use and crime, alternately reveling in the instability and loss of control and fearing and hating it and himself and what he had gotten himself into, again. And of course to cloud those unwelcome latter emotions, he'd take more drugs, which necessitated acquiring more money, which meant risking another stick-up, which brought another rush of thrills and guilt, and on and on.

In the end, just like with the straight routines that he could never quite get the hang of, there was no way he could sustain the crime spree indefinitely. He'd make a wrong move, his luck would run out, and he'd be apprehended. And he'd have a long time behind bars—generally years—to once again ponder how in the world he'd fallen into the trap and let it all happen again.

Jimi has become a virtual fanatic about trying to understand why he does what he does, and about turning his life around. He has immersed himself in therapy, self-help books, and drug and alcohol programs and other rehabilitative programs in and out of prison, seeking some way to break the bad habits and addictions that keep dragging him back into crime and into prison.

Behaviorally, he is a career criminal. Attitudinally, he is not. That is to say, he has been committing crimes off and on for most of his life. But he does not embrace it. He does not accept it as a permanent part of who he is and what his life is to be.

He is not stupid, and he is not evil. Unlike some of the prisoners, he has not internalized a set of values that rationalizes the crimes he commits and the harm he has done to others and to himself. He fully concedes that the things he has done are flat out wrong, and he fully accepts the obligation to change himself to ensure he won't return to such behavior.

He is not stupid or evil, but he is, or has been, weak. And that is what he has been trying so hard to do something about in recent years.

Jimi is a popular, gregarious sort, charming, good-looking, and still youthful enough to draw the ladies. He is generally liked and well-respected by the inside guys and accepted as one of the "Fellahs."* Certainly the PAP volunteers appreciate him and his positive energy.

When he has held a straight job on the outside, his most frequent trade has been, interestingly enough, that of a hairdresser. He would like one day to return to that line of work, and to have his own shop. Whether that ultimately happens depends in part on whether he can re-acquire his license, which was stripped from him—inappropriately, he maintains—by the state of Washington after one of his criminal convictions.

He has significant artistic ability, and once was offered a scholarship to art school. It is yet another opportunity he threw away when the pull of drugs and crime grew too strong.

Jimi is an admitted "nut" about Christmas, in or out of prison. The years he is stuck in prison for Christmas, rather than let it get him down, he devotes himself to making homemade Christmas cards, and putting together little gift baskets of store items and his own works of art. Then, after prevailing upon a guard to let him out of his cell early on Christmas morning, he makes his rounds like a prison Santa Claus, slipping the goodies into the cells of various prisoners while they are asleep or off showering.

He is an extrovert whose joy of life, big-heartedness, and generous emotions are never far from the surface. So too, reportedly, are his less benevolent emotions. Though I have never seen him lose his temper or speak or act toward anyone in a belligerent, hurtful fashion, he admits to having an "Irish temper," and to having had a violent streak when he was younger, which led to frequent fighting.

Another prisoner confirmed in conversation with me that Jimi does indeed have—or at least used to have—a darker, violent side. He spoke in general terms to me of witnessing intense flashes of temper from Jimi, and some serious brawling. "That boy," he concluded, "Years ago—well, there was a lot of anger in him. You didn't want to mess with him."

But at PAP, he was as kind and open and friendly as you could want. And it never came across the least bit phony. I never caught a glimpse of anger or malice that he would then get back under control and hide away. I never saw him putting people down, or behaving in a cruel or unkind way. That just wasn't Jimi.

Rightly or wrongly, I certainly trusted him and felt totally comfortable around him from the beginning.

At the time I commenced these interviews, Jimi was approximately a year away from release. He should have already been out on parole, but because of some infractions he had accumulated earlier in his incarceration, his prison time had been extended.

---

*The elite prisoners. Those at the top of the "pecking order."

The most significant of these infractions was, not surprisingly, drug related. He had (this was at another facility, before his transfer to WSR) exploited a female acquaintance who was on his visiting list. Knowing that she had a romantic interest in him, he feigned a reciprocal interest, and then enticed her to smuggle drugs to him in the visiting room. They got caught.

In the one to two years between that incident and the time of this first interview, he had, according to his own account, been clean and sober.

He often spoke of finally "getting it," of understanding just what kind of damage he had done to people in the past—his robbery victims, the woman he'd manipulated into bringing drugs into the prison, the family and friends he'd disappointed so many times. He knew that he had to follow through on the changes he was feeling inside, to become the kind of person he was capable of being. And he knew that the one thing with the greatest potential to deflect him from that path was drugs.

As his prison time grew shorter, Jimi got more and more anxious but more and more optimistic about how he would fare upon his release. He was doing all he could to set himself up to have the best shot possible on the outside.

He was working as a welder at one of the outside industry jobs at the prison, which put some money on his books, helped him to acquire the work ethic he'd never cultivated on the outside, and gave him contacts that could set him up with a job after his release.

He had a place to live lined up. He would be moving in with his girlfriend Jeannie,[*] an older woman he'd had a relationship with off and on for some years. Actually, he had met her at a drug and alcohol program on the outside during one of his earlier efforts to get clean. She was one of the counselors.

At times, Jimi spoke of prison as having lost any deterrent effect on him, because as much as he disliked it, he knew from experience he could deal with it if he had to.

But I soon discovered that wasn't the whole truth. Jimi did indeed have a deep and significant fear of prison, specifically of a "life without parole" sentence.

To him, there is a huge psychological difference between those who know they are getting out one day, and those who know they are not. As one who was in the former category, his focus was very much on his future life on the streets, all the things he would finally get to experience again or for the first time, all the challenges he needed to prepare himself for. He admired the "lifers" who somehow managed to keep their sanity, and even to stay in relatively good spirits. He wasn't at all confident that he'd be similarly capable of accepting the fact that regardless of how well or how poorly he behaved, of how much or how little he changed, regardless of what kind of human being he became, he would never set foot outside prison again. The whole idea of it visibly spooked him.

---

[*]I have changed the name.

This fear was very real to him, because he knew how close he himself was to being a lifer. He lived every day of his life with people who were repeat offenders to only an equal or lesser degree than he was, and yet who were already doomed by "third strike" sentencing laws to permanent prisoner status, while he would soon be getting another shot on the outside. And certainly if he failed again, there was a good chance that he too would be "third struck" and forced to join their ranks.

Jimi was very cooperative with me about the interviews, as much or more than any other prisoner in the beginning. He was one of the few prisoners who was willing to respond to written questions, which he did on several occasions. And he was always happy to do a taped interview. Often he was my fallback—if the person I had arranged to interview didn't show up for the PAP meeting, Jimi and I would ad lib an interview instead.

He believed in the book project, because he enjoyed talking about himself and prison and crime, and trying to understand it all and help others to understand. He considered our interviews an extension of his therapy, a way for us to explore together some of the things he had to think about and deal with if he were to have a chance to succeed on the outside this time.

At times—such as when we talked about his childhood—my questions met with some resistance. Clearly there were areas that were sensitive for him, that elicited painful and uncomfortable memories. But he acknowledged that that was all the more reason to face up to such matters, and he responded as best he could. He never displayed any hostility toward me in response to my probing.

There is an irresistible genuineness about Jimi, a natural good-heartedness. You know that he's really doing his best to be a good person and to turn his life around for the better. You don't know to what extent he will succeed, or what the ultimate results will be, but his sincerity is palpable, and you can't help but root for him to defeat his myriad demons. Certainly our friendship has meant a lot to me.

I commenced the interview process by mailing sets of questions to each of the prisoners who had agreed to participate. Jimi was the first to respond.

*For what crime are you currently in prison? Tell me as much as you are willing about what you did, the circumstances, etc. If what you were convicted of and sentenced for differs significantly from what you actually did, address that too.*

I am incarcerated for first degree robbery, felony eluding, first degree possession of stolen property, and second degree burglary. I received 116 months total from three different counties. These crimes were all committed while on the run from the law for the burglary.

The burglary was committed during an alcohol blackout. I remember drinking hard alcohol at a neighborhood bar with some drinking buddies. I don't remember leaving the bar. My first awareness begins again when I'm lying in a hospital bed handcuffed to the bed frame. A police officer standing over me informed me I'd been found passed out on the floor of a neighborhood dry cleaners. Over the next few days in jail, I was informed that two other small shops had been broken into nearby.

I had apparently left the bar with the intention of leaving my car at the bar and walking three blocks to my ex-wife's house, whom I was good friends with at the time. Between the bar and her house was a path of destruction in the form of huge plate glass windows broken.

I'd lacerated my right arm pretty badly and the officer told me they'd actually followed the blood from the first break-in to find me in the third establishment lying on the floor soaked in blood.

This would end up being pled down from three counts of second degree burglary to one count of second degree burglary. I received 51 months based on my points, which is determined by my extensive criminal history.

I was employed as a salon manager in Seattle at the time of the burglaries and was able to bail out while I awaited trial. My attorney and I postponed the trial for nearly a year, trying in that year to put together an "intoxication defense." However, I was unable to gather witnesses willing to testify in court to the extent of my drinking that night. As trial drew closer and closer, I began to feel desperate. I'd NEVER turned myself in before and really had no intention of appearing for trial. Running has always been a natural instinct to me, one I wasn't prepared to change.

I threw a party on my birthday in 1990 and smoked crack for the first time in my life on that night. I was hooked from that first hit. I quit my job after 2-3 days of smoking crack, and packed my car and took off. It's all history from there.

I have always allowed myself the freedoms of "natural selection," if you will, whenever I've been on the run. My boundaries expand far beyond those accepted and expected in society. I prey upon those who present an opportunity for fast cash, which is why I've generally resorted to armed robbery. It's fast and easy if one can ignore the intrinsic toll it takes on the conscience. But, the toll has never stopped me from doing what I do to survive while on the run. That punishment comes later, after I've been arrested and have time on my hands to consider my behavior.

My first degree robbery was actually a burglary turned robbery. I was breaking into a salon at about 9:00-10:00 PM. I'd been smoking crack with a couple of girls that day and they asked me to give them perms. I didn't have any rods for perms, so I told them I'd break into a salon to get the stuff I needed. I did that, only to find the owner to be in the salon counting money. I took her purse which contained a 357 magnum, the money she was counting, and the perm supplies I'd come for. I also took her jewelry.

On September 23, 1990, I was driving north on Highway 101 entering Olympia. I was spotted by a deputy sheriff speeding. He attempted to pull me over, and a chase ensued. I drove like a maniac for nearly 45 minutes, nearly colliding with other vehicles or causing collisions several times. I was finally pinned down in a long driveway to a house on the water. The officers knew I was trapped, so they didn't feel the need to enter the driveway. In that moment of time I got out of my car and ran, leaving firearms, stolen property, jewelry, and credit cards in the car, taking only my wallet, stash container with crack, and a lighter with me. I got away from the area and spent the entire day running through the woods. Each time I came out of the woods, it seemed I'd be spotted and chased again. Finally, as night neared, I was spotted in a phone booth trying to use the phone. I was arrested at that point and taken to jail, where my 116 month prison term would begin.

The reality is, I got off easy considering the number of crimes I committed while on the run. I suppose that's the case with most "career criminals." I've been breaking the law since I was a young boy hitchhiking around the country. Again, survival.

So I was given 116 months, but that was actually the sentence for the first degree robbery. All of my other crimes were run concurrently, because the sentencing guidelines lend themselves to that, or did when I fell.

*Tell me about the first time you were ever incarcerated, at least overnight, as a juvenile or as an adult. What led up to it? How did it feel at the very beginning? Recreate it for me.*

My first experience being incarcerated was when I was about 13 years old. I'd been warned several times that I couldn't continue to skip school, which I'd been doing a lot of. I'd begun smoking because of the crowd I was hanging around, and experimented with pot and alcohol. My mother had caught me with pot on several occasions, and she was at her end with answers. She'd taken me to see juvenile counselors and they didn't do any good. Finally, I was taken to juvenile detention by my mother after she found a small radio in my bedroom. Her questioning revealed that I'd broken into some neighbor's garage while they were on vacation and stolen the radio and some tools. Mom drove me to detention and dropped me off.

I was placed in a small cell with no windows and the light on 24 hours a day. I remember feeling very desperate. I cried and cried and cried until the tears turned to anger and hatred toward my mother. I'd lost all trust for her at that point, not recognizing my responsibility in the problems I found myself in.

I was released from detention and returned home, but nothing had changed. I continued to skip school, steal, use pot and alcohol increasingly, and blame my mom for everything.

I would never blame Dad for leaving me a year earlier; he was God to me and he only left because Mom drove him away, at least that was my working belief for years to come.

My several run-ins with juvenile court and detention would leave me quite bitter, misdirected, isolated amongst my peers as well as my family, and totally lost where school was concerned, which was at this stage my only avenue for athletics, the most important gift my father handed down to me before he left.

I continued to have problems with the juvenile authorities that would lead to longer stays in detention, placement in group homes that abused the kids frequently, and ultimately a juvenile work camp far out in the woods where the kids worked in the woods under Department of Natural Resources supervision.

It was at this camp where I met the man who would for years to come be a tremendous mentor to me. He was Arnold Young,[*] a gray haired black man from Chicago who had earned his respect in a fashion I could understand and accept, the hard way. The difference with him was that he'd succeeded. He'd made it to the NBA and wore an NBA Championship ring to prove it.

I was in the presence of a true champion, and not just because he had been a Boston Celtic. He was a hero for giving me his time and understanding my struggles, or seeming to. I would later go live with him for a short time and try to get back on track, but his unwavering support just wasn't enough. I would leave his house eventually, stealing some items on the way out. The items were returned several months later after I'd been arrested again, but Arnold, as disappointed as he was, would later prove once again to be a good friend who cared a great deal about me, as I did him more and more as I grew older and more responsible.

Aside from my relationship with Arnold, my entire juvenile experience with the courts, detention, group homes, foster homes, and camp was negative. I don't have good memories of childhood past the age of 12 or 13, which was when Dad left and Mom began experimenting with dating and dancing until late at night.

The juvenile system really isn't working. The existing juvenile system isolates kids from their families and their communities, forcing them to step outside their boundaries and behave reactively. Even when a child does make a connection, which I believe it's all about—making a connection—these connections tend to be short lived and rarely supported in terms of permanence

I strongly believe in the importance of children making a connection to something, anything. Something that drives them. Something that can be used to teach delayed gratification, something important enough to the child that he or she will want to delay gratification. Of course, this isn't "the answer" to the problems facing our youth today; answers are many, as are problems.

---

[*]I have changed the name.

*Provisions like the "three strike" rule are very popular with much of the public. Some people believe that, if anything, such rules are too lenient and give a person who has already proven himself to be a criminal too many undeserved chances. State and defend your position on such rules.*

My position on the "three strike" law is difficult for me to express in words, written or spoken. Because of my lifetime in the system, I find it difficult to separate my feelings from my knowledge. History tells us this law doesn't work, except as a "red herring." The "habitual criminal act" has been used in nearly every state of the union; in some states, it has existed continuously for decades. For those states, the three strike law is nothing new.

I believe society's response to repeat offenders is natural. The problem is that society is stuck on the idea that prison is the only answer. And when prison fails to change people, as it always has except when education is made available and taken advantage of, society demands longer sentences and tougher time, not realizing what this does.

The idea that we can continue to place bandages on an existing failure only perpetuates, even escalates, the problem. This explains in my opinion the increased level of hate crime, violent crime, and sophisticated crime.

Making prisons tougher with longer sentences and less education seems to be the trend of the '90s. Sending someone away for the rest of their life leaves them with nothing to lose and everything to gain while inside. What effect does this have on the guy he lives with who is getting out in a couple of years or a couple of days, you know, the guy who is getting out next week and moving in with his brother who lives next door to you? Who do you want in your neighborhood? An educated ex-felon who has used his time positively, understands the experience of a victim, the responsibility of a citizen, the value of an employee, and the importance of each member of the community? Or would you prefer the angry, confused, unrealistic convict who's been living with the "life without"* inmate for the past year?

Prison is not the only means of punishment. If one uses one's imagination, it's not hard to imagine alternatives to incarceration that first serve the victim, then the community, then the offender and his family. The process of restoring justice involves first aiding the victim in getting life back to normal, as closely as possible, then aiding the community back to normal, and finally the offender, so that he/she is capable of re-entering society prepared to contribute and bond.

---

*The prisoners use "life without" as shorthand for a sentence of life imprisonment without the possibility of parole.

*Are you disappointed in yourself for being in prison? Do you feel you've disappointed anyone else who's close to you? Whom most? How, if at all, can you make it up to this person or prove yourself to him or her?*

Yes, I am disappointed in myself. I am not the 35 year old male I had intended to be. Not only have I damaged my life irreparably. I've damaged many others' lives as well.

The way the system is set up, I will never have the opportunity to provide assurance to my past victims, so their pain I carry with me forever. I can't tell them I'm sorry. I can't tell them I've spent my entire life in prison growing both academically and emotionally. I can't offer them monetary compensation, except those I'm currently ordered to pay restitution to, which will be handled through the county courts. There is nothing I can do to reassure them that, though I am a free man, they will never have to wonder if I will victimize them again.

Part of the disappointment I experience with this dynamic of not being able to personally participate in the healing process of any of my many victims, ranging from burglary to robbery, is the thought that they will never know that they are not only safe with me in society but instrumental in my process of growing up as a human being. The tragedies that I perpetrated on innocent victims are now the stories that make up the beginning of my journey, which will soon be the platform that takes me on a more important journey, a journey that places me at the podium in front of children who are experiencing the same problems I once experienced.

I believe the giving of myself and the sharing of my painful story will prove effective in the efforts to reach children at risk. It is this effort I would like to give back to all of my past victims.

I've disappointed my mother and father so many times it's unforgivable to anyone but them, but their unwavering support continues. The relationship I share with my family is strong, but I feel a great need to prove that I've finally gotten it right. I understand that I ultimately have to respect myself and value myself enough to get it right for myself, but I feel there is a great responsibility in my hands to behave like a responsible human being and family member. I can't make up the time I've taken away from my mother and father, but I can give them the time I have left without worry that I'll be removed from society again, which will take time to establish.

I feel like "The Boy Who Cried Wolf" whenever I say "I won't be back," so I try and avoid that statement, though that's exactly what I feel.

*If you had all your same good points and bad points except that you never engaged in criminal activity (drugs, stealing, brawling, whatever), would you be more or less attractive to the average woman? Is the "bad boy" appeal a myth, or is one of the incentives in favor of a criminal lifestyle that it's an advantage in getting women?*

The myth that those involved in criminal activity are in some way more attractive to women than those not involved in criminal activity seems a bit abstract to me. I have never been one to date women who were interested in the criminal element. In fact, I would generally hide the facts of my past because I felt it would hinder the process of becoming intimate.

Running the risk of sounding a bit naive after spending 15 years in the joint, I really didn't know such a myth existed. I've always felt that my criminal record would hurt my chances of intimacy. Of course, this would obviously depend on such variables as where I meet my potential intimate partners, what kind of partner I'm looking for, what kind of relationship I'm looking for, and the circumstances at the time. I suppose if I'm on a run (robbery spree), I'm more likely to seek out partners who are less guarded about their partners, in which case my history may seem exciting.

I can't in all honesty say that I've consciously used my criminal history as an advantage or attraction while in pursuit of a female partner or companion. I would say I would much rather have no history of criminal behavior. This is a wish I toy with often in many areas of my life.

# JIMI—February 1998

*"My problems evolved from the absence of my father. I wanted my father back in my life and Mom had very little control over that. In fact, she wanted him back as much as I did."*

After receiving Jimi's written responses to my first set of questions, I responded with some follow-up questions and comments, as well as some questions that opened up new areas.

*Can you give me a little more detail on that first time in juvenile detention? I'm wanting it to be as vivid as possible for readers, so they can put themselves in your place and imagine what it was like for you physically and emotionally. How small was the cell? What did it contain? Were you the only one in it? Was it hot? Cold? Was it clean? Dirty? How fast or slow did the time pass? Do you remember anything else you were thinking and feeling in there besides what you've mentioned so far? How long were you there that first time? Etc.*

I suppose I can best describe it as terribly constricting, even claustrophobic. I remember watching my mom drive out of the parking lot, knowing that she was actually leaving me. That made me feel incredibly helpless.

I remember feeling both very hot, to the point of heavy breathing and sweating, and very cold, to the point of shivering in the single wool blanket. The cell appeared to be clean at first glance, but as I satisfied my boredom I found dirt and dust in every corner. There were places where past prisoners had wiped their snot in corners and on the window sill. The door had been drawn on from the inside, all kinds of drawings. A staff member would walk down the long hallway every hour stopping to look inside each cell.

I was so angry and hurt at my mother that I would not trust her again for many years to come. I was a different person when I finally got out of detention the following week.

Doing time that first time was way different for me than doing time is now. I've learned how to do time and don't experience the same difficulties as I did that first time.

*You made an insightful comment when you wrote about "children making a connection to something, anything. Something that drives them." The only thing that gives me pause for concern is that it seems like some such connections could be unhealthy and harmful. For example, the psychological need for connecting with and being accepted by other people, and for the feeling of having a purpose in one's life is a strong motivation for things like joining a street gang or becoming a skinhead. In cases like those, I'm not so sure I wouldn't rather have the kid just remain unconnected and isolated.*

*It might be that being connected like that just makes one more easily conditioned and influenced by those to whom one is connected. So, yes, being loved and accepted by one's family or by a caring mentor makes one more apt to be willing to try to live up to the strong values we would hope such people would be trying to instill in someone. But it also makes one more apt to agree with them and emulate them even when they're wrong. In some ways it's almost like being connected with people is a neutral condition that makes a person more influenceable for both good and bad.*

*So I think you're right, but I also think that the good you've identified is not an unqualified good, and that, as you know, there's a lot more to this point, a lot more to think about.*

When I said I believe children need to be connected to something I purposefully left out the word "someone." I think the need to connect with someone suggests finding identity in someone else. My experience with mentoring was lasting and positive for me but I believe the connection has to be made to "something" that not only drives them from day to day and teaches them direction and goal setting and delayed gratification but also connects them to society, makes them a part of the community, defines their role in society, if you will. I don't see "someone" serving that purpose. That's not to say I don't believe source figures teach values and ethics by example. I simply mean individuality and the defining of one's self and his/her role in society must evolve out of his/her interests, skills, gifts, etc.

*Your main point against laws that make sentences more severe and add substantially to the number of prisoners who are in prison for life without parole seems to be that it will have adverse effects on the non-lifers (and, therefore, on society once they're released). I don't know that many people will be persuaded of this. I assume that many people would object strongly to the notion that career criminals—who have had multiple chances to turn their lives around already—should not be kept in prison the rest of their lives, but should instead be let loose to prey on society again because otherwise they'd be spending their time corrupting lesser criminals in prison. If all the "life without" people were instead serving twenty year sentences, would that somehow have all that big an impact on whether prisoners like you achieved rehabilitation? It just seems like you're stretching a bit for this point. But tell me more if you think I'm wrong here and that this really is a major reason against laws that increase the number of life sentences.*

*It seems like you're more comfortable arguing in favor of certain carrots instead of arguing against this particular stick. Is the problem that a society that simply writes off and discards a lot of its prisoners—through the death penalty or through life without parole sentences—is unlikely to be the kind of society willing to go out of its way to help the remaining prisoners? When we concentrate so much on the worst prisoners and how to make sure they can never victimize people on the outside again, are we neglecting to address the issue of how best to deal with the other prisoners that even the harshest system would not lock up forever?*

Well, I suppose I am stretching my argument a bit but there is more to my point that I didn't elaborate on. If the system continues to fill the prisons with these "life without" inmates, there are many adverse effects on the system as a whole. However, after I thought about what I had written, I realized that most of these effects could be eliminated if the system were to simply separate the "life without" inmates from the rest of the prison population. So I really won't carry that point further.

I just hate to give in to the notion that we should be locked up forever. My reasons obviously come from the vantage point of living the incarceration experience personally. Having lived the prison experience I recognize the barriers between the community and the offenders, especially the victims and the offenders. The victims and the community have no idea what is happening in prison. By the same token, the offenders have no real understanding of the effects his/her crime has had on the victim and his/her community.

Society is stuck on the notion that the only response to a crime is to lock the offender up. The victim is left out of the punishment process almost entirely, as is the community. It's the system against the offender. The reality is, no one in this equation is satisfied with this response to crime, except of course the system, which generates billions of dollars every year to maintain a failing system.

So my question is: Does locking people up forever *really* restore a victim's life to normal? Does this response to crime *really* allow closure, or are we ignoring the fact that we spend billions of tax dollars every year housing them? I believe there are countless alternatives to incarceration, even those that provide security to the community. In a country that brags that its most valuable assets are its people we continue to waste lives and dollars under the guise of "corrections."

*It sounds like since the system mostly blocks you from being able to make things up to your victims, the closest you can come is to work with children and such to try to reduce the number of future criminals and future victims. It's not a direct payback, but surely it's a valuable one.*

Yes, I would say this has much to do with the possibility that I might have some effect on the number of future victims. It's sad to me that my victims will never know how important their being my victim was, the roles they played in the evolving process of this once offender who has grown into a caring, emotional, loving person who deeply feels the responsibility to volunteer for those who might learn from my experience.

*Approximately how many total years of your life have you spent incarcerated? When are you scheduled to be released this time? Will your release be unconditional and unrestricted, or some form of parole?*

I am 35 years old, and have served 15 years in the adult system and approximately two years in the juvenile system. My scheduled release date is January 11, 1999. Upon my release, I will be required to report to the community corrections office to establish a payment schedule for my restitution. I won't have any supervision at all, which will be the first time since I was about 13 that I haven't had some kind of supervision. My only responsibility will be to make the scheduled restitution payments and to obey the law, which is a responsibility I carry within.

*I want you once again to go back to your first night ever of incarceration. But this time I want you to re-create for me how that occasion was experienced by your mother. As far as you know, what was she doing, thinking, feeling that night?*

I really don't know as I can answer this question. I have problems understanding what my mother was going through, what she was thinking when she dropped me off at the juvenile hall.

I think she was extremely frustrated with me. She tried very hard to figure me out and help me get my life on track after my father left. She took me to counseling and that didn't work. She put me in different schools with no luck. She tried to scare me with a police friend. She tried several things but nothing worked, nothing got me back on track.

That night when she took me to detention I believe she thought she was doing the right thing. I know she had no idea what kind of world she'd exposed me to but there wasn't any way of her knowing that. She couldn't possibly have known what that experience would do to me.

Again, she was at her end with answers and really didn't know what else to do. I suppose she was heartbroken when she drove away without her baby. She loved me very much so I don't believe for a second that she wasn't hurt by leaving me in someone else's care, but she didn't know what leaving me there would do to me and that is her mistake in parenting. That's not excusing my many mistakes in childhood.

My problems evolved from the absence of my father. I wanted my father back in my life and Mom had very little control over that. In fact, she wanted him back as much as I did.

*People often talk about how prisoners corrupt each other, how prisons are like crime schools where people who were bad coming in are worse going out. During your time in prison, tell me about any ways you have done the opposite. Are there prisoners who became better human beings, became less apt to re-offend once released, had their criminal habits and tendencies decreased because you were imprisoned in the same place at the same time?*

This question alludes to the notion that prisons aren't "correction centers" at all, rather "crime schools." The environment has EVERYTHING to do with the product it produces. The fact that prisons can be and often are places where criminal ideas are harvested is a fact that can't be ignored.

My experience in prison has taken me to every major prison in Washington state, including maximum security units called IMU.* The environment in which a prisoner is housed is very responsible for the activities prisoners involve themselves in. If there are no programs that teach personal growth, personal responsibility, and victimization concepts, the only outcome that can be expected from sending offenders to prison is violence, dishonesty, more sophisticated crime and lower numbers of cases of successful re-entry into the community.

The prison environment has become more difficult for me to live in as I've grown. I see the irrational, unrealistic, manipulative thinking more clearly now and it's everywhere in prison. Those inmates who are genuinely involved in change and growth are in an extreme minority in prison and that, from my observation, is not because inmates don't want to learn to live productively in the free world, it's because the prison environment isn't supportive of personal growth type learning. In fact, those who are genuinely committed to growing in prison are seen as "squares." The values in prison are exactly opposite of those in society. What's normal in society is abnormal and sometimes downright dangerous in prison. This makes it extremely difficult to get serious about change in prison.

I like to think that I have been a positive influence on inmates who have crossed paths with me. I am very protective of my time these days. I try not to spend any more time than necessary with inmates who I don't feel are going in the same direction as I am. There have been several inmates whom I've tried to help share my growth with, my experiences. I live and breathe the important issues involved in growing as an offender. Issues such as taking responsibility for my actions, understanding victimization, exploring and understanding

---

*Intensive Management Units. In the state of Washington, individuals who commit crimes and disciplinary infractions while already incarcerated can be sent to special facilities for the worst of the worst prisoners.

where I came from and what got me here, including the tough issues surrounding my childhood, and dedicating myself to contributing to society in the future in more than just a passive way. I believe giving of myself and using my experience as a platform to contribute to society will make this entire incarceration experience mean more to me in retrospect than just a waste of 16+ years.

# JERRY—February 1998

*"I've come to grips with the fact that really I'm paying for my whole lifestyle, and deservedly. If anybody deserves to be in prison, it's me. I mean, I got away with ten times more than I ever got caught."*

Jerry in 1997, when he had hair.

J erry McLaughlin is as dynamic a person as you will ever meet.

PAP, for all intents and purposes, is Jerry's baby. He was present to help it get off the ground in the chaotic '70s. From early on—except for the periods when he was temporarily transferred to other institutions—he has been its leader. At times he is a hands-on ruler. At other times, when he senses that other leaders can maintain what he has built, he steps into the background and lets them handle things, until they fail, burn out, are released, or are transferred. Then he steps back up and does what needs to be done to put things back on track.

Jerry has the biggest say in deciding which prisoners do and do not get into PAP. The people who hold the elective offices in the group are either hand-picked by him, or must at least be acceptable to him. He is our most effective negotiator with the prison staff. Routinely he wins some concession from the administration for PAP that we have been told is simply not possible.

He objects when I refer to him as a dictator, though when I amend it to *benevolent* dictator, the characterization is not so unappealing to him.

He is an excitable, gregarious, fun-loving, hot-tempered man with a controlling personality. When Jerry's present, he'll make sure you know it. In fact, a not uncommon criticism of Jerry is that his persona can be so dominating that some of the other prisoners do not take as active a role in the program and do not express themselves as much as they might in his absence. Often I hear comments along the lines of "Jerry's great! Now if only he'd shut up once in awhile."

He identifies himself, not without some pride, as having been among the hardest of hard-core criminals, a violent, brawling thug who would have been your worst nightmare as an enemy. He often tells our Prison Awareness classes, "Not many children grow up to be exactly what they had dreamed of being, but I did. Ever since I could remember, I wanted to be a criminal, a thief, a con man. And that's exactly what I became. I'm a success story."

Some people end up in prison because they get in over their head in something with ramifications they did not fully appreciate. Or their drug addiction causes them to be desperate enough to take risks they would not otherwise take. Or they lose their temper and commit a violent, out-of-character, act. Or they have a self-destructive compulsion they cannot control.

Not Jerry. "I'm not here by accident," he says. Whatever Jerry has done, he'll have you know, whatever crimes he has committed, he has done so autonomously, with eyes open, and fully understanding the consequences.

But over the years, Jerry has mellowed considerably, and his values have gradually developed in a more humane direction. Those who have known him far longer than I have claim that the differences between the old Jerry and the current Jerry are huge.

When he's in one of his more humble moods, Jerry will claim that really his values have changed little if at all, and that the only reason his behavior has changed is either that he's old and fatigued and just doesn't have the energy and the love of danger that being the toughest son of a bitch around requires, or that he's consciously and strategically behaving himself in order to improve his chances of release.

But there's more to it than that. Always a man of principle, he has allowed those principles to evolve over the years, with the result that he finds fewer circumstances in which he can justify harming others. Always a big-hearted man with a generous spirit toward his friends and loved ones, he has come to cast his net of magnanimity wider and wider. Always a man of keen intellect and insight, he has experienced and understood things that cast into doubt his moral worldview, and he has had the intellectual honesty to let his new discoveries take him where they will.

To see him now is to watch a man struggling with the task of incorporating his new insights into his life while remaining true to himself, his commitments, his past, and his partners. He won't simply turn his back on the principles that guided his life for so many years, and on the people with whom he bonded through sharing those principles. He regards that as contemptible hypocrisy. Instead, he'll graft the old onto the new, and if he needs to overlook the inconsistency here or the convoluted reasoning there in order to do so, he prefers that to what he sees as the alternative—adopting the holier-than-thou attitude of the recent convert who frantically attempts to expunge his sins of the past by eagerly condemning those who still commit them in the present.

Jerry attributes some of his mellowing to the influence of the volunteers of PAP and the other programs. He speaks with considerable emotion about the benefits to prisoners like him of having an opportunity to see ordinary members of the community—"squares"—as fully human individuals, and of coming to understand that not all such people hate him and his kind. He speaks movingly of what an impact it had on him when the only mail he received for long stretches of time in solitary confinement was from a PAP volunteer.

There is no single individual more responsible for the survival of PAP all these years, and for the good it has done in so many lives, than Jerry McLaughlin. He takes great pride in this program and what he has made of it. He is forever working to strengthen and improve it so that it will survive beyond his own tenure at WSR. That is to be his legacy, the positive difference he has made in his world.

Jerry tells me that in the over twenty years he's been the unofficial head of PAP, zero volunteers have ever been harmed by one of the prisoners, including by those who have been released. This is not a trivial point. The outside people who come into the prison through PAP have different motives, weaknesses and vulnerabilities, degrees of savvy, degrees of caution in sharing information such as their addresses and phone numbers, and degrees of willingness to interact with prisoner members who have been released. Yet no volunteer has been stalked, robbed, swindled, raped, assaulted, killed, or conned into engaging in criminal activity. At most, one or two prisoners have failed to repay the twenty or fifty dollars borrowed from a volunteer upon their release.

If anyone were to harm one of us, they'd know they were crossing Jerry, and that would be unwise. Regardless of how much he's mellowed, you do not want Jerry as an enemy.

His attitude toward the volunteers is that of a wild animal toward its young. Allow me a quick story to illustrate:

In my early days at PAP, one of the prisoners invited me and one of the other volunteers to the music room, which is just down the hall from the room in which we meet. We were a little hesitant at first, not being sure if it was within the prison rules for outside people to leave the meeting room. But he cleared it with a guard, and we accompanied him to the music room to hear him and his friends play. Twenty minutes later, we thanked him and walked back to the meeting room.

When we entered, the room was silent, and all eyes were on us. Jerry was standing, and everyone else was seated in a semicircle around him. He had a stern expression on his face. We had evidently interrupted him in mid-lecture. As we took our seats, the unusually grim mood in the room caused my companion to jokingly whisper to me, "This feels like in school, when somebody's in trouble!"

Somebody was in trouble. Us.

For the next ten minutes, he harangued us and all present that no outside member was ever to leave this room during a meeting without his knowledge and permission. "This is a prison!" he declared, "You don't just wander off! Do you know how frantic I get when I count heads in this room and see that two of our people are missing?!" On more than one occasion, he had to pause to keep control of himself and to lower his voice. He assured us he was not mad at us—contrary to the evidence of his demeanor—and that his sole concern was our well-being.

Jerry's blustery style leads many to underestimate him. Make no mistake, he is as shrewd as they come. The more you get to know him, the more you realize that his flashes of temper and the general excess of his personality are strategic as often as not. He has an impressive insight into human nature, and he knows the prison world like the back of his hand. Many times he has said or done something that struck me at the time as clearly unwise, and that I chalked up to his impulsiveness and his tendency for his mouth to jump several steps ahead of his brain. And most of those times, later events proved him right. I trust his judgment now, and require a lot more evidence to side against him.

A solid orator, Jerry takes the lead in many of the Prison Awareness classes, explaining the prison world—the "Land of Oz" as he calls it (and has called it long before the HBO series)—and its upside down values. Invariably his remarks are articulate and compelling, sometimes remarkably so. I've certainly learned from him.

Not that I agree with everything Jerry says. Far from it. We have engaged in some fiery exchanges on several occasions, at times in a way that surprises and concerns people who don't know us well and don't know the relationship we've established. I'll challenge Jerry because I know he can take it. And he'll give it back to me because he knows his verbal aggressiveness doesn't intimidate me. It's our way of respecting each other.

In spite of Jerry's extroversion, I'll always remember an observation Jimi made to me: "I don't believe I truly know him, even after all the years we've been in the joint together. I don't know that anyone does. You think you're getting close to him, but you're not. Not really. I don't think he wants anyone to get too close."

Jerry is serving a life sentence, but not without the possibility of parole. His mind is very much on getting out and establishing a life on the outside, but all that depends on the parole board. At the time that I mailed him the first set of questions for this book, he was anticipating a scheduled parole hearing later that same year.

Jerry is a terrific interview. In spite of his intermittent efforts to choose his words carefully so as not to jeopardize any potential parole, his brutal honesty invariably breaks through. That's just Jerry. He's going to tell you what's on his mind, whatever the consequences.

Once, I was watching Jerry at one of the meetings. He was chairing the proceedings from the table at the head of the room, holding court the way he does, bantering with the fellows in the front row, surveying the room with a cocky grin, bellowing whatever announcements he had for the evening, very much in his element, very much in control. There's an awful lot of Randall P. McMurphy in this guy, I remember thinking. (McMurphy's the protagonist in Ken Kesey's *One Flew Over the Cuckoo's Nest*. You'll recall Jack Nicholson's classic portrayal in the movie version.) The feistiness, the pig-headedness, the scheming, the humor, the boundless energy, the defiance of authority, the ability to inspire or infuriate all whom he encounters, the awareness that he is impossible to ignore, the delight he takes in that awareness.

Life has kicked Jerry McLaughlin's ass so many times in so many ways that he's long since lost count. And he's returned the favor even more times. You'll break his spirit the day he dies, and not a moment sooner.

Instead of writing out his answers—or waiting for me to interview him in person—Jerry chose to make a cassette tape of his responses to the first set of questions.

*For what crime are you currently in prison? Tell me as much as you are willing about what you did, the circumstances, etc. If what you were convicted of and sentenced for differs significantly from what you actually did, address that too.*

The best thing I can do is just kind of run it down to you, and you can be the judge.

I'm in for first degree murder. In 1977, actually on Halloween, I killed a guy who had raped my wife. He was a guy I had known all my life. He was—actually he had been a childhood friend of mine, and I'd known his whole family for my whole life.

I guess, the events leading up to it is, we'd had some problems, you know, we'd beefed a couple times and shit, but I thought we were still friends. I was running a poker game out in the north end of Seattle. It was called a "floater." It was back in the days when you couldn't have no high stakes poker games, and so we kept them moving around all the time, and they'd go, like, 24 hours a day, maybe four or five days long, so you'd move from one place to another.

Anyway, nobody really knew how to get a hold of me, and the reason was me and this same guy had committed a crime, and there was a warrant out for me, but there wasn't one out for him. And, I had started getting a lousy feeling about the guy, so I told everybody I'd left town and gone to Alaska.

Well, the guy goes out, I guess he's out partying, he's drinking some turpin hydrate, and he ends up getting in a fight at a bar. And he shows up over at my house, and my old lady peeps out the door, and she sees Frank[*] on the porch. And, you know, we'd known him. I mean, he was a friend of ours, and so, she sees he's bleeding, so she opens the door to let him in.

Well he comes in, he beats her down, and made statements like, "You're Jerry's most precious 'possession,'" I guess he called her, "And this is the only way I can get back at him," and blah, blah, blah. And, anyway, it was kind of a vengeance rape. And he raped her twice, and it was in front of my kid. And all the time he's thinking I'm up in Alaska.

Well, Laura[†] doesn't know what to do. She calls my brother. And my brother knows how I am. To give you a little bit about me, I think you already know I was sort of a career criminal my whole life. Since I was a kid, I've been involved in crime and shit. So my brother understood that, you know, he had to call and tell me what had happened.

So what happens is he calls and tells me that Frank's raped Laura. Well, I tell him to grab me some, actually, some gasoline and some other things I had him bring out for me.

It's about three – four o'clock in the morning before I finally get word that this has happened. What I was going to do is I was going to go over there and throw a Molotov cocktail at the guy's house, and just shoot him down when he came out. But by the time my brother catches up with me, and I get ready, and I get over there, it's almost daylight.

So, the next day, or the next evening, I caught him. And what happened is I actually lured him to a place. He's thinking he's going there to meet this chick, to sell her some drugs.

---

[*]I have changed the name.

[†]I have changed the name.

And, instead of the chick being there, I was there. And when he realized it was me, we all got in a scuffle.

Everybody's shooting everybody, and he gets shot in the lung and he goes down. And the guy that was with him, he gets shot in the head, but he runs out of the place. So now, my brother's shot, Frank's shot, and this other guy that gets away is shot. And, I'm the only one that ain't shot. [Laughs.]

So what happens is I load the guy in the trunk. He's shot in the lung, and, you know, he's in bad shape, but he ain't dead yet. And I don't want to kill him yet.

See, you got to kind of understand where I'm coming from. I'm an outlaw, and a crook, and the option of going to the police just doesn't even exist. So I've got to handle this myself.

There was never a doubt in my mind that I was going to kill this guy for doing it. You know, people can think of me what they want. But when the evening started out, I was a victim.

Bottom line is, is if you put your hands on anybody in my family, you can expect trouble. And I think you know from talking to me what kind of guy I am. I'm serious about, I feel strongly about, the people I care about.

Anyway, not to justify anything. I planned on killing the guy the minute I found out what he had done. And, I tracked him down and I killed him.

The reason they got me for first degree murder is I had him for seven hours, because I didn't want to kill him until I caught up with this other guy that had gotten away, and I never did. So I ended up just saying, "Well, piss on him," and I killed him anyway. I stabbed him. I took him out into a state park and stabbed him to death, and buried him. And I get away. I go to Florida.

Anyway, when they finally catch up with me and they extradite me back, they got me charged with murder and kidnapping, and first degree assault, and kidnapping of this other guy that gets away, plus first degree assault on him. They got my brother charged the same, and they got my old lady charged.

Well, in order to get the charges dropped against my old lady and custody of my kid back for her, I pled guilty. Because, see, they took our son, and the only way I could get my son back and get custody for my old lady was if I pled guilty to first degree murder.

At the time, that should have only carried about thirteen years—a twenty to life sentence, but it's thirteen years/four months before you're eligible for parole. But in the meantime, they changed the laws, and, now, well, it's been twenty-one years so far.

I'm not trying to justify it or anything. I'm just letting you know how it happened. You know, I'm probably one of the few guys that actually accepts my situation and what happened to me and my life. I knew when I did it that this was going to be the end product of it. I made that choice, and I'm OK with it.

You know, if somebody was to rape my wife again, I'd probably do the same thing again, knowing the outcome.

Anyway, that's kind of the way that I got my beef.[*]

---

[*]Your "beef" is the crime of which you were convicted.

Now, when you ask if the crime I was convicted of was what I actually did, I don't really think so. I think it should have been a second degree murder. There were mitigating circumstances.

Like I said, when the evening first started, I was the victim. And later, the guy's wife filed for victim's compensation, and the state denied it and ruled that no first degree murder ever took place, that Frank had died as a direct result of a crime he perpetrated, to wit, the rape of Laura and the bar fight.

Well, you know, that's like having your cake and eating it too. If the state didn't need to pay them people, why should I be paying the price for first degree murder?

Then again, I don't really think I am. I've come to grips with the fact that really I'm paying for my whole lifestyle, and deservedly. If anybody deserves to be in prison, it's me. I mean, I got away with ten times more than I ever got caught.

So, in some bizarre way, you know, everything you put on the wheel of life seems to come back to you. So, whether I committed a first degree murder or a second degree murder really doesn't matter much. I mean, I've been an outlaw my whole life, and like I said, if anybody deserved to be in the joint, it was probably me.

OK, so that's what I'm in for. And like I said, I got twenty-one years in, and you know, I've made some changes in my life, and I've grown a lot. I think you probably can get an idea of that just from some of the classes we've done together.


*Tell me about the "hierarchy" of prisoners based on their crimes. What crimes garner a person the most respect, and what crimes cause a person to be the most disrespected? Are a person's crimes the sole or main determinant of where he'll be in the pecking order, or is this merely one of multiple factors that determines that? Does this informal system differ from one institution to another, or from one time to another, or has it pretty much existed in this form all over for a long time? Tell me not only about how a person comes to have a certain position in the pecking order, but also why it matters. How does life in prison differ if one is on top in this hierarchy, on the bottom, in the middle, etc.?*

Yeah, you ask some tough questions, Craig. [Laughs.]

OK, the pecking order. It's really not based on a guy's crimes, although a guy's crimes can automatically put him in the lower part of the pecking order. If you're a sex offender, a rapist, you're basically at the bottom of the food chain. If you're a child molester, you're at the bottom of the bottom of the food chain.

The pecking order does differ from one institution to another, but not as far as the crime thing. You know, there's a difference if you're in for a legitimate murder where you haven't killed some innocent bystander. I mean, none of us—we don't care for these guys that go in and whack somebody just so they can't tell on them for a stick-up, or kill a cab driver for a few lousy bucks, or kill the lady that works at a 7-Eleven store.

Them guys aren't much better than the chi-mos[*] really, as far as I'm concerned, and as far as most guys are concerned. They're probably about middle of the line guys, but I think the real deal is that just by the weakness of their personality, by the things that make them do those types of crimes and shit, that'll keep them stuck in the middle of the pecking order instead of rising to the top.

Most of the pecking order is about guys that have a history in the system, that have been confronted by the Man in a situation where, if you would have given up your friends or somebody, you could have got an easy situation or you could have got yourself out of trouble. But you hold your mud,[†] you go to the hole, or IMU, or whatever, and you don't tell on your friends, and if somebody puts their hands on you, you'll get at him.

You don't have to be tough. A lot of times people have this impression that only the tough guys are at the top of the pecking order, but in reality, there's a lot of guys on top of the pecking order that aren't very tough. They've just always been willing. They have a strong moral code.

I think it's pretty much the same as people on the streets. You guys look up to, you know, a police officer that will risk his life to do his job. Well, we do the same thing. You know, if a guy's willing to risk his life for his partners, you know, he gains a lot of respect. A lot of us have all been through riots together, and life and death situations.

You know, it's hard for you to imagine, because you come into this prison, but when we were in real prisons, a lot of us have had situations where if it wasn't for your partners' backing, you would have been the guy who was stabbed to death, you know, and that's how guys rise up through the pecking order.

Sometimes there's a given, you know, like, certain guys have respect coming, because they held their mud through the Sixties and Seventies, even the Eighties, and mostly it's something you have to earn. It isn't just given to you because you're in here for murder, you know, or you're in here for armed robbery, or you're a burglar. Those things automatically set you above a sex offender, but they don't really give you no props. It's all about holding your mud when the chips are down in situations in here. And that's how you get there.

And the way you carry yourself. God, people watch the way you carry yourself. I know guys that are at the top of the pecking order that have never been in a fight the whole time they've been in the joint, because they treat people with respect. But there's always that knowledge that they have to be treated with respect too, you know, and they're not afraid to step up to the plate.

---

[*]Child molesters.

[†]Resist the temptation to better your own position by giving the state information that it seeks.

So, yeah, the pecking order's kind of a funny thing. And it's elusive. I mean, there's guys around here that don't even know where they're at in the pecking order. A lot of guys think that they're the Fellahs.

Fuck, there's a bunch of guys in our club that think they're right on, and, you know, they probably think I'm a lump. [Laughs.] That's just the way it is.

But bottom line is I think most people rise to the top of the pecking order based on the way they conduct themselves on a day to day basis. You can trust them. You know if you tell them something it don't go any further.

I think they have the same qualities that you would look for in a friend, I really do, and that's the honest truth. That's just the way I see it.

You ask how does life in prison differ if one is on top in this hierarchy? Well, when you're on top of the pecking order, it's just a little easier, you know.

Actually, each joint is different. The pecking order thing works a little different in each joint.

See, in a joint like this, like WSR, for instance, automatically the Fellahs that are at the top of the pecking order can get access to PAP. Some of the guys even that aren't in the club, they have access to our office and stuff. They can come out there, and they can hang out and drink coffee and shit, and be a part of things.

I mean, there's money to be made, there's opportunity, you know, criminal and otherwise. There's jobs. A guy comes in, and he's a stand up dude, he automatically has action at getting a decent job, you know. Whereas, if you're at the bottom of the pecking order, hell, you get a job when you're the last guy, the last possible guy that can do the job. You know, you're, like, the one they take only when they have to take you. But if the guy's a regular, well shit, he's got guys that are at the top of the pecking order already in position that are going to try and get him the job. So, it's monetary, and it's quality of life.

You know, in a joint like this, you can use your place in the pecking order, actually to do a lot of good. See, like, some guys would feel like they couldn't go down and talk to the captain, because guys'll think, "Well, shit, he's up there talking to the captain. He might be telling." Shit, I can go up and talk to the captain. Everybody knows I ain't telling nobody nothing. I'll be up there trying to get somebody out of the hole.

Just the other day, one of our newest PAP members was sent to the hole. It was his first dirty UA,[*] but he's out of points, so he can be transferred out of here. So I went up to the captain, and I told him that it was important to us at PAP—our officers inside, plus our volunteers—that we at least throw some support behind the guy and ask the captain, if he's allowed to, to issue an override for him to stay here, that we'll try and be a positive influence for the guy.

So, you know, I used my position in the pecking order, not so much to influence the Man as just my ability to go there in the first place without the other prisoners being suspicious.

---

*Urinalysis. Drug test.

You know, somebody else might want to go up and say the same thing, but they can't, because, "Well, I can't go up there. They might think I'm telling," blah, blah, blah.

There's a lot of different ways a guy could use his position in the institution to do good and positive things, and I think you see a little bit of it.

Here's another example. When I was working up in the phone room,[*] they brought in some young people—some free world people—that they needed us to train so they could work in their office downtown. I had to use my position in the pecking order in order to maintain peace in the room, and keep it kind of separate, and not just anybody could do that. You know, people ride over other people.

So, that's just another way that you can use your position in the pecking order in a positive way. This institution might be the only place that you can do that.

But sometimes you got to be real careful when you're acting as a spokesperson for the population, or, you know, a go-between, because, if things don't go right, they'll always hold it against you. So you always got to think about it before you step up to the plate.

But, you know, number one, if you haven't got respect on the yard, you can't step up to the plate and speak for the guys. So, that's another way that the pecking order works.

*What is your opinion of the way the prisons you have been in deal with visitors? Are your people treated with politeness and dignity by staff? Are they treated rudely or demeaned? Are things set up to make visiting more convenient, or are visits only grudgingly allowed and made to be as inconvenient as possible? Are the rules concerning visits generally pretty reasonable from a security standpoint? Is a reasonable amount of time allowed for visits? Etc.*

OK, Walla Walla's[†] terrible. You know, like, your people'll drive all the way down to Walla Walla from Seattle, and when they get there, they are physically and mentally abused by the staff down there. I've seen old ladies—grandmothers—slammed against the wall and frisked.

There used to be this one bitch there who was, like, on a mission, and, to tell you how bad it was, I was up at the visiting room one night in Walla Walla when a guy's grandmother came in. Now, we're allowed two embraces, one when you get there, and one when you leave. And, they hugged when they came in.

---

[*]Telemarketing company. One of the private industry employers.

[†]The Washington State Penitentiary in Walla Walla is perhaps the most notorious of Washington's prisons. Just as WSR is associated in the prisoners' minds with rehabilitation and is a place that comparatively well-behaved veteran prisoners often end up as a kind of reward, Walla Walla is associated with violence, corruption, brutality, etc.

Well, they were talking, and what had happened is that the guy's sister had died. Well, Grandma started crying, and he stood up, and she stood up, and they were hugging. Only when they got done, they started to sit back down, and this broad went over and cancelled their visit.

You get an embrace when you come in, and an embrace when you leave. They had had their second embrace; they left. They'd only been there about a half hour. Just lost a family member. Didn't matter. Terminated the visit.

That place is like night and day from this place. This place here, your people come up, it's a little hassle to get in, but for the most part, these people treat our people really well. And they treat us pretty good. "Mr. McLaughlin can you do this?" "Mr. McLaughlin, your visitor is here."

Just a week ago, I had a step-brother I hadn't seen in twenty-two years come up. He's dying. He's had three strokes, plus, he's an alcoholic.

Well, he comes up. He hasn't been drinking, but his voice is a little slurred and his movements are different. And, there was some question whether he was sober or not. So the sergeant went out, and he couldn't detect no alcohol on him, and he realized that it was a health issue. You know, and so, before my visitor came in, the sergeant came over and said, "Hey, Jerry, I apologize for taking so long. I guess there was some issue, and I went out there and I realized that he's had three strokes, and I apologize for the delay." That wouldn't happen at Walla Walla.

Clallam Bay?* Well, let's see, Clallam Bay. It was so-so, you know, just such a long-ass drive, and, I don't know, it's just different. They're not as bad as Walla Walla, but they're not as nice as here.

For the most part, I think, a lot of times, our people feel like they're put upon by the administration when they come up to visit, and so, in part, do we. We tend to be defensive of our people and stuff. But when you look at it, in the entire picture, you know, I mean, this is a prison. And when you come up here, you got to expect to be shook down and to be inconvenienced. I mean, that's basic. If they didn't, we'd have guns and bombs in this fucking place. You've got to be realistic.

*One time, a prisoner at a PAP meeting expressed indignation that, in his opinion, his being granted parole was being made conditional on his showing remorse for what he had done and his giving some indication that he has been rehabilitated. As far as he was concerned, he should just have a set amount of time to serve, and once he's served it, that's it. It should be nobody's*

---

*Clallam Bay Corrections Center. Maybe not quite as notorious as Walla Walla, but certainly not a place that is spoken of favorably by the prisoners.

*business whether he's remorseful, whether he's a changed man, whether he intends to resume a life of crime on the outside, etc. On the other hand, I would think that the average person in society would think that these things are extremely relevant, that prisoners should not be loosed back on the public if they show no awareness that their behavior was wrong and no awareness that they ought not resume such behavior. What are your thoughts on this? Is the public correct to make your readmission into society conditional on your satisfying them that you are no longer a threat to others, no longer a criminal? Or is it somehow insulting or inappropriate for them to even attempt to ascertain if you are rehabilitated?*

Well, you know, Craig, I don't know if you heard the whole statement, or if you understand the sentiment I believe this guy must have been trying to express. What you have is a system where the more recently sentenced prisoners come under the SRA.* OK, SRA is determinant sentencing. When you get done with that sentence, whether you're rehabilitated or not, they're letting you back out onto the streets. We didn't decide that; society decided that.

But there's also a small segment of the population in here, including me, that are still under the old guidelines, before the determinant sentencing. We're no different than them other guys; we were just sentenced at a different time.

Now, when we were originally given our sentences, we were afforded an opportunity for rehabilitation. We had ways to prove to the parole board that we were rehabilitated. You know, we had programs that we could go to to get some help.

Now, society has turned their back on us, especially the guys that are under the old guidelines, and have said, "Well, piss on them guys. They don't need education. They don't need work. They don't need the type of programs that existed."

The education, the work, the training, and all the other things that used to be available, was actually guaranteed. You had a right to expect to be rehabilitated when you came to prison. Now they took away all the funding for that. That shit does not exist any more.

Because WSR is the only prison you come to, you're under the assumption that, you know, guys have programs and shit like we've got. They don't.

Plus, even here, society doesn't pay for this shit, like the class that we give, the stuff that we do at PAP. Most of the self-help programs around here, from the stress-anger management to the stock program, are all programs that were developed and funded by inmates. They didn't have nothing to do with the state.

We've done what we could ourselves, in spite of what society has tried to do by turning their back on us. They resist funding for education and the rest of them programs. Well, if you're going to take those programs away, why should you expect us to be rehabilitated?

---

*The Sentencing Reform Act of 1981. This change in Washington's sentencing laws is something that will come up several times in the interviews with the prisoners. Anyone sentenced before the act is an "old guidelines" prisoner; anybody sentenced after is an "SRA" prisoner.

Craig, what I think the guy is trying to say is, if you're going to take all those programs away from us, and you're going to set up a system that's designed to run people through these warehouses—and that's what the SRA does—that isn't on us. We're not the ones that did away with the programs.

See, you asked on this question if society should expect us to come out rehabilitated. Hell yes, I think society should expect us to come out rehabilitated. They should be worried about the type of product they're putting back into the community.

But you know the old saying, "You get what you pay for," and if you're unwilling to make an effort on behalf of rehabilitation, if you're unwilling to spend anything on it, you know, why would you expect anybody to be rehabilitated?

In fact, even the word "rehabilitation" was stricken from the law. The funding for rehabilitation no longer exists. There are no funds for it, period.

There's only one segment of the population that still receives any kind of rehabilitation, or what they call "treatment." And that's the sex offenders over at Twin Rivers.[*]

Nobody's spending any money for rehabilitation. They give us a basic education, an eighth grade education right now, or at most a GED They won't even allow you to fucking try to do anything better than that. We used to have the barber college around here. We used to have a lot of different vocational programs where guys could acquire a skill.

Now you have to go to work in one of the private industries in order to acquire a skill. And that sounds like it would be good, except for guys that come in that have under two or three years. They're not eligible to get into it. You can't get a job around here unless you've got over three years left, and most of the guys when they show up here just don't have that kind of time. So, the jobs fall in the hands of the old guideline guys who are stuck in the system.

You know, I think the guy was expressing a little indignation about society's being blind to this, and obviously in your question, you're even a little blind to it. You in society have the belief that rehabilitation is available for prison inmates. Well, we've got a lot of good stuff around here, but at most prisons, nothing like this exists. Nothing.

And I try to express that in all the classes that I teach. We rock ourselves to sleep when we come up here to WSR. Hell, you can walk in here and go out to PAP, to Lifers,[†] to the

---

[*]Twin Rivers Corrections Unit. Twin Rivers is part of the same complex of prisons in Monroe that includes WSR. It contains a treatment facility for sex offenders.

[†]Concerned Lifers Organization. Lifers is one of the prisoner run programs at WSR. Like PAP, it is not specific to any one race, ethnic group, or religion. And contrary to its name, it is not limited to prisoners serving a life sentence. It has a much larger membership than PAP, as Lifers accepts pretty much anyone who wants in.

Whereas PAP is primarily a social and educational program, Lifers includes more of a political element, writing letters to the governor's office and state legislature, hosting talks and discussions by state

IOAT,* all the rest of that shit. Well, this don't exist anywhere but here. This is like another planet. This might be the best joint in the country.

And how much longer is that going to be? They're moving us into double cells here in about, oh, a month, and their intention is to raise the security level here, make this a close custody institution.

Well, right now, if you look at the close custody institutions, the level of violence and trouble in close custody institutions is, I mean, it's as high as it's ever been. There are stabbings, riots, the whole nine yards.

I'm not saying that this place will just automatically go chaotic when it goes close custody. I think what they'll originally try and do is bring in guys that are trying to program, and that'll be to appease our volunteer base. But eventually, you know, especially when DuCharme† leaves, this place is going to phase out, Craig. You're a witness to the last island of rehabilitation.

And, like I said, the rehabilitation that's here is stuff that we do. Society ain't giving us none of this. I mean, I shouldn't say "society," because you guys are part of society, and without you guys' support, you know, the volunteers and stuff, we couldn't do what we do. And it certainly wouldn't last as long as it's going to last before they finally strangle it.

But the bottom line is, you know, you're talking to a guy that maybe had been out of Walla Walla for six months or something, and telling him about, "Society has a right to expect you to be rehabilitated," and he's been having his ass kicked on a daily basis for the last five, ten years, fifteen years, however many years it's been, and trying to understand how that's rehabilitating.

You know, society's actually out of line in assuming that rehabilitation's taking place if they're unwilling to fucking foot the bill for it. And it won't come cheap. There ain't going to be no easy fix for it.

---

legislators visiting the prison, etc.

Technically, in its very early stages in the '70s, PAP was an off-shoot of Lifers. Since there are no programs that are specifically for whites the way there are programs for blacks, Native Americans, etc., periodically the white supremacists congregate in the racially neutral Lifers and/or PAP and attempt to influence one or the other toward becoming a more racial program. They wielded considerable power in Lifers for a temporary period fairly recently. It has been a much longer time since they were a threat to PAP. Certainly during my time in PAP, Jerry and the other leaders have stood solidly and success-fully against any such influence.

*Indians of All Tribes. This is another prisoner-run program at WSR.

†Superintendent Ken DuCharme, a liberal administrator who played a crucial role in making WSR such a unique institution. He was set to retire shortly.

But what's happening right now is people are turning their back on it. They're assuming that the institution in itself, the harsh punishment, that type of stuff, is going to be the rehabilitation. Well, come on. Two hundred years of tough prisons—you don't think prisons were tough? Shit, prisons were tough when I first got to the joint. All it does is make tough convicts, that's all it does.

And, it's like, every, oh, every twenty or thirty, forty years, society forgets it, and they have to be reminded. And the only way that that happens is they'll close the door on all the rehabilitation, and kick our ass for awhile, until, I guess our life becomes so unbearable, we decide we'd rather be dead than to continue living like this, and then all hell'll break loose, and shit'll happen. And that's what'll bring about change again. Then the pendulum for rehabilitation and stuff will swing back again.

But, you know, I think what you heard out of that guy was just his frustration at, you know, "Why should society expect me to be rehabilitated?" They don't expect it from the thousands of guys that come through this system under the SRA that have a determinant sentence. They get five years, ten years, whatever it is, and when they get done with it, they get out. There ain't no ifs, ands, or buts about it. They're getting out.

And yet you're going to tell other guys that they've got to be rehabilitated, and you don't have any rehabilitation programs available for them. Why would you expect them to be rehabilitated?

It's almost ludicrous to me. I almost agree with the guy.

I think the way you heard it was a little bit different than the way he meant it. You know, I think he was kind of comparing himself to the SRA guys. Why is it just us? There's, like, a couple hundred of us left in the system, and we have to jump through these invisible hoops, with no help from society.

And they took away most of the hoops—the programs—that we could have jumped through anyway. You have to have something to mark. If I go in front of a parole board and say, "Hell, I'm rehabilitated," they'll say, "Well, what have you done?" "Well, I didn't do anything, 'cause there wasn't nothing to do." "Well, then how do we know you're rehabilitated?" It's a big fucking circle; why should I have to do it, if nobody else in the criminal justice system has to? Whatever happened to equal treatment under the law?

I don't want to be treated any better than anybody else. But I certainly don't deserve to be treated any worse than anybody else.

I don't know, I think maybe some time we need to sit down and talk in depth about this. Maybe we can use it as a discussion topic for one of our PAP classes: "SRA as opposed to old guidelines." Or, "Rehabilitation: Then and now." That might be a good idea.

*Compare race relations inside of prison with those of present day society outside of prison. Is there more racism? Less? Do people tend to segregate themselves by race more? Less? Etc.*

You know, it's a strange question. Each one of the institutions in this state has a different chemistry, or a different grouping of people, and wherever you go, the problems and situations are different.

When you're in a real lockdown joint, where guys are doing hard time, and convicts are convicts, and guys are hard, there's a certain amount of racial tension, based on turf really. You know, everything's about the drugs, everything's about the money, everything's about respect. And, when things get out of balance, when one group has it over the other groups, there's tension, and it seems to be drawn along racial lines.

Right now, one of the problems in a place like Walla Walla is you got young gang members, and old guys, the old convicts like myself who really don't understand where these kids are coming from, and so it's like bumping heads for turf all the time.

And young kids, their whole motivation thing is different. You know, the reason they get up in the morning has absolutely nothing to do with the reason we get up in the morning.

So, it's really kind of hard to even say it's just on racial lines. It's more about age.

But, there's different groupings. I mean, a lot of the younger guys weld with the other younger guys, and that's probably the way it should be.

I mean, I'm pretty much a crossover. I grew up in the central district in Seattle; I lived around blacks all my life, in juvenile institutions and in the joint, so I cross over real good.

But, I got to be honest with you, the racial tension exists in prison. But I'm not sure that it's as bad as it is on the streets.

You know, it's different. It's different at best. And, like in an institution like this, it hardly even exists. Oh, there's guys around that don't like blacks; there's blacks around that don't like whites. But they're not a majority and they don't have much of a voice. The guys that are doing positive shit around here are in the majority, so the guys that feel that other stuff, they put it in the background when they're in an institution like this.

Now, it's different at, like, Clallam Bay. At Clallam Bay, you have what they call the "quadrant" system, where you got real small living units, and you're on top of each other all day long. So there are strong racial tensions, but, you know, it's more of a general tension, just based on the close proximity.

You know, like, there's forty of you in a small tank about the size of the room that we have our meetings in, and you're there or in your cell for twenty-some hours a day. You've got a cell you can go to, or you can sit in that big room with all them guys, and that's it.

Just like in a relationship, or a marriage, you know, there's things that people do that aggravate you after awhile. Like with the husband and wife, it's leaving the toilet seat up, or the toothpaste cap off.

Well, that shit becomes real important when you're in real close quarters, you know, under a microscope like that. You're in a glassed-in window with a cop sitting there staring at you all fucking day long. It's a different form of insanity.

And even though there's a lot of tension there, I wouldn't say it's truly racial. Like, some whites might get into a fight with some blacks, but I don't really think it's racial. It's just the conditions that bring out a lot of hate.

You know, 'cause I was hating everybody. I didn't care if they was black or white, sky blue or pink. After about five years up there, man, I was hating.

Soon after I received this tape, I would see the prison from a whole new perspective. Jerry played a key role in that experience.

I mentioned to him I was looking for part time work to supplement my meager income, and he told me about an opening at the prison. It wasn't a prison staff job, but rather a position with one of the private industry employers that uses prison labor.

It was a telemarketing company. Jerry had worked there in the past and had been, not surprisingly, one of their top sellers. They needed at least one outside person there at all times during business hours as a supervisor. At present they had only one full time supervisor, Steve.* Any day he couldn't make it out to the prison, they couldn't work. So they were looking to hire someone to give him a little relief.

Jerry put a word in with the owner and with Steve, and soon I met with Steve and was offered the position. Before I could start, however, the prison required that I go through a week of orientation. All non-prisoner employees of the private industries must attend the first week of the two-week orientation and training that new prison staff members receive. (The second week is weapons training and matters that are relevant to correctional officers only.)

My particular orientation "class" consisted of about fifteen correctional officers (about ten male and five female), three nurses (all of whom smoked, I noted), and two of us civilians who were going to work with private industry employers.

Maybe 75% of the week was taken up with generic litigation-avoidance matters such as workplace safety, sexual harassment, CPR training, etc. that had nothing specifically to do with prison. (The safety video, for instance, was mostly set in an office, and warned us about such things as carrying boxes that are too heavy.) Most of this was predictable and utterly dull.

---

*I have changed the name.

Some of the material more directly relevant to prison was more interesting. Numerous staff members were brought in to address us, and their attitudes toward the prisoners varied considerably.

At one extreme was a no-nonsense woman who made no effort to conceal her bitterness and disapproval as she barked out her warnings about the prisoners and their nefarious ways. "Always remember, you're here eight hours a day and this is just one part of your life. They're here twenty-four hours a day and they spend that time plotting how they can take advantage of any weakness they see in you." Better paranoid than sorry was her message; she did everything she could to convince the trainees to see the prisoners as the most conniving and ruthless of adversaries.

She even tossed in some gratuitous remarks about how WSR's temporary change from one-man cells to two-man cells meant it was hopeless they would ever prevent consensual homosexual activity. She said this with such palpable disgust that I wasn't sure if it was more insulting of prisoners or homosexuals.

Others offered milder versions of her antagonistic message, including one who warned against ever entering prison with a rehabilitative intent. "Virtually every one of these guys who gets out is coming back, and nothing you can do is going to change that. If you even try, all you're going to do is open yourself up to being exploited in one way or another."

On the other hand, there were also messages of a different sort. Don't take it upon yourself to "punish" the prisoners; their being in prison in the first place is itself the punishment. Don't ever give a prisoner a "bum beef" (file a false report of his violating prison rules), even if you are convinced he is a dangerous or evil person but you just don't have the goods on him yet. If you're right in your read on him, he'll get himself into verifiable trouble soon enough and you can give him a legitimate beef. Address the prisoners with respect. Don't verbally abuse and provoke them. Whenever possible, use request wording rather than command wording ("Could you step this way?" instead of "You! Come over here! Now!").

The priorities, they told us, were the safety and well-being of non-prisoners first, the safety and well-being of prisoners second, and the safeguarding of property third. So, for example, you were not to put yourself or another staff member at risk in order to break up a fight and keep a prisoner from being injured or killed. Similarly, if the only way to prevent an escape was to harm a prisoner, then you were to do so, for an escape meant risk to members of the surrounding community. On the other hand, if the only way to prevent destruction of prison property was to harm a prisoner, you were not to do so.

During breaks, I spoke with the correctional officer trainees. The bulk of them came from one of two backgrounds. Several had just done a stint in the military, and this line of work was the closest they could find to what they were used to. Several others had been employed in the timber industry, and were now forced to make a career change due to recent downturns and layoffs. Some of the latter were worried enough to ask when they could expect their first paycheck, as they and their families were already at the financial breaking point.

In general, these new officers were not viscerally anti-prisoner. They were wary, and listened intently to all they were told about what to expect, but only rarely did any of them voice anger or malice toward prisoners in general. At least as often, they made statements that could be construed as sympathetic toward the prisoners.

That they would ultimately adopt the conventional adversarial attitude due to the peer pressure of veteran officers and the hostile behavior of prisoners toward them was entirely possible (though those factors are much less prevalent at WSR than at most prisons). But for the most part they were not entering with that attitude.

The telemarketing room was on the second floor of the cell blocks building. There were about twenty little work stations where the prisoners sat. At one end of the room were two offices side-by-side with glass walls. One was the supervisor office where Steve, and now I, worked. The other housed the master computer that controlled the whole operation and automatically dialed out the calls for all the work stations. (The prisoners making the calls had no access to phone numbers or addresses or any such information about the people they were talking to.) This master computer was operated by a prisoner named Barney.*

Barney was an odd duck. He was reputed to be something of a computer savant, and had managed to make himself highly valuable not only to this employer, but apparently to the prison administration as well. It was understood that he was well "protected" by the DOC. (In that respect only, he reminded me vaguely of the Tim Robbins character in "The Shawshank Redemption" who uses his accounting skills to become indispensable to the warden.)

Barney was a short, roly-poly, fifty-ish man with a brush cut and big glasses. He had a verbal awkwardness and a kind of nervous goofiness that marked him as "off" in some hard-to-specify way. I spoke to him enough to infer that he had at least a reasonably high IQ, and certainly he displayed the attitude that he was superior to the common prisoners, intellectually and otherwise. I had the feeling from early on that there was a lot going on inside of him, most of it not good.

He liked to carry himself as an "old school" con, a veteran who had survived the toughest prisons and maintained his place at the top of the pecking order. He had

---

*I have changed the name.

disdain for the youngsters and the wannabes who didn't properly respect or understand the old ways, or who hadn't earned the status he had.

This self-image was, I found out from PAP prisoners who knew him, largely a crock. To them, his close alliance with the administration made him a quasi-rat. Plus, based on his crime, he had not entered prison with high status to begin with. He had committed murder, which, granted, is usually considered an honorable crime. But allegedly he was a clumsy psychopathic hit man who had shot up a restaurant and wantonly taken multiple lives in a futile effort to kill his assigned prey. Most of the prisoners had disdain for the kind of criminal and the kind of person he was.

Steve was a gangly, middle-aged, low key fellow who mostly got along fine with the prisoners. He seemed neither thrilled nor bothered by my presence. He showed me in his slow, unenthusiastic, repetitive way what I needed to know (which was virtually nothing), and mostly stuck around anyway, making my presence superfluous.

From the very first day, I realized my interaction with these prisoners would be much different from what I was used to at PAP. I wouldn't say it was adversarial per se, but it lacked the underlying appreciation and good will of PAP. At PAP, there was a certain attitudinal presumption in my favor, whereas here they were more neutral toward me.

The workplace atmosphere held a certain tension, and I didn't like it. My duties were pretty minimal—mostly they just needed an outside person to be physically present to keep an eye on things. But I wasn't comfortable in even this mild supervisory relationship compared to the relative social equality I was used to at PAP.

But as time went on, I got along with most of the prisoners there tolerably well, and a few of them I got to know and became friendly with. It helped that one of the workers was a PAP prisoner that I had spoken with several times and liked. It was good to have a familiar face there, someone I could turn to if I had a question or if I sensed some kind of trouble brewing. (Unfortunately, he was transferred to another prison not long after I started.)

Actually, there were several other prisoners there who were nominal members of PAP, but they only came to meetings maybe once a year, because Wednesday was a work day and they chose making money over participating in the program.

What helped even more is when PAP buddies of mine would stop by to say hello. It wasn't every day, but there were a handful of guys who stopped by when I was on my own there, just to have a cup of coffee, shoot the shit for maybe fifteen minutes, and make sure I was OK. I really appreciated that.

(The telemarketing room was at the end of a long corridor. In order to enter the corridor, a prisoner had to be buzzed in from a guard tower. Before letting him in, the officer in the tower would first call us to ask if we wanted him sent through.

So the office phone would ring, Steve or I would pick up, and an officer would say, "Inmate Smith wants to know if you need him to work today," or "Inmate Jones would like to fill out an application," and we would approve their admittance or not.

The exception was Jerry. When he wanted in, the officer would simply call to tell us, "McLaughlin's on his way," and moments later Jerry would stride into the room like he owned the place.)

The longer I was there, the more I settled in and got comfortable. However, two incidents stood out to me as potentially hurting my standing with the prisoners.

The first occurred on one of the first occasions when I was there without Steve. I was hanging out back in the office, as was my habit, rather than circulating around the room looking over everyone's shoulder. I could still look through the glass and have a general idea what was going on, though.

I had noticed that some of the guys had been kidding around with each other, and things were a little louder than usual. A couple of them had been wrestling around a bit, in a seemingly good-natured way.

Prisoners came into the office periodically to get a script, ask a question, or just to make conversation to give themselves a break from the phones. On this occasion, one of them happened to mention casually that so-and-so and so-and-so were getting a little boisterous and that it might not be a bad idea for me to make an appearance on the work floor.

I didn't immediately head out there, because it didn't seem urgent and I was finishing up some paperwork. But the same prisoner came by a little later and reminded me, noting that it wouldn't sound good on the sales calls if the customer could hear these guys carrying on in the background.

So shortly thereafter, I asked the two prisoners in question to come into the office. I told them, "I don't mind you guys talking, but I have to ask you to kind of keep it under control. No big deal, but I've been told twice now that you're getting a little loud and roughhousing out there, so I'd appreciate it if you'd cool it so as not to interfere with the work."

Well, that really set off the younger (he was about 20) of the two prisoners. "Who's the rat?! You mean some son of a bitch really came in here and ratted to you like that? Mother fucker! He better hope I don't find out who it is! Might as well just put a skirt on him!" and on and on.

He went back to his work station shaking his head in disgust. The other prisoner (he was about 35) remained behind with me. He bore a solemn expression. "I have to ask you something, because this could potentially cause a lot of trouble," he told me. "I need to know if someone really told you what you said. Because I doubt we have a rat in here. I figure maybe you said that so it wouldn't sound so much like it was you coming down on us, like you were really just responding to a complaint. If so, that's fine and all, but you need to let me know that now, because I don't think you realize what it would mean if everybody has to distrust each other and think we have a rat in here."

I told him that I hadn't made it up, but that it hadn't been told to me in any particularly ominous way to get anyone in trouble. I said it was more of a general reminder that the supervisor should come out on the floor occasionally to minimize the chances of guys getting too loud. He nodded, but he was not convinced.

To make matters worse, several days later on a day I wasn't there, the owner was remotely monitoring some of the calls from his home (the system was set up to allow this), and he happened to hear the younger of those two prisoners carrying on loudly in the background. He deemed it unprofessional, and sent word to Steve to have him terminated.

My first thought when I found out was that I was going to be blamed for this. I made it a point to talk to the older prisoner, assuring him I'd never said a word to the owner about what had happened on that earlier shift. I explained about the owner listening in and hearing things for himself, and I asked him to relay that to the departed prisoner. He frowned. "If you didn't say anything to get him fired, there's nothing I need to tell him," he said unhelpfully.

So now I had to think there were at least some prisoners speculating about a rat in their midst, or about me making up a story about a rat in their midst, or about me getting one of them in trouble with the owner, or about God knows what. It was a misunderstanding, but one that gave me a vague uneasiness that I had lost some ground with the prisoners.

The second incident involved particularly bad timing on my part. I was routinely five minutes or so late into work. Frankly, given that I was getting little better than minimum wage to make a long commute to a somewhat uncomfortable workplace, I wasn't approaching the job in a maximally responsible, meticulous way. I was considering leaving soon anyway.

But on this occasion, I was more like twenty minutes late. And when I got there, a correctional officer tipped me off that I'd be better off turning around. "Press has been sniffing around," he let me know, "Phone room's closed for the day."

I got a hold of Steve on his cell phone an hour or so later, and he filled me in. A local television station had sent a camera crew to the telemarketing room looking to do an exposé. I don't believe they had anything specific; I think the very fact that the business existed—that a prison would countenance felon telemarketers calling unsuspecting citizens—was something they considered scandalous.

Steve found out in time to close things down, and to send the prisoners away. He told me he'd waited a bit for me, but then left to avoid the cameras, asking the guard to let me know to stay away if and when I showed up. When the people from the television station got there, all they found was a locked door and a darkened room. There were no prisoners and no one from the company to accost. The best they could get—I watched the story on the news that evening—were a few seconds of prison officials stammering and assuring viewers that yes, if the public disapproved of this kind of business operating from a prison, they'd certainly have to give that serious consideration.

Steve said that clearly someone had informed the station about the business and suggested they do a story on it. He asked me where I had been. I told him I was late, that I arrived right after he left. I don't know if he was convinced I was lying, but I know he was suspicious.

The next day the prisoners talked with disgust about the media hatchet job, and about how they must have been tipped off. Though they didn't say so, I have to think some of them made the same connection Steve did, that it was at least suggestive that the day the press raids the place is the day I don't show up for work.

Did these two misunderstandings ruin my reputation in the workplace? Did they have no significant impact at all? Something in between? Given the unfamiliar, paranoia-inducing environment of prison, it was impossible to know.

It felt creepy, not knowing. I felt like I needed to explain myself, but that doing so would only make me look all the more suspicious.

In most other respects, I was getting along increasingly well with the guys, connecting with a few of them. But these two incidents left me very uncertain about where I stood in their eyes.

I didn't have to worry about it much longer. I got fired shortly thereafter. Steve called me at home one day. "What in the world happened yesterday?" he asked me. I had no idea what he was referring to.

The owner, he informed me, was furious. "He says he found out you let Jerry make private phone calls from the office yesterday. The prison can shut us down for that. That's a big deal, especially after we're already getting heat in the media."

The allegation was false, and I told him so. Jerry had dropped by for a few minutes, but I certainly hadn't "let" him make phone calls from the office. And I had been sitting with him the entire brief time he was there, so I knew he hadn't surreptitiously used the phone without my permission. There wasn't even the slightest ambiguity about it; there was zero chance I was guilty.

"Well," he said, "In any case, business is off and we're probably not going to work as many shifts a week as we have been. He said to let you know we don't need you to come in any more. We really don't need another supervisor after all."

I was mildly upset about the false accusation, but not about losing the job. It was actually something of a relief to get out of there, especially in a way that didn't involve a loss of face with the prisoners that could extend to my involvement with PAP.

As soon as I got to the PAP meeting that Wednesday, Jerry let me know (confirmed later by some other prisoners) that it was Barney who got me fired. "Barney lied on you," Jerry told me. Barney had made up the story about me letting Jerry make phone calls from the office, and the owner believed him.

I can't say I was surprised. I had not had an openly antagonistic relationship with Barney, but obviously he was a dangerous kook who was capable of anything.

Why he wanted to get rid of me I'm not at all sure. I wonder if he thought I was getting too close to finding out something I wasn't supposed to know. He had access to the Internet and to the outside world in a way other prisoners did not. He knew everything about that company and its finances. Perhaps he was involved in graft either on his own or in cahoots with the owner. The prisoners had been complaining their pay was short, and I suspect they may have been right.

Jerry told me that serious consideration had been given to retaliating on my behalf against Barney. But in the end, they had decided against it, for two reasons. First, he was such a pet of the administration that anyone who laid a hand on him would be immediately shipped off to IMU or worse. Second, the satisfaction of dealing with him appropriately had to be weighed against the ramifications for private industry jobs at the prison. "These jobs are precious to us," Jerry explained, "They bring money into the joint. These are excellent paying jobs compared to the state jobs. We can't do anything to jeopardize that."

I admit that in a small way I kind of liked the idea that they would even consider avenging my firing, but mostly I felt like this shit was getting way too heavy. I don't come from a world where you talk about assaulting or killing a person because he got you fired from some two-bit job that you wanted out of anyway. You maybe grumble about it, and you get another job. This other stuff was crazy. I didn't want any part of it. I didn't want to have any responsibility for it.

"OK," I said, "I guess I'm a little flattered and all. But if I get a vote, I definitely don't want you to go after the guy. It's not that big a deal. Please. I don't want to take revenge, and I don't want you guys to take revenge."

Jerry corrected me. "No, see, there's a little bit of that—the personal regard for you. But no, that's not what it's about. It's the principle of being a rat and lying on somebody like that. People hate to see that go unpunished. It's not about you; it could have been anybody. It's the principle."

Business did fall off. The telemarketing room reduced its hours, then eliminated whole days. Within a few months, the owner shut it down entirely.

Several of the guys I had worked with started coming to PAP regularly, now that their Wednesdays were free. Two, in fact, joined the book project.

Though I had had considerable uncertainty about how I was regarded by the prisoners in the telemarketing workplace, I will say that after the fact any I encountered were consistently friendly toward me. I'm sure it helped that I went out the way I did, martyred by the wrongdoing of a very unpopular prisoner. "That Barney is a snake," one of them said, "I always knew it, and what he did to get you fired just confirmed it. He's a snake." "I was totally disgusted with the place after what they did to you," said another, "I quit inside a month, and that was the main reason."

At one point, I had a longer talk with one of the non-PAP prisoners I'd always liked. He was an old con, and based on the way he carried himself and whom he associated with, I inferred he had a high position in the prison pecking order.

He was one of the prisoners who had met to decide whether to take vengeance against Barney. "You don't know how close Jerry came to going after him when he found out what he did to you," he confided to me a year later, "Jerry's a very serious guy about shit like that. In fact, years ago, there's no doubt what he would have done. The old Jerry. Barney would have been history. No doubt. With Jerry's temper? No doubt. But that's how much he's changed. He can hold off now. He can control himself. He hated to do it, to let him get away with it, but it's what he felt he had to do. But make no mistake about how Jerry and the rest of us feel about what happened, or about what that piece of shit deserves."

Not long after that conversation, I ran into another of the former telemarketing workers. I made some passing reference to Barney getting me fired, which I had long assumed to be common knowledge, and he looked genuinely surprised. "Barney?" he said, "I doubt it. No, Steve's the one who made that up about you and Jerry to get you fired. You may not know it, but there were actually three or four assistant supervisors before you that were brought in for the exact same reason you supposedly were—to share some of the burden with Steve so he wouldn't have to be there all the time. None of them lasted even as long as you did, because Steve always found some way to have them fired. He was threatened by the idea of having to share any of the authority. He didn't want another supervisor in there."

Office politics, petty dishonesty, conflicting rumors. Nothing particularly unusual about any of that, except that it occurred in an environment where a person could realistically lose his life if he were on the wrong side of the wrong story.

# JIMI—February 1998

*"I remember feeling less than human, as if nobody cared that I was going through this terrifying and lonely time. I wasn't anyone's son or brother in juvenile detention. I was a nobody and nobody cared, or so I thought."*

I n the early stages of the project, Jimi was clearly the most eager of the prisoner participants. While many of the prisoners had to be coaxed to give me any responses—and many others fell by the wayside entirely—Jimi got into the spirit of the project and more than held up his end of the dialogue.

The following is my third set of questions and comments sent in to him, with his written responses.

*Read back over your answer to my question from my most recent set that I sent you where I ask you to tell me about any occasions where you've positively influenced any fellow prisoners. You address several matters related to the question—such as whether the perception of prisons as places where criminals mostly adversely influence each other is accurate, whether prisons provide appropriate programs and such to facilitate prisoners improving themselves, the ways peer pressure can make improving oneself harder to do in prison, how common or uncommon it is for prisoners to work on improving themselves, etc.—but interestingly, you say virtually nothing directly responsive to the core of the question, certainly not with any details. There are no stories about how your example, or your friendship, or your contribution to certain programs or whatever might have had a positive impact on some fellow prisoners and helped them toward a better path.*

*Yet from talking to other prisoners, and even from talking to you in the past, I know that you have been very active in many programs at WSR, and that you have done much to help those around you. It's good to be humble, but don't be afraid to open up to the readers and let them know more about what you're about and how you've chosen to live in there.*

How might my influence have had a positive impact on another inmate's life? Well let me tell you, Craig, this is a hard one to answer, because I can't judge my influence on another human being except by my own perception, which would appear presumptuous. But I'll try anyway.

I believe I have had a positive impact on many inmates over the years, especially so in the past 4 to 5 years. I live my life with patience and genuine concern for others, which has on several occasions rewarded me with heartfelt gratitude from others. I have helped many inmates in teaching my trade (barbering). I was a teacher's aide in a college barber school in Walla Walla.

I have directed inmates in directions I knew to be positive and healthy, mainly because this guidance was given to me from other inmates further along in the journey.

Every year at Christmas I spend what I can afford, even more sometimes, to pass out gifts and send cards to those I've known through my years in prison.

I've reached a point in my prison experience where I seem to live and breathe important issues concerning my rehabilitation. I often find myself passing on to others the information I'm learning, and with those inmates who share the same interests and goals as myself, I frequently engage them for their input, as I like to think they do the same. I enjoy the feeling I get inside when I'm growing, and further enjoy passing the information on.

*Your answers about juvenile detention so far tell me that you believe that even though you were seemingly responding to nothing else, even though your mother was not ill-motivated in turning to that as a last resort, and even though you met a mentor there who was an important and positive influence on you, it still did you more harm than good to be placed in that world. Tell me about why it's so bad. What would have been a better parenting decision from your mother in those circumstances than to do what she did? Besides what an individual parent can do, tell me more about what society as a whole could do that would be a better way of addressing this problem than what it does now with the juvenile detention system.*

What's so "bad" about the decision my mom made and what might she have done better? @#$%+&*! You just love to dig up the tough stuff, don't you Craig?

I suppose one thing I remember feeling more than anything else was the loss of identity. I remember feeling less than human, as if nobody cared that I was going through this terrifying and lonely time. I wasn't anyone's son or brother in juvenile detention. I was a nobody and nobody cared, or so I thought.

I suppose my Mom could have made my Dad take me, or tried to get him to spend more time with me. She could have made me deal with the people whose garage I'd burglarized.

I really don't remember being real responsive to anything except the thought of being with my Dad. I wanted desperately to live with my dad because it was so tough living in a house full of women: my mom, my sister, and her friends who were always staying with us, not to mention my mom's friends who were always at the house. There wasn't any man around any more and that sucked!

The system now is foreign to me; I don't know what they're trying with kids these days, so I really can't tell you what the system now should do. I think mentors are very important, but they have to be delicately matched up with the children. Kids want someone they trust and respect, and in this day and age that's not an easy find.

*What's the most genuinely and deeply frightened you've ever been in prison?*

The most frightened I've ever been was at Walla Walla in 1985. I was transferred to the Walls* for assaulting an officer. At the Walls, I was placed into segregation to await transfer to IMU.

On the morning I was transferred to IMU, I was escorted by four officers to the hospital. I was told I was going to IMU. In the hospital, we were joined by several more officers, including a sergeant and a lieutenant. We waited in an exam room for approximately ten minutes until a door opened up and several more officers entered, literally crowding the room, one of which was operating a video camera.

A male nurse came in and the officers tackled me to the floor and pulled my coveralls off to my ankles. They'd been tied by the sleeves around my waist. I tried to fight, but I couldn't do anything but spit the blood in my mouth on them. The officers pinned me in a bent over position and the male nurse inserted his gloved finger into my rectum and twisted several times before removing it. They didn't offer to let me clean myself. They pulled up my underpants and coveralls and escorted me to IMU. All of this was done with my ankles shackled, hands cuffed to a belly chain.

As if that wasn't scary enough, I was then escorted to IMU, which is total solitary confinement. That experience left me afraid of the system that was responsible for my well being. If they could get away with that, what else would they do?

*How do you plan to spend your very first week or two of freedom when you get out?*

What will I do the first week or two after I get out? I suppose I should know that, seeing how I'm at the threshold of the rest of my life in society.

The first thing I'll do is stop for a freedom meal, probably on the way home. Once home, I'll take a shower and change into some clothes that have never been inside a prison. Next I'll hop on the phone and call about a dozen people and let them know I'm out. Over the next few days I'll be spending time seeing friends I haven't seen in years.

I look forward to sex and know who that will be with, my dearest friend Jeannie. I plan to go to a few AA meetings right away to see if I can find a group I feel comfortable with.

I have wanted to spend as much time with my dad as possible. He is the best friend I have and truest supporter. I have a responsibility as a family member, as a son, to stay out of prison and be there for my family when they need me.

---

*"The Walls" is prisoner slang for the prison in Walla Walla.

I will also be seeking an avenue to share my prison experience with those who might benefit from it. This is something I don't want to waste any time in getting involved in.

There's an awful lot of things people in society take for granted, simple little things like sunsets, quiet walks, stars, bike rides, Taco Bell and Pizza Hut, swimming, driving, etc., etc., etc. I want to feel the experience of being released again, take in the emotions.

# JIMI—March 1998

*"One time I had run away, tried to tell my mom they were beating me up, but my mom convinced me to let her bring me back. She took me back. She asked them, 'Are you beating on him?' They said, 'No.' They convinced her that no, they weren't beating on me.*

*"She wasn't even out of that parking lot, and they were beating the living shit out of me."*

The author and Jimi in 1997.

From the beginning I considered supplementing my written correspondence with taped interviews. There were reasons to prefer writing and reasons to prefer tapes, but ultimately my hand was forced by the preferences of the prisoners themselves. A few of the subjects, like Jimi, were willing to submit to written or live interviews, but most of them much preferred the latter. They procrastinated and took weeks or months to respond to written questions—if they responded at all—but they tended to be a lot better about making themselves available for live interviews.

For several months, I interviewed prisoners on Wednesday night when I came to the prison for the PAP meeting. One of the prisoners—if he remembered—would bring a Walkman with an attachable microphone to the meeting. My subject and I would then duck across the hall into one of the little offices where we could speak in private. (And no, we probably weren't supposed to be doing any of this, but as long as we weren't too blatant about it, the guards didn't get in our business and try to stop us.)

For my first two Wednesday interviews, I followed up with Jimi on our written correspondence.


*After you are released this time, will you return to prison?*

[Laughs.] Well, you know, I don't like to jinx myself. I have told people over and over and over again that I won't return, and I've not lived up to that promise, to my family, for the most part.

I don't even really make a big deal of making that statement any more. My behavior on the street isn't going to change from my behavior now. I've gradually changed my behavior starting about five, six years ago, and I make different choices. I just—I go through a whole different process when I get angry. I go through a whole different process for making important decisions. Things are just much different for me, and consequently, my behavior is different.

And, so, you know, I can say, "No, I'm not going to come back to prison," and I can believe that, but I just don't like to get into all that, you know, because in here, there's a stigma with saying that. In here, unfortunately, people recognize the fact that a lot of people do come back to prison, and a lot of people believe that it's a jinx to tell yourself you're not going to—or to make that statement, that you're not going to come back.

Some superstitions in here are pretty ridiculous. There's one: if you write on the wall of the cell that you live in, you're going to come back some day to see it. That's another one.

And so, no, I'm not going to be back. But I don't say that for the purpose of, you know, gaining anybody's faith or trust in what I'm going to do when I get out. It's up to me, and I'm doing it for me, so—

*On the previous occasions when you were incarcerated, did you similarly believe and state that you would not be back?*

Yeah, yeah. I—

*And what's different about this time?*

Well, the difference is that I felt that just being clean, having a good clear head, having paid my price of doing time, I felt that was the only price I had to pay for committing a crime. I felt that once I paid the price of doing time, it was done; I was all free and clear from there on.

And, you know, there's just a big difference between going to prison, doing my time, and getting out, versus going to prison and packing my time with programs that are going to help me grow, and that did help me grow, and help me learn more about life, and learn more about teaching people.

It's just that the last five years have been a real growing process for me, and that's what's different. The difference is what I've done since I've been in here.

*So on the earlier occasions, you felt that simply being clean, at least temporarily, of drugs and alcohol was the key, and now you feel that was overrated, that—would you say that the drugs and alcohol was more of a symptom than the real problem, or—?*

Well, that's another thing. I had no intention of getting out and being clean and sober. That was—

*Oh, OK. I took your point to be that the reason you thought you weren't going to come back was that you were off drugs—*

No, I meant clean emotionally.

*OK.*

When you walk out of prison, regardless of what you've done in prison, having been away from society for so long, you spend the year prior to getting out, or the six months prior to getting out, getting physically healthy, getting your mind psyched, so when you walk out that front door, you're psyched. You're ready to go. You're feeling good, regardless of whether you're really ready or not, or whether you've done anything to be ready.

So, you feel like you'll never be back. But nothing's changed, except this momentary bit of energy you've got that's going to carry you through, you know, until you go get high, or whatever it is that you're going to go do.

*So the temporary exhilaration of being released gives you a false confidence.*

I think so. Yeah.

*And you feel this time, your confidence is based on something deeper.*

Yeah. I mean, I'm also looking so much further down the road than I have in the past. I've laid out some pretty important goals for myself, and I've laid them out thoroughly and vividly. And I know what I'm going to be doing from year to year to year to year.

Granted, I understand that some things aren't going to happen the way I want, and I've kind of allowed for that in the process of writing my goals. But I have a direction that I'm going in, and I want to get there.

And at the end of that road—you know, twenty, twenty-five years down that road—is my owning and operating a salon.

So, I'm just in the beginning of my journey. You know, there's a lot for me to do yet. Getting out is just going to be a step in getting there.

I think a lot of people set goals when they come to prison to get out. You know, "I can't wait to get out, I can't wait...," but they don't go any further than that. They really don't put a lot of energy into anything beyond getting out, and they get stuck.

When they get stuck, they go to the bag, or go to whatever their addiction was.

*Let's talk about the drugs and alcohol. How big a part of your past was drugs and alcohol? How much was that an explanation for what you did, and to what extent was it a symptom?*

A little of both. I think my big thing, to be honest with you—I played with just about everything except heroin. I began with pot, and booze, and I've pretty much been a drinker all my life, and, for the most part, a pot smoker when I could. I've tried other things, but they never lasted.

But my big thing—what got me in here this time, actually—was crack. I'd tried coke before, but then I went on a three week run of smoking crack, and, you know, I just—I'm an addictive person. I have a tendency to go off the deep end.

And that means anything. I want to do anything to the extreme. Not just chemicals, but, sports, anger—everything I do kind of extreme.

I don't really understand, though, when you say, "Is it a 'symptom'?"—

*Well, I'm saying as an impulsive, addictive youth, would you have simply damaged your life some other way if drugs weren't available?*

Yeah, yeah.

*Or was it really the drugs that did it?*

No, it is a symptom in that sense. Yeah.

*So if society did have some way of keeping drugs away from young people, it wouldn't have mattered in your case. You would have just done something else.*

Yeah. And I did. Frequently. I mean, you know, I'd pack up and go to California just on a whim. I just didn't feel like being home. I mean, a couple of friends of mine wanted to hitchhike down to California, and I did it with them, and this is in the middle of high school.

You know, things were relatively fine. I had my problems, but things were relatively fine at that point. I had moved out of my mom's place. I was living with my dad, and I had a truck, and I was doing well.

But I just took off. I had a truck that wouldn't make it to California, so my friends talked me into hitchhiking down to California.

*Now, are you in danger of swinging too far to the opposite extreme, from being impulsive and free-spirited, to having every part of your life planned out and orderly and rational and predictable and so on?*

I recognize that I live that way now. I'm real picky about where things are in my cell. I'm real picky about my schedule. If something is cancelled, I don't feel good about it. And if I have a couple of hours of free time just to myself where I should be relaxing and maybe catching up on some reading, or not even that, just vegging out for an hour or two, which I could use every now and then, I feel uncomfortable about it, because I've been so busy for the last four or five years.

And, so, yeah, I am. I have to be careful about that.

*And how about not just in terms of day-to-day routine like that, but as far as, like, major life events and decisions and such—?*

You mean—?

*You alluded to it earlier. What if your life after prison doesn't follow the blueprint that you have sketched out so meticulously of having this kind of job, and this kind of relationship, and doing this with your life? What if other things intervene and there are some disappointments or some failures or whatever? Are you going to have the flexibility to deal with that?*

Yeah. I'm doing that right now. That's why I'm in welding school. See, my major, my ultimate goal is to own and operate a salon, and has been for years. Well, I'm in kind of a limbo right now with my barber's license, and here soon I may find out that I'll never be able to do that again.

So, when that became an issue about a year and a half ago, when I realized that that was something that was quite possible, I decided to get into welding school, and now I'm working on my welding certification.

I'm actually enjoying it too. And that kind of mixes with another interest of mine, which is marine engineering.

So, yeah, I'm capable of adapting. I'll survive. I'll be fine. I'm not so worried about that.

*Even if your primary problem wasn't the drugs and alcohol, if it was really more a lack of maturity and a certain impulsiveness, what are you going to do about the drugs and alcohol in the future? Do you have to just go cold turkey and never use again, or can you use responsibly? What do you intend to do, and what do you think you will do, when you get on the outside?*

Well, I won't use anything illegal. So pot, coke, you know, anything illegal. And that's for my own reasons. I believe that pot ultimately—and a lot of people don't agree with this—but I believe that pot ultimately leads to other things.

And I don't mean just because you want a harder high eventually. I mean because in order to buy pot, you got to be around the people that use it to get it. So, you meet this guy, you hang around with that guy, and now you're part of that world.

The bottom line is, I'm going to try my best to obey the law. And the reason I won't smoke pot or, you know, do coke, or do any of that other crap is because it's against the law.

Drinking, I don't know. I don't have an interest to drink, but I've said that before, and I've gotten out and started up again. But I've also been able to be a social drinker for long periods of time.

So, I don't know how that's going to be. You know, I'd like to be able to sit down with my dad and have a beer every now and then. Just, on the weekend, to enjoy a beer with my dad would be nice.

But, you know, anything against the law, definitely not.

And if alcohol becomes a problem, then I'll have to deal with that, with a program or whatever it takes to quit. Because I've got a lot to risk, and I've got a lot of responsibilities that I didn't recognize before.

*So you're not convinced that you're an alcoholic, and that you have to never drink again.*

No, I believe it's a matter of control.

*Because isn't that part of the AA dogma?*

Yeah, yeah. They put these labels on, you know—you're "rationalizing," and you're "giving excuses," and "in denial," and everything.

It all comes down to having control. And, whether it's having control to go to that AA program every day, or whether it's having control to go to church every week or whatever, it's all about having control. Well, if you have enough control to be in a program, then you obviously have some control over your faculties. You're able to make those decisions.

It's all about control, and I don't believe that alcohol is something that one can't control.

*And if they legalize pot tomorrow, you'd feel the same way about that as alcohol?*

No, because pot's a different thing. I don't know; it's been a year now. But I was getting stoned when I was down at McNeil* for about two months. And, it's a whole different thing now, the last few times I got high. It burns you out. The pot's so good, it's—I think I'm too old for it. I mean, it doesn't do to me what it used to do, and I don't enjoy it like I used to enjoy it. It burns me out, it makes me want to eat, and then I want to sleep, and I feel like crap.

And, I just—I had some bad experiences.

*So even aside from the legal issue, you'd probably steer clear of pot?*

Yeah, yeah. That's not to say that I would condemn other people doing it. You know, people are welcome to do their thing. I'm not into the judging and all that, if that's their trip. It's not my bag.

*I want to change gears slightly and address a different matter. We've talked about your most recent crimes that landed you here. And, we've talked a bit about your feelings about the victim. I'm thinking specifically about the woman that you robbed in the salon. Well, first of all, as a bit of background, from what I understand, you've had no contact with her and you're not allowed to have any contact with her. Is that accurate?*

Yeah.

*What are the rules about that?*

That's just part of my judgment and sentence, and it's standard, it's par for the course. Most victims, most crimes with a victim, with an identifiable victim, it's written in the judgment and sentence that you have no contact with that person. For life, if it's somebody you don't know. So, that's written in my judgment and sentence.

---

*McNeil Island Correction Center. Another prison in Washington.

*So even twenty years after you get out, if you contacted her you'd be violating the law?*

Yeah, yeah.

*What is the rationale for that, for those rules?*

I would imagine safety and security for the victim. You know, based on the poor numbers, the terrible statistics for recidivism, I'm sure there's a legitimate reason for there to be a rule.

*So you agree with the rule, or should there be some way of effecting a compromise or an exception to it?*

Well, I think that there will eventually be an exception with mine. Because, I think this victim is clearly someone that I can make feel a little bit more at ease, about the crime, what's happened since then, and the fact that I'm back out in the community.

And I believe, through the prosecutor, I may be able to get an exception to that rule. Or maybe through a mediator, or some type of conference with a mediator, I may be able to have contact with that person again.

*That's very much where I'm headed. What I was getting some background, leading up to, is, what if it turns out that the only contact you'll ever have with the victim is her reading the transcript of this interview? I want you to go ahead and speak to her and say what you would say to her if this were your only opportunity to express yourself.*

Well, I suppose the first thing I would say is that I'm truly sorry for what I later found out, and later realized, was a terrifying experience for her. I didn't realize that I scared her as bad as I did. I found out during the sentencing. The prosecutor made the statement that I had scared her so bad that she wasn't even intending to testify. That was the first time I was really conscious of what I did to her.

And, I was so—in such a state of robbery, of committing this crime, and I'd psyched myself so bad to commit this burglary, which had now turned into a robbery—I was so into this robbery, that I don't even recall what was happening around me. I mean, I hadn't really realized that I was scaring the shit out of this lady.

And she had a pistol. You know, that was another thing—

*Talk to her.*

[Jimi had been fairly upbeat and animated to this point in the conversation. Now his expression was somber and he stared at the top of the desk between us for several seconds, collecting his thoughts.] Well. [Another significant pause.]

I would say that I'm sorry to you, very sorry to you. Seven and a half years have passed. And I've gotten a pretty decent education. I've spent the time wisely. I've been involved in a lot of programs involving victims. I've been involved in teaching. I've had a chance to grow up. I've had a chance to pay society back for the crime that I committed against you.

I've basically become a grown man who makes responsible decisions based on the outcome of the decision. In other words, before I act, I think. And, it matters to me what my behavior does to somebody else. And that isn't something that was always there for me.

I would like to—and I know because of the way the judgment and sentence is set up that I can't contact you, and I can't communicate with you at all. I would like to be able to help you if it's still an issue with you. I would like to be able to help you get through your pain, if you're still having it.

I would welcome—I would offer up myself to you. I'm sure you're still very angry. I'm sure you have a lot that you would like to say to me, and I would be more than willing to offer myself up to you.

I know I hurt you. And there really isn't a whole lot that—because of the way the system is set up—there really isn't a whole lot that I can do, directly, for you to help you understand that you don't have anything to worry about because I'm free.

One thing I hope that some day you will become aware of is, this tragedy for you, and me, has ultimately turned into something that was important, and something that was the beginning of an important part of my life. And I say "important," because this is what turned my life around and, ultimately, taught me the importance of giving back to other people, and, in that process, helping me learn how to become involved in society.

So, I am sorry.

*It seems as though she's the victim that stands out the most in your memory. Is that because she was the most recent, or was—?*

Yeah.

*—there something about that crime that was more intense?*

Well, also, she was a woman, and I'd never had a woman victim before.

*What has been the nature of your crimes before this most recent one? Have they always been robbery and burglary and such?*

Yeah. Burglary, robbery, forgery. This was actually the first robbery that I, the second actually—I had one as a juvenile—but this is the first robbery that I actually got charged with as an adult. Most of my crimes as an adult have been robberies, but this is the first robbery I've ever been charged with. Most of my crimes were—

*The others were plea bargained down to something else?*

Never got caught! [Laughs.]

*Oh, OK.*

I just never got caught. [Laughs.]

*What did you get caught for in the past?*

Burglary. Breaking into a florist shop once when I was drunk. Forging. I forged a couple of checks that didn't belong to me. Possession of a stolen car that didn't belong to me.

*Did you steal it, or just have "possession" of it?*

Yeah, I stole it. I stole it.
And there were several burglaries, breaking into businesses, when I was younger.

*Other than in a physical fight between equals, have you ever physically harmed somebody as a part of one of your crimes? Assault and battery? Murder?*

Well, I have a third degree assault, but it was an officer putting me under arrest. Actually, that was a woman also.
But it was an officer placing me under arrest. She put a handcuff on me, and I didn't anticipate that because I thought she was going to shake me down first, like they do here. But she put the cuff on me. I thought she was going to, you know, start shaking me down, but she reached up and put a cuff on my right arm, and I turned around. I panicked and turned around and started shaking her loose, and she wouldn't let go of the cuff. And finally, through all my jerking and her trying to jerk her hand free from the handcuff—the other handcuff that she had in her hand—she tore a ligament in her finger or something. I took off running and got away, but it ultimately ended up in third degree assault.

*In the course of your robberies, did you use a weapon?*

Yeah.

*Were you prepared to actually use that weapon, or was it merely a threat?*

Merely a threat.

*So if someone had resisted—*

I'd have ran.

*You would not have shot anyone?*

No, no.

*Was it loaded?*

Yeah. [Laughs a little sheepishly.]

*How come?*

There's a whole power trip that goes with a loaded weapon. There really is. You really have to be a very responsible person to carry a loaded weapon, and I don't know that I am that person. Or was.

Because, there's really a control thing. You get this sense of power with that loaded weapon. It's almost like it makes you a couple of feet taller, a couple of hundred pounds bigger than everybody else in your immediate environment. It makes you the most powerful one wherever you go, whether it's walking into a 7-Eleven, or walking into a night club, or, you know, no matter where you are.

If you have a pistol, whether it's on you or in your car, you know that you're the strongest one. You're ultimately going to be the winner of the battle, unless the other person has—

*With the gun, you have the power of life and death over other human beings.*

Absolutely. Absolutely.

*So you did it more for the power rush than because you intended to actually use it.*

I did it for the money.
Oh, you mean why I had a weapon—

*Why was the gun loaded?*

Yeah, yeah.
And also, I liked to go out and shoot it. I mean, I remember once pulling off the road after I'd been driving all night. It was about seven in the morning. It was when I was on my

run. I pulled off into the woods, and I went up ten, fifteen miles into the woods, and I found a nice little grassy area next to a creek. I rocked up some coke, and I sat there and took coke hits—all by myself, smoking crack—and I went ahead and broke out my pistol and went through about forty, fifty rounds, and just had a blast, you know.

So, I enjoyed shooting it too, but I certainly wasn't prepared to shoot anybody.

*Do you think you could have used it in an emergency situation? What if you were holding somebody up and they pulled a weapon on you from underneath the counter or something? Would you have been able to shoot them?*

You know, I would sure hope that I wouldn't, and ultimately, I'd probably be shot. I don't know. I have no way of answering that question. I would hope not. I would hope that I wouldn't shoot somebody. But if somebody pulled a gun on me, while I had a gun on them, it would be at an impasse, and I don't know what would happen. I've never been there before. You know, it would be another stupid, terrible situation that could have been avoided by a pretty simple choice, really, of not doing it.

*So are you going to own a gun when you get out?*

No, no.

*Is that because you're not allowed to, or because you choose—?*

I just don't have any need to. I don't hunt. I can buy my food at Safeway. I just—it's not a part of my life.

*Let's talk a little bit about juvenile detention, because that's come up in some of our exchanges. You're clearly dissatisfied with your juvenile experience, and you've said some critical things about the system, at least as it was when you went through it. I want you to follow up a little bit on that for me, talk about what was inadequate about it, or what you think it needed to be that it wasn't, that would have better addressed the needs of juvenile offenders.*

Well, my experience with the juvenile system—detention—was just that it was so lonely. So, I mean, all of a sudden, you're a young kid with absolutely no one. You're not anybody's son any more, you're not anybody's brother any more, you're not—you're just a member of that little cell block that you're in, or whatever.

My experience with detention was that it was such a lonely place, and what bothers me is that I lost my identity going to detention. I was a pretty bitter kid already, having lost my father. My father had walked out. For some reason, I was bitter at my mom for, in my mind, "running my father out."

So, I was just real lonely, and I didn't feel I fit in with the rest of the kids that were there. That was another thing that kind of bothered me.

*How were you different from them? Why did you not fit in with them?*

Well, I was from the east side,[*] and I was from a pretty well off family. I was the only kid in there that was from my neighborhood, I mean, an upper middle class neighborhood.

Most of the kids in there probably didn't have a mother and a father, which I didn't either any more. Most of them kids in there, their families probably weren't intact. Most of the kids in there probably had been in trouble for quite some time, possibly had siblings that had been in trouble.

You know, I just felt like they were handling it a lot better than I was. I eventually learned how to handle it, but that first time was such a huge—it just changed me forever. That first time I got locked up totally changed the way I looked at things. I was lonely and boxed in, almost in a panic, feeling panicky, crying, just continuously crying, and just boxed in.

There isn't anybody who cares.

At that time, there was a kid there—that later was here, actually—named Dan Burns.[†] He'd done a burglary and killed an old woman. He was fifteen, I believe. And he was really going through turmoil too, because they had remanded him to adult court. For days he was banging on his door and screaming and hollering, and that was just weighing pretty heavy on me too.

You know, it's just that whole isolation. I don't understand how isolating somebody is supposed to help. If you want somebody to be functional in society or in their family, how can you possibly achieve that by isolating them? I know they say, "Absence makes the heart grow fonder," but how does separating people bring them closer?

It bothers me that my mom didn't try harder. And my dad. It really bothers me.

Actually, it bothers me that my mom didn't try harder. It bothers me that my dad took off. Bothers me now. It didn't then, but now it does. It bothers me that he took off, and he gave up. It's not easy to raise a family. I understand that. My mom did everything that she knew to do. But, it wasn't enough.

*I hear what you're saying about parents working harder to solve the problems and keep the family together, but what could the system do differently? I mean, other than just encouraging parents to try to solve the problems within the family structure, once that breaks down and the state does have custody, what can the system do to relieve this feeling of loneliness, that nobody cares, that you're not connected with anything?*

---

[*] Many of Seattle's middle class and above neighborhoods are on the east side, across Lake Washington from downtown Seattle.

[†] I have changed the name.

Well, Craig, I tell you. [Laughs.]

*More and better counselors? I mean, what—?*

Well, I didn't get any counseling. When you go in the system, you don't get counseling. The "counselors" in the system—and I don't care if it's a juvenile system or an adult system—are not counselors. They're people who facilitate your paperwork. That's all. There is absolutely no counseling being facilitated by these "counselors." Not here, not in Walla Walla.

Every one of us has a "counselor" that's assigned to us. The only thing that counselor is going to do—and I mean the only thing they are going to do—is generate your paperwork for you. They are not there to counsel. And, maybe that's a problem.

*And that was true on the juvenile level too?*

Absolutely. My counselor—his name was Mr. Mason[*]—he was a nice enough guy, but, you know, "Yeah, you got to get a GED," you know, "We'll get you in a GED class, and we'll help you get your driver's license." That's it.

That was at Mission Creek.[†] They didn't counsel us. There was no counseling.

*Why not? Too big a workload? They have too many people they're responsible for, or—?*

Well, I don't know. What's too big? I don't know what too big is. I really don't. I have no idea.

I just know that when people think that we have counselors, and they are counseling us, they're mistaken. That's not what counselors do in the system, juvenile or adult.

*Why don't the counselors counsel?*

Well, they're not trained to. They're not trained psychotherapists. They're not trained in psychology. They probably have an associate's degree is what they have.

*So when you were going through the juvenile system, the juvenile offender did not have regular contact with somebody who's actually trained in psychology, or therapy, or counseling of any kind.*

Right. Bottom line.
Does that surprise you?

---

[*]I have changed the name.

[†]A juvenile detention facility in Washington.

*Somewhat. To your knowledge, does it remain that way today?*

I don't know. I have no idea. I'd be surprised, because psychotherapy's kind of exploded in the last, you know, ten, fifteen years especially. In fact, you can probably get it cheaper now, which I'm sure is an issue—money.

But back then, the only time that there was any counseling was a diagnostic period before they sent you from the county jail, or from the detention center, to an institution. The diagnostics were usually done at a hospital in Tacoma. They did most of them statewide, though my detention center, they did their own.

So, I went through a battery of tests for a day or two, and then they sent me on to Mission Creek. But that was it.

*So one recommendation that you have would be to have legitimate counselors, rather than just people who are called "counselors."*

Yes.

*People who actually provide some therapy, some kind of psychological help.*

Yes. Yeah, and especially so in the adult system.

But that's been a pet peeve of mine ever since I've engaged in therapy, is why isn't there any of this in the system? I've learned that there are many reasons.

For one thing, people are paranoid in this system to share personal information. The fear is that the information will be interpreted and used later against them. So, the integrity of the client-therapist confidentiality thing just isn't trusted.

But, it's absent in the adult system, and it's totally absent in the youth system.

I don't know whether juveniles would be receptive to therapy, to be honest with you.

*Would you have been?*

I was once in a group home that was using it. Once a week, we had these groups. And—

*But I thought you said there was none?*

Well, this was a group home, a private facility. I was only there for about six months. It was a private group home system that they had. There were, like, four of them in Kitsap County.[*]

---

[*]A county west of Seattle.

Anyway, they had these groups once a week. They'd pour pitchers of water on your face, they'd spit on you, they made you put a toilet seat around your head, around your neck. They did a lot of things that were very degrading, humiliating. That was during the group.

*The purpose of which was what?*

To get you angry. To get you to let your feelings out. Push you to let it out.

These group homes also were later shut down because they were found to be abusing the kids. And I was one of the ones abused. Not sexually, but I had been beat up on several occasions at this group home.

*By other offenders, or by the staff?*

By the staff. Just the shit knocked out of me, I mean, bad. Bloody, you know.

I ran away one time butt naked. Didn't have any clothes, 'cause he took all my clothes away and made me sleep on the floor in his bedroom. And he got up to answer the door when another kid had snuck out and come back, and I took off.

Butt naked, running out of there. [Laughs.] 'Cause you never know. I mean, they're beating the hell out of you in there like crazy, and you just, you know, "I'm not staying around here. The hell with that, I'm taking off. Clothes or no clothes, I don't care. I'm getting out of here!"

*Did you feel even more lonely and hopeless in those circumstances, when the staff itself, the authority figures themselves, are beating you?*

Yes. Yeah. When I think back, and try and think about the feelings I was feeling when I was getting beat up—very alienated.

One time I had run away, tried to tell my mom they were beating me up, but my mom convinced me to let her bring me back. She took me back. She asked them, "Are you beating on him?" They said, "No." They convinced her that no, they weren't beating on me.

She wasn't even out of that parking lot, and they were beating the living shit out of me. And that night, that was another night I ran away. I took off out of my room.

I remember my bottom lip was huge from getting smacked. I had these men's clogs—in the old days, you know, they had these clogs that were real cool—and I was wearing a pair. And he took them off me, and he hit me in the lip with one. Hit me in the face.

But, one thing I do want to say, one positive experience that I went through when I was in the juvenile system was an Outward Bound course. I went through a 28 day pilot program. It was, like, the first in the state of Washington, and they were experimenting with it. Twenty-eight days in the Alpine Lakes Wilderness area.[*]

---

[*]Alpine Lakes Wilderness in the Mt. Baker-Snoqualmie and Wenatchee National Forests in Washington.

The object was to teach us to push ourselves, to do some things that we were afraid of, to go for things, you know, that we were afraid of doing.

This was basically a hiking and rock climbing trip for the whole 28 days. We had a little solo period, where we had to spend the night by ourselves, and every morning we had to get up and run a mile or two, and dive in a cold creek. And then, at the end of the 28 days, we'd run a ten mile run.

But coming back to the institution was a total drag. I mean, it was like everybody was looking at us, and like we were—it was just a very negative place to go back to after being in such a beautiful place, out in the Alpine Lakes Wilderness area, out in the country. Just the contrast It was a real let down to go back to that institution.

The idea was to eventually get it developed to where the kids would go—after Outward Bound—straight to a bunk in the community somewhere, if not home.

But that program kind of hit the skids for whatever reasons. You know, money probably. I don't know.

But that was a good experience that I had. It really was. And there was group stuff going on there, too. I mean, the guys that took you on these excursions were really into therapy, and they were just the kind of people that are into kind of digging into yourself and looking at things, and—

*So once you got out of the conventional juvenile detention facility, it sounds like these other things you experienced did have some element of therapy or counseling.*

Absolutely. Absolutely. And, you know, there was also a lot of stuff between the inmates that went on. We had to sit down every night and go through stuff. There was a lot of confrontation stuff. Healthy confrontations that we weren't used to. You know, we picked some stuff up.

*So it wasn't like that other place—all that artificial provocation and confrontation of having people throw water on you, and all those games.*

No. Absolutely not.

*It was a more honest—*

Right. There were even times when guys got so mad, they got in fights. But, at night, the idea was that, as a group, we would sit around, and if I had a problem with you, I'd tell you what the problem was, rather than pick a fight with you tomorrow. You know, in the process, I'm learning how it's OK, how I don't have to be afraid to tell you that I don't like you, or that I don't like what you did.

There's a lot of that stuff going on in kids that they don't understand how to express, and what they end up doing is, eventually, reacting to their feelings that get built up.

*When you were beaten by the staff, and you were lying in bed that night thinking about what had happened to you, especially after you had already tried to inform your mother, and she had brought you right back to the place and not believed you, were you thinking or fantasizing about who you can appeal to, you know, "If only so-and-so knew, then this wouldn't be happening"? Were you thinking about your father, or these people's superiors, or God, or anybody else, just saying, "Hey, somebody save me from this!"? "Somebody's got to intervene!"?*

Yeah, but I think I lost that kind of hope early on in my experience with the juvenile system. I lost that kind of hope early on.

Nobody comes to rescue you. They just don't.

And like with that time I was telling you about, I was never laying in bed thinking of anything, because I didn't get in bed that night. The second he busted me in my mouth, I knew that I was going to run away the first chance I got.

Another time, he busted me with a roach,* and he had me scrubbing the linoleum floor with a toothbrush, after I'd done all this other work. And I said, "The hell with this; I'm taking off." He went upstairs while I was vacuuming the floor, and I took off and left the vacuum running. He went up to his bedroom, you know, and I took off down into the woods, and I hiked through the woods for miles, and came out in town.

I was dodging him, and hiding from him, 'cause I saw him. He was down in town now, running back and forth down the main drag, looking for me.

*So every time you were beaten like that, you took off and ran.*

I ran. Yeah. Yeah. I ran.

I got that from my dad. That's what he does. He runs.

---

*The butt of a marijuana cigarette.

# JIMI—March 1998

*"When I first fell—freckle-faced, red-headed kid, with an Irish temper—I was very, very short-fused, but, nonetheless, scared. But I hid the fear in aggressiveness. I responded if I thought somebody was trying to get at me, or somebody was trying to, you know, quote, 'disrespect me,' unquote. I had a false sense of what this respect thing was. So I used to fight a lot. A lot."*

J ust a week later, I sat down for another conversation with Jimi. I was not as happy with this one. Perhaps we were both off a bit. Toward the end of the interview especially, I felt like he wasn't following my questions and was going off on unproductive tangents. Sometimes I tried to steer him back, but sometimes I got caught up in the same kind of stream-of-consciousness rambling. I felt like we were speaking past each. I have edited out more of this interview than probably any other, simply because a lot of it came out too confusing when transcribed.

Still, there is much remaining that I believe helps the reader to gain a better understanding of prison and of Jimi as a human being.

*Let's talk about prison conditions, life in prison. Describe your cell at WSR, how big it is and such. What can you say that would convey to a person who's never been inside a prison what your cell is like?*

My cell is approximately six feet wide, left to right when you walk in. I'd say maybe nine to twelve feet deep. The ceiling's maybe ten feet high.

The cells are double-bunked. At the moment, we've only got one person in every cell, but that'll be changing next month. It'll be two to a cell starting then.

They're what is called "wet cells," meaning that we have a toilet and sink in the house.* A lot of facilities have "dry cells," which afford you a key to your cell, and you would go down the tier, or somewhere in the unit to where there are bathrooms and showers and toilets. Some of the newer facilities are made that way. I don't know why they're made that way, but a lot of the newer ones are.

This facility, here at WSR, is what you would consider the old style of cell. It's bars. Newer facilities don't use bars any more. They're solid rooms, solid doors.

This facility has four tiers. It's four tiers high, forty houses long on each tier. The officers control the cell doors, from the lock box.

*Each one individually, or are they all—?*

Yeah, well, both. Like at chow time, when they call chow, they can press a button and all the houses on one tier will crack open. Or they can do each cell separately.

*The more modern cells that don't have bars, is it thick glass in front so you can see out, or is it all solid where you can't see out?*

---

*The prisoners refer to their cell as their "house."

It's solid, except for a window on your door, and possibly a window somewhere on your wall, facing outside. Generally on the door, there's a window, maybe four inches wide and twenty-four inches high, somewhere in there.

*So the more modern one are actually more claustrophobic, more—?*

Absolutely. Much more isolated. And, much, much quieter. I prefer the bars, even though it's noisier at night.

There's more noise. It's much more open. You're not as closed in. You can reach next door if you want to borrow something or somebody next door needs to borrow something, or a friend a couple houses down needs to borrow something. You can pass it down, 'cause you can just reach right next door. So, there's a lot of advantages to the bars, that I recognize.

*Now, we always hear about how prisons are grossly overcrowded, that people are being released early out of necessity, because there's too many prisoners for the capacity and such. Why at WSR, until now, are there actually two-bunk cells with one person?*

Well, first of all, WSR has a deal with the federal government. These are very small cells. So, when we double up next month, it's going against a federal judgment, though it's since been overturned. But at one time, the federal government came in here and said these cells are too small for two people.

There was also a deal with the community at some point here in Monroe that said that, you know, the population wasn't going to reach over so many people.

And it's not just the size of the cells. The facilities, like the showers, telephones, things like that that inmates are using, when you double up this entire institution, it puts a huge cramp on everything. The weight room, the gym, education classes. It just doubles everything, the use of everything. And it makes it tough.

But these cells here are very small, so two people in one cell is really, really cramped.

*How does it compare with other prisons that have two people to a cell? Are those cells typically bigger than here?*

Well, Walla Walla's got four people to a cell,—

*And what's the size of a cell there?*

They're maybe two and a half of the cells here. They're much bigger. You walk in, and you can barely—by stretching your arms out—you can barely touch both beds with your hands. And then you've got the beds on each side, which are, you know, three and a half, four feet wide, and then, in the back, there's the sink and the toilet. Much bigger.

*To be part of a four person cell the size of the Walla Walla cells, is that more comparable to how much room you have here in a single, or how much room you have here when you're doubled up?*

It's more like the amount of room you have in the single cells here.

But on the other hand, the impact that that many people have on the programs and such is more similar to this place doubled up. 'Cause Walla Walla is pretty crowded.

You got to remember something about single cells: single cells alleviate a lot of tension, and a lot of problems. A lot of problems are derived out of being celled up with somebody in quarters that cramped.

This is the most mellow joint I've ever been in, and there's no one thing you can put it on, but among many things, single cells is one of them. Nobody wants to lose their single cell. Nobody wants to get sent somewhere where it's overcrowded.

And, you know, when I go home at night, I'm by myself. I can think. I can spend my time reading, or writing, or just watching TV if I want to, and what I want to watch on TV. I don't have to share that with somebody else.

Having a single cell is a huge advantage to this place. Huge.

*So it's as much psychological as physical. It's not just how much space you have, it's the fact that you get to be alone, and you have some privacy.*

Absolutely. Absolutely. I transferred from Walla Walla to Clallam Bay after many years at Walla Walla living with three people in a four man cell. In close custody at Clallam Bay, they were singled up. Even though they had two bunks, they were single cells, like here, only one person living in each cell. And they were wet cells, but they were the solid cells that I talked about before.

And I was in heaven, even though some would say that's the worst joint in the state because of the way they run it. I loved it, just because it was a huge relief to finally be able to have my own cell. I can shut everything out. I can get away from the prison crap, and grow, and think, and do things that the prison environment is not conducive to.

*So if you had a choice between being in a small cell by yourself, or being in one that's even two and a half to three times that size with another person—?*

Hands down, small cell by myself.

*You'd rather be by yourself in the small cell.*

Yeah. I would. In fact, I would probably—I'm down to ten months left—I would probably rather stay in the hole in a single cell here until I leave, instead of going back to Walla Walla.

There's tension there, there's overcrowding, and just having to live with those kids, you know, that's just not my bag any more. Being in a single cell means everything in the world to me.

*What time in the morning do you get up?*

Six o'clock.

*Does everybody have to get up at six o'clock?*

No. No. They serve breakfast at about six-thirty, six forty-five, somewhere in there, and my alarm goes off at six o'clock.

*So, is it optional, that if you want to eat breakfast, then you have to be up by then, but you can skip that if you want?*

Yeah, I don't eat breakfast. I just get up and make a cup of coffee, and clear the cobwebs. [Laughs.]

*So people could sleep in until noon.*

Oh yeah. Yeah. They're aren't enough programs or jobs, there aren't enough things available for everybody in the institution to be fully programmed. It would be ideal to think that everybody could be placed at any one time in the program they want to be in, or that they need, but that's not the case. So, there are a lot of people that are part time programming, or they have a job, you know, later in the day, or they're taking a couple of classes that classifies as their program.

*What are the restrictions on your schedule? What are you required to do at certain times?*

Be back at count. The first count is at six o'clock in the morning. There's an informal count at around eleven o'clock, eleven-fifteen in the morning, and that's the time that most everybody has to go back to their house, unless you're working in industries, and then they take an industries count out there. There's a count at four o'clock, and then there's a count at nine o'clock, and then there's an informal count at about ten o'clock, or ten-thirty. The night shift officers come walking around.

*So, for the one at six o'clock, you're locked in your cell anyway, right?*

Yeah.

*So they just come around and count people lying in their beds?*

Right. Yeah. It's a rule that you're supposed to be showing skin, but they don't make a real big deal of it. I've never heard them stop here and wake somebody up and tell them to show some skin. At Walla Walla, though, they'll wake you up. But they've had experiences there where dummies were placed in the bed.

*So, you have the counts, and then the meals are at a set time—*

Meals are a set time.

*Is there anything else that's mandatory, that you have to work your schedule around? Is the rest of the time your own?*

Well, there are things that are at certain times, but optional whether you're involved in them. Things like, you know, your mail. You've got to get your mail in the box in the morning by the seven forty-five gate, because they pick it up right after eight o'clock.

We're allowed to order commissary once a week. You've got to get it in there—your order form—at a specific time during the week, otherwise you'll miss it for that week.

Payday's generally once a month for everybody. There's a couple of different pay periods, based on where you work.

Each tier has a different day for laundry, personal laundry. In each unit, there's a set of washer and dryers, and then there's a couple of guys that work, doing just the laundry, and that's their paid job. Like, my day on my tier is Tuesday. I take them my blue bag down there on Tuesday. All the C unit personal laundry bags are blue. They know by the color coding what unit it goes to.

*Now, is the degree of freedom you're describing typical at all institutions you've been in?*

Well, you mean degree of freedom as far as partaking in—?

*As far as how much of your time is your own, how much of your time you're not required to be doing something, or be in a certain place.*

No. I mean, for instance, Walla Walla is a good example. Here, if you want to go to yard at seven forty-five, right after chow, and stay out there until, you know, they call yard in at about ten-thirty, you can. But at Walla Walla, there's no morning yard at all, except on the weekends. There's just not enough room, so they go in shifts. Based on what side you're on determines what time you get to go to yard. You go to yard at night today, and day tomorrow, or day today, and night tomorrow. Protective custody has the yard in the morning.

*What I'm getting at, though, is, for instance, if one is in the military—and I've been fortunate enough to avoid that my whole life—but if one is in the military, it seems like almost none of your time is your own. You get up at a certain time, everybody has to get up at that time, you all get lined up, and you're told, "We're going to do this for one hour, then we're going to do this for two hours, then we're going to do this for two hours," and your whole day is following someone's orders and doing everything in unison, and you have little time to yourself, and then you're back in your bed at a certain time. Now, it sounds like prison is dramatically less regimented than that, that in at least that respect, you have a lot more freedom in prison than in the military.*

Yeah.

*A lot more time to yourself.*

Yeah, that'd be a correct assessment. Absolutely. Much, much more.

But, you know, reasonably so. Those who control us, the people who hold our freedom in their hand, day to day, out on the main line, are people who have no more education than a high school education, no more experience than an orientation class. Some of these kids that are coming in here and working can't be more than 18-19 years old, literally. Never in a million years would they get the respect that your drill sergeants and your officers get in the military, that they've earned in the military.

So, that type of control just wouldn't work.

*If they had the personnel for it, like if they just used retired military officers or something, should prisons be run like boot camp? Would it be better for discipline and such, or is that a bad idea?*

Well, it's a hard call. They have a boot camp here in Washington, and I got to see it first hand when I was down at McNeil Island. What the public thinks is going on there is much different than what's really going on there. You hear "boot camp," or you hear, "work ethics camp," and you're thinking that these guys are getting up, doing calisthenics for two hours in the morning, and they're running a mile every morning, and they're "Sir, yes sir!" and it's nothing at all like that.

A lot of it is just a show for the media. Typical of what I saw happening there was, a friend of mine that works for the road crew, he had been digging a ditch to put some pipe in, and the media was going out there that day. He'd been digging a ditch with a back hoe, and when the media got out there, they took a picture of all these work ethics camp inmates standing next to this ditch with shovels, and they hadn't touched that ditch. Then they put it in the newspaper: "Work ethics camp inmates working, digging ditches." They hadn't been. They weren't doing anything like that.

All of their time is taken up, and they have some good classes. A lot of those guys can learn, if they want to learn. But one of the flaws in that program is that the people who are running it don't really have the control people think they do. I mean, these guys go out to work every day, and then they come home and they go to class. And they're not allowed to smoke, or drink coffee, or cuss, or talk back, or anything. Well, we had a couple of them working in the marine shop where I was working. You think I'm not going to let a guy smoke? You know, he asks me for a cigarette, I'm not going to give him a cigarette?

You know, the rules just weren't enforced universally everywhere on the island, that level of control just wasn't there. So, really that program was a joke.

I'm not so sure that that's the answer anyway. I'm more towards an education type thing.

But obviously some people, I believe, are just flat out recalcitrant. They don't want to learn, and so be it.

*Can anything reach people like that?*

Time. Probably.

*Think some of them will mellow with age?*

Yeah. Yeah, I think most do mellow with age. That doesn't mean even after they've mellowed that they aren't willing to commit crimes to get high, though.

Mellowing is maybe deciding that you no longer want to hurt people, or you discover that you have compassion for people. That's all fine and dandy, but that doesn't mean, because you have compassion for people, that you're not willing to do a crime that you don't understand is actually victimizing somebody, or a group of people, or a community. You know, a lot of people in here would consider most property crimes as flat out victimless.

It's weird, how you see it. But when you really, really look at victimization, you understand how many people are affected when you commit a crime, you realize that victimization is a lot more than just a one-on-one crime against one person. I don't think a lot of people have looked at it in that detail.

*I noticed in your written answer to my question about when you were most afraid in prison, it was an act of brutality by guards. Have you ever been fearful of other prisoners,—?*

Yeah.

*—such as when you first came to the joint? Was that an issue?*

Yeah. When I first fell—freckle-faced, red-headed kid, with an Irish temper—I was very, very short-fused, but, nonetheless, scared. But I hid the fear in aggressiveness. I responded if I thought somebody was trying to get at me, or somebody was trying to, you know, quote, "disrespect me," unquote. I had a false sense of what this respect thing was. So I used to fight a lot. A lot.

But the fear wasn't so much that I was going to get hurt physically, 'cause I really didn't care about that. Once I got in the mode of fighting, it didn't matter. I feared that I was eventually going to be looked at in a certain way, or I was going to be taken as weak. I had to prove myself, and so, you know, I fell into what people normally fall into when they come to prison. What people think of them is important to them, and they try and influence what people think of them, by their actions, or their words.

*One thing I've sensed from talking to the prisoners is a definite sense of loyalty, an "us" against "them" kind of attitude, and I wonder if some prisoners have lost the ability to see people as individuals, to recognize that some guards are sons of bitches and some of them are OK, and some prisoners are sons of bitches and some of them are OK, and to judge everybody as an individual. It sounds as though there's more of a tendency to think, "Well, he's a prisoner, so he's one of us." People that I've talked to have even defended very violent, predator-type prisoners who are committing homosexual rape and such. They say things like, "Well, that kind of thing goes on and that's their bag. That kind of thing goes on, and we don't like it, but hey, you know, those are the breaks." It's sort of like, prisoner wrongdoing is winked at—*

Sure.

*—like that's OK, but—*

But this guard's a bad guy, because he's—

*Right, because he's a guard, and—*

He's a guard, and he does his job and he goes home and raises his kids beautifully,—

*Right.*

—And he's a father, and is, yeah, contributing to the community.
Terrible, awkward standard, yeah.

*To me, at times it almost sounds analogous to racism or something like that, where if you're a member of this group, then you're OK, but if you're a member of that group, then you're not. If you're white, you're OK; if you're black, you're not. If you're an American, you're OK; if you're a foreigner, then you're not. There's this kind of group loyalty thing going on, where people aren't judged as individuals.*

Sure.

*What are your thoughts on that?*

Well, what you can't really tell is how genuine it is. In other words, you can never get an honest, true, sense of people's attitude towards other people. Because in prison—though not so much here at WSR—people aren't going to admit that, you know, this officer is a likable guy, or I have respect for him. Generally speaking, you're not going to admit that, regardless of how you really feel.

There's a very strange standard in here. The set of values in prison is so awkward. I realized that several years ago. It was sick, and I couldn't believe it. It actually never dawned on me, and finally I was awakened to it. Something that's very common in here is you hear somebody that's in here for murder pointing at somebody, or talking shit about some guy that went to PC* because they raped somebody, or told on somebody. Well, those aren't good things, but murder isn't so swell either. You know what I'm saying? [Laughs.] So, there's a very, very twisted standard in here.

Something else I was going to say about that is a lot of people are so caught up here in what other people think, that they literally cannot grasp what it means to take ownership of, and responsibility of their own feelings, and their own actions. By that I mean, if I tell somebody, "I'm not going to do this just because you want me to do this. I don't feel like doing it, and that's why I'm not going to do it. I'm sorry that you want me to do it, but I'm not going to do it for you." Their only vision of this is that, "This guy isn't doing something that I want him to do. He must not have respect for me." That's real common in here, taking everything as personal, as disrespect. In fact, that's real common with a couple of guys I know well.

*Now, who's more capable of rising above these feelings, in your experience? Have you known more prisoners or more guards who were capable of rising above the "us versus them" mentality and just being genuine human beings, and treating people as individuals?*

It's pretty equal. It really is. You know, there's a few here and there on my side, and there's a few here and there on their side.

---

*Protective Custody. Prisoners in protective custody are routinely derided by other prisoners as weak or evil or both. They are the prisoners who fear for their safety if left in the general prison population—primarily sex offenders and those who have snitched on other prisoners (as well as those simply rumored to be these things, or falsely accused of being these things).

*Well, it seems like as long as both sides are caught up in this "us versus them" mentality, then you really can't see any promise on the other side, and there's no incentive to be a decent human being toward the other side. I mean, why should a guard treat you decently if whatever he does, he's going to be hated just as much as if he were the worst bastard in here? And vice versa. Why should a prisoner be cooperative or be a decent person, or treat a guard with respect,—?*

Well, I'll tell you what, though—

*—if they're going to hate you no matter what you do?*

There is incentive. And, hopefully I can say this without sounding too biased, but there is incentive on our side of it at least. But that is because we are the controlled, the powerless. I've seen time and time again, guys—inmates—actually reaching out, as a group, to communicate with the administration and with the public. PAP's involved in all kinds of groups and clubs where we're trying to reach out like that, and communicate.

The only positive thing that the administration does towards us is they may offer a program here and there, but hell, I can't even really think of anything that isn't generated by the inmate population. I mean, whatever the administration offers, they have an agenda. Their agenda is satisfying somebody, whether it's somebody in the capital, or somebody in the public that's been screaming about something and they can say, "OK, well, we're going to add a program."

*But, say, two new guards start tomorrow. And one of them is a real hard-ass, he's not honest with the prisoners, he wrongs them, within or outside of the rules, and he's just a bastard to be around. And the other fellow's a little more liberal. He's not a saint, but he's a mostly decent guy, he's mostly straight with you, treats you right, and he does what he's got to do to do his job, but he's mostly an OK guy. Are they both going to be regarded equally as the enemy?*

Nope.

*Or will there in fact be an ability to see that one of those guys is a decent human being, and one is a bastard?*

Well, if the officer that is a bastard to be around likes being a bastard to be around, then regardless of what we do, you know, he's going to do what he wants to do. But, it's going to be a lot easier for the guy who's a little bit more liberal, maybe not so rigidly adhering to every single rule. You know, maybe willing to let you in and out of your house so you can go take a shower in between gate times. Little things like that mean a lot to us. And they're recognized, too. They get respect from us.

*So there is an ability to appreciate that?*

There is, but how they receive it, or whether it matters to them, is up to them, and we obviously don't control that. But we perceive it. We appreciate it. We recognize it. They get respect, from most of us, when they are a little bit more liberal, a little bit more respectful, and a little bit more understanding of our plight, if you will.

*But it sounds like one of the things that you learn early on as a prisoner is that your first loyalty has to be to your fellow prisoners—*

Yeah.

*—and most of the convict code of unwritten rules reflects that.*

Yeah. But that's—unfortunately, that's the devil right there. I mean, for me, for years, that was the devil for me. That is the source or the reason for why I got in so many fights. That's the source of why I lit fires in the joint, had weapons in the past—

*What's the source? Be more specific.*

The source being that it mattered to me what other people think.

Well, it doesn't matter to me what other people think any more. So a guy could come up and call me a PC punk, rapo,* whatever—I'm not [laughs]—but a guy could come to me and say whatever he wants to me, in front of whoever he wants, and now, I'm able to say, "OK, who is this? First of all, do I care what this guy thinks? And second of all, even if everybody in this whole institution believes him, do I really care what they think?"

Now, I have the luxury of having that choice. Because I'm going home. There are other things that are more important to me.

But there are a lot of people that aren't going home, and this is it forever. So what their name is, or what their name means, is a big deal. Their reputation, whether somebody can work them, you know, their honor. Honor means everything.

My name is established. If I need anything right now, I can get it. I'm out of a bag of coffee; I can get it. If I need a carton of cigarettes, I can get it right now. And it's nice to be able to do that. If I was using dope, I could go get a fifty paper of heroin, probably, if it's here.

You know, my point being that the guys that aren't ever getting out, or that have so long that they're not even thinking about getting out, well, they're in a different frame of mind. And that's why I said earlier that it would be important to try and separate those guys from guys that have a release date in their head.

---

*Rapist.

*Now, why wouldn't you fear having a bad reputation? Even though you're scheduled to get out in a few months, if everyone thought you were a snitch or whatever they may think, wouldn't you be afraid of getting a knife in your back, or just something happening to you?*

Maybe. Or maybe not, just because I've made a name for myself. [Laughs.] Maybe it's easy for me to say that now. I mean, I've been through all that, and I've earned my name, and I've even had skeletons in my closet that I've had to live with.

So, it's not like, you know, what the hell am I trying to say?—maybe I've earned my name and my reputation, and I respect my fellow inmates, and I hope that I have their respect, and I've even got some good friendships in here, some very good friendships in here. But, I'm at a point where what they think of me isn't what's important. What's important to me is my movement in my life, and my experience—

*But, presumably it's only not important to you because it was important to you before. I mean, it sounds like the reason you have the luxury of not playing the game now, and not playing strictly by the convict code even at its most ridiculous, is because earlier in your time, you did play by the code, you did play the game.*

Yeah.

*And you got a reputation. So, if you had been this enlightened the day you entered prison, and said, "I'm not going to play the game," from day one, would you—?*

Guys do it.

*Would you have been able to survive at all?*

I'd have been able to survive, yeah, but I wouldn't have been one of the Fellahs. And I have the luxury of saying I am now.

Some of my friends and the people who I hang around with, and the people who I talk to in the joint, are people that are in here for murder, are in here for the most serious crimes. These are guys that grew up in the Sixties and Seventies, even the Fifties, in Walla Walla, which, you know, back then was tough.

When you think of prisoners, and you think of convicts, these are guys that were all that at Walla Walla back then. And they're not that way any more. They're older, and they're mellower. I associate myself with a group of what you might call, like, our "rat pack" of guys. There's about, probably, forty or fifty of us that fell around the same time, and were at Walla Walla all through the Eighties and Nineties, and some of them before that. All of us know each other, and know each other well. We've all worked together, we've all lived together, we've all played together, and we've been seeing each other's faces for years, I mean, day in and day out.

# BILL—March 1998

*"I have heard people say that if they were given a life sentence, they would commit suicide. I tell them, 'Why wait?' Someone so dependent upon external experiences to make their life worth living would be better off on the hara-kiri express anyway."*

Jerry and Bill in 1997. (Photo courtesy of Linda Coleman.)

Bill* is a true prison veteran. He has been incarcerated for the bulk of the last fifty years in prisons and jails around the country. He is, admittedly and unrepentantly, a career criminal. A thief, specifically.

Bill is a close friend and confidante of Jerry's. For the temporary period that WSR went double celled, they were cellmates.

Bill served as president of PAP during part of the time that I was a member. Even when he did not hold a formal office in the group, he was one of its more influential members. He is not the type to call attention to all he does for the program, but when you deal with him, you figure out pretty quickly that he is one of the few responsible guys who is willing and able to get things done.

When I, or other outside members, have initiated PAP activities, auxiliary programs, etc., Bill has lent his support, though often in a behind-the-scenes manner. It's a daunting task, given the apathy and inertia of much of the membership, and the uncertainty and inconsistency in what the administration will allow. Bill will see to it that the proper paperwork is submitted; he will provide information and reminders to other prisoners during the week; he will feel out the administration to ascertain what ideas might or might not fly; and in cases where a certain level of prisoner participation in an activity is necessary to its survival—where what we need more than anything is "asses in chairs," as Jerry puts it—he will be there.

Bill is a soft-spoken, gentle person. (Most of the time, anyway. When he's committing crimes or attempting escapes, he's not quite so harmless.) When one of us refers to him with irony as "Wild Bill," he'll gently correct us: "That's '*Mild* Bill.'"

He has a wonderful deadpan wit that likely goes over the head of many in his audience. He has a muttering, dry style (he's compared it to that of Popeye), and if you listen closely you'll hear some gems. Sometimes all he has to do is open his mouth, and he'll get Jerry laughing in anticipation, which in turn can get me and the others going. "That's my cellee," Jerry will say with a broad grin, "I know how his mind works."

Bill is clearly among the most literate of the prisoners I've met. He has written poems, short stories, song lyrics, and novels. He will not uncommonly bring up various authors and their works in conversation.

He was already well into his 60s when I met him. He'll joke about aging, but I don't think it sits well with him. Some old people probably don't feel the loss of their youth as much because they never did a whole lot with it when they had it. But Bill has always squeezed all the adventure he could out of life, always exercised his capacities to their fullest. He knows what he's lacking as his mind and body betray him.

He'll lose his train of thought here and there, and has to work a little harder to concentrate and remember things, but I haven't seen anything more severe than that. If he's on the road to senility, I'd say he's traversed less than 5% of it so far.

---

*Bill has chosen to be identified by his first name only.

Still, I think he rebels even at these beginnings of mental deterioration. I once observed him lose his temper and storm out of a PAP meeting. He'd had some momentary difficulty grasping what someone was saying to him, and he felt he was being teased about it. To me it seemed innocuous, but it was enough to send him out of the room in anger and disgust.

Physically, Bill is a good-sized man who could certainly still handle himself if someone made the mistake of testing him. But I'm sure he cut a much more imposing figure twenty or forty years ago.

Bill had a hell of a time figuring me out when we first encountered each other. We joke about it now, but those first few meetings he eyed me warily. He couldn't fit me into any of the categories he was familiar with from his many years of incarceration. What was I doing volunteering at a prison? Was I a naïve do-gooder? Religious missionary? Gay guy? Wannabe criminal? He just couldn't get a fix on me.

For a time, he even entertained the notion that I was an undercover cop, sent in to infiltrate the group. "You were always listening so closely," he said, "Taking it all in. Paying a little too close attention."

Even after several years, he'll still occasionally ask me in all seriousness, "Why do you come out here?" In other words, "What's in it for you?" I answer as best I can, and he studies me closely. Then he acknowledges my answer with a nod and an "Mmm hmm," and goes on his way. It still doesn't quite add up for him.

Bill is typically an eager enough conversationalist, albeit in his low-key sardonic way, but once the tape recorder was running, he played things as close to the vest as any of the interviewees. He has consistently adhered to the convict code for decades, and one of its most important tenets is to safeguard confidentiality, to know when to keep your mouth shut. Bill's responses to my questions tended to be careful and controlled. He rarely took advantage of opportunities to spell out his thoughts in detail, to engage me in debate. Much safer to say too little than too much.

Bill was one of the few prisoners who was at least as willing to engage in written correspondence with me as to do taped interviews. He is experienced and comfortable with the written word in a way that few other prisoners are.

In his correspondence, you will note that he sometimes peppers his answers with the heavy slang of a Jimmy Cagney prison movie. It's a persona he turns on and off at will to amuse himself. He's just having some fun, trying to make the book a little more colorful. He's also capable of speaking and writing in as urbane a style as you'd like.

His outlook on life is bemused and cynical. He chuckles at what he takes to be my more moralistic questions and comments. He simply doesn't look at the world in such terms, he'll tell me. He lets me know such an approach is bound to be ineffectual with him, as well as with the vast majority of the other prisoners.

Yes, Bill is quite proudly amoral. An amoralist who wouldn't double-cross his partners regardless of how much he would profit, or who will put together a "welcome basket" of coffee, cigarettes, and candy for a new prisoner who arrives empty-handed. An amoralist who will write a letter home for a prisoner who is too mentally unstable or illiterate to do it himself, and who is as courteous and gentlemanly to the volunteers on Wednesday nights as anyone there. An amoralist who will keep up the spirits of those around him with his humor, and who will put in the extra work that almost no one else will to see to it that PAP survives.

So I'll keep working on him, trying to convince him there's something wrong with helping oneself to other people's property. And he'll keep resisting. And in the process, we'll share some good times, have some laughs, and maybe gradually come to understand each other better. For while I will never concede that his career choice is an ethically acceptable one, Bill is someone I am genuinely fond of, one of my favorite people out there.

Here, then, is my first set of written questions for Bill, and his responses.

*For what crime are you currently in prison? Tell me as much as you are willing about what you did, the circumstances, etc. If what you were convicted of and sentenced for differs significantly from what you actually did, address that too.*

I am enclosing a "rap sheet" which explains all that and more.

[Later I asked Bill to supplement the official documents he provided to me with his own version of the events, which he did. Normally in this book, I do not include the perspective of law enforcement, but since Bill specifically gave this material to me as his response to my question, and because we later refer back to it, I will quote from it at length here.]

OFFICIAL VERSION OF THE OFFENSE

On April 1, 1983, a burglary alarm was sounded at Sound Services* in Longview, Washington. Based upon that alarm, an officer was dispatched from Sound as well as a Longview Police officer. When the Sound officer (a retired Longview Police officer) and Officer Burleson† arrived at the scene, they approached

---

*I have changed the name of the company.
†I have changed the name.

the house together. Upon arriving at the house, the defendant came around the corner leveling a 9mm Browning semi-automatic pistol at them. [Bill] grabbed Security Officer Jenner* and ended up sticking the gun in his ribs and used him as a hostage or shield in an effort to get the uniformed police officer to leave so that he could make good his escape. During the course of the negotiations, [Bill] threatened both Officer Burleson and Security Officer Jenner repeatedly with the pistol. He was able to make his way down the driveway toward the street, using Jenner as a shield and a hostage. During this event, another uniformed officer was able to get behind [Bill] and get him into a cross-fire between Burleson and himself.

[Bill] was taken into custody and was searched at the scene. In addition to the Browning 9mm semi-automatic pistol which was fully loaded, the officers found a .38 cal. Derringer on his person. This weapon was also loaded.

After [Bill's] arrest, it was determined that the house had been forcibly entered through a sliding glass door at the rear of the house. Nearby was found [Bill's] vehicle, a 1977 Mercury Marquis bearing Nebraska license 2——. This vehicle was impounded and a search warrant was issued on it. Found in the vehicle, among other items, were a .38 cal. Colt Cobra, stolen from a police officer in Georgia, a pair of hand-cuffs stolen from the same officer, and a .45 cal. Colt semi-automatic pistol. Both guns were loaded. Also found among the defendant's possessions were license plates from Iowa and Washington issued to this same vehicle. [Bill] told us later that he had resold the vehicle to himself in these states

*I have changed the name.

under various names in an effort to get license plates and titles which corresponded to the VIN number on that vehicle. In addition, he had identification for various other names. He had a Nebraska driver's license under the name of [alias], and passports made out to [three more aliases]. He had a Colorado driver's license and identification belonging to [another alias], and a Mastercharge card. [Bill] also possessed a "super ear" listening device which he indicated he had planned to use at a later time for bugging a security company.

In addition to the bugging-wire-tapping equipment, the defendant had a CB radio in his car and the holster or carrying case to a portable scanner which he indicated to other officers, was on loan to an un-named friend at the time of this burglary. A single-bitted ax found in the vehicle appeared to have safe insulation material on the blade. [Bill] indicated that this was probably what the material was. Among his personal effects were a large number of magazines dealing with coin collecting and miscellaneous jewelry.

[Bill] played games with the Longview Police Department for several hours after his arrest. At one point, he told the officer his name was John Doe and he desires to be booked as that. It took considerable effort in questioning him and running teletypes before his eventual real identity was discovered. It was discovered that [Bill] had warrants out for him in other states, most of these for escape, as well as a Federal UFAP warrant.

[Bill] apparently had connections with a bondsman known as Paul Gunn* in the Vancouver-Portland, Oregon, area. Mr. Gunn alleged to have done business with [Bill] before and has

*I have changed the name.

some trust in him even though the UFAP warrant
was outstanding.

In his interviews with law enforcement officers here, [Bill] expressed a willingness to
shoot it out with police but the arrival of
the last armed officer behind him was too great
a chance to risk a gun battle. [Bill] at all
times was obviously willing to use the loaded
firearm that he had in his possession. His only
reason for surrendering was his belief that he
would not survive a gun battle.

[The paperwork Bill provided to me also contained the final disposition of the case.]

[Bill] was charged with first degree burglary and first degree kidnapping on April 4,
1983. On April 7, 1983, [Bill] pled guilty to
both charges, containing allegations that he
was armed with a deadly weapon and a firearm at
the time of the commission of the offense. The
court entered firearm and weapons findings and
sentenced [Bill] to concurrent life sentences
on both charges.]

*I think a lot of people would look at you and say, "Wait a minute. This isn't somebody who's too young, or too dumb, or too strung out on drugs to know better. What's he doing in here?" What has society, or the prison system, or you done wrong to explain why a grown man with obvious intelligence and talents has not "gone straight" and spent his life in more productive ways than committing crimes and languishing in prison?*

That old dock-walloper/philosopher, Eric Hoffer, said in *The True Believer*, "Attitudes structure situations." The reverse of that adage is also true.

My earliest memories are of the police being the enemy. I was arrested at age 6 (1939) for stealing postcards and selling them in taverns. All of my values, problem-solving skills, education and social perspectives were acquired while I was in custody.

I seemed to have a natural aptitude for getting money illegally so I never developed any work ethic.

What the hell, the justice-system is based upon adversarial encounters between prosecution and defense. The prison-system is designed to stifle accepted norms and mores of behavior. To give a fellow prisoner an item of food or to lend him a book is a punishable act. Guards tend to be nit-picking and antagonistic. The line between "them" and "us" is maintained at every level of the judicial system. "Getting away with it" becomes a way of life for prisoners.

That attitude carries over upon release from custody. A prisoner hits the streets broke, alone, and eager to catch up on the hiatus of action. He wants to be like everyone else who is living a middle-class life style. This means acquiring the wherewithal to get a car, decent living quarters, and any and all other accouterments necessary to pursue his hard-wired gonadic quests.

Got to get the cash in a flash—continue till captured—get released—jump back on the merry-go-round. Our prisoner has long since lost all fear of capture and incarceration. Ambition, experience and absence of fear equals escalating criminal activity.

Languish is not a word I'd choose to describe doing time. The stigma of being a criminal has lost its sting. All that is really lost in prison is the ability to travel and express oneself romantically. Everyone has to be some place.

Prison to a convict is like a small town to a hick. "Nothing ever happens around here." Not true for *all* prisoners. The prisoner's creed is, "It's not where you are, but who you are."

Besides, if you have lived by the code, the more often you come to prison, the more friends you acquire.

*Compare friendships made in prison with friendships made on the outside.*

Harry Browne, in *How I Found Freedom in an Unfree World*, maintains that one should never go out of character to make friends. If you do, you risk spending virtually all of your time with people you have nothing in common with.

A prisoner serving a long sentence will spend more time with his close friends than he spent with any friend, lover or relative in the free-world. For instance, my best friend in this place is with me six-to-eight hours every day, and when WSR double-cells, we will cell together. We're talking maybe twenty hours in each other's company each day. Can you think of any other situation where you spend 600 hours a month with anyone?

I have been in six prisons. In each prison there were one or two people who could use my money as their own and count on me to back any play they may initiate up-to-and-including….

When I am free, any of those dozen-odd people are welcome to sleep under my roof, eat at my table, and use my car, cash and wardrobe as they see fit. There are two free people, both women, who are in that same category. I believe that extreme conditions tend to mold lasting friendships. Prison certainly qualifies.

*What about prison do you think would come as the biggest surprise to people who have had no prison experience at all?*

I think the biggest surprise about prisons for free-world folks would be the way prisoners accept the loss of freedom. I have heard people say that if they were given a life sentence, they would commit suicide. I tell them, "Why wait?" Someone so dependent upon external experiences to make their life worth living would be better off on the hara-kiri express anyway.

Many people are surprised by the apparent normalcy of prisoners. I have had prison officials tell me that after reading my record and then talking to me in person they cannot believe it is indeed the same person. Public persona vs. private reality is not unique to prisons, but it seems to be more pronounced in a prison setting.

*Prisoners often talk about WSR as if it were dramatically different from other prisons. Describe what is different about WSR compared to other places where you have been incarcerated.*

WSR! This is a very soft camp. To be able to talk to our volunteers and sponsors, to have the freedom to use the yard and gym all day, to have an excellent library, good food and living conditions makes WSR pretty unique.

I have been in prisons where there are no paying jobs, yard is one hour each day on a cement basketball court, you never see the night sky for many years and there is no contact with people who do not work for the prison.

All Southern prisons feature long sentences, brutal physical labor, corporal punishment, bad food and no pay. Many big prisons—San Quentin, the Texas Prison Farms, Reidsville, Georgia (my last escape) and many more—experience mayhem on a daily basis and murder several times a year. This is the garden-spot of prisondom.

# BILL—March 1998

*"Escaping is more attitude than mental prowess or physical strength. The first and most daunting step is to be cognizant that you are putting your ass in serious jeopardy. The second step is to empathize with the people who want to keep you caged. Ask yourself, 'If I were he and he were me, would I be aware of this attempt and would I have a counter move to thwart it?'"*

I wrote back to Bill with several follow-ups to my initial questions, as well as some new questions. He mailed me a response almost immediately.

*What more can you tell me in your own words about your most recent offense that landed you in prison? Any time I see something labeled an "official version," I know I'm not getting the full story. You mentioned in conversation, for instance, that the implication that there were only three or so cops there was false, that in fact there were over a dozen arrayed against you.*

I had left a load of merchandise with a fence in Oregon and, having some time to while away until I got my money, I went to Washington to look at a score. It wasn't kosher, so I thought to pay my expenses with a quick burg or two.

I set off a silent alarm of a type I was unfamiliar with. Initially, there was one cop behind the place and two approaching from the front. I chose to jack up the two rather than the one because it was more convenient to my car and I figured the one in back for a shotgun. I made the uniform lay his pistol on the ground and got the mufti-guy around the neck with my pistol in his ribs. He made a play for the gun and I placed it on his temple.

This place was just a couple blocks from coppo-shoppo, so before I progressed much further, I was ass-deep in SWAT-teamers. I am sometimes a bit reckless, but I was never suicidal.

The total count of involved fuzz-folk was sixteen—including the two I was brow-beating.

After the third warning to put the pistola on the sod, I figured I had gotten all possible mileage out of the stand-off and complied with the demand.

I made my phone call to a bondsman friend of mine and engaged the cops in a long-winded conversation (with the emphasis on the first syllable) to try and maintain the status quo until the guy could get there to post my bond. He tried to post the required 50K and they raised it to 100K. I copped a quick plea to get transferred out of that jurisdiction before the teletype could dump aspersions upon my sterling character.

*It looks like from your record that you've escaped on multiple occasions. How common are escapes? Are you better at it, and able to pull off escapes in ways that other prisoners couldn't, or do a lot of people get away like you did?*

Escapes are like the Thomas Alva Edison quote regarding genius: "One percent inspiration and ninety-nine percent perspiration." Very few prisoners have the grit and determination to escape, because that act puts one in much the same status as a six-point buck in deer season. In many instances, an escape gives the authorities carte blanche to make an escapee start his sentence over. If you have several years served, it doesn't count. You have to go back to the starting line and begin anew.

It does require some ingenuity to escape. There are but four methods to beat the first obstacle—climb over, dig under, bore through, or bullshit your way past. The latter is the most effective ergo the most desirable method. There is still that "moment of truth" to be faced, but the odds are much better when one makes his play away from the shadow of the gun-towers.

Escaping is more attitude than mental prowess or physical strength. The first and most daunting step is to be cognizant that you are putting your ass in serious jeopardy. The second step is to empathize with the people who want to keep you caged. Ask yourself, "If I were he and he were me, would I be aware of this attempt and would I have a counter move to thwart it?"

*When I read your account of the impact of environmental factors from childhood and from incarceration on the attitudes and behavior of yourself and other prisoners, I find most of it quite plausible. It makes perfect sense that if people are confined in places with perverse modes of behavior and value systems, they have to be affected by that. On the other hand, it's the kind of account that I think would be more convincing if it concerned other people or even your past self instead of your present self. That is to say, once you're aware that certain of your beliefs, attitudes and behavior are the result of factors such as the prison system's being intentionally designed to warp people and stifle their sense of right and wrong, then why retain those beliefs, attitudes and values? Once you're self-aware enough to explain these things in terms of your past and your environment, then the explanation undercuts itself.*

Just as the escapee must use empathy to anticipate the reaction of the cop, I would suggest that *you* use empathy to understand the answer to this question regarding anti-social behavior by people who are aware of the high-risk and low-yield of criminal lifestyles. It is true that we learn by our mistakes, but what we learn and how we use that knowledge depends upon the structure of our value system.

So, Craig Convict, you're getting out next year after serving 12 years. Has the system made a believer of you or are you going to get back on the high-wire? Sure, prison is pathetic and boring. So is the menial life you're returning to; at least in prison you have the excuse that they are holding a rifle on you to make you live on the brute level. If you are content to flip burgers and live in squalid conditions, what was the point of leaving prison?

*You state that the "stifl[ing] of accepted norms and mores of behavior" in prison is not some sort of unintended byproduct of the system, but is in fact intentional. Could you elaborate on this? What do prison officials do that has the goal of warping prisoners morally and encouraging them to adopt value systems that do not fit with those of society? Why would they pursue such a goal?*

Of course the reason the administration plays the petty tyrant, calls you an inmate, keeps IMU filled to capacity for petty offenses, encourages ethnic dissension, and makes eye contact with staff a punishable offense is to discourage unity among prisoners and to keep the majority of prisoners servile abject rule followers.

It is simply a management tool. If there were any solidarity, it would be extremely difficult to keep a million Americans locked up and another million plus under the onus of judicial blackmail via jails, probation, community-placement, etc.

Prisons are good for the economy and the social structure, but there is a saturation point. I figure that at around five million incarcerated and ten million under the imminent threat of being slammed. Perhaps I'm wrong and Keynesian principles apply. "Spend your way to prosperity," with currency being convicted undesirables. I know that is a digression, but it may anticipate a question you have for later.

*"All that is really lost in prison is the ability to travel and express oneself romantically." This is quite an attention-grabbing sentence. I have mixed feelings about it. On the one hand, I want to say it's a useful reminder of how most of the truly important things in life are things that are a part of you in any circumstances; that material possessions, creature comforts, common freedoms, etc. can easily be overrated and can distract us from the things that really matter. On the other hand, it could be a therapeutic self-deception. One way to adapt to adverse circumstances is to convince oneself that they're really not that bad after all, regardless of whether this happens to be true. Is the reason you don't miss what you lack in prison that those things aren't particularly important or desirable after all, or is it that to obsess on what you lack would serve no useful purpose but would just drive you crazy or make you miserable?*

No, I don't think that my attitude about prison being just some place to be is sour grapes. Of course, if I had the chance to live a more "normal" middle-class life, I'd take it.

# 130     PRISON CONVERSATIONS

"Take" is the operative word, though. I don't dread prison to the degree that I'd inform on a friend or relative to get out. I would not kill a guard to get out.

I have lived an extravagant life style, and I don't recall that I went about daily life with a permanent feeling of elation. Life is food, water, and air. All the rest are abstractions and creature comforts which we use to feel superior to the rest of the animal kingdom. I certainly enjoy no immunity to that vanity. I *am* aware of it and sometimes amused by it.

*Approximately how many total years of your life have you spent incarcerated? Realistically, what is the earliest date you could be released this time? The latest? Will your release be unconditional and unrestricted, or some form of parole?*

I have not been legally free since the winter of 1969. I had three escapes during that time and IT WAS GROOVY!!

I doubt that I will ever get out. A conservative estimate would be that I have done more than half my life under lock.

*What is your take on "victims' rights?" It seems very popular nowadays to assert that society bends over backwards to ensure exaggerated rights for suspects, defendants, prisoners, etc., and in the process gives short shrift to crime victims. Is this accurate? Is the system so soft on criminals as to, in some sense, favor them over their victims?*

Victims Rights is another Law Enforcement and Judicial System propaganda device. It is a good vehicle to dehumanize and demonize high profile defendants. Media coverage of that vituperation and righteous indignation against conceived monsters tends to stigmatize all prisoners, thereby justifying whatever zealots deem appropriate to do to "bad guys" and "scumbags"—two current buzzwords.

Soft on crime—my aching arse. Everyone I know is serving at least triple what was required when they were hard on crime.

# BILL—April 1998

*"'Coddling criminals.' That's always seemed
like a pretty good idea to me."*

Bill and Jerry in 1997.

Shortly after I received his second set of responses, I had the opportunity to sit down with Bill for a taped interview.

*Bill, just following up on some of the stuff we've done in writing, as you have described it, the criminal lifestyle is clearly a hard habit to break. It's the so-called "revolving door" phenomenon. When prisoners are released, they often just resume the lifestyle that they're used to and comfortable with, and then they come right back here if they get caught. From society's standpoint, what can we do about this revolving door problem? What could the system do differently that would result in fewer people falling into the habits you've described?*

I don't really see any solution.

Sociologists have been working on this for a long time. What do they call it?—"self-perpetuating institutions," I think.

I don't think stopping it is what people are looking for anyway. I think they're probably looking to increase the prison population rather than stop these guys from coming back.

I don't think it's a communist plot or anything like that, but it's good for the economy, and good for society.

These places are really geared to take away from the values, you know, the mores of society and things of that nature.

If there is a way for penology to do something for the crime rate and lessen it, I don't know. I don't know what it is, and I don't think anybody else does.

*So you're saying that they don't have a solution, and if they did, they probably wouldn't want to implement it anyway, because they want a lot of people in prison.*

There's a lot of reformers that would like to see things changed, and it is pretty much done on a right wing/left wing basis. The left wing wants to help people that they consider need help—the social aspects of things. And the right wing just wants to grind them. It's been that way ever since I was a kid, and before then.

My theory is that when the Berlin Wall crashed, that took the boogie man away. You know, J. Edgar Hoover was a past master at that. They'd say, "Did you misappropriate funds? Have you been taking credit for things you shouldn't?" and he'd say, "Is that a Communist behind that bush there?!" They had Big Brother behind the Berlin Wall, and then that caved in.

You have to have a boogie man, a scapegoat, and we kind of became that. Police departments got into public relations. They know how to appropriate money, and they know they have to demonize, dehumanize a certain class of people.

It's not that anybody I know personally doesn't have it coming. If I was a parole board member and a guy like me come up, I'd say, "No, I'm not going to turn you loose on those people. Man, look at your track record."

But it's good for the economy to have a large prison population. It gets fruit pickers off the street and stuff like that.

*Elaborate on that. Why is it good for the economy? Because, I think most people, looking at it superficially, would say that it's obviously undesirable for society to encourage crime and prison terms. Why would we want people out there robbing and killing, and then put them in prison and have to pay a fortune to give them room and board and such? I mean, it seems like a net loss for society. Why do you feel it's in their best interests?*

Do you know what the budget is for the prison system? I don't know; I haven't been interested enough to look it up. But I know it's a whopping amount of money. And where does that go? That goes to the grocers, and, you know, the wholesaler for this, and the wholesaler for that. It sounds cynical, but there's a lot of brother-in-law deals in there. Like this upcoming construction they have planned for here. Some brother-in-laws will do pretty well on that, I'm pretty sure. Wait and see what the price tag is on that.

When I was at the medium security units at the Walls, they brought in a crew to fix the showers. These guys are former guards that had retired, and they bring them in to set up.

The one guy had a lunch bucket the size of a pick-up truck bed. And they'd sit up there at this rotunda. They had this wing closed off so they could repair the shower. They were down there about two weeks, and I thought they were retiling that shower, and when they finally cleared off and went to the next tier, I went down there to take a shower.

What they'd done, they'd replaced the tile around the faucet, you know, about three pounds of tile total. The story was that they got a hundred and eighty thousand dollars for that. Somebody supposedly saw the bill.

So, yeah, there's plenty of graft and corruption.

*I can see how it could be in the very narrow economic self-interest of some individuals and institutions that can make a dishonest buck off of certain contracts and such, but do you think it's in society in general's economic interest to have a lot of people in prison?*

Well, yeah, I think that if you count the amount of people that are employed at the correctional end of it, and at the judicial end of it, there's a lot of people making a lot of money off of this. Right now we're at full employment—the Keynesian point of full employment I think is four and a half percent—and that's about where we are.

Of course when Reagan come in, he incorporated the armed services into that. I don't know if you're aware of that, but that's when they started counting people in the armed forces as employed, so the unemployment figures would come out lower.

But I think it would put a dent in that if they didn't put all these people in prison. If everybody'd go honest and stop doing things that put them in the penitentiary, they'd have to make more laws. I think the engine's feeding itself. I don't think it's close to saturation yet.

*So there'd be no productive use for all these extra people.*

No, I think that you wouldn't have to bring any Mexicans up to pick the crops.

I wrote a term paper on that one time, based on that—the economics of prison, you know, starting from the county jail and all those people that are employed, and all the supplies they use, mattresses and tear gas, and this and that. You're talking about a million people locked up in the United States now. It's quadrupled since the last time I checked a few years back.

*You made a kind of facetious remark that you're not alleging a "communist plot," or anything, so I took that to mean that you're not appealing to some kind of simplistic conspiracy theory.*

No, it's not like everybody's just saying, "Well let's do this and make some money." Like I say, the police and the prosecuting attorneys, you know, it's their job to get people into prison. And they have the public relations now and know how to use it, and it's all on their side.

*Well, to what extent are the people in the system conscious of these goals that you're describing? To what extent are people consciously thinking, "Let's pretend we're trying to cut crime, but let's really try to put as many people in prison as possible"?*

If they want to cut crime, you know, they could legalize drugs and put people on maintenance for drugs—the real bad dope fiends down there beating those old ladies in the head, stealing TVs and selling them. They could reduce the crime rate by a whopping percent, just by doing that. But I don't think it would appeal to the right wing of the Christian Moral Majority, and whip up the troops.

It's just that, right now, we're it. We're who the bad guys are. You see it if you watch TV. Those two buzz words—"scumbag" and "bad guys"—if you watch TV all day without hearing those eighteen times, I'd be surprised.

So, it's not that they're saying, "Let's put everybody in prison," but public opinion wants it, and—

*But to what extent is it a conscious, cynical strategy where they're intentionally trying to put a lot of people in prison and pretending otherwise?*

Well, starting with the politicians, and down to the prosecutors, what you have is an adversarial thing, and it's their job to get as many people in prison as possible. The sheriff and the police want promotions, and they want bigger police forces, and the NRA's all for this. They swap out with the police departments to get their agendas going, put money on people who are right thinking, you know, right wingers. So that much is conscious. That's just a scam.

They bugaboo people, tell them, "How would you like these guys in your neighborhood? These guys'll be getting out, moving next to you. We need harsher sentences, and more prisons." I believe that much is conscious.

But I think the public is duped quite a bit. You know, every time the politicians get on there, talking about, "I'll put my trust in the intelligence and the common sense of the American people," well, if they ain't laughing up their sleeves on that one.

*Clearly the general public isn't in on the plot. They're not consciously saying, "Let's put as many people in prison as possible for the economic good of society." They want less crime.*

Well, yeah, but when they go to the polls, they've been had a little bit, propagandized, you know, by the people that have the money, that get on the media, and the ones that can get on there free, like the police. It used to be that they always accused the press of slanting to the left, but it's pretty well slanting to the right now.

Course, it's always been cyclical. I've been around long enough to see that. In the Fifties, they wanted to pound you. In the late Sixties and Seventies they wanted to "coddle" you.

"Coddling criminals." That's always seemed like a pretty good idea to me.

*Why don't you talk a little bit about the prison rules and procedures, and the motivations behind them, because in some of your written responses, you indicated that they're intended to warp the prisoners' values and make them not fit for law-abiding society later.*

Well, that's like if you come in here and don't have anything, and I think you're a pretty good guy, and I say, "Well, you know, Craig's a solid guy. He never snitched on anybody, never raped nobody's baby, and he just come here from the county jail. Let's get him together a little package with some coffee, and some cookies and stuff." Hell, it's against the law. They'll have fourteen charges on you for that. They got little three digit numbers they put up there until they run out of space on the paper for that. They'll take you to court and find you innocent of some of them and guilty of some of them. They never find anybody innocent of all of them.

*Now clearly they have at least an alleged reason for that rule. They wouldn't say it's just a matter of, "We want to stop these people from being generous toward each other, and try not to let them be friends." I mean, they'd say, "Well, this is the only way you can prevent people from being extorted. If somebody steals something from someone, and the person's scared to accuse him of it, the only way to prevent that is to say: if you've got somebody else's property, even if that person claims he gave it to you, then we're not going to honor that. We're going to assume you stole it." I mean, on the surface, that's a plausible justification for having that rule. Why do you feel that that's not an appropriate rule?*

Yeah, in the past that's been used to exploit people, and even what they call the chicken hawks[*] would get the young guys by giving them candy and stuff like that.

But, you know, if I subscribe to a newspaper, and say we're both from Portland, Oregon, and I get the Portland, Oregon paper and loan it to you, we're both subject to a week in the hole for that, get fined fifty dollars, lose thirty days of good time.

I think that they just take it to such extremes, you know, ridiculous extremes. They have enough people telling them what really goes on that they don't really think if I loan you a newspaper that I'm trying to exploit you in some kind of way.

Now, I've been on the other end of that. I have exploited people. I've loan sharked, run poker games, and stuff like that. That's legitimate if they bust me. And they have a couple times. At that other place, I had a hundred dollars in loose scrip, and you're only supposed to have five dollars in loose scrip. You can have a hundred dollars on your books, but you can only carry up to five dollars, because that's how much you could have got in change at the store.

So they found a hundred dollars in my cell. I don't have any beef about that. But if they find a guy with six dollars and twenty-five cents, you know, it's kind of ridiculous.

*It seems almost like you're advocating letting the guards have more discretion, that they should be able to use common sense and say, "Well, you know, if it's not too far beyond the rules, then we should let it go," but do you trust them to use common sense like that?*

Well, no. No I don't. Especially the new guards.

You know, you have to have some rules. It is a prison. But the one we were talking about earlier, some of that is just that they want to keep you off balance, off your guard so you don't coalesce into some kind of a formidable union-type thing. They have to discourage that.

I've never seen it here, but I've seen it in other prisons, where they'll encourage racial strife and things, to keep guys from, you know, getting too strong. They pit people against each other.

*What do they do that would encourage that kind of stuff?*

Well, they'll just say, "Man, I just heard that nigger say some pretty terrible stuff about you. It's none of my business, but I just thought I'd tell you to be on your guard, man." And then they tell the same thing to the black guy about you. And then it's the Mexicans.

Then they encourage stool pigeons. They're a law enforcement tool, and they try to get people to believe that they have to do that.

Any time they see a guy get his head a little bit above the surface, well they'll snatch him up, lock him up in the hole for a year or something.

I don't really know if there's anything to do about that either. [Laughs.]

---

[*]Homosexual predators in prison.

*Well, I think the public would say that those rules all sound very plausible from the standpoint of security and such. I mean, it doesn't sound like the only reason the institution would have those rules would be because they're trying to warp people morally, and make them unable to function in normal society when they get out, and so on.*

Well, I'm not saying that it's a conscious effort. But, the way they force you to interact with people in here, if you did that in your neighborhood, you'd be a hateful son of a bitch. A guy comes up and says, "Could I borrow a cup of coffee?" and you say, "Get out of here before I call the police!" [Laughs.]

They don't want too many fast friends in here. And they don't want the guards to get too friendly with us.

The new guards they've just indoctrinated, you notice it when you go through that metal detector. When you go through it, if you were a blind man you could tell how long that guy's worked here by the way he shakes you down. If he squeezes your socks [demonstrates by meticulously patting down his legs from the bottom up] and, you know, fluffs your hair, then you say, "Now, this son of a bitch hasn't been here two weeks yet." If the guy says, "Go on, man," [demonstrates with a dismissive wave to pass on through], he's probably ready for retirement. And there's all kinds of things in between.

*One of the things we've written about in our correspondence is that a lot of people who've never experienced prison assume that it's this horrible thing, and they say, "I'd rather kill myself than be in prison, especially for a long time, for a life sentence." And you wrote about how, in reality, a lot of prisoners adapt quite well, that they're mostly normal people, and more or less content with their lot. How common is it for prisoners to adapt so readily like that? Do most people who go to prison fit in fairly well?*

Well, most guys that are, you know, criminals or even borderline criminals that steal for the money, for the living, they know this is a part of it. They're raised in the system.

And after you come to prison the first time, you don't really have the fear any more. It's not what you thought, you know, that when you first get inside the walls, everybody's waiting with a big knife to sodomize you or kill you or whatever.

So you're watching the ball game, or you've got this coming up, and there's little entertainment things, and distractions. It's pretty much like you're outside, but you just don't go home at night. You have your friends and your little social thing.

Really, except for a few, like I said, of the abstractions, you're pretty much living as good as most people. Probably better than some.

*Now these people who assume it's going to be horrible and that they'd rather be dead and all that, if someone like that actually does get convicted of a crime and get sent to prison, what usually happens to them? Is it a self-fulfilling prophecy? Do they have as much trouble adapting as they thought, or do they end up seeing it's not as bad as they expected?*

Yeah, I think most do. Like you, you'd probably say, "Man, I'd hate to be in this son of a bitch. I can go home. I can leave here tonight." But if you got here, you'd make three or four pretty good friends, with like interests that you have.

People can adapt to damn near anything. You can sleep down by the river and it doesn't bother you, or stay in a Holiday Inn and it doesn't bother you.

Some of the ones you see get here, you know, they think it's like their life is coming to an end. But this is just a different form of society. There are primitive societies and sophisticated societies, and this is probably somewhere between the two.

*So you find that not that many people who actually get to prison, are in despair, and suicidal, and that kind of thing.*

Not unless when they first come in—if they've done something that's horrified their own family and stuff, and they feel like they've done something they can't live with, well they might be. But, if a guy's in here for sticking up a delicatessen or some kind of theft, where he's not a pariah in this place, then no, it's pretty easy to adapt.

Some people are just a little flaky anyway. You know, they can't take this, can't take that.

As far as this doubling up, just tonight I heard some people—some people you know quite well—sounding like an old married couple. "Man, you put this stuff on the shelf! I want to put it under the bed!" and back and forth. You know, they give us foot lockers to use, so I called to them, "Ah shit, just throw the stuff in your foot locker and shut up!"

*What do you think's going to happen with that? Are tensions going up due to the double celling?*

Yeah. Have you seen the cells in here? Two people living in that space is hard, unless you're a pretty adaptable person. There will be a lot of fist fights, and I won't be surprised if before a long hot summer's over, they'll burn this son of a bitch down, to tell you the truth.

*So you think it could really get out of control, full scale rioting potentially?*

I mean, it's only been a couple days, and already guys are hollering, "Hey, shut up man! I'm trying to sleep, you know?" It's twice as noisy, and confined a lot closer. You can't have the privacy to use the facilities. Guys that had little comfort zones—you know, whatever they did, they read or watched TV—that's kind of gone by the boards.

*So even though for the most part you got to choose who you were going to room with, it's still causing a lot of tension.*

Of course, you know, Jerry, now, he's done twenty-one years straight, and I've done probably thirty-five years, and we're used to bad conditions, down in the hole so many times. This is a pretty comfortable little place for us, like living in a submarine.

*How much of your thirty-five years have you had a cell to yourself?*

Not much. I've been in dormitories, and mostly double cells.

*Walla Walla is what, four to a cell?*

Four to a cell. Usually three, because they weren't that crowded. It's a four man cell with three people in it, four bunks. And they were as big as this office, so it wasn't too bad.

*You mentioned, in response to my question about what would people be most surprised about concerning prison, that prisoners seem so normal. You know, they'd talk to prisoners and they'd say, "Hang on, this is just a regular guy, like I'd meet out on the streets." Why do prisoners seem so normal?*

Well, it's just that when they're not doing what they do, when they're with their peers, they're pretty much the same as anybody else.

Before I got to prison, I thought Humphrey Bogart and Jimmy Cagney were in here, beating tin cups on the bars and all that shit.

Granted, there's always a violent atmosphere in here. A lot of these guys are in here for murder, some of them for brutal murder. But they don't have the incentive to do that. Whatever drove them to do that isn't present any more. They're just like a bunch of guys that are in any big institution. It's like an army post. You make friends, you do this, you get interested in that—who won the ball game, who won the Academy Awards, what's for dinner, and things like that.

*So for at least most of the prisoners, their crime was somewhat out of character, or aberrational. Most of the time, they're just like the guys you'd meet down at the local bar, or the military post, or whatever.*

Same thing. You know, they have the same interests, and likes and dislikes.

*So if I just took somebody at random from the general population in here, would they seem surprisingly normal to me?*

Well, another thing is that when they took the money away from the mental institutions, they let quite a few people out of mental institutions, and they end up in facilities, lockdowns. So there are a few more nuts than there were in the old days.

But generally speaking, you know, eighty percent of the population is just average people that ran up against some problems. A lot of these guys were workers, mill workers, agricultural workers, fishermen, loggers, and that's what they're thinking of getting back to. When they talk to you, they got pictures of their wife and kids, and that's what they want to go back to.

*I think this brings us back to a point you were making earlier about demonizing criminals and convicts, because I think a lot of people would be surprised how normal the prisoners seem. Because there is a tendency to oversimplify, to think the good guys are on the outside and the bad guys are on the inside, and they're just like totally different species. You know, they're animals, they aren't like us. They don't have normal human motivations and normal values and such.*

Did you ever read a book called *Kind and Usual Punishment?*

*No.*

That'd be worth reading. This woman interviewed dozens of people, sometimes surreptitiously, and she went to parole board meetings, and conventions and things. And some of the ridiculous things—like one guy, one of the wardens, said, "Those criminals don't feel pain like other people do."

Anyway, she told about this one guy who was a warden for the federal system, and he was kind of a traveling warden, and when they wanted to appropriate money or they had some agenda, they wanted to get something done, they'd send this guy around, and he was an expert at making the people riot. They'd tear the beds up and burn the place, and that's so they could appropriate more money.

*How did he make people riot? How did he provoke them?*

Well he'd just come in here, and whatever little things you had going, he'd say, "That's out! You're not doing it any more! We're cutting this out! We're cutting that out! And you guys that have been going to yard, you're coming in at three o'clock in the afternoon." Confrontation.

One thing about these guys in here, they probably accept confrontation a little quicker than people in the free world. So their response is pretty standard, and they know what it'll be. They say, "Shit, let's burn this son of a bitch down then if they're going to do us that way!"

And that's what they do, and so then the guy can go on to the next one. Might not be the next day, but, you know, eighteen months down the road, they'll say, "Well, go over here. Go over and aggravate those people." He makes people go off. Maybe they need new equipment, they need to hire new guards, they need to remodel the prison, or build a new prison, but they'll send him in to stir things up so they can justify getting the money they need.

*Let me make one more quick pass at the first question. So you don't have any specific ideas or conclusions about how the system could be better. We talked about that it probably wouldn't be improved, because there are certain interests in the system that would prefer to keep a high prison population for their own economic benefit. But leaving that aside, assuming instead that people did have the right motives and they did want to cut crime, you don't see anything they could really do about the revolving door, about—?*

No, though of course what they did have, what they just took away recently, was better education and more job training. If they take these guys that could stand it—which would be about half the guys in this prison—and take them out and make a lot more camps, where people are out working instead of confined and idle, I think that might alleviate some of it.

Yeah, I think maybe if you let people live more like you want them to when they get out, and give them a way to earn some money, and save a little for when they got out. Then, you know, instead of making it all stick, make some of it carrot. I think that'd probably help.

*So in general, do you think that a fairly soft prison with some programming and work opportunities like WSR—especially the single cell version of WSR—will have a lower recidivism rate than a place like, say, Walla Walla?*

Yeah. But I also think a lot of these guys are bullshitting themselves.

We used to call it "riding the Bible." You know, everywhere they go, they got the Good Book under their arm, and when they get out, boy they ain't out a half a day, and they're getting drunk, and got them a pistol, and looking for something to steal. So, you know—

*Are they fooling themselves, or are they con men who are fooling the administration and the public?*

A lot of it's self-hypnosis.

They have unrealistic expectations about what's going to happen when they get out. They think it's going to have a Hollywood ending. They're going out to their little wife, and they're going to live happily ever after.

Like the guy who says, "I'm one of the few guys in the world that's such a great lover that these women never cheated on me or anything. When I get out, I always put them to the test. I ask them, I say, 'Baby, was you true while I was locked up?' And every time they tell me, 'Yes, Daddy, I was.'"

*There you go. [Laughs.]*

But, you know, guys forget that their people have another life besides them. They're out there earning a living, you know, and having a social life. And this guy comes out, plunks down in the middle, and he wants to be the center of attention, and have everything revolve around him. When it doesn't work out that way, he goes off the deep end, "Well, I can't make it this way, like a god damn square. I'll go—"

*You also mentioned that one of the advantages of WSR is the fact that there are programs involving outside people, like PAP, where you can interact with somebody other than other prisoners or state employees. Why does that matter to prisoners? Why is it good to have programs like this?*

Well, just, personally, it's something to look forward to, to go and chat with somebody about something besides doing time, and get other perspectives. And the fact that a lot of them are female too. That doesn't hurt either. In these joints you never used to see a woman. They didn't have no women guards. Of course, that's a mixed blessing too—women guards.

*Is the presence of females frustrating, because you can't actually do anything sexually with them, or is it better than their not being here?*

No, I'm comfortable talking to women, and I miss it when I can't talk to them.
And who knows what fantasies a guy might have about one or two of them.

*One thing you said that was interesting in one of your responses—I made a note of it—you were talking about the revolving door, and why people come back to prison, why they re-offend, and you said, "If you are content to flip burgers and live in squalid conditions, what was the point of leaving prison?"*

Yeah, that's it.
If you can't live better by getting out than you live in here, you damn near would be better off just staying. If it's about comfort and living conditions, why would you put yourself through that?

*Well, because it's not about that though. There's the obvious response—it's better to flip burgers for minimum wage because you're not victimizing people, and you're not doing morally wrong things. That's what makes it better. It may not be better in terms of your housing, or what food you're eating, or material stuff like that. But, I mean, isn't that a relevant difference between the two cases? Isn't a burger flipper at McDonald's better ethically than a person who's—?*

[Laughs.] It never seemed like that to me. That was never a part of the problem where I was concerned, the moral aspect of it.

You know, that's what you do; you're a thief, a burglar, a stick up man, whatever. Like they say about the credit card, "Don't leave home without it;" I always figured I was going to get mine one way or another.

*Yeah, but how can you just say, "That's what you do"? I mean, obviously you're capable of drawing moral distinctions, because you do it all the time. You wouldn't snitch on somebody, you're not going to kill a guard to escape, you're not going to go murder some old woman or something for no reason. So it's not as if you're some psychopath who can't make moral distinctions. You're an intelligent person with a conscience. You can make rules for yourself. Why don't you make that kind of rule here? Why don't you draw a line here, where you can see a distinction between working for a living versus burglarizing and victimizing people? Why doesn't that bother you to live that way?*

[Laughs.] Well, I guess because I've always done it. Like these guards say, "It was good enough for my pappy, it's good enough for me." "See, that's why you can't give that guy that newspaper, because I'm in the same boat on a different level. We do it this way because we've always done it this way."

*Are you bothered if I challenge you on stuff like this?*

No, no. I don't mind answering. I'm not thin-skinned about too many things.

Yeah, you know, I can see that some of my stuff's off-center. I've had women ask me, "Well, why don't you live a decent life? You could do this, you could do that…"

But what it probably is is instant gratification. "Well, man, I could get that little thing if I had the two years to spare, but I want it now." By "now," I mean before breakfast.

*Right. But hopefully that's not an absolute. You wouldn't go for the instant gratification if it meant snitching on a friend, or killing somebody, or something like that.*

Well, yeah, and in fact, I was thinking about this time I went and rung a doorbell somewhere in Indiana, and this old lady let me in the house. She's got this big old honker diamond ring on, must be five carats, and there's sterling everywhere and everything.

So this old lady is taking me all over her house—she must be seventy-five years old—and she's showing me pictures of her son, and I'm thinking, "Boy, I'd like to have that ring!" But she's an old lady, and she's living by herself, her son's gone somewhere, and she's got trouble with her hip and everything. I thought maybe I'd come back when she wasn't there and take what I wanted, but I wasn't going to threaten her and tell her, "Hey, take that ring off your finger!" you know. I just said to myself, "Jesus Christ, if I do this, shit, I'm just a lousy son of a bitch."

So, there are times that I'll let the money go rather than put somebody through something like that.

# RICO—April 1998

*"My intention was not to kill. My intention was to hurt.*

*"And, I just didn't stop swinging."*

Rico in 1997.

Rico\* is one of the more complex of the prisoners that I've met at WSR.

At first glance, he comes across like a glib, slick con man, someone who is very much in his element in prison. He fits the stereotype of the street savvy criminal, though he also displays an ability to interact just as smoothly with the "square" world. (One of our volunteers remarked that Rico is the one prisoner who could sell a used car to anyone.)

However, the more I observed him, and the better I got to know him, the more I realized how incomplete and misleading such initial impressions of him are.

For one thing, he is not a career criminal. Other than some apparently nickel-and-dime level buying and selling of illegal drugs, he committed one crime, one horrific crime. Granted, he learned the criminal code of conduct at a very early age from his family and from his neighborhood peers, but he did not pursue a criminal lifestyle.

At times he seems almost as extroverted as Jerry, but I learned this doesn't come naturally to him. For all his skill at addressing a group, giving a presentation to a class, circulating around the room and "busting chops" (as he calls it) with considerable verbal dexterity, it's all a performance. At heart, he is an intense, sometimes brooding, private person. The slick persona is something he chooses to adopt intermittently for certain purposes, but it masks a deeper, more serious self.

Once I realized that, I wasn't at all surprised when he later told me how intimidated he had been by the notion of joining PAP, and how reluctant he had been to interact with strangers from the outside world. Other prisoners had had to really twist his arm to get him to join and participate.

Far from being caught up in a criminal lifestyle, Rico is adamant about rejecting crime. He attempts no justifications and makes no excuses for what he did. He knows it was completely and unambiguously wrong, he accepts responsibility for it, and he is willing to accept whatever punishment society decides he deserves—up to and including execution. If and when he is given another chance on the outside, he will take it with whatever conditions it includes.

Even amongst the more civilized prisoners of PAP, this attitude of forsaking crime is uncommon. It means admitting fault, experiencing remorse, and making deep and difficult changes. It's far easier to go along with the crowd and do what the vast majority of one's peers in prison have done—continue or commence a criminal lifestyle. It takes considerable skill and strength of character to resist that pressure, while sustaining the respect of one's fellow prisoners as a solid convict.

Rico not only refuses to succumb to that peer pressure, he also refuses to facilitate others' doing so. He won't trade crime stories with other prisoners. He won't join in

---

\*Rico has chosen to be identified by his nickname only. The nickname "Rico" is derived from his Puerto Rican ethnicity.

the common prison ritual wherein repeat offenders are welcomed home with open arms. He doesn't believe in the message that prison is the one place they can always expect to be loved and respected. He has nothing but disdain for so excusing and encouraging what he regards as gross and blameworthy failure.

Rico is engaged in a difficult balancing act. He adheres to the convict code. He minds his own business and does not side with the administration and its rats. Yet he openly rejects much of what his fellow prisoners stand for and the path they've chosen in life.

As a result, there is at times a certain aloofness in the way he interacts with other prisoners. He is trusted and accepted, yet there is still that sense that he is not fully one of the "Fellahs." There is not quite the camaraderie, not quite the commonality of interests and values.

"Rico is about Rico, number one," says one of the prisoners, which is to say that his primary focus is on himself, and not on his fellow convicts collectively, as the convict code would require of the ideal prisoner. I don't know that Rico would disagree.

For long periods of time, he "disappears" into himself. He stops coming to meetings, and when the other prisoners are asked about him, they respond vaguely that you don't see him around much. His socializing drops to a minimum. He goes to his job, works on correspondence classes in his cell, accepts visits from his family (some time after arriving in prison, he married a woman he'd known on the outside, and they're raising her daughter together), but otherwise he remains alone with his thoughts.

He states openly that he will not maintain connections with other prisoners once on the outside. No matter how close the friendship on the inside (and he has had some strong friendships), he has no intention of maintaining it once one or both of them is released.

When Rico takes part in any collective activity with other prisoners, it is sporadic and on his terms. If it isn't conducive to his getting out and staying out of prison, or beneficial to others in some way (such as his work in a program that counsels at-risk youth), then it does not interest him.

He jumps in and out of PAP. When I took the class and during my early time as a volunteer, he was one of the leaders. After that, he has more often been out than in. When he feels that the group is not consistently serving good purposes but is succumbing to the individual agendas of the less scrupulous prisoners (e.g., when too many of the prisoner members are treating PAP as nothing more than an opportunity to try to persuade a woman onto their visiting list), he stays away.

Rico is mostly a cynic when it comes to the prospect of prisoners succeeding on the outside without returning to crime. He sees how few of them have made the effort to turn their lives around. He sees them trying to con everyone—including themselves—into thinking that they're really sincere about going straight, and then he sees them come back at the next turn of the revolving door.

I think a handful of guys in our little group are good bets to make it on the outside, but I'm sure if I were exposed to the general prison population and saw all the things Rico has seen over the years, I'd end up cynical too. How can you not expect the worst from people when you see so much failure, so much dishonesty, so much weakness? And the brutalizing nature of modern prisons—where "rehabilitation" is a politically unpopular notion to be scoffed at—does nothing but push people farther and farther into this morass of anger and egotism that virtually guarantees recidivism.

Jimi was the one exception to Rico's cynicism, the one time he let himself believe in a friend. Years ago, when Jimi was last released, Rico thought he had so much going for him, and was such a good person at heart, that surely Jimi would stay clean and build a successful life on the outside.

But sure enough, soon after Jimi's release, he got back into drugs and alcohol, re-offended, and returned to prison. And that was it for Rico. He tells me it broke his heart the day he saw Jimi back in prison, and he vowed never to let himself get his hopes up again.

Now he just does his own time and concentrates on saving himself, and doesn't let himself get emotionally involved in other people and their situations.

At least that's what he claims. I have heard him speak of the necessity in prison of cultivating a moral detachment, an apathy toward the plight of one's fellow man. To do otherwise would be to risk driving oneself crazy opposing the injustice and cruelty that one is powerless against. He says he has become a cold, unfeeling person in prison.

I don't buy it. The evidence indicates instead that Rico is a naturally caring, moral person. He has to consciously constrain his emotions so that his concern for others does not distract him from getting his own life in order, but that hardly makes him a cold-hearted brute. For a person who had really succeeded in shutting himself down emotionally would not lament it the way he does. He certainly would not devote himself to causes such as helping troubled youths avoid prison.

One of my first encounters with Rico came during the Prison Awareness class I took before I became a volunteer. In the group discussion, I asked a number of hypothetical questions about prison life, how someone such as myself would fare in prison, etc.

After the session, as we were getting ready to leave the facility, Rico sought me out. With a look of urgency, he implored me to think twice about whatever I was doing that might lead me to prison.

Clearly he had surmised that my questions could not be purely hypothetical. To him, I seemed just a little too curious about certain things.

I assured him my questions had nothing to do with my own situation. He looked at me uncertainly. If there was even a chance that I wasn't being straight with him, he had to warn me of the peril I was in. "It's not worth it. I don't care what you're doing, or how small the risk is of getting caught. It's not worth it," he said. "Don't be misled if we joke around sometimes in the class, or it looks like we're getting along and having a good time. I hate this place. Every guy in here hates this place, and we hate every day we spend here."

Since then, I've known there's a lot more to him than just a smooth-talking con man. And I've certainly never let him get away with the absurd claim that he has ceased to care about people and has let his heart grow cold in prison.

Rico will practice his verbal dexterity on you for fun, but when it's time to be serious, he has no tolerance for bullshit. He won't give it, and he won't accept it.

As with all of the interviewees, I submitted a list of written questions to Rico. And as with many of the interviewees, he didn't get around to responding in writing, and asked if we could do a taped interview instead. So we did.

*The first of the questions I mailed in to you—which you've now had a chance to think about—had to do with your crime. I don't know how much you want to say, how comfortable you are talking about it, but let's talk about it insofar as you are willing. What are you in for? And tell me if what you were convicted of differs at all from what you really did.*

No, I was convicted for exactly what I did. I had no problem admitting what I did.

Prior to this incident and what led up to it, I'd never even had a traffic ticket.

I lost my focus with alcohol and cocaine. And because of my insistence on messing with that alcohol and cocaine, on the day of my thirty-fourth birthday, an argument broke out. I walked into something that I shouldn't have seen. Actually it was a domestic thing with a live-in girlfriend. I walked in on her and her lover. And, I didn't know how to react other than violently, and I took her life.

*Why do you attribute this to your involvement with alcohol and cocaine?*

Because—it's not that I attribute it to it, but I think that had I been—and then again, I don't know how I would have reacted if I were straight. You know, hindsight is always twenty/twenty. So, I probably would have acted the same.

I do know that the situation—the relationship—wasn't a healthy one. It was a turbulent relationship. Had I been thinking rationally and not been so dependent on drugs, I would have left the relationship. I would have left the situation.

*So your involvement with drugs affected whom you were with, and what kind of relationships you had with people and such.*

And my environment. I stood as close to the drug as I possibly could.

*So were you a different person socially, after you got involved with drugs? Did you start running with a different crowd, as they say, or—?*

Well, I got dumber as I got older. Instead of getting wiser, I just got dumber.

I got to the state of Washington after an eight year military contract, and I got a job with Boeing just to see—'cause I was going to give the Navy twenty years. But I was making good money there, so I stayed.

I was single, had no responsibilities, and I decided I wanted to make friends. And I made friends by showing them what real cocaine was all about. You know, I'm an East Coast guy, so I went and got the East Coast cocaine, introduced it to these guys, and all of a sudden, Rico was a hit. I had all kinds of friends.

*Had you gotten involved with drugs and heavy drinking in the military, or was it after you got out of the military?*

No, the drugs were after I got out. In the military, I drank. I drank hard; I worked hard. The advantage in the military is that you can go through a good drunk for maybe four or five days, then you go out to sea for about thirty, forty-five days, and, you know, you're fine. You don't think that you have a problem, because, like I said, you work hard, you party hard.

But when you come back here to society, and you're doing Lunchbox Joe, and you're working, you're putting in your forty, you know, and you have the resources to buy alcohol on a daily basis, and to use drugs on a daily basis, well, that's what I did.

*How old were you when you started using drugs?*

I smoked pot when I was in high school. I used to do pot. Smoked hash when I was in the Mediterranean. Liked beer. Liked drinking rum.

But none of that was ever a hindrance. It was later I got into it heavily. When I got out of the Navy, and this stuff was readily available, I started using. I started using more routinely than I did in the past.

I just enjoyed using. I enjoyed being the life of the party.

*Why was it more available now than in your past?*

More available, or maybe just more appealing. I didn't like my situation. Like I said, I was in a strange state. I was alone. And the quickest friends you make—for me anyway—were the people in the bar scene.

The people in the bar scene, the guys that I worked with, were into alcohol, were into cocaine. And, you know, you want to be one of the guys, so I got involved too.

Where I started using real heavily was when I got involved in a relationship that I wasn't happy with. And instead of being a man, and walking out of it, realizing what the situation was and dealing with it, I just let it do me. I stayed in a relationship where I was very unhappy. I just diluted it with the alcohol and the drugs.

I was working; I was making good money. So I didn't consider myself a junkie. I wasn't mainlining anything. I never put a needle in my arm. I had money coming in. I never stole from anybody. So I was one of those quote-unquote "sophisticated junkies."

All I was doing was just bullshitting myself. Straight denial.

*Prior to the murder itself, had you committed any crimes at all? I mean other than the actual illegal drug use itself of course. Did your lifestyle lead to any crimes other than the murder?*

No, no. I was law-abiding. I was raised by poor but dedicated parents. I have a brother who's a judge in Florida. I have a sister who works for Merrill Lynch. I'm the only idiot in the joint.

I had all the opportunities. All the opportunities. My parents put me through private schools. I had a decent education. I had all the opportunities to be a productive citizen. I just wouldn't take heed to the signs.

I caught nine grand mal seizures. OK? While I was messing around with alcohol and cocaine. Two in one day. And I still wouldn't stop. It's the madness of addiction.

But I'm not blaming my murder on the addiction. I'm not saying, "Oh, well, it was because of this," you know. I should have gotten out of the situation. I knew what was happening.

The ironic thing about the whole thing is that three months prior to the crime, I had gone to the Ballard Care Unit,* completed their twenty-eight day program, sat my girlfriend down, and told her, "Listen. This relationship is obviously not going anywhere. We both are seeing other people behind each other's back. We've disrespected each other numerous times. I think we need to count our losses and, you know, part as friends."

I really wanted that. I really felt that. But she cried, and told me she loved me, and wanted to have my babies, and I fell for it. Man, I fell for it hook, line, and sinker. It wasn't but three months later, man, that I took her life.

*What's the Ballard Care Unit?*

The Ballard Care Unit is a drug program. It's a drug treatment program where you go for twenty-eight days. The first week or so is detox. The next week is group therapy, and that kind of stuff.

---

*In Seattle.

And, man, I gave it a valiant effort. But, you know, it pissed me off, because it cost me ten thousand dollars to go through the program, and I wanted a doctor to take a magic wand and say, "Ding! You're cured." On the twenty-eighth day, I found out that sobriety was my own responsibility. That pissed me off. [Laughs.]

*For most people, is it rare to go through just one program like that to get off drugs and alcohol and succeed on their first try?*

It all depends on how bad they want it. You know, various people have to go through various things. The only thing I regret about the fact that I am now sober is that a life had to be taken. That's the only fucked up part about me being sober today. Because, I mean, if I wanted to chase the bag in the joint, I can chase the bag.

*And you don't.*

I don't. I choose not to. I don't miss it. I don't even miss it now.

Like, I think about before, and the craziness, and all that stuff, and I kick myself in the ass, like, "Man, how could you have been so stupid?"

And it's just, you don't think for nothing else but that. When it grabs hold of you, that's all you live for.

That's all I wanted to live for. Let me not generalize. Let me just say, that's all I wanted to live for. That was where my happiness was.

*How old were you when you started using cocaine heavily?*

About thirty-two.

*And how long after that started did the murder occur?*

Two years after. I was doing cocaine to be productive at work. And I was drinking a fifth of alcohol to bring me down. I would drink a pint of alcohol before I even brushed my teeth, so I wouldn't have DTs.

*In the average day during that period of your life, how much did you drink?*

I drank about, I would say, two fifths a day. And it wouldn't take me but maybe a couple of days to knock out an eighth of cocaine. And that's just straight snorting. Just snorting.

*I'll show my ignorance of drug matters here. How much is that? I mean, would that be considered a very heavy quantity of cocaine to use in one day, even amongst serious cocaine users?*

Oh yeah. Oh sure. For a layman, it would bury him. You would have to work your way up to that.

Not like it's any accomplishment to get there. But, that was the level of my addiction.

*How much did it cost you to buy that much alcohol and cocaine on a daily basis would you say?*

Oh, about two hundred and forty for the eight ball, and twelve dollars for both bottles.

*You were making good enough money to cover that?*

I was making good enough money, and I was also supplementing my income. Everybody I worked around wanted it, wanted what I had, so they supplied my habit, you know.

*So in addition to being a user, you were dealing as well.*

The law of the game.

*Was your live-in girlfriend as heavily into drugs as you were?*

No, no. She knew my weakness. She knew that as long as I was high that I'd stay home.

No, she was an intelligent woman. She worked for the Department of Justice. She was a conciliator for them.

You know, at one time, we loved each other very much. I can't tell you where we both lost our focus.

But she was a self-admitted enabler. OK? And, she traveled a lot. But she made sure that when she was gone that I was quite readily supplied. She'd call home and there I was, in my basement, watching the game, stoned or drunk.

*How long were you with her?*

Approximately three years.

*So from before the cocaine habit started.*

Yeah, very much so.

*So you come home one night, and your live-in girlfriend is with somebody else.*

It wasn't even at night, it was during the day. On the day of my birthday.

*Was he someone you knew?*

He was somebody I had seen, somebody that I was made aware of.

*Was he somebody that you already were aware that she was cheating with?*

I had been told that. I had been told that.

*So it wasn't a great shock that it was—?*

Well, what it was is that I was born into a Latino traditional family, and I bought into this machismo thing. I was taught that there's no greater disrespect, even to where some people may look at me and say, "Well, you know, she had that coming."

No, she didn't have that coming, and I know that now. I mean, the difference between before and today is that today I probably would just take a twenty dollar bill, give it to the guy, and tell him, "Go get yourself a real piece of ass."

That would have saved me from having to do three hundred months.

*Were you stoned on cocaine when you arrived home that day?*

Oh, it was my birthday. Come on. I was already flying high.

*Had you just come home from the bars, or where had you been?*

No, no. Because, one of the things about me is, as long as I had the drug, and as long as I had the alcohol, the bar never saw me. I was one of those in-house, stay-at-home junkies.

*So tell me what happened. You get home, you catch her with somebody else. What ensued?*

I didn't even hesitate. I didn't have a gun—you know, I don't believe in carrying guns or any of that other stuff—but being from the city, you have a pipe, a bat, or something by the door. That's for protection from intruders. At this particular time, I had a pipe. And I used it.

*Was your first instinct to use it on her, or on him, or both?*

Well, he ran like a bitch. I mean, if he really felt something for her, he should have protected her. But he just ran, and left her alone.

He later came back and testified against me.

*How did he get away? Was there another door, or—?*

Yeah, there was an exit,—

*He went out the back door?*

—and he found it. Yeah.

*Could you have caught him if you had concentrated on just him?*

You know, it was a moment of rage, and evil, and darkness that just was so overwhelming, that had anybody else been there—if there had been more people in the house, they would have been hurt.

I just lost it. I just lost it. I lost it.

*So if she had been closer to the exit, and made a quick getaway, and he had tripped or—*

It would have been him. It would have been him instead.

*You were just equally enraged at both.*

Oh yeah. Very much so. Very much so.

*And how did you feel when you actually struck her? Did you immediately wish you could take it back? Or did you feel a triumph that you were doing what you needed to do? Or, what did you feel as you were doing the act?*

When you're doing the act, you feel like there's a great—you're getting even. You know, when you're doing the act, you feel like you're getting even.

Once it's over with, it's all about, "Oh shit! What have I really done here?"

*Was it over with one second later, or three days later, or—?*

No, no, no—

*When did the aftermath of it begin for you emotionally?*

No, 'cause I turned myself in right away. They didn't have to come looking for me. They didn't have to find out what happened. You know, it wasn't a thing of where I had to go get a Dream Team or anything like that to protect me or get me off. I told them straight up.

*How long did it take for you to feel regret and to realize you had—?*

Well, as soon as I found out. As soon as I realized what the hell I did.

I mean, the impact of it, I drank everything else that was in the house, I snorted everything else that was in the house, I smoked everything else that was in the house. Then I called the cops.

*When you struck her, were you intending to kill her, or was your rage more general, just, "I'm going to strike out at her," period, or was it, "I'm going to kill her"?*

My intention was not to kill. My intention was to hurt.

And, I just didn't stop swinging.

*Where did you strike her?*

I started at the head, and ended at the head.

*When did you realize that she was dead?*

When she was down.

*So you realized that you had gone too far, that—*

Oh yeah.

*—you had done more than just hurt her?*

Exactly.

*Had you ever done anything remotely like this before?*

No, no.

*Had you ever attacked someone at all like this?*

I have a mother. I have a daughter. I have a sister. OK? I have no history—quite contrary to what the media has portrayed—I have no history of domestic violence. I have no history of hitting women.

*You mean what the media have portrayed about criminals in general, or about you?*

Oh, about me. About me.

*I'm unfamiliar with these stories. I haven't read about you in the media.*

No, no. What, are you kidding me? They say I was abusive, and I was this, and I was that, but they fail to mention that she wasn't no woman that was dependent on me. She worked for the Department of Justice. Our friends were marshals, FBI agents, cops. If she ever, ever thought for a minute that she was in jeopardy, or had ever gone to work with a mark on her face, I would have been in the joint a long time ago.

*How do you cross that line, if this is the first time you'd ever done anything like that? How do you push yourself past that line? There must be an important psychological barrier that has to be overcome, for a person that's never been violent to that degree, never struck somebody with that kind of force, in that kind of rage. How do you do that for the first time?*

It takes—there's a lot. There's been a lot of hurt. OK? There's a lot of hurt that's going on inside your life, there's a lot of hurt going on inside of you, and you don't share it with no one, and it builds, and builds. And it doesn't get any better, and all you're doing is diluting it, and covering it up with alcohol, and covering it up with drugs, and covering it up, and covering it up, and covering it up.

And all you're doing is blaming, and not taking responsibility for any of it, but blaming it on that particular person, then when something like that occurs, and you snap, you just—it just happens. It's not something that you calculate, or something that you want, you know, to manipulate, to ponder upon and act upon.

It didn't take but more than a minute for all of this to happen. I mean, it was over in a minute. If that long. You see, you react, bang! That's as long as it takes.

It's just many years of not being able to release, to express, to let that bullshit go. And it all manifested itself and blew up.

*So it sounds as though your behavior was an aberration, that you had never done anything like this before. Would you say that you're equally unlikely to ever do it again?*

There's no doubt in my mind. I will not do another minute, another second, of prison time for anybody. For anybody. OK? I mean, it took for this to happen for me to have to take a look at myself, for me to have to look at all the garbage and all the shit that I'd been holding inside of me. And it hasn't been easy for me to shovel that shit out, and realize what it is that I have to do.

# RICO—May 1998

*"No one really knows the type of energy that's expended when something of that emotional nature happens. I mean, I was in a state of mind that I never, ever want to be in again. Never. Hopelessness. Anger. Evil. I mean, evil. A strong sense of evil.*

*"When all this was going on, I felt all of that, and then it stopped, and it was finished, and she was laying there. It was, like, there and gone. And what was left was just an empty shell. That's what was left."*

About one week after our initial interview, Rico dropped by the telemarketing room where I had recently started working part time as a supervisor. He asked to speak to me in the office.

He seemed bothered by something, and was a little more awkward than usual getting his words out. I soon gathered that he was having second thoughts about the book project.

It turns out he had been talking to his brother—the judge in Florida. "He says I'm crazy to be involved in this. He says I hardly know you. That you could use that interview for God knows what."

I was a little taken aback, but I quickly reassured him as to my intentions. For several moments, we spoke over each other. "Well, I don't know what he means, but—," "I just have to know I can trust you," "I'm going to use the interviews for an oral history book like I said," "I just have to know you're being straight with me," "It's not like I have some ulterior motive," "Because you know if you're not," "I mean, your participation is totally voluntary," "I'll come after you," "You know me well enough by now to know what I'm about."

But wait. Had I been threatened in the middle of that? I heard it, but it didn't really register, because we were talking at the same time.

We spoke a little while longer, and he seemed satisfied with what I told him. We talked about a convenient time for the next interview, and I told him I'd mail the raw transcript of the first interview to him before we got together for round two. We shook hands.

It was really only after he left that it dawned on me he'd told me he'd come looking for me when he got out if I crossed him.

The more I thought about it, the harder it was to…suppress a grin. "That son of a bitch," I thought, shaking my head.

Come Wednesday night and the next PAP meeting, I sought him out and commenced giving him the business. I tried to feign anger, but soon we were both busting out laughing. "Man, coming at me with the 'tough convict' routine," I said in mock indignation, "I'll come after you! I'll find you!' Jeez!"

"No, man," he said through our laughter, lifting his hands up in a defensive gesture, "No, it's not like that."

We settled down and had a good talk. Whatever doubts his brother had suggested were allayed, and he was still agreeable to a follow-up interview.

This is one of those things that's hard to convey to someone who doesn't know these guys, doesn't know Rico. Why wasn't it the least bit intimidating to have this convicted murderer sit there and threaten me?

Well, I suppose because he's not a murderer. Not to me. He's Rico.

A murderer is a frightening abstraction. Rico is a man. A man who has spoken to me from his heart. A man with whom I have developed a certain mutuality of trust and respect.

Is it possible that Rico would harm me in the future? Sure. Barely. I'm not losing any sleep over it. Many of the people I know on the outside are at least as likely to harm me as he is, and some no doubt are more likely.

Three weeks after our initial interview, Rico and I taped a second conversation.

*Well, first off, let me ask, since you received a transcript of the first conversation that we had, did you have any follow-up remarks, did anything jump out at you that you should have said but didn't, or that you wanted to change, or talk about, or elaborate on—?*

No. I just hope I didn't sound too matter-of-fact, or like I didn't care.

I've just accepted my role in what I did, and I've taken responsibility and accountability for what I did. And sometimes, in discussing it, since you've already thoroughly dealt with the whole grieving process to get to the acceptance level, you get to the point of where, you know, you just say it like if it's an everyday event. And, reading the transcript, I was concerned that that was what I displayed. But that's not how I feel.

You know, I wanted to give you the facts as accurately as possible. And as far as the facts are concerned, the way I portrayed them was accurate.

But as far as how I feel about the whole thing, I couldn't have made a dumber mistake in my life.

*Why don't you give me a little bit of a history, then, about your emotions concerning the event? Because you're saying now it's been so long ago that you've already been through the various stages of acceptance and such, so now you can speak of it without intense emotion, positive or negative. It's just a part of your distant past. But what about the feelings you were experiencing back then? What were you like emotionally, in relation to this event, five minutes after, a month after, a year after, etc.?*

After the event? Or a little bit of history prior to the event? Or both?

*Mostly the aftermath of it. Because I think we got—though obviously a lot more could be said—we got a lot of the build-up to it last time. What about the emotional aftermath? How did you react emotionally to the event, and how did that change as more time passed?*

You know, the strangest thing about this whole thing was that even though I've never felt such darkness in my life, and even though it left me emotionally drained—like I'm sure you've heard guys in the class speak about the first thing we want to do when we land in jail is just shut down and sleep—at the same time it was like a release of a lot of pent up anger and resentment that I had.

It was a temporary thing. But, I've often thought about it, man. It was crazy. It was a bursting out of a lot of negative energy pent up inside of me for such a long period of time.

I was in the suicide tank of the King County Jail,* 'cause I was overwhelmed once I had realized the full extent of what I had done.

I had erased any possibilities of ever being back with my family. 'Cause I have a very law-abiding family. Very, very traditional type of a family. They had denied my request for me to come home a week prior to this event, so I had erased them from my life. I had—

*What do you mean by "erased" them from your life?*

I didn't consider them family any more. One, for them denying me to come home, and two, for the disgrace and embarrassment that I had put on them, from my actions. I had also met the victim's family, and knew them very well.

During my whole period in the suicide tank, it was just, you know, overbearing, because all I could think about is the family having to fly over and have to deal with what I did. It was a period of my life that I didn't want to deal with. Had I had an instrument or anything that would have taken my life, I would have used it at that particular time.

*Would you say you kind of shut down emotionally and were numb, or would you say you were feeling intense negative emotions?*

A combination of both. I was numb, because I had never, never been in trouble with the law before, never been in that type of environment before. It was my thirty-fourth birthday, and I'm in the King County Jail with a murder beef.

And at the same time, the intense emotions of the impact of what I had done was beginning to come in. I was coming off the high of cocaine and alcohol, and the more reality started to set in, the more I wanted to do away with that reality. I didn't have the drugs any more, so the next thing I wanted to do was just take my life. It took for me like about a good month or so of drying out, being sick and the whole bit, before I decided to accept the responsibility.

And that's when I told them that there wouldn't be a trial. I was very cooperative with the cops, with the detectives. I was very cooperative with the prosecutor. I told them exactly what happened.

---

*King County is Seattle.

Even though it wasn't a murder in the first degree, because this wasn't something I premeditated, they charged me as such. But I wasn't going to put the family through a trial. I pled guilty.

I didn't drag her name through the mud or bring any dirt into it. I took full responsibility and said, "This is what's happened. This is what I did. This is the weapon. Here I am." They didn't have to come looking for me. I didn't try to hide it. I accepted my twenty-five-to-life sentence.

*Why did it go down as a first degree? It seems to me it would be categorized as second degree, just the way you've described it.*

Right, and had I had a lawyer, I mean, a paid lawyer, a reputable paid lawyer, I would have had second degree. But I had a public defender, and, you know, they're overloaded with cases, and the best thing that they can do is get a guy to cop. I of course was a willing participant, because I didn't want to have the family go through a trial.

But, their case was that I had sixty seconds to ponder upon and act upon what I did. And in the state of Washington, if you've got sixty seconds before the act, it's premeditated. So that's how they got first degree murder.

*Did they threaten you with more? What worse could they have done if you had insisted on going to trial? What were they holding over your head?*

Well, what they held over my head was—and I found out later that they couldn't do it, but I didn't know that at the time—was, "You either cop to first degree murder, and take these three hundred and eight months, or we're going to go and ask for life without."

*So it would have been the same crime, just a different sentence.*

Just a different sentence.

*It would have been first degree murder in either case, but—*

Exactly.

*—their offer was to give you this sentence of "only" x number of years versus life without parole.*

"We'll give you a little bit of hope, as opposed to no hope at all," was what they were telling me. So, even though I wasn't going to take it to trial anyway, it was a no brainer. I chose to take the three hundred and eight months.

*Now, it sounds like your emotions were based on two distinct factors. You felt one way about your own self-interest, your own future, your own predicament, but you also had emotions to deal with about the crime itself, feelings about what you had done.*

Right.

*And you said as to the first, you were numb. In contemplating your own future, and the "What have I gotten myself into?" kind of thing, you were more numb toward that. But you did feel a lot of emotion about the event itself, and what you had done. Tell me more about that, and how that changed over time.*

Well, once I had decided that to take my life was not going to do anybody any good—except maybe the victim's family, I don't know—but once I decided that I was not going to take my life but was going to take full responsibility for what I did, then I decided to go all the way. I decided to find out why I did what I did. I decided to find out what was it about me that caused me to do what I did.

I like women. You know, come on, I'm not one to be beating women. If I had a history of that, then that's something to look at. But I didn't.

But I wanted to find out, you know, once I decided to take responsibility, I took a good look inside myself. I didn't like a lot of what I saw. So I started shoveling up a lot of garbage that I had walked around with.

I was molested when I was a seven year old boy, repeatedly, by my mother's brother, and it was a secret I kept away from my mom and pop for like about twenty-five years. I didn't think they were going to believe me anyway, so in order to maintain the fact that I am a man, and be secure in my masculinity, I had to hide it. I bought into that macho role, even more so than anybody else who thought that they was macho.

So, my thing was I needed to change my whole way of thinking. I needed to grow. I needed to get away from that conditional way of thinking that I had been brought up with. I needed to challenge myself and say why is it that it was fine for me to treat women the way I treated them—either emotionally abusing them, or sleeping with somebody else, or doing whatever I wanted to do with other women—but when it's done to me, I react the way I reacted? I didn't like it. But it was all right for me to do it, you know.

I wanted that balance in my life. I wanted to be able to say, "Hey, wait a minute, man. If it ain't good done to you, what makes you think it's good done to the next person?"

Well, it took for me to look inside myself and really start shoveling a lot of crap out. A lot of crap. A lot of anger. A lot of resentment.

Me and my father never really saw eye to eye, you know. I always say that our love is best served from a distance. My father taught me the streets. My father taught me how to lie. My old man taught me how to manipulate, and he taught me how to do these things to my own mother, while he was going out there and doing all the dirt. Then he went and decided he wanted to hit the church road.

Well, it was too late for me. I was already on my path. I have a brother who's eleven months and three weeks younger than I am. However, that guy decided to hit the books. Before, I had my father's acceptance because I lied for him, I cheated for him, I manipulated for him, I covered his ass. Now all of a sudden, I'm a piece of shit, he's a church-going whatever he wants to call himself, and my brother can do no wrong. And from then on, he always put us in those categories. So I got used to living on my own and doing my own thing.

So I carried a lot of shit inside of me.

I was always the type of guy that I wouldn't ask for help. I was too proud, too macho, even though I was wandering, and never was able to do a lot of things. And here I was in the joint in a maximum security place in Walla Walla with a sentence of twenty-five to life.

I made a conscious decision that I was going to grow the fuck up. Later for family. Later for my past. Later for what I've learned growing up. Later for what I've seen. Later for all of that. What can I learn from dealing with Rico?

And I've learned a lot, man. I'm getting ready to be forty-five years old, and it's just while I've been in the joint that I can actually say that I'm now beginning to like who I am. I was never able to say that. I didn't like who I was. So I hid it. And I hid it well. I was a master at that, you know.

And to some extent, I still am. But now I don't have to use it. Now I like meeting people who are genuine, who are candid. I hate manipulation. I hate lies. I don't want to be part of that. I've been part of that; I've contributed to that. I've done my share of that. Now I don't want no part of that. Now I want to stay focused. If anything, I want to be able to help guys not have to tune up their old ladies.

So I don't want—Teresa* was her name—I don't want her life to go in vain. I don't care if I have to stand up in front of a thousand women who have been tuned up by their husbands. I'll let them know, "Hey, I fucked up. You know what I'm saying? But what do we need to learn?"

And I'll stand up in front of another thousand men and tell them, "Hey, we don't have to go this route. It isn't worth it." Because it's going to eat you up alive. You wake up every morning, looking at those bars, wanting to kick yourself in the ass, if you have a conscience. If you don't have a conscience, then you don't give a damn. And you're not going to grow.

*What does it mean to "tune up" a woman?*

To hit a woman. That's, I guess, prison jargon. You hear it talked about that way in here.

But I need to sharpen that stuff up, because, God, I don't need to sound like that.

---

*I have changed the name.

*So initially, you were traumatized and depressed to a suicidal degree over what you had done.*

Very much so.

*And then you made a decision to try and understand yourself, rather than punish yourself, and to dig into yourself psychologically and therapeutically, to understand, and that's how you—*

I did it by reading. I did it by researching. I did it by watching. I did it by listening, which I had a hard time doing all my life.

And I'm still doing it. I'm receptive to change. I'm receptive to being open. I'm receptive to a different shade of perspective besides black and white.

You know, now I can hug a man and not feel that I'm being gay. I can cry, and not feel that I'm being weak. I can show weakness at one particular time, and know that I can be strong at another. I don't have to be this firm, strong guy, never showing weakness, or never showing tears, or never showing anything else.

I had my perspectives on what a man was all about all screwed up.

*Her name was Teresa?*

Her name was Teresa, yeah.

*This may not be important, but I did notice that—in looking over the transcript and in our, conversation so far today—you never did mention her by name. It was always "the woman I was in a relationship with," or "the victim," etc. Do you think there is any psychological significance to that? Do you think that it means anything that you didn't mention her by name?*

I think it's more the fact that the more open I am about the situation, the more real I keep it, the more therapeutic it's going to be for me, and the more I'll grow..

I don't want to get over it. I just want to get stronger about it, if that makes any sense. I want to get to the point where I want to be able to talk about this genuinely and candidly, in hopes that other guys don't have to do the same shit, man.

You have guys in the joint, a lot of them with prestigious positions in their lives who had never put their hands on a woman, and then all of a sudden, a situation comes up and bang. A person they once cared for in their life is dead. And they couldn't tell you why. This place is filled with them. And they're the best inmates or convicts that the institution has. They're never a management problem. But on that one occasion, something made these guys snap.

*If it's therapeutic and beneficial to deal with it openly, then I would think you'd be more inclined to talk about her by name and personalize it.*

Well, sure it's more therapeutic if you talk about her by name. I mean—

*But my question was why did you* not *talk about her by name?*

I wasn't ready to with you. You know what I'm saying? If you noticed, I had to come back and ask you what these tapes were all about, and what you would use them for.

When we first started the interview, I thought we were going to take some baby steps. But you went straight for the jugular. [Smiles.]

*Let me ask you something else that occurred to me when I was thinking about our earlier conversation. I thought you struck a very delicate balance that I'm sure is very difficult to achieve. You were somewhat critical of Teresa without condemning her, without relieving yourself of responsibility, and it reminded me of the fact that in our society today, not only do we demonize criminals, but we tend to deify victims. We regard criminals as absolutely evil and irredeemable, and victims as flawless and pure, and it's considered the worst in bad taste or immorality to criticize victims in any way. Well, in real life, people who commit crimes are flesh and blood people and a mixture of good and bad characteristics, and people who are victims of crimes are the same.*

Right.

*I felt like you were kind of trying to be careful about how you said it, but that you did achieve an interesting balance where you were able to present her as human and flawed, but without implying, "She deserved it. She was a bad person. Here's what justifies what I did." Talk about that a little bit. How do you feel about pointing out the flaws of someone you murdered, knowing that that could make people's skin crawl to read that?*

Well, it's not so much about people or how they'll react. I know what she was all about, but I try to keep away from bad-mouthing somebody whose life I already took.

First of all, Teresa didn't have this coming. OK? So, for me to say any derogatory statements against her, on top of taking her life, to me, would be twice as bad.

She wasn't no angel. She had her flaws. She did her deals. But I had a choice. I should have gotten out of the situation. But I chose not to. So, because of that, I'm in the position that I'm in right now.

But, for me to sit here and elaborate on the different things that she had done, you know, at the present time, I'm not prepared to do that, because it almost sounds like I'm justifying what I did, and I'm trying to stay away from that.

I guess if it was a situation where you and I are just talking, just kicking it, and stuff like that, it might be different. But, for the purpose of the interview, and the book, and the recorder, you know, I don't feel we need to go there. It would be different if you and I were just sitting over a beer and talking, just two guys openly discussing relationships or discussing our past, or something like that, then I'd have no problem doing that. But, under this present forum, I don't think it's the time and place for it.

*You mentioned your family several times, and your feeling that they had rejected you a week earlier by not letting you come home, and your anticipation that they would reject you because of the crime you had just committed. So you were assuming that there was this permanent rift with your family. What turned out to be the reality? How, in fact, did your family react, and what kind of relationship did you have with them after this happened?*

Well, I couldn't have been any better on target.

I've never asked those people for anything. Since I was thirteen years old, I've worked. I've always been self-sufficient. Seventeen years old, I went into the navy. I've been, you know, emancipated and self-sufficient, on my own, my whole life.

I ask them for one favor one time, tell them I need to come home and get my life together. But by that time, they were Christian community members in a prestigious position, with a son in the prosecuting attorney's office, and they were in good standing with the community. They certainly couldn't have a son come back with a drug problem. I mean, that would tarnish their reputation. So, they told me no.

*You're originally from New York, right? Were your parents in New York when you asked to go back and stay with them?*

At that particular time, yes.

I found out later that they had solicited the advice of my now-judge brother during that time about what he thought, and he concurred with their decision.

So I had no problem, you know, predicting how they were going to react. My mom, when I was at the King County Jail, wrote me a small paragraph, apologizing for not realizing the extent of the seriousness of my request, and that was it.

I spent the next five years with no mail, no phone calls, no visits, because that's how I wanted it. I didn't want to be bothered. And it was the best five years of my life.

They've tried to establish some kind of contact since then, but I haven't seen them since. You know, I'm cordial, I'm respectful to them, but I've grown to a totally different level.

*So, you've had contact with them by phone?*

I talk to them maybe on Mother's Day, Father's Day. Nothing of real substance.

I get more love and consideration and substance from a gentleman like yourself, and from the volunteers than I do from my own family. But those are genuine people. Those are people who don't look at the bars; they look through them. They look at the individual. They don't look at the act; they look at the individual.

There's a saying, "Those who judge, don't matter. Those who don't, do."

So, the most important thing to me right now is to maintain my focus. I've made so many mistakes in my life in the past that now I want to maintain my focus, do whatever it is that I have to do to be a productive citizen, and keep that balance as a man, and be true to my word, and don't get caught up in none of this garbage. I deal with it every day, and, you know, I think we have a power that we don't recognize or that we take for granted, and that's the power of choice. And I like that power, for myself. Not speaking for anybody else.

*That reminds me that I wanted to ask you something about the immediate aftermath of the murder, and it has to do with the power of choice. OK, you're an alcoholic, you're a dope fiend, you've just committed murder—*

All that.

*—you're psychologically messed up—*

All that.

*—why didn't your instinct for self-preservation kick in? Why didn't you run or hide? Why did you turn yourself in? I mean, I think I'm a reasonably good, albeit flawed, person, with at least some degree of courage, but if I was facing life in prison or the death penalty or even a long prison term, even if at some level maybe I deserved it, I think my self-preservation, just my animal instinct, would kick in and I'd have to try to avoid it if I could avoid it. Why did you not try to get away?*

I think as soon as I saw her lying there, and I saw exactly what I had done, I knew I had fucked up, and I wasn't in no mood to run. I'd been running from myself, you know. I wasn't in no mood to run.

I didn't do the noble thing. I didn't go right to the phone. I finished off every ounce of drug and every leaf of weed, and every ounce of alcohol that was left in the house, to build up the courage, and numb myself, and dilute the emotion of what was getting ready to happen.

Once I did that, then I made the phone call.

*Any second thoughts about it, you know, five minutes after you hung up the phone, did you kick yourself and say, "Man, now I'm going to prison. I could have avoided this!"?*

You know what? I wasn't even thinking about prison. I wasn't. I wasn't thinking about prison, I wasn't thinking about the courts, I wasn't thinking about none of that process. I was just so caught up in that event, and what had just transpired, and the energy that was released and at the same time magnified that anything could have happened to me at that particular time and I wouldn't have cared. I've never, never felt any lower or darker in my life.

*Well, you said it wasn't a noble act. Was it a courageous willingness to do one's duty in spite of the horrible consequences that might ensue? Or was it an act of self-destruction—"I don't care about myself any more. I'll go ahead and make the choice that brings about terrible things like prison, because what the hell, I'll just destroy myself that way"? I mean, were you trying to do the right thing by turning yourself in, or were you trying to hurt yourself? Why did you turn yourself in?*

I turned myself in because that was the thing to do. But I wasn't even giving it all that—I had just taken the life of somebody that I had at one time really cared for. So, run for what?

If I had premeditated this, then maybe it would have been different. But that's not how it happened. I blew up.

No one really knows the type of energy that's expended when something of that emotional nature happens. I mean, I was in a state of mind that I never, ever want to be in again. Never. Hopelessness. Anger. Evil. I mean, evil. A strong sense of evil.

When all this was going on, I felt all of that, and then it stopped, and it was finished, and she was laying there. It was, like, there and gone. And what was left was just an empty shell. That's what was left.

And, my nature is, you know, come on, I've never been in trouble before. For murder? Well, I got to call this in.

I'm telling you, I felt nothing. I felt nothing.

They come in. "Did you kill her?" "Yes I did." I didn't ask for Miranda rights or anything. "Where's the weapon?" "Right there." "Why did you do it?" Explained it all to them.

*If you were totally drained and numb, it seems like you would have been too passive to turn yourself in. I would understand why you wouldn't have run, or had any elaborate plan about escape, but it seems like you would have neither run nor turned yourself in. You know, maybe just sat there almost catatonic with no energy, no ability to do anything—*

I did for awhile. I did for awhile.

*But to turn yourself in requires more of an active choice. It's not a product of passivity and not giving a damn—*

Come on, you pick up the phone, dial nine-one-one. "Show up at such-and-such a place. A murder has been committed." How much energy does that take? Especially when you're blind drunk and have done cocaine and weed. How much energy does that take?

*It takes more psychological energy than not picking up the phone.*

[Shakes his head.]

*How do you feel about it now? Do you have a certain pride that you did the right thing by turning yourself in?*

I think it's the least I can do, you know, for Teresa, for her family. I mean, the papers smutted me up anyway, but that's not what matters to me. It was the least I can do. My goodness.

As far as what I thought about it and stuff like that, I never gave it any thought. I never patted myself on the back, or anything like that.

It isn't, like, "You did the right thing." The right thing? The right thing was to leave the situation when I needed to. That's the right thing. The right thing was to say, "Hey. Check this out. This relationship ain't going nowhere. I recognize it for what it is. See ya." That's the right thing.

*Ever regretted the decision to turn yourself in?*

No, no, no. The decision to turn myself in? No.

*Never were sitting at Walla Walla wondering—?*

No, no. It made the grieving process and everything else easier. I just wanted to let the courts do their thing. I didn't have the resources to fight it anyway.

This was a highly publicized case. I mean, my brother was a prosecuting attorney in Queens District, New York. Teresa had worked for the Department of Justice. They were treating it like I had killed a cop. They had smutted me up all over the newspaper. Some of her friends were saying that I was constantly beating her, and all this other stuff.

*Had you ever struck her before this incident?*

No, no. Come on. She was one that if I ever would have touched her, she would have picked up that phone. Teresa wasn't no weak woman. She wasn't no weak woman.

She was a good woman. She didn't take no shit. She just felt that what was good enough for me, it was good enough for her. If I was going to cheat, she was going to cheat. I just wish that she would have kept doing it behind my back, and not flaunted it in my face, you know.

*How long were you in the King County Jail?*

The murder happened October Fifth. By February, I was already on the bus on my way to Walla Walla. And that includes a long month Christmas break and a long month sentencing break. That just goes to show you how quick that process was.

*So from October until February you were in jail. Had you ever been in jail before?*

No sir.

*Tell me how you experienced jail initially.*

To me, and I'll be very honest with you, having come from Puerto Rico to Harlem to the Bronx, and having had to fight, like, every other day in Harlem and in the Bronx going to school when I was a kid, I just switched modes. I was ready for whatever was going to happen.

*So jail was new, but tough, dangerous, gritty situations were not.*

I didn't sweat the load as far as the game was concerned.

You know, one thing about convicts and criminals is they can read a person real well. They pick their spots. They know, as soon as a person walks in that tank, who's a mark and who isn't. A mark being somebody that they can manipulate, they can intimidate, you know.

I'm facing a first degree murder beef, and could care less. You know what I'm saying? I assure you I wasn't no mark. So, I fell right on in.

*What did you do that enabled them to read you as not being a mark?*

I was only tested once. I had to kick cocaine and alcohol cold turkey, and I was sick. Funny thing about it is, if you're a junkie, for some reason they'll generally leave you alone. But if you're a guy who comes in with some petty crime, or they see you on the phone whining to your girlfriend all day every day, they can spot a mark, you know. You come in whining and stuff like that, come on. They'll test you.

But I think it was my first day there. And I didn't even want to eat anyway, because I was so sick. I couldn't eat. But I left for a minute and when I came back, my meat was missing out of my tray. And I let the tank know how I felt about it.

*What did you do or say?*

Well, I told them straight up, I said, "I don't know who took it, but I know you guys know who took it. OK? If you're such a mother fucking man, then why don't you take it in front of my face, and then you can have all the meat you want. You know what I'm saying? Here I am, I'm calling you a punk, all right, and hope you don't like it." Sat down, ate my meal, and I was left alone.

*You weren't frightened at all in that situation? You weren't bluffing?*

Bluffing? No.

*You weren't secretly hoping that they would not call you on it?*

No. See, where I grew up, you don't sell woof tickets,* if you're not going to back up your play. If you're going to sell a woof ticket, and get your ass kicked, then you're worse than the fool that stole your meat and kicked your ass. You know, if you're going to come out there, and display that, and say that, and not back it up, come on. [Laughs.]

Yeah, you'd really need your ass kicked for that one. No, you just don't do that.

*No one ever messed with you after that?*

No. And the thing is, I wasn't no tough guy. But, neither is any of these other guys. If a guy sees that you're going to fend for yourself, they're going to leave you alone. I assure you. I assure you. It's those that don't fend for themselves that get picked on. But I don't care how skinny, how white, black, brown, purple, OK?, or what your features are: If you fend for yourself, you get the guy's respect. If you don't fend for yourself, you might as well roll over. It's the law of the game.

*Is the only way to fend for yourself with violence or the threat of violence?*

You're not going to go in there and say, "Please don't kick my ass." That's not the way it works, you know. [Laughs.]

There's a lot of attitude, a lot of stress going on, a lot of emotions, locked up in one tank, a lot of diverse people from various backgrounds locked up in the tank, all together. You know, attitudes are going to clash, and you either learn to deal with it, recognize it for what it is, or get ready to fight.

You know, show a little respect. If you're going to use the phone, and there's only one phone and about twenty-four dudes, use it for about ten, fifteen minutes, and let the next guy get it. Don't hog the phone up for about two or three hours, when you only have ten days to do, and there are guys in there doing life on the installment plan. It's not too smart.

So, it's not a matter of being a tough guy. It's a matter of just fending for yourself, and showing the guy that you'll fight back. If you're a guy who's going to at least give him a fight, and the other guy isn't going to give him a fight, then I don't care how tough he is, he's going to pick on that other guy. 'Cause he knows with you he's at least got something coming back at him.

It's all a part of the game.

---

*To sell a woof ticket = To talk in a tough or threatening manner.

# LARRY—May 1998

*"I can apologize until I'm blue in the face. I can tell the victims' families that I'm sorry, but, you know, how far does sorry go? I mean, they don't know how I feel. You can't express the remorse that you feel. I mean, at least I can't. I cannot ever tell those people how bad I feel."*

O f all the interview subjects for this book, Larry Sullens is the one I had the least opportunity to get to know well on an individual basis. When I first approached prisoners to ask them for their cooperation in this project, Larry was a fairly active member of PAP. He even ran for one of the elective offices, though as he was not one of the hand-picked candidates of Jerry and the inner circle, it was one of those symbolic efforts that at most adds some slight patina of democracy to the proceedings.

By the time my interviews were in full swing, however, Larry had all but dropped out of the program. He'd come by once or twice a year, and I'd wave to him on the yard once in awhile on my way to a meeting, but that was about it.

So my impressions of Larry are considerably less deep, less confident than those I have of the other prisoners appearing in this book. Still, I have interacted with him enough to make at least a few observations.

Larry is a decidedly jovial person. I seldom see him when he does not have a smile on his face. He is quick to laugh, eager to see to it that the people around him are having as good a time in life as he is, equally socially comfortable with his fellow prisoners and with us outsiders.

Because the only side of Larry I see is the jolly, friendly, open, good fellow, it surprised me when he disclosed that he had buried that element of his personality in the aftermath of his crime, and in the difficult process of adjusting to prison life. I don't doubt that Larry was as depressed, anxious and angry during that period as he says, but it's hard for me to even picture. It isn't the Larry I know.

Judging from Larry's account of his pre-prison life, he is possibly the second most "square" of my interviewees, behind only Jeff, whom you will meet shortly. He had a largely conventional, largely successful, life. He was raising a family and operating his own business—a martial arts school.

And then greed took over. The lure of easy drug money took him deeper and deeper into a new and dangerous world, until what had started as small scale involvement in "victimless" crimes ended in multiple murder.

Larry is a "lifer," or more specifically a "life withouter"—a prisoner serving a sentence of life without the possibility of parole. He works full time, seemingly just to keep busy and productive, as he has little to gain financially from it. Most prisoners who work, especially those with outside industry jobs, accumulate enough money to help their families on the outside if they choose, or at least to buy themselves some of the few "luxuries" available in prison—perhaps a radio, a television, or some non-cafeteria food. But in Larry's case, nearly all the money he earns is immediately confiscated to pay the court costs, victims' compensation, etc. imposed upon him as part of his sentence..

His court-imposed monetary obligations are such that regardless of how long he survives, or how many years of that he works full time, he will never come close to satisfying them all. Rightly or wrongly, the system has ensured that not only that will he spend the rest of his life incarcerated, but he will do so with minimal opportunity to lessen the degree of his deprivation.

I am not the first writer to have had the chance to interview Larry. He tells me that many years ago, while incarcerated at Walla Walla, he and two other prisoners allowed a reporter access to them and their lives, for a story about life on the inside.

The reporter, Larry says, presented himself as if he intended to do an honest and sympathetic account of life as a prisoner. But instead of presenting the facts, the reporter chose to write a fanciful and melodramatic account of the three prisoners as a sort of violent prison gang, terrorizing and extorting their way to domination over various weaker prisoners. Larry was chosen for the role of "enforcer" in this instance of imaginative journalism, perhaps because although short in stature, he has something of the stereotypical prison bodybuilder physique and is an accomplished martial artist.

I can't say for sure that the story the reporter wrote was false, but it sounds nothing whatsoever like the Larry that I have spent time with. Furthermore, by coincidence, one of the other two prisoners in this alleged terrorist trio happens to also be someone I know—a former PAP member. I find it equally unlikely that he would have been involved in the activities alleged in the article. Indeed, he is one of our rare—and hence greatly treasured—PAP success stories. He's on the outside now, married, working, and doing just fine as a law-abiding citizen.

Given that Larry had been burned in the past, I would have understood if he had turned me down. But he was quite gracious about agreeing to participate in this book project.

Larry is a bright and likable man who got way too deep into something whose ramifications he did not fully appreciate. When the situation became overwhelming, he tried to solve his problems with a gun, with tragic results. Now he deals every day with the consequences of his actions, remembering the lives he took, and the life he gave up.

Larry responded to my initial questions several months after I mailed them to him. In the interim, I conducted this interview on tape with him. Unfortunately, after this interview and the aforementioned written exchange, I received no further material from him until well over a year later.

*Larry, I know you're in the process of responding to some of my questions in writing, so rather than go into those matters in this interview, why don't we try something a little different? How about if I toss out some common beliefs about prison—?*

OK.

*—that the public has, and you respond to them? Tell me if they're bullshit, or if they're true, or what you think of them.*

OK.

*Well, I think it's commonly regarded in the general population nowadays—and this may not have been as true thirty or forty years ago as nowadays with the country drifting so far to the right—that prisons are much too soft. Allegedly, prisoners really have it easy in here compared to how it should be. Especially compared to what you did to your victims, you guys are being treated wonderfully. Actually, the most common metaphor used, or the most common comparison, is a luxury hotel. I've heard that numerous times on TV, personal conversations, classes I've taught. People say, "It's just like staying in a luxury hotel except you can't leave. It's like they just lock the doors of the hotel, but you still have all the amenities. It's a pretty easy life." How would you respond to that?*

[Laughs.] Well, I would say it's not a hotel. It's not even a motel.

I guess you'd have to make that comparison separately for each place where I've been. I won't even use Walla Walla as an example here yet. That was the first prison I went to. But before that, I was in jail. I was in a small jail in Okanogan County, and that was basically my first taste of being locked up.

*Where is Okanogan County?*

In Washington. It's right by Omak. It's the largest county in the state, but it's probably the most poverty-stricken also. It's basically all Hispanics, apple orchards. You kind of get the picture there.

But, anyway, it was small, and so they weren't really concerned a lot with overcrowding. I was in the lockdown area. Basically, that was five guys in one area, and each guy had their own cell. They actually locked down within that area. So it was a little extra security.

So besides my cell, I had a room to go into, kind of like a day room. You'd eat your meals, and you'd go to this day room.

We had jail clothes, but they also let you keep whatever other clothes you wanted basically. I mean, if you wanted to have a pair of sweats, or a sweatshirt, you could have that in there. And they had recreation for one hour a day.

I thought it was kind of neat because they'd come around and ask you what you wanted to eat. For breakfast they had the same thing basically every day, you know, hot pancakes, hot cereal, some juice. They never had coffee; they always had tea or juice. But they'd ask you sometimes what you wanted for lunch, 'cause it was a small jail and they had a lady that cooked there, and she'd come and say, "What would you like today?"

*So Aunt Bee would bring her picnic basket, and—*

Yeah.

It's up in the north part of Washington, and kind of out in the sticks, and all the guys would get together and decide we want hamburgers or pizza. And we had commissary also.

*Did Walla Walla turn out to be pretty much the same deal?*

Oh, hell no. [Laughs.]

*[Laughs.]*

Yeah, that's what I'm leading to.

So I was there for a year, and I kind of got used to this. You know, they asked me what we like, and it wasn't too bad a time or nothing. I was stressed out 'cause I was waiting for my trial, and going through all the preparations for that, but I wasn't stressed out about the jail.

But after I was convicted, they put me on a little van with about five other guys, and they shipped me from there to a receiving place in Ellensburg, where we had a sack lunch and we got on the chain. The chain went from there to Wenatchee, and I spent the night in Wenatchee.

Now, Wenatchee—here's the big change—there, I went to a cell that was basically made for twenty people, and there was at least sixty guys in there. It was just overcrowded, beds everywhere in this tank. There was nowhere to walk; it's just all beds. And all these guys are in there. It was just a madhouse.

So it's kind of crazy. I was, like, "Wow! Look at this!" And the food comes, and it was slop. It wasn't even edible. I don't even remember what we had, but I remember I didn't eat nothing that night.

*Now is this another county jail?*

Yeah, and what we're doing, we're en route to the Shelton R-Units.[*]

*OK.*

For some reason we spent the night there. The next morning, everybody gets on the chain bus, we go right to Shelton.

---

[*]The Washington Corrections Center in Shelton is a hub of sorts for the Washington prison system. The Reception Center (R-Units) is where new prisoners are processed and evaluated. When prisoners are transferred from one prison to another, they also go by way of Shelton.

That was another big eye-opener there. We got there, they give you your bedroll and all that stuff. Things are a lot harder, there's some fights going on, and it was just a total switch.

I'd been kind of relaxing a little bit, in this little old county jail, and now all of a sudden it's real live prison. And I'm now exposed to a greater variety of races that I wasn't exposed to before. In Okanogan, it was mostly Hispanics, there was a couple of Native Americans, and I was the only white guy that was there. There were two others I'd seen, but they weren't in my pod. And there were some women upstairs, and once in awhile we'd see them.

But, now I'm in this place where it's just a madhouse, and there's gangs. That was my first real exposure to gangs, other than seeing them on a street corner, driving by or something.

So, here, you get up in the morning, you have to get out of bed, you have to go to breakfast, you have to sit where they tell you to sit. You come in, and you take the first available seat to your left. So that was a big change, right there, just having everything so strictly controlled.

OK, then after being there for thirty days, I went to Walla Walla. And I don't know how people can say it was a motel or a hotel. The only thing that I can say is that you do have the option of buying a TV, and a radio, so you do have that luxury. I guess you'd call it a luxury. And, it's pretty nice to have a radio and TV to pass the time.

Other than that, there is no other luxuries. Other than what you can buy on the store, on the commissary, and your TV and your radio.

And musical equipment, if you're into music. You can have a keyboard or a guitar. I have a guitar. Passes away a lot of time.

*What about a weight room or recreational facilities?*

Well, they're there, but you pay for them just like anybody else does, and you got to put aside time to get there if you're going to school or working, you have to put away some time to get in there.

And, the main thing is you don't get really big from working out, 'cause the food here doesn't have the proper diet of proteins and carbohydrates—

*Then how do prisoners get so big?*

Most guys, it's just genetics. I mean, you look at me. I'm kind of stocky, but I'm not going to get any bigger than I am now. And I've been lifting weights for ten years. Since I first fell, I started doing push-ups and working out, and I lifted weights, and I'm as big as I'm going to get. I'm not going to get any bigger than I am now. And I've tried. [Laughs.]

I've tried eating as much food as I can take in, and it's just basically impossible. If you know anything about nutrition, you're just not going to get any bigger.

Now, like, at some of the camps, you can get some supplements. So, there are ways of getting bigger. But those guys are also out there swinging the pick-hoe and planting trees, and they're doing some serious work.

*What do you think when you hear the media and people talking about how easy life is in prison?*

I just think those people have never experienced it.

It's not easy. The hard thing is you're removed. You're removed from society. That's the number one goal they want to do is remove you. You are removed from a lot more than what people think.

I mean, I hear on TV, I see every once in awhile there's people on there, and they say, "Well, they should be doing hard labor, and they shouldn't have TVs," and all this stuff. Well, there's guys in here who do hard labor. There's guys in here who work just as hard as anybody does out there, and they only make 45 cents an hour. So, there is hard labor, but they get paid a little money.

You got to remember that some of that money that they get paid goes to restitution fees, or it's mandatory money that comes out for victims' comp. So if we weren't working, they wouldn't be getting that money either. So, there's kind of a two-way street there a little bit.

I mean, with us working, we get a little bit of money we can send home and help support our families, buy a little commissary, save up for a radio or a TV, help pass away our time, and they get money from us as we work. So it works for everybody, you know. If we weren't working and partly paying our own way, they would be griping that they need more money for this and that, and people's taxes would be going up, or however they decided to get the money.

You know, from my perspective, it's not a hotel. I'm removed from all my friends, my family. If it's a hotel, it's the noisiest, most open-doored one I've ever seen in my life. There's no privacy. You know, there's no privacy. At a hotel, you got quiet. You can shut the door, put the "do not disturb sign" out, and you're OK to go until the next morning and you get your wake-up call. Here, in the middle of the night you could be woken up, because somebody's being arrested for something.

There's just constantly something going on. The guards are walking by all night long. There's just numerous little things that you wouldn't think about that disrupt you. You might just fall asleep, and they come and cuff up the guy next door and it wakes you up. Ten minutes later, they come by count and they can't see you so they wake you up. You fall back asleep, they come back by again and wake your cellee up because he has to go to work. I mean, there's all those little tiny things that you kind of wouldn't think of out there, but they add up, and you're losing your sleep, and you have to get up the next day and go to your job, if you work.

And at WSR here, you have to work. Work or go to school. If you don't work or go to school, you're not programming, and they move you out. But at Walla Walla, there isn't enough work for everybody, so there guys stay up all night long, and it's a madhouse. It's noisy. People are playing dominoes and cards all night. It's just loud.

So for people to say that it's a hotel, or an easy life—for some of the hardened criminals who've been in prisons all their life, it might be easy. But for the guy just coming in, it's not easy at all.

It wasn't easy for me. It took me a long time to adjust to it. And even now, I still have problems with it. I sit down and think a lot. I won't ever be out there to see my daughter. I see her when she comes in and visits. That's the only time I see her.

Or my parents, and my friends. And that's the main thing that's really hard to accept.

No matter how you look at it, there's no way that you can compare it to a hotel. It's just not that easy. They don't cater you. You know, the food isn't that good. You get your three meals a day, but I'm telling you, it's not that good. [Laughs.]

*Just to play devil's advocate, when I listen to people who have anti-prisoner attitudes, and complain about how it's too soft and all that, there seem to be two common comparisons made. One is that they're offended that a prisoner's life should ever be better than the life of somebody who hasn't committed crimes. So they look at people in ghettos, or people who have to work three jobs to put food on the table for their family, and they say, "Well, unless the prisoner has a worse life than that, then there's something unjust here. 'Cause here's a fellow who never did any horrible crime, and he has just as much trouble having his sleep disturbed or—*

Right, right.

*—"working so much, or having so little money," or whatever.*

Right.

*And the other comparison is, a lot of people have an emotional belief in the principle of retribution, that there should be some rough equality between what you do to others and what's done to you. Certainly when I was teaching and I talked to my students, if I made any kind of a pro-prisoner point, or if I said anything about the inhumanity or the tough conditions or unjust conditions of prison, the most common response was, "Well, they've still got it a lot better than their victims do,—*

Right.

*—"cause their victims are dead or they're crippled or they're destroyed emotionally, and until the prisoners are suffering more than that, until they're worse off than dead people, they have no grounds to complain." Now, how do you respond to that? Do you think prisoners, or you specifically, should have to be as bad off as your victim for justice to be served?*

I don't think that they need to be as bad off. I mean, I kind of have a belief that there is a line there where guys maybe have it too good compared to their victims, but at the same time, two wrongs don't make a right.

Things happen in people's lives, and sometimes you have to sit there and say, "Well, this happened." There might not have been a reason why. It might just happen because somebody was wigged out on drugs or something and it was just a bad situation. Things happen. Or it might have been planned, and therefore, that would be worse.

But, I can't look at my own situation and say, "Well, I made a mistake, so now I should be punished to an extreme."

I'm living with my mistake every day, and that's really a hard thing to even come to terms with. I mean, I'm not ever getting out. It took me a long time just to get to where I could cope with that, and get back to just being the guy that I was before I fell, where I could accept things on an up-and-up level, and I can start joking around again, and just be myself.

There was a time when I was real stressed out, and I couldn't handle the idea of doing that much time. It was really hard. And I put on a game face—a mask, you know—and I was actually hiding my feelings.

I don't have to do that so much any more. I mean, I still do it occasionally, and it just happens, but there's a side to my personality where I like to joke around and have fun, and I've always been like that. And that's the side that I'm saying I'm getting back to.

But when I hear people saying, "Well, that guy killed someone; he deserves to die," when I hear that, I don't like that, because every case is different.

One of my victims I meant to shoot, because we got into a confrontation and there was guns on both of us, and it was either him or me. Now I accidentally shot somebody else that was in the line of fire, and I felt really bad about that. But there was nothing I could do at that time. I mean, it happened, and I can't change that.

I can apologize until I'm blue in the face. I can tell the victims' families that I'm sorry, but, you know, how far does sorry go? I mean, they don't know how I feel. You can't express the remorse that you feel. I mean, at least I can't. I cannot ever tell those people how bad I feel.

And they don't really care what I say. They're just upset that I removed somebody out of their life, and it was a violent act. From their side, they're saying, "I don't care what happens to you. I just want you to be miserable." Because they're also hurt, and I understand where that comes from, how they're hurt, because I know how bad I feel for creating that circumstance.

But I don't know what to do. I don't know anybody that's been in prison that can sit down and tell their victim how sorry they are, and it would really make a difference to that person. You understand what I'm trying to say here? I mean, it's hard to even explain here, or put into perspective I guess.

*And your suffering, or being executed, would not undo—*

No, it wouldn't.

*—the wrong anyway.*

No.
So, that's what I'm saying: Two wrongs don't make a right.

There was a time when I actually thought I was going to get the death penalty. I thought they were going to try for it. And the prosecutor just finally said, "There's no way I can get the death penalty on you, 'cause you basically never were in a criminal lifestyle."

At that point, I was relieved. But originally, when I thought about the death penalty, I thought, "Well, that'd be the best route to go. Just get it all over with. Everybody'd be happy." But then I thought, well, no, because then my family'd be upset, and my daughter'd be upset, and my friends, and now they'd all be victims, too.

So, you have your victim, and if something happens to the person who created the circumstance, then you create more victims. So it just keeps going on. It's like a domino effect at that point. If you keep pushing it and pushing it, nobody's going to be happy in the end. The victims' families are still going to be victimized and they're traumatized by it, and if you go further than that, then the other side ends up becoming victims too.

And they're already victims anyway. 'Cause as soon as I went to prison, my daughter became a victim of me not being there for her. So it just goes on.

I mean, it kind of upsets me when people say those types of things, but there's also a part of me that understands that, 'cause I know that if—

*Yeah, that's what I was going to ask next, is—*

—somebody would have killed somebody that I knew—

*Sure, let's talk about this, because I know in some of the group discussions we've had with the prisoners, a pretty fair number of them—probably a majority—are pro-death penalty. Now, some of our outside members were quite taken aback by this, but it didn't surprise me at all.*

Right.

*The prisoners tend to be in favor of revenge, they're in favor of using violence to solve their problems and to retaliate against wrongs that have been done to them and their loved ones. Rightly or wrongly, that's the mentality of most prisoners, it seems to me. They punish through violence, so how could they consistently oppose the state doing the same thing? But, what about you? If someone close to you was murdered, would you want the murderer to pay with their life?*

Before I came to prison, I think I would have been more prone to go for the revenge factor. Revenge equal opportunity. Now that I've been through it, I don't know. I mean, it's more of a situation now where I would think that I'd have to weigh the pros and cons of the whole situation.

But there was a time when that was my belief too. Before I came to prison, I thought that if somebody killed somebody, then they deserved to die too.

*What pros and cons would you have to weigh? What do you mean?*

Well, now that I know, now that I've been in that situation, I would say if somebody close to me—I'll just say my brother—if somebody killed my brother, I would want to go after him. I'd just do it. I don't know if I'd kill him, in that situation, or if I'd just hurt him, but I would think that I would go after him. Even right now, if I was to get out, if something happened to my brother, I'd—

*Are you just saying that you'd be so overcome with emotion that you'd do that, or are you saying that doing that is justified?*

I would think that that would be justified. Because I don't have a lot of faith in the system, in the police and all that. I mean, they might get the guy and all that, but they might not, and then you never know what punishment they'd give him. That's why I say I can understand how the people feel.

*So your victims' families, you not only think that their desire for revenge is understandable, but also that it is justified, that they would be correct to come and kill you, or to harm you.*

Yeah. I do. Even when I was on trial, there was—

*Well, what happened to "two wrongs don't make a right"?*

Right. Well, it's there, but you got to still understand the emotional side of it. I mean, you get caught up. That's all that happens.

When I was at trial, the guy that I shot, his brother got all upset, and he was coming at me over the chairs they have there, and they had to stop him. And I was, like, "Wow!" He sprung, and he was coming, and I really didn't know what to do even. [Laughs.]

You know, I was, like, "Well, this is it." I thought he was just going to pounce on me, and I didn't know what was going to happen. But they stopped him at that point, I thought, "Well, that's the same thing I would have done." There's nothing different at that point that he did that I wouldn't have done myself.

So that's why I'm saying I can understand. I understand where people come from.

*But you're saying more than that you understand. You're saying that you agree with it, and those are quite distinct. So let's draw that distinction again,—*

Right.

*—because I want to make sure I understand your position.*

OK. I understand the emotional side that makes people want to have the revenge.

*Understanding is different from agreeing with it, though.*

Right.

*So if your brother was murdered, say, you might well go after the perpetrator and deal with it through violence—*

For me it would have to be at that moment. I mean, I wouldn't—

*But are you merely predicting that emotionally that's how you would react, and you wouldn't really be able to control yourself, or are you saying that that's the correct thing to do?*

No, I'm not saying it's the correct thing to do. I'm saying that I can understand, if somebody was in the situation, and the emotional pressure got to that point, and they burst out and reacted, but I'm not saying that I would stalk the guy down, and hunt him down. That's not what I'm saying. I'm saying if I was in the courtroom, and it just all built up—

*So you feel that seeking revenge in that way is predictable and understandable, but ultimately not right.*

Yeah. I think it's more of a human reaction, actually.

I just recently saw a thing on TV where these people burst out in court and attacked the perpetrator. I was amazed, because these people just lost it. They were coming through the bailiffs, and attacking the guy while he's cuffed up, and throwing chairs at him, and I was, like, "Wow!" and that's kind of what I'm saying. They're there at that time, and they're caught up in the emotion.

But, for me to say that I'd go out and stalk the guy down, or whoever it was, no. And that's what I mean by two wrongs don't make a right. If I had time to sit there and say, "OK, you know, they have the justice system to deal with it," then that would be the other side of what I said earlier, even though I don't have a lot of faith, personally, in the system.

Although, they seem to get guys and detain them, whether they're right or wrong, or if it's the right guy. They do have a way of getting their man. [Laughs.]

*So you don't think that you deserve to die. You don't think that you deserve to suffer equally with your victims. But do you feel that in some other sense, you have a debt to repay to society or to the victims' families? Do you think that you're under a heavier obligation than an ordinary person off the street to, you know, contribute something positive to society, or to try and make up an infinite deficit in effect? Or do you think you have no more and no less obligation than just any other adult human being, who should live a good life and should be productive and so on?*

No, I think everybody has an obligation at that point. I've tried to do things that didn't necessarily have to do with the victims' families, like, when I went to Walla Walla, I got involved with a community program that helped kids, making sponsor signs for the youth football league. And from that, they generated money to buy uniforms and repair the stands, et cetera, et cetera. But, that was just something I got involved in to give back to the community.

Now, I pay restitution. You know, what little money I get from my job—I make twenty-six dollars and fifty cents a month—they get fifteen to sixteen dollars out of my check. That's what they get each month. So it's more than fifty percent of what I make.

If I knew the money went directly to the victims, I'd be a little more agreeable to it, trying to maybe work a little more towards that, but the money goes back to the court. I don't know where it goes from there. I know for a fact that a large part of my restitution is for the court, the court-appointed attorney, and court costs, not the victims.

And, to me, that's not right. Even though I should pay it—theoretically, it's only right that you pay it back—but the problem I have is that there's so many guys who don't have that same requirement. It's not equal across the board.

Just as an example, if you took five guys right now that are in here for first degree aggravated murder, I'd be willing to say only one out of five—I don't have the statistics; I'm just using it as an example—would have restitution that would be payable back to the court. And even that person might not have to pay it back till a later date, and it might not even be a substantial amount. For example, I know one guy who's in for two murders that only had to pay victim's costs of seventy-five dollars. That's it. He didn't have no court costs.

Now me, I've got a hundred and ten thousand dollar fine, plus they add interest on it.

[At this point, I suffered my first tape malfunction of the interview process. The next approximately fourteen minutes of our conversation were lost. I pick up the transcript where the tape resumes.]

*Larry, are you a bad man?*

No. I'm not. Not even in here. I don't portray to be a bad guy. I stand up and walk tall and proud, and do my own thing, and if anybody gets in my face, I'll get in their face right back. But I don't portray to be a bad guy, or a bad ass.

*I don't mean "bad" in the sense of tough or a bully, but "bad" in the sense of, are you an evil man?*

No. I never have been. I've never been an evil person. I don't think you'll find anybody that knows me that would say otherwise.

I didn't really live a life of crime or violence. I was involved in martial arts, as an instructor, but I wasn't a guy that went around and kicked people's butts because I knew a martial art, or nothing like that.

My school was family structured. My main goal was to have families. You know, a dad and his kids, mom and dad and the kids, the daughters and the moms, the brothers and the sisters. My school was a family-oriented school. I had about three hundred and fifty students there in Snohomish.* And I had another school in Bellevue for awhile.†

*So you still have self-respect. You feel you're a good human being. You're not constantly punishing yourself. You don't think you're evil.*

Well, I went through a stage. I did. I tried to make sense of what happened. And, I thought that I had just gone loony bins, and went off the deep end. I couldn't understand what had happened. It took me a long time to understand why I even got involved. I blamed myself for everything.

Dick and I had worked for a person who was importing drugs, and we made easy money by making deliveries.‡ I mean, we were the middle guy. Take the money, pick up the drugs. Or take the drugs, pick up the money. Vice versa. And, we got paid each night. We were making three to six thousand dollars, depending on how far we had to drive. And, it was never very far. I mean, a forty-five minute drive at the most, one way. So, that was pretty good mileage, pretty good money. [Laughs.]

But what I'm saying by "blame myself" is that I was making good money with my school, and I had good clientele, where I didn't need to be doing this. But I got caught up in the easy money, and some things happened where I got in too deep, and I knew I was in too deep at that point, but I really couldn't get out.

*Sounds like kind of a slippery slope, like you made some fairly small mistakes based on greed, but once you had made those little mistakes, then it was hard to avoid a little bit bigger mistake, and a little bit bigger mistake,—*

Right, right.

*—until eventually there's a couple of dead people.*

---

*A Washington town northeast of Seattle, near Monroe itself.

†Eastside Seattle suburb.

‡This is one of the people Larry ultimately murdered. I have changed the name.

Well, actually, the little stuff was going on, and then a big event happened, and I was in. And the big event was when we were making a delivery and a guy tried to rob us, and that guy ended up getting killed by the people we worked for. So, at that point, I knew I was locked in. I couldn't get out.

That was when I discussed with my wife about getting out. She said, "Yeah, we need to." She worked for Nordstrom, accounts payable supervisor. High position. She had a chance to go to Connecticut to open a new store. We were going to move, thought about it—

*So you weren't going to starve without the drug money.*

Oh no, no, I wasn't going to starve without the drug money. That was just icing on the cake, I guess you'd say.

*Just greed.*

[Laughs.] It was. It was greed. I'd have to say it was. It was paying for my little toys. I owned a motorcycle, owned cars, you know. It's pitiful. [Laughs.] I admit it. I just got caught up in that, and I was liking that lifestyle, having that money.

*What about the person you are today? If, all of a sudden, you were let out of prison, through some clerical error or something, and you walked out and you were just a free person, and nobody was the wiser, would that be a good or bad thing for society? Are you a threat to anyone? Do you feel like you'd be a good citizen?*

The only way it would be bad is if the victims' families found out, they'd be really hurt. They would be devastated. They'd say, "Man, how did he get out? We thought it was over, that he was gone. We put him out of our mind. We forgot about him," and now it's, all of a sudden, it's a reminder. "Now we know he's out. Oh my God!"

And they probably think I'm some monster or something, which I never was in the first place, to be honest with you. There just were circumstances that came into play, and it could have happened to anybody, basically.

I mean, if you were in that situation—not saying that you would have gotten yourself into it in the first place—but let's say you were in my shoes, you might have done the same exact thing as I did. There was an argument. I had a weapon; he had a weapon. He pulled the weapon out, and shot. At that point, I had only two alternatives: Get shot or shoot back.

And I would say that most people would have shot back. I mean, I would have to say that if they said they wouldn't, I'd almost have to call them a liar. I mean, maybe they wouldn't, but your primal instinct to stay alive kicks in.

I told that to the judge, which was a really bad thing to do. [Laughs.] I won't do that again ever.

# RICO—June 1998

*"One thing about us is we're good character readers. We know it if a guy's coming from the heart, or he's just trying to feed us a line of bullshit. And when you know a guy's coming from the heart, you kind of draw up to that guy."*

The author and Rico in 1997.

I developed individualized questions for each prisoner. One of the questions I initially sent to Rico was the following:

*Clearly for some prisoners, it's very important to them to live by the "convict code," to be regarded as "solid cons," etc. I don't just mean that they abide by the code because it can be dangerous not to, but that they mostly agree with the code and base some of their self-esteem on their living up to it. However, you've expressed obvious disdain for this attitude on occasion. Tell me about this.*

Rico let me know the next time I saw him how impressed he had been by the question. He said he was taken aback that I had read him so accurately.

In our first two taped interviews, we stuck mostly to discussing his crime. In this our third interview, I decided to follow up on this matter of the convict code.

In contrast to his earlier acknowledgement of ambivalence about the code, once the tape recorder was running he took a quite different tack. The more I probed him about this matter, the more defensive he became. He was not about to admit he ever made any compromises with the convict code, or had any doubts about it.

It created an interesting dynamic. I felt comfortable pressing him on it, because I knew from previous conversations that he is capable of taking a deeper, more nuanced approach to these matters. But he remained true to the role he had chosen of the solid convict who sticks by his fellows and his code and won't let someone like me put words in his mouth.

*Rico, why don't you give me a brief summary of where you've been and for how long, since your time in the King County Jail? Where did they send you from there, and then where'd you go after that? And, how'd you end up here?*

OK, I spent four months in the King County Jail. I pled guilty to first degree murder. I went from King County Jail to Shelton. I spent eight weeks at Shelton, where they were testing and classifying and going through the medical process that they put a new arrival, a new inmate through.

And then from there, I was classified because of my crime—my time structure, and also my conviction, Murder One—I had to do five years mandatory at a maximum facility institution. And Walla Walla was, at that particular time, the place to go. So that's where I went.

I spent approximately eight years in Walla Walla. I got my medium custody after five years, and that medium custody made me eligible for a transfer. But I really wasn't looking to go anywhere until I found out about WSR. I came to WSR approximately three years ago.

And here I sit. I have four and a half more years to do.

*Do you anticipate that all of that will be at WSR, or will they ship you out somewhere else before your time is up?*

You never know. You never know what policies or procedures somebody in Olympia is going to draw up tomorrow. So, you know, they could say, as to where before it was five years that a guy had to do in a maximum security joint, now it's three years. Or whereas before you could only get minimum custody with two years left, now you can get minimum custody with four years left. So, it always changes. You never know.

One thing you will know is you're going to do every single day of your time. You're not going to get no early outs, that's for sure.

*Don't you get time off for "good time"?*

You get a third off or a fifth off or whatever they have regulated at the time, but as far as, you know, "You've done good. I think your programming methods have proven to us that you can indeed make it back into society. You have shown remorse. Your actions have shown that you are rehabilitated, and you will not present any problem to society," absolutely not. They're not going to take any of that into consideration.

*So once you factor in the good time, and you subtract that from the sentence, what's left is a minimum. You can't improve on that. You can stay longer than that, if you screw up, but you can't do less time than that.*

No. No. That's the Washington way.

*Each time you move from one institution to another, do you have to go through Shelton?*

Yes, unless you're already at a related institution. Like this particular place in Monroe has three different commands. It has Twin Rivers, it has, now, the Farm,[*] and also WSR itself. That's three commands under one supreme command. So if you're going to move to do a lateral transfer from one of those to another, then you don't have to go through Shelton. But if you're going to another institution, another facility, another location other than this command, then, yeah, you're taking a beeline right to Shelton.

---

[*]Known colloquially as "the Farm," the Minimum Security Unit (MSU) is part of the same complex of prisons as WSR. It is a work camp that includes a dairy farm.

*You've mentioned to me that you were wary of PAP and some of the programs when you first got here, and that you had had some anxiety about whether to join or not.*

Right, right.

*Why did you feel that way?*

Well, it goes back to when I first got to Walla Walla. I chose not to have any communication with my family. I chose not to have any communication with the outside world. I chose not to have mail. I chose not to write. I chose not to make any phone calls. And the reason that I chose to do that was because I wanted to get to know who this guy was. Who the hell was Rico? Why was Rico always running? 'Cause Rico was running.

Rico was living, but Rico was just existing. There was no purpose, I felt, for my life. Here I was 34 years old with a murder beef. And I knew that I had better potential. I knew I had better decision making skills. I knew I had a lot that I can offer, but I never went that route. I never did that route.

I was always living a lie, OK? I was always being somebody, trying to be somebody that I wasn't. I learned those skills real well. And I wanted out of that. So when I decided to take responsibility for who I was, and for what I did, that's when I started to look inside this guy, and really find out who this guy was.

So it was then that I said, "OK, this is where I'm at. This is what I've got to deal with. This is the hand that's been dealt. I'm going to play it. And when I say 'play it,' I'm going to look at who this guy really is." And when I took a good look at who I was, I didn't like it.

So I went through all kinds of different denominations, and I started reading the Word, I started reading the Koran, I went to Jehovah, I went to—all over the place. I was searching. I was doing a real search of self-discovery. And I started reading. I got involved in reading about the self. I got involved in reading about what a real man was all about.

Because I bought into that whole macho thing. OK? But I started educating myself. I started going to school. I started taking college credits. I started doing things that I never thought that I could do, because, one, I never tried, and, two, people were telling me I couldn't. So, when I started doing these things for myself, and I started receiving some praise, and I started seeing some good marks, and I started being treated with encouragement and support, and some genuine love, rather than the manipulating, lying, cheating, and all the rest of the bullshit that I was involved in, I started feeling better about myself. I started treating people better. I started trusting.

And I started believing in myself. And I started liking this guy who I was. I really started to like who the hell I was. And I was like, "Wow! You know, I don't like why I'm here, and I don't like where I'm at, but I like who I'm beginning to be." OK?

So, when I came over here, and I saw people coming in and interacting and stuff like that—I never had that. I never had that from a genuine sense. You know what I'm saying? I never sat down and just spoke to somebody—there was always some motive, some ulterior motive, or it was just hanging out just to bullshit. I didn't want that in my life any more.

And since I stood away from it for so many years, I didn't know how to do it, one, sober, and, two, genuinely, and honestly, and sincerely. Those were all new tools that I had developed, but I developed them with people that I was comfortable with, not people that I didn't know. So I didn't feel comfortable, you know.

But they pushed me, "Come on Rico." I'm like, "I'm not comfortable, man." But they knew what I was capable of. I had even done a TV project in Walla Walla, and a whole bunch of other stuff. I was cool around that environment, and around those supervisors, and those educators, and those counselors, but when it came to actually dealing with society, with strangers, in a whole totally different form, I had never put those skills to practice.

So my first instinct was what my first instinct was all along: to run. Don't feel comfortable? Run. So, I got the hell out of there, and I stood away from PAP for awhile. But they kept after me, "Come on, come on."

So I started off with the Prison Awareness classes. And then I started hearing some feedback from the classes, and then I started establishing a rapport with some of the people. And that brought me out, made me that much more comfortable, and helped me see that I can indeed establish a relationship, and I can use these skills, and at the same time, be me. OK?

I know I got a little long-winded in that answer, but you hit a nerve there. [Laughs.]

*How did you initially get involved with the supervisors and the educators at Walla Walla that you mentioned? They must have been strangers at one time.*

Well yeah, but it was easier, because I knew them through my work, and it was easy to go to work. I've always had a good work ethic.

I coached various softball teams, hooked up with people that way. I had four back-to-back championship softball teams in Walla Walla. And I had some straight killers on my team. OK? I mean, people would tell me, "If you can coach those guys, you can coach anybody."

But it wasn't that. It was the fact that I was always somebody who, instead of forcing, I was just showing and guiding and saying, "Hey, you know, you can do it this way." And I saw some guys who needed more help than I did. And when I was learning these skills, I was sharing it with them.

One thing about us is we're good character readers. We know it if a guy's coming from the heart, or he's just trying to feed us a line of bullshit. And when you know a guy's coming from the heart, you kind of draw up to that guy.

The educators, through my work, saw that I had something to offer, something that I didn't see. They helped guide me into different areas that I wanted to get involved in. The Director of Education interviewed me for a cultural thesis that he was doing for his doctorate, and in that process, he had asked me about the English as a Second Language program, and I had shared with him what I thought about the program and what I thought about the school system and what they can improve on and what needed to be done and the whole thing, and he challenged me to become one of his teacher's aides. That was an area that I really didn't think I'd ever see myself in. But I took it.

And that really helped me, because here I was—not a teacher, 'cause I never called myself that. I always walked that thin line, OK?, where I was always willing to help, but I never put myself on a pedestal.

But my Latin brothers would come in, and I was like, "Hey, check this out. You can do it this way. You can do it that way. You can do it this—," and you're talking to a bunch of proud Latinos in there that are checking you out. You know? But I never implied that I thought that I was better than they were. So that helped me out.

So, you know, when you get evaluations and people compliment you, and instead of degrading you, they're supporting you, it does a lot for a fellow's self-esteem. And when you receive it, it's that much easier for you to give it.

I've been treated a whole lot better by yourself and the volunteers in many areas than—I can honestly say—by my own family.

*What classes are still available at this institution?*

GED. They have GED. They're trying to get high school classes right now. They still have some of the vocational training courses. They have absolutely no college credits, none.

*Why is that?*

Because they took the two year degree program out. They just stripped it clean.

What do they do out there in society when they need money? Where do they go? Whose money do they take? Education. They did the same thing here.

*Do you think the prospects are good for returning college-level classes to this institution?*

I think the prospects are good, if you get legislators to look at these studies that they do, that they spend so many thousands of dollars to put together. If they start looking at these studies, and paying attention to these studies, then, you know, it'll happen.

But as long as the climate is such that the media and everybody else wants to portray fear and anger and vengeance, and as long as that train is still running, then we're not getting nothing. And as long as they can continue getting votes on that train, then they're going to ride it for all it's worth.

*So to return to what we were talking about, when you arrived here, it isn't that you weren't interested in PAP and programs, or that you distrusted the people in them, or had any negative feelings about them; you just weren't sure that you could handle it.*

I didn't know how to act.

It was easy for me to go inside a group drunk, stoned, high, to make an ass of myself, be the life of the party, not talk of anything of substance. I had plenty of experience with that.

But to sit down and articulate and talk to you and deal with you from the heart, that didn't exist back then with me. I didn't know how to do that. I didn't know how to be open. I didn't know how to share. It was taboo for me to let you inside my world. I was a whole lot more comfortable locked up in my own shell, being miserable by myself.

I had to tear down a lot of walls, brick by brick, in order for me to get to the position where I can sit down here and articulate with you and be open with you honestly and sincerely on what's going on in my life, the mistakes that I've made and where I'm at today. It took a lot for me to get there, you know. And, I couldn't just go into a room and say, "OK, here's my new skills; I'm going to try this." I didn't feel comfortable. I didn't know where I fitted in.

I turned from an extrovert to an introvert. I used to be a guy who was very social, but then I turned inward.

Now that I know everybody in the group, I'm very social again, and I'm letting people inside of me, letting people see me, letting people see the real me. My thing now is that as long as I keep it real, there's no problem.

*How were things for you in the very beginning, when you finally did decide to join PAP?*

Well I was nervous. I was nervous. I didn't talk a lot. I was observing. You know, I wasn't looking to catch. I wasn't—

*What does that mean?*

"To catch"? Well, you know, hook up with a woman, have a woman write to me. It didn't interest me. It didn't interest me. Guys wanted to set me up with different people. I didn't want that. I wanted solitude really.

I wanted solitude, because I didn't want to be sweating the phone. I didn't want to be sweating visits. I didn't want to be sweating whether or not I got a letter. I didn't want none of that. I wanted to deal with this—I had enough problems dealing with this knucklehead. I wanted to put him back on track. But I wanted to put him back on track honestly.

That's why, to some extent, I have to be very careful, because I've made so many mistakes in the past that now I'm so rigid, and so hard on myself, that, it's like, I don't want to try to be Mr. Perfect either.

But now I'm at the point where I want to have that balance. I want to keep my focus. I don't want to use the past as a hitching post; I want to use it as a guide post. OK? But I'm going to keep on going forward. And I'm going to be genuine about it. If I got something I need to share with you, if I got something I need to say to you, I'm going to try to do it in a very tactful manner, you know, be honest and open, instead of just carrying a grudge around, wanting to hurt you or despise you. You hold a grudge, you hold yourself.

There's been a lot of things I've had to learn, you know. I didn't know nothing about forgiveness. "Forgiveness? Fuck that asshole!"

My family. I've had to really work with the things that happened to me in the past, things that happened with my family. I had to get to a level where I had to understand that, hey, they're human beings, they made mistakes, they're not perfect. And, again, this is the hand that I've been dealt. Deal with it. Move on. Be better than that. And that's where I'm at.

*How many years did you not have mail and phone contact?*

About five years.

*Does that mean that even if a letter arrived for you, you refused it, or did you just not happen to get much mail?*

I didn't happen to get much. I used to get, you know, mail for my birthday, for Christmas, and stuff like that. I just thought, "Well, OK, you wasn't interested when I was out there."

*Did you write a single letter during the first five years you were locked up?*

No.

*Did you make a single outgoing phone call?*

Nope. Nope.

*One thing I wanted to talk to you about is that you strike me as having maybe achieved a kind of balance that I would think is fairly difficult. On the one hand, you have the "Fellahs," who are at the top of the food chain because they live by the prison code, and everybody looks up to them because they're good criminals. They know all the tricks, they conform to the code, and they fit perfectly into this pecking order. At the other end, you have people who have violated the code or that just don't have the social skills or whatever, and they're distrusted and ostracized, they're punished in small ways and occasionally major ways. They're at the bottom or outside the pecking order. It seems to me you're somewhere in between. It seems like you get the respect, but you're not a total believer in the code, at least insofar as wanting to identify yourself as a "convict" or as a "good convict," you know, to be one of the boys. Tell me something about your attitude toward all that.*

Well, I'm not interested in being a convict. But I learned at a very early age to mind my business. I came from Puerto Rico to Harlem. My father was in the game, you know, and he told me at a very early age—I think I was about six or seven years old—that the biggest beef a man can get is for being a rat. I remember that like if it was yesterday. OK?

I've seen a lot of things in my life. I grew up in New York City. So, I know how to fend for myself, and I also know how to mind my business. What a guy does is his business. So, I like to think that the reason why I'm respected is because I fend for myself, and because I hold my mud.

I mind my business. I don't go around telling. I don't go around spreading anything around. I don't go around getting into other people's business. I do my time. I do my program. What the guy does to the left or to the right of me, that's on them. OK?

*What if other people are involved?*

What do you mean "if other people are involved?"

*What if the guy to your left in doing his own thing is victimizing others? Then does it become your business?*

Is victimizing others? What do you mean? I'm not too clear on the question.

*Well, you're saying that, that what everyone does is their own business—*

Is their own business. That's their business.

*But what if what a person does is victimizing someone else?*

If the guy he's victimizing lets him victimize him, that's his problem, not my problem.

*What if it's not a question of letting it happen?*

You mean violates him, rapes him or something like that?

*Could be.*

Well, it depends on the situation. I'm not going to let nobody jump on one of my partners. I'm not going to let nobody violate any of my partners. OK? There's a circle there.

But a one-on-one? I'm going to leave it alone. But I'm not going to let nobody rat-pack anybody around here.

Now, as far as that's concerned, you know, some people classify it as being a "convict;" I classify it as being somebody who is going to stand up, not only for himself, but for his partners, going to have his partners' back. And in an environment like this, you can't do it alone.

*Now is the "no snitching" rule something that primarily applies to prison, or do you think as a general rule—?*

It applies on the streets too. I mean, come on.

*So if I go home today and find that my home has been broken into, am I doing something ethically wrong if I call the police and tell them?*

Absolutely not.

*Then why isn't that snitching?*

That's not snitching, because it's your house that was violated.

Now, if I know who broke into your house, and I tell, that's snitching. You have to understand: I have that "don't get involved" mentality. OK? A person comes into my house, he's got a problem. He goes into your house, that's your problem. Like it or not, that's my mentality. I'm not going to be nobody's hero. I'm going to take care of mine though.

Now, as far as being a "convict," and coming back and forth from the institution, I'm not about that shit at all. If you hate this place so much, if you're going to whine about this place so much, if you curse these pigs out so much, and you hate it so damn much, why the fuck do you keep coming back? I ain't got time for that. But while you're here, you know, you do yours. Whatever that guy's doing next door, that's his problem. As long as it doesn't affect you, doesn't affect me, that's on him.

*What if I go home tonight and I see someone breaking into somebody else's house, and I call the police, or I tell the owner of the house, or, you know, I reveal that information. I say, "I just saw John Smith breaking into that house over there at such-and-such address." Is it wrong to do that?*

I'm not going to tell you that. If it's right for you, then it's right for you.

What are the police going to put in the report? "The informant…" OK? The police give you that tag. So if you feel right with it, that's fine with you, but that doesn't necessarily mean that it feels right for me.

*So if you were on the outside and you witnessed that, you'd keep your mouth shut.*

If it's your house, Craig, and me and you are tight, and somebody's breaking into your house, I'm going to be there for you. If I don't know you from Adam, that's on you, partner. They can drive that truck up and take that house.

*Why don't you care about a stranger? It's still a human being. They shouldn't have their house broken into.*

I would imagine so, but I can't go around—and I'm sorry—caring about every single individual. All right? Because right now, I have to take care of this person right here. And already having a record, I ain't telling the cops shit.

*Is living by the code in here a matter of survival and self-interest, because the consequences of not doing so would be so bad, or is it actually a matter of principle? Do you think it's actually ethically correct to live that way?*

There's very few people that live by the code any more. Not in this joint, not in the other ones.

*Here's what I'm getting at: There are things that a person might do if they're in an unusual, dangerous environment like a prison, things you might do just to save your own ass. Or there are things you might do because they're right. And I'm trying to figure out which one this is.*

*Let's say I find myself stuck somewhere in the middle of nowhere with a bunch of vicious racists, and in order to not be killed by them, when they start talking about "Nigger this," "Nigger that," maybe I start talking that way too, just so they think I'm one of them, so I can save my ass. Is that analogous to living by the convict code? You're with a bunch of criminals, you better act like them and be accepted by them? Or is it actually a matter of principle, that a good person won't snitch on people, and an ethical, honorable person will do the things the convict code requires? Which one is it? Is it principle, or are you saving your ass by doing it?*

You have people who do them both.

*Why do you do it?*

It's principle. To me it's a principle. To me, you just don't tell. To me, you man up. That's me. OK? That's how I was raised. That's how I've done it all my life. To me, you man up.

You feel you got to tell, then you deal with the consequences. People can justify just about anything they do. If it works for them, fine. But deal with the consequences. You know, don't whine about it.

To me, it's clear-cut. To other people, it may not be. But to me, it is. You know, you tell, you got a snitch jacket.* A guy comes up with paperwork saying, "Hey, this guy told on me," then you're a rat. It's as simple as that.

---

*One's "jacket" is one's file, or record of past behavior. More generally, one's reputation.

*Tell me more, though, about why it's wrong. I understand why it would be in your self-interest not to get that label. But I'm trying to understand why it's wrong. If I see someone being wronged, or if I myself am being wronged, why do I have an obligation to the wrongdoer to keep that secret? Why am I not allowed to tell anybody, if he's doing things he shouldn't be doing?*

If it's happening to you?

*Yeah, if somebody's trying to rape me or something, why can't I say that that's happening? Or if I see him robbing or killing somebody else, why can't I say, "He's robbing and killing somebody"?*

You can if you want to.

*But why is it wrong to do so?*

It's wrong, because for me, it's wrong for the way I think. OK? Because for me, it's the way I've been raised. If somebody's trying to rape me, I take that raping feeling off his ass. Not by telling on him. By trying to take his head off. I assure you that that man will not come back trying to rape me again. Or to even think about it.

Now, if you want to tell on him, then he's going to go and tell everybody else you ratted him out. So on top of you being a punk, you're also a rat. Now if you want to do that, that's fine. They have places for you. They call them Protective Custody, where you can eat popcorn and drink pop all day, if that's what you want to do.

*Well, now we're back to self-interest though. I want to stick to principle; I want to know why it's wrong.*

But do you see what I'm getting at? It's up to the individual. You know, you may say, "Well, why is it wrong?" Well, God! If a guy's trying to violate you, he's disrespecting you.

*I don't mean why is it wrong for him to try to violate me. I mean why do I have to keep it secret?*

You don't have to keep it secret. You straighten his ass out.

*I don't see how that's going to work in most circumstances. Maybe in a very artificial situation like a one-on-one in prison, you can say a person has to fight his own battles and handle the situation himself. But you're saying that in all situations, even outside of prison, your values preclude revealing wrongdoing. But are you telling me that, for instance, if the press reveals wrongdoing, then they're doing something ethically wrong? If they reveal—*

You take, you see—

*—political corruption, or—*

You're taking this to a whole totally different level.

*That's what I'm wondering about. I'm trying to get to the level of principle. Why is it wrong, if you witness wrongdoing, if you're aware of wrongdoing happening, why are you under an obligation to that wrongdoer to keep secret his activities?*

I'm not under an obligation to the wrongdoer. You see, that's a play on words.

If I'm coming home, and somebody's breaking into a car, I'm not going to stop my car and roll down the window and say, "Hey! What are you doing?" Especially in today's world. Because, chances are, that guy may be packing, and will blow my head off.

Now, why did he blow my head off? He blew my head off because I stopped and didn't mind my damn business. OK? Now, if I'm married and with a kid, that means that they are without a husband and a father, because I decided to be a hero for Joe Blow, who's a human being that I didn't know.

So we can go on and on about different scenarios, but the bottom line is, if the individual feels that that's what he has to do, then by all means, do as you feel you have to do. You have no obligation to nobody but yourself. But don't whine about the consequences, is what I'm saying.

*I think you have every right to whine about the consequences.*

[Laughs.]

*If you do something which is the right thing to do, and you suffer for it, you have every right to whine about the consequences, because you've been treated unjustly. So if, in fact, I should reveal wrongdoing when I see it, if I should reveal—*

In a perfect world, I would agree with you.

*And that's all whining is, is pointing out that the world's imperfect.*

[Laughs.]

*[Laughs.]*

Thank you very much. [Laughs.]
We got into a good one. We got into a good one.

*Yeah, I think this is an important distinction though, and I come back to my earlier example: If I'm stuck in the middle of nowhere in rural Idaho or something with a bunch of vicious, violent racists, white supremacists, I may have to behave in ways that I don't believe in. I might have to pretend to be a racist or whatever, in order to save my ass—*

To save your ass! Sure!

*But I would never call that "principle." I might say it's an excusable lack of heroism, or lack of extreme bravery, but there's no principle involved. If I'm pretending to be a racist, I'm just saving my ass. I'm not doing the right thing.*

Yeah, but, you know, the scenario that you're giving me, I mean, if I'm over there in Idaho, and I'm smack in the middle of a damn Klan deal, and they throw a hood on me, then I'm going to curse every Puerto Rican out I see also, until I get the hell out of there.

*Right. But when we behave that way, we're behaving with—*

With survival skills and our mind.

*—with an excusable level of cowardice. Now, we aren't behaving according to principle.*

Here we go with the play on words again. I mean—

*I think that's an important distinction, because you can approach it either way. There are people who believe in the convict code and the "don't snitch even in extreme circumstances" rule on its merits, as a matter of principle. They do it because it's the right thing to do. And in fact, even if they were going to suffer for doing it, they'd still do it, because it's the right thing. There are other people who've learned, "Jeez, I better do this, because this is the way it's done around here, and I'm going to get killed if I don't live this way while I'm here." And it seems like, to me, you're sort of in between, that you've learned to live that way because you have to, but you also say you believe in it on principle.*

Do you actually think I need to save my ass around these guys? Do you think—?

*You've said yourself that if someone behaves contrary to the code, that there would be serious consequences.*

Well, if I ratted on anybody—and I've told this to people—if anybody can bring up any paperwork, anything like that showing I ratted, then take my head off. Because that's what you got coming. OK?

So, again, what goes on in a cell next door, or right in front of me over there, you know—I've had it happen. I've had the cops come and say, "You seen anything?" "Absolutely not." And I didn't do it because, "Oh, well, if I say something, I'm going to get my ass kicked." I did it because, hell no, I didn't see nothing! I ain't been seeing anything. It wasn't because, "Oh, if I say it, I'm going to get beat up."

I believe in it. I believe in it. I believe that people should mind their own business. I believe that whatever goes on in Craig's house is Craig's business. And whatever goes on in Rico's house is Rico's business. And if Craig wants to violate this person, and this person lets him, that's that person's business.

So, you know, as far as the words, and the principle, and the this and that, I do it because I believe it. I mean, and that's as a matter of life, just as much on the outside as inside here. I really firmly believe that.

*Well, I believe that one of the most effective weapons against wrongdoing is precisely the light of exposure, and that if I see you being harmed, if, say, something's happening in here—they're taking away your educational programs, or they're going to shut down PAP, or somebody's lied about you in your file and that's affecting your parole, or something like that—I feel no obligation whatsoever to keep that secret. I'll broadcast it to the world. I'll say, "Rico's getting screwed.*

Well, we're talking about a totally—

*"Someone is wronging Rico, and I ain't going to keep it secret. Here's what this guard is doing, or this other inmate is doing, or this warden is doing, and—*

No, Craig.

*—they shouldn't be doing it."*

# LARRY—June 1998

*"She was in the line of fire and got struck in the kidney by one of the shots. She lived for maybe ten to twenty minutes. Time was distorted to me. I really have no idea how much time elapsed. I tried to help her as much as I could. I got a blanket and a pillow for her. She said she was cold. I tried to get help. They had the CB radio disconnected. There are no phones in the area. I didn't want to leave her there. She just faded."*

About two weeks after our first taped interview, I received in the mail Larry's responses to my written questions.

*For what crime are you currently in prison. Tell me as much as you are willing about what you did, the circumstances, etc. If what you were convicted of and sentenced for differs significantly from what you actually did, address that too.*

I am currently incarcerated for two counts of first degree aggravated murder, one count of first degree attempted murder, and one count of first degree arson.

I was involved in drug trafficking. My involvement was basically pick up and deliver (a middleman). I worked with a friend of mine (Dick). In November of 1988, Dick was supposed to make a delivery. $150,000 in cash and a key (kilo) of heroin. A few days later, I got a personal visit from some of the guys I worked for, not a nice visit either. They wanted to know what was up and where their product was. I had no idea. And I hadn't seen Dick in days or heard from him. I finally got a phone call from Dick, short message—"Meet me ASAP at the cabin." The cabin is a small 'A' frame we built in Okanogan, WA., whereabouts only known to a small handful of people. Okanogan is approximately 260 miles northeast of Everett.*

I had to be present for a school testing on Saturday. My Taekwando students were testing for new belt ranks. I left later in the afternoon to meet with Dick. I arrived at the cabin around 11:00 or 11:30 PM. Dick told me he didn't make the drop and wanted to keep it all. He had been doing some of the heroin, so he was very hard to talk to. I just wanted to get the stuff back to the people we worked for, before they really got pissed. We argued about it for maybe 10 minutes or so. Dick pulled a gun out from under the pillow by him and fired twice at me. I dove over to my gym bag (I had my gym bag with some clothes so I could stay the night) and pulled out my gun and fired 6 times rapidly in his direction. Once I realized my gun was empty, I reloaded with my speed loader.

Dick had been hit twice. His wife Debbie† was behind him, maybe 6 feet, reading a book while this was going on. She never concerned herself with our business. She was in the line of fire and got struck in the kidney by one of the shots. She lived for maybe ten to twenty minutes. Time was distorted to me. I really have no idea how much time elapsed. I tried to help her as much as I could. I got a blanket and a pillow for her. She said she was

---

*Northside Seattle suburb.

†I have changed the name.

cold. I tried to get help. They had the CB radio disconnected. There are no phones in the area. I didn't want to leave her there. She just faded.

I saw flames on the other side of the cabin. A kerosene lamp was broken on top of the wood burning stove. I can only guess it had fallen from the book shelf just to the left of the stove. Maybe caused by one of the shots from Dick?

I was in a panic. I grabbed my bag and ran to my car. The door was locked. My keys were in the cabin on the coffee table. I ran back. The wall was engulfed in flames and smoke filled the room. I grabbed my keys and turned around to leave. Blair,* Debbie's daughter (Dick's step-daughter) was there. She was up in the loft asleep. I didn't even know she was there. I told her, "Come on!" But she didn't want to leave. I didn't realize it at the time, but I was still holding my gun. Maybe that's why she didn't want to go. I reached for her and she freaked out, hitting me and yelling. I slapped her with my left hand, trying anything to get her attention. That only made it worse. I grabbed her by the arm to pull her out of the cabin and a shot went off. I had grabbed a hold of her with my right hand, still with the gun in it. As she pulled away, the gun fired. I thought she was dead. She collapsed on the floor and I saw blood on her chest. She didn't move. I ran to the car and drove home. I don't remember ever crying that long in my lifetime.

The next night I was arrested. The officer called on the phone and asked my wife to have me come out. She came and woke me up. I got on the phone. Same deal. They asked me to come out to talk about a homicide. As I looked outside, all I could see was red and blue lights, police cars, a SWAT van, and a lot of officers and one dog. To keep it short, I walked out the front door, complied with the officers' instructions to get on the ground, etc. I was taken into custody. They drove me to Snohomish County Jail, took statements. I didn't know at the time, but I basically told on myself. I tried to explain what happened. They didn't care. I learned Blair was in the hospital. She had a gun wound. The bullet had grazed her and she passed out. I was relieved she was OK. I spent two days at Snohomish County Jail, then was transferred to Okanogan County Jail.

The prosecuting attorney looked into filing the death penalty. After learning I had no prior record and was in good standing with the community, he decided not to file. He offered me a plea bargain of 54 years (one count of first degree murder).

During my trial, the DA told the jury and all who watched that I owed Dick money, which was sort of true. I was purchasing a business from him. But if you look at the books, I was never late on a payment to Dick or the lease on the building space where my Taekwando school was. So the DA was wrong. Next, he said I burst into the cabin shooting everyone, again not true. Even Blair testified as to what she heard—Dick and I arguing, etc. Then they tried to say I burned the cabin to cover evidence of a crime. They even went as far as introducing my transcript from Everett Community College. I was in two law classes in

*I have changed the name.

1983. The DA said I knew how to cover up a crime. Well, I hate to point it out, but the first week of class, they teach you that a fire doesn't cover up a body. So once again he was wrong. They just wanted to make up something ugly to make the case stick in the minds of the jury and the people.

I pled not guilty, because of the circumstances and I didn't initiate any of the shooting until I was provoked to defend myself or be shot. I never planned to go to Okanogan to shoot anyone.

*Think back on what you believed about prisons and prisoners before you ever set foot in a prison. What turned out to be the single biggest difference between those early beliefs and reality?*

I believed that all prisons were filled with dangerous people of all kinds—murderers, rapists, robbers, etc. And they are, just not everyone in prison, as it turns out, is a bad guy. There are a lot of people in prison for soft crimes. Money laundering, for example. Bad checks. (Oooh, scary.)

I felt all prisoners got nothing and had nothing coming and most certainly don't deserve anything.

I believed in the TV stereotype.

The biggest difference for me now is I see and live the prison life. People in prison are the same as people outside—good ones, bad ones, leaders and followers, those who get caught and those who don't.

Some things you hear about, if they want you to, and others you don't. Example—you never hear of a stabbing or a drug overdose on the news or in the paper. Once in awhile a riot or disturbance, escapes yes.

Not all people I've met in prison were or are guilty of the crime(s) they are here for. Some are here for a crime, but not necessarily the one they did (maybe karma).

There are some who made bad judgment calls, like a robbery, who may have gotten a lot of time and would never do another crime, while there are some who have done terrible crimes and will do very little time, get out, and do more.

Basically I believed the stereotype. Now I find humor in the media stories.

*What are some of the things you miss most about the outside world?*

I could make a huge list ranging from seeing the refrigerator light come on when you open the door to walking in the zoo, but my top five are:

1. I really miss teaching kids at my Taekwando school. They were unbelievably fun. (Adults too.)
2. I miss the relationship I had with my wife. We had a lot of fun times and quiet times together.
3. Hiking and biking. Riding with friends on weekend camping trips.
4. Going out for a drive any time, both cars and motorcycles (bicycles also).
5. Being with family and friends. Holidays, parties or whatever.

*Summarize for me what you take to be the main elements of the unwritten "code" of behavior that prisoners have established for themselves. From what you've observed while you've been in prison, and from what you've been told of even earlier times, how has this code changed, if at all, over the years? Is there a difference in the rules and expectations themselves? In how tightly they're enforced and how easy it is to get away with violating them? Have you seen any significant differences in the code from one institution to another?*

The unwritten code…

For me, it might differ a little, because I have my own code I go by. However, it's not very different. First of all, you never tell on anyone, not even a guard. I mind my own business.

I watch my brothers' back. Those are the people I know who would watch mine.

Then there's the pecking order(s).

The first criterion is your crime. It's not right, but I think it's been around as long as the Ten Commandments. You automatically are in a better standing if your crime is:

1. Murder, any type, except baby killing and grandparents.
2. Any crimes from assaults to embezzlement.

The worst is:
1. Rape.
2. Child molestation.
3. Killing babies can fall in here.
4. Rats. No one likes a rat, not even guards. I can't comment for everyone, but most, me included, just can't stand them. Personal reasons. You can ask.

The code is generally the same wherever you go.

There has been a change. In the 1970s – 80s, rats and rapists would of either gone to PC or would be beaten, stabbed, no ifs or buts. Now they walk main line like everyone else. But let it be known, if there was ever to be a riot, they're all targets. They don't get any respect from any of the other cons.

The code is not really enforced. It just happens. If someone violates the code, one of his partners may put him on the spot—"check him" as we call it, or put him in check. Then he might have to deal with the situation.

*As far as you can tell, is it at all common for people to be imprisoned for a crime they did not commit, or is that almost unheard of? If there are such cases that you are aware of, is it usually a person who was living a criminal lifestyle, but who happened not to commit the specific crime they finally pinned on him? Or are there people who are even more fully "innocent," and end up in prison because of a case of mistaken identity or the like? To put it another way, in your opinion, if a person stays out of trouble and never breaks the law in any significant way, is he at any risk at all of being incarcerated?*

I don't know a lot, but I do know it happens. I know of one person here that didn't do the murder he's here for. I did know a fellah that made a deal to get out of an aggravated murder with the police, so the police department would not be embarrassed. He only did seven years.

But yes, we're all innocent!

We've all seen it one time or another. Recently on TV, two men were released after DNA proved to be someone else's in a rape case. The men did ten years or more, now they're free. They were found guilty by jury, but they were innocent.

There have been cases where the DA will add crimes to an individual because his crime had the same MO. This makes his points go way up, and then so does his sentence. It forces a plea bargain.

People are always at risk of going to jail wrongfully. Wrong place, wrong time, mistaken ID, color of clothing, car, bearded or bald. Who are people going to believe, the arresting police officer or you? In court, the DA is like a God. He would never lie. People are fooled all the time.

# BILL—June 1998

*"I would guesstimate that the prison nut base has at least quadrupled in the past two decades. You don't have to be crazy to come to prison, but if you are you'll feel right at home here."*

B ill remained one of the most cooperative of my subjects. I could always count on him to respond promptly to my written questions, or to allow me to tape a conversation with him. This, my fourth interview with him, was by way of written correspondence. (Bill did skip one of my questions. I asked him how illegal drugs are smuggled into prison. One can't give away professional secrets after all.)

*I've heard a lot of comments about how the newest generation of youth offenders are somehow more violent, more unpredictable, more remorseless, etc. than previous generations of newcomers to prison. Any truth to this, or have prison veterans always lamented the deterioration from the "good old days" of their own romanticized past?*

No. The current crop of gangsta brats are no more fierce or combative than youthful offenders of the past. The only difference is that street gangs are more prevalent than in former times. When several members of the same neighborhood end up in the same big-yard, they tend to get a false sense of security from having help to deal with violent encounters. This tends to encourage verbal confrontations initiated by a gang member who is relying on more backing than he will actually receive in a blood-letting situation.

When I hit a county jail at age seventeen, an old con told me that the new crop of prisoners just didn't measure up to young thieves from his generation. This was in 1950. That theory is still bandied about the cell-block as a self-evident fact.

*What is IMU? Describe it for me, and tell me any personal experiences you've had with it.*

IMU (Intensive Management Unit) is a system to soften the pate of hard-headed convicts. Like many penology or law enforcement projects, it got its start and funding by legislative misinformation. The supposed purpose of IMU is to keep violent assaultive prisoners isolated from the main prison population both as a safety precaution and as punishment for prisoners who assault guards or use deadly force against fellow prisoners. In fact, most IMU cells are filled with prisoners who committed minor infractions or who had snitch-kites* dropped against them (usually unsigned kites) by "reliable informants." IMU is no-frill treatment: twenty-three hours of cell confinement with a one-hour combination shower and exercise period. Many nut-cases are lodged in the 12-man pods. When there is

---

*A "kite" is a note or letter. In this context, it means a prisoner has informed on another prisoner in writing.

any disturbance, pepper spray is used to quell the noise. Participants and non-participants receive equal doses of chemical quietus. These 96-man units are kept filled to capacity with a long waiting list of people who are in solitary awaiting their turn. IMU is a Ponzi scheme perpetrated by the gaolers.

*Are crazy people less likely nowadays to be separated from the rest of the prison population? How does their treatment differ from in the past? What types of offenders, if any, currently get some form of treatment rather than punishment?*

Many of the facilities to house and treat psychopaths and social non-copers had their funding axed by the Reagan gang in the early '80s. As you are probably more aware than I am, city streets are teeming with wackos. The court dockets are far too crowded to split hairs about mental competency in the majority of court cases. After all, how sane does a fellow need to be to walk the big-yard? DOC has a few facilities for folks weird enough to be conspicuous in a crowd of misfits. It is moot whether those spaz-wits get treatment or mistreatment. There is some funding for compulsory self-help programs but those are a joke. I would guesstimate that the prison nut base has at least quadrupled in the past two decades. You don't have to be crazy to come to prison, but if you are you'll feel right at home here.

*Have you found prisoners to be any more or less inclined than the general population to see things in "political" terms? How would you describe the political opinions of prisoners??*

Of course the overwhelming majority of prisoners are of a liberal bent. "Do I favor coddling criminals? Bet your arse I do." You will have noted that a pretty shrill dynamo-like whine emits from Wallsville. Most prisoners feel that they deserve to have courts and appeals courts exert to the max when the written law favors their rosy view of the merits of their own particular case. Any politician who wants to relax penalty phases or give early release breaks is a cool campaigner. Right-wingers are all pinko-commie-queers. Most prisoners have no real clue as to the mechanics of achieving political goals.

Perhaps surprisingly, many prisoners have extreme right-wing feelings about punishment, which does not apply to them. I believe some of that myself. The only cure pedophiles and stool-pigeons need is a nice thick hemp rope and a tall tree.

Most convicts believe in the "pendulum" theory of public opinion on crime and punishment. Have you noticed how phallic a pendulum is? Now I want to review those bastards' central file.

# BILL—June 1998

"*I think there ain't nothing these bastards can do to me or for me that would much change my outlook on the way things are. I've got my own outlook on what the world is, and what values are, and they're not going to change that. Like I said, they could treat me real good, make the warden my chauffeur, I'd probably put him in the trunk, steal his car.*"

J ust a few days later, I had the opportunity to follow up with Bill in person.

*Why don't you tell me a little bit about how things have changed over the years in prison, Bill, given that you've been in and out of the prison system for literally decades. What are some of the main changes you've seen over time?*

Well, it was real hard in the early Fifties, and all through the Fifties really. There were a lot more murders and, you know, mutilation and mayhem in the penitentiaries then than there are today. They softened up from the late Sixties—Sixty-eight, Sixty-nine—to almost Eighty, when Reagan took over. Again, I don't blame him personally for that really, but when Jimmy Carter was in, he had a kind of a liberal slant on how to treat prisoners. And by some coincidence, we got a lot of peanut butter on the line.

But all during the Seventies, they tried the social programs a lot more. They stressed rehabilitation, education. Especially here. This was kind of the keystone state for it, Washington state.

They had furloughs. You could go home for the weekend. And a lot of guys did, and did what they were supposed to do. A lot of guys went out and shoved half a drug store up their ass and came back in. So, I think the right-wingers even kind of went along with it, 'cause they figured we'd fall on our ass if they give us enough rope, and that's pretty much what happened.

So, anyway, when the right-wingers got in again—Reagan twice, and then Bush—that was twelve years headed in the other direction. You know, do away with rehabilitation, education, and go back toward punishment. And then that leads to a lot of unrest in the prisons.

This place is kind of—like I said before—it's kind of a garden spot of prisons. They have all these programs and they had the single cells. But they're getting away from that. I think once they go close custody, well, that'll probably kill these programs, and this'll be just like any other joint. You know, they'll probably have mysterious fires, and guys getting knocked in the head here and there and shit.

*You said there was more murder and mayhem in the past, in the Fifties and such. Do you mean that the guards and the employees—the staff—were able to wreak mayhem on the prisoners, or do you mean prisoner against prisoner violence?*

Well, yeah, prisoner on prisoner. You could get killed for little or nothing, you know, a two packs of cigarette debt, or what they call now "dissing" somebody, which wasn't current then, but it amounted to the same thing. If you just insulted somebody, made it look like they were less than they claimed to be, that could get you killed pretty easily. It was a prestige, esteem, thing. Or, a lot of times, it was over homosexuals and all. Who had the right to have certain homosexuals.

I was in Quentin from Fifty-eight till Sixty-two, and in one three month period, we had twelve murders. So, that was, like, one a week for three months. And countless people got piped and stabbed, and lived through it. So, that was kind of the way it was. You pretty well had to sidle down the wall, and watch your ass a little bit, and be careful what you said and who you associated with, a lot more.

But prisoners ran the god damn things then. They did all the labor. You know, in a wing like we're living now, there's probably sixty cops involved in just pulling those bars and stuff three shifts. In the old days, they'd have had two cops in there, and the prisoners would have the keys and let the guys in.

And the prisoners would do the laundry, they'd do the maintenance work. Now the way they do it, they take two cops, or a free man and a cop, just to change one light bulb. In the old days, a prisoner with a utility belt would fix three toilets, change two light bulbs, fix somebody's wiring, might dab some paint on something that needed it, and put a window pane in, you know, all in the morning. It'd cost the state a dollar eighty or something. Now it'd probably cost four thousand dollars to do all that shit.

But that's one of the big changes, is that they don't utilize the convict labor any more. Of course, the outside industries they have here makes a difference, but in any of the penitentiaries, there's a hell of a lot of talent that's lying idle that they could utilize and, like, cut this cost by I don't know how much percent, but I'd guess that they could run it for fifteen percent of what they're running it for now.

*Why do you think they don't do that?*

I think it's a social program myself, a full employment program. That's a good part of it. They don't really need these cops here. Like, today they said—they made an announce-ment—they said they weren't going to open up the pill line. They said, "The pill line will be delayed because we don't have any supervisors." There's two mess halls, and each one of them has got eight cops standing there watching you eat. So they're way the hell overstaffed, and they're saying they don't have any supervisors.

That is one of the big changes. You know, these are good jobs and good benefits for sitting on your ass all day in a tower. Guys like to do these jobs 'cause they're easy, and they say they're dangerous, but hell, those guys aren't in any danger in this day and age.

*So you never have any kind of riots or attacks on guards like in the past?*

No. There used to be. Like in Quentin, there's five tiers, and if a guy would come in, a new guard, just a real prick or something, somebody'd just drop a forty pound marble tomb block behind him from the top tier. The shit would just explode and make a hell of a noise and, you know, he might get nicked with a couple of those flying rocks, and he'd see that was kind of telling him, "You fuck with us, and we'll fuck with you." And usually it worked.

But now they have these god damn IMUs, and they've quartered most of these penitentiaries. And I imagine that's what'll happen here; they'll put quadrants in this son of a bitch. One set of prisoners that can go to yard all day, and another set that can't. And one group that can work in industries, and one that can't. That'll create some dissension there too.

*Just in listening to you, from my perspective, I'm not sure which is worse: having the prisoners in control and having the high degree of murder and mayhem and anarchy, or having the guards be totally in control and having excess personnel around watching everything you do and controlling every move you make. They both sound like hideously unnatural and inhumane conditions, and, not really preparing people for the outside world. What do you think? I mean, do you think either of those environments is the least bit conducive to people improving themselves and making it on the outside?*

Well, that brief window that we had all during the Seventies, it was at least a window for people that wanted to avail their self of—which probably wasn't that big of a percent—but, the people that did want to take advantage of that, it was there for them. They could get a degree in four or five years, and get all the education if they wanted. They could do this and that, and they got good visiting and things.

So, that was there for them, but it's not going to make any difference. You know, it depends what your goal is. If you just really want to isolate a son of a bitch cheap, you can put him in a drawer like at the morgue and, you know, put him on an IV and render him unconscious, if you just want to store him. Probably a hell of a lot cheaper.

They get bonuses for cutting these food bills and shit, so I say, "Well, hell, just don't give us anything, you know. It's a hell of a lot cheaper."

I was a youngster when I was at Quentin, in my, like, early to middle twenties, and I was scared about half the time. God damn, nobody wants to get stabbed to death, and it was there every day. But it didn't stop me from doing what I was going to do. I still ran a poker game, took what I wanted to take.

I'm probably the least likely son of a bitch to ask what you can benefit from in a prison. It's a prison, you know. Like I say, we're all sociopaths.

[Laughs.] I don't believe I said that, though I'd rather be called a sociopath than an inmate.

*What does it mean to you to be called an "inmate"?*

I won't answer to it. I equate it with a mental patient. That's what an "inmate" is. What the hell else is an inmate?

"Prisoner"! I'm a prisoner. That's what I consider myself. I don't consider myself a "convict," which is kind of a bogus tough guy term. I never subscribed to that shit. You know, "We're tough. We're convicts. These other bastards are just residents or inmates." That's just blowing smoke up your own ass. If you can picture that.

*[Laughs.] So, you think "prisoner" is the neutral term?*

Yeah, that's what we are. We're prisoners. You know, we're in prison. That's what the hell a prison is, to hold prisoners, not to hold inmates. If they want me to be an inmate, I'd probably be in bed with cloth slippers by my bed, you know, getting medication and shit.

*During what era were prisoners the safest?*

Oh, shit, probably now. See, even when it was wide open, when they were letting people out on furloughs and shit, Walla Walla was the murder capital of the world. They had a little place they called Blood Alley there. It was a blind spot from all the gun towers. It had the distinction of having the most deaths in the smallest area, you know, for a certain period of time. So, you could lose your life pretty easy in that place.

So, I think, probably, it's safest now. But, they could make the whole god damn world safe if they just handcuffed everybody to a big anvil, both hands and shit, if all you're worried about is making it "safe." They could just use "super prisons"—one man cells, and you never see the guy in the next cell. The Russian system. *Darkness at Noon*. Did you read that, *Darkness at Noon?*

*By Arthur Koestler, yes. Do you think that's the way they've achieved higher degrees of safety, by decreasing freedom even more?*

Oh yeah. Yeah, that's really what it is.

All the politicians say, "I never doubt the intelligence of the American people," you know, but they're really saying, "You stupid son of a bitches. Man, you're going to go for it again." I mentioned earlier that they've kind of won the public relations war. Being soft on crime or something is—you know, I heartily subscribe to coddling criminals myself—but I know it's not fashionable to say, "Hey, take it easy on them guys! They're human too!" They say, "You fucking commie! We're going to string you up too!"

Yeah, if safety's all you want, that's the way to do it. Or maybe just have those holes in the ground like the Chinese had, with the bamboo and shit, you know. A dug out trench. Assuming you don't ever want these guys to get out.

But, you know, that's overblown too, what these guys in PAP tell you about, "We're going to be your neighbor again," and all that. A guy's not going to do anything different if you slap him around every day and kick him in the ass, or if you give him angel food cake every day. They're going to do the same shit when they get out that they're going to do.

*You don't think the way people are treated has any effect at all on their behavior in the future?*

Oh, to some degree, but not to the degree that they say it does. You know, if I get out tomorrow, I'd probably be looking for some easy money. I wouldn't give a shit how nice they treated me.

I'm just not going to go out there and live low class. I'm not going to do it. No matter how nice you are, or how mean.

'Cause I've had it both ways. I was in a Texas joint, picking that cotton all day in that heat. I said to myself, "Well, what'll I do when I get out?" I said, "Well, hell, I might try stealing for awhile." You know, same thing when I was at Walla Walla in the Seventies. Same thing when they put me out in that halfway house. I said, "Well, 'halfway' my ass! Where's the airport?"

*Why is that, do you think, that your environment had no effect on your intentions for the future?*

Oh, shit, I was just into it too far, you know. If you've done this shit for thirty, forty years, you're sure as hell not going to change.

*You think it's too late once you get past a certain age, if you're deeply into the lifestyle?*

Oh yeah. They wear some of these guys down, like there's a couple guys in here that have been thieves all their life, and they start learning all the words to "Old Rugged Cross" and shit like that. They're bullshitting their self. They're not going to change. Dope fiends aren't going to do anything but go out and be dope fiends.

You know, if I did say, "Ah shit, I'm going to get out there and straighten up," and I went out there and got me a job, worked my way up to manager of Burger King or some shit, then I'd say, "Man, I'd sure like to have a this-or-that. Well, fuck, why don't I get it then? It's not that hard." That's probably what I'd do, take some kind of a short cut.

*But it's clearly not because you're an unprincipled person, or a "sociopath" as you put it, because if you were, then you wouldn't adhere to any principles at all. And yet there are obviously principles in here that are important to you.*

Yeah.

*Important ideas you have about loyalty, and friendship, and not snitching on people, and stuff like that.*

Yeah, but I just have a different view of property. [Laughs.] Never could understand that concept of property.

You know, I'm being half serious. Even as a kid, I'd say, "This guy owns this house? How the hell can he own this house? How can he own this piece of land? That god damn land's been there for twelve billion years, or whatever the estimate is. And, this guy's been there for thirty years."

So then I extrapolate that to his jewelry box.

*Yeah, a lot of the guys draw that distinction about different levels of crime. "Well, I'd never go kill an old lady or something, but property's different. I don't really hurt anybody; I just steal." Is that the way you feel, that there are some crimes that are OK, but there are certain lines you don't cross?*

Yeah, but as far as hurting anybody, you don't normally give a shit. You might halfway think it's funny. You joke about it. Like, you see some guy that you clipped, and he's got his wallet, and he's looking, and he's running around, looking up and down to see what happened, where his money went. You're driving back by, and one time we said, "Look at that guy, man. It looks like he's trying to pump new life into that wallet." You know, you don't really give a shit that the guy had to save up or sell something to get that money.

*Why don't you give a shit about that?*

That's it, because you don't know the people and they're just—it's a kind of a "them" and "us" thing. It's just like scoring a goal in football or something. You slipped in and made the goal and got away. It's a kind of relief that you got away without the consequences.

*You have a feeling of achievement?*

Yeah.

*I partly agree with the distinction of different kinds of crime. I'm glad that some of you even who are so incorrigible about the property crimes clearly have standards about not harming people and not killing them. On the other hand, I think even those fairly minor crimes still matter. I mean, I was the victim of a fairly trivial crime: I got my car stolen last year. And it still matters. You know, you're still wronging somebody. It still is a significant inconvenience. It caused me a lot of emotional distress. It caused me a certain amount of financial harm. It would have been a lot worse if the car hadn't been recovered, but it still matters. And it bothers me that you can say that you don't care when people are harmed that way.*

No, you really don't care. Or at least for me—I'll talk about me—it's a kind of a joke. You're betting your ass, and this time you got away with it, like I said, and it's a pretty good feeling of relief. You got the reward, you can go do what you want to do, you got the money, you got the jewelry, whatever. You can go on your little spending spree, go to Vegas, go take this girl on a trip or whatever it is you want to do. It's there for you, and you feel like, maybe, the fox that did get the grapes. And that guy you stole from is just some son of a bitch that wants to call the police on you and put you in jail.

I had an old thief tell me one time, he said, "If you're ever going to clip somebody, and you get a twinge of feeling sorry for him, imagine when you're up in that god damn defendant's bench, and he's up there on the witness stand saying, 'Yeah, that so-and-so! He's the one robbed me!'" So, you set yourself against them. And when you grow up a poor kid and shit, you kind of think all those guys that, you know, got good jobs even, are rich son of a bitches that have contempt for you. That kind of sets the pattern for the rest of your life.

Later on, you realize, "Hell, this is just some poor schmuck, you know, working at the god damn post office. Sure he gets a new car every two years, but his ass is in a path this wide. You know, he's going down the furrows there, and he ain't got any more choice than you got when you're locked up. I mean, he misses a month's work, he's fucked." But even after you realize it, your patterns and standards are set.

I think most guys have what they call "walking around sense" that you can see that, by some standards, what you're doing is wrong, whatever it is, you know. If you go into a supermarket and eat a god damn peach, then the cost's going to be passed on. So you're just kind of fucking society in general.

And I can feel sympathy, if I find out something about somebody, that they're in bad shape, or that the loss hurt them some way. I never made it a point after I got to be an adult to give back identification and shit, but sometimes I'd see something, you know, get somebody's wallet, and I'd see something in there that'd personalize it, and I'd throw the thing in the mail box rather than throw it in the river. So, I think that's what it is, is that as long as it's not personalized, it's all right. You can justify it.

*So if it's somebody you have a personal connection to, you have a lot more trouble victimizing them.*

Yeah. There are places you draw the line.

I've found people's wallet in the supermarket a couple times and given it back to them just like that, but that wouldn't stop me from stealing it the next day. I have the same instincts as you do. I wouldn't feel right keeping a person's wallet I found. But when you're out hunting, they're fair game again.

So it's a complicated thing, you know. A little more complex than it looks on the surface.

*Now we've talked a little bit about whether the environment, the prison environment, can change that at all. You feel that, with a few exceptions, it really doesn't matter that much what the prison environment is like. People are pretty much going to do what they're going to do.*

Yeah, I don't know. I think the majority of them, yeah. I think there ain't nothing these bastards can do to me or for me that would much change my outlook on the way things are. I've got my own outlook on what the world is, and what values are, and they're not going to change that. Like I said, they could treat me real good, make the warden my chauffeur, I'd probably put him in the trunk, steal his car.

*Don't you think it would change, at least a little bit, where you draw those lines? Maybe push those lines back a little bit?*

Oh, I don't know.

*Maybe if you got more into the habit of seeing people as individuals, as human beings, then once you're on the outside, you'd be more inclined to say, "Wait a minute. This is a real person. I shouldn't be hurting her."*

Well, say, like, it's the volunteers I know from PAP, or even just the one time only students that come up for one of the classes on a Saturday or a Tuesday. I couldn't rob those people. If I got out, and I was trying to get away or something, and I see their car, and I knew it was their car, I'd say, "No, not this one. Might be a little more risk, but I'll just wait for somebody else that I don't know."

So, that's what it is. If there was some way they could personalize that shit to you. I don't know how they'd do that, though.

*Yeah, what do you think it would take? Maybe, like you were saying, in your case, it's too late, because the patterns are so strong, but what do you think could have happened in your past, or what could happen with fellows who maybe haven't been robbing and such for as many decades as you have? What could happen to make them see even strangers as human beings with rights not to be victimized?*

I think maybe if you could get some kind of a victim awareness thing, but not the way they do it here. This is total bullshit they have here.

*How do they do it here?*

Well, they just harp quite a bit on how people feel that get robbed and that shit, but it still doesn't personalize it for you. You know, the theory that I'm familiar with is to have the people that you robbed confront you, which is all right, but you've already robbed those people, so they're immune anyway. You're not going to double back on them.

But that's usually for if you've done something violent to them, you know, if you've raped them or beat them on the head or something. But, say, if you and I had met and I'd stole your diamond ring and your silverware, I wouldn't have any qualms about laughing about it while we were in the same room and shit. I'd say, "Yeah, I hope you got good insurance back on that shit, 'cause I made mine, you know."

So I don't really know what the answer is. It's kind of like religion. If there is something, I don't think the human mind can get around what it is. And I think that's probably the same with this shit. If there is an answer, I don't think we're probably capable of coming up with it.

*Tell me more about the victim awareness type programs. Do you think they're mostly manipulative, phony, dogmatic, or what? What rubs you the wrong way about them and doesn't seem effective?*

Yeah, most of these are started by people that are looking for a way to make a living, and that's what they come up with. They write a program, and they've got statistics to back up this and that.

Some of them are in it for more than the money, but they've still got their own agenda, they've got their own viewpoint, and they just try to mold you into that. I don't think too many people start out and say, "What can I do here to save humanity?" It's, "What kind of god damn program can I put together to make a decent living, and maybe not have to work too hard, and get a little prestige at the same time?"

*Do you think they're patronizing?*

Yeah. Pretty much, yeah. It goes back to the inmate thing. They say, "Here, you three inmates there, you got to do these forty-two pages," and the only right answer's the one they think is right. There's no room for individuality there. You just say, "I'm a bad boy, because..." whatever it is.

*And if you've memorized their dogma correctly, then you pass and you get the reward.*

Yeah, you could sleep in class, as long as you know in the end to tell them what they want to hear.

*What do you think could be done differently? You said if they had a different kind of victim aware-
ness program instead of the kind of bullshit version they have now, it might work. Any ideas what
that would look like?*

I think that these god damn prisons have to be pretty much obsolete, except for, you
know, people who are damn near criminally insane, violent.

More work programs. I seen one town—I forget where the hell it was now, some little
town—they were going to do that. They were going to take them, do reforestation, do clean-
up on lake fronts. I think that's probably the thing to do. If you haven't killed anybody, or
you're not a threat maybe to do violence to somebody, then, Jesus Christ, why not use all this
manpower to go out and do shit that needs to be done for the ecology and things?

I think maybe that might be an answer. Give a guy a minimum wage job doing that shit.
Make him responsible to report somewhere. Or even live in a god damn dormitory and shit.
I don't think these god damn warehouses are ever going to be the answer.

I don't think it's possible—even if they had some reformer politicians—I don't think
you could get anything like that through to stop locking these people up, because it's full
employment, and the support for these things is enormous.

*Do you think it's the "pendulum" theory, that right now we're in a harsh period on criminals, and
maybe ten, twenty years from now, it could be real liberal again?*

Oh, yeah, you know, everything's got a beginning and end, and I think this son of a bitch
here's getting so top-heavy eventually they'll have to find a way to stop it. Yeah, whatever the
year span is that they're doubling the prison population, that can't go on, unless they get some
monster fertility program and start having kids like rabbits.

There has to be a saturation point. I can't imagine that that's over fifteen or twenty years
away. They're building new prisons, but how many prisons can the two million people that'll
be left on the outside afford? That's what it's going to boil down to.

*Now, if you say the dogmatic, patronizing, victim awareness type programs for the most part
probably don't work, and we need some other way of humanizing strangers, humanizing victims,
so that you're more hesitant to victimize them, what about more neutral programs, like PAP itself,
that really aren't trying to force you to learn certain dogma? Or just social programs in general
where you interact more as equals with regular people from the outside? Do you think in some small,
indirect way, that they increase the tendency of guys on the inside to see even strangers as human
beings that they shouldn't victimize?*

Yeah, it's surprising how limited your association with what we call "squares" is. Everybody
that I associate with knows that I'm a burglar, and always have, you know, over the past thirty,

forty years. They either like that or they don't associate with me. And so, except on a real casual basis, I don't encounter those people.

I mean, unless I'm laughing up my sleeve or something, in some situations. I went with this one woman, her son was an IRS agent, and, you know, I'm on an escape out of the swamps down in Georgia, and I came up in her town in Nebraska. Her family and everybody in her circle was heavy into the Humane Society. So we go to this party at the house of the president or chairman or whatever of the Humane Society.

So, you know, everybody's sitting, having a few drinks, looking out of the corner of their eye to see who this woman's new boyfriend is. Actually I'd known her since we were kids, but the people there didn't know me. And the hostess puts me on the spot and says, "Bill, what do you do?"

I told her, "I'm a seal hunter." [Laughs.] Boy, everybody just stopped midway at that. And then my friend told them, "Oh, don't listen to anything this bastard says." [Laughs.] "He'll tell you anything."

*[Laughs.] Did they find out your true profession?*

No, they never did. They were mighty curious. One of them says, "You know, I don't know what that guy does, but I don't think it's legitimate."

*[Laughs.]*

"He's gone all the time. He's got big cars and things."

But, that's really the only time I ever interact with people that work for a living and shit, and have probably the good values, or the accepted values.

*What effect do you think it has when prisoners are given an opportunity to interact with "squares" like that?*

Well, I think you find that most people are cool. And, this group here, you know, PAP, it's like anybody else. They have certain people that are more capable of coping than others, but there's nobody in there that you can dislike.

People in there are trying to do something, for whatever purpose. Maybe they're writing a book or something. But they come in and they're wanting to spend their time, you know, like we're doing here, and that has to mean something. At least you know those people are guys you could have a beer with.

*What is the general view prisoners have of people who come in from the outside for these programs?*

I think a lot of the guys are there to try to catch and shit like that, a good many of them. You know, people can say that's right or wrong. And some of them have done it. They've pulled wives and sweethearts and shit out of that.

*It doesn't seem to be as advantageous any more since they changed the trailer rules.* You can't have sex anyway, even if you meet somebody and get married.

Yeah, they took away a good part of the incentive.

*Yeah.*

You get all the problems without any of the benefits.

*Right.*

What was it that one guy said? "You know, sex is different when you're married. Then you have a partner." [Laughs.]

*[Laughs.] What do you think prisoners in general think of the folks who come in from the outside? Is there a general view that they're dupes or suckers, or are they appreciated, or what?*

I think all the guys I consider regular guys, I mean, Jerry and all the guys in the club and shit, they appreciate everybody coming in. We do try to discourage guys from just coming in looking to catch. There's nothing wrong, if you meet some woman, and like her, then hook up with her and shit, if it's a mutual thing, but if, you know, you want to honey bee it—go from flower to flower—and shit like that, that's a little bit too much.

*What about prisoners who aren't in the programs, prisoners who don't partake of things like PAP? Do they kind of look down their nose at the outsiders, or at you guys who do program?*

---

*Prisoners who avoid infractions long enough can earn "EFVs"—Extended Family Visits, known colloquially as "trailers" or "trailer visits," which are multiple day visits from immediate family in trailers within the prison walls, including conjugal visits with spouses. However, the DOC has recently tightened the rules governing EFVs, most notably by making "new" spouses ineligible. Now, you have to have been married to the person before you came to prison or before the rules were changed in order to be eligible for conjugal visits. The prisoners are quick to point out that the DOC has thrown away a very valuable tool in controlling prisoner behavior. Sex is such a powerful carrot that even the long shot that a guy might one day find a woman willing to marry him for conjugal visits has made many a prisoner think twice about committing infractions that could cause him to lose that small opportunity.

No. These clubs, especially this god damn club, is the hierarchy of this god damn joint. You can probably see that. What ten or twelve guys in there say is, is. So, I imagine most guys, they wouldn't mind getting in the club, but we have a membership limit of fifty, and there's a waiting list. A lot of guys can't qualify. They can go to the Lifers. They have a little lower standards, but they still have some standards.

I imagine most guys would like to be let in this club, but for some reason or other, they can't qualify. The people who wouldn't want to do this are probably a real low percentage.

*I've wondered sometimes about the inside membership of P.A.P. I mostly like the guys who have chosen to be in it and have been accepted into it. But then I wonder about the people who are excluded. I'm sure some of them are excluded for reasons that, you know, even in my eyes they would be bad guys. Maybe I wouldn't want to rub shoulders with them. But I know that my values and my reasons for exclusion aren't going to be identical to those of the prison hierarchy.*

Yeah.

*And I know that the guys at the top have their own sets of values that sometimes I think are bullshit. So there must be good people that I wouldn't mind rubbing shoulders with that I'll never meet in here, because Jerry and you guys don't accept them as equals.*

We're not going to let them in. That's just the way it is. In any place, you know, they got people that say this and that, and it's just about got to be that way.

I'm pretty hidebound about that shit myself, even if it's a guy that it might have just been one moment of weakness in his life. They got him in there and scared him, and he testified against his partner. But you got to go on past performance, especially in the criminal world. You know, that son of a bitch that did that once, he's never going to get the chance to do it to me. At any level, even a real minor level.

A lot of the guys now, they're real forgiving, a lot more than they were twenty years ago. So they'll let a guy like that hang around. Or a guy that's got a sex beef or something. If I'm in a crowd and he comes to me, it's "Keep on stepping," so they have to double back after I leave.

It's not that, you know, I think that I'm some kind of a real nice guy or anything, but there's people I don't want around.

*Is it the special circumstances of prison that makes snitching so unforgivable, or in general is that, in your opinion, just a horrible thing to do?*

Yeah, it's always wrong.

*Even on the outside?*

Even when I was a kid in school, you know, that son of a bitch—we called him a tattletale then, instead of a fink—he wasn't appreciated. We're into some little thing that we're going to do, and here's a son of a bitch that's going to tell on us for doing it.

*I'm curious about this, because I've talked to a couple of the other fellows about this, about why there's such an intense dislike and absolute ostracism of people who are perceived as snitches. I'm curious how much it extends outside of the prison environment. I mean, what do you think, ethically, about, say, an employee of a corporation who blows the whistle when he finds out that they're doing illegal things. Is he worse than a murderer? Or what do you think of Woodward and Bernstein revealing Watergate secrets? Is that a morally horrible thing to do?*

Oh no, that's cool. Like if you seen a robbery, and call the police, you know, see somebody getting stuck up, and you call, that's what you're supposed to do. You're a citizen. You haven't chosen to side with me.

But if we're out there riding in a car, and you say, "Let's go make some easy money. Let's break into a place," and we do it, then if you tell on that, well then I'd say it'd make you pretty worthless.

But if you see somebody breaking into your neighbor's house, and you call the law, that's what you're supposed to do. You're not a criminal. But if you're a criminal, and chose to be a criminal, and then you want to kiss the Man's ass, and make it miserable for everybody else, well, you know, anything bad that happens to you, I'd applaud it.

If we stole together, and I'm over at your house, and we're thieves, and, you know, we burgled twelve places, and then you call the cops because somebody's breaking into your neighbor's house, I'd say, "Well, you lousy son of a bitch, man." But, if you're not in the life, those police are there for you. That's what they're there for.

*Are there any such distinctions to be drawn within prison itself?*

No.

*OK.*

It's, like, say if I've got a trailer visit coming up—I just married some new wife and we've got our first trailer visit—and they take me in and say, "All right you son of a bitch, who do you want to go to IMU for two years, the guy that did this or you?" I'd say, "If you don't mind me making a personal observation, you can suck my cock."

*[Laughs.]*

[Laughs.] And if you do anything else, well, you know, fuck, you're not fit to live with. We might not do anything physically violent to you, but you sure as hell ain't going to eat at my table.

*Let me give you an example, because I've used something like this example with other prisoners I've talked to, and I want to see how you respond. I'll give you two cases which, to the layman, seem totally different ethically, like there's virtually no comparison at all, and yet by the letter of the convict code you're describing, it seems as though they would have to be treated the same.*

*Case number one: Let's say that I go to prison, and maybe I am in the lifestyle. I've been out robbing, and conning people, and doing drugs, and whatever. And I come to prison. And I observe you involved in something that's technically against the rules. Maybe you smuggle some drugs in or something. And I run and tell the staff. I run and tell a guard secretly, because I expect it to benefit me. I don't care what happens to you. Maybe I even exaggerate, maybe I even lie about what you're doing. It may not even be true what I'm saying. So, I go and rat you out, just out of self-interest, just to save my own ass, and maybe get a few advantages for myself, or just out of malice toward you. Because that's the kind of person I am. That's case number one.*

*Case number two: Let's say I come to prison, but not because I have a lifestyle as a criminal. Maybe I did one thing when I lost my temper, or maybe I'm even here falsely. You know, maybe I'm even here as an innocent person by some mistake or something. But in any case, I haven't really chosen a criminal lifestyle. And, I'm placed in prison, and somebody victimizes me, or tries to. Maybe some big guy's trying to rape me, or steal from me, or whatever he's trying to do. And, even if I wanted to get violent about it, I know I have no chance in the world to defend myself against this guy who's, like, twice my size. Or maybe there's even more than one guy. So to get violent myself or get him before he gets me isn't a realistic option. And, in those circumstances, as I'm about to be raped, or killed, or whatever's going to happen to me, a guard or somebody stumbles into the situation and asks, "What's going on?" He sees the situation and asks "What the hell is happening?" And, let's say I just speak the truth. I don't make anything up, I don't exaggerate. I just say, "You all placed me in this cell, against my will. I mean, you've placed me in this dangerous situation." And I tell him truthfully what was being done to me and by whom. I just speak the truth. And because of that, those guys get in trouble. The alternative was that I just die, or get raped, or whatever.*

*Now, to me it seems like those two cases are hugely different, and yet, under the convict code, are they both equally bad cases of snitching? Am I equally a bad person in both of those cases?*

Yeah. Yeah, there's no distinction there. You can't go do that, man. You have to figure some other way.

The accepted way is, say you're in with a big guy, and you're in the cell at night, and you say, "Well, you know, I like you a lot, and I wouldn't mind doing this, but I'm not going to let you drop me. But if you wait till tomorrow, and you buy me a couple candy bars and treat me right…," and then just wait till you get to something blunt to hit the son of a bitch on the head with, or throw flaming gasoline on him or something. [Laughs.]

*[Laughs.]*

Whatever you've got to do, you do. Or if the cop comes by, and he says, "What happened here?" You say, "Well, something like this!" and you just—pow!, "You son of a bitch! Fuck you, copper!" and spit on him, whatever. They'll take you and put you in the hole. You haven't given up anything. You got out of the situation, and you haven't told on nobody.

*Why is that? Why am I obligated to take punishment upon myself when it's someone else who's guilty of the wrongdoing, it's someone else who's trying to treat me in a horrible and inhumane way? Why should I suffer for that?*

Well, it's because you're part of this god damn conglomerate. And if you want to walk with these guys, you have to do this. We do it. And if you're not willing to do it, well, you don't measure up. Uncle Sam doesn't want you. Stay the fuck away from us.

*How do you personally feel about that? Surely you're capable of seeing that the two cases I laid out are different, that the person is guilty to a different degree.*

Yeah.

*How do you feel about treating those two people the same?*

The guy wouldn't be welcome at my table. I wouldn't talk to him, if for any reason, he went to the Man. It just isn't how you deal with it. You forfeit a lot when you come in here, and you have to live by a certain code, and if you don't, well, fuck, you're outside the code.

There's no exceptions.

*How do you feel about the person who was doing the victimizing? Is he welcome at your table?*

No. It depends on what he's doing and everything. You're not immune from getting robbed, just because you come to a penitentiary. I mean, that doesn't give you god damn carte blanche to keep your money. So, if a guy pressures you, like, "How much money you got?" and that, that's different. I've seen a lot of guys do that. They just prey on those fish. But it's up to you to get the guy off your ass without going to the Man.

There's no situation that justifies bringing the police in.

But if the guy's going to beat somebody up and rape him, well, he's a fucking rapo, man. You know, he can't come around me. If the guy sodomizes his cell partner at night, he's just like any other rapo to me.

But now, if it does come to where the guy gets raped or something, and he sticks a knife in the back of that guy's neck, well then, I'd probably buy that guy a pop next time I see him. "Way to take care of it, buddy."

*It's just interesting to me, and I guess appalling at some level, but fascinating that the lines are drawn where they're drawn, that a person who stabs somebody in the back of the neck in a revenge killing is OK, but if he just simply speaks the truth and says what's being done to him—*

It's because these guys are here to stop us from getting out of here, and if they see us getting out, to kill us. And it's their job to get us and write as many charges as they can on that piece of paper and put us in the hole for as long as they can. They're the fucking enemy. When you go to them, you're with them, you know.

If you can get out of the situation and come to some guys for help, and if you're a young guy, and say, "You know, I'm not afraid to fight, but this guy wants to fuck me. I'm not—"

*So, it's not snitching if you tell each other, only if you tell a guard.*

You can come get some help, yeah. Get somebody to intercede. Say, "Hey, man, this guy's all right. You fuck with him, you fuck with us," you know.

Sometimes it turns out that the guy wants to do it anyway, but mostly not.

*How would a nonviolent person fare in prison? If somebody came here with Martin Luther King-Gandhian type principles and said, "I don't intend to harm any other human being. I'll turn the other cheek."? Do they have any chance of surviving?*

Oh yeah. I think Jerry said one class that some guys can come in here and never have to do any violence to anybody. Only thing is, people are not sure if they will or not, but they're pretty certain that they might if it starts. They get by.

I haven't had to do anything to anybody in the last twenty years.

*What if there is no mystery about it? What if I come right out and say, "I'm not going to do violence to you, no matter what"? What if that's just my moral or religious principles? Could I survive?*

Yeah, but you better just hang around the church. [Laughs.]

Pacifists, you know, that's all right, but where are you going to draw the line? Are you going to let a guy take your cake and supper every night, and make you wash his socks, to keep from getting beat up?

But, yeah, if a guy don't want to do anything unless he's forced into a situation, then how he handles that is up to him.

But, I was kind of an admirer of Gandhi, the way he did it, you know. Takes more balls than I got to take that shit without wanting to get back at them, do them some physical harm of some kind. Yeah, I think he's probably one of the great guys of the century. Top five or something.

*I've always wondered what would happen to people like that in prison, because, for instance, back in the '60s, you had people coming to prison on principle, people who were civil rights marchers,—*

[Laughs.]

*—and anti-war protesters, and such. And, most of them were just the typical yahoos who happen to get involved in some cause, but some of them were actually people of principle. They were moral and religious people, and pacifists in some cases. And, I always wondered, what happens when they get in with the regular prisoners?*

Oh, they'd probably be all right. Flower children type and that. The only thing is that, if they don't believe in property, they'd probably do well, because they won't end up with much, if they're not willing to defend it. That's what it boils down to.

Yeah, I don't know. Maybe I don't remember how tough it was when I was twenty years old, but it's kind of an unforgiving thing, you know.

*So you can recognize the distinction as a layman, that—*

Oh, yeah.

*I mean, you can imagine how somebody who isn't in the prison culture would feel about, say, someone who's an innocent man or whatever, and he's sent to prison, and, as an alternative to being raped and killed, he reveals what's being done to him. I mean, it doesn't seem like a morally awful thing to do.*

No, it's just that, like I said, you've got to think if that guy did it once, he can do it again. I say, "Well, what happened?" "Hell, some guy was going to rape him. He told on him." I say, "Well, you know, the son of a bitch ain't never going to get the chance to tell on me, man. I don't want him around me."

Because that's really what it is, kind of a self-protection thing. You don't want a son of a bitch that's got a history of cooperating with the police in your circle. I do believe in past performance as an indicator of future performance.

# BUCK—June 1998

*"You know, when you take a human life, it's like no other crime. For me personally, it's like I'm bonded to her for the rest of my life. And sometimes that motivates me to be a better human being, actually."*

The author and Buck in 1997, with Jimi clowning in the background.

W hen I joined PAP, Buck* was in the middle of a one-year term as its president. He subsequently served a second term—reluctantly, as no one else
was willing to accept a position that entails a fair amount of work and grief,
while garnering only minimal appreciation.

After his second term ended, his work schedule kept him from coming to most
of the meetings, so I did not see him as often as I did most of the others. But he
remained a member in good standing, and he continued to help organize and stage
the Prison Awareness classes for the community.

Buck is a quiet man, humble and unassuming. He does not have a threatening
"tough guy" air about him, yet he certainly would not shrink from a fight. He is not the
most extroverted or verbally flashy of the prisoners, does not call attention to whatever
book learning he has acquired through the minimal schooling available in prison and
through self-study. But he is a person of a certain intellectual and emotional depth.

He does not make it a point to broadcast his religious convictions, yet his Christian beliefs are a very important part of who he is. He has looked askance at me when
I've made remarks that indicated how unappealing I find religion to be.

He is a young white male who shaves his head, but as you'll discover, he is
decidedly not a "skinhead." He is one of the few prisoners who seems universally
respected by all factions, all races. When I have heard non-white prisoners make
occasional allegations about subtle racism in PAP's admissions practices, Buck is
routinely excepted from such criticism.

Buck also seems to be an exception of sorts in another way. The prisoners we
meet in PAP—and I'm sure this is even more true of prisoners in general—tend to
have quite self-centered personalities. They have been socialized in a world where
those who do not constantly assert themselves and take care of "Number One" are
run roughshod over.

One of the ways this self-centeredness manifests itself is in their conversational
style at the meetings. One of our volunteers noted to me that when a prisoner and
a volunteer talk, the conversation nearly always ends up being about the prisoner
and what's going on in his life. Other than superficial greetings and vague pleasant-
ries—"How are you?," "How's work?," "Whatcha been up to?," etc.—the prisoners
only infrequently show much curiosity about us and our lives. (Now, I should point
out that there is a partial explanation for this that does not imply any excessive
egotism on their part. I believe many of the prisoners are sensitive to doing or saying
anything that could seem the least bit threatening or suspicious to an outside person.
The last thing they want to do is come across like a potential stalker by showing undue
curiosity about the lives of the volunteers. So I suspect they're consciously avoiding
prying into anything that might be considered too personal.)

---

*Buck has chosen to be identified by his nickname only.

But in any case, as this same volunteer observed, Buck is a pleasant contrast to the norm. If anything, he's rather reticent about calling attention to himself. And he seems genuine in his fondness for the outside people and his interest in their well-being. As she told me, she always feels that he cares about us as individuals, that he truly appreciates our being there, that he doesn't just see us as an audience to whom he can talk about himself or complain.

Jerry believes that one of the most important purposes that PAP can serve is to give prisoners the opportunity to handle responsibility, to develop leadership skills, to become more comfortable opening up and expressing themselves in a group forum. Buck is an excellent example of this. Serving as PAP president was a wonderful opportunity for him to grow. He's tasted the self-satisfaction that comes from being counted on as someone who can lead and get things done. (I later learned that he was disappointed when we took our questions or concerns to one of the other PAP leaders. He wanted us to recognize that we could come to him when we needed something.) He is not intimidated by speaking in front of a group. His social skills with non-prisoners are now, I am told, far better than they were before I knew him.

Buck has quite literally grown up in the system; he has been imprisoned continuously since his early teens for a horrendous crime that weighs on his conscience to this day.

One wonders how he would fare on the outside. On the plus side, at this stage of his life, he is a mature and stable person who respects himself and others. His prison jobs have given him a good work ethic and specific skills that make him highly employable. I have never heard him say anything that would even imply that he would find it appealing to live a criminal lifestyle.

On the other hand, the world outside of prison would be utterly foreign and perhaps intimidating to him. His social style, his verbal style, his body language, his values, every instinct he's developed since adolescence came about through a process of adaptation to the artificial world of prison.

Somehow he has emerged from it all as a decent human being, not a violent thug, not the institutionalized monster that stereotypes the long-term prisoner. But can he balance a checkbook? Drive a car? Find his way around the Internet? Behave appropriately on a date? Avoid being ripped off by a slick salesman? Handle office politics? Budget his money? Understand what does and does not constitute a threat or an insult in a non-prison context?

As important as any other difference between his inside life and his outside life will be the ways in which he is perceived by others. In prison, he is a person of considerable stature. People trust him, respect him, regard him as an honorable man by the prevailing standards. He knows he is so regarded, and greatly values that.

As an ex-con on the outside, Buck will routinely be feared, reviled, distrusted, discriminated against, shunned, stereotyped, and hated. Given the nature of his crime, a good percentage of the people he will be living amongst will believe that he has no right to be alive, let alone to be living freely in their community.

He has had the resourcefulness to make the journey from boyhood to manhood in an environment that makes such a journey a truly treacherous one. But he has not completed that journey. In many respects that we take for granted, his life experiences ended long before his childhood did. On the outside, he would be a boy trying to live as a man, trying to survive long enough for his dormant and unused capacities to catch up with the parts of him that have matured and developed.

I did not have an immediate rapport with Buck. Neither of us are particularly gregarious; we are both better listeners than talkers. At the meetings, we'd chat a bit, but typically did not gravitate to each other or get very deep conversationally when we did talk.

For the book project, he was one of those who didn't respond to my written questions. Then once his schedule changed to keep him away from PAP meetings it was not easy to arrange taped interviews with him.

But on the two occasions we did have a chance to sit down alone together with the tape recorder running, I was quite pleased. He was thoroughly cooperative, never defensive in the face of my questions. His demeanor was kind and easygoing. He took the project and the questions seriously, and at times his responses displayed a profundity that I had not anticipated.

The more I've gotten to know Buck, the more I've come to appreciate him. Somehow he's managed to develop a basic gentleness and decency, without it rendering him the least bit weak. He's earned my respect.

*I'm going to start with the question that I've typically asked everybody, and that'll get the ball rolling, and then we can talk about other stuff as it comes up. What crime are you in here for? What did you do? Is what you were convicted of, in fact, what you did?*

Well, yeah, what I was convicted of is what I did, without a doubt. I don't never deny what I've done. I'm in here for first degree murder and first degree armed robbery. I robbed a store. I shot the manager, which was a lady. Mary Anne Benson.* Never forget her.

*How old were you?*

I was fourteen at the time.

---

*I have changed the name.

Why'd I do it? Pretty much, 'cause I wanted to do it, you know, just to rob. I mean, it wasn't the first store I robbed. Eventually, it just progressed—my way of life at the time, or my attitude and anger I had—and I shot her.

*Were you working as an individual robber, or part of a group?*

Actually, there was two of us. Yeah. But I did the shooting.

*Had you done a lot of robberies and crimes before this incident?*

No. I mean, it was like, three months prior, I started to get into crime more heavily. There was a lot of family problems, I had a lot of anger, and I just didn't care about life. It wasn't a financial reason. It wasn't for drugs. It was more me, anger, you know, not really caring about anybody, let alone myself.

*Were you a drug user at the time?*

Marijuana user.

*But it wasn't a big part of your life. It wasn't a motivation for your crime.*

No. No. And it wasn't like I was a criminal. I just got caught up with the wrong kind of people.
But that's not the reason I'm here. You know, my family is not the reason why I'm here. I mean, there's certain things in society that brought me to certain situations, but I'm responsible for being here.

*Were you in school, or had you dropped out?*

I dropped out.

*At what age did you drop out?*

Fourteen.

*Oh, OK. So just recently before the crime.*

Yeah. I felt like, well, nobody really cared if I dropped out or not, so I just quit school. You know, moved out from my mom's house.

*Where did you live?*

I lived with a friend and his sister.

*A friend of about your age? Just another youngster?*

Well, he was a little older. Yeah. He was seventeen. His sister was eighteen.

*How did your family react when you dropped out of school and moved out?*

Didn't like it. But, my mom was always kind of liberal, and it's kind of like, you know, "If that's what you really want,…" And I took that to mean she didn't really care.

*Do you think in retrospect that's accurate?*

No. But, you know, it's kind of like, "If I'd known then what I know now, I'd never…," you know what I'm saying?

*So you think she did care, but it was just her style to allow a lot of freedom?*

Yeah, and I think she was kind of tired, you know, 'cause she raised us kids all by herself.

*How many kids?*

Three of us. Three boys.

*So your father was not in the picture when you were growing up?*

He was, but he wasn't. When he was in the picture, he was more of a negative than a positive. Yeah.

*So roughly how many places had you robbed prior to the incident?*

Six. Yeah.

*Did you have a weapon with you every time?*

Not for the first two.

*What did you do there? Did you pretend to have a weapon?*

Yeah.

*The old hand in the pocket kind of thing?*

Yeah, and my friend had a baseball bat and stuff.

*What went into your decision to obtain a gun, and use a gun for the later robberies?*

I don't know. Get it from TV? Oh yeah, got to have a gun. You know, me with my warped sense back then, I wanted to see what a gun would really do.
If you ask me, did she any way provoke me? No.

*Had you ever used a gun or handled a gun prior to needing one for the robberies?*

Rifles, you know, when I was a kid. Hunting and stuff.

*Never a handgun?*

No. No.

*Did it turn out to be fairly easy for a fourteen year old to obtain a gun?*

Yes.

*How did you get a gun?*

Actually, from one of my friends. From a friend of a friend, who got it in a burglary in Oregon.

*Did you have to pay much for it?*

What was it? Forty bucks? So, not much.

*How did you feel going into the stores with a gun, compared to the first couple that you had robbed without one?*

Like it was power. You know, like everything in the world is cool.

*So you really did feel different, more powerful, an exhilaration—?*

Well, yeah. But, you know, at the time, I had a real warped view of the world.

*Not uncommon, though, because I think a lot of people with a gun feel exactly the way you're describing.*

Yeah, especially when—see, I was looking at a gun as a weapon, more of an offensive thing than a defensive thing. Me having a weapon was strictly offensive. It wasn't—for me—for defensive, you know, like most people with a good sense of balance in life will own a weapon for.

*Right. I think it's kind of a myth that people own weapons for that reason, though. I think if guns were in fact intended to be used for defense, then it would mostly be the weaker members of society that would rush out to get guns. It would mostly be females who would have them, and elderly people, and so on. But in fact, the most common people to have guns are single males concerned about their virility and wanting to be tough. You know, so. [Laughs.]*

Yeah.

*It's usually not weak people who need it to defend themselves.*

Yeah.

*Tell me how things went down on the occasion of the robbery when you shot this woman. Give me a description of what happened.*

Well, we walked in the store.

*What kind of store is this?*

It was like a mom and pop store.

*Like a little grocery or something?*

Yeah.

*Where at? In a small town? Big city?*

Vancouver, Washington.

*Oh, OK.*

So, it was small—well, medium, for the state of Washington.

*This is southern Washington, just over the border from Portland, right?*

Yeah. And, me and my friend went in to rob the store. Found out, in the process of robbing it, that my friend knew the lady that we're robbing. She recognized him. So, me with my warped sense, I think, "Well, she knows us."

*So she can identify you.*

Yeah. Sometimes I like to think that's why I shot her. Sometimes I think I just shot her to shoot.

Either way, it's kind of like, my attitude is, you know, I took human life. But I like to—everybody wants to justify why they did something. So sometimes I want to say there was a reason. But I took a life, either way.

*So give me some more details. You go into the store together. You have a gun. Does your friend have a gun also?*

No, he didn't, as a matter of fact. Probably because I didn't trust him with a gun.

*Was he your age?*

No, let's see. I was fourteen. He was almost eighteen.

*He's not the fellow you were living with though, is he? The seventeen year old—?*

No, no.

*So you go in, and, are you holding the gun on the woman?*

Yeah.

*She's emptying out the register—?*

Yeah, and she gave us the money, without a doubt. She gave us the money.

*How much money did you get in the robbery?*

Only eight hundred and thirty-seven dollars, I think it was, and change.

*And then your friend says something about knowing her—?*

Well, she says something to him.

*Oh, she said something to him.*

Yeah.

*What'd she say?*

"Brad,* why're you doing this?" And then I was, like, "What?! You know her?!" And he was, like, "Well, yeah, but I didn't know she was working here." I'm, like, "Ohhh," you know.
Then I shot the lady, and we left, you know. I shot her through the neck, and left.

*Was there any other conversation? Did you say anything to her? Or did she say anything to you? Were those her last words, what she said to Brad?*

Yeah, I think what happened was that I turned to him, and asked him, "Do you know her?" "Yeah." You know, and then automatically, I just turned, and I shot her.

*What was your immediate reaction or emotion after you fired the shot?*

Well, I think, right at the first, I was, like, "Why? Why'd you do that?" You know what I'm saying? Then, it was, like, "Well, you did it." Then, you got to justify it: "Well, you had to." You know what I'm saying?
But first thing you want to do is grab the bullet back, in midstream. You know, but you did it.

*So, as soon as you pulled the trigger, part of your reaction was to wish you could undo it.*

Yeah. And then the next thing's, like, for me personally, I had to justify why I did it.

*How did Brad react when this happened?*

---

*I have changed the name.

Personally, I think to this day he thought it was a good idea.

*So he didn't seem shocked, or disapproving, or anything?*

No. No.

*And you think if he had been holding the weapon, he would have done the same thing?*

Yeah. I think as much as I was unbalanced, he was a little bit more unbalanced than I was. Even to this day, I think that.

*Whatever became of him?*

Well, when we first got incarcerated, he went to protective custody, because he told on me, and stuff. So, he went to protective custody. And, I think at the time I did harbor an anger towards him.
Actually, he's here now.

*Oh, he's here in this institution?*

Yeah. And they asked me when they moved him in, you know, moved him into this prison, which was after, like, thirteen years, "Are you two going to be compatible? Because, we'll put him on the next bus out if not," and I said, "Yes, we're going to be compatible."
I mean, we ain't going to be friends here or nothing like that, but I don't harbor no anger towards him now.

*Is he a fellow that you had been close to? Were you good friends with him?*

No. He's somebody I met, like, through a friend. Yeah.

*And you had done some of the robberies with him, but he wasn't somebody important in your life.*

No. And to this day, he's still not. I mean, he's important to my life, because he's part of my history, but he's not someone I was ever close to. He's not important as far as my future.

*Right.*

You know, or my present neither.

*So, did you immediately flee the scene, or—?*

I fled the scene.

*—or did you stay at all to see if she was OK, or if she was dead, or—?*

No, I left.

*So you saw her drop and you assumed the worst? Did you assume she was dead, or—?*

I assumed she was dead.

*Did you know where the shot had hit her at the time?*

No, but I knew it hit her in the upper region of her body.

*So you knew she was either dead, or at least seriously hurt?*

Yeah.

*So what'd you do?*

Ran out of the store, you know, ran, actually, back to the house, packed everything up, and then went to Oregon.

*So, at that age, you didn't even have a getaway car or anything. You couldn't drive.*

No, no. Hopped on the first transit over to Oregon. Yeah. And, actually I was going to leave Washington permanently, but I came back in the state and went to my mom's, and that's when they arrested me.

*Why did you come back?*

Had to say goodbye to Mom. I didn't know I was wanted at the time neither. It's not like I knew I was wanted and I was going to get caught, you know.

*So as far as you knew, they had no way of knowing who had done it. They weren't looking for you. They had—*

Yeah. Yeah, when I pulled up at my mom's, they came out of everywhere—bushes, vans.

*How did it come to pass that Brad told on you?*

Well, first of all, he told his friend. And you know McGruff? The crime dog? You know what I'm talking about? They got the McGruff Crime Stoppers?

*Right, right.*

All right, well, they had our crime, you know, where they were saying, "If you know anything about…." Well, Brad told his friend about what we did.

*Just bragging?*

Yeah, boasting. And his friend turned us in.

*Oh. Did he get a reward from the McGruff program, or—?*

Yeah, he got a reward, and he was in some other trouble that he got out of. Yeah, you know, that he got away with 'cause he told.

*Did Brad benefit at all from what he did, or was he just bragging, not intending to benefit from it?*

No, he wasn't intending to tell, but, see, they arrested him first. 'Cause they didn't know me, you know, his friend didn't know me. And then Brad told them about me.

*Oh, OK. So, he told his friend, but then later, he also told the police?*

Yeah.

*Did they go easier on him because of that?*

Well, yeah, in a way. But they also took it easy on him because eventually, after I pled guilty, I told them, "Hey, he didn't do it." 'Cause I'll own up to what my mistakes were. I won't try to put it on somebody else.

*But, normally, does it matter who pulled the trigger? I thought in a situation like that, that you'd be equally guilty, even—*

No, it doesn't. He's been down eighteen years too. He was convicted of first degree murder too. Yeah. And armed robbery.

But the parole board eventually is going to probably let him out before they let me out, because I was the one that did the shooting.

*OK, so it might make some difference in the end.*

Maybe. But I think he's not as positive about life as I am. When you see a shrink, you know. Yeah. You know, I've done more positive things in prison than he has. Like, he's always just been a porter, you know.

But, I mean, I think it would be fair to let him out before me. Because I did the murder.

*Tell me more about why you did it. You said earlier that some of it was just a sort of generalized anger, or not caring about life, or—*

Well, you know, I was one of them kids—See, I can understand when them kids, they just explode, you know. Do I condone it? No. Do I believe they're harmful to society? Most definitely. But, see, I understand them, because I was there. I mean, at the age of fourteen, I didn't care about if I died or not.

*What had been that bad about your life that would lead you to feel like that?*

There wasn't a lot of love in my family. My mom worked a lot. So, we were pretty much on our own. I never felt love when I was a kid at all.

I also lived with my father for a time. See, my father, he's a criminal. He's always been a white collar criminal. Embezzlement and stuff like that. He's done time in prison.

Then when my dad got tired, I'd go back to my mom's, you know, then I'd run Mom so ragged she'd send me back to Dad.

*What were you like as a kid, that you were running people ragged?*

I wasn't very respectful, to anybody. I think it was my way of getting attention. 'Cause my brother, my older brother, he's very intelligent. And he never had to work at it. Me, I always had to work for every grade I got. I had some jealousy towards him.

Then my other brother, he was, like, the baby of the family.

But I lived part time back east in Waterbury, Connecticut with my dad, and part time out here in Vancouver, Washington with my mom. So, it's kind of like, I always felt, well, they don't want me. Neither one of them wants me.

*When you think about your childhood, and when you think about what happened when you were fourteen, does it still feel like you're talking about yourself, or can you detach from it, where it almost feels like a different person? I mean, is that you who did those things?*

Oh, it was me, without a doubt.

*So it feels the same as if you were talking to me about a mistake you made last week.*

No, it's kind of like, however I've changed, that's still who I was, it's what I was. It was the lowest part of my life, how low I can go as a human. But it was definitely me.

And I don't detach myself, because I've grown so much from there. You know, I've learned so much, just looking at how I felt about being not loved and, you know, how much price I put on what other people thought of me. You can't detach yourself. At least I can't.

And the lady, you know, Mary Anne, it's kind of like, I still live with her, because I think about her all the time. You know, when you take a human life, it's like no other crime. For me personally, it's like I'm bonded to her for the rest of my life. And sometimes that motivates me to be a better human being, actually.

*Do you feel you owe it to her, and her memory?*

Yeah. To treat people a lot better than I did.

*I think that's one of the most common questions people have about criminals, especially people who commit murder, is, how do you feel in retrospect about the victim? Is it something you think about a lot, or is it something you just push out of your mind and you're cold about it, and you don't care? It sounds like, for you, it's something that really sticks with you.*

Well, to me it does. I don't really know if the shrinks think that's healthy or not, but to me it does.

I mean, it's not like I dwell on it twenty-four hours a day.

*Right.*

Does it come into my mind every day? Well, it does most days.

*How does it mostly feel to you? Is it just a real sense of frustration that it can't be undone, or—?*

Yeah. It's not so much about how I threw my own life away. It's more about how I took a life. You know, it's never about I threw my life away.

*So you don't sit around thinking about, "Boy, I wish I hadn't spent all these years in prison. Look what I did to my life." You think about her.*

Yeah, because, whatever I done to my life, I done. You know, it's like, yeah, I made a mistake that I'm going to pay the rest of my life for.

Memories of her will never go away. Me being in prison is never going to go away. I mean, because, it's going to be a part of my past. Just like, when you went to college, that's part of your past.

That one instant changed my life forever. You know, it's something I've grown from. It's not like I figure, well, I threw my life away. In some respects, you know, I hate to say it, but it's helped me be a better human being. Because I was in a worse spiral than that.

*Do you think that actually being apprehended and imprisoned for it made a positive difference, or do you think that just the enormity of what you did would have had the same impact on you and jolted you into turning your life around if you had gotten away with it?*

No. No.

*You don't think you would have regretted it as much and turned your life around in response to it?*

Well, even when I got in trouble, when I was a kid, for stealing cars, it's kind of like, all them slaps didn't mean nothing. I mean, they go away. I'm not talking about physical slaps; I'm talking about, you know, from the juvenile system, just slapping my hand and saying, "Don't!"

Me getting away with it? No, that wouldn't have helped. No.

*So—I just want to make sure I'm clear on this—the actual punishment for it, being stuck in prison for all these years, was a necessary part of shocking you into a realization of what you had done and the need to improve and all that. It wasn't the enormity of the crime itself, by itself, that did it; it was that coupled with your being in a place like this.*

Well, see, it's hard to say, because I never had that opportunity, but I've had this opportunity.

*OK.*

You see what I'm saying? I might have, but then again, I only know the way I did react in this one instance. So, maybe. I don't think so, but maybe.

But do I think there's something wrong with our juvenile system, and adult system? I definitely think when a fourteen year old commits murder, he should be put away. For the rest of his life? I don't know. You'd like to say there should be a panel of, maybe, judges, psychiatrists, to judge him in maybe thirteen, fifteen years, you know, maybe even ten, you know, to judge him. To judge what he is then.

*In a sense, you could say the same thing about other ages too, though.*

Yeah.

*Someone who commits murder at age thirty, certainly there's a reasonable chance that at age forty-five, that he may be a sufficiently different, improved person that you might want to give him a shot.*

But, see, when you commit a crime that young, you're dealing with an adolescent mind. I mean, because, like me, being that young, I didn't even know what life was. So, it's kind of like, you're dealing with two different minds, two different ways of thinking. I mean, if he committed a crime when he's thirty, then something's definitely wrong with him. But it's definitely something different when a fourteen year old commits it.

*How old was Mary Anne?*

Thirty-two.

*Oh, so she was quite young.*

Yeah. Mother of two.

*Oh.*

And, you know, that's another thing. That always hurt, 'cause I knew how I'd feel if some-body took my mom.

See, me and my mom didn't have a close relationship when I was a kid, but we do now. Because, now we're on the same page. You know, when I was as an adolescent and she was an adult, we weren't on the same page. Because what she told me had no bearing, it was untruths to me. Now that I'm older, it's like, shit, that makes a lot of sense. Like with most of our parents, when we're youths, you know, we don't listen. "Come on, you ain't going through what I'm going through."

And my mom, you know, she used drugs and stuff, so, I mean, I was introduced to them early. I could smoke marijuana in my house when I was, like, thirteen years old, you know, without no problem.

*Would you be a liberal parent like that? I mean, if you get out, and you get to be a parent?*

No, no.

*You're not going to be like that?*

No. I'm a good listener, and I'll understand. But I'll still tell them, "No, you can't do it." But you also got to practice what you preach. You can't tell them no, and then be doing it yourself.

Yeah, I don't know. I would not be as liberal as my mother was, by no means. No. But I would not be as hard as some parents. I'm very understanding.

*As I noted earlier, I think a lot of people are very curious about whether you think about your victim or not, whether a murderer puts that behind them or it's something that's on their mind a lot. I think a lot of people jump to the conclusion that people who commit murder don't give a damn about the victim, and they're cold and unfeeling about what they did. I've always wondered, though, what is it that people want from the murderer? I mean, if, hypothetically, the person did care, how is that supposed to manifest itself? What would you say if the public challenged you on that, if they said, "Well, you're a murderer and you don't really care about your victim"? You know, what are you supposed to do or say in response to that?*

Well, you know, most of the negative comes from not knowing. They're not in the position to understand.

You know, when I was first incarcerated, I thought it was just between my victim and me. Then later I realized, there's the family too. What I did affected all their lives. So it they wanted their pound of flesh, or they wanted some retribution from me, then I could understand it.

But I also know that her husband—I didn't find this out until, like, five, six years ago—he's a Christian person, and he's already forgiven me. At least that's what he said in the paper. Because, unfortunately, he was burglarized by some kids, and they wrote up a story in the paper about him being "twice a victim," you know.

Thank God, he's already said, "I've forgiven him."

*Do you respect him for that, or is that a sign of weakness for him to do that?*

No, I respect him for that.

*Do you think you'd be capable of that, if someone murdered someone close to you?*

I'd like to think now that I could. Yeah. At first, no.

But you see, me, I have a convict mentality, but I don't. For most convicts, it's like, "No, you can't forgive. You've got to get your retribution." But, me, how can I do that, when I did the same thing?

*So you understand the desire for revenge, but you don't really agree with it.*

Yes. Yeah.

And, see, I don't put myself above other criminals. It's more that I don't understand certain criminals. I think for a lot of us, our thought's negative towards them, because most of us don't understand them. You know, what you don't understand, you hate. Or, you want to disassociate yourself from them.

But I can't put myself above them. I took a human life. Most of the victims of the criminals that get looked down on are still living. You know, they can get help, maybe, and move on with life. My victim never will.

*Well, what is the appropriate response to your crime? Is it retribution, in the form of taking your life for her life, or something else? What do you owe the victim, or the family, or society? How can you make it up?*

Well, see, we get caught up with, it's me against the state of Washington, 'cause my victim's family very rarely comes into play. So, it always feels like what does the state of Washington want from me? Which isn't even necessarily the citizens of Washington, just whoever's in the legislature or government—what they want.

*Right.*

So, I don't know. The way I thought back then, no, you can't take my life, you can't take nothing of mine. The way I think now, they did have a right to take it. That is, if they had said so in the beginning, not after eighteen years.

*I'm a little confused. Do you, now, believe in the principle of retribution?*

No, but, see, I understand it.

*Right.*

You know, would I forfeit my life for it? No.

*Well then, what should you do?*

I mean, should I be a slave to their people? Well, no. But, how much suffering do you want? See, that's what it is. That's why I'm having trouble, because I've never really been a victim in my life. I've never been a victim like that at any time. So I don't know what that feels like, and how much retribution you would want, as a victim.

*But is that really who's most qualified to answer this question, the people who've been victimized? Granted, they're the ones who've had the most intense experiences and emotions about it, but if anything, that might sway their judgment, sway their reasoning, you know, if they're too emotionally involved.*

Yeah. Because a lot of times even they don't know exactly what they want. They just know they want their pound of flesh.

*Yeah, so is that really the only group we should consult in deciding issues of justice—the people who've been victimized? It seems to me that they might have the most skewed judgment.*

See, one thing is, I'm not a big believer in this restorative justice either. I don't think it'll work, because you can never get two parties that are equally willing to cooperate to one goal. Because, in our society, we always try to win. And me being subservient to anybody would not be a winning situation for me.

But do I owe society a debt? Yes. But it's nowhere near what I owe to the victim's family. See, I do realize that I caused my community harm. But I don't think it's anywhere near the debt I owe the victim's family.

*But what can you do about that debt, the bigger one to the victim's family and the smaller one to society?*

Well, I mean, do they want me to stay the rest of my life in prison? See, I don't know.

I mean, of course I want out of prison. Everybody does. But I don't want out just because I want freedom and stuff. I think I'm a mature adult now. I think maturely, and I think positively. And, I know what I want.

But, see, that's all about me.

*Right.*

You know, that's all about what I want. But the victim's family, I don't know what they would want. See, I'm having a hard time with that one.

*What are they entitled to from you, not so much what they want?*

Well, they're entitled to the rest of my life. I took a life. They're entitled to the rest of my life.

Now what does that entail? Me, I'm dead set against the death penalty, because I think it's wrong. Most people want to preach the Bible to me about the death penalty, but I think that ain't right neither. It says "Thou Shalt Not Kill," you know. It doesn't say, "Kill for this," and "Kill for that."

*What do they preach to you from the Bible? What do they say?*

Well, you know, "an eye for an eye." The old sayings.

*Old Testament.*

Yeah, they don't want to even look at the New Testament.

*Yeah, as far as I remember my Bible, the New Testament directly supersedes some of those Old Testament rules.*

Yeah, but you'll still hear them preaching in church that the death penalty's fine. I mean, that's what they're trying to preach to us in here. But it's the same with slavery, you know.

But I think if the victim's family said, "Hey, spend the rest of your life in prison," well, that's their right, but I wish they would have told me that in the beginning, 'cause I would have planned my whole life in here differently.

*How so?*

Well, not so much plan it differently, but I would have never had so much hope. You know, the tunnel wouldn't have gotten as bright. I wouldn't have dragged other people into my life on the pretense of me being released into society.

*We're talking now about hypotheticals, about the victim's family deciding that they want this, that, or the other thing from you. In reality, though, what's going to happen? In reality, are you likely to be released, and if so, approximately when?*

About Two thousand one or Two thousand two. So I'll end up doing twenty-two years. But then again, we're back to a parole board that must decide if I'm fit, so it may be longer.

Actually, some people think the parole board is just here for punishment, that as long as your punishment's done, they have to let you out. But it's never like that. They're also protecting society in their own way.

I don't have too much problem with the parole board. It's just that I wish they could know people a little more than they do.

*Yeah, how well do you think they do their job? When you see the people who get parole, and the people who get turned down for parole, do you usually agree or disagree with the judgments that are made?*

Actually, they're pretty close.

*So they do a pretty good job?*

In my estimation. This is strictly my estimation.

*So most of the people you see them letting out are people you think probably aren't really threats to society any more, and most of the people they keep in, you think it's probably better they stay in here?*

Yeah, because I'm judging from what the people are like in here. And I know a bunch of people—they're under the new guidelines, so they don't come under the parole board—that I wouldn't let out when their time is up, but those are the new rules. I know which ones are coming back. I love some of them dearly, but I know.

*So you have a pretty good sense of whether a person's going to make it on the outside?*

Well, yeah, if I know them.

*Are you ever really surprised by somebody who makes it or somebody who comes back here you didn't think would come back here?*

I've yet to be surprised by someone who failed. I've been surprised one time by somebody that made it that I didn't think would. And he was a friend of mine.

*But of the people you knew well, you're generally not surprised.*

No. Just the one guy that surprised me that made it. And he was a real good friend of mine, you know.

*And he's still doing OK on the outside?*

Yeah, he's been out for years. I mean, he's been out, like, six years. For the first year and a half, I was still thinking he'd be back, but he's been fine.

We used to walk the yard all the time, and he'd say he was going to make it this time, but, you know, I didn't know if it was for my benefit that he was talking. But I think he got out and realized, "Man, there's a better way of life than being incarcerated, than walking this silly track that we have out here."

*So you think he changed more after he got out?*

Yeah. I think he learned to hang up the drugs. I mean, 'cause he wasn't a big drug user in here, but he was a recreational one. And I didn't know if with the bigger supply out there, that he would be more of a user.

Yeah. I think he learned to hang up the drugs.

# JIMI—July 1998

*"Being on the run is very liberating. I mean, don't get me wrong. You don't have any barriers. You're just out there. There's no rules to live by. There's nobody to listen to. No appointments to make."*

Once Jimi realized that many of the others weren't bothering with written responses, he too got a little lazy about responding in writing.

He remained as eager as ever, however, to contribute to the project through taped sessions.

*Jimi, let's start with some of the questions I mailed in to you recently after our last session. One of the questions was about your mentioning that you didn't get caught for most of your crimes. So, about what percentage of your crimes would you say you were apprehended for, and convicted and served time for?*

One percent. Probably less. Very few of my crimes.

*How many crimes have you been imprisoned for?*

Nine.

*So less than one percent would imply that you've done more than nine hundred crimes.*

Easily. I can remember in a summer, I did seventy burglaries with a couple of friends.

Matter of fact, I went to the bank one day with my mother, and there was an easel from the sheriff's department in the bank that showed a bunch of snapshot photos of all these houses that had been ransacked. And it had a big headlines over the top of it, "East Side Burglars!" and "Beware!" and "Watch Out!" and all this crazy stuff. I was looking at this thing and I was thinking, "Jeez, this is me!" [Laughs.] I was so scared that my mother was going to somehow make the connection. She didn't, for probably another month, but that was my first spree of crimes.

*How old were you?*

Sixteen. [Laughs.] I was young. Yeah, that was my first spree of crimes that I had ever done.

*So you think you've done somewhere in the hundreds? Total crimes?*

Easily. Oh yeah, easily. I've gone on robbery sprees where every town I've stopped in, I've done a robbery, maybe two. I've done a robbery getting away from another robbery before.

You know, when you're on a spree, or when you cross that line, where you've chosen not to live by the rules—and for me, that means running—well, I don't run to get somewhere and live by the rules. I run, and in doing that, my boundaries are way out there. I don't have any limitations of what I'm willing to do to survive.

Robbery became what worked for me. It was quick, easy, fast money.

So, yeah, when you're in that mode of doing crimes to survive, and you're living in this subculture, and you're living underneath the world that's going on out there, the normal world, and your life is at night, you know, there are no boundaries.

Crime is what happens at night. They say there are two people out at night: cops and robbers. That's true, for the most part.

*Now, when you've freed yourself from these restraints, and you've gone on a robbery spree, and you haven't felt constrained to play by the rules, does that make it easier to disregard rules across the board? Because, I notice it doesn't seem to be an all or nothing thing for you. When you go off on a spree like that, it doesn't seem to suddenly eliminate your inhibitions against murder, or rape, or certain kinds of violence, and so on.*

I think for a lot of people it does. I think it does. I think most people that are in here for murder aren't "murderers." They're people who have murdered. They're people who have found themselves in a situation where they've murdered. It's a very small percentage of people, from my experience in here, that have some need to murder. You know, your serial killers. It's a very small percentage of the murderers in this country, or at least those that I've experienced.

People who have murdered are people who have found themselves in a situation where murder became a split second reaction of anger, or self-defense, or whatever their situation was. I've never found myself in that situation. I thank God. I've always told people that had I ever been faced with the choice, in a robbery, if somebody had ever called my bluff, I would probably have ran, rather than shot somebody. Just because I've never felt like shooting somebody was an option.

Maybe that's because of the way I was raised, or whatever. I know that kind of sounds contrary to my point about having no boundaries when I'm on a spree. But, I believe that when I'm out on the run, my boundaries are pretty far out there, and I could just as easily be caught in a situation where I had to murder.

I know I keep going back and forth on this thing. [Laughs.] But some of these murder cases that I've heard of, I can't see myself, in the same situation, doing what they did. And so, you know, everybody's different, and everybody reacts to things differently, and fortunately for me, I haven't reacted violently, as far as doing physical harm. My harm to my victims and to society has been emotional.

*Like you say, you seem to be arguing both sides here, and I'm getting a little confused. Let me approach it again. Do you think that law-breaking in one area tends to spread to other areas, or are they totally separate? When you're in that mode, that frame of mind, where all of a sudden the rules against stealing other people's property don't count—when you're on a spree—does that also make you less respectful of other rules and other laws? Because it seems like it doesn't. It seems like you still have your usual inhibitions against murder and rape and most immoral or illegal things.*

Well, I still drive by the speed limit. I still wear my seat belt. You know, I don't walk down the aisle in a grocery store stealing things. So I suppose not. I never committed rape.

*So you still operate under certain moral and ethical constraints.*

Sure. It's a money thing for me. Not being able to wait. Not being capable of delayed gratification, I guess is what that's all about. It's always a money thing for me.

*Did all the money go to drugs?*

A lot of it. Once I go. Drugs or alcohol. I mean, there was only a three week period of doing coke, but all of the rest of the times, it's been primarily alcohol.

Being on the run is very liberating. I mean, don't get me wrong. You don't have any barriers. You're just out there. There's no rules to live by. There's nobody to listen to. No appointments to make.

But you're not getting anywhere when you're doing that. Nonetheless, once you've done it, and you've felt it—once I ran, I felt liberated. I felt, "Wow!" you know, a lot of pressure off my back.

*That kind of thing is very desirable, very intoxicating. I've done the same thing, just without the crime.*

Sure.

*I mean, I've thrown off all my responsibilities, as far as just quit my job and everything to go and travel for months, just wander around and see different places. No alarm clock. No appointments.*

Right.

*No job. No classes.*

Right, the very same—

*It's a—*

—exactly the same—

—wonderful feeling, and that's one of the things that I value about life is my brief periods of freedom like that, where I don't have to be somewhere at a certain time every morning to work for somebody else or do something I don't want to be doing.

Right.

So, you know, in my own way, without the robberies and such, without the guns, I've done some of the same stuff. So, yeah, I agree. It's very exhilarating.

Right.

Did you accumulate quite a lot of money through these hundreds of robberies, or were they mostly very small time things?

No, you spend it as fast as you make it. You spend it the same way you make it. You make it illegally; you spend it illegally. You know, you make a bunch of it; you spend a bunch of it. If I make ten thousand dollars on a robbery, it might be gone a week later. If I make—

What do you find to spend ten thousand dollars on in one week?

Hotels. Clothes. Something for my car. Girls. Whatever they needed. Clothes for them, you know. You can spend ten thousand dollars quick. You really can. And, just out partying around, hotels, you know, booze, and out eating. When you're on the run, it goes fast.

Don't get me wrong, I didn't make ten thousand dollar hits on a regular basis. For me, a five hundred dollar robbery was a good robbery. That was good enough to keep me for a couple days.

But you can easily spend ten thousand dollars in a week. Some people spend more.

Jewelry, there's another thing. You can spend it quick. [Laughs.] When you don't earn it, you spend it quick

So most thieves don't budget very well.

No. I suppose maybe the smart ones do, but how smart are they really?

[Laughs.]

The thing that kills me is these guys that are sitting in here, and they're talking about getting that one hit. They're going to get out and get that one hit. And then they're going to go straight. Or the guys that are going to get out, they're going to grow one crop of weed, sell it, and then they're going to go straight.

Well, come on, man. Think about that for a second. Jeez, I mean, these are either people who have never experienced one good hit, or they're delusional.

*Why is it that you were caught so few times, like one percent of the time or whatever it turned out to be? Were you just that good, or is the system that inefficient?*

The system's that inefficient. I did crime since I was thirteen, fourteen. I started doing little things, then got up to more. The thing is, is once I start doing crime, once I commit a crime, or once I go on the run, I'm doing crime all day every day. I mean, I'm doing so much of it, that by the time I'm caught, everywhere I've gone, I've done crime.

And I think that's the case with most people that have been criminals most of their lives, that have been breaking the law most of their lives. Lots and lots of crime.

Even counting the little shoplifting—I can remember when I was a kid, for awhile there, when we were getting into drinking, we'd go up to 7-Eleven and steal a couple bottles of Mad Dog, you know, me and my buddies. Before that, it was stealing candy. You know, after candy, it went to cigarettes. After cigarettes, it went to booze. I mean, it started when I was a kid. And I've been doing a lot of it ever since.

*So even though losing your inhibitions about committing one type of crime doesn't necessarily jump to other crimes—I mean, being willing to commit robberies doesn't make you willing to murder or rape or whatever—it sounds like if you stay within the same crime, like robbery for instance, that the more of it you do, the easier it is to do the next one.*

Yeah, that's very true.

My first robbery was very hard. I had to actually sit outside for the longest time working up my nerve. I knew somebody was in this building. It was a tavern. And I knew somebody was inside. I didn't know if this person was armed. I didn't know if the money was in the safe. I had some inside information that this person was not going to put the money in the safe, but was going to drop it off at the bank that night, but I didn't know for sure.

I had to sit outside the building, outside that door, before I kicked it in—I sat outside that door for about ten minutes, actually bringing up energy and psyching myself up to be an asshole. You know, actors do it, I can't remember what it's called, but actors, you know, they psych themselves up to play a part—and I literally had to do that. I was that scared.

And now that I think about it, I sat in my car for about a half hour before I even went up and waited at the door. So, you know, I had to actually turn myself mentally into this other person, and then when I went in there, I was somebody I had never been before. I talked to this guy with absolutely no respect. I treated him like shit. I was screaming and yelling, and trying to scare him, and make him think I'm crazy. You know, it was really weird.

But after that, what's weird about that is that after that, I kind of honed that energy and that aggressiveness to a calmer image, still aggressive, but with an appearance that I was a little smarter, maybe a little more aware of the situation that I was in, a little more in control of the situation that I was in.

But that first robbery, I wanted him to think that I was completely out of control and I would blow him away in a minute, which I wouldn't have. Far too scared, I'm sure. Unless, you know, maybe—I don't know.

*You were just a teenager?*

First robbery? No, I was older. I was in my twenties. I was twenty-six.

*Twenty-six?*

Yeah. Twenty-six, my first robbery.

*So before that, you had only done burglaries.*

Yeah, burglaries and forgeries. You know, it's all stealing. But, when it escalated to robbery, it was after my first bit down.* So, I was twenty-five or twenty-six.

*So you're using "robbery" in the legal sense of stealing directly from a person, rather than just stealing property, like, from a building.*

Yeah, exactly. Yeah.

*How did this first robbery victim react to you?*

Well, scared, but he calmed down as the thing was happening. The whole thing went down in about two minutes. I mean, he was, you know, panicking, "Don't shoot!" and, "You can have the money," and all that. But as he calmed down, he started trying to talk me out of it, and telling me that it's not worth it, and trying to tell me, you know, that it can't be that bad. I think he even offered me a job. He even told me, you know, "It can't be that bad. I can put you to work."

*Now was he just bullshitting you to try to save himself and his money? Or—?*

I don't give a shit what he was doing;—

---

*I.e., first prison term.

*—do you think he was sincere—?*

—I wasn't interested in no job! [Laughs.] I just put a gun on him.

I had no idea. I didn't know who the guy was. I just had some information on the guy, you know.

*You knew from some employee or something?*

Yeah. Exactly. Yeah.

*How much money did you get in your first robbery?*

Four hundred dollars. It was supposed to be in the thousands, and it was four hundred measly dollars. In fact, I ended up taking his tip jar, and the tip jar had almost as much as the robbery. [Laughs.] Jesus! That was crazy! I think I totaled four hundred dollars for that robbery. It was crazy.

But, you know, when you're on the run, that's four hundred dollars cash, and that's the hotel for the night, that's drinks all night at the bar, that's a full tank of gas, and I'm off to the next town. Four hundred dollars isn't a bad night's work really.

*Do you think it's typical for most people who commit crimes that they only get apprehended for one percent, or a small percent like that?*

Yep. I even asked around, because you asked me a question like this in writing. Some people said a twentieth of a percent. You know, one guy said a twentieth of a percent. Other people said less than that. Then I heard ten percent, and when I dug a little further when they said ten percent, they said, "Well, maybe it is more like one percent or two percent."

*I would have thought it would be pretty low, but that seems like an exaggeration, because, I mean, one percent really is one out of a hundred, so if you've been imprisoned for half a dozen crimes, that would be, you know, six hundred crimes you've committed.*

Yeah, but think about it. I mean, now I'm talking about every crime. I'm not talking about just felonies. I'm talking about every crime in the span of my life. Everywhere I've gone, I've done crime. I lived in Ohio for awhile; I did crimes there. I lived in California for awhile; I did crimes there. When I was working as a security guard in California, I was doing crime in the mall I was a security guard at.

I've always done crime. I always have. I've never been connected to what's outside those walls. I've always been connected to what's inside of here. There's no connection to anything for me out there, other than family. I'm not a part of it.

In six months, this is all going to be something very new again. I'm not a part of them out there.

I kept two very separate lives on the outside, even when I was working: People that knew where I've been, and people that didn't. And the people that knew are generally people that party and are a little more liberal, and pot-smokers, and, you know, partiers.

So that's something that has to change. I've got to be connected out there.

*Do you think that the reason such a tiny percent of crimes result in punishment is because it's an unavoidable part of living in a free society? I mean, we don't live in a police state, where every move you make is monitored, and where the accused has no rights and is assumed to be guilty. Or do you think that even in a democratic, free society, that if people were more competent and more efficient, more crimes would come to justice, and come to punishment?*

No. Yeah, it would have to be a police state.

*So this is part of the price we pay for freedom, is that only one or two percent of the crimes that get committed lead to punishment.*

Well, yeah. I mean, I don't know that you can take this one percent as the general consensus of everybody in the system, but people who, like me, have been committing crimes since they were a kid, yeah, it's about one percent.

I hear China has a pretty serious crime problem over there too, and they are a police state. So, I don't know that that would be the answer either.

You know, I got no solutions. I'm merely a problem-maker. [Laughs.]

*I would think it depends on the type of crime, too. If you're talking about burglaries and such, then somebody can do a lot of those. But if you're talking about, say, murderers, I certainly hope it's not the case that every person who's been convicted of murder actually committed—*

Absolutely not.

*—a hundred times as many as he was caught for.*

Right. Other than, you know, your serial killers. They're a whole different breed and there's not many of them, there really aren't. But, people who have murdered, like I said, aren't murderers per se. I mean, you put the title on them because they've committed a murder, but generally that's the fact. They've committed a murder. Or, a couple of murders in one specific incident. These aren't people that have repeatedly murdered and murdered and murdered. Those that have repeatedly murdered are a whole different group of people. That's serial stuff. Man, that's a whole different ball game.

If I take away the little stuff—stealing candy and stealing cigarettes and stealing booze when I was a kid—when I take away those little things when you're a kid that maybe some people accept as no big deal—I don't hold that to be true; I don't think that's acceptable behavior—but when I take away those smaller, minor misdemeanor-type crimes, the percentage of how many crimes I've been caught for compared to how many crimes I've done goes way up.

*If we limit it to felonies, what do you think the percentage would be?*

[Laughs.] Well, maybe not "way up." Probably ten percent. I've been convicted for nine, so we're talking about ninety. Ninety felonies. Ball park.

*Does it concern you at all that the system is this inefficient, for your own future? I mean, you're in a situation where maybe you have too much of a safety net in effect. You can misstep—in fact, you could misstep ninety or ninety-five times perhaps—and still stay out of prison. Would you be better off psychologically if you knew that one mistake would really be costly? Would that better enable you to avoid that one mistake?*

No. I don't trust the system as it is anyway.

Other than one relapse where I used almost two years ago, I've been clean, and very serious about growing up, making the right choices, getting the connections to society, with my family, setting some goals—I've been very serious about all that for probably four or five years. Maybe six, seven years actually, now that I think about it.

But, I've been walking on eggshells that whole time, and I'm walking on eggshells right now. I've got six months left to go, and I'm not doing a damn thing wrong. They can go in my house, they can come get me, they can give me a UA, they can do whatever they want, and I shouldn't have a thing to worry about. But, I still worry.

I was standing outside in the smoking area today, and three cops came down. And whenever there's three or four of them together, you know they're coming to get somebody. Well, instantly my heart started beating a little faster, even though I know I'm clean.

It's just incompetence. It's the system. I don't trust the system. And I don't trust the system out there on the streets any better than I do in here.

*That makes it even worse. That means that your potential to come back to prison is only very loosely connected with what you do on the outside. So, the threat of punishment really doesn't provide much of a deterrent, much of a factor for you to stay clean.*

The threat of punishment doesn't provide any deterrent whatsoever for me. It never will. The change is my being connected to society, this connection I'm talking about that's very important to me. It's not only a connection to society, but it's a connection to humanity. What my role is, as a human being, in this world, on this earth, to everybody. How my being on this earth for however many more years I'm going to be here, how that affects humanity.

And that's a much bigger picture than I ever used to see. I am part of the world. I am part of life. And that is what is important to me now, that I am part of something. What I do affects people. When I victimize somebody, it doesn't just affect the victim; it affects everybody involved in their lives, and the list goes on. There's a ripple effect and it goes way out there.

My family. What I do affects my family. What I do affects my friends. Now that I'm older, I see I'm connected to much more than I ever felt like I was connected to. And that is what makes me make the right choices as opposed to the wrong choices.

I'd love to be on a robbery spree, be on a Harley, but what it would do to my family, what it would do to the people who I victimize's families, you know, it's just a huge cycle that I don't want to interrupt any more than I already have.

*So you're confident enough in your principles and your maturity and your strength that, to you, if you had a zero percent chance of being caught or a hundred percent chance, it wouldn't really matter.*

Absolutely. It has nothing to do with them any more. 'Cause I'm very welcome in prison. I'm happy here. I shouldn't say I'm "happy" here, but I am accepted here.

Actually, there are times when I am happy here. I have some very close friends in here. I'm somebody in here. You know, I've never been anybody on the streets.

I've never even thought for a second—when I'm getting ready to do a robbery, when I'm getting ready to take off to go do crime—I've never said, "Wait a second. Better not do this. I might go to prison." Come on, that "deterrence," that's bullshit.

*Has it ever deterred you from any other crimes other than robbery, like if—?*

Yeah, rape, actually.

*That's been specifically the threat of prison, rather than just your feeling that rape is not right?*

Well, I mean, walking around with a hard-on on the streets sometimes, all of a sudden the thought of rape comes to your head, and you think, "Hell no! I'm not going to the joint with a rape beef!" That's the only one, though.

And, for some reason, I've never given myself permission to murder. I've always been able to make that connection, with murder and what it would do to my family. So, that's always kept me from committing murder. I've never really had a reason to murder, either, but whenever I've thought murder, I've always thought, boy, that'd crush my family.

So, I don't know why those two things—oh, I know why rape. I just wouldn't ever do that, just because of what that means in here, if I should get caught.

*That's interesting, because that implies that the severity of the punishment really does affect its deterrence value. Because rape, in effect, is much more severely punished, maybe not technically by the state, but if you count the treatment by other prisoners, a rapist faces much harsher conditions in prison than do people convicted of other crimes. That would imply that if we could somehow make every criminal's life as unpleasant as what rapists go through in prison, then there'd be more deterrence.*

Well, that may be true. And it may be true that prisons are far too easy, that it's way too easy doing time. You know, there's a good argument there, and I don't know that I would necessarily disagree.

But if hard time isn't coupled with some type of education, then you have bitterness and anger, and what you have is a product that comes out angry, bitter, not any smarter than they were before. Craftier, but not any smarter.

*So even if the severe punishment deters more people, the drawback of it is that the ones it doesn't deter, it'll make even worse. Those who do commit the crime in spite of the deterrence will be embittered and made worse by the punishment.*

Sure. Then you're also going to have a harsher prison system that you have to manage, too. There's another problem.

*So, does it take more resources to have an even more inhumane prison system? I mean, in a place like this, the prisoners to some extent can govern themselves. They can have minimal supervision. But I would think in a more severe prison system, people have to be watched more closely, and you have to have a higher ratio of guards to prisoners.*

Yeah. But then I think it all depends on what we're talking about, though, as far as hard time. I don't know that you would need more manpower if you're talking about a lockdown situation, like IMU. I mean, one officer in IMU can run three pods, which is several hundred inmates, actually. So, I don't know, as far as manpower, what that does.

But one thing that happens in a harder joint is you have a lot of violence, and that means you need to have a response team. So who knows what all the dynamics are of a higher security facility.

*I want to move to a couple of the questions that I submitted in writing that came to mind as we were speaking. You've told me that the fact that you were apprehended and imprisoned, and forced to confront what you had done, and forced to be in a place where you really don't have many options, is a key part of what's turned you around. You've told me that because you don't have much freedom, and because you are coerced into thinking about yourself and your past and your future, that that has compelled you to get your life in order, and that you don't know that you would have made the same tough choices if you hadn't been shocked by that experience.*

*But if that's the case, then it seems like one could say, "OK, from what Jimi's telling us, clearly the system works. Prison does have a tendency to put people back on the right track. It stops them from their crime sprees, and, for some of them at least, it puts them in a situation that forces them to think and to change their life for the better." So should we conclude that prison works?*

Well, that depends on your standard. If you're building a product, and you send it out there, and it gets recalled, and then you build it again, and it gets recalled again, and then the third time you send it out, it's OK—and you consider that a success—then fine. But, this is my third time down as an adult. Counting my juvenile record, you'd have to say the system failed with me five, six, seven times. It wasn't until I grew up that things changed. For whatever reason—whether it's my having contact with my fiancée, or being opened up to psychological ideas, or my education—whatever the reason, I grew up.

When I fell this most recent time, I remember telling my dad, "Look, there's something wrong with me." [Laughs.] "I don't know what it is, but there is something wrong with me. I cannot believe I fucked up again. I need to figure out what it is that's wrong."

*Was it the shock of being in prison, and the conditions of being in prison, that compelled you to that realization?*

No, no. It was the shock of—my father told me, on the morning of my birthday, that he was very proud of me, and that he hadn't been that proud of me since I was a little boy, and that I was doing better than I'd done in years. And then that night was the night I relapsed into coke and, and went on a three week run, robbing. At the end of that three weeks is when I called my dad, and said, "Hey, I'm down for robbery. I just got busted. I'm probably going down for ten years."

It crushed him. And I realized there's something fucking wrong with my thinking.

*If you had not been caught, would you have still grown up and still made the improvements you've made?*

I don't know. I honestly don't know.

When I first got out of the joint after my second prison sentence, shortly after that, I got busted passed out in a building, like I wrote you. I was drunker than shit, passed out. I woke up, I was in the hospital. They were stitching me up and there's cops standing all around. I bailed out the next morning, and then I went home, I called a private rehab place, and I got some help. That was the beginning of my journey to sobriety, and learning how to work a program, and understanding what addiction's all about.

And though I relapsed to coke for that three week period, that's not to say that my sobriety is gone. I'm sober. I'm happy to be sober. Then later, years down the road, I relapsed again, to weed. Not a big, major deal, but I did relapse. But, that's not to say that I am forever lost.

So, I don't know. I may have. I don't know for sure whether, if I'd have gotten off, whether I would have stopped getting in trouble from that point on, or whether it would have been later on down the line.

So, I can't answer. I have no idea what would have happened there.

*What would be your answer in general to the question of does the present prison system work?*

Growing up works. Educating people works. Even punishing people works. But locking them up, and not educating them doesn't work.

I think people that are locked up should be forced to go to therapy. I think kids that are having trouble in school should be forced to finish school. You know what I'm saying?

*Does it work when people are forced to do something like that?*

Well, I don't know. It gets them a degree.

*I taught for a number of years, and my experience was that any student who was in my class because it was a requirement was almost always a bad student, was difficult to teach, and didn't get much out of the class. So, I mean, for me, it was always very hard to justify paternalistically forcing people to help themselves. I mean, you give them the opportunities, but when you compel them to go into AA, or take this class, or do this program, or get this therapy, or whatever, I've always been skeptical that that helps many people in that situation. But, what's your experience with that?*

No, you're right. [Laughs.]

*[Laughs.]*

You're right. It doesn't help. I just get frustrated. [Laughs.]

Because, I have the same argument about the drug treatment here. So, you know, you're right about that. That's just me talking out of frustration over the failure of the system.

The system doesn't work. It doesn't. But that's not to say that there aren't a lot of people that are getting out of prison and staying out of prison. Unfortunately, society doesn't see those numbers. Ever. When was the last time you heard about the numbers in prison of people that have gotten out and stayed out? Or that the recidivism rate is down? Or that this guy got out of prison, and he's changed his life around? When was the last time you heard about something like that? Well, there's a lot of people who have gotten out and are doing fine. I mean, a lot.

*People are programmed to disbelieve all that even if they are told, because they have it in their head that once you've committed crimes, once you've been to prison, that establishes that you're one of the bad guys. And anything you do from that point on will be interpreted according to that assumption. So, if you seem to be turning your life around, it just means you're real shrewd at pretending to be a good person, but we know you're actually a bad person, and so on.*

Right.

*I'm convinced that most people—it's not a matter of whether they have the facts in front of them or not, because even if they have the facts, they'll interpret them according to those assumptions, and they'll twist them to fit their presuppositions anyway.*

Sure. Which is ego, if you really get down to it

*The need to see others as inferior and more evil than oneself?*

Or not having the willingness to change their mind, to accept information that would change their opinion, that would show them that they were wrong about a guy.

You know, it's sad, but yeah, I agree. I agree. A lot of egos out there. It's unfortunate, because, I think, personally, I am a very emotional person. I'm very perceptive. I am perceptive of other people's feelings. And even though I've victimized people all my life, I am very aware of, and I care about other people's feelings. You know, I think I'm a good person. And I care about people. And I like to do things for people if I can. I'm on a good path, of growing up and doing good things with my own life.

But there are a lot of people that may never know that, just because of those biases. The ego. They're not willing to change their mind.

And, you know, tough! I'm at a point where it doesn't matter to me any more. I'm not going to go out there and try to convince everybody that I'm a changed man. I can't do that.

*As long as you know, I guess that's the important thing.*

Right.
And my dad. He's got to know.

*One of the other questions I submitted in writing had to do with the fact that here at WSR, there seems to be a lot more going on than at most prisons. You have programs, there are jobs, maybe a little more access to yard or recreational things, certainly more outside people coming in for various reasons to interact with. But what about at a more typical prison, like Walla Walla or one of the others? Because Jerry and them are always saying that this is really unique, the WSR situation, that we shouldn't generalize from WSR to think that this is what prisons in America are like, because they're not. So, assuming that's correct, what about those more typical prisons? How do people spend their time? Is it boring? Are you more apt to get into trouble, or be more restless? What do you do with your day?*

Well, for the most part, just like you people on the streets, our lives are basically centered around our jobs, whether you're a tier porter that works three hours a day, or whether you're a welder that works eight hours a day, or, you know, whether you're working in an institutional laundry, whether you're working in the kitchen—

*So do most people at other prisons have some form of job?*

Yeah. Or that's the attempt, anyway. There aren't enough jobs to give to everybody, but you could also be taking classes. The post-secondary education has dropped dramatically in this state to where you mostly only have that which supports the institution, like welding class at a place where prison employers need skilled welders. But at least there's still some education. There's still English as a Second Language; they offer that everywhere. There's GED classes. So most everybody's life still is centered around either work or education, though education has been limited drastically.

But even given that, whether you work three hours a day or whether you work eight hours a day, you've got the rest of the day for your time. At other institutions—most of the other institutions in this state anyway, and I believe everywhere else they're doing it too—they've got controlled movement, and they've separated the joint into halves or quarters or thirds. Like at Walla Walla for example, they've separated the joint in half. That means, half of the joint has access to the yard in the afternoon, half of the joint has access to the yard in the evening. The next day, it switches. So that means three hours of yard a day.

OK, so other than work or school and those three hours of yard, can you say pinochle? [Laughs.] Or, five card draw. Or chess. Or reading. A lot of cell time.

Probably the biggest time consumer, and the biggest controlling tool that any institution has, is television. People waste a lot of time watching TV. When I started studying is when I really realized how much time I gave that TV. I watched a lot more TV than you'd think.

*What would happen if, starting tomorrow, they decide to take the TVs away, if they just say that it was a mistake to let prisoners have them, that it's too much of a benefit to them, and that the prisoners need to be punished, so we're going to take all the TVs away?*

A lot of people would have nothing to lose. Now, maybe not here, 'cause there's still a lot going on here, but at Walla Walla, that place would go off. If they took TVs tomorrow, then tomorrow night Walla Walla would sit down. I guarantee it.

*What does that mean?*

The prisoners wouldn't go to work the next morning. They would have to run the kitchen themselves. They would have to run the laundry themselves. The prisoners would be throwing toilet paper out and catching it on fire. They'd go crazy.

And DOC recognizes that. They use it as a tool, a controlling tool. It's a way of keeping people occupied. When I go to my cell, my TV is on, whether I'm watching it or not. You know, it feels awkward not to have my TV on sometimes.

*Does mass disobedience often take the form of something as passive as a sit down strike or something like that, or is it usually more violent rioting?*

It didn't used to, but it is now. That's the way they do it now. You know, every once in awhile, several guys will clock an officer or something, but it isn't the way it used to be. They just don't go crazy and burn up a building like they used to do.

*So now there's actually more of a civil disobedience or passive resistance in prisons, compared to the past.*

Yeah, that's kind of the way to do it. You sit down and you don't go to work, and you make them understand—I mean, you just make them run the institution if they want to. They're going to hear your demands, or they're going to hear your requests, you know.

*Why do you think that changed? Why is there not the rioting and the violence any more?*

I'll tell you several reasons why they don't set the joint on fire like they used to. One reason is 'cause it costs you money now. You get infracted, it costs you money. Another reason is 'cause you lose good time, whereas you didn't used to. Now they—

*There used to be no ramifications if you used violence?*

Well, they didn't have cameras. They didn't have surveillance to see who was doing what. Now they have cameras everywhere in the joint. There ain't hardly any blind spots but a few in the whole joint. So, now they know who's doing what. They can tag you for it.

*Are we on camera right now?*

[Smiling.] No. We're not. This is a blind spot.

*Uh oh. [Laughs.]*

But, they may be listening. [Laughs.]

*OK.*

You know, they've gotten more sophisticated. And the punishment has gotten harsher. They can fine you. They can stick you in IMU. You know, do an eighteen month program in IMU like I did and you never want to go back. IMU's crazy.

*So now you're more likely to get caught for violent resistance and the punishment is more severe. The consequences of violent resistance are worse now than they used to be.*

Sure. Which leads to the deterrent thing. [Laughs.]

*We're running pretty low on time; let me jump to one more question. Many times I've heard you or other prisoners make disparaging references to the "kids," to the youngest inmates, to the "gang bangers," you know, that they're more animalistic, more amoral, more out of control, wild, unpredictable. Not only do they not live by society's rules, but they don't live by the convict code or any kind of criminals' rules either. Allegedly, this generation of young people is a lot worse in those respects than previous generations. Is that true, in your opinion, or is that just what each generation says about the next generation—they always think the upcoming people are worse than they were?*

Yes and yes.

*Tell me more.*

Well, I mean, I believe both are true. It's true that the kids are that way, and it's true that that's what generations always say about upcoming generations. I don't necessarily think that the earlier generation is always wrong to think that about the newer generation. I think it's a reflection of society.

*So are you saying that the kids today are worse, but maybe not as much worse as people make them out to be?*

Well, everything has evolved. What kids are willing to do to commit a crime, the kinds of crimes kids are committing, their feelings about crime and their victims. I think they're maturing younger.

*What do you mean by "maturing"?*

Well, I think maturing in their criminal sophistication. Maturing in their—

*Not maturing in a positive sense.*

Right. Unfortunately, probably not. But some are, you know. I mean, kids I think are being forced to make choices at a much younger age, so a few of them are probably learning to make responsible choices, being more mature in a positive sense, but mostly not.

But not only have the kids evolved, the system has evolved to where they're punishing kids differently now. They're punishing them with more time, they're punishing them for simpler crimes, they're punishing their more serious crimes more harshly with longer adult terms. So, I think all of the above is true. I think it's a reflection of the changes in society, basically.

It's all going to pot. [Laughs.]

*Are the young gang bangers—as seems to commonly be alleged—more intimidating, more scary, more unpredictable?*

Yes, yes, and yes.

They're more scary, in that I don't trust what they're thinking. I don't know what they're thinking. To be honest with you, there's very few of the youngsters that I'm in contact with, that I eat with, or that I hang out with, and I do that as a mentoring opportunity. But, those that I'm not in touch with, or that I don't communicate with, I'm kind of afraid of them, just because of what I hear, and, you know, the time they're getting, the crimes they're committing.

When I was seventeen years old, man, I was committing crimes, but not like they do now. They've got kids that are doing robberies and killing four or five people in a robbery with two or three of their buddies. I mean, you see it on TV too. The media gives it to us left and right.

But the murders that are going on out there by these kids. These kids are just going crazy out there, man. So I think, yeah, I think children's crime has evolved. It's gotten worse.

*How much of the public perception and what you're describing in the media is a racial thing? I think sometimes when people—especially on the outside—dismiss young people, and speak disparagingly of them, and talk about them as being "animals," or say they're "wilding," I think mostly they're picturing teenage black males in gangs, and so I think there can be a definite racist edge to that.*

Really? I don't see that. I'm not picking up that perception from the media.

Don't get me wrong, this is a very racist society we live in, both on the streets and in here. So you may be right, but I just haven't picked up on that in the media.

You know, in here, people from different racial and ethnic backgrounds generally stay very separate from each other. There are those that cross, and, you know, that's OK. It's not a big deal for those that cross; they usually aren't hassled for it. But for some reason, those barriers, that separation, exists between groups.

# JERRY—July 1998

*"But there's some times that, like, when they've kept you awake for days and stuff, you're not really afraid of dying. Death is not something that you're afraid of. You're afraid that you'll learn to accept and like what they're dishing out. That's a bigger fear than dying."*

Except for Jerry, the prisoners in this book doing time for murder—some of whom have been introduced and some of whom you'll meet shortly—either fully acknowledge that their murder was wrong, or deny that they committed the crime at all. Jerry is the only one who admits his crime, but maintains that what he did was justified.

I wanted to dig deeper into this, so I followed up in a series of written questions. He did not respond. Maybe my questions were too personal, or maybe he was just procrastinating.

In any case, he readily agreed to let me interview him on tape, and he put no restrictions on what I could ask him.

In our first taped interview below, I mostly raised new issues. But in later exchanges, I did take the opportunity to ask him more about his murder.

*Can you clarify some terminology for me? We hear about "IMU," "solitary confinement," "segregation," "the hole." Are some of these different names for the same thing?*

OK, some of them are the same thing. The way it works is that when you're first infracted, they put you in what they call "the hole" now. Basically, you go to the hole, and it's kind of a staging place. Actually if you receive anything less than a thirty day sentence, you stay in that first phase—the hole—which is not in the IMU unit in most institutions.

But if you receive a more serious infraction, the hole is just the first phase on the way to IMU. IMU involves a transfer to another facility. IMU is an Intensive Management Unit, and it's more closely controlled. It has its own system, its own captain, its own lieutenants, shift lieutenants, the whole nine yards. It's actually a separate institution within an institution.

Once you get there, to get out of there, you have to go through a whole re-classification process in order to get back into a mainline institution. In other words, it has to be approved by Olympia before you can return to a mainline institution, even though just on the other side of the wall from you in IMU is a normal joint. Transferring out of IMU is like transferring from one institution to a different institution.

And the same holds true when placed in IMU. The sentence has to be approved from Olympia. And then you go.

Most sentences, they do what they call "Ten-Twenty-Referred to Ad Seg." That means you got ten days of isolation—which is like a blackout cell in the hole—twenty days of segregation—which is just the regular hole, and there's other guys on the tier you can holler at—and then they refer you to Administrative Segregation.

So when you go to the Ad Seg committee after those thirty days in the hole, if they decide that you're a threat to the orderly operation of the institution, that you've been involved in whatever nefarious activities, they'll put you in IMU.

Now, the shortest shot you can get at IMU is six months. And you're only eligible to try and get out every six months after that. You go to a review every thirty days, but that's only for different levels within IMU, not for transfer out. Because they have their own sentences in there.

Say, if you throw some food on a cop, or some feces on a cop, or something, you'll be in a strip cell at Level One, you see. And whenever you get out, even to go the shower, you will remain in restraints. When you go get on the phone, you will remain in restraints. You'll have to wear them while you're out of your cell, even to use the telephone. Plus, you got nothing in your house. No books, no nothing. You can't order no commissary or anything.

Get to Level Two, you can order some commissary. Not all of it, but some. You can order a bar of soap, some toothpaste, a small selection of, say, candy bars, and that might be it.

Then you get to Level Three. And you're allowed to have maybe a radio. And, a wider selection on the store.

Then when you make Level Four, you can have a TV, if you have one or buy one.

But beyond that, your living conditions will stay pretty much the same. It's constant. You're in a cell that the light stays on twenty four/seven. You only get an hour and ten minutes a day out of that cell. That's all you're guaranteed. You get an hour of recreation, and ten minutes shower. The rest of the time, you are in that cell. Period. There's no ifs ands or buts about that. They feed you in the cell, the whole nine yards.

*Is it one person to a cell?*

One person to a cell. They did double up for awhile, but control became an issue. You know, they couldn't, like, run in and goon a guy. They'd have to fight two guys. It makes it rough in close quarters.

*What's the purpose of having the light on twenty-four hours a day?*

I don't know what their purpose is. They've never let me read their post orders why they do it. My guess is, from reading stuff that I have read, about Hitler, the Nazis, isolation deprivation, sleep deprivation, mind-altering situations—that describes IMU and our daily life.

In other words, it's the hand that feeds you. You become dependent on them for your mail, for your information, food, everything. And you're almost thankful for anything that they do for you, even though it's stuff you have coming. But since they don't do it very often, when it does happen, you're thankful for it. Although you had it coming all the rest of the time too.

But the reason that they leave the light on is basically because you become more wore down. You don't sleep well. You don't hit REM very well. You actually do a lot more fantasizing when you're deprived of REM sleep. You do daydreaming type things. I can't say why they do it, but the effect that it had on me was almost a drug-like effect. You're wore out a lot.

They actually will come by and hit the door at calculated times, you know, every hour, every two hours. And they make a lot of noise. The whole thing is set up with these real high ceilings, and it echoes. So when the door comes open for the guard to come in and make the rounds every hour, or every half hour, it goes KEESHKACHOOK KAKEESHKAKOO behind him. And then he comes up to the next one: KAKEESHKAKOO. So you're awake by the time they get in there.

You never get any more than a half hour into your sleep, before they're doing that. Some places, like here, we can get ear plugs. But in IMU, you can't have ear plugs. And there's a reason. They want to keep you awake. Plus, like in the daytime, if they keep our sleep out of whack, you become more docile. You're trying to catch a nap. You're trying to go to sleep. You're not asking them for something every time they come in.

On the other hand, they'll ease that door open when the medic comes by for sick call, so you don't hear it. Right? Then they won't make all that noise. Many's the time you'll miss your chance to tell him, "I got a sore throat," or whatever, or, "I need some ointment. My face is starting to break out," you know.

So that's why I think they do it. You know, just part of that tearing you down, wearing you out. After a couple years, you're wore out.

*Does it work? Does it make people more docile? Or does it backfire?*

It backfires in cycles. In other words, like, on a day-to-day basis, it probably works. It builds up, you know, and you become more and more docile.

But there seems to be a cycle to it. Because pretty soon, you're not sleeping, and you're not even trying to get that sleep during the day that they want you to get. You're just kind of waiting. And you're thinking. And you're plotting. And the guard's done something to piss you off, and you're trying to think of some way to get even with him.

Or maybe even it's another prisoner. They got guys in there that are in the hole, or in IMU, for no other reason than that they have mental problems, and the symptoms of their mental condition is contrary to the smooth running of an institution. So they slam them in there.

I've known guys that actually have the ability to beat on the wall twenty-four hours a day, for a day or two, and then rest for maybe four or five hours, and then give you another twenty-four hours of beating on the wall. They'll lay on their back and put their feet to work, and then switch around and work their hands. You know what I mean? One after the other. Sometimes their head. And it's almost like torture.

So now you're trying to think how to do something to him. But, the guard comes by, and he's the first person you have a chance to do something to, you know.

No, it doesn't make everybody docile. They have to subdue a lot of people a lot of times. They have to use the stun gun, the bean bag gun, the goon squad, the fire hose, gas, which are all things that they've used on me. Except the stun gun. Never been shot with the Taser. But gas and the bean bag gun, and hot water and cold water. All those things. [Laughs.]

*What were you doing to deserve this?*

Well, different things. There's a lot of times I brought in on myself, and a lot of times they start out on a couple of guys they're having problems with, create a situation, and decide to take everybody's mattress, take everybody's shit. And then they're gooning all of us.

*For what reason? If you're all separate, in separate cells, why are they collectively punishing you for what one person's doing?*

Because somebody's screaming obscenities and shit, and they can't tell who it is. They decide it's everybody. Or they find a homemade weapon, so they take all of our stuff.

Because even though we're separated and there's no connection and stuff, we manage to make certain connections, you know. So they may not know where something came from.

As hard as they try, we try. So, we always find a way. There's the old fishing line, even the mail system. I mean, there's a lot of ways we use. We do things, you know.

*What's "the old fishing line"?*

You take a thin, thin thread of your clothing and unravel it, and you tie it to something like a comb, or a small piece of plastic, something that will slide, you know. It can be a section of a little plastic book cover, you know, and there'll be, like, tape in the book cover so you can tie it down, make it so it's weighted, and it'll fit out through the crack in the door. They're electric doors, so they'll always have a crack for the slide to go on. There's no other way to do it.

Then, I can flick my line out, and another fellow can flick his out, and they cross, and he fishes it in. Then, in the middle of my line will be whatever it is I'm passing to him, you see.

So they'll come in and strip everybody's stuff. Well, if you ain't done anything, you know, and you don't want give up your TV and your mattress and stuff, sometimes you might just decide, you know, "Hey, you got to kick my ass to take this shit!" Because like I said, you been in there for a year and a half, two years, you're sick and tired.

You know, bottom line is there were some guards that would do shit like push a tray too far in so it don't balance—Voom!—food goes on the floor, they say you did it on purpose. Now they can strip your stuff, or they can put you on Nutraloaf.

Neutraloaf is a wheat germ substance that is almost unbelievably rancid. There's different kinds. Walla Walla's has the consistency and temperature of a steamy turd, a soft steamy turd. They wrap it in a piece of cellophane, so that you can see it. It's brown, it's soft, and it smells like shit. And you have to eat that. That's all you get, two times a day, until they take you off the Neutraloaf.

All they have to do is say that you did something, in order to do that to you. Say you're asking the guard, "Hey, how long till I can get my yard?" "Eh, don't worry about it." "What the fuck you mean,'Don't worry about it'? I'm the next guy out! How much longer is it? I ain't got a clock. What time is it?" Well, he didn't like you talking to him like that. So he sabotages you at lunch, claiming you threw your food on the floor. Bam! You're on Nutraloaf.

Well, I'm sorry, I'll shit in a cup and wait for a time when I can get it and sling it on him. You know what I mean? 'Cause I know that he's going to want to come in and kick my ass. And when he comes in, they're going to kick my ass, they're going to use the hot water, the spray or whatever, but every once in awhile, I can get off a shot. Every once in awhile, you get a little satisfaction. And that's all that's really important.

*So you can't win, but you can have some satisfaction.*

Oh, yeah. Yeah. You can never win, and you know that going in. But every once in awhile, just to know that you're alive, and that you count, and that he has to think about it the next time he does something real shitty to you, you will do something.

It's important, because after awhile, they quit. They didn't bother me much. They tortured people they thought they could torture. They literally torture people that they think they can torture. They'll tap at the window, playing games with people. Some of those nut cases? Oh, tortured them to death!

But they didn't bother me much, after awhile.

*So when you resist violently, instead of just making them angrier and making them retaliate more, they back off?*

Well, it's not a matter of backing off because they're scared. But if a guy knows that I don't care, that I'll throw shit on him, and I'll trick him, and I'll wait a month to do it, then he'll think twice before he fucks with me.

You know, fuck with me when I'm doing something wrong, and I'll accept it. If I'm doing something wrong, I've got no problem with it. But I'm not the one to torture just because you're having a bad day, your wife didn't give you none, or just because you're being encouraged by your peers.

They do that. They encourage each other. Like, maybe the guy might be all right on a shift when he's by himself, but he gets with a couple other guys, and he might be the worst dick there. You know what I'm saying?

Well, you got to make him respect you. And if the only way you can do that is, like, plot a month, plot a year, and then do something to him, they'll know better then. They won't stalk you. They'll go stalk some of them other guys that might not really be serious.

You have to give them something to think about.

*Why don't they just get angrier at you and retaliate all the more if you do those things to them?*

Oh, they do for a moment. But then you do it back. I mean, it isn't all one way. There can be an opportunity to do bodily harm. If you harm me, I'm going to try and do you. You know, I'll give exactly what I get. I wouldn't let nobody torture me without putting up a fight.

*I'm just curious why it doesn't escalate, because it seems like—*

Because there's witnesses. See, when they come for you, they have to bring a camera. OK, and there's other staff that are witnesses. And hey, they don't even trust each other.

If they thought no one was watching, they'd kill us. Given an opportunity, there's two, three people on duty all the time that would go ahead and kill you.

I've taken a whupping where they were going to kill me, but another officer came in. I was in a confined area, no windows, just two security doors at opposite ends. It's almost like a little hallway, with one door to population and one door to segregation. And they were doing a pretty good number on me. But somebody came through that wasn't part of their clique, that they didn't know or trust. So they quit kicking my ass. They quit.

But they may have been going to do me that day. They've killed some of my friends. Beyond a shadow of a doubt, they've killed some of my friends.

But there's some times that, like, when they've kept you awake for days and stuff, you're not really afraid of dying. Death is not something that you're afraid of. You're afraid that you'll learn to accept and like what they're dishing out. That's a bigger fear than dying.

*How do they beat you? Do they hit you with weapons, or their fists, or—?*

That particular time, they were just using fists and boots.

*How many of them were there?*

Three of them. There was actually four, but one was watching the wrong door. That's how come I got saved. You know what I'm saying? [Laughs.] Guy came through the wrong door.

*What did they do to you?*

Oh, they fucked me up. Closed my eye. Had blood running out my ear, thought I might have something wrong, you know. Gave me a pretty good monster stomping. They were probably going to do me, if they hadn't been spotted.

But I mean, I've had them choke me, you know, the sleeper that they put on you. I've had them choke me out. Then, like, when you're starting to wake up, you have this quiver, you know, and they say, "Oh, you want some more!" and choke you out again.

They did it to me three times, every time I started to come to. Each time, I thought, "Well, they killed me. They murdered me."

We had refused to lock up, and there was three of us out on the tier. They came down the tier and we fought them. They had to retreat the first time and go get some help, and then they came back and kicked our ass.

I thought they killed me. Choked me out. They were using clubs then, too.

*Did they ever break any bones?*

Yeah, ribs and stuff like that. Yeah.

*So you've had your ribs broken in these incidents?*

Oh yeah. A rib broken, shoulder out of socket. Yeah. Yeah.

*Do they kick you in the nuts, or go for the most sensitive areas to try to injure you?*

Oh yeah. Yeah. All of that. All of that. You know, but when you're in the middle of it, it isn't as painful as people think it is.

*Because you've got your adrenaline going and everything?*

Yeah, you've got your endorphins working and stuff. You're not in near as much pain as people think you're in.

The nut shot still hurts though. [Laughs.] You know, 'cause I've never been kicked in the nuts in the middle of a fight. It's when they have you already in restraints and they'll have your hands behind your back, and you'll be bent over, and they'll have their hand in your hair. And the guy trailing you will get you. See, that's why a lot of times, we make them carry us, 'cause you don't want to spread your legs. You keep your feet together. You know what I'm saying? Make them drag you.

*And you said all this is being videotaped when they come for you like that?*

Well, actually, like, during Big Red* days, it wasn't. But since they started IMU, when an incident happens, when they have to go in and subdue somebody, they're supposed to have to take the camera. And you got to remember, there's other guys in there that are a witness to this. And other cops too, and they don't know how they're going to hold their mud.

But hell, they're the ones that keep the cameras. We don't get to videotape them.

---

*Another nickname for the Washington State Penitentiary in Walla Walla.

*Do you think it works? Is there still a chance of someone just being beaten to death in those circumstances, or are they afraid to do that because of the cameras?*

Well, case in point, you seen on *Nightline* what they did with video cameras running in the Texas joint when they brought them guys down there from Missouri or Kansas or wherever. They didn't mind, you know. I mean, they sicced the dog on the guy. [Laughs.]

There's no telling the depths of stupidity of some of these. They're as bad as the criminal that goes out and videos their crime. You seen that. These guys are the same way.

Sometimes they aren't thinking, and let's face it, once their adrenaline goes, there's no guarantee that they'll stop. And how hard do you have to hit a guy with your baton to kill him? It could be one blow. It could be five blows.

I know that they've got a video somewhere in their archives with a guy hitting me about five, six times to the head and shoulders. Good, wholehearted swings. Wham! Wham! Wham! With a baton, when I was already in handcuffs.

*What's the purpose of doing it when you're already in handcuffs?*

His adrenaline was going. Maybe I kicked at one of them or something. Who knows? I don't even remember. I do remember the explosions though. Five or six times. Back of the head, shoulders. Hard.

*Were you knocked unconscious by it?*

No. I can take a shot.

*You've got a hard head.*

Got an Irishman's head. I wish I would have been unconscious. Yeah.

*Do you feel more pain afterwards, when you're recovering?*

Ooh, yeah, when they get you into that strip cell. They leave you in restraints of course. You ain't coming out of them cuffs for awhile. And, you know, you're laying there wishing you could rub something. [Laughs.] Got a head you can't rub. Yeah.

But, you know, when you're in there, you almost have to laugh at yourself. When you find out that you ain't dying, you almost have to laugh.

*You've had friends actually killed in those circumstances?*

Oh, for sure. Beyond a shadow of a doubt.

They were exposed once, in the Seventies, what they were doing to our friends, up on the third floor, which was a mental ward. If you wasn't cooperating in those days in Big Red, they would put you up there for observation. Well, like, in a seven, eight year period, probably fifteen guys "committed suicide" up there.

I mean, come on. They didn't commit suicide.

Then, they had orderlies that were in PC that rolled over on this one doctor,[*] named Dr. Tucker,[†] and started telling them about the atrocities that he and the others were doing up there. None of them guys had committed suicide.

What happened is that the testimony of the orderlies that were working for this Dr. Tucker and the rest of them was discounted because they were convicts and weren't to be believed. Bottom line, the guy was fired for one day, and immediately hired back. That was the punishment. He was never found guilty of any of that stuff. But everybody on the yard knows what they did. We all knew.

*Did it stop after it came to light like that?*

It stopped after it came to light to a degree, but not completely. Later, there was a guy named Kurt May,[‡] he was the Bellevue Sniper. Wins a million dollar lawsuit. Four guards had held him down and run a night stick up his ass. Right? He wins a lawsuit over it. He won his case, and he also gets a transfer out of Walla Walla to here. Plus he just got married.

And just when he's getting ready to collect the million dollar settlement, he commits suicide in his house in the middle of the night. Give us a break. [Laughs.] Give us a break. Nobody believes that anybody that just got a million dollars, just got married a month or two before, just got the transfer he wanted, is going to commit suicide. It would be like, you know, doing it when you're at the top. No. It didn't happen.

*How do you fake a suicide? How do they make it look like suicide?*

When you're in the hole, you know, they've got control over who your neighbors are. Maybe they filter out the neighbors, put them on the other tier. Go in there in the middle of the night and hang him. How hard is it?

*They can make it look like he hung himself?*

Sure. Four or five guys subdue you, and they hang you. And the guys that come up from the mortuary, the funeral home, they'll say you died from whatever they're told to say you died from. You know, they're the ones that make that call. There is no watchdog beyond that

---

[*] "Rolled over" on him meaning informed or ratted on him.
[†] I have changed the name.
[‡] I have changed the name.

that goes in and makes sure that this wasn't murder. There is no—like in a regular police force—there is no internal affairs. They don't have that. They police themselves.

*In a case like that, where the orderlies are prisoners, and they reveal what was happening, and they get the doctor in trouble, does that count as snitching according to the convict code?*

No, see, these guys were PC anyway.

*Well, say, hypothetically they weren't. Assuming they didn't already have that in their baggage, if a person blows the whistle on this type of wrongdoing—if he's telling not on a fellow convict, but on administration people who are torturing and killing convicts—does that count as snitching? Would that be looked down upon?*

Well, it probably wouldn't be looked down upon by most. But I wouldn't do it. To me, it's still snitching. I could never take the stand, even in a case like that. I ain't going to take the stand on anybody. Creator'll get you, or some of that guy you tell on's family will get you.

Now, if they murder a guy, I'll tell that guy's family, and I'll tell the Fellahs on the yard, but I ain't taking the stand. I'll tell my people. But I won't tell the Man.

Because I don't think there would be much point, number one, you know, just like happened in that case. They told on the guy, and he lost his job for a day. Whatever that means, maybe he lost his seniority. And really he only lost the job through being dumb enough to have PC convicts for crime partners. They were actually helping him kill the guys.

*So the code doesn't just apply to loyalty to one's fellow convicts. You're also not supposed to tell on other people.*

Yeah.

*Even the enemies of the convicts.*

You never take the stand. Never take the stand. You can't do that. Not any "old school" convict. That's not how you're taught.

Long time ago, case in point. In the old days, before computers, you could tear up a parole hold. So, I go to a bondsman, have a bondsman pay off a sergeant up there in the King County Jail to tear up a parole hold, so I can bail the guy out. And we bailed him out. Cost an extra five grand. Some time later, the guy's back in jail, we pay the sergeant, he takes in some hacksaw blades and everybody escapes. Six, seven guys, they escape out of there.

Well, I guess somehow or other, this thing comes to light about our paying the sergeant and some cops up there. Right? This is, like, in the late Sixties, or early Seventies, and by now I'm doing time myself. So they come to me in here, and they offer me a deal. I could get out.

I could go home. I was serving a fifteen year sentence, but they were going to let me go, if I give up the cops that helped with the escape.

Can't do it. Wanted to spit on them for asking me. I was insulted to my very core. These guys were my crime partners actually. I don't care that they're cops. What in my jacket would make them believe that I'd tell? That I'd feather my bed with the misery of somebody else? Not going to happen. And most of the guys that I truly like and love in this institution feel the same way. You know what I mean?

I'm not here to police the world. I'm not my brother's keeper. I'm my keeper. I'm not going to bear witness against nobody. I don't think Jesus Christ would have appreciated a Judas. That's where all that came from. You know, the lowest form of treachery is betrayal of one's own. I mean, you can't get no lower than a Judas goat, can you?

*Does this apply beyond the convict life?*

It depends. To me it applies, because of the life I chose. It would be different if I was a tax-paying citizen, and I'm out there working hard, and I had never committed a crime, and never relied on the silence of anybody else.

In other words, if you testify against me, you're not a rat, Craig. You're not a rat, because you've never been a criminal. You're not a criminal. You do not walk in the shadows. That's not your responsibility. Your responsibility is to bear witness. You see what I'm saying? I would think less of you if you didn't. People that refuse to testify because they're scared or whatever, they don't get any respect from me.

Now, if you refuse to testify because it's against your moral beliefs, I'll stand behind you. But if you refuse to testify because you're afraid, then now you're not supporting the rest of the people of your peer group. In a different way, now you're the one doing the same thing as Judas did to Jesus. You're turning your back on your own.

*It's an interesting distinction, though, because then you're drawing a solid line between two types of people: the people who commit crimes and the ones who haven't.*

Exactly.

*And once you've crossed that line, it sounds like you can never cross back. Because you're saying, even after you're back out in the free world, and you're not pursuing a criminal lifestyle, you'll still always be in that second category. You'll always be with the people who've committed crimes. You'll always be loyal to them. You can never rat out anybody, even if you're not a criminal yourself any more.*

See, it depends on what you mean by "be loyal to them." What does that mean? Does it mean that if they needed me to, I'd drive down, pick them up, and take them away from the scene of a crime? That I'm not going to do. But, bear witness? No. They can count on my silence for the rest of my life. Because it would lend a lie to all my life if I broke weak now.

*So, you feel this connection, this loyalty to all wrongdoers? What if you were in a situation where you became aware of some kind of corruption or law-breaking by your employer, or by a politician, or something like that? You wouldn't tell anybody?*

Hell, I'd try and get some! [Laughs.]

*[Laughs.]*

I'd cut myself in!

*You could never be an investigative journalist, for instance. It would be a profession that would be ruled out by your principles. You could never tell anybody about wrongdoing.*

I could, though. I could expose it to the light of day. Like, in a journalistic way? That wouldn't bother me so much. But, just like a journalist, I would never take the stand. I'd never give up my sources. I mean, I wouldn't have a problem with that kind of exposure, no.

But talking about exposing somebody, understand this: If I see somebody assaulting a woman or some old man, I will jump on him. See, the difference is, a lot of people will see that and call the cops, but I will slam on the brakes, grab my lug wrench, and do battle with the guy, jump in my car, and try and get away before the Man gets there.

*But an individual as a vigilante can't right all the wrongs in the world.*

I'm not saying—

*So, isn't it impractical to think that you can counter, you can protect—?*

No, I wouldn't—

*—your fellow citizens without the help of the police?*

I'm not even thinking along those lines. What I'm saying is if I see that type of a crime being perpetrated, I will take an active part against it, as it happens. I will not drive by and leave somebody, you know, like the woman that gets beat to death after fifteen witnesses have seen her being beaten, because they were afraid to get involved. A couple of them eventually called the cops or something, but by then it was too late. Well, I'm not that guy. I'll go over and kick the dude's butt, or do battle with him.

*Right. But what if—?*

I would involve myself at that level. But, I'll try and be gone before the police get there.

*But what if you can't realistically do the job by yourself? What if you find out about an intended attack on a woman? Maybe there's a group of people who are going to attack her within the next hour, and you hear them on the phone or whatever. You know that they're plotting something. You know they're on their way over to do something. And you don't have time to gather up your vigilante buddies, and—*

Well, no, see—

*—you go—*

—No, no, no, see—

*Well, let me finish—*

—see—

*—the question though. Let's say the circumstances are such that you can't intervene violently yourself. You can't just go protect her and be the hero, and you can't gather up enough other vigilantes to come over and protect her. You can either let it happen, or you can call the police. What would you do, faced with that choice?*

Well, no, you're setting up a scenario that just can't happen.

*Why is that?*

It's an impossible scenario. Number one, I can always intervene. You know what I'm saying? I can always intervene.

*You can prevent every wrongdoing that you become aware of?*

No, I mean, if I was aware of somebody going to commit an atrocity.

You got to understand now, if somebody was going to go over and whack some broad because she testified against him, and she was a cohort in crime, well, I wouldn't lift a finger. That's not my problem. She entered into that life, and she knew the code, and she broke it. That's on her. I wouldn't waste my time.

What I meant was, like, somebody assaulting a total stranger. I wouldn't have to know him, for me to get involved. But I still wouldn't take the stand.

Now, I might—like, if somebody was killed and I knew about it—I might go find relatives of that somebody who was killed and tell them. You see what I'm saying?

*So you'd tell another private party, but you wouldn't tell the state.*

Yeah. That's because I believe people have a right. I don't think governments have a right. I don't think they have a right, really, to do a lot of the things that they do. I think they've gone way above their right to interfere in our lives for a long time.

*You kind of pushed my example to the side as not being possible, but why is it not possible? Why couldn't there be a case where you become aware of upcoming violence against somebody that you can't individually prevent without the assistance of the authorities?*

But, then I'd just have to say, "Well, shit, there's nothing I can do about it."

*So you wouldn't tell the police, even to save a life.*

No! I'm not calling the cops, ever. Wouldn't call the cops, ever. You know, I didn't call them when my wife was raped. I just wouldn't do it. There's a lot of other things I might try and do, so that I can sleep at night. But, calling the cops just doesn't happen to be one of them.

You know, if somebody does something wrong to me, I will decide the punishment. I'm the one that's going to decide what I think is fair and just if you do something wrong to me. I give you, and all others, that same right. If I transgress on you, I will not whine, snivel, or complain about whatever it is you do to me, including kill me. Might come back and haunt you, but I won't whine, snivel, or complain. You got that right, if I transgress that far.

I've made transgressions. I've done things that required retaliation by somebody if he had any sack at all. And they retaliated. I never thought, and they never thought, of going to the Man over it. Come on! But if I transgress against you and you retaliate, I got nothing to complain about. I had that coming.

*Have you transgressed against people to the extent that you deserved to be killed for it?*

No, I don't think so. I don't believe so.

You know what? This sounds corny, but I try and deal with people fairly and honestly. I don't even rip off dings,* I mean, prey that's out on this yard. Never have. A lot of guys thought I would, because of the way I carry myself, but I never have. I actually have a pretty

---

*A "ding" is a mentally handicapped or insane prisoner, or just a prisoner who is in some sense too weak to cope with prison.

good reputation for being honest and trustworthy. My word you can count on. I don't think I've done anything to deserve to die for.

But I killed a guy whose brother might have a different opinion. You know, I killed the guy raped my wife. But it's still his brother. And he's a killer. He'd like to whack me if he could.

But here's another example of what I'm talking about. There was somebody that the brother had moved on previously,[*] and he was doing time for it. This guy that he had moved on had kind of told, and kind of not told—one of those type things. So now the brother—my arch-enemy—needed an affidavit from the guy, retracting his story.

In effect, this guy who told is my ally, since he's the enemy of my arch-enemy. You know, war makes strange bedfellows. But that doesn't matter. When they came to me, through a third party, and said, "Hey, we need this guy to retract what he said, man. Do you have any influence with him?" I went and used my influence with the guy to get the affidavit, because it's the right thing to do. He had no business telling in the first place.

But that isn't going to stop the brother from wanting to kill me. The one has nothing to do with the other.

*And what was your motivation in helping him in that way?*

'Cause it's the right thing to do.

*You would have done it for anybody in that situation.*

I'd do it for anybody. It's what we do.

*Was the affidavit you influenced him to supply honest?*

I don't know. That isn't my problem.

*So you were required by the code to lie, or to encourage someone else to lie?*

I would lie, cheat, and steal—

*You said you deal with people honestly.*

Yeah, but, I mean, to get somebody off, unless the guy was a rapo, a chi-mo, some ghastly deed. But if he was just out trying to make a living, no. I would try and help him, if I could.

Now, would I myself lie for the brother? No, I wouldn't. I owe him nothing. But I owe our code at least to tell this guy what's the right thing to do, and that's to not tell.

---

[*]"Moved on" meaning attacked.

See, they had a falling out, and they stabbed each other. They ended up stabbing each other. OK, well, when thieves fall out, it takes two. They had issues. And to bring the Man into your issues, after the fact, is wrong. And that's basically what I told him. I said, "Hey, you plan on trying to kill the guy at some later date. I plan on killing the guy at some later date. But you're supposed to be a convict, and you know what you're supposed to do. You know you're not supposed to let the Man execute our sentences. That's just not what we do."

Does that make sense? In a bizarre, left-handed sort of way?

*[Laughs.] If qualified in that manner.*

Don't let this get into the hands of a shrink. [Laughs.]

*[Laughs.] So, as part of the code, you would lie for a fellow convict?*

Oh yeah

*To get him off.*

Yeah. Now, I wouldn't tell on anybody, regardless of who they are. But the only person I'm going to lie for is a stand-up convict. I ain't going to go in and lie for a piece of shit. I ain't going to go in and lie for a guy that might roll on somebody else. I ain't going to lie for a guy that commits some atrocities against mankind. Ain't going to do it. But if a guy's a solid convict, and he needs me to say, "Yeah, I was there. I know he didn't do it," then I'll do that for him.

*And you don't have any problem doing that?*

No. They don't have any problem with writing me up and lying on it. They don't have any problem with locking me up for two years with no due process in the hole. They don't have any problem with kicking my ass, gassing me, and shooting me with bean bags.

*Well, how does—?*

Hold it. OK, these are the same people that initiate false charges when we're in prison. See? And they don't mind lying, cheating, stealing, in order to do us. Well, we have to lie, cheat, and steal to do them back. I mean, you know, let's face it: They're not being honest and forthright. Why would I? It's like I'd be playing with glass cards, you know. Get in a poker game, and they can read them from that side better than I can.

*It still sounds like a "two wrongs make a right" situation. You're saying that because you've been wronged, because they're such bad people, and they do—*

Craig,—

*—wrong things to you and your fellows, that it's OK for you to be a liar.*

—if you were in the Land of Oz, the world would be upside down. And that's where we are. We're in the Land of Oz, and those rules hold true here. It might be repulsive, appalling, and all those things, but that's our reality.

And all these guys that might come in here and try and tell you that that ain't their reality, they're just blowing a lot of smoke up your ass. "I don't get high any more. I don't do this any more." They're blowing smoke up your ass. That's because they ain't become honest with themselves. You know what I'm saying?*

I ain't been high in a couple years now. But I don't walk around, like, "I'm this better person. I've gone through this moral transition. I can never again do any wrong." And, they're out smoking weed, and their first plan when they get out is to have a drink and blah, blah, blah. They're setting their self up for failure. You know what I'm saying? It's all bullshit. But, they've been lying in here for so long, that even when they got you in front of them—a guy they ain't got to lie to—they continue. That's the bottom line. I just don't happen to be a liar.

What I do when I get to the streets, the way I'll try and live my life, is not going to be the way you live your life. But it's not going to be the way I used to live my life either. I have to set up a whole new set of rules to live by. And I'll live by those rules as hard and tenaciously as I've lived by my old set of rules. It's like rewriting a constitution, or my Bill of Rights. I'm giving myself permission for what I will do and what I will not do.

But it won't be a set of rules that applies to mainstream America. I can't be that guy. Never will. An alcoholic will never be a good bartender. I will never be a model citizen. I will live within the laws, so that I never have to come back to prison, but I won't call nine-one-one.

If we sat down and went item by item, the things that I give myself permission to do in here, in my new rules for my life on the outside, I'll have an opposite to that. But it ain't going to be your opposite to that.

And that's where I think most guys make a mistake. Because I used to make that mistake. All my plans for getting out, and all my plans for success, were really plans for failure. They were designed to fail from the door. The speed and the level of failure was only dictated by opportunity and chance. And that was it. Because there was no plan for rejoining the world.

---

*I believe that this odd non sequitur where Jerry contrasts his willingness to be frank with the tendency of other prisoners to tell me what they think I want to hear about their drug use was his first attempt to tip me off that Jimi was not being straight with me. At the time he said it, I didn't really make that connection. Or maybe I made it very vaguely, because you'll notice that subsequently I ask him if he was referring to anyone in particular in his remarks. He denies it, but in the light of later events, I came to disbelieve his denial.

You know, I don't want to change the world, move the world, or even impact it. I want to be able to sit by the road, and watch it go by, and have the freedom of choice to do some things with my life. But that doesn't mean nine-one-one or any of the rest of those moral leaps that people want us to be able to make that we just can't. Or the moral leaps that some guys would like to pretend that they've made, that they haven't. You know, they'll dial nine-one-one on somebody else, and then burglarize his house while he's in jail.

*Now, when you talk about the guys who are pretending to be more reformed than they are, the ones who are saying they don't get high even though they do, or they're saying they're going to live a certain way in the free world even though they probably won't, and so on, do you have someone specific in mind, or are you just saying that in general, guys—?*

No.

*—tend to deceive themselves and others, and to overrate their chances on the outside?*

Yeah, I wasn't hitting on nobody in particular.

*Because, I mean, there's a lot of guys who present themselves as significantly reformed. Are you telling me to not take what they're saying seriously?*

No, no. A lot of them are reformed, or believe they are. A lot of them believe they are. But there's so many other patterns in their life that they're not honest with. And until they are, it doesn't matter.

You can dress up a pig, put make-up and a wig on it, and it's still a pig. You know what I'm saying? All the education, all that other stuff—no. Until you go back to the root and find your fundamental lousy thinking, the way our thought process keeps us down, you're going to be repeating the same patterns.

Like, I was a crook long before anybody even used drugs. See, so I had been on a wrong thinking life long before drugs. A lot of guys say, "Well, if I quit using drugs, then I'll be all right." "If I quit robbing banks, then I'll be all right." Yeah, quit robbing banks, quit using drugs, but if that safe was open, they would till tap a little bit, because their fundamental thinking hasn't changed. You know what I'm saying?

You have to go all the way back and—boom!—and say, "OK, what I'm going to do is I'm going to make a commitment each day to try to live my life so that I'm not violating anybody else. I won't be put upon; I'm not going to tolerate that. But I'm not going to put upon anybody else. I'm not going to shoplift anything, because it affects the people I just stole it from, it affects the customers that have to pay more to cover the costs." All these different things.

You know, when you say there's no victims to selling drugs, or to any of the things that you do—look, be honest with it, and say, "Well, no, there are victims for almost everything we do. Even some of the right things that we do, there'll be victims for." And admit that, and get that out of your life, and make a commitment each day, like when you wake up.

Every day when I wake up right now, I say, "Man, I feel like a million bucks. I'm going to have a good day." Even if I don't. That's how I try and start every day.

When I get out, same thing. I'm going to start each day, saying, "Man, I'm going to live it right. It's another day. I'm going to get it done again today, like I did yesterday." You know what I mean? "And I'm going to try not to look at my watch when I see that safe open at Safeway."

It's all about the little instincts that we have, with our whole lifestyle. If I'm absolutely positive that nobody will catch me stealing this money—there's no cameras, there's been fifty other people come through here, and nobody even knows I was here—can I leave that money there? That's a battle that I'll have to fight within myself, just like I'll have to do with drugs, I'll have to do with alcohol, and I'll have to do with all those things.

It's a day-to-day fight. But if you fight them little fights all the time, you ain't going to find yourself in the big ones. You're not going to be plotting to rob a bank. If I'm trying to live with some moral justification when it comes to the little stuff, I can't possibly be giving myself permission to plot a bank heist at night.

*Let me ask you a related question. And I don't want to get trapped in the issue of whether to tell or not; we'll just assume you're not supposed to tell. But I'm curious about how you assess the actions of others, ethically. It seems to me that sometimes when you guys talk, there is almost an exaggerated loyalty toward fellow criminals or fellow wrongdoers. If somebody is victimizing somebody else, there seems to be almost too much tolerance of that, or even, like, a celebration of it, an attitude of, "Well, if he can get away with it, more power to him." Do you think that that's a common attitude?*

No, I don't think so.

*And again, I'm not talking about turning the guy in or not turning the guy in. I'm talking about what do you actually think of him as a human being? Let's say somebody's running a scam from inside. Because things like that have happened, here or at other institutions. Let's say that some clever prisoners with limited access to phones or computers, maybe through their job, are able to perpetrate some kind of scam whereby they're victimizing somebody for money or for some other purpose.*

For money?

*Yeah, let's say they steal money from somebody on the outside through some con or some trick. How do you feel about that?*

I don't feel anything about it.

*Why is that? Don't you think it's wrong to victimize people like that?*

It would be wrong for me to do it. I wouldn't do it, and I wouldn't let it be done to me. Nobody's going to take my money. And I expect other people to look out for their own money. If you're not looking out for your money—

*Well, that's—*

No, that's not my responsibility though. How is that my responsibility?

*I'm not saying it's your responsibility—*

Yes you are.

*—to stop it from happening. But it can be your responsibility to have an opinion about it. How to act on that opinion is a different question.*

But my opinion about it is almost non-existent.

*But why should it be non-existent? I mean, you're—*

Because, hey, the guy—

*You're blaming the victim. You're saying that if somebody gets robbed, well, it's their fault; they should have protected themselves.*

No, not just should; they need to protect themselves. The guy that comes up with a scam to embezzle some money from in here, well, yeah, more power to him. You know, he's—

*Why "more power to him"? He's—*

Because he's a criminal. I mean,—

*But he's—*

—listen,—

*—wronging somebody who doesn't deserve to have their money stolen.*

I understand that. And that's why it's wrong for me to take it.

*Well then, why wouldn't—?*

See, 'cause I've made that connection.

*Then why wouldn't it be wrong for anyone to—?*

Because it's not right for me to police the world.

*I'm not asking you to—*

I told you, I'm not my brother's keeper

*I'm not asking you to police the world. I'm not asking you, "Would you stop him?" I'm not asking you, "Would you tell on him?" I'm not asking you that. But you're saying that you don't even disapprove of what he's doing.*

No. No.

*Why not?*

'Cause I don't. Don't you see what I'm saying?

*No. You—*

I just don't.

*—lost me on this one. This part you're losing me on. Why do you not disapprove of victimizing somebody like that?*

'Cause that's not really even victimizing him.

*Oh come on, Jerry.*

Come on.

*You know better. Property crimes aren't victimizing?*

Well, yeah. Yeah, there's a victim. I mean, like, if my grandmother was robbed, or her money was embezzled, I'd certainly go punish whoever took it. And I expect those people to do the same thing.

But that's for them to do, not for me to do. I have to do mine, and they have to do theirs. And the dude that comes up with that scam knows that when he does, he's running the risk of taking money from the wrong person. If he takes it from the wrong person, they're going to whack him.

*Well, I hope you think it's wrong for some reasons beyond that he might get whacked for it. Things can be wrong for reasons other than that they might provoke retaliation.*

But, hold it. Hold it. It's only wrong for me. Doesn't that make any sense?

*No. A principle's a principle. Once you recognize that it's wrong for you to do something, you are implicitly recognizing that it's wrong for anybody to do it. If stealing is wrong, then stealing is wrong. It's not personalized.*

But, it's my principle for me not to do that kind of scam. That doesn't mean it's OK for me to make another guy live by that principle.

It's the same way you're trying to make me grab onto one of your principles with this conversation. It would be wrong for you to do that, or to think less of me because I don't go along with your principle, just like it would be wrong for me to try and convince you that it'd be all right to go out and steal that money. You see what I'm saying?

*You can disapprove of certain behavior that other people do without—*

No, I don't have that right.

*But you yourself do it. You disapprove of—*

I don't have that right.

*You disapprove of rats. You disapprove of people who commit rape. There are numerous behaviors you disapprove of.*

Well, I have a right to disapprove of atrocities against man. I'm sorry.

*Then why can't—?*

'Cause I don't think what you're talking about is an atrocity. I just don't have a problem with somebody trying to get some money. I just don't have a problem with that. You know, if they ain't taking it from me, I ain't going to worry about it.

You got to understand. If you came to me and told me that you had a scam, I'd stop you. I'd say, "Hey, I don't want to hear about it." I'm not interested. It's none of my business. My life is on a need-to-know basis. But if later, you were indicted, and I found out what you did, I wouldn't think bad of you.

But if you were doing kiddie porn on the Internet, I'd hate your fucking guts. Now, those are my values.

*So, it's not a matter of whether you have a right to judge others or not; it's a matter of the specific act in question.*

Sure.

*You disapprove of kiddie porn; you don't disapprove of stealing. It's not about a person's moral principles only applying to their own behavior. Because your believing that kiddie porn is wrong means you think it's wrong for anybody to do it, not just that you think it would be wrong for you to do it.*

Sure, but you were trying to make me make a moral leap that I don't have in me. I don't have a moral problem with that guy taking somebody's money. I don't have a problem with that. Them people he's stealing it from should have a problem with it, but I don't have—

*Well, here we go again. Why should they have a problem with something if they're not being wronged? Because according to your value system, it would only be wrong for you to steal from them, not this guy.*

They should have a problem with it, not me.

*But what I'm saying is that nothing wrong is being done to them, according to your value system. According to what you're saying, it's only wrong for people who disapprove of stealing to steal. So anybody else who steals isn't doing anything wrong.*

I'm not being wronged by it, so I'm not going to lose any sleep over it.

*You're not being wronged by kiddie porn on the Internet either, but you're capable of disapproving of that.*

Yeah. That's different. Children are at stake. People that can't take care of themselves are at stake.

There's a big difference. If you was doing it for money, it's one thing. If you're doing it for pleasure, that's another. It's a whole different thing. If somebody does it to extract pleasure out of the misery of some other humans, that's wrong. You know, and I have no problem having an opinion about that.

But am I going to worry about somebody taking some money? No. I ain't going to worry about it. But he ain't going to tell me about it either, 'cause I'm not going to allow him to involve me in it.

*Well, I can see why you wouldn't want to tell on the guy, and maybe even why you wouldn't want to get involved to stop him or something—because those are separate questions—but I'm a little surprised that you're not able to step back from it and see that it's wrong, and to disapprove of it.*

Hold it. I know that it's wrong. And in a way, I disapprove of it. In a way, I disapprove of it. But would I voice the disapproval, or have a problem with him or anything? No.

I don't have the right, like I don't think the cops have the right and the courts have the right, to get in the middle of people's lives. We need to look out for our own. I always looked out for mine, never asked anybody for any help, not looking for none. You understand what I'm saying?

So, what am I going to do? Run over there and say, "Give that money back!"? Come on.

See, you're misunderstanding what I keep trying to tell you. It would be wrong for me. I recognize that it's wrong for me to do it.

*Now, you continue to make that distinction with some acts, but not others.*

But that's because I can only concern myself from now on, from this day forward, with what Jerry does. And with how the world is interacting with Jerry.

Jerry has not done real good in life. Jerry hasn't done real good. And I need to worry about that. I don't need to worry about making those moral leaps, or dragging out that stuff about myself—I don't need to do that. I need to survive each day, and try and be a better human being all the time.

And, if at some future date, the kind of thing you're talking about comes to appall me, or to aggravate me, well, then, that's where I'll be at that date.

*Right.*

You know what I mean? 'Cause however far I still have to go, I'm still five million miles from where I was ten years ago.

Right now, in 1998, it would be wrong for me to embezzle somebody's money. That's the best I can do. I can't worry about anybody else, or anybody else's problems. Not now. Jerry's got to worry about Jerry's problems. 'Cause I got a boatload of them.

# JIMI—September 1998

*"You know, if you've been in the system for a long time and established your reputation, you get here and a hundred guys welcome you with open arms. You're loved by a lot of people."*

B y the time of this interview, Jimi's January release date was drawing close. It seemed every time I saw him he was visibly more excited about it. He had some anxiety, but most of his excitement was positive. More and more, our conversations focused on his impending release and his plans for life on the outside. I looked forward to discovering what form our friendship would take away from the controlled and artificial world of the weekly PAP meetings.

At the same time, I was receiving what I interpreted to be warnings not to get my hopes up about Jimi's chances of success. It was apparently part of the code, though, not to talk down a fellow convict or lessen his chances of receiving support on the outside, so everything I was told was vague, and they even avoided using Jimi's name, so as to keep open the possibility that they were talking about someone else, or making broader points about prisoners in general who have a problem readjusting to life on the outside.

Jerry dropped several hints that Jimi was not being straight with the volunteers and was not as ready for release as he was letting on.

It got to the point where I was reading between the lines of almost everything Jerry said. At one meeting, he was speaking to a group of us about the positive role PAP and other programs have had in many prisoners' lives. He made the point that it would be a mistake to see PAP's success or failure purely in terms of the recidivism rate of its released members, and especially in terms of how any one person fares on the outside. For one thing, he reminded us, PAP and its volunteers provide an invaluable morale boost for prisoners whose sentences will never allow them to be released. It also provides an education to those members of the community who are willing to enter the prison and see for themselves what it's really like.

My immediate thought was, OK, so what's the "real" reason he said that? He knows that we've all grown fond of Jimi and are rooting for him to make it this time. Is he anticipating Jimi will fail and that those of us who have supported him will feel betrayed or demoralized enough to give up on the program?

Or was there no connection whatsoever?

Similarly, Rico was noticeably unforthcoming about talking up Jimi and his prospects on the outside. When I asked him about it, he implied cryptically that things were not as they might seem. Was he simply expressing a general skepticism based on Jimi's failure the last time he got out? Or was he alluding to some more specific present evidence?

Others made similar comments here and there, but again nothing directly derogatory about Jimi.

I found myself avoiding doing anything that could be seen as encouraging them to violate their confidentiality customs. So, like them, I tended to approach the subject gingerly, to avoid speaking of Jimi by name, to stick to hypotheticals.

I did, however, feel that I needed to get a clear answer to at least one question. To both Jerry and Rico, at different times, I stated that though I respected their code regarding talking about Jimi behind his back, I did need to know if we outside members were at any risk whatsoever of being harmed or conned if we provided friendship or support to him once on the outside.

Absolutely not, they assured me. On this issue they were crystal clear. Jimi was a good guy and a solid convict, they told me, and he was doing his best. His feelings for me and the other volunteers were genuine; we were not putting ourselves at risk by remaining in his life after his release.

So what was it that they were hinting at? About the only information I could glean from them was that he was not as free from drugs as he was telling us. But they offered no details about how much he used or how recently.

I asked Jimi himself about these matters, of course without being specific about who had said what to me. He responded with what I took to be a bit of a guilty smile (though was even that interpretation based on the vague warnings I'd been receiving?), "Oh yeah, but I told you about that," he said, "That was back at McNeil Island when I got in trouble over that."

"Have you been off drugs since then?" I followed up, "Because that's not what I'm being told."

"Sure, yeah," he said, "Except, you know, that time on my birthday. I did relapse there. But I'm clean now." In the last interview, he had indeed mentioned a relapse two years ago. Perhaps they were one and the same. Or maybe he wanted me to make that connection, so I'd infer that the drug rumors about him were "old news." In any case, I decided not to pry any further.

The following interview took place on an evening where I had another prisoner scheduled—a new interviewee—but we had miscommunicated on the date, and he didn't happen by until fairly late in the session. (His brief interview that night follows as the next chapter.) In the meantime, Jimi graciously agreed to fill in. I had nothing specific prepared for Jimi. But I generally preferred a natural conversation over a tightly organized formal interview with detailed notes anyway, so we went ahead.

*Tell me a little bit about the different kinds of prisoners there are. I take it there are different cliques, different categories. How would you describe some of the main types of prisoners?*

Well, I suppose, similar to what is outside the walls, there are groups of people that are segregated, separated, by financial status. There are groups of people that are separated by race.

There are the same separations that there are out there, but we tend to categorize people first by their beef, and the bottom of the pecking order is obviously child molesters and rapists. And, ironically, at the top of the pecking order—those who get the most respect in prison—are murderers. And then, everywhere in between—

*Does it depend whom they murder, and the circumstances and such?*

Not generally, no.

*So if you got drunk and strangled your wife, it would be the same as if you had some heroic shootout trying to protect your partner in a bank robbery or something?*

Well, you know, probably not. I mean, but it depends on the character one puts forth once he gets here. It depends on who he identifies with once he gets here. It depends on the heart that he shows, or the balls that he shows once he gets here, what he's willing to do to establish his respect once he gets here.

Those things sometimes have just as much to do with how you're perceived as your beef does. Like, I had never murdered anybody, but I'm cliqued up with the people who are murderers. All my best friends in here are murderers.

Even though I'm not a murderer, my friends have always been murderers, and that probably has more to do with the type of time I did when I first fell. I was not who I am now. And so, because of—call it a "reputation"—or the stupid things I did when I was young, reacting with anger, a stabbing here, fighting endlessly, and getting into it with the cops, and all that kind of crap, that kind of stuff earned me some respect in here. And so, over the years, I became trusted by those at the top of the pecking order.

I think it has a lot less to do with who you murdered or how you murdered than it does what you do once you get here. But, for some reason, murderers are generally at the top of the pecking order, unless there's something funny with the beef, unless it's a murder-rape.

But quiet as it's kept, there are even those where the rape part of the murder is hidden. It's not talked about. Nobody knows about it. I'm sure there are plenty of people among the Fellahs—the clique at the top—that have those kind of beefs. It's just that nobody knows it.

*Oh, so people don't always know each other's crimes? At least not in detail?*

No. It used to be a standing order that you dropped your paperwork when you walked into a house. At Walla Walla, when you moved into a house, you had to show your paperwork, meaning your judgment and sentence. I remember for years, whenever we had somebody come into our cell, we wanted to see their paperwork right off the bat. If they had a funny beef, they were moving out. If they had a real funny beef, they were moving out right then and there. I mean, we made them just walk out of the house and say they refused to lock up.

*But nowadays, you don't see their paperwork?*

Well, for a long time here at WSR, with single cells, a new guy wouldn't be moved in with somebody who could demand to see their paperwork; he'd just be placed in his own cell.

But in general, I don't get caught up in that any more, because I don't get to know new people. I'm guarded of the people I get to know. New people come off the chain, I don't know them, I don't want to know them. I haven't gotten to know somebody new in years, unless it was somebody that was cosigned by the Fellahs. Somebody that they could say, you know, "Hey, this is so-and-so, my brother from Walla Walla. Everybody knows him. He's a good guy."

You know, if you've been in the system for a long time and established your reputation, you get here and a hundred guys welcome you with open arms. You're loved by a lot of people.

*Well, let me give you a little more background on my question, or a little more explanation, when I ask about the different types of prisoners there are. I get the sense, as an outsider, that, first of all, WSR is somewhat different from the typical prison, and—*

Sure.

*—the people we meet in PAP are somewhat different from the typical WSR prisoner. It seems like, typically, what we're seeing is people who have at least a pretty good reputation as far as not being a rat, not having a bad beef, and they're mostly at or near the top of the pecking order. And, they have some social skills with outsiders. They won't embarrass the other prisoners by being included. Now, that's not going to be typical of all prisoners in this institution, and especially in other institutions. So it seems like there are whole types of prisoners we just don't see—*

Yeah.

*—in PAP. For example, in addition to the kinds of people we meet in here, there are—well, you've touched on some of them—there are the people who are excluded from the pecking order—the untouchables, the outcasts, like the rats and the rapists. We don't see them. What about predators inside the prison who victimize other prisoners, and really aren't very safe to have around the public? What about the people who've been defeated by the predators? The punks, the people who've been, you know, conquered by the predators within the system, and therefore don't get much respect either? Or people who don't play the game at all? Are there people who are sort of outside of this kind of group? Not because they're bad guys or they have bad reputations—they're just kind of invisible people in the system, and they have their own values or lifestyle or whatever, and they would never be involved in something like this. They would never be in the "in" crowd. I mean, talk to me about the different groups, different types of prisoners that I wouldn't encounter as a PAP volunteer.*

Well, first of all, nobody's invisible in here. Everybody in here has a life. Everybody in here has a story. And, everybody in here has something going on in here.

There are a lot of little cliques in here. You got people that hang out at the chapel—people that are susceptible to being victimized, people that have ratted, people that have raped. The chapel is almost a haven for people who are not accepted, or people who are frowned upon,.

It's just that in PAP, we're real guarded about who we bring in here, as a lot of the clubs are. But, if you wanted to see an entirely different type of inmate, the place to start would probably be the chapel. And, you know, right or wrong, that's just the way it is.

But walking that yard, you see people cliqued up everywhere. You see very few people walking completely alone. I mean people that just stay by themselves, stay alone. There aren't very many people that do that.

*Because they figure out that it's not safe to do so, or—?*

No, not really. It's safe to do that here. There's no threat here, unless you disrespect somebody of course. Obviously that's a threat. But, this isn't like Walla Walla, where, you know, somebody that knew you in the county could say you told on somebody, and then you have guys come after you out of the dark with a shank. It's not like that here.

But you're right; you're just looking at one sort of group in PAP.

And other people may not even see us as the top of the pecking order. We're at the top of the pecking order from our perspective. But nobody victimizes us. We've learned to manipulate the system. We cumulatively have a lot of years experience in the joint, so we know how to manipulate the system to get what we want, which, in reality, you have to do. Otherwise, you don't get anywhere in the joint. You don't get in and out of your house unless you know how to manipulate the system.

But, there are many cliques in here, and many different types of people, and it's just like out on the street.

I mean, you've got groups of kids that are into playing hacky sack. You got a bunch of Spanish-speaking prisoners. I mean, the most obvious is the racial groups. There's the Mexicans, the Indians.

You know, you got a bunch of little white kids that are like surfer dudes and skateboarders. You got a couple other guys that are real serious about basketball.

There are black guys that identify white. They hang out together. And, you got a bunch of white guys that identify black, and they kind of kick it with only blacks or a certain few white. You know, you're talking about a large number of different subgroups, different subcultures.

Then, you do have people that have been victimized. And people who have been victimized will continue to be victimized. No matter how they're victimized, they'll always be targets.

And you have people that are predators that, strangely enough, get a weird kind of respect. Not necessarily a respect for what they are, but there are guys that are, that are—that it's just kind of accepted that that's the way they are.

See, I have one guy in mind that, you know, we almost like him. We've known him for years. He's been in the system for years. But he's a serious predator on kids. Kids come in, and he wants one. He's never getting out, and that's what he lives for, to have a young pretty kid in his house, for sexual reasons. You know, in this backward world, it's OK. I mean, it's not really OK. I don't enjoy it. It's not something I condone. But, we kind of look beyond it, ignore it.

*Even if it's non-consensual, it's OK by prison standards?*

With him, it's not non-consensual. He makes it consensual.

*What does it mean to say that he "makes it consensual"?*

Well, he makes it worth it. With money. Financially takes care of them, looks out after them. These are kids that are scared, so, you know, he moves them in his house. He buys them all the store they want. He's got an outside industries job, so he has plenty of money to spend on them. He buys them clothes, and, you know, pampers the hell out of them.

Obviously this is somebody who has homosexual experience to draw from, so he sees something. I mean, these kids that he picks are kids that he either thinks they can be prey, or he thinks they're potentially homosexual or bisexual or whatever. He doesn't just see a good looking kid, and go after any good-looking kid. I think he sees something that he can take advantage of, maybe just some weakness. I don't know. I don't know. I can't read his mind. It's weird. It's really weird.

*But you feel it's consensual?*

I believe he makes it consensual.

It's not something the kid would probably do on the street. I don't even know that though. I really can't say even that. I know the kid doesn't move out. He builds a relationship with the kid, and they end up being together for a long time. I mean, for years. So, I don't know.

*It seems like it's in kind of a gray area, because I think you described it as victimizing, and yet you also say it's consensual.*

Yeah. Well,—

*So, maybe, are the circumstances coercive? Rather than the specific guy being coercive?*

Sure, in another place, another time, the young person might never even think twice about something like that, would never even consider it, but under the shadow of fear, who knows? I don't know.

There's really an attitude of "survival of the fittest," or "natural selection" around here.

*It seems that there's a definite disrespect for people who can't defend themselves in a sort of macho, physical violence manner. You can have just about any other flaw, and it's no big deal. But, if you're not willing and able to defend yourself through violence, then you're not going to win any respect in this place.*

That's true. Violent place. A lot of violent people. And I suppose violence, or the threat of it, is the core of what puts you at the top of the pecking order, if you really examine it. Everybody I know of that's at the top of the pecking order is potentially violent, or has been.

*One of the reasons I'm thinking along these lines, it seems like a lot of the prisoners excluded from PAP—some of the people with "funny beefs" and that kind of thing—are people we wouldn't really want to associate with anyway. I don't know. But it strikes me that potentially good people would be excluded also. I'm thinking of a person who entered the prison system basically nonviolent, not so much through being a coward or being effeminate or something, but just nonviolent by choice, just because of his moral philosophy, his religious philosophy. Somebody who was more inclined to speak the truth than to play games or learn how to play games, and learn how to hide things, and all that. But somebody who valued truth and nonviolence, I don't see him doing very well here. I don't see him becoming accepted. I don't see him being in PAP, or being at the top of the pecking order.*

We've got them.

*You've got some people you would describe that way?*

Sure. Sure. Absolutely. Jeff.[*]

*How do they survive?*

Jeff committed a heinous crime. But, Jeff is very non-violent. Jeff is basically a citizen who committed a crime. He doesn't care about the pecking order. I don't even know where I would put Jeff in the pecking order, 'cause he doesn't care. He doesn't care about a pecking order.

Jeff and I have always been really good friends, 'cause we were cellees for a long time. I've always respected him as somebody that lived in the free world and got a college education. He was somebody far from those who I had hung around with all my life. I learned a lot from him, you know, we've always been friends.

But Jeff doesn't care about the pecking order. And there are others.

---

[*]Jeff has not appeared yet in this book but is one of the nine prisoner interviewees.

*How do people like that do it? Because we were just saying that you're not going to win any respect and get into a group like this if you're not violent, or at least have the threat of potential violence going for you.*

Well, I'm not so sure that I was saying that you're not going to get in PAP. I'm saying that people at the very top of the pecking order tend to be that way, but he's not at the top. I mean, he doesn't care about the pecking order.

*OK.*

But, he still has my respect. He still has the guys in PAP's respect.

Actually, there's a lot of people out there that aren't in the pecking order, that nobody knows their beef. They're the loners that you talked about. And they've got my respect, and they've got our collective respect from on top of the pecking order or whatever, just because they're another man and they're in here and they get that respect.

But, you lose the respect when someone finds out you've ratted, or someone finds out you've raped, or someone finds out you've done something heinous or been involved in some, you know, heinous crap.

Respect is different, though, from friendship or brotherhood. I mean, people get automatic respect in here. But respect just means you get your space; I get my space.

*How do you avoid being victimized if you're that kind of person?*

I don't know. Jeff's never been victimized.

I think, minding their own business. That's something that gets you respect in and of itself—minding your own business, doing your own beef.

You know, a lot of times, just the fact that you're hanging with some dings, or some rapists, or some known rats, that in itself will exclude you, just because you're hanging with them.

This is a twisted world. I mean, it really is. You know, how anybody could expect to come to prison and gain a solid foundation of values, and a solid foundation of beliefs and goals—it's impossible. You can't. I mean, those are things you get over years and years of growing up, if you ever get them at all. I don't know.

Some would say that those of us that have been in prison the longest are the most recalcitrant, instead of growing up in any positive way. I don't know.

*What do you think are the long term consequences of developing the kinds of values and lifestyles and habits in here that they have to in order to survive? What does this life do to people long term?*

Well, my first time down, you know, I came to prison, and I didn't understand responsibility. I didn't set goals. I didn't know how to be responsible.

And I came to prison, and I didn't have to be responsible, for the most part. My rent was paid. My tuition for what schooling was available was paid. My food was paid, laundry was paid. Everything was paid for. I didn't have to do anything, except lock up at night.

So, I came to prison because I couldn't walk down that straight and narrow line. While I'm in prison, they didn't give me any skills to learn responsibility, and then they expected me to get out and walk down that straight and narrow line that I couldn't walk before, and now it's even straighter and narrower than it was then, because I'm on parole. I couldn't walk it before, what makes them think I can now? Especially now that I've, you know, learned to be crafty, and have learned more than ever not to delay gratification at all.

Prison is a terrible place. It teaches people way wrong things. Way wrong things.

*Give me some specifics. What is it about prison that doesn't teach you to delay gratification?*

Violence is the answer. Violence is how you respond to things. That's one thing that's real common in here. Something goes wrong, you either react verbally violently or physically violently. That's just the way. For years, that's the way I did it.

Maybe prison didn't teach me that. But, I think prison did teach me that, actually. I came to prison fighting, and thinking that that was what I had to do, 'cause I was young, and red-headed, and freckle-faced, but it got me on the top of the pecking order, I guess. [Laughs.]

But, until several years ago, I didn't know anything about setting goals, and how to get there. It was day-to-day, living from day-to-day, and, you know, the things that I've learned, I've had to learn on my own. I've had to put myself through school, and I've had to grow up, and take some programs, and learn about addiction, and learn about anger. I mean, there's a lot of things I've done.

*Well, you mentioned that one of your problems was not being responsible enough to walk the straight and narrow and fulfill your responsibilities on the outside, and that prison certainly didn't help you with that. It sounds like violence is another good example. But if one of the things we object to about people, and one of the reasons we put them in prison in the first place, is we don't like their tendency to use violence to solve their problems, isn't prison an environment where you're taught precisely that—to use violence to solve your problems?*

Well, yeah, the environment's conducive to that. Because of those in the environment, that's the way—"when in Rome"—I mean, that's the way.

But I don't think it's the statement of purpose of the Department of Corrections or anything.

*Well, let's talk about that. What do the prison authorities do that fosters or discourages violence? Could they and have they created a less violent prison atmosphere?*

They've done a pretty good job, for the most part. What they did years ago was, in Washington state anyway, they divided the institutions in half or in thirds, and they added to their payroll. So, they've got more people, more officers, and they've divided the inmates up, so there's less inmates together at one time. And, now, in any joint, they can respond to a fight immediately. I mean, there's very few places where you can fight and get away with it for more than, you know, a minute, if that.

*A lot of damage can be done in a minute.*

Yeah, well, I'm not saying violence doesn't happen and it can't happen. But they've tried to get to the point where they at least can decrease it. They started taking away your good time, and over the past ten, fifteen, twenty years, they've done things to respond to the violence. Compared to twenty years ago, it's not as violent as it used to be. Not nearly as violent.

*On the whole, do you think it's still advantageous to be a violent person in this system?*

Not at all. Well, it depends on what you're talking about.

*Well, let's say we have two people admitted into the system, one of whom tends to be a very aggressive, violent person, used to using violence to get his way, used to victimizing people, used to not taking "no" for an answer, and the other person is maybe a little more passive, a little more nonviolent, tends to shy away from confrontation like that, tends to be a somewhat rational, reasonable, calm person. Who's going to do better in prison?*

In prison? Now, are you talking about to meet their release date, or are you talking about survival while they're in here, and live comfortably while they're in here?

*Talk about both.*

Well, the person who is nonviolent is obviously more likely to meet his release date. He'll get out when he's supposed to get out. The guy who's violent is going to lose a shitload of good time. He's going to do a couple of programs in IMU, which is six months at a shot.

But, as far as how the two will live, well, part would depend on what kind of support they have from the street. But if neither of them have any support from the street, the guy who's violent's going to make out ten times as well as the guy that's nonviolent. I mean, make out in terms of getting things done, getting personal clothes, getting into a program or a job he wants, you know, being involved with groups of people where he's in on things, he's getting things, he's able to maneuver, and get things done, and come and go as he pleases.

The violent person's going to get along that way. He's going to be able to manipulate the system much easier.

# 9—September 1998

*"It used to be, someone stepped on your shoe, and you're just, like, 'What are you doing, man!?' But now, it's, 'Step on my shoe, hey, I'll blow your head off!' It skips over the whole process and takes it straight from Point A to Point Z. There's no reason to argue any more. There's no reason to fight. You just settle it with your gun."*

9 in 2001. (Photo courtesy of Linda Coleman.)

Gerald, or "9-0" (Nine Oh)* as he's called, is an African American product of the ghetto. He became involved with street gangs—"9-0" is a nickname derived from the name of his gang—from a very early age. The things he experienced and perpetrated as a child would be overwhelming and traumatic to me even as an adult, but to him, crime and violence were simply an everyday part of childhood. Out of necessity, his street smarts developed at a much more impressive rate than his book smarts. As he approached manhood, he seemed well-positioned for a successful life of crime.

But it was not to be. For many on his path, the end comes abruptly by way of a bullet from a rival gang member. For 9, the end came a little differently. He was apprehended and imprisoned for his criminal activity. Often this means a temporary, enforced timeout until the revolving door opens back up on the outside and one can resume one's chosen lifestyle. But in 9's case, the severity of the crime of which he was convicted resulted in a sentence of life without the possibility of parole. His career was over before it ever really began.

That was many years ago. 9 is an adult now. By the time I met him, he had already been incarcerated for over a decade.

It's impossible to spend much time with 9 and not find your thoughts going to what might have been. Had he had the opportunity and the willingness to devote his intellectual gifts to something other than crime and running with gangs, there's no limit to what he could have accomplished.

There is something special, something different about 9. He is one of those rare people that you just sense is capable of greatness (including great evil).

I first met 9 not at PAP, but at the telemarketing job. He was one of our prisoner employees. He was a PAP member, but had not been attending since I had joined, due to the Wednesday night meetings conflicting with his work schedule. Later, however—after the telemarketing business closed down—he became a somewhat more regular attendee.

I found him immediately likable, as I'm sure most people do. Part of his appeal for me is his obvious intelligence. (I'm drawn to intelligent people, because I believe that morality is rational and that, all else being equal, the more intelligent and insightful a person is, the more capable he or she is of understanding what one ought to do and why. Granted, dumb people can have good hearts, but their goodness is the goodness of the well-behaved cocker spaniel. We can be grateful that they've been influenced in a harmless direction, but that's different from the autonomous moral development that is available to a thinking, rational being.)

One small example of how sharp 9 is: One time I was sitting with him at one of the Prison Awareness classes. I asked him if he was going to speak, and he said no.

---

*9 has chosen to be identified by his nickname or first name only.

There had been some talk of his doing a presentation on volunteer programs, but they had assigned that to someone else, so he had not bothered to prepare anything.

Given how haphazardly organized these things can be, later in the session they told him that they needed him to cover that topic after all, and to do so immediately. He was completely unfazed by this. He promptly got up, ad libbed a twenty minute talk that was as good or better than any of the others that had been prepared and rehearsed, adeptly handled all audience questions, and sat back down.

For most people, speaking in front of a bunch of strangers is a harrowing experience, even given the chance to prepare. To be asked to speak extemporaneously in such a situation typically inspires nothing but terror. But for this gang member, this convicted felon, this long-term prisoner with only minimal opportunities to socialize with non-prisoners for over a decade, it was a walk in the park.

It was not just that he had the social presence and rhetorical skills to win over the audience in that situation. The actual content of what he had to say about the programs was compelling, logically organized, and well thought out. So in terms not only of style but of substance, we were listening to a very bright, dynamic person.

But I also was told by many people that 9 had a well-deserved reputation as a consummate con man, so I was just a bit wary of him.

He is a charmer all right. He has a generally ingratiating style about him, at least with outside people. He is polite, friendly, quick with the compliments, quick to agree with you.

He has an instinct for showing whatever side of himself he senses will be perceived most favorably by his present company. His machismo tempered with sensitivity and vulnerability enables him to be quite the ladies' man. With older people, his deference and good manners, coupled with his diminutive stature and sometimes boyish nature, place him comfortably in the son or grandson role. (We not uncommonly refer to him as a "good kid" and the like. He's no kid; he's a grown man.) Most of the other prisoners perceive him as a solid convict who is tough and courageous enough to stand up for himself and not betray his partners.

So was he being calculating in the way he presented himself to me? Did he quickly pick up on the fact that I'm a sucker for brains, and that I respect people with depth and a conscience, and did he then emphasize those aspects of himself when communicating with me?

I don't doubt that there was some of this going on. It seems to be in his nature to do what it takes to win people over to his side, as one never knows who could prove to be a useful ally for some future purpose. I have no reason to believe he'd choose to be different or more genuine with me.

Yet, it's more complicated than that. My take on 9 is that he is all that he presents himself to be; he is merely selective about what he shows to whom and when. (Which

I'm sure could be said of any of us to some degree; he's just more skilled at it.) I'm not convinced he's a phony in any more nefarious sense than that.

Allow me to cite a couple of reasons that I do not perceive his admittedly slick nature too negatively.

For one thing, in spite of his reputation as a schemer, almost everyone seems to have a favorable view of him.

Steve—the telemarketing supervisor—was the first one who warned me that 9 is adept at playing every available angle. But at the same time, he had a clear fondness for him.

As far as I know, none of the female volunteers whom he's sweet talked ever later denounced him for manipulating them or trying to get them to take risks or do anything wrong for him.

When I mention him to staff, their most common reaction is to grin and roll their eyes or shake their head, as if to say, "What a character!" This is hardly the reaction I'd expect if he were some evil, violent person who made their jobs more dangerous.

Plus, if he were some sort of phony, the other prisoners would see through him pretty quickly. A person who only *pretended* to be loyal, or willing to fight his own battles, or be someone the other prisoners could depend on, wouldn't get away with such a charade for very long. But in 9's case, other prisoners accept him as a solid convict.

Granted, some prisoners have animosity toward him for taking a stand on certain racially-charged controversies, but I have never heard any accusations that he has done anything to earn their disrespect. 9 has not only survived in prison, but has risen to a position of some leadership. Thus have his peers expressed their judgment as to his character and trustworthiness.

Also, I've known him for multiple years now, and he's never harmed me or maliciously used me.

My second piece of evidence that 9 is something more than some amoral hustler is his ongoing relationship, and now marriage, to a former staff member at another prison. You'll be reading much more about this woman and their relationship as you get to know 9 through the interviews, but here's a preview:

Given his reputation, when 9 developed an alleged friendship with a staff member, and eventually claimed to love her and want to marry her, many assumed he was engaged in some sort of con. Certainly the prison administration did everything in its power to break them up and to ascertain what he *really* was up to.

Well, here it is, years later, and no one's found the ulterior motive yet. Nothing in the way he's behaved toward her, as far as I'm aware, indicates anything other than that he sincerely cares for her and is grateful for her presence in his life. When he speaks of her, it is with seriousness and with love. She's obviously touched something deep inside him, something that would presumably not be present in the first place if he were nothing more than a conniving egoist.

In stating my opinion that 9 is not just conning everyone, I don't mean to imply that there is not a dark side to him. He comes from a brutal and terrible past, partly of his own making and partly not. I don't know that he can ever fully overcome that. I'm certainly not convinced that he has yet.

I believe 9 is all the good things he seems to be. But I also believe that much of his goodness is potential, that he still has a lot of growing to do. For instance, despite his being a caring person in many respects, in our interviews I perceived his attitude toward his murder victim to be dismissive and unfeeling.

Also, while he has acquired some amount of self-education in prison, there are many, many gaps in his knowledge. I get so used to thinking of him as an intellectual, that it can still surprise me when he displays a total lack of awareness of some mundane fact that all "educated" people presumably know, or more importantly, when he shows that he has not outgrown some ignorant attitude, such as his unfortunate affirmation of African American racism toward Asians, or his sometimes cavalier attitudes toward women.

Perhaps in the beginning, 9's embrace of violence and crime was reluctant, a necessary evil, in his eyes, to surviving a dangerous childhood. But eventually that embrace was an eager one. His slight physical stature marks him as an underdog, but guns have provided him a way out of that role. He has known the exhilaration, many times over, of instilling fear in others, dominating others, exercising the power of life and death over others. Despite what he now recognizes about the ethical ramifications of violence, when he recounts the violent triumphs of his past, he does so with an unmistakable relish.

When 9 spoke to me of overcoming his fear of guns, and coming to "love" them, his arm lifted instinctively, and his hand took the shape of one holding a gun. (Not thumb side of the hand up, as I assumed from television and movies is the way to hold a gun, but palm down.) There was indeed something loving in the gesture, something comfortable, something familiar. Something chilling.

I sense that there is a part of 9 still capable of violence and brutality, and still capable of liking it. Yet, I cannot help but continue to harbor high hopes for him. Maybe I'm just not willing to admit that he (or society or whomever you want to blame) could piss away such potential.

As things stand now, 9 will likely never leave prison. But whether on the outside or in whatever more restricted ways are available to him on the inside, it is imperative on him and on all of us who might have any influence on him, that he continue to grow and to channel his vast potential for good. People like 9 don't come along often enough that we can afford to waste them.

9 was one of the last people to join the book project. I sent a set of written questions to him, and we also arranged to get together for taped interviews during some upcoming PAP meetings. This first interview was conducted immediately after the Jimi interview of the preceding chapter. We followed up the next week with a longer interview. Days later, I received 9's responses to my written questions.

*Just as a starter, where does "9-0" come from?*

Well, I was born and raised in California. "9-0" is a symbol of the area that I grew up in.

*A symbol of the area?*

Yeah.

*How so?*

Well, you know, it's from "9-0 Crips," or "Rolling 90 Crips." It's the name that I was given growing up in the gang lifestyle.

*Is the "90" geographic, based on 90th Avenue or 90th Street, in LA?*

Yeah, 90th Street. Everyone receives nicknames of course, and, by my tattoos, people automatically started calling me "9-0," because I have a "90" on my right arm. That's a name that has been sticking with me ever since I was a teenager.

*How do you feel about that name?*

Well, I'll always be proud of it, because it means to me my survival and my being able to be the man I am today. But, of course, if I could go back to when it began, there's quite a few things that I would change, because they've done nothing but cause me harm.

*How do you mean, caused you harm?*

Well, you know, what it represents. Of course, it always brings instant enemies, people you come in contact with, knowing what it represents. It's pretty much equivalent to the way a Nazi symbol on a guy automatically, to me, you know, symbolizes racism or someone that dislikes blacks. It's the same with my tattoo. Any time I come across people that know that

I'm associated with the gang lifestyle that that tattoo represents, it's always meant giving me a hard time. It's never led to a positive outcome.

*Is this antagonism mostly from people in other gangs, or people who are anti-gang?*

Well, both. Anti-gangs. People from other gangs. And, people that's not a part of any gangs, but are just, you know, adults or elders that know that it's a terrible way to grow up, because it leads to nothing but destruction. And, those are the ones that I mostly get ridiculed by, as a whole.

But, like I said, it'll always be something I'm proud of, because they wasn't there at the time that I was involved in the lifestyles that I lived in. And that's what made me proud.

*So, when you look back on your gang past, and your survival, and the things you had to do to survive, you don't see it as a negative thing that you shouldn't have gotten into, or something you've outgrown, or something you reject. You have a certain pride still, associated with it.*

Yeah, that's a good question, because that's something I've thought about. I'm twenty-nine years old now, and I look back to when I was eleven or twelve. You know, my friends was my family, being that I was an only child, but not living with my mother or father. My friends were the only family I had. Anything I did that was to protect the safety or solidarity that I had with these certain individuals, of course, is something I've always been proud of, because I've risked my life, and they've risked theirs for me. That's what make me proud. Without their support, I probably wouldn't be sitting here talking to you today, because of the incidents that I've been involved in. But, in retrospect, you know, I'm also not proud of having gotten involved in it, because I should have had the intellect back then to separate myself from that type of environment that would have led me into the position I'm in today.

*So, you think it was avoidable to go down that path?*

Yeah, now that I have the education and understanding that I do now. At the time, when I was committed to it, I didn't have a clue as to the things I know now. But if I'd known then what I know now, of course, yes, it was a terrible mistake, a stupid mistake.

*Now, what could a child do in those circumstances who didn't have much family support? You say you were an only child, not living with your parents. You were in a bad neighborhood, a violent neighborhood. What better choices did you have at that time that you wish you had done instead of become involved with a gang?*

Well, number one is stay in school. As long as I committed my time to my academics, and focused on my intellectual skills and staying in school, of course, that would have led me down a path where I could have been attached to something that would have then geared me for higher education. And higher education would have carried me through high school and hopefully off to college, where I could have been in a productive area, rather than selecting my friends in the bad neighborhood in which I lived. Simply because I lived there, that didn't mean that that should have been an area that I hang around. I mean, I can live there, and hang around with people in another area that are committed to education. They're the type of people I should have surrounded myself with, rather than the violent and the gang members.

*Now, if you excluded yourself from the violent and the gang members, would that be safe for a child in that position in that neighborhood? Could you have survived if you didn't become part of the "in" group, part of the violent people?*

I don't know. That's a good question. There have been some survivors, of course. There have been some other ones that was not as fortunate. There are success stories of people that survived who didn't go down that road, or some that actually got involved but then backtracked and reversed into the direction of education, who are now successful. I mean, you know, you got the NFL, the NBA, various sports, certain scholarships, and they found their talent in the midst of realizing that this is the wrong path.

Yes, I could have survived. I mean, at the very least, you know, I could have encouraged my grandmother, say, "Look, we got to move away from here." Growing up in an environment with no family, just pretty much my grandmother who was ill and poor, we were kind of stuck there. But, I'm sure there were some opportunities there for her to find a way to separate and move out to areas where there wasn't as much violence.

So, yes, there were alternatives. It wouldn't have been strictly my decision, but I could have influenced her, because she would have heard me if I would have explained to her what I was going through.

*So you were living with your grandmother most of the time you were growing up?*

Yeah, she's who raised me.

*Was it just the two of you?*

Yeah, pretty much. You know, I seen my mother every couple years, and I had cousins that came around a lot, but it was pretty much the two of us.

*What happened with your parents? Why weren't they in the picture?*

Well, when I was born—I was actually born in Augusta, Georgia, right outside of Atlanta—my mom was wanted by the cops, and when she birthed me, I was born as a breech baby, and I remained in the hospital six months after I was born, and in that time, she disappeared, running from the cops. That's what placed me in the custody of my grandmother, who lived in LA. I didn't see my mother again until I was around eight years old.

*What was she wanted for?*

Well, everything that you could think of: drug dealing, promoting prostitution, robbery, you name it. She was an outlaw. And, my father ultimately started doing time for being her co-defendant, and I didn't see him until I was around ten, after he had served time in prison.

*Did you ever establish any kind of significant relationship with either of your parents?*

With my mother. After I got locked up, my father died in the process of coming up here for me to finally spend time with him for the first time. I mean, I had met him several times when he came for my birthdays, but if I add up all the time I spent with him over the years, it would probably equal out to be three days. I'd never spent more than two hours with him at one sitting.

As far as my mother, yeah, I spent a significant amount of time with her after she finally left the drugs alone. She actually at one point turned her life over to God. I was in her custody for a short time until I got out of control, and she ventured back into that lifestyle. And, we also established a relationship after I came to prison, but ultimately, she died while I was here, of a drug overdose. So, we never had a chance to reach that level of a proper mother and child relationship.

*At what time were you back in her custody?*

Well, when I was sixteen years old, I was back in her custody. I lived with her for maybe three or four months, and that's only because at the time I was in trouble, and my grandmother was really ill. She was in the hospital, and, of course, you're living with your grandmother like that, someone has to take custody of a child, and my mom tried to straighten her life out to accommodate me in her house, and her life.

But she couldn't fake it. She couldn't be the motherly figure that she wanted to be. She knew she couldn't handle it. She ventured out, and that left me pretty much by myself, and I went back to the same type of lifestyle that had led me into trouble.

*So, who failed first? I mean, when you went back into her custody briefly and she was trying to get her life in order, and had found religion, and was more or less sticking to the straight and narrow, or trying to, did you screw up and then that kind of put her over the edge, or did she screw up and then that kind of left you without any supervision, and you screwed up too? I mean, which came first?*

Yeah, which came first? She screwed up first. You know, it resulted from her getting married. She committed to a guy she had known for years. Actually, when she left my father, that's who she got involved with, and they got in trouble in Vegas and ventured up to Seattle.

He was in the criminal lifestyle, of course, so when she tried to do her thing—the straight and narrow—in the same household, he was still doing all the corrupt things. And I seen it.

Ultimately, she chose him over me. I mean, she pretty much put me in a position as, where, "Yeah, I know I didn't raise you like I should have. I know you're my only child. But, you're not going to cause disruption between me and my husband." And, I understood that. And, I told her, I explained to her, I said, "Hey, you know, I didn't ask to be brought into this world, so I'm going to make the best life for me, whatever I can, despite whatever you do. If you choose him over me, so be it." And I left.

The next time I saw my mother, it was behind bars when I was serving time for my murder.

*And she's passed away since then?*

Yeah, she passed away in Ninety-four. Drug overdose.

*And your father died when?*

My father died in Ninety, from cirrhosis of the liver, from drinking.

*And your grandmother that raised you, is she still alive?*

No, she died during the time of me going to trial, facing this murder charge. But she didn't have a clue what I was in jail for, or that I was even in jail. In fact, my mother actually lied to her, because we knew it would have broke her heart.

But I want to say that she raised me well. Anything wrong that I done stems from nothing she did. In fact, it was the opposite of anything she ever taught me. I was more worried about disappointing her than anything. That's why I didn't want her to know. And, she died without knowing that I was doing time, that I was in prison. All she knew was I up in Seattle.

*What did she die of?*

Well, she was on a respirator for a long period of time, because she had breathing problems. So respiratory illness is what resulted in her death. She had seizures as she grew up. She used to be an alcoholic.

But, she was pretty much straight and narrow. I mean, she broke no laws, committed no crimes, other than drinking alcohol. That was the only problem she ever had.

*When did you first get involved in crime?*

Well, I was involved with it quite a few times as a youngster, because of the people I was hanging around. I was pretty much an accessory to it.

I never had a feeling for it. I never did enjoy it. It was always, like, "That's not right," or if I see someone hurt, I'm, like, "Wow," you know, "That's wrong," except when they were causing a threat to me or the people I'm closest with. But ultimately, going out and offensively creating problems, that was something I never felt strongly about. But, then, obviously, to hang around the fringe of those that was actively involved in it made me a part of it, made me an accessory to it, even though I never liked it.

Our way of having fun was committing crimes. But, I always had a belief within myself that as long as I didn't actively participate, then I can wake up tomorrow morning and feel comfortable with today, because, hey, I violated none of my morals. You know, I felt OK.

But even so, there were some things that I would actually question my even being around them, being a part of at all. But I was in a position where I couldn't do anything about them; I couldn't prevent them from happening if I tried. If I had made an effort to stop them from happening, that could have resulted in me losing my life. So, I was in a terrible position there.

*If you didn't enjoy it, then why were you involved in it?*

Well, once I had made a commitment to the 90s, or the people I associated with, there was a rule, like, "Once you get in, you couldn't get out," and you'd be construed as a traitor or someone that would be detrimental to what they represented if you tried to leave. But, I felt that, OK, if I was to be a part of this, I still wouldn't be active in some of the things they did. Unfortunately, that still made me a part of a lot of things that happened that bothered me. But I just kept my mouth shut; that was pretty much the way I was raised, and I've been taught.

And in the end, it resulted in me heading right down that same road that they were on, doing what they were doing. Didn't want to do it, didn't even like seeing it, but ended up doing it myself.

*You say you can't really get out once you're in. So, even if you don't leave as a traitor in the sense of jumping to another gang, or going to the police as an informant, or something like that, even if you just voluntarily stop being a member, you're saying even that is impossible.*

Well, yeah, in a sense. But maybe not so much any more, because, you know, this is a free country. If I had decided to get up one day, and my family could move me to another side of the earth, well, that's nothing nobody can do anything about, and then I'd be pretty much out.

But we didn't. We couldn't afford to do that, to move away, to separate ourselves from that. I was stuck in an environment where I pretty much didn't have too many choices, after I made that first wrong choice.

*So you couldn't just go to them and say, "I've changed my mind. I mean, I'm going to keep living in this neighborhood, and I'm not going to be a traitor to you guys or anything, but I just don't want to be a part of what you're doing any more. I'm going to live my own life, and go to school."*

That would be suicidal, because then they'd see you as weak, you know, "We're going to start treating you like the enemy then, because it you're not a friend, you're a foe." That's the attitude they have. If I was to try to disassociate myself from them, they'd think I'd adapted to the beliefs of everybody else that was so strongly against them, and meant them harm, and I'd have been treated like an outcast.

Living in the neighborhood as an outcast is not a very good thing in Los Angeles.

*So, it's worse than never having been in it at all.*

Yes, by far. By far. Because, once you sign on the dotted line, so to speak, you know, you're stuck with that contract for the rest of your life. That's a tail no one ever gets rid of as long as they live, except for a few that do the right things to go back and try to make an effort to teach guys not to get involved. You know, ex-members who return to try to teach young people about positive alternatives to the gang life. But that's really the only way that you can prevent that tail from following behind you anywhere you go in life.

*What age were you when you first became involved with a gang?*

Even at six or seven years old, my friends and I were a part of it, but I was probably eleven when I became actively involved. I officially became a member when I was thirteen.

*And when's the first time that you committed, or were an accessory to, a crime with a gang?*

[Laughs.] That's a good question. It was during that time period, between eleven and thirteen. In fact, it might be earlier than that. As far back as I can remember. Not even a teenager yet.

*What kind of crimes?*

Well, robbery, snatching purses, you know. Burglary, stuff like that. It was nothing with, like, violence involved, except when you'd snatch a purse, or hit somebody and take something they had on—snatch some gold jewelry. Those are pretty much what we did at that age.

Then, of course, you graduate to, like, selling drugs, or trafficking drugs, being involved with every part of the drug game. I was involved with that. Stealing cars. Those type of activities I was involved with.

*And, you say you really didn't enjoy it. How did you feel about these activities when you were engaging in them?*

Well, you know, after the fact, it didn't bother me, because then I was safe, and, "Hey, it's over with." But, in the process, you know, I was always the scared one. I mean, I'd rather rob than shoplift. That's how nervous I am. That's the kind of attitude that I've always had. Rather than going in and trying to sneak and do something—I'd just get too nervous. I'd give myself away. I'd rather just go in and say, "OK, I'm taking this!" and do it and run. That's the approach I have to a lot of different things.

But, as far as, like, going out, stealing cars and snatching purses, I was always the person behind the scenes, encouraging someone, "Snatch it and I'll pave the way for you, and we'll run." I never had the guts to actually do it myself, because I was worried about the consequences and the repercussions.

But, mostly, I think I was worried about disappointing my grandmother. That was the thing that, actually, was always sitting in the back of my mind—disappointing her, because I know she taught me better. So, I was the manipulative one.

*I'm surprised that you can remain so much on the periphery of these activities as a member of a gang, especially early on when you have to prove yourself. So, you're saying that you weren't personally doing much of anything that was violent or criminal, but you were just sort of around, on the fringes, when other people were doing it. How did you get away with that? Why weren't you expected to do whatever violence is necessary to get the job done?*

Well, say for instance, you're in a fight at school, and there's, like, five on five. I mean, you could be the one that's rooting everybody else on, but after the fight is over, you would say, "Yeah, did you see me hit the guy over the head with the books?" "No, I didn't see it," but, hey, we was all there, and they seen you there, so they don't know any better.

But, now, that was at a young age when I avoided doing a lot. But as I grew up, as I became fifteen, sixteen, I couldn't stand on the sidelines any more. But even then, it was pretty much a defensive thing. I mean, it wasn't like I was going out to create, like most of them were. I was now actively involved, but not to the extent that I was going out creating it.

You know, I'd be at a party, and some of my friends would initiate something, and there'd be an outburst. And that would put me right in the middle of it, down in the trenches, involved with everyone else. But I was always leery of going out and creating or instigating something like that, because I knew, not only could I lose my life, but I could also lose someone else of value to me. And I wasn't even as worried about something happening to me any more; I was more or less worried about what I'd have to do to somebody.

You know, being a small guy, there's always that challenge. Even when it ain't a challenge, you see it as that. And there's the thing that I not only have to represent myself as a man, but I have to represent myself as a gang member. If I was huge, or a big guy with muscles—I feel like a lot of those guys never get approached and never get, you know, provoked. But as a smaller guy, someone that everybody feel they can take advantage of, that is what got me involved in a lot of different incidents that I wish I had never been involved in. I'm just fortunate I'm alive today to speak about it. Came out on top, so far.

*At what age did you first start carrying a weapon?*

Fourteen.

*Knife? Gun? What?*

Gun. I mean, I've always had a knife, you know, a little pocket knife. I always wanted to be a little Cub Scout type. My uncle gave me a knife when I was little, but I carried it around as a showcase rather than as a weapon, because I knew the guns were the one. I couldn't take a knife to a gun fight. I mean, everyone else carried guns simply as neutralizers.

My first gun that was given to me was a thirty-eight. A friend of mine, who's now dead, he gave it to me, because he was worried about some of the things that were going on at that time in LA. He suggested to me, "Maybe you'll need this."

I used to be afraid of guns, growing up. I always thought that just picking one up, it might go off.

Then, I think I became attached to it, because I felt safe with one in my possession. It came to where I couldn't go anywhere without one. That's how I went from not liking them, or being afraid of them, to loving them.

*Did you carry a gun all the time after that?*

All the time. Didn't go anywhere without one. A lot of times, I took one to school.

*Was that fairly common in that area?*

Oh yeah.

*A lot of people had a gun all the time?*

Yeah. And it wasn't even so much being worried about threats to me, but a lot of people—and on some occasions, I have this attitude—have the mentality that you ain't hip unless you got a gun.

*A status kind of thing.*

Status, yeah. You're a gun carrier, then, hey, you're a lead guy. You're the one that people recognize, or are going to have to recognize.

It used to be, someone stepped on your shoe, and you're just, like, "What are you doing, man!?" But now, it's, "Step on my shoe, hey, I'll blow your head off!" It skips over the whole process and takes it straight from Point A to Point Z. There's no reason to argue any more. There's no reason to fight. You just settle it with your gun.

If I approach you in the alley, and you give me some type of response that's aggressive, hey, I hope you got a gun. 'Cause I got one. That's the attitude.

But, even when I acted first, I still felt like I was pretty much on the defensive. I would act first, simply because I was worried about being second, being too slow to react. You know, knowing that if I let him act first, it might be too late for me to react.

Because you could see the violence in their face. I've gotten used to it. You can see it, especially when you know this person has got a reputation for doing a lot of violence. If I knew that I would be nothing compared to the victims he's already caused, then in prevention of me being a victim, I'd know that I had to make him one before I allow myself to be one.

That was my approach to a lot of it. But that's the LA approach with every gang member that speaks honestly to you. That's what it is.

*Now, do you have to be willing to threaten with a gun to let him know that you're capable of protecting yourself, or do you have to actually shoot somebody in that situation?*

Well, it's a common rule that you never pull out a gun unless you actually use it, because you put somebody else in a position now to where the next time they see you, they going to use theirs.

But I've done both. I've used it to threaten, pretty much, like, "Hey look, you don't get away from me, this is what I'll do." But I try to avoid that. Because if I pull it out, that's just a common rule. That's just an automatic rule. If I don't use it, tomorrow when I see him, he will use his. He going to blow me away. And, I can't run from everybody in the town that's looking out for me, and I don't want to have to go out looking for this guy to eliminate him, simply because of what he's capable of doing to me.

*So, we've advanced past the knife stage on the streets. It's kind of pointless carrying a knife any more. Everybody's got guns now.*

Oh yeah, unless you're going out to the woods, or going camping. That would be the only reason. A knife is unheard of.

*How old were you the first time you shot someone?*

First time I shot someone. OK, now, that's a good question, because I really don't know. I've been in positions where I got a gun and am in the middle of a shootout at a drug house, and people got shot. But I couldn't tell if any of my shots hit them.

But the one that I actually know for sure that I hit, I was fifteen. The first one that I intentionally shot, that I know I shot.

*Tell me what happened and how you felt about it at the time.*

Ha, yeah, that was one that was an incident that started from a party. I was dating this female, this former girlfriend of this guy that belonged to another gang and was a huge drug dealer I knew about all of my life.

He winds up going to jail. He was significantly older than me, too, and she was about seven years older than me as well, but she liked me. I got involved with her, while he was gone in jail. She was pretty much nothing but a sex toy, and she was gorgeous and all my friends liked her. We were together for a few months.

He, of course, eventually got out of jail. He beat the crime, and he got out of jail. Well, some of his friends had been explaining to him that, "Hey, look, 9-0 has been fucking your bitch," and he put her on the spot where she's, like, got to choose.

Well, of course, she made it look like it was all my fault, "Hey, I'm in love with you. Yeah, you know, he was doing this, doing that," so, there was no way for me out of it. I mean, I could go to him, say, "Hey, she's lying," but, of course, he would have believed her first.

But he knew that I knew that they were involved. If I hadn't known, he might have let it go, like, "Hey man, you know, you were doing no differently than any other guy would that think this lady was single." But he knew that I knew she wasn't single. So it was, like, "Hey, you knew this was my woman when you did this. You took advantage of me when I wasn't around."

So I and a few guys went to a skating rink one night, and him and several of his friends, their intention was pretty much to bum rush us, to attack us. But, I knew about it in advance. I found out about it.

*So, his group, his gang, was going to ambush you and your friends.*

Yeah. They was going to come in, pretty much to beat us up. There was no intent, I don't think, to kill us, because only one of them I knew for sure had a gun.

But, I found out about it, what they was planning on doing that night, through a girlfriend of his girlfriend, who told me what their intent was. So, when they arrived, I was waiting for them. My friends were on the inside; I was still on the outside.

I shot him. I was drunk, and it was actually my intent to destroy him. Because, I knew that just by shooting him, he'll be back tomorrow. And next time, rather than coming to look for me to fight, he going to be looking to kill me.

See, a situation like that, by me shooting him caused a big uproar between his gang and the gang I grew up around, because it looked like we now have a big problem between our gangs. That was a small incident that escalated into something to make rivals out of two Crip gangs. But that's the kind of scenario that happens a lot. Little things get taken to that level many times.

*Give me more details about when you shot him. What was the situation?*

Well, it was a Friday night, around one o'clock in the morning. You know, I was drunk. He was high class, you know, the nice cars, all the money, the jewelry. Sitting out front, waiting for him to come, I had been drinking. I don't drink, but I was drinking just to get my adrenaline to flow, and to have the nerve to approach the situation.

When I shot him, I actually aimed toward his head, but I ended up wounding him in the shoulder blade, and through the shoulder and the neck.

*Were you hiding somewhere?*

Yeah, there was, like, several cars on the side of the building, and I was beside the cars. And, it was dark, so no one saw me or could make out who I was if they did see me. I was leaning up on a car when I seen him drive up. I knew in order to go in the skating rink, they had to come around the front and walk past me. So, I stayed on the side of the car waiting for him, then I called him out.

He didn't hear me; his buddy heard me. "Somebody's calling you." And then, of course, he couldn't really see me in the dark. I don't think he knew it was me. He asked me, "What's up?" and I said, "I need to talk to you."

"Who is this guy?" he says, "Who is that?" I said, "Hey, you know who it is." And, he walks toward me, and I said, "You got a problem with me?" and I approached him with the gun.

He said, "What are you talking about?" I don't know what I would have done if he would have said, "Hey, look, man, look, I ain't got no problem." But, I knew what his intent was whatever he said, so really, rather than take any chance for his friends to go in their pockets or anybody to pull out a gun to blow me away, I had to act first. So I pulled the trigger.

*You were with your friends?*

Well, I was with my friends, but I was outside at the scene by myself. They were inside.

*Why were they inside, instead of out there with you?*

Well, because I knew that, you know, growing up in LA, even though this is just us two people, really the whole gangs almost are involved. So, it was my understanding that some of his friends would have probably been in that skating rink to call him on the telephone and say either we're down there or we're not. So I needed my friends to be inside, just pretty much as a decoy, so his friends would see them. Because if they had told him, "No, they ain't here," he probably wouldn't have committed himself to coming down.

*How many people were with this guy when he got out of his car?*

It was two other people.

*Just three guys?*

Three guys total.

*Three guys were going to be enough to beat up your whole group?*

Well, I mean, not so much the whole group. It was just the people I was with. He knew the common group that I hang around with was two other people, pretty much my best friends. So, he knew how many to expect.

*I was picturing bigger groups. So, really you were just two groups of three.*

Yeah, just groups of three.

You know, but they was going to come in, and they knew if they beat me up, they got to beat the other two up, because that is the ritual. If I go down, we all go down. That's the attitude with all gang members in LA. With anybody I'm associated with or I hang out with or I go places with, that's our pretense. When one go, we all go.

*Now, when you shot him, why didn't the two people with him retaliate?*

Well, for one, I would have blew them away. I mean, I'm drawn down on them, finger on the trigger with the gun cocked, and they knew that all they got to do is buzz and I'm going to blow them too. Because they had nothing in their hands, so they would have had to reach.

What they should have done if they was smart, they should have came prepared. But they was planning on going in the club, and they couldn't have nothing in their hand when they walk in; you got to have it disguised. So, when I aimed at him, you know, they were there too. And, of course I told them, "Don't go for anything!"

*Now why didn't you feel you were just digging yourself in deeper by shooting this guy, just making it escalate? Because now you've got the two guys he was with, and the rest of his gang for that matter, who are all going to be trying to kill you.*

Everybody else, yeah. And that's pretty much what resulted. I mean, I knew that. But I also knew that my gang had my back. I knew that I was well protected with them. I mean, just by my being willing to stand up to that guy that night, all I had to do was go back to my neighborhood, and the word would have got out, they would have known, like, "OK, now the 90s is having problems with the Golden 30s, and this is what it's all about."

Now, we were well recognized, one of the three top gangs recognized in LA, so they'd know that in order to deal with me, hey, man, you're going to deal with all of us, and risk losing a hell of a lot.

But, then before it went any farther, the word came out that it was all about a female. That is what watered it down a little bit, because, it ultimately got other people involved, and they said, "Man, you mean to tell me you're going to try to take advantage of a young guy, simply because he fucked your bitch, and you're going to go out there and cause some problems with this?"

That's ultimately what pretty much saved me, or part of what did. So, fortunately, it ended up resolving itself.

# 9—September 1998

*"And my reaction—and this was my common reaction when I was in this kind of danger—was, 'Hell, if I die, I die.' Just ready to accept the loss of my life. And, as I've grown up, I've come to realize that that was probably the most—no, it was the most—stupidest thing I ever thought, but that was my attitude."*

9 and I resumed our conversation at the next PAP meeting.

*Last time, we mostly were talking about your childhood experiences, and your early criminal career. And, you told me of the first time that you shot somebody with the intention of killing them—though you didn't actually kill him on this occasion, is that correct?*

That's correct.

*You tried to,—*

Yeah.

*—and struck him where? In the neck?*

Yeah.

*Was he seriously wounded, or it just grazed him, or what?*

Oh, it was serious. Not to the degree where he was, like, in the hospital paralyzed, or nothing like that. Rather than breaking any ligaments, it, like, went through muscle. It was on the left side of his neck, and it pierced right through.

But I wasn't aiming at his neck. I was aiming at his head. Just a bad shot.

*Now, did he go down when he was hit, or—?*

Oh, he went down. He backed up, grabbed his neck, went up against the wall, and slid down the wall. And, I had the opportunity to walk up and kill him, because his friends that was with him dispersed, and—

*Oh, so they weren't standing there frozen.*

No, they—

*They had taken off.*

Yeah, they just dispersed. Actually, I gave them an opportunity to get away.

*Oh, OK.*

If they would have stood there acting like they were going to go for weapons, which I'm sure they probably had, I would have blown them away, simply because I was afraid for my life, more so than I was afraid of doing something to them. But they dispersed.

*Now, if you had intended to kill him coming in, then why didn't you shoot him a second time?*

I wasn't looking to actually murder him. I mean, I wasn't. I've always believed that it really takes a sick individual to commit murder, unless there's some justifiable reason to commit it, like to save your own life.

I really wasn't even enemies with him. I mean, I had no grudge against him, only that I knew he wanted to do something to me.

I felt that because I was under a threat, I was allowing myself to shoot him, and if it would have killed him, so be it. But when I realized that he wasn't dead, and he'd gotten my point, I felt like I could be safe once I got back to my neighborhood. That was my thought at the time.

*So, you didn't feel that by wounding without killing him, that you'd just be creating an even more bitter enemy who'd have reason for revenge.*

Only because I knew I was under the security of my neighborhood. Even though I know that's an insidious thing to think, but that's the logic I used at the time. My friends told me I should have killed him. But it wasn't my intent to actually go out and kill this guy, not over a female. That's what the bottom line was all about. And, I think that is what discouraged me from actually doing it. Now, if he would have actually done some harm to me, and I felt bitter about that, then, of course, I probably would have had no problem doing it. But behind a female, I didn't think it was worth it.

*So, you did not feel that your neighborhood would protect you if you didn't shoot the guy.*

No,—

*You're saying only if you shoot him and at least wound him, then they'll rally behind you and—*

Well, yes—

*—protect you from his and his gang's revenge.*

Right. You know, because I would have been viewed as a coward or someone not worthy enough to be a part of that group or fraternity if I had wanted them to protect me without first confronting him myself. But by knowing that I was serious business, that I was seriously able to represent what we all represent, I've shown enough to warrant their support.

Anytime someone from a certain area go out and represent something to show the strength of their neighborhood, you're doing your duty. Even though my reasons were selfish reasons, you know, they understood the reason why I done it, and gave me that support, and let him know that if he even come near me or come touch me, then there's going to be hell to pay.

And I knew that was going to come about. That's probably the reason I didn't kill him after I had wounded him.

*You mentioned last time that you were not any kind of a big drinker, but on this occasion, you felt you needed to be under the influence of alcohol to build up your courage to do this.*

Yeah.

*Talk about that. What was it about shooting him that required you to have alcohol?*

Well, I remember my thoughts. I mean, I used to have some of the stupidest thoughts, and I had them frequently. Knowing what I was about to be around, and the people that I was about to be around, I knew what was capable of happening in this situation. And my reaction—and this was my common reaction when I was in this kind of danger—was, "Hell, if I die, I die." Just ready to accept the loss of my life. And, as I've grown up, I've come to realize that that was probably the most—no, it was the most—stupidest thing I ever thought, but that was my attitude.

But, now, I was nervous, is the reason why I drank. I mean, I felt by getting drunk, I would be calm, you know, I wouldn't be so nervous. A nervous reaction is usually a late reaction, and I didn't want to get caught in that predicament.

And it was also my conscience, I think. I think I wanted to water down my conscience to where it wouldn't bother me as much to pull the trigger to blow this guy away. If I was sober enough to think rational, I might not be able to do it.

*So you think you were nervous both about your own physical safety and about the moral act of shooting another person?*

Yeah. My physical safety, and the moral act.

Plus, I knew I was in a lot of danger of getting caught. It was in an area that I knew was going to be crowded, so I knew that once I did it, they automatically are going to know who done it. And there I'd be, headed for jail.

But I was damned if I did and damned if I didn't. If I don't shoot him, then I'll be viewed by everybody as the coward, and my neighborhood would think that I just embarrassed them all by not doing what I should have done. So I felt I had to go through with it.

And, the alcohol is what, like, put me in a position to be able to say, "Well, hell, you know. Have no feelings. Just come out and do whatever you have to do, and, in the end, you can blame it on the alcohol."

So, I think I did it to calm my nerves, and to water down what I was really feeling.

*When the effects of the alcohol wore off, did the emotions kick in? Did you feel a certain fear in retrospect of what you put yourself into, or did you feel any conscience kick in, or what happened?*

I think it was both. I think there was fear, because, for one thing, I didn't know if he was going to live or die. I mean, I imagined he would be going to the hospital, but I didn't know what condition he was in. I knew I shot him in the neck, but not really if it was through the throat or not.

I was worried, because I knew, from that point, I couldn't just go hang out or go where I wanted to without always watching my back and, you know, observing everybody, because they knew who I was, and I could have been a target. But, I made it be known to everybody in my neighborhood what I had done, which they had already found out as soon as I done it by phone calls anyway.

But, you know, it's just an ordinary thing that happens in that lifestyle. I mean, it was one of three incidents that happened that same day.

But the thing that weighed down my mind afterwards is—I've always had the conscience to think, "Where am I headed? What am I doing? Why am I even doing this? What will be the cost?" This was something I didn't want to be a part of any more at that point, because I was worried about disappointing my grandmother. Because, like I said, she taught me far better than that. I think I was more worried about her than anything, knowing that she was ill, and knowing how she worried about me. I mean, if she seen me with a scratch on my hand, she'd almost faint. So, I could imagine if she heard something like this. She would just, like, be totally depressed.

I don't know. I think all of it affected my feelings about what I'd done.

*You mentioned that this was one of three incidents?*

Well, yeah. It could have been more. But that particular day, I remember two other violent acts involving friends of mine that got into several shootings, like one at another club. Rival gangs, you know, gang-related incidents. So, that was common in California.

*So, this really was nothing out of the ordinary.*

No, it was not out of the ordinary. The only thing that was maybe out of the ordinary was that these things all happened on one day, rather than, you know, spaced apart more.

But, I remember that day, you know, that while I was mostly worried about myself and what I had gotten myself into, I'm also meanwhile worried some other people that got caught in some situations that they didn't want to be a part of.

But, it's a frequent thing, especially when you're young—and all of us were young—it's almost like, that's your ambition, to go out, get caught up in something, and represent. Let everybody know what you're about. You know, it's almost like flexing your muscles.

*Now, what are you going to say to people who stereotype black people, or poor people, or poor black people, that hear your story, and will say—it'll just confirm their opinion—that "Jeez, these young black kids. They're like animals. They're just off killing each other. They have no morals."? Or, "It's ordinary for them to be shooting each other; they have no respect for life," and all that? How do you respond to people who are going to draw that kind of racist conclusion from what you're saying?*

You know, if I was to stand before those type of people and they brought up the same question you just brought up to me, I couldn't ask them to understand, because they would have to live there and experience those areas themselves. I mean, it's almost like asking someone that hasn't ever been locked up before how to understand doing time. That's impossible.

But, what they do have to understand is that young people that grow up in those areas usually, a lot of times, don't have any choice. They're put under great pressure. I mean, that's where peer pressure's at its highest. And, usually, the situation that you're placed in in those areas is where you have to choose to be a part of them, or you almost have to choose to be away from them entirely. I mean, if you don't choose to be with them, you pretty much have to relocate. You have to be able to afford to be elsewhere.

But, if you choose to be a part of them, hey, you're accepted, you're protected. Now you're just one of the family.

But, rather than just stereotype people like that, and automatically assume that, "Hey, this is the only thing he knows. It's a common trend among black people," consider the situation that he was in as he grew up, as I explained for my situation. A lot of times, it's not his choice. It's something that he had to do in order to survive. Or he'd be another statistic. A young dead black man parked in the cemetery somewhere that probably couldn't even afford a funeral.

But, a mistake is only a mistake until you're old enough to know better. Then, it's a bad decision. And, until he become an adult and mature, only then if he still show them same traits that he learned to survive back then, then he deserve to be stereotyped, because now he has the knowledge to know better, to be a better person. But, if he shows that he's able to mature above that, think back, and learn from his mistakes, then give him a chance. Because, not only would he try to prove to you that he earned that chance, I think he'll be more or less trying to prove it to himself, to work, to show exactly how far he's come.

So I'd say, don't be so quick to judge those people, simply because of the areas they were raised, or the people they're around.

*Are the people who can turn their life around after that kind of upbringing the rare exceptions, or is it fairly common that people can mature and grow up and have decent values after going through that terrible kind of childhood in that kind of neighborhood?*

You know, that's a good question, and I can only answer that question as a matter of opinion. I've seen it both ways. I don't know which one happen more, which one happen less.

But, I compare it to a person that's doing a lot of time in prison, and getting out, and expected to be a productive part of society. It all depend on what he did during that time while he was incarcerated. It's the same as what that person learned as he grew older, being a part of that lifestyle. If he adjusted to what is best for him, and figured out a goal and aimed for it, and did what he had to do to get to that point, then, yes, it happens a lot.

There is a lot of athletes that's actually gang members. I mean, ESPN highlights a lot of it with all different sports. I mean, hey, there's ex-gang members that have Super Bowl, and NBA Championship rings. And some actually have become educated growing up in the projects and become doctors. And other people too, but they were given a chance. And—

*But not all pro athletes have turned their life around. Some of them are just rich criminals now, instead of being poor criminals in the ghetto. They have—*

You're absolutely—

*—Super Bowl rings, but they also have the same morals they had when they were fifteen.*

You're absolutely right. But what I measure is a person turning their life around once they're given a chance. Most gang members are never really given a chance. If someone live that lifestyle, people usually don't give him a chance, because they figure it would be a waste of time. But once given a chance, then that's my measure of success, because that's all I really ask for for myself. And if I fail, then, hey, I had my chance.

But, that's what I measure as someone has turned their life around: being in a position where they have an opportunity to change and then taking advantage of that.

*So, if you had the opportunities, if there are people who've tried to help you, or you have the wealth based on your athletic success or whatever it might be, and you still don't turn your life around, then you're worse than the fellow who never had a chance.*

Exactly.

*So, Mike Tyson is more reprehensible to you than a fellow who's still stuck in the ghetto and never really had any opportunity at all.*

Exactly. Exactly.

I mean, it's the same as the parole board. Some people are given opportunities to show they've changed and some aren't. There's people that got horrendous beefs and that's getting out. And there's guys that turned their life around ten years ago that can't get a chance, like Jerry McLaughlin, for one.

I mean, yeah, you know, when you get a chance and don't take advantage of it, you're worse than the person that never got it.

Give that opportunity to someone that is going to take advantage of it, and might put himself in a position to come back to help the next person out, to give somebody else a chance. But, when you get out and you abuse that opportunity, when you get out and get caught up in your same situation again, you're making it less likely that the next guy will ever get the opportunity you just got. You're destroying people's faith that a person in that position can turn his life around.

That's why I appreciate it when someone gives me an opportunity, and I want to respond in such a way that they'll be encouraged to come back and help someone else out. I don't want people to lose faith in us because of what one of us does.

*Now, you mentioned the option of leaving that kind of neighborhood entirely, that if a family maybe has enough money to escape, they can move to more of a middle class area, or at least some place that's not totally entrenched in gang warfare and such. How are people who take advantage of that opportunity perceived by the people who are left behind? Is that kind of family seen as cowards, or traitors to their neighborhood, traitors to their race?*

No, not really. I mean, the youngsters probably would view it that way. But the elders would say, "Hey, man, good luck."

I mean, see, the thing with gangs in these areas in LA that's not shown in the media is that some of those families in those neighborhoods see the gangs as being in the role of police. They see the gang as protecting the neighborhood and not allowing nobody to come over there to do nothing to them. You know, because the actual cops don't fill that role. When they come to the neighborhood, they probably do more damage than anyone.

That's the way some of those elders view it, so they actually support a lot of the gang members. "Hey, this is our neighborhood. This is what we defend. It's our turf." The same as all countries protect their territory.

*That's interesting, because that's the way organized crime is perceived in a lot of white, ethnic neighborhoods. That's how the Mafia is seen. People know they have to be careful and respectful around them, that they're dangerous and everything, but, in a sense, they're protecting the neighborhood. You know, they provide some order and stability to the neighborhood, and they keep outsiders from doing any harm. So, they're sometimes seen in a semi-positive way, the way you're describing with the gangs. Maybe mainstream society is less inclined, as outsiders, to understand that in black neighborhoods, they can perceive gangs the same way that the Mafia is seen in some white neighborhoods.*

Right. And, you know, the only thing the media shows is the violence, the murders, and the stuff like that. But what they don't show is the fact that a lot of those same people give back to those communities, give back to those neighborhoods, and look out for those families. I mean, to an extent, they're accepted and respected for whatever reason. Yeah, there's a bad side, but there's a bad side to everything.

But, you know, to view someone who leaves as a traitor—someone that gets out to go and find help elsewhere—no, not all people would see you that way. I mean, you'd probably be viewed that way by some, but what do you care? You're gone anyway. These are people you don't plan or hope to see again in your life. These are the people that you're running away from. What do you care what they think?

*So, are these typically the only options available to a family in that kind of neighborhood? You can either try and escape, if you've got the financial wherewithal, or you have to adapt to the lifestyle and join a gang, and seek that kind of protection and that kind of acceptance from your peers? Is there any alternative? Can you be strong, can you be independent, can you—?*

Yes.

*—be respected without joining the gang, without joining that lifestyle?*

Yeah. I mean, it's possible. You can. It happens. I mean, you know, just because one person grows up a gang member, that don't mean that his father or his brother who also lived in that neighborhood did as well.

There were people that was viewed as, you know, elders that we respected that actually preached against gangs. In a church, say, an adult would come up and preach on how bad the gangs are—preach to the gang members. And they respect that. Because, he's entitled to his opinion.

Yeah, you can be strong. They have to see some other opportunity, you know. Like, they got rap artists now. A lot of gang members, or people who would have been gang members, have actually shown their talent through rap music. A lot of it is out of control, and I'm not a big rap fan, but they've found ways to get involved in the system, to make the money, to make it work for them, and then to give back to the community.

So, rather than going and doing drive-bys, hey, make a tape, see if we can get it on wax and make some money off of it. Those are some of the strategies that, you know, people are getting themselves involved in. Even, professional fighting, and sports like I mentioned, and stuff like that. Those are other opportunities.

*Now, you mentioned that prior to the incident where you shot the guy in the neck, you had been involved in other gunfights, but you had no way of knowing for sure if any of your bullets had actually struck anybody.*

Yeah.

*You had been in group situations where gunfire's being exchanged. Tell me about that.*

Well, one time, we were at the movies, and, it was, like, a Friday or Saturday night—I can't remember. And I was young. I couldn't have been no more than thirteen, fourteen then, but I was hanging around people that was older than me, like, sixteen or so. And I had a gun, even at that young age—though now, they're carrying them at ten and eleven.

But, this one in particular that I remember, we were at the movies—Greek Theater in LA. I was standing with a few females, talking with some of them, and there were a bunch of guys around. And some people walked up.

Now, when you go to a movie, you're ending up there with Crips; you're ending up there with Bloods. You don't know who you're in line with. This is a theater that's located on the outskirts, away from anybody's neighborhood, so you're subject to run across any rival gang.

And, we ran into a few. I had a couple friends who, of course, any time they see someone that's from a rival gang, they always got to be the vocal ones. See, I can keep my mouth shut, just ignore them like they don't exist, but when groups get around each other, they end up flexing their muscles to let them know, "Hey, fuck your set! My set's bad!" I mean, especially when you're around women; it's almost like an ego check. You're going to stand up, you know, like most men do, and represent yourself accordingly, or look weak in front of those females.

So, it turned into a shouting match or an argument, and then, of course, fights break out, women get pushed. One of my buddies got into a fist fight with one of them. He beat him up, knocked him up against the wall.

Well, what we didn't know was that one of them had got away, and come back. We were busy focusing on the fight, but then we looked back, and I heard people say, "He got a gun!" So, we scattered. Everybody went to our cars where we had left our guns, reached up under the seat or went in the trunk and got our guns out.

It turned into a big old shoot-out. Everybody shooting, everybody targeted. I mean, windows were shot out of cars, people hiding behind cars, people gunning after them. Some people got shot. Even a couple of guys I was with got shot. One got shot in the leg. One got shot in the shoulder.

But, it was wild. All you know is that you got whatever gun you can get your hands on, and you're aiming at a target, and these guys are shooting at you and you're unloading at them.

Now, some of their guys got shot, but how can I say if I'm the one that shot them or it's the other people in my group who shot them?

But there's been a number of incidents where I've been involved with gang warfare. I can't always remember all the details that led up to it. All I know is I was there at a time when something erupted. It's usually something disrespectful said or done.

And, it's not fighting any more. First thing you do, you pull out a gun. Or, he pulls one out, you draw down. It just turn into a shooting. One guy might shoot and duck, run, and somebody be chasing after him, shooting him. Retaliation.

*Was that the first time that you ever fired a gun at another human being?*

The first time I ever fired a gun at another human being, I think I was twelve and a half. That's the first time I actually fired at someone.

A friend of mine—Cedric[*]—he had a thirty-eight. It actually was the first gun I ever shot. He showed me how to use it, what to do with it. It was his gun. He used to go outside in his backyard and just, like, shoot in the air. I was scared, because I was worried about what it was going to do to me—knock me down—how powerful it was, how loud it was. I was afraid of guns when I was younger.

And, it's almost as if, when I got this gun, and I started shooting it for the first time, I felt what it's capable of doing. I felt powerful. I felt like I could be in control, and not worried about anything.

Due to my size, I'm always confronted with situations that I have to defend myself against getting beat up. I mean, somebody always feel like they can bully you, and I've always suffered that as a kid, growing up. Everybody was bigger than me. "Fuck him!" you know, "I'll push you down!" and, I went through that a lot at a young age.

But, at one point, I realized I wasn't going to put up with that any more. Having this gun compensated everything that I lacked when I was young. So, I knew this was something I always needed.

The first time that I shot at a person, I was not quite thirteen, I don't think. I was maybe twelve and a half. It was in front of a grocery store.

I was shooting at him, but I wasn't actually shooting at him. I was just trying to scare him. Then, my friend told me who he was, and how "that son of a bitch" was somebody he was looking for anyway. "Shoot him!" he says, and I shot at him.

Stupid kid. Twelve and a half. Didn't know any better. Looking at it now—I'm twenty-nine—stupid as fuck. But—

*So, you were shooting at him before you even knew who he was?*

---

[*]I have changed the name.

Yeah. [Laughs.] I mean, you know, aiming at a person, trying to scare him. It was dark, about eight o'clock at night.

*Just as a kind of prank?*

Just a kind of prank. But then, the guy that was teaching me how to shoot, knew who he was and recognized him. "Ain't that such-and-such? That son of a bitch! Hey you!" And he looked, and spotted us. "Shoot him!" So, I'm shooting at him.

That was my first experience ever shooting at a guy. I probably shot everything around him but him.

*But you were actually trying to hit him.*

I was trying. [Laughs.] I was trying.

*How far away were you?*

Maybe fifteen yards, twenty yards. I'm not good at measurements, you know, but, about fifteen, twenty yards. A maximum twenty-five. I could see everything he had on. I seen his eyes and mouth open, so it was close enough that I should have been able to hit him.

*What goes through your head? I mean, I know you were just a kid at twelve and a half, but what goes through your head, to pull the trigger and actually try and shoot somebody you don't even know?*

I don't know. I think it's the affection of being accepted by somebody you really respect. That's what I think it was. I knew this is one person that's going to go back and tell some of the people that I really looked up to, "Hey, this is a tough guy here, man." I mean, just the feeling of being accepted I think is what I enjoyed the most.

But then, you know, as I grew older, of course, I looked back and thought, "How could I even think some bullshit like that?" But, it took a lot of travesty in my life to actually come to that. But, I remember at that time, I knew that's something I wanted to identify with, because people appreciated me.

*And it's strong enough even to take the life of a stranger.*

Yeah. I mean, I wasn't considering the consequences at that time. I didn't even know of any consequences. I thought it would be hip to be accepted by these guys. If they talk highly of you, hey, everybody else will recognize you too. Identity crisis, I think I was suffering from as a kid. I was an only child, and these were the only people that I knew, so automatically I just wanted to fit in. And I thought that was the way.

*Is there much awareness, political awareness, within a community like that, in terms of people kind of standing up and saying, "How come we're shooting each other? How come our anger and our violence is directed inward, toward each other, toward our own community?" I mean, why is so much of the violence self-inflicted in that kind of neighborhood?*

You know, that's a common question I hear all the time, especially since I've been locked up. Everybody here know where I'm from, and the area that I'm associated with. That's a question I've been faced with year after year after year.

I don't know that there's so much political awareness, but, then again, yeah, there is some. We have, like, Representative of California Maxine Waters in Congress, you know. Or Jim Brown, who, of course, is a famous NFL star, but he's an advocate of all these different programs.

They walk the community, and they have different programs to stop the shooting, and they deliver the message, you know, that black-on-black crime ain't the answer, it's nothing but genocide. We're doing nothing but killing each other. Your brother shouldn't be your enemy, you know. This is something they always preach.

And, for the longest time, I used to believe that my own people were my enemy. I mean, these are the people that you're surrounded by every day that's targeting you, beating up on you, abusing you, or doing something to somebody that you care about. The white man ain't coming to the neighborhood and shooting up my buddy, or shooting up my cousin, or doing anything to me. Why should I be treating him like he's my enemy? Or anybody else for that matter?. The people that inflict all the wounds and injuries on me is my neighbors, the people I'm surrounded by or I'm confronted with, the people I associate with, which is the blacks.

But, you know, the political advocates are out preaching now and showing you that stupidity is the reason why you're shooting at each other. Different trends have set in, like since the Rodney King incident. "Hey, look what the cops did to this guy! "Yeah, but you done no different to the brother that you done something to." And people start to see, and they start having, like, treaties.

There's a lot of people that's pushing away from the gangs, or that's working to stop a lot of the black-on-black violence.

Actually, the biggest problem now is the youngsters that can't let go, or that still want to be accepted like I was when I was a kid. But it's always up to the responsibility of the elder to stop it. It's our job to stop it, to stop the guys that came up after us. It's our responsibility. They can't think as maturely as we're able to now. When they get to our age, they'll be able to think that way, but right now, we're the only ones able to stop it.

Unfortunately, a lot of times the prominent people that's in those positions to speak out and tell about the problems, the youngsters or the gang members aren't going to listen to them anyway, because if they are able to listen, they probably would listen to their fathers and their parents, which they don't do. But someone they can closely associate with has the best chance of getting through to them.

But they're beginning to listen, because it's not as nearly as bad as it was not too long ago. They're gradually coming around.

Plus, you know, there's new laws coming out about gang-related activities. They got the RICO act, the gang task forces. In Washington, you get an additional five years if you were part of a gang when you committed the crime you did.

So people are either becoming afraid, or they're more aware, so it's decreasing.

But, you know, it's always going to be there. You're never going to get rid of that core. It can flourish one year; the next year, it can die down and be mellowed out.

But, yeah, people are aware.

*One thing that's puzzling, looking at gangs and gang warfare from the outside—I mean, sometimes I can understand why people are trying to kill each other. I'm not saying I agree with it, but at least I understand the differences between different groups. I understand the incompatibility, the hostility, between Christians and Jews, or Christians and Moslems, or, I don't know, rednecks and hippies, or even white and black—people from different backgrounds, different values, different lifestyles, different political causes, different ideologies. I understand why they're shooting at each other.*

*But what the hell's the difference between a Crip and a Blood?*

[Laughs.] Well, originally it was always just simply the Crips. The leader of the Crips—the person that actually created it back in the Sixties—he's on death row right now.

But, the Crips was always just one huge family, you know, that identified with the color blue. The name came from the fact that back then it was hip to walk with a cane—"cripple"—the same as you see some fraternities do today. The saggy clothes, you know, all that originated back then.

So at the time, there were always nothing but Crips; there were never no Bloods. Bloods came about as part of the Crip gangs that didn't believe, or trust, or agree with the things that other Crips did. Like, now, some of our biggest enemies is other Crips. So we treat them as Bloods. So, a Blood is the exact opposite of a Crip. I mean, if there's—

*So Blood is a splinter group from the Crips?*

Splinter group, yeah, that's what I was trying to say. That's what it originated from, like you said. There was the one party and then the second party came out of that. One believes one way; one believes the opposite. The people that don't agree any longer with the main group, of course, then they splinter off and become another group. Then the people that come along in the future, they have to choose which one to be a part of. This one or that one; it all depend on their beliefs.

It's really not so much beliefs, though—

*Yeah, is there any ideological difference? I mean, it sounds kind of arbitrary, like there wasn't much ideology behind the split. What are the actual ideas that are different between Crips and Bloods?*

Neighborhoods. Areas.

*Just geography?*

Bottom line, it's geography. I mean, they got some Crips and Bloods sets, like, the only thing separate them is one small street. I mean, like, if I sit on this side of the street, I'm in a Crip neighborhood; if I sit on the other side of that street—I'm in a Blood neighborhood. Everybody live on one side, it's all Crips; everybody live on the other side, it's all Bloods.

That's not always the case, though. You know, it's unfortunate but I once lived in a Blood neighborhood. So, I didn't spend much time at home. [Laughs.] But, you know, I once did, because, unfortunately, at the time that's where we were able to afford to live.

But, that's what it is. I mean, the high school you go to. Like, Crips only go to this high school; Bloods only go to that high school. That's how far out of hand it is. If you go to this high school, these are the people you associate with, these are the people you're around all day. You know who your enemy is, and if you're proud to be a part of this high school, and you're proud to be a part of this neighborhood, then we know what you represent, right? Of course, people identify with that.

*So, it's just kind of geographical coincidence? It doesn't sound like there's much to it.*

There isn't much to it.

*I mean, the reason, you know, communists and capitalists are shooting each other is because they have vastly different ideologies about society and about how things ought to be. What you're describing sounds more like Michigan versus Ohio State.*

Yeah, a rival and an arch-rival, you know.

*You just have a loyalty to your geographic entity—your college, your state, your city, your neighborhood, whatever it might be. I don't know, but to me, that seems like such a trivial difference to be killing each other over.*

There's a lot of other different personal reasons for a lot of different people, but yeah, that's the bottom line of what it's really about. As a whole, that's how it originated, as I explained to you. And just as you said, it's trivial. People didn't agree with the way the people represented themselves, or what they believed in, so they separated themselves.

And once you're separate, or once you walk away from the Crips, then, of course, you'll be treated as an enemy. So you might as well be one. So, they created a gang of their own—the Bloods. That way they know they're not going to be just a target. If you surround yourself with people that believe in the same things you believe in, then, hey, you got some defense, you got security against the Crips that's going to come after you for being an outcast.

*So, in your case, when you became a Crip, was there any choice involved? Did you have to sit down and say, "Gee, should I be a Crip or a Blood?" like choosing whether to vote Democrat or Republican?*

[Laughs.]

*Or is it just a matter of, "This is the neighborhood I live in, the high school I go to, therefore if I'm going to be anything, I'm a Crip"?*

I was fortunate, because, I was placed in a situation where the only people I was surrounded by was pretty much predominantly Crips. I was never in a situation where I was surrounded by Bloods to allow me that opportunity to have to decide. I was fortunate enough that I was surrounded by nothing but Crips, and I never had to compare the two. I mean, my friends were Crips. They were friends before they were anything.

*Why is it "fortunate" to not have a choice?*

[Laughs.] Well, you know, we know who's the more powerful, who's the most dangerous, who's—

*So, the Crips are the more powerful? They outnumber the Bloods? Bloods are just a smaller outcast group?*

There's a lot of them, but, yeah, Crips outnumber them, you know. Actually, the Mexicans outnumber us all down there in LA, but the Crips outnumber the Bloods.

But, when I say "fortunate," you know, I don't mean that in terms of comparison, but then again, yeah, I probably do. It's a matter of being proud of who I am, proud of being the person that I am today. I have no problem about the way I grew up any more, because it turned me into the person I wanted to be, which I am now.

It's almost like a white person saying that they're proud to be white, or a black person saying they're proud to be black. I might say it's "fortunate" that I'm black, meaning that I am proud of who I am. And that's the reason I say that.

Of course, a Blood would probably say "fortunately" as well. But I'm fortunate that I chose to be a Crip, because it meant my having the friends and the solidarity—the understanding that we had as friends. Before we were Crips, we were friends.

*The Mexicans and other groups, they all have their own gangs?*

Yeah, they have their own. That's a totally different part of LA. That's a totally different ideology.

*So, the Crips and Bloods are specifically black gangs, pretty much one hundred percent black?*

Oh no, not one hundred percent. Maybe eighty-five, eighty percent. There's a lot of Mexican Crips, a lot of white Crips. I mean,—

*OK.*

—there's some whites, Mexicans, a lot of Samoans. A lot of them are Bloods too. I mean, like, they got certain parts of California where the area is nothing but all Samoans. Like, SOS—Sons of Samoa—they're a Blood gang. So, yeah, even though they're Samoan, they're Bloods and they hate Crips.

See, there's an interesting difference between the streets and prison. On the streets, when you have a problem with somebody of a different race who's also in a rival gang, it's seen as a gang thing rather than a race thing. You would think that, you know, the blacks would come together if a black man was fighting a Mexican, or that all blacks—Crips, Bloods or whatever—should come together against whatever race that's trying to destroy them. But it's not seen as a race issue. If it's a black Crip in a fight with a Samoan Blood, then the Crips of all colors support the Crip and the Bloods of all colors support the Blood.

But then, it's different in prison, like in California. It's the funniest thing; in the prison system, when any time there's a race versus race, the Crips and the Bloods and everybody else come together. They put their rags down, they ignore who they are, or what their gang affiliation is, and they only see themselves as black. After the incident, or the uprising, or whatever, and everything's mellowed back out, the Crips go one way, the Bloods go another. Isn't this amazing?

*That's interesting.*

Yeah. It could be the same black and the same Samoan, but now since they're fighting in prison, it's viewed as a race thing rather than a gang thing. The blacks come together with the blacks, and the Samoans come together with the Samoans.

*Sometimes it seems like people are only able to come together and put aside their differences when a crisis is obvious to them. I mean, maybe in a prison riot or something, people will show some solidarity and stop fighting amongst themselves, but when it's a more subtle threat, like the Establishment just gradually beating you down every day through the socioeconomic system,—*

Right. [Laughs.]

*—then people will still just bicker amongst themselves instead of banding together.*

Right. We can only band together in a crisis. Rodney King proved that. All of a sudden, everybody put the guns and weapons down against each other, and started targeting Koreans and everybody else. Burning up stores, you know. But after the cops got control of the city back again, and things calmed down on that level, the blacks was back to the usual gang versus gang, fighting amongst themselves. No more unity.

That's amazing. I cannot explain that to you. Please don't ask me, 'cause I couldn't.

*Can you articulate the resentment that is present among at least a fair number of people in the black community against other ethnic groups, like the Koreans—other non-white, non-power-elite groups, like Asians and such? Why is there so much animosity?*

Oh, that's easy. [Laughs.] That's an easy question there.

OK, imagine this: I mean, we had a Korean War back in the Nineteen fifties, and then the Koreans are defeated and come here, exiled from their own country. The slaves had come to this country four and five hundred years ago, and they was responsible for building a major part of it, but now it's the Koreans who just got here that get money every month. They get a place to stay. A lot of them get cars. And a majority of the businesses on the street corners in LA are owned by them, whether it's a liquor store, a laundromat. And, when blacks walk into these stores, in their own neighborhoods, the Koreans treat them like animals. They start watching them, observing them, distrusting them like we're all criminals.

So, now, the blacks feel like, we have never got no compensation, like they did. I mean, the American government goes and blows up their country, and then turns around and gives them compensation for it, gives them a place to live, gives them affordable housing. And here there are blacks, you know, dying on the streets, suffering from drugs and all the problems. And the blacks feel that white America have never given us our forty acres and a mule.

But who are they to think they're going to come over to our country—not speaking as a black American or a white American, but just as an American—and get better treatment than the people who've been here three or four hundred years? You were just recently allowed to come over here, and you get better benefits than me? That is the resentment.

The Koreans own all the stores, like I said, in the neighborhoods. They own the stores on the corner. There's an incident happened back there, right before the Rodney King riots, like, several weeks before. The incident where a Korean lady shot a black girl coming into a store over a bottle of orange juice. She shot her in the back of the head. The Korean claimed the girl tried to steal the orange juice. She wasn't trying to steal it; she had a pocketful of money.

But the Korean lady got charged, got convicted, and they gave her three months probation. That was the bitterness. That is why they tore it down. That is why they targeted Korean stores.

*How factual is it, and how much of a myth is it, that immigrants are given all these advantages?*

Oh, it's—

*Because I've known some immigrants, and I don't know that many of them were being given a whole lot. Most of them had a pretty difficult existence.*

OK, Japan. Take the Japanese. They're still paying these people for living in concentration camps back many years ago. What have the blacks ever got for living in the way we lived? As slaves. I mean, we still have difficulties going to the banks to get a loan. That's why you hear the jokes about black people can't have credit.

How do the Koreans get their money? I mean, they can't even afford to live in their own country. How are they able to afford to get over here and buy a store? I mean, that should be common sense to America.

Now, white America—and I hear it all the time—talks about that black people are just bitter. Yeah we're bitter! Because if anybody ever deserved an opportunity to afford something, it's us, because we helped build this bastard. But foreigners come over here that can't even afford to live in their own country—they're coming here because they're desperate and they don't have anything—and now they can afford a store? And we can't even afford a home?

Where's that money coming from? The government.

# 9—September 1998

*"As a whole, my being honest can sometimes discourage a friend or loved one from being supportive because they are afraid they can't withstand the long term commitment required to remain a part of my life. Therefore manipulation and deceit is sometimes necessary due to the fear of not even being given a chance before the person is overwhelmed."*

Less than a week later, I received in the mail 9's responses to the first set of written questions that I had submitted to him.

*For what crime are you currently in prison? Tell me as much as you are willing about what you did, the circumstances, etc. If what you were convicted of and sentenced for differs significantly from what you actually did, address that too.*

I'm currently serving time for aggravated first degree murder. The summer of 1987, I was with a few friends looking to buy beer, underage, in need of someone of age to purchase it for us from a mini-mart. I was in a conversation with several people across the street from the mini-mart. Moments later I heard screaming and yelling, looking up to notice that the person I arrived with was chasing a stranger and headed my way. I had no idea as to why he was chasing this person. I assumed that the guy he was chasing was a purse snatcher or thief of some kind, so I grabbed him and tackled him so that my buddy could catch him.

After I helped my buddy catch him, he ultimately slit his throat, killing him dead by several stab wounds. Witnesses testified that it was he and I both who attacked and killed the individual, thus making me the accomplice.

I actually had no idea that it was the intent of my buddy to rob or kill this guy, otherwise I would've ignored his effort and stayed clear. Unfortunately, my innocent action unintentionally aided in this killing.

We were abducted and sentenced for murder, with the State claiming that it was our intent to rob and kill this guy! It was not my intent, nor was I aware of what was going to transpire as a result of my buddy catching him. I was convicted for being an accessory to the murder, even though it was known that I didn't actually commit it.

I was placed in a position to either testify and finger in court the person who actually committed the murder (my co-defendant), or face life in prison as being a part of the murder myself. I pled innocent, said I was unaware of anything or anyone, and ultimately was convicted as an accomplice.

*Tell me about the first time you were ever incarcerated, at least overnight, as a juvenile or as an adult. What led up to it? How did it feel in the beginning? Recreate it for me.*

The first time I was actually incarcerated was for assault with a deadly weapon. I was with an acquaintance at a bus stop awaiting a bus. We both had been drinking (socially). He was nearly 10 years older than me.

I walked to the corner to see if the bus was coming, and turned back only to see three guys and one female beating my buddy down, stomping and kicking him. I ran towards them, threatening everyone involved to get off him. They ignored me, so I pulled out a knife. He was nearly unconscious.

It was four white people beating him, not saying that makes it a racial issue, but it was, because my buddy asked them for the time and received racial slurs as a response. Stupidly, my buddy struck one in the face, and that resulted in all of them beating him down.

While I was standing there, threatening them all with a knife, one approached me, threatening to take my knife and kick my ass as well. This was in the downtown area of Seattle. I backed up hoping they would retreat, I could help up my buddy and leave.

Although a non-drinker, I had drank that night and I'm sure my thoughts and actions were influenced by alcohol. As soon as the one who approached me turned away, I went on the offense and attacked him with my knife, stabbing him in the neck. The remaining three ran across the street and I attempted to help my buddy off the ground.

Before I knew it, a fat white man wearing only shorts (who owned the antique store that we were in front of) came outside with a gun, put the gun to my head and detained me until the police arrived. While awaiting the arrival of the police and paramedics, the guy I had stabbed was beating me while the antique store owner held me at gunpoint, until the sirens were heard. He then lied back down on the sidewalk as the police drove up.

I was 18; he was perhaps 35. I went to jail for assault with a deadly weapon, which was my first time.

I was nervous, scared, especially being in an "alien" state where I knew nobody, only those few I met while I was here. I didn't know what to expect, or how serious the charge was. I didn't know that I couldn't claim self-defense, since it's basically unheard of in Washington.

After being there for a couple of days I became more relaxed because I was surrounded by those in a similar position as me. I was released in five days, promising that I'd return to court on the scheduled dates. But I never did, thus having a warrant out for my arrest.

*How much contact do you currently have with friends and family in terms of mail, phone calls, visits, etc.? Has the amount of contact been pretty steady during your time in prison, or has it varied much? How important is such contact to you, and as far as you can tell, how important is it for prisoners in general? Do you feel you can be totally honest with your people about your life in prison and how you're dealing with it, or do you have to be selective about what you tell them, and what side of yourself you show them?*

I have limited contact with friends, but none with friends I had at the time of my arrest. I'm the only child of my parents, raised by my grandmother, until at 16 I moved out on my own for good. My parents are both dead, as well as my grandmother. They all died while I was incarcerated.

I have a couple of friends I've accumulated since I got locked up that I communicate and correspond with, but not often.

My current fiancée is my best and only friend that I have in life. She is dependable, reliable, and has been steady for the past 6 years. She's a former employee at Clallam Bay, where we met, and now the biggest part of my life. She's my entire world.

Contact with friends and loved ones is the umbilical cord for remaining alive and sane while doing time. In my experience, it's easy to notice who has family support and who lacks it by the attitude of the individual. Having such appreciated contact is the incentive to allow one to remain hopeful and inspired, the motivation to stay focused and positive, if for nothing else but out of gratitude for the support and friendship.

For some, being honest is the easiest and best route to discuss prison life, depending on the attitude of the recipient. But for others, like myself, I'm selective because I refuse to subject those in my personal life to my feelings and emotions of dealing with time. It's an unnecessary stress factor, one that only causes pain and worry, especially when there can't be nothing done about it.

I express positive things, and appreciate sharing the simple things that mean a lot to me, but I avoid showing the "bitter" and angry side of me because it reflects onto the person or people you're a part of. Besides, it takes away the integrity and discipline within the relationship, and provokes hostility where there should be love and understanding.

As a whole, my being honest can sometimes discourage a friend or loved one from being supportive because they are afraid they can't withstand the long term commitment required to remain a part of one's life. Therefore manipulation and deceit is sometimes necessary due to the fear of not even being given a chance before the person is overwhelmed.

One has to be a different kind of person in prison than with your people. One's morals and discipline is raised to an extremely higher level in prison where respect is the biggest and toughest demand. Almost anything can be deemed as disrespect, including things that one would not even consider if on the streets. And disrespect in prison is life threatening. Even a stare or gaze is considered as disrespectful, where on the streets it's only being "nosy," and is ignored. But not in prison.

It's almost a must to have multiple personalities in prison, in order to get along with everybody, and yet to still be presentable to those "outsiders" that's a part of your personal life.

*Tell me about prison jobs. How do job opportunities differ from prison to prison? How much choice is involved in whether to work and what kind of work to do? How do you get paid, and how much? Is it the kind of work experience that will make you more employable once you get out? Are most prisoners who work employees of the state or of outside industries, and what are the pros and cons of both? When there are more prisoners than jobs, what determines who gets the jobs? Give me any other information you can about prison jobs besides what I happened to ask about here. Tell me about your personal experience with prison work. What jobs have you had on the inside?*

Prison jobs varies. Job opportunities differ in every institution, especially the three I've been housed: Clallam Bay, Walla Walla, and WSR.

Clallam Bay predominantly has institutional jobs. State prison jobs are generally about $50 a month. It only has one industry job, building chairs, but even the fortunate few (perhaps thirty inmates) who hold those jobs cannot receive a pay rate over $1.00 an hour, because that industry is still DOC owned, with headquarters as the employer. Most every other job available there only pays between $0.38 and $0.42 cents an hour.

Walla Walla has one private industry—Earth Ray (sewing)—and that pays minimum wage. That has a private owner, and approximately 20 inmate workers. The remaining jobs are those $50 a month institutional jobs.

WSR offers the best job opportunities in the state, having six private industries, paying a minimum of $5.15 an hour, with multiple opportunities that benefits a worker when he's released. Redwood (making clothes), Micro-Jet (cutting metal with water), A & I (making window blinds), Elliot Bay (brewery material), Washington Marketing Group (telemarketing), and Compu-Chair (making chairs), are the private industries with private owners. The remaining jobs are institutional jobs paying the same wages of $50 a month.

Most prisoners work for the state because there's not enough private industry jobs available for the number of prisoners. The choice of jobs depends on an individual's capabilities, or having someone available that has influence with the immediate boss. An applicant is interviewed, but his prison profile can either help or hurt his potential hiring.

Most managers are aware of prison life, who's acceptable and who's not, and rather than hire someone detrimental to the morale of their effective workers, the applicant will get overlooked.[*]

All jobs get paid monthly, with all private industry jobs losing a 35% deduction for cost of incarceration, mandatory savings, and victims compensation, plus the usual taxes,

---

[*]I.e., employers do not hire known rats or sex offenders, because other prisoners would refuse to work there or would constantly clash with them.

social security, and money taken by the government first. If you owe restitution to the court, that's another 20% deducted from your check.

Some jobs offer experience that would make you employable when you reach the streets, and here at the Reformatory, some jobs require classes and training before hiring that provides you with skills that would also be recognized and considered on the street. Welding, drafting, and sewing is among the skills that would make one employable.

The pros are that an employee can afford to help his family financially, can afford the necessities to make life in prison more comfortable: personal clothes, shoes, TV, radio, food, personal hygiene items, etc.. Everything costs money in prison, often even more expensive than on the street. It allows a prisoner to be responsible and teaches him to manage money and be helpful to his family and loved ones.

The cons are he's required to work more for less pay than society, and then loses most of even that money back to the state for various reasons. The highly paid staff stand and watch the inmates do their job, and complain about the inmate being overpaid. For example, in the kitchen, the prisoner assistant cooks prepare and serve the meals and clean up afterwards for $0.38 an hour, while the officer only oversees and follows the menu, while being paid a good salary.

When complaints are made, the prisoner worker is blamed, not the staff member. That goes for nearly every institutional job.

Both institutional and state employers demand an extreme amount of work from the prisoner, especially those with the highest pay (minimum wage) and consider it a privilege for a prisoner to have such a "luxury" job. The threat of imminent firing is constant because there's quite a few awaiting the "good" jobs, and prisoners are viewed as nothing more than inmates, even though they produce more money for their employer than do his employees on the street. There's less overhead capital and more profit in prison, and the employer doesn't have to provide the same benefits and wages that he'd have to pay his employees on the street.

As for my personal experience with prison work, I wasn't willing to alter my entire days and program around a job as my priority. I didn't feel the need to have to explain to my boss the reason I chose to go to a visit, as they expect you to arrange your visits around work schedules. My visitors' schedules come first, especially considering they find the available time to come see me.

I've worked numerous prison jobs, some only to remain active, programming, and occupied. Kitchen jobs are mandatory at each institution for ninety days upon arriving off the chain. I've been a kitchen worker, librarian, tier porter, chair maker, telemarketer, tutor for GED students (teacher's assistant), etc.

*What are some of the things you miss most about the outside world?*

The things I miss about the outside world is too numerous to list.

The ability to be social with all genders, without the threat of being accused of fraternizing, too personal, or assuming a motive for my reason for talking to someone from the outside.

I really miss having the ability to come and go as I please, venturing into the world to discover life in its totality and the experience of growing up with opportunity.

The simple things, such as: answering a telephone, shopping, going to the park, seeing the Christmas lights glow at Christmas, or just playing in the rain without being assumed that I'm under the influence of drugs.

Celebrating holidays with a big dinner and loved ones around to share the feelings of a family.

I really miss most of all being there when I'm needed most for those who really deserve my presence and help when I can give it.

I miss having a pet, or just the smell of traffic on a busy day with gas fumes in the air.

I miss life with opportunities available for me to explore and learn along the way. I miss meeting different people that I'm not forced to be around everyday, all day. I miss going to the movies, football games, or just talking on the phone, late at night.

Of course, I miss sex, but also the comfort of a significant other without limits, at a time of my choosing, and not under constant surveillance with rules governing our closeness.

It's an awful lot I could ramble on about, but the things I most need and miss are the things that make me feel human, feel complete, and believe that life is worth the memories it creates.

# JEFF—September 1998

"So I get back in my car, and I'm driving around Hope, this little town. It's just a little bitty logging town. And they've got this neon sign at the edge of town, when you're driving out of town, that says 'Leaving Hope.'

"Yeah, I'm looking at this sign, and it's midnight, and it's raining, and I'm all fucked up. You know, and that just did it. I had to pull over, and I lost it right there.

"I cried. I started crying and everything. You know, 'cause that's when it finally kicked in, the reality of what's going on. It took that long. Before that, I was still in that shock period."

Jeff in 1997.

Jeff,[*] for better or worse, is PAP's resident "square." He is a college-educated, middle class professional white male who was never part of any kind of criminal subculture. He is the farthest thing from a career criminal. He is someone who was fairly "ordinary" for most of his life, until in a moment of insane rage, he destroyed two lives, one with finality. He is in the middle of a decades-long process of rebuilding the other—his own.

Jeff doesn't "fit" in prison. Most of the prisoners hate prison and would love to be just about anywhere else, but at least they are surrounded by their peers. They live among people with similar worldviews and similar values, people who have had similar criminal experiences, people whom they accept and who accept them. Jeff is a lonely outsider in their land.

At times during the interviews I sensed he wouldn't mind being perceived as a little more of a tough guy, as a member of the convict inner circle. For instance, when I asked him about the possibility of his re-offending, he gave a coy response in which he purposely left the door open. Instead of simply saying that he had no intention of engaging in criminal activity and leaving it at that, he got cute and attributed the unlikelihood of his returning to an American prison to his possibly leaving the country, or to his thinking through any potential future crimes well enough to enable him to avoid capture.

Sorry, but I don't see him as an international criminal mastermind. He's done a remarkable job of surviving in what has to be a nightmarish world for a person of his background, but he hasn't conquered that world, he hasn't achieved a position of leadership in it, he hasn't been fully accepted into it.

But ultimately I don't think it's all that big a deal to him. He might flirt with the idea of being admired as a "solid convict," but it's not his major concern. When he is properly focused, Jeff is about more positive things than that. He works a full time job and saves his money responsibly; he maintains as healthy a relationship as he can with his people on the outside; he participates in several of the programs available at WSR and uses them to grow and develop as a person as well as to interact with outside people; and he looks within himself to seek to understand why he committed the violent act he did and how he can avoid anything like that ever happening again upon his eventual release.

Because his background and his social style are so contrary to the prison norm, he is perceived by some of his fellow prisoners as aloof, as thinking he is better than them. (This is not a universal perception by any means; for instance, some of the guys in PAP are friends of his and think highly of him.) Jeff denies feeling superior to his fellow prisoners, and I believe he is sincere.

---

[*]Jeff has chosen to be identified by his first name only.

I sympathize with him on this, because it's hard to deny that kind of allegation without seemingly affirming it. When he speaks favorably of those who could be considered his social or educational inferiors, it has a patronizing feel to it. Whether he denies or acknowledges elitist attitudes, he's trapped in a verbal minefield.

In our interviews, Jeff showed a willingness to talk about his horrific crime, even though doing so shows him at his worst. I appreciate that. If we are ever to understand how such crimes happen and what can be done to make them less likely, it is imperative that their perpetrators frankly and thoroughly share with us their perspective on what happened and why.

Jeff's account of his crime is a harrowing one. More than once when I was listening to the interview tapes and typing up the transcripts, I had to stop because the enormity of what he was describing unnerved me.

Jeff can never turn the tape off. He murdered his wife. His crime is a part of him and will remain a part of him until the day he dies.

I don't know how a person copes with the knowledge that he has committed such a crime. During our talks, there were moments when Jeff was emotionally open about it. At other times, there was a coldness, a detachment that was vaguely disturbing. For example, Jeff believes his murder should fall under one legal category rather than another. To explain why, he contrasted the way he killed his wife with alternative scenarios that would have constituted "aggravating circumstances." Now, his legal claim might well be one hundred percent valid, but I got a chill listening to him describe hypothetical ways he could have tortured his wife before completing the murder.

Jeff's demeanor in the interviews—as it is in general—was friendly and cooperative. He comes across as a decent guy who is doing his best. Once in awhile he was a bit evasive or wanted to engage in some verbal sparring with me, but mostly he approached the interviews with a positive and open attitude.

After a very, very long time in prison, Jeff will eventually be released. It is understandable that people would be alarmed by this, and would perceive someone who committed such a violent act to be a menace to society regardless of how much time has passed. But however we might respond to the matter emotionally, it is worth reminding ourselves that a "crime of passion" murder like Jeff's is virtually never repeated, so any fears we might have are all but groundless.

The drug addicts, the career thieves, etc. are long shots. You hope they'll stay out when released, but you know they'll probably get right back into their comfortable criminal lifestyle instead. But the person who never lived such a lifestyle is highly unlikely to repeat the one time in his life that he snapped and murdered a loved one.

It's hard for me to imagine myself in the shoes of most prisoners. Their background, their habits, their attitudes are foreign to me. When I look at Jeff, though,

I see someone a lot more like me, at least on the surface. Watching him makes me wonder how similar my life would be to his if I somehow ended up incarcerated.

Rico tells me a story to illustrate Jeff's peculiarity as a prisoner: There is an understanding that a pack of cigarettes or something of similar value is expected by the prisoners who do the laundry if you want yours done properly. Jeff refuses to go along with this. So Jeff's laundry is returned to him in a wrinkled pile, whereas Rico's is consistently well laundered and neatly folded for him.

Says Rico, "I keep telling him, 'Everybody's got a hustle. There aren't enough outside industry jobs to go around. Everybody else has to find themselves a hustle. This just happens to be their hustle.' But he won't go for it. 'I'm not going to bribe them; it's their job. I'm not going to bribe somebody to do their job!'"

Rico tells it with a tone of frustration, but I think he also feels some admiration for a person who refuses to ever fully conform to prison expectations. Rico won't brag about it, but he'll watch out for someone like Jeff, and see to it that his prison naivete doesn't get him into too much trouble.

I hear a story like that and I laugh, but I also cringe in recognition. I'd be as ill-suited to all this as Jeff is, and just as likely to stand on principle when it makes no sense to anyone else. I don't know whether I could survive as long or as well as he has.

Jeff is one of those who procrastinated most about responding to my written questions. He proved very agreeable about getting together for taped interviews, however, and ultimately I got as much material from him as from any of the participants.

The following is our first taped conversation.

*Jeff, I'm just going to go off the printed questions I mailed in to you, that you've already looked at and had a chance to think about. And, then we'll just kind of ad lib it from there. Why don't you tell me about the crime that you committed that landed you in prison. Give me the story behind that, and we'll talk about that for awhile, as much as you're willing to say.*

Do you want the long version, or the short version?

*Give me the long version.*

We might be here awhile.

*That's all right. Tell me the whole story.*

Well, interestingly enough, it was this week, nine years ago. I used to live over here in Snohomish, just next door. Another bit of irony there. When the gates open, I can see my house out there. There's this really big tree on the hill, and I used to live right next to it. It's the biggest tree up on that hill. So, I know right where the house was.

*So you can just about see your house from prison?*

Pretty much. I mean, when they open up the gate down here, when they have trucks coming in, you know, you can see out there. We kind of sit up on a hill here, so you can see a lot.

Anyway, just to give a little background, I'm from Utah, was raised in Utah, but I wasn't raised a Mormon. I ended up meeting my wife —who was a Mormon—there, and we moved to Texas to work in the oil business down there in Houston. We were both geologists.

So we moved down to Houston, and ended up getting married while we were living down there, and I started going to church with her, just because it seemed like the thing to do. She was Mormon and I wasn't, and I thought I'd check it out, even though I grew up around it my whole life, and I knew that it was rampant with hypocrisy. I just never realized quite the extent.

*Were you of a different religion, or a non-believer entirely?*

Pretty much agnostic. My father was a Mormon when he was a kid, and then he sort of fell off the wagon. I never was really raised in any church.

*Did you come from a middle class background?*

Yeah, my father was a chemical engineer. We were middle class, upper middle class.

*Which is a contrast with most of the people that you're rubbing shoulders with in a place like this.*

Yeah, yeah, I mean, my family was well-educated. I have two degrees from the University of Utah: geophysics and geology. My brother is an environmental engineer. And my mom went to school also. So, yeah, you know, I wasn't living a life of crime or any such thing. I was a taxpayer and a law-abiding citizen.

But, anyway, so we lived in Houston, and the Mormons that live in Houston are much less hypocritical, because they're such a minority that they have to practice what they preach. I mean, they have to live their religion, because there's such opposition from the Southern Baptists and Assembly of God and all those people down there.

So, I kind of became—oh, what's the word?—I admired their sincerity, because I'd grown up around Utah, where there's such hypocrisy, where all my friends were Mormons, and they'd all smoke dope and drink beer, and, you know, talk bad about the church. Whereas down there, these people actually were sincere.

So, I ended up joining the church, in Houston. Then, we got really tired of living in Houston. Moved to Snohomish. And I got a job working in computer programming in Bellevue, doing software engineering and computer graphics. I had been doing computer graphics with geophysical applications for the company I was with in Houston. So, I just used those skills for a different application, which was actually working on tank simulators for the M1 tanks. They have a big tank training ground down in Fort Knox, Kentucky.

*What year did you move up here?*

That was Eighty-seven.

*How old were you at the time?*

I guess that would make me twenty-six. Yeah, we moved here in Eighty-seven.

So, we lived here a few years, and the more I got into the Mormon church, the more I realized that I was not cut out to be a Mormon.

I want to make clear, I'm not blaming my crime on the Mormon church; I'm just giving you some background.

The bottom line is I got in too deep. They have all this heeby jeeby doctrine—I don't know if you're familiar much with the Mormon church—but, you know, they have their temples, and they have these ceremonies, and they got all this weird stuff. You know, they're very nice on the outside. They're very family-oriented, and they don't smoke, and they don't drink coffee, and it's a very wholesome, pleasant church. Right? But, when you get into the doctrine, I mean, they got a lot of weird stuff.

So, initially I was attracted to the nice family atmosphere, and very wholesome, and, you know—'cause I never really had that growing up, where you have all these big family picnics, you know, with kids running all over the place, and stuff like that. My parents, they weren't much for that. My dad didn't like the big family outings.

So, I joined.

*Your wife was a member all along.*

Right. And, I joined the church for social reasons, and then ended up getting into you know, the serious stuff. But the more I went on, the more I realized it wasn't for me.

*What parts of it bothered you? What made you realize it wasn't for you?*

Just their bizarre doctrine. I mean, they believe that everyone is going to become a god, on their own little planet. I mean, and they're rather arrogant as to their views on everyone else's religion. You know, like, "Well, these people are so lost and confused. They just don't know what they're doing." That's why they've got missionaries running around the world.

As I say, they're good people, but they're very caught up in their own selves. I mean, they think they're the ones, you know, just like every religion does.

*It turns out there's a little more to being a good person than not drinking coffee. [Laughs.]*

Oh, yeah. Well, but that's the kind of thing you'll hear growing up in Utah, people saying, "Well, my kids don't drink coke!" or bragging "My dad doesn't drink coffee!"

*So they must be good people. [Laughs.]*

Yeah. I mean, he might be boinking the neighbor's wife, but.

*Right.*

So anyway, in Nineteen eighty-nine, my daughter was born—Julia.* So she's nine and a half now.

*She was the first child of your marriage?*

Yeah, yeah, the only one.

So, also in early Nineteen eighty-nine, I was laid off from my job as a computer programmer, because they lost their contract with the Army. At that time, in Nineteen eighty-nine, the economy wasn't as good as it is now, and jobs were a little tighter. When I got here in Eighty-seven, it was pretty good, but in Eighty-nine, and Ninety, it really slacked off. So, I had trouble finding another job.

I finally did though. I went to work for another company in Bellevue. They're a huge government avionics contractor.

The atmosphere was totally opposite from what I came from. I had had my own office, my own computer, my own computer lab. Now I was in this very oppressive environment, a sea of gray cubicles. It's the difference between a small, human-oriented company, and a big company that's very government oriented.

*So prison wasn't your first experience with a huge, gray, dehumanizing institution with little cubicles.*

---

*I have changed the name.

Yeah. So anyway, I was under a lot of stress when I got laid off. We had just bought a new house over here in Snohomish. Just had a new baby. Just got laid off from my job. And, I was having real problems with the church. I was really stressing.

So, as the summer went on, I went to work for this company that I really didn't like, all the while looking for another job. And, there was one really excellent opportunity that slipped through my hands. I won't go into that story, but I set all my hopes on this job. It was a technical support person for computer sales, where I would do demos and stuff like that, and you do a lot of software installation and get your own car and stuff like that. I pretty much was given the job, but then the guy ended up going to another company, so I was left out in the cold.

So, at this point, I became quite depressed, and my wife and I actually got into counseling, marriage counseling, because my marriage was suffering quite severely.

*In what way? Were you losing your temper with her or—how was your marriage suffering?*

Well, no, I'd just take off for the weekend, wouldn't come home. You know, I'd go rock climbing. I was a real outdoors person. I'd go on trips up in the mountains, and stay up there for a few days. You know, stuff like that. So, yeah, there wasn't any abuse or anything, though emotionally what I was doing was abusive.

So, my marriage is falling apart, I hate my job, I've got my new daughter, and I've got this house that I can't afford. You know, and all this stuff's building up.

And, I'm in the church, and they're telling me what a rotten person I am, because I'm not doing their thing. And, I just lost it. I came home one day and got in a big argument with my wife, and I killed her.

*Big argument about what?*

Same old stuff. I mean, nothing in particular. Just, you know, "Why aren't you here? Why don't you come home?" that kind of thing. You know, "Why aren't you here, instead of out running around?" I wasn't being unfaithful, but I just wasn't there.

*So, it was nothing out of the ordinary. It wasn't a different kind of fight, or a more intense fight.*

Well, it was the only fight that got physical. You know, it got physical, and I stabbed her.

*This was the first time it got to a physical level?*

Yeah, yeah.

*Had there been a lot of arguing, a lot of conflict before that that just didn't get physical?*

No, I mean, because I was the kind of person that held everything in. I wouldn't yell and scream. I would just go away. And, you know, that's not real healthy, because you just get to the point, and then you blow up. Sometimes it's better just to get it all out instead of hold it in, 'cause that doesn't do any good.

*Well, what was happening with you emotionally? What made this different? I mean, I understand the general circumstances you've sketched out, but on that precise occasion, how did you feel emotionally that was different from how you had felt on previous occasions when she was upset about your leaving and taking off for awhile?*

Well, I don't know if it's a chemical thing or what, but when your stress reaches a certain level, it's like you become a different person. I mean, it's like people who drink too much, and they're like a whole different person. I mean, I wasn't drinking, but it's like I was. You get imbalanced chemically.

You know, I became this different person. It's, like, where you just don't care about anything. It's, like, I don't even know who this person is. You know, that kind of thing.

*Did you feel out of control of what you were doing, or how would you describe it?*

Yeah, it's like I was watching somebody else do it, like I was another person.

If anybody was surprised, it was myself. I mean, you know, of course, everybody else was, too, including my wife. She never suspected. I never suspected.

As I say, I was in counseling. But this counselor we had was actually worse than not having one at all, because she wasn't really qualified. She was a social worker or something, and she was a do-gooder, and—

*Where was she from? Was she from the church?*

Yeah.

*OK.*

And that was the first mistake—we got a counselor through the church. She was way out of her league, I mean, with my problems. Of course, she didn't know that, and I didn't know that, but, if we had someone who was qualified, maybe things would have been different.

Because I had told her I was feeling suicidal. I mean, I had told her. But she didn't take me seriously. I told her I was going to go jump off Snoqualmie Falls and all this stuff, which I had thought about. But she didn't take it serious.

*So even before this happened, you had thoughts of suicide.*

Oh yeah, yeah.

*Had you had thoughts of violence toward others, including your wife, or was it always suicidal, always toward yourself?*

It was mostly myself, yeah. That day, I actually went and bought a shotgun, 'cause I was going to kill myself. I got the shotgun, I drove around, and I couldn't do it. You know, I had this gun, but I couldn't bring myself to do it.

So, I'm driving around and around and around. I end up going home, and my wife wasn't even supposed to be there. She was supposed to be out somewhere else. I didn't even know she was going to be home.

So, I got home, and she's home, and, you know, I'm in a state of mind where I just almost killed myself. And that's not a good state of mind. I mean, suicide and homicide are real close, you know. I mean, if you can kill yourself, you can kill anybody.

And, so—what was your question? You had a question there. I was going somewhere with that.

*Was there an actual decision made to kill your wife, or was it so totally spontaneous that it wasn't really a decision?*

Well, that's the whole reason I went to trial was, you know, in this state, the definition of first degree murder is that you premeditated for at least a moment in time. If you think about it for a moment in time—however long a moment in time is, nobody knows—if you think about it for that long, it's first degree murder. In most states, there has to be some sort of planning, like, if I went and bought a gun and shot her with it. That's premeditated, because you've got to do a certain succession of events. But, you know, we just got in an argument, and I grabbed a knife and stabbed her.

Yeah, I had to reach over and grab a knife, so there was that decision process right there, but, in most states, that would be second degree murder, because it's a spontaneous thing.

*So, it wasn't, like, when you were driving around, you were thinking, "I'll either kill myself or maybe I'll kill my wife instead."*

No. No, because, it was only when I got home that I focused all of that anger on her.

She didn't deserve it. I mean, she didn't have it coming. You know, she wasn't cheating on me, or anything like that. She didn't deserve it.

But, somehow because she got me in the church and all that stuff, it just all of a sudden computed as "All the problems I'm having are your fault!" you know. That transferred that anger onto her, and she became the recipient of it.

*When you grabbed the knife, were you thinking, "I'll just kind of harm her or shut her up or get her out of my face with this," or were you literally thinking, "I'll kill her with this"?*

At that time, I mean, if you're to that point, there's no stopping. You know, it's not, like, "Well, I'm just going to cut her up and make her worry a little bit." No, it was nothing like that.

There's no conscious thought there. I mean, if there was conscious thought, I would have took her up in the mountains, in the wood chipper, and she'd be in a hole and I wouldn't be here. You know, I mean, that's the bottom line. There's a hundred thousand ways to get rid of somebody, other than the one I chose. I mean, a knife is not a clean instrument.

*But when you had the knife, and you decided to use it on her, you were thinking in terms of actually taking her life.*

At that time, yeah. I mean, at that point.

*In deciding where to plunge it in and such, you were trying to kill her.*

Yeah. Yeah, as I say, when you reach that level, yeah.

*And you'd never done anything remotely like this in your life.*

No. No, I mean, I never was much for getting in fights or anything like that. And maybe I should have, because that's a release, you know, of anger, and I just never learned how to release anger at all.

You know, in here, I've become much better at coping, because I know how I work. I understand it. But out there, I didn't have a clue. Nobody had a clue, including this counselor that should have had a clue. You know, if I had had a good counselor that recognized that there was a real problem here, hopefully it would have been worked out.

*So you just associated her with all the negativity in your life, with the church problems, and the money problems, and all that.*

Yeah, I mean, that's what happened. As I say, there wasn't a conscious decision to do that, but that bit of anger there just triggered the whole thing. You know, like, all of a sudden, I viewed her as the source of all of my problems. And, you know, it was, like, "Well, I'm not going to kill me; I'm going to kill her."

But as I say, I didn't go in the house with that intention.

*So, you're arguing and you just reached over for a kitchen knife or something that was lying there?*

Yeah, it was on the counter there.

And, as I say, in this state, first degree murder is premeditation for a moment in time. I went to trial over that. I never claimed that I didn't do it. You know, I called nine-one-one not too long after and told them I did it.

*Yeah, take me through that. OK, so you grabbed the knife—Or, I'm sorry, did you want to make a point?*

Yeah.

*OK, make a point about the first versus second degree murder, and then we'll go back.*

Yeah, so, I went to trial. I was arguing second degree murder; they were arguing first degree murder. That's the only reason I went to trial. It wasn't that I wasn't guilty. It was just the degree of guilt, the intent.

*It sounds like the way they define it, second degree murder would be virtually impossible.*

In this state, it is. I mean, in that room there [motions across the hall to where the PAP meeting is being held], there's probably twenty first degree murderers and two or three seconds. I mean, the only guys that get second degree murder are guys that were, like, getting robbed, and they killed the guy, which in a lot of states would be justified as self-defense and they wouldn't do any time. Whereas in this state, you get second degree murder for defending yourself.

There's no way they can get first degree out of those cases, but they can get a second degree out of them, even though, you know, somebody's mugging you or robbing you. They say, "Well, you should just hurt them enough to get them off you." In this state, you know, you can't really defend yourself.

I mean, I've got friends in here—there's one guy, he got attacked by three guys, ended up killing one. They gave him second degree murder and first degree assault, even though they were mugging him, trying to take his money.

Another guy had a couple of muggers coming at him, and he pulled his gun out and shot one.

OK, that one's a bit excessive, since the mugger didn't have a gun. [Laughs.]

*Right. The punishment should fit the crime, and mugging shouldn't be punishable by death.*

But what's amazing is this guy he shot, the bullet went through the guy's throat and out the side, and missed everything. If it would have hit his spinal cord, it would have killed him, but it went out the side, and didn't really hurt him too bad.

He got a second degree assault, and did a year and a half, which I find truly amazing.

I mean, the time structures are another whole story. There's guys—

*Well, let's not get off on tangents with these other guys.*

Yeah, and there's a guy in here that robbed a bank, killed a teller, and got less time than I did.

*Right. Let's go back to where we were.*

OK.

*OK, so you're arguing. You grab the knife. And then what happened?*

Then I stabbed her. About fourteen times.

*So are you saying anything to her at this time? Are you hesitating? Is she saying anything? Is she screaming? Is she fighting?*

Well, see, it's just an act of rage. I mean, you know, when someone gets in that state, there's no stopping. It's like an animal.

*What resistance did she put up?*

Well, you know, naturally, she's not trying to get stabbed.

*Is she more surprised than anything, or what?*

Well, yeah. I mean, sure, yeah.

*It's not like you've been abusive in the past.*

No, no, no. I never hit her at all.

So, yeah, she's totally surprised.

*So, this is totally out of character.*

Right. As I say, that's why nobody had a clue, including myself. And, you know, that's unfortunate, because if there had been an event, if I had hit her in the past or something, then that might have been a good thing, because maybe I would have got help or something. But, it never got to that point. I'd never hit her or anything.

*So, in your mind, this is all one action. It's not like each time you're stabbing at her, you're making a separate decision.*

No. No, not at all.

*It's all just one thing that overwhelmed you all at once?*

Yeah.

I went to trial, because the only deal they offered me was first degree murder with a top end of twenty-seven years. That's the only thing they offered me. If they would have offered me second degree, I would have pled guilty right off the bat.

*It seems to me to be more of a sustained series of actions. That's what I'm curious about. I mean, if I'm driving down the highway and somebody cuts me off, and I'm short-tempered or whatever, and I take a shot at him spontaneously, that's one quick action. It takes, like, one second to do. But, if I chase him for thirty seconds or a minute or a minute and a half, taking several shots at him along the way, to me that just seems different. To me, that does require more of an intent.*

Well, it depends on your state of mind. I mean, I don't know if you have ever been in a situation like that, you know, where you're just in a state of blind rage. You know, it's toxic.

*Yeah.*

It's toxic anger. You know, there's ten guys in that room that can tell you the same story about the situations they've been in.

You're not stopping to think, "Well, OK, I got to do this and that." I mean, there's none of that.

That's interesting that you say that, because, I got convicted of first degree murder, plus I got an exceptional sentence due to "deliberate cruelty," because there was fourteen stab wounds. And, their argument was very similar to what you just said, that, "Well, this takes a significant amount of time," and blah, blah, blah.

But, you know, it wasn't like I was sitting there and burning her with cigarettes or something.

I mean, granted, murder in itself is deliberately cruel. I mean, that's inherent in the act of murder, is it's cruel. There's no way around it, whether you're shooting or strangling a person, or whatever you're doing. The act itself is inherently cruel.

Another thing is, whenever you go to trial, they always want to give you as much time as possible, because they want to make you pay for making them go through a trial instead of accepting their deal. It's, like, "Well, this guy cost us $300,000 in his trial, so we're going to make him pay."

It's a true story. There's all kinds of guys in here that took a deal. The guys in here that went to trial, they got three times as much time.

*So they never offered you second degree, or you would have taken that.*

Yeah.

*What was the best you could have gotten without going to trial?*

Twenty-seven years. With a third off for good time, I would have done eighteen. As it is, I got forty. So I've got to do at least twenty-seven. So, in essence, I don't have any good time. I mean, that's what it boils down to.

So their argument was that fourteen stab wounds is excessive. You know, but unless you understand the state of mind of the person at the time—I mean, yeah, if you take someone, you stab them, and you watch them squirm around for awhile, and you stab them again, and you kick them a few times, then yeah, you're torturing them.

But, you know, if you're just going crazy, there's no conscious decision there.

*So, you're in this rage, this kind of detached state where it almost feels like another person is doing it, and—*

Yeah.

*—you're sort of watching yourself do it. Tell me how that changed. I mean, how did you come out of that, or how did you feel immediately after it happened? Tell me what was happening inside you emotionally during and immediately after your stabbing your wife.*

Well, once it was over, I had the conscious realization of what's happening, you know, what's going on.

*Immediately?*

Yeah. Yeah. I mean, it's, like, the house is covered in blood, you know, and you got a dead body on the floor. It's, like, "Damn," you know. I mean, it's like waking up out of a nightmare.

*So, was it all at once like that? A—*

Yeah—

*—fairly sudden realization?*

Right. I mean, as I say, it was like having a bad dream, except it's real.

And, my daughter was in the house. She was only nine months old at the time. She was just a little baby.

*Let me stop you for a moment, because I want to hear about that, but let me just follow up—*

OK.

*—on this. So, is that why you stabbed her fourteen times, instead of thirteen or fifteen or twenty or five or zero? Is it because you were in this rage, you were kind of out of control and everything, and at some specific point, the realization kicked in, and that's when you stopped?*

Well, to tell you the truth, the knife bent. Or there would have been more. But, after fourteen, the knife hit bone or something. It was a cheap kitchen knife. I mean, it wasn't a big knife.

*So that kind of compelled a temporary stop.*

Well, yeah, it's, like, you know,—

*And then, once you had to stop for that reason, then the realization of what you'd done kind of kicked in.*

Yeah. Yeah, you know, there probably would have been more. To answer your question, that was why I stopped. And then, when I realized what I'd done, I was more shocked than anything. I mean, that first emotion is shock, like a "How did this happen?" kind of thing.

And, as I say, my daughter was in the house. So, I'm, like, "Well, what do I do with her?" So, I put her in her crib, and I left. I jumped in the car. I panicked and took off.

I mean, we're kind of out in the country, so there's no neighbors or anything that really heard anything. Actually, one of our neighbors heard some screaming, but didn't really attribute it to anything. So, nobody came over or anything.

So, I jumped in the car and left. And, I drove to Canada, you know, 'cause I'm, like, freaking out.

*Did you have any money or anything with you, or any possessions?*

I had a few hundred dollars, and I grabbed a sleeping bag or something, you know, just something I could grab. I mean, it was, like, a five minute thing—grab this and this and this, and leave.

*What were your plans, to the extent that you had a conscious plan at all? What were you intending to do?*

I was just interested in leaving. I was, like, "Well, Canada sounds good." I mean, everybody goes to Canada, right?

So, I drove all the way to Canada, to Hope, British Columbia.

Have you ever been to Hope?

*No.*

It's a nice town. You ever see the first Rambo movie?

*No.*

No? Well, that was filmed there.

*OK.*

But anyway, so this happened in the afternoon. And when I got up there, it's, like, midnight. But my daughter's still in the house. And, you know, I'm very conscious of this fact. So, I check into a motel there, and I'm planning on calling somebody, you know, the cops or something.

So, I'm agonizing over this decision of, do I call somebody? What do I do?

So I get back in my car, and I'm driving around Hope, this little town. It's just a little bitty logging town. And they've got this neon sign at the edge of town, when you're driving out of town, that says "Leaving Hope."

Yeah, I'm looking at this sign, and it's midnight, and it's raining, and I'm all fucked up. You know, and that just did it. I had to pull over, and I lost it right there.

I cried. I started crying and everything. You know, 'cause that's when it finally kicked in, the reality of what's going on. It took that long. Before that, I was still in that shock period.

So, I drove back over the border. I drove all the way back to Everett.

*So you had actually gotten a motel room in Hope.*

Right.

*But you didn't make the call from there.*

No. I thought about it, but I didn't. I got a hotel room, but I couldn't sleep or anything. So I sat there for awhile, then I drove around town, got some coffee and stuff. Then I saw the sign, and that was it.

And all this time, I've got this shotgun with me, 'cause I was planning on killing myself.

*Any trouble getting over the border in both directions with a shotgun in your car?*

Well, of course, I didn't tell them I had it. I mean, you've driven across the border.

*Yeah.*

So you know.

*They typically don't search, yeah.*

Yeah. But, you know, I'm still conscious that my daughter's in the house. I didn't want to just kill myself with her still there. I had to do something, call somebody or something, 'cause it might be days before somebody goes over there.

But instead of calling, I drove all the way back to Everett, checked into a hotel room there, and took the shotgun up into the room. My plan was to call somebody, and then I was going to blow my brains out.

So, I got a hotel room. This is eight o'clock in the morning by now, next morning. And I call nine-one-one.

Because I couldn't go back to the house. I mean, I was going to go get her, but I couldn't do it. I couldn't go back. I was just going to go get my daughter, and take her somewhere. But I couldn't. I couldn't go back to the house.

*Did you consider taking her from the beginning, when you initially left?*

I was just so panicked that I thought it best just to leave her there, you know. I wasn't in any state of mind to take care of a baby.

So, it was eight o'clock in the morning. I check in the hotel room. I call nine-one-one, say, you know, "Go to this address. There's a little baby there that needs some help. And, there's a dead woman on the floor." Or, well, I didn't say that. I said, "There's a little baby there that needs some help, and," what were my words? I guess my words were "I think I killed my wife," and to check on her, and the baby. And they said, "OK, we'll check on it." Then I hung up. Didn't tell them where I was.

So, I'm sitting there with this shotgun. You know, and I'm, like, "Now, what do I do?" How much time do we got? Do we have a few minutes?

*Yeah.*

OK. So, I'm sitting in there, and, you know, it was just like in the movies, where I've got my big toe on the trigger, and I'm sucking on this shotgun. It's not a pretty picture.

I'm sitting there, and, it's like I had this vision. I mean, you know, I wasn't ever really religious, even when I was Mormon. But, I had this vision of despair. I mean, you know, the Catholics tell you when you commit suicide, you're going to Hell and all that, and I never really bought that, but I sat there, and I had this vision of, like, you know, the blackness and the mist, the blackness and just the most awfulest thing you can imagine. I saw that. I don't know if that was just from religious scare stories or what, but, I'm, like, in this trance.

I'm sitting there, and I, like, snapped out of it. I'm, like, "Fuck," you know, "What the fuck am I doing?" So, I'm, like, "Well, this is out. I ain't doing this," you know. [Laughs.] That wasn't happening. I mean, it almost did. It came that close.

So, then I'm sitting there in a hotel room, going, "Well, now what the fuck do I do?" you know, "I got to get out of here." So, I'm getting ready to leave. And the phone rings. I'm, like, "Uh oh," you know, "Who's this?" So, I answer it, and it's the cops. 'Cause, you know, nine-one-one, of course, traced the call.

*OK.*

So they knew I was in the hotel. They figured out where I was.

I've been in there for a couple hours by this time, and I'm looking out the window, and there's a SWAT team out there. I mean, a SWAT team. You can see them. There's guys hiding behind the cars and shit.

You know, and the cops are saying, "This is Officer So-and-So. Are you Mr. —?" I said, "Yeah," you know, "Yeah, yeah, yeah." And I asked him, "Did they go to my house?" and they said, "Yeah, we got your daughter, and she's OK. And your wife's not OK." You know, they broke it down to me.

So, they said they had a SWAT team out in the hall, and they told me to turn myself in. They had cleared that whole floor of the hotel. They've got the SWAT team set up in the hall, plus what I can see out the windows, you know.

So I talked to the guy for about a half hour. I said, "Well, what if I just run out in the hall with my gun?" 'Cause he asked me if I had a gun, and I told him I did. I said, "What if I just run out there with a shotgun?" And he said, "Well, we're going to shoot you." [Laughs.]

'Cause at that point, it's, like, well, I couldn't bring myself to do it, so let them do it, you know.

But I didn't do that. I turned myself in.

*Why did it take a half hour? What was going through your mind? What were you talking about?*

Well, I didn't want to go to jail, you know. Of course, nobody wants to go to jail. So, I'm, like, "Well, I can still kill myself. I can still do this." I've got the shotgun. You know, I'm thinking, "Or I can jump out the window." I was only on the second floor. Of course, there's a hundred cops out there, so that wouldn't be such a good idea.

But, I mean, I was in a very fucked up state of mind. And the cop's trying to talk me into giving myself up. You know, they got the cops that know how to talk to you, the negotiators, the hostage situation guys.

And I was asking them about my daughter, and making sure she's OK and stuff. You know, they said she was all right.

It took that long for them to talk me down, you know, to where I'd come out, because I was still in a pretty agitated state of mind.

*And then you gave yourself up?*

Yeah, yeah. They took me to jail.

*How does that work? Do you toss the gun out first, or come out with your hands up, or how do you turn yourself in?*

Well, they wanted me to toss the gun out, and I said I wasn't doing it.

*How come, if you're turning yourself in anyway?*

Well, I don't know. I just—

*Just being ornery?*

That gun gave me security for some reason.

So, then they wanted me to come out with my shirt off. And I said, "Well, I'm not doing that either." And they said, "Well, just come out," you know, "You got to stick your hands out first, then you got to come out real slow," you know, "And turn around, and then you got to lay down," and then, of course, they jump on you. They've got a little barricade at either end of the hall, with their little shield and all the guns, and, I mean, you're not getting any shots off.

*So even if you jumped out in the hallway with your shotgun blazing, you wouldn't have been able to hit anybody anyway; you're just going to be dead.*

Right. Basically, yeah. I mean, they got their bullet-proof jackets on and all that stuff, so, yeah, they would have mowed me down pretty good.

But, I always wondered, you know—because they were at either end of the hall—I wondered what would have happened if they had had to shoot me down. They would have been shooting right at each other.

But presumably they thought about that before they set that up.

*Were you afraid of dying at that point, or were you just dreading prison?*

Well, everybody's afraid of dying and afraid of prison.

*But, I mean, did you think that dying was a realistic possibility in that situation, that the cops might kill you, or—?*

Oh, sure—

*—were you more focused on prison?*

No, I was more focused on dying. I mean, prison, I hadn't even got that far yet. Because, when you're sitting in jail, then you start thinking about prison. But, when you're not in jail, prison's, like, "Well, that's where somebody else goes," you know, "I'm not going to prison," you know, "I'll get out on bail or something. I don't deserve to be here," that kind of shit.

But yeah, dying was a serious possibility, because I almost did it to myself. And then, they certainly would do it.

But, they talked me out of it, so here I am.

*They took you off to jail from there?*

Yeah, they throw you in the car, and handcuff you. Due to the nature of my arrest, they send you right to the shrink floor, where, you know, you get suicide watch and all that stuff. They've got a twenty-four hour watch on you. So, I didn't go right into the tank where they throw the drunks and everything else, you know, which was good, because I'd never been in jail before.

And Snohomish County Jail is much nicer than King County Jail.* I mean, just going right into, boom, something like King County Jail is—I mean, I haven't been there, but I understand it's really not pleasant.

*So, you'd never set foot in jail, or prison, or juvenile detention, or anything in your life?*

No, no. Got a drunk driving ticket once. That was about it.

*But didn't do any kind of time for it? Just got a ticket?*

Yeah.
Nope, never went to jail. Got caught shoplifting once.

*As a child?*

Oh, a teenager. Yeah, stealing stuff.
But no, I'd never been to jail before. And so, I say fortunately I didn't go the worst route. At least I eased into jail. I was on the best floor, and I didn't go into general population until after awhile. And even in general population in the Snohomish County Jail everybody gets their own cell. Whereas in King County, they just throw you in a big room with, you know, forty other guys, and it's not nice.

*Well, let's go back to right after the crime occurred. Now, once you realized what you had done, and you woke up from the nightmare in effect, then your instinct for self-preservation kicked in and your first thought was to escape. You know, "How can I get out of here, get away from this situation, not go to prison," and so on.*

Right.

*When did a feeling of regret or guilt kick in? When did you feel bad about what you had done, rather than just panicky for your own situation?*

Well, when I was in Canada, that's when that first started. You know, when I turned around and came back. And then, of course, once you get to jail, then the whole thing starts, then the reality really sets in.

---

*Suburban Seattle versus Seattle itself.

*So it really does take a certain amount of time.*

Well, it does, because, you know, if you've got a SWAT team outside your door, you're worried about them. You're not worried about what happened yesterday; you're worried about what's happening right now. I mean, I was just sucking on a shotgun, you know. I mean, those situations took priority over anything that happened the day before.

Once you get somewhere where you're stopping for a minute, like, in jail, or when I got to Canada, it's, like, I'm sitting there, "Well, now what do I do?" That's when it all starts, you know, realizing what I'd done.

So as I said, I knew my daughter was still in the house, and that I had to do something about her. I couldn't leave her there.

*You didn't have to drive all the way back to Everett for that, though.*

True.

*Why didn't you make the call from Canada, and if you were going to kill yourself, kill yourself in Canada?*

I considered that. But my original intention was to go back to the house to get my daughter. But once I got to Everett, I couldn't do it. It was, like, "Well, I'll check into the hotel here," you know.

My original intention was to go back in there and get her.

*Yeah.*

But, I didn't.

# JIMI—September 1998

*"I'm not coming back. And you hear that a million times over and over again. But, I'm going to show you."*

We were now less than four months from Jimi's scheduled release. It was hard not to be drawn in by his growing excitement.

*Jimi, why don't we talk today about leaving this place, which you're intending to do quite soon.*

[Smiles.] I am.

*I know that's uppermost in your mind right now, getting out of here and getting started on the outside. Tell me what it's like, being this close to getting out. What effect does it have on you emotionally to know it's so close?*

Mixed emotions. It's very exciting. You know, I pretty much stay in a good mood now. It's real exciting to think about the freedom to do what I want.

Something that's really exciting this time, being my third time of being released from prison, is that I don't have a tail.* No supervision. Which means it's up to me. I'm responsible to myself. And, ironically, I think that's a good thing. You know, maybe somebody that wouldn't know me might not think so, but it's tough being under supervision. I think I'll actually respond better to just being responsible to myself.

It's also scary, because, as confident as I feel, my plans were all put together in here, not out there. So, it's a whole different world out there, and the reality in here is much different.

It's easy to sit in here, with a clear head, you know, very little going on compared to what's going on out there, physically and mentally healthy, and to set goals about your life, for your future when you get out. But, getting out and doing them is a whole different thing, and you're going to run across obstacles that, you know, you may not have visualized, or you know, you may not have been cognizant of when you made these plans in here.

But at this point in my life, I'm not tripping over it like I used to. I'm thirty-six years old. I'm not scared like I was in the past. I'll just do what I have to do. I know that I don't have any shots left.

*You've been scared in the past, anticipating getting out?*

Sure, sure. Oh yeah. Not anything that I would share with anybody, but scared that, you know, "God, am I going to get it right?"

---

*I.e., he won't be on parole, in work release, etc. Straight from prison to the streets.

But the reality was that I hadn't done any work. I hadn't done anything to understand who I was, and what got me here, and, you know, the kind of behavior that I'd been doing to get into prison, and where I learned it from. There's a lot of stuff I had to learn this time around that I probably should have learned the first time around, but maybe wasn't old enough to.

But, you know, I'm much more focused on the excitement.

I was going to say that not only am I responsible to myself, but I'm responsible to my family, I'm responsible to the people that are close to me, especially my father. You know, obviously, if you don't love yourself, and you don't respect yourself, then you're not going to be any good to anybody else.

I'm not coming back. And you hear that a million times over and over again. But, I'm going to show you.

And normally I don't tell people, "Well, I'm not coming back." You know, I've told them that too many times before. So you're not allowed to print that. [Laughs.]

*[Laughs.] Why do people think they're going to make it, and then they don't?*

Ah, they lose focus of where they've been, lose focus of being in the joint, lose focus of the consequences, lose focus of where they're going. After you've been through this experience, you're not really afraid. Like, I don't have the fear that you have of getting arrested.

*So it loses its deterrent effect—*

Absolutely.

*—once you've experienced it.*

Absolutely. I don't have the fear of losing my freedom.

*So, you know you can survive in this environment.*

Absolutely. I can go to the worst place that Washington state has to offer—Walla Walla, the pit—and be welcomed with open arms.

I mean, I'm not saying that's what I'd be thinking. But, obviously, I don't have the same deterrent for walking the straight line and obeying society's rules and laws that you might. It's different for me. I have to have a different incentive. I have to understand a responsibility to myself, my father, the community that I'm involved in, not a fear of punishment.

*Now, the prison environment is something that you can survive, and you will have friends if you go to any Washington prison. There will be people who know you and respect you, and you'll be OK. But isn't it still a huge step down from freedom on the outside?*

Absolutely.

*So, in that sense, isn't there still some deterrent? Wouldn't you still be a lot worse off if you fell again than if you avoided prison?*

Yeah, you'd be a lot worse off, but we don't always make the right decision, the decision that's in our interest, based on that.

*But does it retain any of its deterrent value because of that? Or is it totally lost?*

Well, you know, there's some, but not much.

See, something I had to recognize for me—I can't say this is a problem for everybody—but, for me, my problem is that I run from things. And it can be as small as a traffic ticket that I haven't paid. Or, it could be missing an appointment with my parole officer. Or, a relationship that I'm trying to get out of. Instead of getting out of it responsibly, I'll pack my car and take off. Or I have in the past.

And once I take off, I'm out there. And, you know, God forbid what happens later. [Laughs.] I survive however I can once I'm out there.

So for me, running has always been my problem. I run. That's always been my problem.

*Isn't there still the comparative difference though? So, even if prison isn't a nightmarish place that you fear, isn't it still sufficiently worse than staying out and staying free that it should deter you?*

Well, I think it's a different deterrent. It's a different fear. Should I fall again, I would be afraid of what it would do to my family. I would be afraid of, you know, what my friends in here would think of me. I would be afraid of losing the freedom, 'cause that hurts.

There's not much focus, or much weight put on your loss of your liberty. That's why people in society keep asking for more punishment for us. They're forgetting that they've taken our freedom away as our punishment. "Well, let's take their weights away, and let's take their cable TV away, and let's—," you know. They keep adding on more and more punishment. But, you know, just losing your freedom hurts. That hurts.

But a good example of how you lose your fear of prison would be, when I fell the very first time, I fought tooth and nail for months in jail to get out of this prison sentence. I was willing to go to trial, willing to do what I had to. It just went on and on forever, and I didn't take a plea bargain until I saw that there was no way that I wouldn't end up going to the joint anyway. I did not want to go to the joint, because once you crossed over and you went to the joint, it was, like, "Man, you're one of them!"

Every time since then that I've fallen, I've pled guilty. "Let's go. I want to get out of jail and get to prison. Send me to the joint, you know, where I can do my time and get it over with."

So, no, I don't think that prison is really a deterrent any more. I mean, obviously, it hurts to lose your liberty, your freedom. It hurts, whether it's your first time, or your fifth time. So, there is some deterrent still there. But I just think it's different. What you lose and how you react is different when it's your third or fourth time down, or even your second time down.

*Is the lack of deterrence of repeat offenders in any way a flaw in the system that could be corrected, or is that a lost cause, and we should focus on other ways of keeping people from coming back?*

Well, I've never not done a crime because I was going to go to prison. I've never stopped and said, "Wait a minute. I could get sent to prison for this."

When I do a crime, I'm in survival mode. I'm doing whatever I got to do.

And actually, yeah, I might be thinking, "Oh my God, I could go to prison. I could get a ten year beef for this. I could get a fifteen year beef for this. I could get third struck here. You know, what am I doing?" But, you know what? All that might even go through my head. But it doesn't matter. I talk myself into doing the crime.

Once I'm committing crimes, I'll talk myself right into it, just so I can get the money I need, and I can get on about my way, and I'll block out all the crap that comes with it. That's why, you know, being on the run is a head game for yourself.

*Do you think there's anything that the state could do differently, or the prison system could do differently, that would make people stop and think, or is that a lost cause?*

Yeah, I don't know. Deterrence, I don't know.

I've never believed in the whole deterrence thing. Deterrence works for a child that's grown up and learned to look beyond his nose, and been taught that from the get go. I wasn't. I wanted it now and I had to have it now. I was raised that way. I was spoiled, and so I didn't understand delaying gratification. I didn't understand working for what I wanted. I didn't understand sacrificing. I didn't understand any of that. So there is my flaw.

For a child who was raised in a good home, and taught to delay gratification, and be responsible, then deterrence might apply.

*But for people like you, it doesn't work.*

No.

*Let's go back to what you were saying about people who do end up back here, lose their focus. Why do people lose their focus? Why do they go astray and end up back in a place like this?*

Well, I suppose at the top of the list would be drugs. But then you would have to answer the question: why do they relapse, or why do they resort to drugs?

There's a lot going on out there, compared to in here. In here, my laundry bill's paid, my food is fed to me, I have a bunk, I have a measly old job where I work five hours a day or whatever. As small as this life is in here, it is a life. But everything is taken care of in here. Compared to having to do all the running you have to do out there, man—you got to keep appointments, and you got to be here, and be there. You've got to be responsible. There's a lot going on out there. There really is.

And it's been so long since I've been out there, that I can't even name it all right now. I can just remember how hectic it was at times. And it just seemed like there was so much going on. You're always trying to catch up. You're always behind, and, it was just real frustrating.

And, when I finally did take off, it was easy. It was, like, schwooo, "Wow, let's go!" and I went on a three week run robbing, where I didn't answer to anybody. Slept in a hotel every night. Robbed. That was it.

*And you think you'll avoid that this time.*

Yeah.

*And, it's because of internal changes in you.*

Yeah. Well, several changes. I mean, yeah, internal. But, they come from several different sources. First and foremost was probably a four to five year relationship that I engaged in with Jeannie, who now is a very dear friend of mine. She pointed me in the right directions, as far as books to read and such, and we went through a lot together. She's a psychologist, and she actually gave me, if you will, therapy, for four to five years, over the phone, in letters, and in visits.

*What kind of books have you found helpful? Are you referring to self-help books, or psychology books, or—?*

Psychology, yeah. Understanding behavior. The books I read in my psych classes.

I was going to say, my education is another factor. I ended up having a real interest in psychology when I was getting my Associate's degree. And, man, I must have took five or six psych classes through my Associate's degree.

*Was this in Walla Walla, or where?*

Yeah. Yeah, at Walla Walla.

*Are these correspondence classes, or actual on-site classes?*

No, that was when they still had academics.

*So, is the main problem with most people who re-offend that they don't change for the better while they're in prison to prepare themselves for getting out?*

Some try to. Some start to.

But nobody's getting any deep-seated therapy in here. Look, you can go through Breaking Barriers,[*] and you can go through Toastmasters, and you can be in PAP, and you can even get an education. Well, at least you can get your GED, and you can go out there and get a welding certificate, or a computer certificate.

But what does that teach you about why you're here, where you came from, where you learned to do the things that you do to get here, identify the patterns of behavior, identify cycles in your life that lead you to keep making the same mistakes? Until you identify what all this stuff is, then you're still susceptible to the same behavior. You haven't identified it. So it's still there. It's still a habit. It's still a pattern for you.

So, I mean, we're talking serious therapy. And nobody gets it in here. And people in here need it. Or they need some type of directed counseling, some type of counseling that is actually giving them direction on where to look, and what to look for, and, you know, digging deeper here and there. 'Cause without it, you're going to have the same behavioral patterns.

I see it in here on guys that I've known for ten, fifteen years, doing the same stuff, running the same games. It's just the same old crap. Hearing the same stuff come out of their mind, out of their mouth, and, man, it's old.

*So, was it just kind of a lucky break for you that you fell in with somebody who's knowledgeable—?*

Very lucky.

*—about such things, and—?*

Very lucky.

*—was able to give you therapy, in effect?*

Yeah.

*So, formally there is no opportunity for that kind of counseling or therapy in here?*

---

[*]A self-help program.

No.

It's tough, yeah. They don't offer one-on-one counseling. Or group counseling, which would—if you could find a good group that you trust, then some of these guys could probably learn some things. But they don't offer any of that in prison.

Which is kind of interesting, 'cause we're here for thinking disorders. We're here because we think wrong. And we act on our thoughts the wrong way. And, you know, if we don't learn about it, we don't understand where it comes from, then where does it go? It doesn't go anywhere. Keep doing it all of our life.

*How did you luck into connecting with a person who could give you therapy?*

It was when I quit drinking on the street.

That morning after I had passed out in a building and ended up being arrested for breaking and entering, I said, "Man, I need to get some help. I've been drinking too much." And I had. For a couple months, I'd been just plowing down the booze.

So, I called this treatment program, and put myself through outpatient treatment. It was a private, outpatient treatment program, and Jeannie was my therapist there. She was my one-on-one counselor. We had groups three times a week. Then, every week, we'd have a one-on-one. She was my personal counselor for the one-on-ones.

And she was good. And we connected, and—in more ways than one. [Laughs.] Actually, though, it stayed professional. Just a good friendship. It wasn't until, you know, about five or six years later that we shared with each other that there were more feelings there, which, that far down the road like that, it was OK.

*And people don't have access to that kind of thing in here.*

No, they don't. We've got a guy in here that's supposed to be teaching drug treatment, and he's so busy, he can't even get your one-on-ones in, and he's, he's—ah, it's ridiculous, man.

*Why do you, or did you, drink? And why did you do drugs?*

Well, I drank socially, in the beginning, but then it later developed to where I would drink to punish myself. I would drink to forget about—I have a hard time with—I panic. I think that's why I run. I have a tendency to panic when I feel pressure, and when I feel, you know, the world caving in on me, whether it's from a responsibility, whether it's from other responsibilities. So, my answer was to drink.

As far as where that comes from, it could come from anything. Drinking was what my dad did, when we had problems. Drinking was what my peers in my childhood—or at least in my teen years—did. They drank. So, I learned that that's just what you do. I mean, when it gets tough, go tie one on.

I would also reward myself. When I was doing good, I'd reward myself by getting drunk. [Laughs.] I pretty much had an excuse to drink all the time.

*How does drinking constitute a punishment, in those cases when it does?*

Because of what I know will happen. Spending my money when I know I shouldn't. "I don't deserve this. I'm not worth it. I'm going to go get drunk. I don't care if I can't afford it. I don't deserve to have it," you know. Just having shitty, low self-esteem.

I mean, as years go by, I begin to think that I can't not drink anyway. I mean, drinking is part of my life. And, it was just, you know, a habit. That was just how I would react to life's circumstances, life's situations.

*In a way, you associate it with escape, with your tendency to run.*

It's a release.

*So, getting drunk when you have a problem is similar to hopping into the car and just driving away and not dealing with it.*

Yeah.

*How is it going to be different this time? Do you feel that you have the maturity and, for that matter, the contacts with other people that, if you find yourself falling into that mode, you can turn to someone for help? So, could you pick up the phone and call Jeannie, or your father, or me for that matter, just any friend on the outside, and say, "I'm feeling tempted just to take off and drive away, 'cause I screwed up at work," or, "I just smoked dope and I shouldn't have, and I'm starting to feel like I'm falling into old habits"? I mean, would you reach out to another person now?*

I've got ten people right off the bat I could name, yourself included, that I know I could call, and be honest with. There are at least that many people in my life that I can be completely honest with about all of that. So, yeah, I have a good network of people that I can contact should anything like that happen.

But another thing is—

*And you wouldn't feel embarrassed—?*

No.

*—to say, "I'm screwing up, or am on the verge of doing so. I need some help. I need somebody to talk to"?*

No. This is less about embarrassment than it is about fear. This time I don't have to worry about a parole officer saying, "Well, come on down and see me. You're going to jail." I don't have to worry about that.

I was just talking to somebody about that this morning. If I was to be out somewhere and I had a couple drinks, and I felt like shit about it, well, you know what, I'll go catch an AA meeting. Or I'll go call Nick, or I'll go call Danny.* Or I'll call my dad and say, "Man, Dad, I screwed up," you know. I don't have a problem with that.

And what's nice about it is then I knock it off, I brush it off. I get up, and I walk. I'm responsible to myself now.

So, yeah, that's very important. Very important. To have a network of support like that.

*So, you used to have more of the fear factor, that, "If I screw up, there's a parole officer looking over my shoulder who I have to constantly report to, and he's—*

Absolutely.

*—always trying to figure out where I am and what I'm up to."*

Absolutely. Absolutely. I haven't been without supervision since I was fourteen. This'll be the first time since I was fourteen that I don't have supervision.

And, there's another point that I was going to make—and don't get me wrong when I say this—but, I want to say that I've always been a loner. And that doesn't mean I haven't had friends, but what I mean is, in all my adult years, I've had two separate groups of people. And neither of those groups really knew all of me. The group of people that knew I'd been to prison, well they didn't know what I wanted, and what I was afraid of, and what I was striving to do, and they didn't understand the other side of my life. They didn't know about all that.

And then I had the other side of my life, such as my work life. The people in that life, or in that circle, they didn't understand that I'd been to prison. They never even knew.

So, I had two separate groups of people that I gave my time to, but neither one of them knew me completely, to where I was open and honest with them completely.

So, in that sense, I've always been a loner. But I've opened up quite a bit in the last, well, the last eight years, since I've been down on this beef, and since I've been involved with Jeannie. Learned to be a little bit less secluded. Opened up.

*When you look at your fellow prisoners, can you spot who's kind of got their life back in order and who hasn't, and who's going to make it and who's not, at least the ones you know fairly well?*

---

*These are two ex-con friends of Jimi's who still live in the Seattle area and were reportedly doing well and staying clean on the outside. I have changed the names.

*If I picked out twenty people that we know from PAP, and I said, "What if these twenty people got released tomorrow?" Could you tell me, with some degree of confidence, which ones would be committing crimes again within a few months?*

No.

*So it's that hard to predict?*

I couldn't do it with any kind of confidence. I could give you my gut, but I think there's very few, unfortunately, that have clicked on why they're here.

Now, I'm not counting the people who have committed one crime—generally a murder— one crime of passion. Never been in trouble before, and then here they are, and they're going to get out twenty years later. I'm not counting them, because their numbers on repeat offenses are real low. They generally don't come back.

But, I'm talking about people who have been repeat offenders. You point out twenty repeat offenders to me, I couldn't tell you. I could listen to them for an hour and guess, but that's all.

And probably eighteen of them are coming back. Or are staying within the system, in some sense, whether they're coming back to prison, or just going in and out of jail for little things. Or maybe just being addicted for many years to come. I don't know a whole lot of people that I could actually say, "Well, he's not coming back." There's only a handful of people in here that I know of—of the repeat offender type—that I think have gotten it, that it's clicked with them.

*So if the superintendent came to you and said, "You now have the authority to release any ten people in here that you want, and the only condition is that if any of them re-offend, then you have to serve their punishment," or something like that, you couldn't pick out ten people that you could say, "Yeah, I'm going to pick this guy; I'm going to bet on this guy"?*

I wouldn't. I wouldn't take that chance. Wouldn't even think about it.

*It's a depressing idea that eighteen out of twenty would come back, or whatever it might be.*

Yeah, well, I'm not saying I'm right, but that's how I feel.

*Yeah.*

That's based on my experience in the system, which is sixteen plus years. That's what I see.

You know, we don't give much publicity or much media attention to the people that do make it. But, the numbers of those that don't are stunning. Recidivism is real ugly.

*Is there any hope, or anything you can say of a more positive nature? Because people are going to read this, and their reaction is going to be, "Well, that's what we've been saying all along, that most of these people are a lost cause, and they shouldn't be let out, because they're just going to re-offend if they are let out. So keep them locked up and throw away the key."*

But that's not what I'm saying. I'm not saying any of them are a lost cause. I'm saying, as long as they're not getting what they need, they're a lost cause. And, you know, when I talk about therapy, I mean therapy with integrity intact. I mean therapy with the integrity of the therapist-client confidentiality intact. That's something that inmates worry about.

*Sure.*

They worry about revealing things, being open and honest with a psychologist, or a psychiatrist, and then having that information put in their file to be judged at a later date. And that happens. I mean, people have lost out on being paroled based on things in their file that they said to a psychiatrist during an evaluation.

*You mentioned that other than your first time down, you've wanted to get out of jail and get to prison. Why is that? Why do people want to avoid jail and go to prison?*

Freedom. You have more freedom in the joint.

*Compare the two for me.*

Yeah. You have more freedom. You know, it's just easier. You have better visits, more access to the phone, you can wear your own clothes. You know, probably all the things that they say, if they took them away, then we wouldn't want to come back.

But we're human beings, and we adapt to whatever we have. And, no matter what it is that we adapt to, they're going to want to keep taking more. Then every time society takes more, we adapt to that.

Like, it was just two, three years ago that they took this thirty percent,[*] and all the inmates were getting ready to riot all across the state. I mean, it was insane. Everybody was, like, "No way! They can't possibly do this! Are you crazy? You're going to take money out of the money that my family sends me?" And our people, our families on the street, were upset about it.

---

[*] In Washington, 30% of all prisoner income—pay from their jobs, money sent in from their people on the outside, etc.—is confiscated by the state.

But, here we are three years down the road, and who cares? You know, people still complain, but they just have thirty percent more sent in when their people send money from the outside. So we've adjusted.

*But returning to the jail versus prison comparison, why is it that jail turns out to be worse than prison?*

You got to understand, we're living here for a long period of time. Jail's temporary. But, you know, there's guys in prison that are doing life. The rest of their life. In here.

Well, what has a guy like that got to lose if he doesn't have a TV to go home to at night? What does he have to lose when some sucker out on the yard says something out of his neck to him, and his honor is on the line? "Oh, wow, dude just called you a punk!"

Well, you know what? If you say no more TV, and no more clothing, and no more visits, and there isn't anything left to lose, that guy on the yard's a dead man. The guy's got life without, you know, and when they take him to ad seg, and make him do a program in IMU, it wouldn't be no different from what he's already doing here.

You know, it's like losing your freedom on the street. You go to jail, you lose your freedom, and everything that comes along with freedom—your ability to drive, to travel, whatever. Well, when you go to the hole in here, you have to lose something, too. You lose the ability to wear personal clothes, the ability to walk around without handcuffs, the ability to watch TV. You lose a lot.

And you have to. You can't have it be just as bad out of the hole as in the hole.

All this stuff in here is management.

*So, they want you to have stuff that you care about losing when you're in prison.*

Sure.

*But why don't they want you to have stuff you care about losing when you're in jail?*

I think that's the whole thing with knowing it's a temporary layover. They don't care.

There's so many people in jail. There's way more people in jails than there are in prisons. They're just constantly going in, day in, day out. I think it would be impossible, logistically, to have inmates having their TVs, and inmates having their clothes, and inmates having jewelry, and inmates having schooling. You just couldn't do it, 'cause inmates are going in and out every day. You don't know whether you're going to be there, you know, in a month or in six months.

*Is some of it intentional, based on wanting to put pressure on people to plea bargain? If jail is really bad, then people will want get sentenced and go to prison?*

Some think so. I don't subscribe to that. It sounds paranoid to me.

*Yeah.*

But there are those that do.

*I have a friend who has twice been arrested for trivial things, and had to do a few hours in jail each time, and he wanted to know what advice you would give to somebody who is basically a law-abiding person, and is unlikely ever to do serious time anywhere, but might, you know, get into some minor kind of trouble, or might by some error, end up in jail, just for a brief period, like, say, overnight, or for a few days. What advice would you have for somebody like that?*

You mean, when he gets to jail, or—?

*Yeah. I mean, how should he conduct himself, or what should he be concerned about, or is he in any danger?*

Yeah, it depends on what county he's in, though any jail is potentially dangerous. But there's a big difference between some of these jails nowadays, you know, where they've got these closed door cells, and some of them probably single cells, compared to something like King County. King County's got just a big floor, with maybe ten, fifteen beds in it, and even those are just cement slabs. But, there's probably forty or fifty guys in that tank. So there's, you know, thirty guys on the floor, and only ten or so who get a bed. It's cramped. It's packed. I mean, you're right between two guys; you have no idea who they are.

So, yeah, I mean, it depends on where you're at.

But in general, what you have to do is stay to yourself. Stay to yourself. Mind your own business. And if it feels like somebody's invading your space, then you have to bite, and you got to bite hard. [Laughs.] Don't avoid that, otherwise people will continue to invade your space.

*And that's even if you're going to be there briefly, if you're there for, like, a few days.*

Well, if you—

*You still have to worry about that kind of thing.*

—want to make your few days more tolerable, it's up to you. [Laughs.] You know, there are all kinds of people in jail, including predators. They prey on your food, they prey on you, they prey on the attention they can get for, you know, giving you whatever kind of hard time they can give you. Jail's not fun. Not at all.

*And you should keep to yourself. So, you shouldn't seek out ways to connect with people who might be—?*

That helps.

*—quality people?*

Well, when I say keep to yourself and do your own thing, that doesn't mean you shouldn't find somebody that you can clique with, and, you know, talk to, and maybe play some cards with. That helps. That does. In fact, it always feels better to do that.

*What kind of people are most at risk? I think he was concerned, because he's kind of a yuppie and he looks like one, and he's soft in the sense of not being used to that world.*

But there's a lot of guys that are in there like that. There is. There's more than you think. I mean, if it's King County, there's typically, like, one or two per tank.

Now, when I say there's a lot of guys, I mean in the grand scheme of things. But they're still a minority. He may well be the only yuppie in that tank. So, yeah, you want to be careful, and you want to maybe find somebody that—

*Are people like that a special target? Is he at more risk because recognize him as vulnerable and out of his element?*

Sure. Sure. He would be. Anything that looks like weakness is going to be a target.

*I told him that he has to be careful of going to the authorities about anything, that that's going to get him in trouble, especially if he intends to be there any length of time. I suppose if he's there overnight, who cares, but if he's going to be there for any length of time, then he's got to be careful not to be perceived as taking his problems to the guard, or anything like that.*

Yeah.

*Would that be one of the main things to avoid?*

Yes, but you also make a good point that it depends on how long he's going to be there. The reality is that he's a citizen. He lives by the laws and the values and the norms of society. So, if he's going to be there for a day or two, and he's in trouble, then he needs to go to the authorities. Bottom line. They'll put him somewhere where he's all by himself. It may be boring, but he'll be safe. And, the reality is, out in his world, that's what's right. He's allowed to seek that kind of help.

*So, it's only those who've chosen a criminal lifestyle that have to live by the code.*

Sure.

*Not so much the outsiders who fall into that world temporarily, or by accident.*

Yeah.

*You know, talking about people who are new or temporary arrivals to this world, can you still remember how it felt for you when it was all new? Can you kind of sympathize with people like my friend who've never been a part of this world before, and understand the kind of intimidation the prison system, or going to jail, represents for people like him?*

One of the most traumatic experiences I've had in my life is something that I still haven't even dealt with. I mean, it hasn't ever been fully resolved. And that is concerning my mother driving me to detention and turning me in when I was thirteen or fourteen. I think I wrote you and told you about this story.

*Yeah.*

I still haven't resolved that. If I spend some time and really think about it, it breaks me down again, and I'll cry.

It was just a terrible, terrible experience being locked up. And I was young.

I wasn't around anybody else though. When I was locked up, I was locked up in a cell by myself. And maybe I was more afraid of that, you know, the isolation. But, I didn't have to worry about, you know, anybody harming me or anything, 'cause I was locked away.

But, the experience was huge. Huge. I mean, so huge that for years I hated my mom. I didn't trust her. I thought all women were scum, and they couldn't be trusted.

I mean, for years, all this stuff was going on inside me, and I didn't even realize it, until I thought about how I acted in relationships. You know, I just kept diving out on them. Couldn't trust them.

*So, it certainly didn't do what it was intended to do. It didn't put you on the straight and narrow, and—*

No. It made me very angry. I was a very angry kid from that point on.

*So you just took it as an act of hostility, that you were being harmed unjustly.*

I was very angry that she had done that to me, rather than that I had done it to myself. Nobody pointed out to me my own responsibility. Nobody pointed out to me what my thinking was, or what my thinking could have been. They just locked me up.

*Has it made you unwilling to do what your mother did? I mean, if you found yourself with a teenage child who was totally out of control, and you had tried everything you could, and he was still getting himself into trouble, and you saw him going down the wrong road—he was into drugs and maybe committing crimes or whatever—could you see turning him in and putting him in that world?*

No.

*You would do anything to avoid that.*

Anything. Anything to avoid that.

I'm pretty patient with kids, too. The experiences that I've had with my godkids have been great.

I had a friend at McNeil, and his old lady used to visit him with her three kids. Those kids just loved me. Every visit, they'd come and, you know, spend the day at my table. They wouldn't even visit their mom's boyfriend.

For some reason, I get along with kids. I'm real patient with them.

No, that would be the last thing I'd ever do to a child.

*So, what would you tell somebody who was in a situation like that? Somebody that came to you and said, "My kid is totally out of control," and they described their child, and it sounded to you like they were describing you when you were that age. And they said, "I've tried everything I can. I think I'm just going to turn him in and have him put in juvenile detention"? What would you tell that person?*

I'd tell them about my experience. I'd tell them what it did to me.

# HENRY and 9—October 1998

"We had a thing, back then, a slogan. We'd say, 'Each one, teach one,' you know. We felt it was our duty to take the kids that were coming in at the time and teach them what they needed to know. Because institutions are a pretty hard place to survive in, especially at that time, and especially Walla Walla. So, the ones that we would recognize as being worth saving, we would more or less take them, put them under our wings, and try to get through to them."

Henry in 1997.

During my brief stint working inside the prison for the telemarketing company, one of our prisoner employees was Henry,[*] a smallish, older African American man with a graying beard, a ready smile, and a twinkle in his eye. He was easy to get along with, and a good worker. Henry was a member of PAP, but I really didn't get to know him well until the telemarketing room shut down and freed up his Wednesdays to attend meetings.

It wouldn't have occurred to me before then to approach Henry about the book project, but after I brought 9 aboard he strongly urged me to ask Henry to participate as well. He sold me on the idea.

Henry, it turns out, is a mentor of sorts for 9. During the time that WSR went to two-man cells during renovations, Henry and 9 were cellees. 9 speaks of him with the utmost respect and admiration, and regards him as having been a huge and positive influence on his life.

Since then, the more I have gotten to know Henry, the more I have come to share 9's high opinion of him.

Henry has been incarcerated for decades on multiple life without parole sentences. He's been through the wars in tougher prisons during tougher times than today's WSR. He has done what he's had to do not only to survive in the system, but to win the acceptance and respect of his peers.

Whether in spite of or because of his longevity in this most brutal of worlds, there is a palpable dignity about him. When he looks at you with that kind smile of the gentle sage, you find yourself unconsciously adding a "Mister" to his name when addressing him.

He is a nonviolent, non-confrontational man nowadays, partly because he's already established his reputation and partly because WSR is a slightly less inhumane environment than the typical prison. Don't mistake that for weakness, though. He is a proud man, with a no-nonsense manner. Henry has no trouble standing up for himself if he feels he is being disrespected.

His philosophy is a stoic one. He preaches a message of adjusting to your circumstances, and taking advantage of the available opportunities to improve yourself. Even if your lot is to be in prison for the rest of your life, you accept that with serenity and with dignity, and you make the most of it.

He's the first to admit that he does not always live up to his ideals, but I doubt there are many of us who could do as well in his situation.

Though Henry appreciates the admiration many of us have for him, he is not arrogant. If anything, he is inclined to laugh it off or make a self-deprecating remark when we give him the "wise man" treatment, like we expect nothing but profound thoughts from him. Indeed, his book knowledge does not seem unusually extensive,

---

[*]Henry has chosen to be identified by his first name only.

and though he is intelligent, he does not stand out as remarkably so. When prompted on complex or abstract matters such as privatized prisons, the economic and political implications of prison labor, philosophical issues about punishment, etc., he will offer opinions, but one does not get the impression such matters are his primary focus.

Henry's wisdom is of a more immediate, practical nature. It is the product of a long life filled with more than its share of challenges and tribulations. It is the product of meeting those challenges and tribulations firmly and responsibly and with eyes open, so as to learn from them.

His life experiences have qualified him as a teacher and role model for many of the younger prisoners. Among his greatest assets as a teacher is an almost limitless patience. Given the way the prison environment pulls people away from the path of growth and maturity, Henry knows improvement takes years and comes only after the lessons that setbacks and disappointments teach.

So he keeps preaching the message, living the message, and he accepts and works with people in spite of their failures. Every so often, he sees somebody handling a difficult situation with responsibility and maturity, and he knows he had a role in that.

9 adores Henry, but he's been far from the ideal student, especially in the early years of his incarceration. I once asked Henry, "How did you know not to give up on 9?"

"I don't give up on people," he replied.

Henry maintains that while he was involved in the incident that resulted in his receiving multiple life sentences, he is not guilty of the crime for which he was convicted. I tend to be more comfortable with prisoners who admit their crimes, accept responsibility, and express remorse, but I can't condemn Henry for not doing so, since I am not privy to what really happened. If, as he claims, he didn't commit the crime, I wouldn't want him to feign remorse just to impress people.

For a long time, there was no realistic hope that Henry would ever leave prison. But like so many prisoners, he's spent years and whatever money he could find making appeals and trying to get his case reopened and his sentence reconsidered. Shortly before this first interview, he received some potentially good news. As you'll read in the transcript, his case had finally taken a turn for the better.

Despite this successful battle, the war was far from over. No single ruling was going to free him. If he was ever to leave prison, it would come at the end of a long process of more rulings and appeals and delays and defeats and victories. But at least for the first time since his original sentencing, it didn't seem like such an extreme long shot that he would one day leave prison a free man.

9 tells me that he and some of Henry's other friends have a tougher time with the emotional roller coaster of Henry's case than Henry himself does. In an unusual reversal of roles, Henry finds himself counseling *them* to avoid the high hopes and disappointments of this process.

Still, there's no question that it weighs on him, and he admits that. As much as he tries to keep a positive attitude, the cumulative effect of the suspense, delays, and defeats can get to him. I suspect that preoccupation made him less inclined to give a lot of himself to this book project. I'm told he is self-conscious about his written English, so we were limited to taped interviews, and I was able to secure only two of those with him. I did, however, have many conversations with him off tape that deepened my understanding of prison and thereby indirectly contributed much to this book.

I just cannot see Henry choosing to lead a criminal lifestyle if and when he is released. Of all the prisoners I grew to know, Henry may well be the one I would rank as the least likely to re-offend.

In our second interview, I asked him about this very issue of whether he would re-offend if he were released. In the pause before he answered, we looked at each other, and smiled at each other. For the benefit of the readers, he gave a straight and thoughtful answer. But for me, any answer beyond what passed between us in that momentary silence was superfluous. At his present stage of development, Henry's about as inclined toward criminally victimizing others as I am. I know it, and that smile told me that he knows that I know it.

This first interview with Henry was actually scheduled as an interview with 9, but he brought Henry with him, so I had the opportunity to converse with them jointly.

This was one of my most enjoyable interviews. Listening to their banter and seeing the obvious fondness and respect they have for each other was simply a delight.

Henry deserves no small share of the credit for any good that 9 has done with his life or will do in the future. He is a role model and a teacher for those who will listen. Because many of those he influences in a positive direction have been or will be released from prison, I have to believe his efforts have helped to avert a considerable amount of crime and damaged lives. Society owes a debt of gratitude to this convicted murderer.

*Well, this was intended to be a conversation with 9, but we have a surprise guest, a pleasant surprise. Henry has dropped in to join us tonight. Let's get a little background on you, Henry. How long have you been incarcerated on this particular beef?*

Henry: Twenty-one years.

*How many of those twenty-one years have you spent here at WSR?*

Henry: Going on four.

*Where'd you spend most of your time? Walla Walla?*

Henry: Walla Walla, yeah.

*OK. How long have you known 9-0?*

Henry: Since he was a baby. [Laughs.]

9: Yeah.

Henry: How long have you been down? Twelve years?

9: Yeah.

Henry: Yeah. Known him twelve years.

*How'd you meet?*

Henry: Well, he came to Walla Walla as what we categorized as a "lost soul." He was involved in his little gang activities. That was his mindset at the time. But he was still just a kid when he came into the institution. And, some of us more or less took him under our wing.

We had a thing, back then, a slogan. We'd say, "Each one, teach one," you know. We felt it was our duty to take the kids that were coming in at the time and teach them what they needed to know. Because institutions are a pretty hard place to survive in, especially at that time, and especially Walla Walla. So, the ones that we would recognize as being worth saving, we would more or less take them, put them under our wings, and try to get through to them.

*Now, this is just something you guys were doing informally—*

Henry: It was voluntary, yeah.

*—on your own; this isn't some kind of state program or official prison program.*

Henry: No. Oh no, no, no. The state was the one that was just throwing them in there. So, I mean, it was up to us to see to it that they survive. So, and that's how I met him.

I took to him then, as I do now. I had a great deal of liking for him, because I saw even back then that he had a lot of potential.

*So, he comes in on a murder beef, he's involved in gang activity and such; what did you spot about 9-0 that told you he's one of the ones that can be saved and should be saved?*

Henry: Well, first of all, he had the gift of gab. Secondly, the thing that I recognized and appreciated most about him was he also had the foresight to listen. He was very attentive, as he is now [laughs, looking at 9]—he hasn't changed. He would listen.

You know, we all understood that most of the youngsters that came through weren't like that. You'd say something to them and they would agree—"Yeah, you're right. Yeah"—and go right on doing what they were doing.

But, then, we also had the wisdom enough to know that a lot of the things that they would say that they would not do any more, really, in their form of life, and the way their life was structured, if they were put in a certain position, they had to react in certain ways. We understood that. We would make allowances for that.

But we also respected them for the fact that they listened when we told them, "Hey, OK, if it's anything that's gang-related, keep it with the gangs. Don't bring it to the old timers. Don't involve us." Because we were the ones that were going to have to step up, and go to the administration in order to let them know that, "Hey, things are all right. You know, it's over with." So they were respectful enough for that, and we respected them for that.

And we respected them for their lifestyle, because we knew that it was their type of lifestyle, as we had ours, you know. We had no problem with each other.

*Clarify that a little bit for me, when you say that you were in the position that you guys would have had to go to the administration to tell them everything's OK. What do you mean?*

Henry: Well, if there had been an altercation as far as gang violence and stuff, they couldn't very well go to the administration and say, "Well, it's OK," you know, "It's straightened out," or, "We've resolved the problem." The administration wouldn't listen to them.

But, if three or four of us old timers went and said, "Well, OK, we've talked to these guys. Now, that's over," then even if they didn't just take our word for it, they would listen. And most of the time, their response would be, "Are you sure?" "Yeah." "Well, all right. All right, you guys go on," you know.

*You didn't want them to involve you guys in what they were doing, or even to keep you informed in detail what was going on, because you wanted to be able to go to the administration and say, "As far as we know, there's no problem"?*

Henry: No, no, no. It wasn't that way. No, not—

*OK, I'm still misinterpreting your point then.*

Henry: It wasn't that we wanted to be able to go to the administration, no. The thing of it was, see, at Walla Walla, they have a thing there to where anything that happens, if it happens on a scale of more than two people, they categorize it as being "racial," or "racial conflict," or "gang-related."

9: "Riot." A "riot situation."

Henry: Or "riot." Yeah, they declare it as a "riot situation."

So now, say if four or five of the Crips had an altercation with four or five of the Bloods, and they had their altercation maybe in the gym or wherever, and the police maybe didn't catch it. But, the word got back to the administration. And we knew, by being old timers, that OK, their next move, in order to say that they were making the institution secure is going to be to lock it down. To avoid that, we'd say, "OK, look, Associate Superintendent, this is what happened. If they had an altercation, it's over with now. That's done." You know.

*Right.*

Henry: "That's taken care of."

*So, you'd tell them, "It was overblown. It's not what the rumors said it was. There's—*

Henry: Right.

*"—no reason for a lockdown."*

Henry: Yeah, yeah, so there's no reason to lock everybody down, and make everybody suffer for what eight or ten guys have done.

*Yeah.*

Henry: But it wasn't that I would go to 9, or to any of the others, and tell them to stop, or say, "Hey, what's going on, man?" You know, because if they tell me, I wouldn't understand it anyway, because they had their own little lingo, they had their own little logic, they had their own little signs that they used, you know, and I wasn't aware of them. So, I would be out of place even trying to intervene in their conversations or their activities.

I mean, our whole thing was, once they got there, there was maybe twelve or fifteen that we really put a lot of effort into salvaging, as far as knowing that, "Hey, whatever he's caught up in, this is really a nice young man," you know, "But, hey, OK, he's involved in this. We understand he's involved in it, and he has taken this as the way of his life, so we can't just tell him, 'Hey, man, get out of that.'" It doesn't work that way. We had sense enough to know that.

But, we also know that, hey, inside of him, he wants to be left alone. He wants to do his own time. He doesn't want to be involved in conflicts every other day to where he has to go and maybe, say, strap up, put a knife on, or when you go around the corner, peek to see who's there and all. We know that he didn't want to be in that situation. So, therefore, we would put a lot of effort into teaching him, "Hey, it doesn't have to be this way. But, in order for it to change, you have to be the one to change it."

"Well, what am I to do?"

"Well, hey, look at me. I'm doing the rest of my life here. I don't have to live like that. You don't have to live like that either. All you have to do is be your own man."

*Let's get some background on you, Henry, so—*

Henry: Sure.

*—we can understand how you came to be the person you are, how you reached this stage of life.*

9: [Laughs.]

*[Laughs.]*

9: Yeah, that'll take awhile.

Henry: [Laughs.]

*You say you've been down for twenty-one years on this beef?*

Henry: Yes.

*Were you in prison before that, or was this your first time?*

Henry: No, this is my second time.

*OK.*

Henry: My first encounter with prison was here at WSR in Nineteen fifty-nine. I came in here at nineteen years old for a robbery. And, I got out, and I stayed out, until I was thirty-eight years old. And, I came back to prison at the age of thirty-eight, and I've been here ever since. I'm fifty-eight years old now.

*What can you tell me about your current beef? Is it something you're comfortable talking about?*

Henry: I have no problem talking about my beef. I mean, I'm serving the time for it, so I don't have no problem talking about it.

Even though I've broken the law, I haven't done anything to where I feel that I should be just totally ashamed of it, you know, as with crimes that violate kids or women.

I'm in for murder. In fact, I was charged with five counts of first degree murder. It happened in Nineteen seventy-eight. And, there was another individual involved.

We went into an apartment. And, there was people there that had had an altercation with this friend of mine that I wasn't aware of. Consequently, it came out to where there was gunfire. I was the first person shot. Twice. From what I understand, it's supposed to have been an accident. I wasn't supposed to have been shot, but I was.

*Who was shooting at whom?*

Henry: Well, my friend was shooting at the guy that was standing right next to me. That's how I supposedly got shot.

But, anyway, five people wound up dead. And I was charged with five counts of first degree murder.

*You were there for what purpose?*

Henry: Well, I was there as more or less a mediator. What it all started from was a drug deal. And the drugs that was supplied to my friend—according to him—was bad drugs. So, the thing of it was, I got involved because I knew both parties very well. My involvement came about when my friend asked me, "Hey, come over there with me. I'm going to go over there, and I either want my money back for these drugs, or they're going to give me a new supply."

So I said, "Well, OK, no problem. Come on" What I didn't know was that the night before, there had been a big altercation about these drugs, and guns had been drawn and all. I wasn't informed of any of that. So, me, the good guy Henry, I say, "Hey, come on, let's go. We'll straighten this out."

And I go over there, and here I am.

*So there were two of you, and how many of them in the apartment?*

Henry: Six.

*Two against six?*

Henry: Yeah.

*Everyone armed?*

Henry: No. No. No, everyone wasn't armed. In fact, there was only two people that had weapons.

*Oh, OK. So your friend was one of the people doing the shooting.*

Henry: Yeah, he had two weapons. So he was really armed.

9: [Laughs.] Really armed.

Henry: Yeah.

*So you just kind of got caught in the crossfire.*

Henry: Well, yeah, I did. I did. But, I mean, I don't blame no one for that but myself.

*Now, how did you get charged for the murders? Simply because you were present, and therefore an accomplice in some sense?*

Henry: Yeah. And see, all my life, through my growing up, and people that I've been associated with, I've been a person who knows that, hey, you don't talk. Even if you have to go to jail, hey, you go to jail. You don't talk. You just ride it out.

*So you would have had to sell out your friend.*

Henry: I would have had to sell out my friend. Yes.

*I see. So you didn't actually shoot anybody.*

Henry: I never even had a weapon. If I had, I should have shot him, because he's the one that shot me.
No, I didn't have a weapon.

*So basically, you had to either live by the code and take the fall, or you had to rat out your friend.*

Henry: Yeah. Yeah, I rode it.

*What happened to him?*

Henry: He's dead now. He died about six years ago of cancer. He died at Walla Walla.

*Was he serving time for the same incident?*

Henry: Oh yes. Yeah.

*Did he get a life sentence also?*

Henry: Yes. Yeah, and his just came up short, you know. I'm still here chugging along. [Laughs.]

9: [Laughs.]

*Why did it go down as first degree? Did they claim that you guys intended to kill them when you went there?*

Henry: That's the prosecuting attorney's thing, yeah.

*OK.*

Henry: Yeah, his thing was, "OK, you were there. You knew what was going on, and then even after it went on, you did not report it." Because, yeah, the thing I did was, I went home and had my wife patch me up, and I got in the bed and passed out, with two bullets in me.

But, for one time in my life, I was really glad to see the police, when they came and arrested me, so I could go to the hospital. In fact, one of the bullets had lodged on my spine.

Yeah, that was the first time in my life that I can think of that I was glad to see the police, so I could go to the hospital. [Laughs.] That was two days later.

9: [Laughs.]

*Did the prosecution claim that you had actually fired some of the shots, or did they just deem that irrelevant, and say that because you were there, that makes you responsible?*

Henry: Well, there was one guy that lived, that was shot five times, but he lived. And, he was part of the prosecuting attorney's team, and he said that he believed that I also engaged in the shooting.

*Oh, OK.*

Henry: But, they asked him, "Did you see him with a gun?"
"No."

Once he was shot, he just fell down and played dead, and he heard everything else that was going on in the house, so they asked him, "Well, did you hear him say anything about it?"

"No, I didn't hear him say a word."

"Did you hear the other guy?"

"Yeah, I heard everything he said," and he told them everything he said, exactly as it was, because, I mean, I was there also. But he didn't claim to hear nothing from me indicating I had done any of the shooting.

When I came out of the apartment, there was a girl there. She took my clothing off of me to find out where I was shot, because I kept sticking my finger through the hole, trying to figure out where it came out in my back, and I could never find where it did.

So, I was tripping. You know, I'm halfway in shock.

But anyway, she testified that when I came out of the apartment, I had no weapon. And she was right there at the doorway when I came out.

*So, you didn't do any kind of plea bargaining? You went to a full trial?*

Henry: No, I didn't do any kind of plea bargain.

*Did you have your own attorney, or a public defender?*

Henry: No, I had an attorney, if you want to call him an attorney.

9: Same one I had.

*Really?*

Henry: Yeah, the one that has about two or three wings now in the Washington DOC.

9: You might want to note for the record that Henry also just overturned his case, based on everything he just told you.

Henry: Yeah, I just had my case overturned in the Ninth Circuit Court, last January.

*And the grounds were?*

Henry: Well, the grounds were that this guy—well, part of it is because the sentence that I was sentenced under was unconstitutional. Because, actually, see, I was sentenced to life without the possibility of parole before the law was even on the books. They were talking about it in Olympia at that particular time, but they hadn't put it on the books yet. But they gave it to me.

Plus there was a lot of more complicated issues to it.

*So, you were sentenced to be in prison for the rest of your life, but now it's been reversed, so you have the potential to actually get out of here.*

Henry: Right. Yes.
I have a life sentence now. It started out with the death penalty.

*Oh, really?*

Henry: Yeah, they tried me for the death penalty, but they couldn't get that.

*So the prosecutor sought the death penalty, but the judge gave you life without parole.*

Henry: Yes.

*And now this reversal should reduce that to just regular life,—*

Henry: Right.

*—with the possibility of parole.*

Henry: Yes. So, now I'm waiting for it to be reduced for me to go home.

*And if it's reduced like that, what would it be reduced to? Are you already over what you would have had to serve?*

Henry: Well, according to the old guidelines, yes, I would be eligible for parole, because a life sentence meant twenty years, which was a mandatory thirteen years and four months. Well, I've done twenty flat. So, yes, I would be eligible to go home.
But, there's a catch to that also. There was five counts of murder. So far, they've taken two of them completely off of me, so I have three now. So, now, the three remaining life sentences are also being litigated in court, because the judge never stipulated how they were to run. When he sentenced me to life without the possibility of parole, he didn't specify it on each count.

9: Consecutive versus concurrent.

Henry: Right. So, now, that's being litigated in court, as to whether, if the judge doesn't stipulate it, then is it just one sentence, or three, one after another?

*OK.*

Henry: [Laughs.] It's complicated. I'm fighting. It's a fight.

*Are you optimistic? Do you think you're going to be walking out of this place fairly soon?*

Henry: Well, you know what? The statement that I have made to all my family, loved ones, and close friends, is that I might give out, but I'll never give up. And that's true. I wake up each day with that affirmation in mind. Yes. I might give out, but I won't never give up.

I'm not trying to be in that one hundred and ten percent of the guys that are in here, saying, "Well, hey, I shouldn't be here," because I did break the law, to a certain extent. But to be in here for the rest of my life, no, I don't feel that I'm going to do that.

But, it's not something that I go around crying about each day, because I'm still alive. I have a life here, you see.

You know, he's my cell partner. [Motions to 9.] And like I tell him no less than once or twice a week, "Hey, we're here. We can make a life here. If not better for us, then for someone." I don't let it get me to the point to where I would ever give up.

Oh, don't get me wrong; I don't walk around here just being a jolly good guy every day. You know, I have my moments.

*Sure.*

Henry: But I try to make most of my time be constructive. I try to do positive things all the time. I try to uplift other people. Whatever I'm involved in, I try to make sure that it's something that's of a positive nature, and if it's not, I won't participate, you know.

*When you spotted 9-0 and kind of took him under your wing at Walla Walla, did you see a lot of your younger self in him? Was there any similarity there?*

Henry: Yes. Very much so. We laugh about it now. [Laughs.]

9: [Laughs.]

Henry: Very much so. In fact, I have a son that I compare him to in a lot of ways.

Like, the other night, we were talking about something [laughs], and he asked me about something, and I refused him. You know, I'm on the bottom bunk and he's on the top, and I can't see his face. He's just laying there, and he asked me something, and I refused him, and the way [laughs], the way he said what he said, he was just like my son.

It wasn't what he said, but how he said it.

*Right, right.*

Henry: He said, "Why not?" [high-pitched, plaintive tone] you know, [laughs], like that.

*Yeah.*

Henry: And we laughed, you know. And then, it took him awhile to get it out of him because we were laughing, but he wanted to know, "Why are you laughing like that?" So, I explained it to him, "Man, you sound just like my boy—Little Henry—you know." And that's just the way I think of him.

*Yeah.*

Henry: I mean, hey, I love the guy. You know, I love him. He's just like a son to me. Because, I have more time to spend—quality time—with him, that I would love to have with my son, and my kids on the streets, but I don't have that. So, then, what I do is I utilize that through him. I mean, we spend a lot of quality time discussing quality ideas, you know. And that makes me feel good.

*Did you have any kind of mentor or role model like that yourself in your early period in prison?*

Henry: At first, all my role models and mentors were hustlers, pimps, you know, the Cadillac drivers, the guys with the three piece mohair suits and the Stetson hats. Guys that hung in the pool halls.

I mean, I had family. Don't get me wrong; I had a beautiful family. Mother and father, you know, they were ideal family people. But that wasn't for me. I mean, after I got to the age of fourteen, I was more or less allowed to just do as I please, because I was arrogant enough to get away with it.

I did have the sense to continue with my schooling. But I was doing all the other things. I was selling drugs, I was with the fast girls, I was gambling, and all this, and so, my thing to my parents was, "Hey, you don't have to do anything for me. I can take care of myself."

"Well, if you feel that way, then you can't stay here and not abide by our rules."

"Well, hey, fine, thank you. Do I have permission to leave?"

"Yes."

"Well, thank you very much!" So I was gone.

*You mentioned you had the early beef for robbery, back in the late Fifties.*

Henry: Yeah, Fifty-nine.

*And then you were out until you were thirty-eight years old.*

Henry: Yes.

*At which time you were convicted of murder.*

Henry: Yeah.

*During the time in between, when you were on the outside, were you pretty much living a criminal lifestyle that whole time?*

Henry: No. I was working. I worked for the federal government.

*OK.*

Henry: Yeah. I have an extensive work record working for the Hanford Nuclear Energy Commission as a radiation monitor.

*So you've had periods of mainstream work like that, and periods where you were doing the drugs and the criminal activity.*

Henry: Well, at times, I would even be still involved with the drug trade as I was working. You know, my thing was not so much the use of drugs. My thing was, I was more or less carried away by the money—you know, the selling part of the drugs. In fact, I never even realized that I had a drug habit until approximately a year and a half ago, when I came here and I went through the chemical dependency class and found out. And then I realized, well, I admitted to myself, that I had a habit.

All my life, I've never really indulged in any drug to excess but one. I've tried every type of drug there is, but I have never really been deeply involved with any drug other than marijuana. I loved marijuana. [Laughs.] I used to smoke it every day. But I never admitted to myself, or to anyone else, that I had a problem with marijuana until I went to the chemical dependency class here. I had never gone to a chemical dependency class, and I had had, oh God, I would say twelve, thirteen, fourteen marijuana beefs at Walla Walla, you know. But, hey, during that time, all that happened if they found it in your pocket, they'd take it and then put you in the hole for two days. You'd come out, and you'd go on about your business.

So, I never had no chance to really just reflect on what had happened to me, until I went to this class. And then, you know, I came to the conclusion that I had a problem with it. I was willing to accept that, and I did. And I have had quite a few chances to smoke weed here.

If you offered me some heroin or cocaine or something, you know, that was always just a wasted offer, you know. It just doesn't turn me on. But now, I turn down weed too, and I have no problem doing so.

In fact, a guy asked me today, you know, and I said, "No thank you." I don't have no problem doing that now.

But that class helped me quite a bit, because it made me realize that, hey, I don't need marijuana to be Henry. I had been indulging in marijuana since I was twelve years old. I mean, frequently. You know, I would make sure I had some every day, 'cause I would buy it by half pounds. [Laughs.]

The only thing that I can't shed, or that I have not been able to shed so far, is cigarettes. [Laughs.] Anything else, no problem, you know.

*Henry, how do you explain how you became the person you are? You know, how you have the positive focus, and the desire to be constructive and to help other people, given your past and your environment in here and such? What do you attribute it to?*

Henry: You know, to be honest with you, I'd have to say that what I attribute it to explains why I know it's so important to be a role model or a mentor to young people that come into prison, 'cause that's where I got mine.

Because, see, when I first came into Walla Walla after the murder conviction, I was bitter. I mean, I hated the world.

When I got off the chain bus, I saw about three guys that I knew, that had been in there with me in Fifty-nine till Sixty-two. They had been in Walla Walla for years. They were old timers, and they knew me from back then. Plus, I had been to Walla Walla on visits since then, you know, to the functions up there off and on, because I had a couple of brother-in-laws that stayed in there. So me and my wife would go up there to their little Black Prisoners Club functions and stuff, and I knew quite a few of the guys in there.

But when I got there, my whole thing was this: OK, I'm in prison for the rest of my life. Now, I've been able to protect myself out there in the world for all these years, and I'll be damned if I'm going to come here and let myself get relaxed to the point where something happens to me. My thing was, if anything would have rose to the level of a conflict, I was going to act first.

And I'm thankful to God, I pray to Allah that I didn't kill nobody there, when I first got there. Because that was my intention. I think if anyone would have just crossed me in any kind of way to where I'd have felt threatened, my first reaction would have been to strike first. Because that was the law of the land at Walla Walla at the time. Hey, you kill or be killed, you know. And I fit right into that mold at that time.

But some of the prisoners had started a program a few years before I got there. It was a separate program from the whole institution. I mean, they had a tier, all to themselves, and that was it. That's where they stayed.

So, I was out on the yard one day, and a couple of the guys that I knew, the old timers, they came up to me and said, "Come on. Come with us."

"Where are we going?"

"Come on."

"Ah, I don't want to hear that shit, man, I'm going to smoke this joint."

"Bring your ass on here, or we're going to kick your ass right now!"

"What are you talking about?"

Well, I knew these guys, for them to say that, and the way they did, they weren't bullshitting, you know. So, reluctantly, I went. I go down there, and they tell me, "This is your cell."

"What do you mean? I live over in Six Wing."

"This is your cell! This is where you're going to stay. You're going to the program."

And that's how I started becoming aware of me. That's where I first learned who I really was. I stayed in there for eight months straight. Daily classes, from eight o'clock to three o'clock, every day. [Laughs.]

But it was nice, because, you know, you could invite your wife to come in on the weekends. Your wife could come spend the whole day with you down there. And, it was an eye opener for me.

So, that's where I got my start to realizing that I didn't have to be the way that everyone else was in order to survive. And that's what I teach others now.

*How did they know to pick you, that you would benefit from this program? They spotted something in you like you can spot in a younger man now?*

Henry: Yeah. Yeah. I mean, and the amazing thing—see, that's the difference between a convict and an inmate. A convict doesn't go by color. Both of these guys who first brought me into the program were white. So, it wasn't like they were black guys looking out for a black guy. Both of these guys were white guys.

And that's what started me to changing my whole idea about who I really was, and what I really wanted to do. And from that day on, I've always maintained the attitude of, "Hey, each day, if I can do just one thing to better myself, pretty soon I'm going to be the best that I can be." And I do that. I haven't reached that pinnacle yet, but I'm trying. Every day, I try to do something better than I did yesterday. Or try to come up with something that's more positive, not only just for me, but for anybody that's around me. I try to keep people around me in a positive light, you know.

I mean, it's kind of hard sometimes. [Laughs.]

*[Laughs.]*

9: For the record, he's laughing at me. [Laughs.]

Henry: [Laughs.] Yeah. Yeah.

*Well, I want to hear some of 9-0's impressions of those early days between the two of you also, how he saw the beginnings of your relationship. So, was Walla Walla the first institution you went to—?*

9: Yeah.

*—after the county jail and Shelton, or whatever are the usual first steps?*

9: Walla Walla, yeah, the "Big House" as it was known.

I'm an only child. I don't have any brothers or sisters. I really didn't have nobody to look up to. I'd always had a problem listening growing up, because I never had no one that could teach me the things that I wanted to be taught, that I've now learned that I really wanted. I was hungry for it.

But, entering Walla Walla, you know, I was nervous. I'd heard all the rumors about it. I was scared.

*Now, was your attitude entering Walla Walla that, because you're a young guy, you're alone, you're scared, "Jeez, I better find some Crips and get with them. At least those are people I can trust. That's my group"?*

9: I was hoping for that of course. I knew that there's a lot of Crips, that I was recognized amongst all the Crips that was in there at the time in the state. So, anywhere I went in the institution, I planned to run across someone that knew me or knew of me.

Being the size that I am, and hearing all the rumors about prison, you know, I figured they're going to approach me wrong, and I knew that I got to prove a point from the first day. I got to make an example. I got to show that I'm not going to be somebody that's easy to be taken advantage of. I'm not someone that's going to be punked. That was my mentality.

Of course, when I walked off the chain, the first person that I actually saw was this guy that'd been locked up thirty years. Huge. I mean, the guy's my height, but his arm is as big as my waist.

Henry: [Laughs.]

9: I'm, like, "I hope this isn't all the people I'm going to come across here, because my plans to come and prove a point have failed already." [Laughs.]

I mean, but I came across some people that I didn't know, but who knew of me. Apparently, you know, some people knew me before I even got there, knew of the 9-0 name. And, I was approached by several guys that I had no idea who they were, but they walked up to me, introduced themselves, and told me who I was, you know, "I heard you were 9-0. My name is such-and-such." And, I was skeptical, because that's the normal rule when you enter a prison, you know. You're apprehensive about people that you meet.

*How did they know of you?*

9: Well, you know, usually in the prison system, your name gets to the institution before actually you do. Like, for instance, with Henry. He could be leaving tomorrow, but people wherever he's going will know that he's on his way.

*Why did they seek you out when they learned you were on the way? Were they Crips and they wanted to protect you?*

9: Well, it was actually Crips looking to identify with me. God knows that's one of the first things to do when you come to prison; you're looking for something to identify with. So they pretty much softened my arrival. You know, "Hey, listen, my name's such-and-such. I'm this and I'm that. I'm a Crip. I heard you're this. Man, you know, if you need anything, let me know. What are you doing tonight? Let's walk in the yard and talk."

And some of the people I first met there, I still know to this very day, even here at this institution. The actual first person that walked up and introduced himself that day is someone that I have since maintained a friendship with for the past twelve years.

But, actually, you know, it was after I got comfortable with my surroundings and knew what was going on that I came across some elders, like Henry, and his co-defendant. I used to work on a job crew with his co-defendant, at first having no idea of the connection between the two. And his co-defendant was somebody I came to totally dislike, I mean, totally despise. He done some things to me that I took offense to, till I ultimately lost the job where I worked with him.

At that same time, I was involved in a lot of incidents, a lot of violence, like Henry said, a lot of gang activities. I was in and out of the hole all the time, fighting, cussing out police, refusing orders. It was the older guys like Henry who played the role with me of explaining to me, "Look, youngster, in order for you to do time, as much time as you got, this should be your focus." They pretty much drew the diagram of the way my attitude should be, as opposed to the way it was, the things I should be focused on, considering the things that I'm doing, the time that I'm facing. They jacked me up, set me down, and explained it to me, the same way they done with Henry when he first arrived. But I was a lot younger than he'd been.

*How much of your initial violence, and incidents and infractions were unavoidable, given the nature of the institution and the people you were with? You know, unavoidable in order to protect yourself and to establish the reputation you needed to? And how much was unwise and excessive, and something you should have been steered away from?*

9: No, in the beginning, it was all necessary, and it was all unavoidable, because that's just what you have to do to establish yourself, not only for yourself, but for the people that witness you. I mean, pretty much you establish yourself to be known as, "Hey, he's a no-nonsense guy. He's not going to be approached."

And not just by convicts or inmates, but by staff as well. I'm not going to be disrespected. You're not going to talk to me any kind of way. I mean, I'm in here for breaking the law. Don't think I'm going to stop now. And that's just the way that you have to get established in order for you to be productive throughout your time here. Because you establish respect, but not just from the people that's locked up with you, but also from staff.

You know, the same way Henry said, you know, that he's able to go in front of administration and defend some of us that's in the hole. That's only because he's established there. Any Walla Walla senior staff knows him, knows what he's about, knows he's a no-nonsense guy, and if he step up and stake his word on something, they value it. Simply because, they know him, and they trust that.

It's the same thing with me. I wanted to get that, and that's how you establish that in the beginning. You don't want them to misperceive you as weak.

*How did you establish your reputation in the early going?*

9: Well, I was in a lot of fights, that's for sure. I was involved in a lot of gang activities, of course. I was well identified amongst the Crips.

*Were you kind of seeking that out to make your name, to make your reputation? Were you inciting violence, so they would see the kind of tough guy you were? Or were you just reacting when things happened to you?*

9: A lot of times I was reacting when things happened to me. But a lot of times also I was involved in some things because—it wasn't trying to establish a name for myself, because I came from an environment where my name was already established. But what I wanted to prove is that, you know, I'm somebody that, when the times get rough, I'm willing to put forth my effort to cover your back. I mean, the solidarity, the trustworthiness, the loyalty, to know that any time, in any circumstances, any situation, that you can count on me. And that's pretty much the establishment I was trying to make.

You're not so much looking for friends, but you're looking for camaraderie. And, I want to put that out there on the table, so any time, anybody in the back of their mind, when the times get rough, they can think back and they'd say, "I know that 9-0 will be one that will be down for the cause." And that's what you represent when you do these things. Not so much you're trying to establish your name, but, you know, you got a choice there. Either you're going to put yourself out there in a position where they can trust your loyalty or how well you're going to handle yourself, or you're going to show that you're weak, you're a coward, and you're not trustworthy, and then everybody surrounding you is your enemy.

*Now, before you had actually established that you're someone who is willing to protect himself and use violence if necessary, and you're not a coward and so on, were there attempts to feel you out, to victimize you, to see what you're all about?*

9: No, I'm fortunate. I believe that I'm fortunate to this very day. I believe that I was one of the last of the fortunate few that was taught by people like Henry and quite a few of his friends. You know, they spotted me out, they pulled me up from all angles, and talked to me. Obviously, all of them, I think, had the same identical opinion of me, for whatever reason, I still don't know. [Laughs.]

But, they gave me the wisdom to know, "To do time, and you got a lot of time to do, this should be your attitude. Not the one you got."

I'm sure there's quite a few that probably would have tried to test me, but they felt like if they would have made an attempt, they would have been disrespecting the people that looked out for me, such as Henry.

*Wasn't there an incident, though, that you were telling me about off tape recently, where they tried something and you had to defend yourself?*

9: In prison?

*Yeah.*

9: Well, I was involved in a lot of violence in prison, but not where I was, like, attempted to be raped or nothing like that.

*No, I don't think it had to do specifically with rape. I just remember there was one time that you were telling me a story where you felt you had to use what would seem like excessive violence against somebody, just to prove that people aren't going to be able to take advantage of you, that they aren't going to be able to victimize you.*

9: Oh, you're talking about the incident at Walla Walla, when I wound up in IMU for two years. Of course you'd remember that. [Laughs.]

Henry: [Laughs.]

9: You know, that's actually the incident that placed me in isolation, in IMU for a long time. That's the one that erupted on the school floor.

*What happened there?*

9: Well, a guy had come off the chain. He was a rival gang member. I had been there for a couple years already. Walla Walla had separated the Crips on one side predominantly and the Bloods on the other, and they had put this guy on our side. So, all the guys on the other side, which were the Bloods, told him, "You know, if you want to get over here, get into an incident with the Crips. That way, when you get out of the hole, they'll separate you to us." It's a common strategy. Any time, even nowadays, when they separate somebody, that's all they got to do to get placed where you need to be.

Well, this incident here, the guy takes off on me. Just walks right—

*Just to interrupt for a moment, I know this is a naïve question, but why do you have to go to that extreme to be transferred? Why can't he just say, "I'm a Blood; I belong over there"?*

9: Well, then, you'd be like a coward. You'd be snitching yourself off. I mean, it's almost like a protective custody situation.

*Oh, OK.*

9: But, yeah, like, sometimes they probably do. But, the institution will say, "Well the hell with you. You're going where you're going anyway." You don't have those personal priorities, even though it was a common thing for them to assign the different gang members to different sides, but—

*Right, right.*

9: —it wasn't total. We still got some of theirs mingled with us on our side, and some of ours over there.

So, but, here's the situation. He was there, despite whatever his efforts were. In order to get out from over there, if he went to the administration and asked for it, they probably would have denied it, or he would have been seen as a weak punk.

*OK.*

9: They told him the wise thing, the convict thing, to do was to take on one of us. "When you get out of the hole, they'll separate you, put you over on our side." So, he chose me.

*So, he figures, "Here's a little guy. I can take advantage of him."*

9: Yeah, he thought something like, "He's little enough, I can probably whip his ass,—

*[Laughs.]*

9: "—and at the same time get a reputation for kicking his ass, 'cause he's 9-0." He knew it's something that a lot of them wanted to do at the time.

Henry: Can I interrupt here?

*Yes Henry.*

Henry: Not only that, but also, during that time period, there was also certain officers would put people in certain predicaments, knowing what the outcome is going to be, because there might have been a guy that maybe told an officer, "Hey," you know, "Eff yourself!" or, "Up your mama's nose!" or whatever. So, then, if he figured that, "Well, OK, I can't really do nothing to this guy myself, but I know what to do." Then—boom—they put him in a situation where he get his head peeled off real good.

And, some guys have really been hurt behind that, too. I know of a couple of incidents where guys have gotten killed, put in situations like that by the police.

*They just put them in with a rival—*

Henry: Right!

*—gang.*

Henry: With a rival gang, knowing that eventually, maybe not today, but tomorrow, he's going to get checked. So, that happens. That used to happen at Walla Walla. I don't know what happens up there now, but—

9: Probably still do. Probably still does.

Henry: It probably does. That's their tactic. I mean, they still got the same police.

9: It even happens here. I mean, you go to the hole—

Henry: It happens here.

9: —for something, and they know what's going to happen if you get back out on the main line back with the guy you done something to to get sent to the hole, and you might not be liked by the administration or the police down there, and they'll say "Send his ass back out there!"

Henry: Yeah.

9: Get your ass whupped. That's whupping someone's ass by proxy. Somebody else doing it for you.

Henry: Yeah. Yeah, they do that.

9: It's a common thing. We know it exists.

Henry: Yeah, we do.

9: We've seen it exist. But, in this case, you know, I don't know what all happened, but he just chose me. And, he blindsided me. I mean, totally. He was taller than me, but he didn't weigh a whole lot more than me, so I was fortunate he wasn't a huge guy.

But, I mean, I kind of lost it. I remember flashing in my head, like, "What the fuck?" because I realized the same way he snuck up on me without me actually knowing, he could have had a knife, he could have had anything. He could have ended my life. That punch could have been a knife. You just don't let somebody sneak up on you like that.

*Where was this taking place?*

9: In the kitchen, in the chow hall, in front of everybody in the prison in there.

*OK.*

9: And, that's the way he wanted to do it. You do it that way, and you get caught by the police.

Henry: Oh yeah.

9: That's the way. You want to get caught.

*So he wanted to start a fight that would be broken up fairly quickly.*

9: Fairly quickly, to save him an ass whupping, plus, he'd go to the hole. Then, when they ask, "What happened?" "Hey man, I got into a rival gang. I told you not to put me over there with no Crips." And, the next thing you know, "OK, we'll send him back to the other side." That was his strategy to get to the other side with his friends.

*OK.*

9: What it wound up was, I stomped him out. I mean, I literally lost it. Stomped him with my boots.

*So first he blindsides you.*

9: Yeah, he blindsides me.

See, at Walla Walla, it's a practice that you sit at a table with everybody that you trust. I watch your back, the person sitting in front of me watch my back, and these two do the same. Anybody that walks up around this area that's suspicious, you know, he's being watched by everybody in that area. It's just a common thing, because there's so much violence there.

But, this guy managed to sneak up, so everybody around was upset because it could just have easily been them attacked. It didn't have to be me. Why were we all sleeping? How could we all have missed that?

But, I got a hold of him, because he was trapped. He didn't have nowhere to go, simply because he was stuck in that row where he had had to sneak up just to get to me. And there was no way out. Even if he had tried to get out, somebody would have grabbed him. But fortunately, I got my hands on him fast enough.

*So, did he throw a punch, or did he hit you with a weapon, or what did he do?*

9: No, he punched me in my face. I remember I was cutting up my fish. It was at dinnertime. I'll never forget it. And he walked up, and all I remember was a blindside—pow!—in my face.

*He didn't knock you out or anything.*

9: No, thank God, he didn't knock me out. He stung me. I mean, it hurt. But, before I could actually feel anything, I was out of my chair, had my hands on him, because he hit me, and like an idiot he stood there. He should have kept coming with more.

*He stood there admiring his work.*

9: Yeah, just, like—pow! And, I think he knew he was stuck, because everybody around him was, like, "What the fuck?" Now he was trapped in an area, like, anybody could have hit him. But, I got my hands on him first. I got him on the ground, and I beat the hell out of him. I mean, I literally put my knees in his chest, and even a cop got hit.

One cop came up, stuck his face down on the floor, telling us, "Break it up! Break it up!" because they didn't put their hands on you at that time. Sometimes they did, but a lot of times they'll tell you, "Stand for a shakedown!" hoping you'll break it up. Because if they touch you, it can create a riotous situation. All he got to do is grab you the wrong way, and some other convict jump up, like, "What the fuck you doing? Why you trying to hurt him?" Boom! It explodes. So that's a sensitive situation there.

But we both went to the hole. Of course, as it turned out, the cops in the kitchen had viewed him going all the way around just to target me, and they knew what his intentions was. So, I got out the hole, but he didn't.

Then I found out the people that was responsible for it was the guys on the other side who told him what to go do. And, the very next day,—

Henry: [Laughs.]

9: —up on the education floor, I went up there with my cellee. I knew a lot of those guys from the other side had this one particular class. So me and my cellee, which happened to also be a Crip out of LA, we had our minds made up. "Grab your stamps. Grab your phone book. Let's go," because we knew we were going to be shipped out of there after what we planned to do. And that's the last time I seen Walla Walla.

We tore it apart, the education floor. I was trying to send out the statement then that, you know, "Just the same as you sending somebody to beat me up, after I finish him, I'm coming to see you."

And when I had one of them down, I stabbed him with a compass.

*So you went to the education floor, and how many people were there that you were seeking out? Was it just one guy, or a group of people?*

9: Well, it was actually two in particular that we was looking for, but they had five of their friends with them, so it was seven against us two. But most of them were cowards, and we knew it. I mean, we'd known them throughout our time there.

But there was one I had promised that, "If I ever catch you in an area where I can get my hands on you, I'm going to whup your ass," and that was the promise I made to him. 'Cause he come off the chain with the same attitude I had, but you know, he was a Blood, so it was "Hey, fuck Crips!"

*So you went in, the two of you, and you beat up as many of the seven as you could grab, and—?*

9: Well, I had—

*—wrecked the place, or—?*

9: Yeah, you know, there was a huge one that I was kind of worried about, thinking that me and my cellee were going to have to work together to take this big guy down, but, I mean, I was actually like a deer in headlights, staring at the way my cellee was beating the hell out of this one guy.

And, the next one, he got up, came toward my cellee. I said, "No, you belong to me," and I hit him with everything. Chairs, desks, globes. I mean, literally there was five Mexicans had to pull me off of this guy. I was trying to strangle him, after I stuck him in the chest with a compass. But the rest ran.

*Why in the world do prisoners have access to a compass anyway?*

9: Well, you know, they got—

*That's the equivalent of a knife.*

9: Well, you know, I guess they used it for their class, like a drafting class. They got drafting tools that are sharp like that compass they had in class.

You can make a weapon out of anything. But this was a compass. It had a blunt end, but—

*Were you intending to actually kill any of them?*

9: No. No, I wasn't even thinking about killing any of them. That wasn't even on my mind. I wanted to damage one bad enough to leave my mark. But, I mean, I was just in a state of rage.

My mind wasn't made up to kill nobody, because I was already in a fucked-up situation already, and that wasn't my mindset. But had it came down to it, to either my taking his life or him taking my life, without a doubt I would have tried to kill him.

*Henry, what was your reaction when you found out about all this, that he was attacked and then retaliated the next day in such an extreme manner? I mean, how did you assess all that when it was going on?*

Henry: Well, now, that wasn't the first incident like that that had happened in the institution. You know, I'm not saying he was involved in all of them [laughs], but that was more or less an ongoing thing between the Crips and the Bloods, you know, at that time.

So, it didn't strike me as anything worse than what we had come to expect. I viewed it as, "OK, hey, it's still going on." The same old thing, you know.

*So you weren't disappointed in him. You weren't thinking, "Oh, I thought we had gotten past that point. I thought—*

Henry: Oh no.

*—I had gotten him away from that."*

Henry: Oh no. Not at that stage. No, no.

9: [Laughs.]

*[Laughs.]*

Henry: They were really still in the middle of it, at that stage. Yeah. Like I said, it was either on the school floor, in the gym, or out in the yard, or wherever. You know what I mean?

Actually, I'll tell you what. It got to the point to where they were involved in so much stuff—spontaneous things—so often, until where the old cons would say, "Well, you know, I want to make this move here. I want to do this, but them guards—," and someone would say, "Well, hey, just wait a few hours. You know, those kids are going to have all the police occupied. Then you can go do what you wanted."

9: [Laughs.]

Henry: [Laughs.] You know. Yeah, really. I mean, it was one of those things.

And, you know, I didn't see him no more until he came here.

But we've always had a respect for each other. I mean, don't get me wrong, it wasn't that every day I'm on him, "Hey, don't do this! Don't do that!" No, it wasn't like that. But whatever he was doing, or wherever I would see him, he would always acknowledge me with respect. And I would always reply in kind to him.

And actually, we never really would just sit down and just have a real good long conversation with each other. But we'd say things to each other in passing. I mean, he knew who I was. I knew who he was. I knew what he stood for. He knew what I stood for.

But now, there was times, you know, they'd be doing something, and I'd have to say, "Hey, come on you guys. This is not worth it. This is the wrong time," or, "Hey, here come the police!"

"Thanks, old man," they'd say, you know. They were gone.

9: "O.G." [Laughs.]

Henry: [Laughs.] Yeah, "O.G." It took me the longest time to figure out what that meant.

*What does that mean?*

Henry: "Old Gangster." [Laughs.]

*Oh, OK.*

Henry: [Laughs.] Yeah.

9: That's a respect term, where you're respecting—

Henry: Yes.

9: —your elders.

Henry: So, I mean, then when he came here, that's where we really got to where we just—

9: Bonded.

Henry: We bonded. We just bonded with each other.

*How much time passed between when you met at Walla Walla, and when 9-0 went off to IMU?*

Henry: When did you go to IMU?

9: In Nineteen eighty-nine.

Henry: Eighty-nine, yeah.
And you came here in what?

9: Ninety-six.

Henry: Yeah.

9: All them years I—

Henry: Seven years.

*And when did you first enter Walla Walla?*

9: Nineteen eighty-seven.

*OK, so you had roughly two years where you were sort of a mentor to him, but not real close.*

Henry: Yeah.

9: Right.

*Then he goes away, and, like, seven years later, you get back together—*

Henry: Seven years later,—

*—and establish a closer relationship.*

Henry: —here he come out on the yard.

9: You know, after I left Walla Walla for that incident, you know, and he was still up there during those years, I wind up coming here, and I was only here six months before I got kicked out of here and went to Clallam Bay. And, I did IMU stints up there that he was even hearing about up at Walla Walla, like, "God damn! Damn that kid!" [Laughs.]

Henry: Yeah. Oh, I always knew where he was.

9: All the time.

Henry: I knew where he was, and I knew when he was getting out of IMU, and when he'd go back.

*So you kind of were aware of each other during this time.*

Henry: Well, I was aware of him. He wasn't aware of me.

9: Yeah.

Henry: Because my program was still going as it had always been, you know.

*Was there any direct contact? Did you write to each other or anything during this period?*

9: No.

Henry: No.

9: No, but, see, the incidents that I was in was such big issues that it could hit the mainline, like, "Man, did you hear what happened over at Clallam Bay. That damn 9-0 done did—"

*"9-0 is up to it again!"*

Henry: Yeah.

9: Yeah, and, you know, you'd hear this, and,—

Henry: Oh yeah.

9: —like, "God damn!"

Henry: I knew where he was, you know. Yeah, I knew where he was all the time.

9: In Ninety-six when I got here, you know, I heard his voice. I was on the stairs above him, and I was sure I'd heard him. I asked a few people that I knew, "Who's all here?" They named me down the list.
And then, they mentioned his name. I said, "Henry here?"
They said, "Yeah, Henry been here for the last year." First thing I do, soon as the gate count, I come out. There he was. Embrace. "How you doing?" I mean, I ain't the same little short midget that I was back then. I got a beard this time. A moustache now.

Henry: [Laughs.]

*[Laughs.]*

9: You know, and from the point that I left him last time to the point that I met him this time, I had suffered a whole lot of adversity, and I matured a hell of a lot through a lot of turmoil. And, when we bonded, he finally had the chance to groom me. He explained to me the importance of me and my ideas, my thoughts, my plans, and my maturity level. He pretty much made it definitive for me to understand who I actually was. And, he shared a lot of wisdom with me.

He even made some hell of a predictions to me, and I thought, "OK, maybe he's just having his senior moments." [Laughs.] But it turned out to where he was right, but hey, he never told me, "I told you so."

But he showed me something, he enlightened me on some issues, some things that I should focus on, and I'm fortunate for that.

And that's one of the reasons why I endorsed him for this project when I talked to you in a previous conversation. One thing I admire about myself is that I've always had the intellect to understand wisdom when I see it, and to respect my elders. And one thing you got to realize, Craig, that back twenty-one years ago when he fell, Walla Walla was rated as the highest murder rate in this country. And when you look at someone, to survive those times, and still be as rigid of a man as they are today, I mean, every bit of a man to his core, you can only salute him and hold him in the utmost respect.

[Turning to Henry] Because you had to be one of the strongest men I've known. To be able to survive all that, to turn out to be the person you are today, I'm fortunate just to know you.

But, share with me that knowledge that made you to be the type of person you are, despite losing your freedom, despite how society has treated you. To hell with all the issues. To hell with all the laws. For you to have this whole understanding about life in general from the position that you're in, share that with me.

[Turning back to me.] Because, being honest with you, if I had to spend the rest of my life in prison, Henry would be somebody I want to be when I grow up. Just his thought, just his intellect, just the person he is. And, hey, he would be my ultimate goal.

But his insight, just sharing the way he has right now, if I was to have that on the street, if I got out, I mean, I'll be the best that I can be. And I recognize that. All of my friends recognize that, from Henry. All the youngsters, including the gang members, recognize Henry.

There's some in his age group that's here that's been locked up an equal amount of time that's lost that status. And that's why you have to admire someone with the pedigree, the type of understanding that he do have.

He showed me some things that as a young man I feel privileged just to have learned from him. And I'm still growing.

# JERRY—October 1998

*"Actually, even when I was young, and I was gambling with my youth, with my behavior, when I decided I'd rather use drugs, or I'd rather be assaultive, or I'd rather do this, I knew back then that at some point in the future, I was going to have to reckon with that. I was going to have to pay for that."*

Jerry in 1997.

My previous taped conversation with Jerry came during a particularly stressful time for him. He had just had a hearing before the parole board that would determine his future. If they decided in his favor, he'd soon start the transition out. If they turned him down, he was looking at multiple additional years behind bars. They might even find a way to never let him out.

I'm sure the wait wasn't easy on him, but he seemed to be coping well enough. He continued to come to the PAP meetings every week, and to play a prominent leadership role. He went through with the interview with me, and in spite of the fact that I challenged him and we got into some intense exchanges, he remained very much in control of himself.

Shortly after that, though, there was evidence that the stress was getting to him. At the PAP meeting one week after that interview, our usual group of thirty or so prisoners and volunteers were having a discussion about the next Prison Awareness class. Jerry seemed edgy and out of sorts all night.

Several times he snapped at people with little or no provocation. He would sit silently brooding with a frown on his face for several minutes at a time, and then utter a few defiant sentences against something that someone had just said. The logical relationship between his remarks and the statement he was reacting to tended to be tenuous at best. Somehow he was interpreting whatever people said as an attack on him, or on prisoners in general.

Just when he looked on the verge of blowing his stack completely, he would regain control, quiet down, and simmer for awhile. His violent temper is what he was best known for in his younger days, but it had been largely stored away in his recent, mellower years. I had never seen more than the mildest flashes of it in the fairly brief time I'd known him. Was that about to change?

In the course of the discussion, one of the volunteers made a perfectly reasonable statement that just as the prisoners ask us to understand that some of their hateful attitudes and violent behavior are a predictable result of being brutalized by the system, so too is it true that some of the objectionable behavior of the guards can be understood in light of the violence, disrespect, and hatred directed their way by some prisoners.

Jerry reacted to her with his angriest, most paranoid denunciation yet. "How dare you try to justify…?!" and he was off. As soon as I could get a word in, I attempted to defend her against the bizarre spin Jerry was putting on her words. (It was particularly ludicrous that he would interpret this particular volunteer as arguing in favor of treating prisoners badly. You'd be hard pressed to find any of our outside members who was more pro-prisoner in her attitudes or had volunteered more time and effort to this group than she had.)

The situation was escalating. Perceiving that he was being attacked from two sides now, Jerry hesitated for a moment. Then he made a cutting remark or two to me, and once again willed himself back from the brink. He returned to his stony silence, staring glumly at the floor before him.

But this time, he couldn't just sit there and listen to the outrages he perceived being uttered around him. Seconds after the exchange, he abruptly got up from his chair and took several steps toward the door. He paused, changed his mind, and circled back around to the opposite side of the room. The discussion continued, but I kept an eye on him. He was lingering by the coffee urn now, surveying the room.

I couldn't take it any more; I had to talk to him. He said nothing as I approached him.

"What in the world's gotten into you?" I said. I again tried to paraphrase the point I was sure she had been making, and to tell him I found his negative interpretation of it implausible.

He quickly cut me off. He didn't raise his voice to where others could hear us, but he was definitive in tone. There was a clear anger in his words, albeit still a controlled anger. "Don't tell me what the bitch said!" he warned me, "I was sitting there listening to her with my own ears! I don't need you to explain it to me, like I'm too deaf or too stupid to understand what I heard!"

"I'm not saying you're stupid," I said, returning to my point. I sensed the confrontation diminishing my articulateness.

He was having none of it. He raised his hand in a gesture to silence me, and he let me know that our conversation was over by telling me, in not a hateful, but a measured, deliberate tone, "Fuck you Craig."

He wasn't going to let me in, at least not tonight. I shook my head and returned to my seat. I noticed him head out the door moments later.

On the long drive home, I found myself unable to stop thinking about his puzzling behavior. How could he have interpreted things the way he did tonight, to react to us like that?

And why did it concern me so much? That evening an awareness gradually came over me that Jerry was someone who truly mattered to me. I clearly regarded Jimi as a friend, but I hadn't yet made a personal connection like that with any of the other prisoners. The more time I spent with Jerry, the more I was coming to understand—despite our many differences—what an extraordinary person he was, and the more I was developing a respect and fondness for him.

Arriving home, I still couldn't get the night's events out of my mind. By coincidence, I had a nearly-completed letter to Jerry on my computer concerning some suggestions for PAP. I sat down and added several pages to it.

I had to let him know that I wasn't backing down. Even if I hadn't been able to articulate my points well in person, I had a good case. In writing, I described the meeting and his behavior from my perspective. I listed and explained his many unwarranted remarks, and I speculated that perhaps his "off night" was an understandable consequence of waking up every day wondering when the parole board was finally going to inform him of his fate. I stressed that my disagreements with him in no way reflected a low opinion or lack of respect for him—surely he had to know that already, right?—and made clear my sincere wish that our exchange did not mark a rift between us.

The next week was one of the infrequent PAP meetings that I had to miss because of another commitment, so I did not return to the prison until two weeks later. I wanted to see if Jerry had settled down enough to talk things over, and to see how he had taken my letter.

The first news that greeted me was that Jerry had been turned down for his parole, and that apparently he had known for awhile. He had probably known the evening of his bizarre behavior, but had chosen to keep it to himself.

Jerry was absent that night and Bill explained that he was taking it hard. He was feeling a need to step back from his commitments and re-assess what he needed to do with himself. For the time being, Bill told us, we would likely not see Jerry.

9 was one of the prisoners most disappointed by the parole board decision, and apparently one of the people Jerry told first. We crossed the hall to the office to talk about it for a few minutes.

It hit 9 hard because, as he expresses in the interviews, he deeply admires certain of the "old cons" who have remained true to their principles and lived a life of integrity, even behind bars. He obviously sees Henry that way, and Jerry is another. He gets caught up in their struggles to gain release after decades of incarceration. His own sentence does not allow for the possibility of parole, so perhaps he craves a vicarious taste of freedom through them.

9 told me that Jerry had been tipped off by whatever source that what sunk him was his failure to commit to a counselor that he would never drink again in his life. Instead, he made a commitment to never *abuse* alcohol, but he didn't rule out one day having a beer or two and watching a ball game. This was not the answer they were looking for. (Jerry's precise history with alcohol I do not know. I do recall, however, asking another prisoner—someone who had known Jerry for a long time—whether he thought Jerry would return to crime and violence if released from prison. "If he doesn't drink, absolutely not. If he does drink, absolutely yes." For what it's worth, I later found out this prisoner was something of an enemy of Jerry's.)

I sat in the office alone for several minutes after 9 left. The tape recorder was there, but I didn't have it in me to try to recruit any interview subjects just now.

Instead, I tried to articulate some of what was going through my head. I thought of writing another letter to Jerry, but instead turned on the tape recorder and ad libbed some remarks. Nothing very profound, just my disappointment over the news, my faith in his strength to maintain himself in spite of it, my sincere wishes that he return to us soon, etc.

Then I crossed the hall back to the meeting room, and one by one asked the half dozen or so volunteers who happened to be in attendance that evening whether they'd be willing to make a similar statement onto the tape that we could give to Jerry. They were all glad to do so.

I gave the tape to Bill. "I know your heart's in the right place," he said, "But I know Jerry, and this isn't really the kind of thing he responds to. He's got his own way of dealing with things. But you're a bright guy and you can read people and situations. I won't tell you you shouldn't do it."

Jerry, in fact, did not stay away for very long. Within a few weeks he was back on a semi-regular basis, and not long after that he was back to his old position of prominence in the group.

And in speaking with him, I gained insight into why he had taken some time away. He said it wasn't a matter of being depressed, or needing time to himself, or anything having to do with his emotional state like that.

Instead, it had to do with the delicate balancing act he performed. On the one hand, he wanted to behave himself and avoid any infractions that could jeopardize his chances of regaining his freedom. On the other hand, he wanted to maintain his position at the top of the pecking order, and to fulfill certain self-imposed obligations toward his fellow prisoners, and indeed toward us. For among the commitments he took most seriously was to head off even the slightest risk of harm coming to any of the volunteers from any prisoner, on the inside or after release.

He felt it was a reality of the prison environment that living up to his commitments meant using violence or the threat of violence, thus risking his other goal of earning parole. For a time he had been able to pursue both goals simultaneously, but the balancing act could not be maintained indefinitely. His reputation bought him some time; people knew to think twice before crossing him, knew from his past what he was capable of. But the more time they spent around the newer, mellower Jerry, the more chance they would take certain risks that would once have been unthinkable.

Jerry could survive as a voluntarily declawed lion for only so long. Being turned down for parole meant staying out on that tightrope awhile longer. Sooner or later he would be faced with a choice: Either take action in a way that would put him at odds with the administration and eliminate the hope of regaining his freedom, or betray the code he had accepted to live by. (And if it did ever come to that, there would really be no choice involved. Jerry was fully committed to the former as the lesser of the evils, and was prepared to accept the consequences.)

One way to lessen the chances of being faced with that choice was to pull back from certain commitments and certain entanglements in the lives of other prisoners and outside folks. The more people depended on him and the more obligations spun off of this, the harder it was for him to keep to himself to do his own time and to stay out of trouble. One such commitment was to the safety and well-being of the people of PAP. Was it time to relinquish his role of guarantor, to warn us that he could no longer afford the risks?

No, he determined. At least not yet.

He'd continue to walk that tightrope to freedom, where leaning too far to one side meant being perceived as weak, and leaning too far to the other side meant suffering the consequences from the authorities.

For a time, he said nothing pro or con about the letter I had written to him. Weeks or months later, he made a joking reference to it. We had had a minor disagreement over something in front of some people, and he tossed an arm around my shoulder and laughingly said, "I got to be careful not to be too hard on Craig here. He'll think I don't like him any more, and he'll send me a ten page letter about it."

He also didn't mention the tape we had made for him in the aftermath of his parole hearing. I eventually brought it up to him. Had Bill been right, I asked him, that he didn't connect with that kind of gesture?

He frowned and waved off Bill's remarks. "Of course it meant a lot to me, and of course I appreciate it," he said. Then he reminded me how often he'd stressed what it meant to a prisoner to know people care. And he retold the story of his time in IMU when mail from a PAP volunteer had sustained him during a tough period.

I decided to make his parole hearing, and the sentencing and parole system in general, the opening topic of our next taped conversation.

*Jerry, I wanted to follow up on one of the issues that has come up in our earlier conversations, and earlier correspondence. Why don't you explain to me the distinction between the old guidelines and the new guidelines for being paroled or getting out of prison in the state of Washington?*

OK. New guidelines. The SRA—Sentencing Reform Act—of Nineteen eighty-four created a system of determinate sentences. There was a grid set up, and a point system set up, based on your prior convictions, the severity of the crime, weapon or no weapon. The grid sets a range for your sentencing. You receive that sentence, and upon completion of that sentence—those months, however many months it is—you automatically get out, and there is no tail. No parole. No supervision. You did your time, you were done. Bam, you were out.

At some point—I think it was in, like, Ninety, Ninety-one—they decided that they needed to make a little bit of a change, and so starting then, certain guys have what they call "community placement," which is a form of parole, a form of supervision.

But your total sentence still stayed the same. In other words, if you received a hundred months, and you got out in eighty months, you'd have twenty months of supervision. So your determinate sentence of a hundred months total doesn't change.

Or a fine. Say you owed some money. You pay off that fine, you might be off supervision, but they'd monitor you for those additional twenty months, or until you paid off all that fine. And in that time, if you got, like, a dirty UA, or you did something that they thought was a violation, they could put you back in jail for thirty days, sixty days, something like that.

OK. An old guideline guy, we received an indeterminate sentence.

*This is anyone sentenced before the Nineteen eighty-four reforms?*

Right. Nineteen eighty-four. Sentencing Reform Act. Everybody that was sentenced prior to Nineteen eighty-four received a maximum sentence, and the minimum sentence was determined by the parole board. And the parole board originally would base their minimum sentence kind of on, like, a rule of thumb. Like if it was your first offense, and it was a property crime, and blah, blah, you know. They would give sentences based on informal rules, so you kind of knew what to expect. It would be, like, a five year sentence, and you'd do three years, four months on it.

*So, it was just kind of an informal understanding; they weren't bound to that, but they usually paroled people at about that time.*

Yeah, about that time.

Say the judge gave me twenty years. I go to the parole board. The parole board would give me five years. So, now, really I got five to twenty. 'Cause you owe that twenty no matter what. But if you earn your good time, they'll parole you after three years, four months of that five.

*When do you go to the board?*

You go to the board, like, six weeks after you get to the R-Units.[*]

*OK, so almost immediately after the judge makes his determination of the maximum, very shortly after that, the parole board sets your minimum.*

Yeah. They'd break out your jacket, and your criminal history, and everything. And they would set a sentence on you. After the completion of that sentence, then you'd be paroled.

They could parole you. They didn't have to.

*OK, so it means you're eligible for parole, but—*

You were eligible. They never had to parole you, but for the most part they did.

---

[*]The aforementioned Receiving Units in Shelton, a Washington prisoner's first stop in the prison system after his conviction.

This came up when they were arguing it out in the federal courts. The Attorney General of this state, the picture he was trying to draw for his argument that they weren't treating us old guideline guys unfairly by keeping us in prison longer than if we had determinate sentences like the SRA prisoners was that we never had any realistic expectation of ever getting out anyway. But that's not true.

In fact, the practice of the parole board was to see you six months prior to the expiration of your minimum sentence, and to set conditions with you. If you didn't get no more infractions, if you did these things, if you jumped through these hoops, you'd be released. And you'd go back for a ten day parole hearing later to determine if you'd met the conditions. They'd say, "OK, you completed it," and within ten days, you'd be on the streets.

But, when you got to the streets, that's still part of your sentence. You're on parole, and that's part of confinement. See, it's just confinement in the community. You're still carrying out a sentence. At any time, they can take you back.

Say there was an allegation made against me. And they couldn't prove it in a court of law. But they had a preponderance of the evidence. In other words, the fact that I was in the area, capable of committing the crime—they could violate my parole and send me back to prison. In the old days, if you just had association with other convicted felons, they could send you back to the joint.

They would reset a new minimum term. So, say you get another nickel, you'd have to do another three years, four months on that.

*Can they go above the original maximum?*

Not above the original maximum.

*Unless they actually try you—*

Unless they—

*—all over again.*

Unless you were convicted again.

*OK.*

They'd have to—

*Not just by a preponderance—*

—convict you of a new beef.

*—of the evidence; you'd have to go through a whole, real trial, with real standards.*

Exactly. Case in point. I get fifteen years maximum for a seventy-five dollar set of tools in Nineteen sixty-seven; in Sixty-eight, I get to the joint. I do my minimum and I get out. Me and my old lady have an argument. I end up going to Alaska. I'm working on a fishing boat. I get in a fight up in Alaska. I don't get in no trouble, but I get booked in.

OK, so that's how they found out I was in Kodiak. Boom! The cop comes out onto the boat, and says, "Hey, Jerry, man, there's a warrant out for your arrest." You know, boom! So they extradited me all the way back to Washington, and got me for leaving the state without permission, change of marital status, change of address, and failure to report, and sent me back to prison for another, you know, couple, three years.

I get out again, and this time, an informant says that he went to my house to buy some drugs, blah, blah, blah. So they kick down the door, but they don't find nothing. They don't find nothing. They send me back to prison for violating my parole, even though I didn't get convicted of nothing new.

I get out of prison again. I get pulled over in Seattle, and in my wallet is a receipt from a place in Alaska, in Fairbanks, Alaska. The cop knew I was on parole, so he turns it over to my parole officer. They revoked my parole again for leaving the state without permission, and sent me back to the prison, back to the joint again, and gave me a new sentence.

All of it within that fifteen year stretch. You see what I'm saying? So as long as you're alive and that time hasn't run out, you own that tail.

Right now, I have a life sentence. Right? I have a twenty-to-life sentence. Under the old guidelines, that meant thirteen years, four months.

*So, life was the maximum set by the court, and twenty was the minimum set by the board.*

Well, actually, in a murder, first degree murder, by statute you must serve twenty years, less good time, consecutively without relief. What that means is that you have to pull thirteen years, four months without any break, either from bail, or escape, or anything. You have to serve that before you're eligible for parole.

Then, again, the practice of the parole board was, after you served all but six months of your thirteen years and four months, and you had certification of your good time, they would see you, with the intent of setting some goals that you could achieve for parole.

The average stay in prison at that time for first degree murder was about sixteen years. That's all documented, historical fact. But that doesn't exist any more. In the interim, Nineteen eighty-four comes along—the Sentencing Reform Act—and that all went off the board.

Then in Nineteen ninety-one or something like that, the state lawmakers passed a law that ordered the parole board to give us remaining old guideline guys a sentence that was consistent with the SRA sentences.

*What was your new sentence?*

Well, I mean, it keeps on growing. I just went to the board again—

*But, I mean at that time, when they had to give you a definitive sentence consistent with the SRA sentences?*

They gave me twenty-six years. If I had committed a first degree murder under the SRA, twenty-six years would have been my maximum. That's the longest they could have kept me. Supervision—no supervision, that's as long as they could have kept me.

But when they gave me a re-sentence of twenty-six years, they also kept the old sentence, which is a life top. See, even though they said re-sentences "consistent" with the SRA, they didn't say to give us exactly the SRA sentence. So, even as I reach the end of the twenty-six, they can still give me more. They can still continue to give you more time.

*But doesn't that make the twenty-six year sentence meaningless, if it's really just indeterminately long?*

When they argued it in the U.S. Supreme Court, they argued that the re-sentences were consistent with the SRA, because now we have every reasonable expectation of getting out.

Well, every harvest is in its own season. It is just now bearing the fruit of the lie. Just now, are we arriving at that end of the lie.

The lie is that we have any realistic expectation of ever getting out, unless we, like, jump through some magic hoop, attain some level of—what? what is a monk trying to do?—you know, spirituality or something. I don't know. Divine intervention? Luck?

You know, the general consensus is that they will continue to release just enough people to be able to say, "We are letting people out," but at the same time, to maintain enough people to warrant their continuing funding.

We are their sole reason for existence. The SRA prisoners don't come under the parole board. We're just a small group of prisoners. There aren't many of us left. We're being managed by a parole board that is paid an exorbitant amount of money to manage the smallest group of inmates. And there is no justification.

But there is no sympathetic ear. There is nobody willing to say, "Well, jeez, it isn't right to treat these guys like this." Nobody will step up to the plate and say, "Well, you know, one murderer ought to be treated equally to any other murderer." You know what I'm saying? Nobody will say, "Wait a minute, we can't treat these murderers like this while we're letting these murderers go." Who gives a damn about murderers? To find anybody that was politically secure enough to champion that cause is impossible. That person doesn't exist.

*So, if I understand correctly then, before the SRA reforms in Eighty-four, the parole board had no disincentive to letting people out when their time came, because they were going to continue in existence and continue to draw a salary anyway. So, they could let you out after thirteen years or whenever you would normally get out. But ever since the SRA changes kicked in, and no new prisoners were any longer coming under their jurisdiction, now they do have an incentive to keep you in prison, so that they can continue in their position and continue to get a paycheck and so on.*

Exactly. Exactly. And to, like, lend emphasis to the argument, the lowest rate of recidivism for any single group are the old guideline convicted murderers. They return to prison at a lower rate than any other group of criminals. There is no other group less likely to re-offend.

Yet, the board's argument was that these criminals of yesteryear are so much more sophisticated than the killers that we have coming into our system now that they can't release us. What Kit Bail[*] actually said—was quoted in a newspaper as saying—is that even though she had been instructed by the court to start letting us out, and was in contempt and was being fined at the time, she said she answers to a "higher power." And her higher power has told her that it's her job to protect society from our ilk.

*So she was practicing civil disobedience from religious motives?*

Yeah, yeah. She said her higher power wouldn't allow her to release us.

And then in the legislature, you know, you've got Ida Ballasiotes.[†] She's just strictly hate motivated. But she's actually had to back off of her stances a little bit, because people are starting to realize that, you know, it's one thing to champion a cause, and another thing when it's all hate motivated. It outweighs good reasoning, you know. It outweighs good lawmaking. It outweighs justice.

Justice is, like, blind. That's why the lady wears a blindfold and holds the scales, because it's got to balance out. But this lady's peeking out from under it, and she's got her thumb on the scale, you know. And she has that influence, and so we're stuck.

---

[*]Chairwoman of the parole board in Washington until 1999. A rape victim. A former nun.

[†]Ballasiotes is an infamous figure amongst the prisoners. After her daughter was murdered, she became the most visible conservative activist for harsher treatment of prisoners in the state of Washington. She has since been elected to the state legislature, where she continues to concentrate on crime and punishment issues. The prisoners in PAP are of course sympathetic about her loss—the perpetrator is decidedly low in the prison pecking order and they have as little use for him as she does—but most of them regard her as an unreasonable zealot who has an insatiable appetite for taking revenge against all prisoners collectively for her family's tragedy.

*Now, what is the parole board supposed to go by? Leave aside what they really go by. I mean, we're theorizing that they're inclined to keep you in here unjustifiably for their own paycheck, but, leaving that aside, what are they supposed to go by?*

Psychological evaluations and—

*Let me ask you this way: Are they supposed to go by what you've done in prison, or are they supposed to go by a prediction of what you'll do on the outside if let out?*

Oh, basically, the prediction of what you might do when you're released again.

*OK.*

Based on maybe, oh, an hour worth of interviews with the psychiatrist. He'll make a determination, and put you into a group of moderate, to high, you know, chance of recidivism. It could be based on—I don't know what exactly.

But maybe based on, OK, like, if your parents were alcoholics, or—

*Right.*

—you have no job skills. You know what I mean?

*Right.*

They take this little information, and they make a judgment on the future. They look into their crystal ball, and make a decision. And they speak with you maybe an hour, two hours tops. That's it.

*And these sessions must bear almost no resemblance to real therapy, or real psychiatry, because the prisoner knows that he's not talking to a psychiatrist the normal way; he's trying to bullshit somebody so he can get out of prison. And they know that too, so both sides are playing a game.*

Yeah.

*So, it's nothing like a doctor-patient relationship,—*

No.

*—where they're really trying to understand you, and you're trying to be honest, and—*

No. See, and at one time, when we were first under the parole board, we actually had counselors that lived up to the name of counseling. They tried to work with a guy. If a guy had mental health issues or problems or something, they'd try and work with him.

Now, under the streamlined system with the SRA, those positions are no longer necessary. There isn't any funding for treatment.

The only kind of people that get any kind of treatment in prison whatsoever are sex offenders. And that's special funding, and special institutions. It's obligatory that they take these programs, and it's obligatory to the state that they give them these programs. But that's the only section of the inmate population that is recognized for treatment.

*Why did the sentencing reform have any impact on whether you have proper counselors or not?*

Because there was a determinate sentence. By making the sentence determinate, society said, "I want this man put away for fifty-seven months." You know what I'm saying?

*So, they're no longer saying, "We want him put away until a professional judges that he can safely be released."*

Yeah.

*They're saying, "Just put him away for this period of time, and that's it."*

And that's it. Yeah.

*So they don't need anybody to find out if a guy's sane or dangerous or whatever. He's just going out the door when it's his time, no matter what.*

Exactly. And the people that have assumed the position of "counselors" are actually line bulls* that have graduated from block officer, to sergeant, to a counselor, instead of going to the lieutenant slot.

And when they go in as counselors, their sole purpose is to gather information. They don't counsel you. The most they do is push your papers through when it's your time. See, 'cause there's a set system. An SRA guy, when it's his time to get medium custody, he goes to a medium custody joint. And when it's time for him to move on from there, then he goes to a minimum custody joint. Somebody has to say, "OK, this six month period is complete. He's got this many points," so they can push the paper, and he can go on to the next stage of his sentence. That's all the counselor really does.

---

*Correctional officers.

There's only x amount of beds in any of those other facilities—the minimum facilities, pre-release or work release. There's only a small number of beds that are set aside for the guys that are under the old guidelines. And only when that bed is available will one of us be allowed to go to it. But the SRA guys move through the system according to whatever their determinate sentence says.

In other words, we're stuck in line behind a group of people that can crowd in front of us. Guys that have committed murder—first degree murder—are transitioning out to the streets because their determinate sentence is ending. A guy that killed a woman and the fetus in a satanic sacrifice type murder is hitting the streets. He's already started the phasing out program, and he's got, like, ten years less than I got in already, and he's actually going to get out.

It's just a matter of he arrived at this point of his sentence, and it comes up—boom—and he's got to go to here, and then there, and then back to the streets.

But they don't have to release us or to start us on the transition through lower custody level facilities. If there's no room for us, they have the discretion to keep us old guideline guys where we're at.

The truth of that bullshit's just now coming clear, you know, 'cause now some of the worst SRA murderers are getting out.

*Now, I know it's your position that there's an unfairness of having dual systems, where some guys are under the old system and some guys are under the new system at the very same time. What if we did have just one system for everybody equally? If you had to choose between only those two, what do you think is more fair? What do you think is better from society's standpoint? Do you think it makes more sense to say, "Jerry McLaughlin's going to be in prison for twenty years, period"? Or does it make more sense to say, "Well, he'll be in prison somewhere between twelve years and the rest of his life, depending on, you know, what we judge as we go along"?*

Well, actually, there should be a form of merger. There should be a maximum penalty that a guy can pay. And a guy should know what it is that he's facing. By the same token, you leave a window of opportunity where a guy can earn off of his sentence by his behavior—participation in programs and stuff—so he can be released on early parole. That's the whole point; it's early parole, so a guy's got to earn it.

And, you know, there's still a mandatory sentence. There's still a minimum. You got so much time that you have to do. "OK," the state says, "This is what we demand from you for our pound of flesh, something between this much and this much. If in that time you've done enough work on yourself to deserve to be out early, we're going to let you out. If not, we're going to keep you until this latest date. But when that date comes, your pound of flesh is paid." You know what I mean? "And, if you cross that line again," you know, "We're going to…"—whatever it is. The punishment can be increased—whatever it is.

You know, 'cause that's the whole thing. There's got to be a way to know. There's got to be a conclusion to what it is that I owe you.

It'd be like if you went to the bank, and they say, "Oh, don't worry about the interest. Don't worry about the term of the loan. The payments are only this. Just keep paying that each month and we'll let you know when you're done."

*Well, are you describing a hybrid system, or are you really just describing the old system? Because under the old guidelines, there was a maximum, wasn't there? It's just that in a case like yours, you have life. So, in that sense, there's no maximum.*

Under the old guidelines, you had a maximum sentence, and when you got to that, you were done. And that I agree with.

*So really, you like the way the old guidelines work, except for a life sentence, because that's open-ended; they can keep you forever.*

You know what? Even guys with a life sentence were better off under the old system. Like I said, when the parole board knew that they had a job either way, they treated us more fairly.

Now they've taken that abuse to the point of screwing around old guideline guys that aren't even in for murder. Guys that haven't killed anybody are doing just as much time, or doing way more time, than SRA murderers of today are. And they're still in the system right now. They're not getting out. There's just no real good reason for it.

*Let's personalize it a little bit. I know this year you went before the board again, and you had some hope that it was actually going to go your way. Tell me about that process, and how you responded to each stage, and, you know, your thoughts and emotions about it along the way.*

Well, my particular series of events was really kind of stressful, because, for one reason or another, they kept postponing my board date, you know. And, I had been focusing on bringing a lot of positive things into my life, and getting lined out, but at the same time,—

*What does "getting lined out" mean?*

Getting things in a row. Getting things lined toward the street, with the hope that I could show them a path that I was on, that my completion of a journey would be one of low risk to them. 'Cause what you have to do with the parole board is, number one, you have to relieve them of responsibility, of liability. You have to have completed enough things that they can say, "Well, listen, you can't sue us. He completed this, this, and this." So you have to take that liability issue off.

*You're being realistic, but you're assuming they have a real desire to let out guys that are going to make it. You see what I'm saying? In other words, you assume that they truly believe that the guys that they're letting out, let's say, are the guys that are most likely to make it.*

I had to set up things for my future that looked solid, and since I've done so much time all my life, and I've had to have a lot of restrictions in my life, I had to show them a future that had a lot of structure. And, I thought I had laid it out pretty good. I thought I had a pretty good line.

*What did you lay out for them? What kind of things were you setting up?*

OK, I had a job lined up working for Richmond Moving and Storage* that provided me not just a decent living, but a real nice living, especially for a guy in my situation. I had a place called Loma House,† which would have offered me residence. That's a retreat that is run by the Lutherans now. It used to be part of the Catholic Archdiocese, but the Lutherans bought it, and they run a retreat up there in Issaquah.‡

They would have afforded me an opportunity to, like, take care of the place for the first month, till I got my feet on the ground and get my job down at Richmond. Then I could have continued to live there, doing work around the place, for about six months. At the end of that six months, certainly with my income and stuff, I could have lived anywhere I wanted to.

I also had a checking account, an IRA account, and credit cards. I had established all the things necessary to make sure that there would be no desperation in my life.

*Right.*

I hadn't over-complicated my life by taking on a wife and a family, and kids or anything. I tried to keep it as simple as possible, and I thought it was a pretty good plan. Most everybody thought it was a pretty good plan.

*In all honesty, deep inside, what did you think your chances were, at that stage, before you met with the board?*

Not real good.

*Really?*

Not real good.
You know, my hopes got up. I mean, hope springs eternal. But I'm a realist. I knew.

---

*I have changed the company name.

†One of the halfway houses where prisoners can go when transitioning to the streets.

‡An east side suburb of Seattle.

Actually, even when I was young, and I was gambling with my youth, with my behavior, when I decided I'd rather use drugs, or I'd rather be assaultive, or I'd rather do this, I knew back then that at some point in the future, I was going to have to reckon with that. I was going to have to pay for that.

And so when they turned me down—I got to say, I'm kind of proud of myself—I didn't have a hostile reaction to it. In my gut, I didn't have much of a moment of anger. I didn't feel like going to get high. I didn't feel like assaulting anybody. I didn't feel like quitting anything.

I said, OK, it's like feeling somebody out in the first round of a fight. I understand now what they're working on. I have a better insight into them; they have a little bit into me. It's up to me, the next time I go, to have improved on that. You see what I'm saying?

*This wasn't your first time before the board, though. Right?*

First time in ten years.

*OK.*

And when I went to them before, it was for what they call a "Duration of Confinement" hearing, which isn't about getting out. That was about receiving that sentence that was supposed to be consistent with the SRA.

*So this was the first time that you had a chance to get out.*

First possibility of parole.
I knew better than to expect to get out the first time.

*How did the meeting go? What happened with the board?*

Thought it went well. I thought it went well.

*Did they ask you questions? Who was there? What was it like?*

Yeah, there was Kit Bail, and the other lady, and my nephew, who was representing me. He was my attorney. And, he spoke eloquently and let them know that I had community support, and that, you know, my family weren't just all criminals. He deported himself real well. And I had two counselors up there, my old counselor and my new counselor. They both did me pretty good. They both did pretty good.

Like I said, Kit Bail knows me. I'm an old con.

*How does she know you?*

Oh, you know, for years she's been on the parole board, like, forever.

*So she knows you from ten years ago when you were—*

Yeah, from even before that, you know. She's been on the board for twenty-some years. So she knows me. They review our cases all the time. They review our jackets every two years.

So, you know, for me to come up there and say, "OK, I've been good for a couple years. Let me go," was kind of a wishful thought. No matter how much my volunteers seem to think that I'm a lot better guy, I got to admit—I mean, she has to deal with reality.

The reality is I've been a very bad guy. You know what I mean? I haven't just been the run of the mill bad guy, you know. I didn't accidentally get in trouble. My cellees didn't cause me to get in trouble. I usually generate, mastermind, and create a lot of my own trouble. So, I got nobody to blame. I mean, it would be hard for me to sit there and be mad at people for doing what I knew full well they were going to do at some point, you know.

And, what I hope, though, is that in the fashion that I took it, in the things that I'm going to do in the future, that when I go again—it's like when you're trying to line something up. That's why I called it the line, when I'm laying it out. When the line gets long enough, you can stand behind it and you can see where it goes. See, when it's a short line, you can't really tell where it's pointing. But when it's a long enough line, when you've set enough good things in a row, people will have to acknowledge it. As winding as my past has been is how straight my future has to look. Otherwise, they're not going to let me go.

*You say they may be justified in not being convinced that you're a good enough guy now to make it, but what's the reality? Are you in fact a good enough guy to make it on the outside?*

Oh, I think so. I think that it's so new that I've arrived at that place in my life—but, yes, I do. I really do.

But, that's neither here nor there. If I tell them, "Hey, I'm ready. How come you can't recognize that?" well, that's ridiculous. Let's be real. I mean, for fifteen, eighteen years, I was a scoundrel and a scalawag. What the hell, now I'm a saint? No, it ain't working like that.

But I am ready. I think I'm ready. Don't get me wrong, I'm not ready today. But if I had gotten parole, I wouldn't be out today. I'd still be a couple years from the street. See? But I'd be beginning that process.

And, it's just like anything else. You don't get everything all ready right now, because, if we're going fishing, the bait spoils. You know what I'm saying? The lines get tangled. Our reservations are cancelled. The charter's gone. Whatever. That's if you plan too far in advance.

*But does that analogy really hold? I mean, is it a mistake to become a better person now instead of waiting until just before you get out?*

No, no, no. No, that's not what I'm saying. Like,—

*Or just become a less dangerous or violent person who doesn't get into trouble?*

Oh no, that's not what I mean. No, see, 'cause, like, it's one thing to be a better person. Personal and spiritual growth should be ongoing, all the time. I mean, who can quit growing? Who's really, like, the best they can be? I don't know anybody like that yet. I've never met anybody that was the best they can be.

What I mean is, you said, am I ready for parole? Well, there's things that I have to do to ensure my security, which include some structure, which include financial, which include community support, which include all these things. Now, if you put too many things out there, and it's projected way out there in the future, well then when you get to there, a lot of those opportunities, the people that offered you the jobs are gone, the business is closed down, the home isn't there any more. It's not realistic to set up all the details too far in advance.

*So you're talking more about practical, logistical things you're setting up, and—*

Exactly.

*—not so much your own internal growth and changes.*

That's right.

The guy in here is really ready to go. The guy in here, the guy that lives inside Jerry, he's ready.

I mean, now, there's a lot of Jerry Mac the Convict still here, but Jerry McLaughlin lives in here also now. And, as I get closer to the streets, I can shed more and more of Jerry Mac.

But not all, because I still have to continue to survive in here. I still have to maintain harmony right here, in this office, between a bunch of these guys. And Jerry McLaughlin just couldn't do it. Jerry Mac can. So I got to keep him present.

But as I go through the system, as I transition towards the door, I can leave more and more of him behind, and put more and more of those other things into my life that are positive, that are productive, that are designed for success.

You got to have a plan for success. I'm not just going to get lucky. My luck hasn't changed just because they're letting me go. You know what I'm saying? Luck is the residue of design. I have to have a good design in order to have good luck.

*What kinds of things did they ask you in the meeting?*

A lot like just what we had right now. [Laughs.] All this stuff we're talking about. Yeah.

*Like, what plans have you made, what have you got set up,—?*

Yeah. Yeah, asked me about my future plans and stuff. They wanted to know what I'd be doing in the future, or what assurances I could give I wouldn't offend and stuff.

I thought I covered them all pretty well. And, actually, basically what they said is, "Well, you know, that's all fine and well, but at this point we still find you unparoleable."

*How were you informed of their decision?*

Well, I seen it on a computer, like, three weeks later.

*You were in an office somewhere or something?*

I was in the office. Had him punch it up on the computer. They sent me a letter, like, a few days later. Yeah.

*Were there any reasons given?*

Not really. I mean, it was kind of ambiguous. I couldn't figure it out. They didn't identify anything specific. They just said, because of my infraction behavior, you know, because of my history, "We feel that," you know, "And we recommend that you continue blah, blah, blah."

So, that's that.

*Did they—?*

"We feel you need some more time."

*—mention anything specific about violence, or drugs, or alcohol, or anything?*

Well, just that I shouldn't do it. [Laughs.]

Actually, they did make a point about that. See, like, during my interview with the shrink, the shrink said, "Do you have an alcohol problem?"

I told him exactly this. I said, "I've never had an alcohol problem. I've never had booze in the house." I had a bar, and I had sealed bottles, you know, like the brown jug from Kentucky. I bought them from wherever I was at, all over the country. They were, like, memorabilia. They weren't to drink. The thought of opening one of those to have a drink was ludicrous. I wouldn't even think of it.

I've gone weeks without having a drink. I never thought of myself as having an alcohol problem. But both my parents were alcoholics.

I have used drugs, and I have abused drugs, and at different times in my life, I've abused alcohol. But I never went out and accidentally got drunk. Every time I went out to get drunk, it was by design. We'd say, "Hey, let's go. Let's get plastered," you know, and we would. 'Cause that's what young men do. Or at least that's what we thought young men did.

I told him, "But since my parents were both alcoholics, I'm intelligent enough to know that I'm predisposed to be an alcoholic, and that those things will probably cause me trouble, if I allow them to." I said, "I have no intention of getting out and drinking. But after I've been out three or four years, if I felt secure in who I am and in my surroundings, I wouldn't mind having a beer and shooting a game of pool with the fellows, you know. That'd be nice."

They took that statement, which I just gave you almost verbatim, and they said, "We do have some concerns that he plans to experiment with alcohol after about three years. Once he gets off parole, he plans to experiment with alcohol."

*Now did this teach you the lesson to be a better bullshitter in these meetings with the psychiatrist?*

Well, of course, next time I go to the parole board, I'll be president of our chapter of Alcoholics Anonymous.

*You'll be even more guarded in what you say to them?*

Well, you can't be president of AA and ever expect to have a drink again.

*[Laughs.]*

Yeah, I mean, the fact that I'll be conning them does not diminish my personal growth.

*Right.*

What it is, is that I have to overkill. I cannot be honest. I cannot be straightforward. I have to bring a certain element of deception to the thing.

*So you have to simultaneously grow and improve as a person, and convince them that you're doing so. And those really are separate things. Because you can grow and become a better person, and be honest and genuine about it, and they might not assess it that way. Or you can totally bullshit them and not improve yourself at all. But you're trying to do both.*

Yeah. Yeah. Yeah, that's exactly what I'm saying. The truth, even though in my mind it's good enough, is obviously not good enough for them. The truth is not going to set me free.

But, you know, if the truth of the matter is I'm a better person, then that's the truth. I don't know how any one or two people can sit in sole judgment, and make a determination that I should not be free based solely on the fact that, at some point in the future, I'd like to drink a beer. Now, who could do that? What pompous pile of crap could convince himself that they were that righteous? I just can't even fathom the personality that it would take to be that person, you know.

So, like, getting back to what we were saying before, they are going to let out certain people, a certain number of people, and that's it. Regardless if somebody more fit, better, comes along after they've let out that number. I believe they reach a number. They do it by a number.

*Like an unofficial quota.*

A non-official quota that keeps the U.S. Supreme Court from saying they're not doing it. You know what I mean? And that's that. So, luck, of when you go to the board, is going to have a lot to do with it. I hope I arrive at the right time, that they're able to give me a fair judgment on my next time. But if they don't, I have to assume I just arrived at the wrong time, and hope my luck is better next time.

*How long do you have to wait for your next time?*

They haven't told me yet.

*Oh.*

Three or four years. I don't know. Something down the road. Maybe not that long, you know. Things change. It's actually a fluid system that we're in, you know. You never can tell. I'm always an optimist. If I ever lost my optimism, it'd be hard to take.

*I think there's obviously a reason to be skeptical that the board can really assess your life and your future and come to a very sound conclusion about what you're going to do. I mean, it's a lot of guesswork. Even if they were doing their job responsibly, it's still difficult, it's still a lot of guesswork. You know, leaving aside whether they're corrupt and they're purposely not letting people out. Because they just don't have that much evidence available to them.*

No, and the evidence that they used to have has stopped. They no longer have that source to draw from. Now, they've got simply your infraction record. You can be infracted because a guard don't like you. You can be infracted based on "reliable information."

*And by "reliable information," you mean "reliable" in quotes, not really reliable information, in other words.*

No, no. That's what they call somebody that—

*They* call *him—right.*

—has been telling. He's a "reliable informant." One of their rats, their known informants. They call that "reliable information." "We've received reliable information that Mr. McLaughlin is doing this." Well, it could be coming from a guy looking to create an opening for himself where I work. I could be out of my job out there. That was what the guy was really after. See? I'm down in the hole. I'm being investigated.

The other day I received a "suspicion UA." I haven't been dirty in over two years, but I received a suspicion UA. Now, I came up clean. But the clean result ain't going to show up in there. The fact that I came under suspicion is what'll be in there. You see what I'm saying?

What happened is that I cut my hair, and my behavior, in their opinion, had changed, because I cut my hair. And they got a new policy out—a prisoner makes any drastic changes, UA him. OK, but it ain't written down there that that's what it was. I got a verbal confirmation that that's what it was, but it isn't down in writing. So when the parole board sees it, they're going to see that I came under suspicion, you know, and figure if there's smoke often enough, some place there's got to be a spark. They'll think I'm just slick and I'm getting away with it.

OK, so, I have to outlive my history. You know, I almost have to outlive the people who judged me in the past, and maybe get a new deck, to be judged a little bit more fairly.

*Now as hard as it is for outsiders like that to try and judge you and your future, how good are fellow convicts at judging that kind of thing? I mean, you're a pretty good judge of character. How well can you predict what your fellow prisoners will do when they get out? Do you—?*

Pretty good.

*—have a pretty good sense of who's coming back and who's not?*

Pretty good. Yeah. Yeah. I know the guys that are real with their effort. And I know the guys that aren't. I know the guys that are fooling themselves.

See, there's a lot of guys that are making an effort, but they're fooling themselves in other things that they do, and I can see it, you know.

I see them when they drop their guard, you know, and they say, "Oh man, I'm just chippy with it. A little bit came in; it got offered to me. It was free," but, all these million excuses, you know, "Hey, but when I get out, man, it ain't going to be like that."

Well, when you get out, it's all free. There's nobody around. There's no gun tower up there to stop you from getting it. Nobody's going to be watching you, you know. Especially the SRA guys that are going to be done, with no supervision. They don't have a parole officer that's going to come out and piss test them every week or whatever. They're not going to have to get on the lie detector machine. None of those things.

*Are you surprised very often when you see someone come back?*

No. Just happy to have them back.

*OK.*

Company, you know.

*Yeah.*

Sorry sometimes. Like, if I really care about them, I'll be a little bit sorry that they came back.

*Sorry, but not surprised.*

Very seldom surprised. I don't remember the last surprise I got.

The surprises I get are pleasant ones—the ones that stay out. You know, those are the only surprises. And it's not that many. It's not that many.

A lot of guys from my generation are starting to stay out now, because they're older. They're wiser, sharper.

Some of them aren't no better. They aren't no different in how they see the world. But they've changed enough to where they can stay out of trouble.

You know, like, we run counter to society. Well, you don't have to agree with everybody to get along with everybody. Sometimes you just got to keep it to yourself, you know. And that's kind of where a lot of guys get to eventually. Like, "OK, I really don't feel that I did all that much wrong, but…."

See, there's a lot of guys that have committed crimes that are not just criminal by nature, but immoral by nature. You know what I'm saying? Well, I'm not talking about those guys that have molested children and such. I'm talking about guys that robbed a bank, stole some money, were grifting, sold drugs.

You know, in today's society, people are starting to draw a moral/immoral line where, you know, "You're selling to kids, blah, blah, blah." But, in our generation, if you got into selling drugs rather than robbing somebody or hurting somebody, it was actually kind of stepping up. You know, you left that violence stuff behind, and now you're into a more peaceful existence. But you're still running counter to the society.

Well, when that guy quits doing that, it isn't because he comes to a moral conclusion that, "Hey, it was wrong for me to sell this pot." You know what I mean? "And not give Uncle Sam his share," you know. Like he ain't been getting his share every time I buy a pack of cigarettes or something to eat somewhere.

But, you know, you say, "Man, I just can't have this in my life, 'cause I want to stay free." Now, they might still smoke a little bit of weed. Some of the guys might use a little bit, you know. But that's all. They've learned how to co-exist in a system that they don't fully agree with. So, some of those guys are starting to stay out. But, they haven't gotten that much better.

Some of my friends, though, have changed morally. I got some serious outlaw friends that have found new life. One of them has a ministry. Mike Madison.[*] He takes a lot of convicts' kids on camping trips. He's a guide and stuff. He used to do marriage counseling here for relationships, working on relationships. That's his ministry.

I got another friend who's like a poster child for Narcotics Anonymous. Don Merchant.[†] He's turned his whole life around. He owns a home out here in Snohomish, and he was working a drywall outfit for an older guy, and the guy got so sick that he retired and now Don runs the drywalling outfit for him.

And these guys are both killers. They're guys that have held court, both on the streets and in the joint. They were considered dangerous men.

*How are these fellows regarded by the veterans who are still on the inside? Are they seen as going soft? Are they squares that sold out? Or are they respected?*

Nah. Their names still make some of them tremble. These guys I was just talking about, Merchant and them. No. They're like old folk stories, you know, when you talk about the days, about guys that were holding court in the yard.

*But how is their present turn interpreted? How do people regard what they've done?*

They still bow down. Yeah, they still bow down. They can go anywhere.

*Do people emulate them. Do they want to make changes like that in themselves?*

In a joint like this, yeah. We've been interested in showcasing a lot of our successes, and guys like this are perfect for that role.

You know, but not everybody that claims to have reformed is going to get respect like that. You take that guy from Florida—Dave the Blade[‡]—that says he found God. Well, hell, he was a piece of shit in the first place. He wasn't respected. I did time in Florida. He wasn't respected

---

[*]I have changed the name.

[†]I have changed the name.

[‡]Jerry here refers by nickname—which I have changed—to a Florida murderer who had recently been in the news.

by the guys in Florida. He was a piece of shit. He took two girls out and murdered them, after he made them partner to his crime. He's the one that let them know in the first place, and then murdered them to keep them quiet. Man, he's a pile of shit and nobody really respected him anyway. You know what I mean? How hard is it to murder some women anyway?

The guys I'm talking about never murdered no women. They murdered men that they had grievances with. You know, there's a difference. They gave no quarter and asked for none.

And every time somebody gets out—one of the Fellahs, a good dude, gets out—these guys are the first ones to meet him and try and get him into something positive now. They work hard at it. And nobody, not even the guys in the bowels of the institutions—Walla Walla, Clallam Bay—would ever put their mouth on a bad word about these guys.

*Are they more highly regarded than if they had gotten out and continued in a criminal lifestyle?*

Sure. Sure. We admire them.

*People are proud that they made something positive of themselves?*

Sure. You know, everybody likes to think that eventually, like, they too can turn it around. These guys were the extreme.

Most of the guys in the joint are just cannon fodder. They're following along, and they're doing what their friends are doing and stuff. OK, well, these guys weren't those guys. These guys were doing whatever the hell they wanted to do, and other people emulated them. They didn't look to anybody for approval of what they did. They did what they wanted to do.

*Is that one of the things you look for? The people who are most likely to make it on the outside and to turn their life around in a positive way, are they the ones who were leaders and individuals, even when they were bad guys?*

Yeah. Not the guys that just get out and don't come back. Some of them are followers. But the guys that get out, and do well, and stay active and proactive, and do positive shit with their life, and make a positive mark in the world, every one of them that I know of was a leader in the joint.

*Let me ask you something I asked Jimi. Let's say you were on the verge of getting out. And somebody came to you with the following deal: "We're going to let you submit a list of ten names of prisoners currently at WSR that are incarcerated with you, and we'll let all ten of them go free. And the only condition is, if any of them re-offends, you have to serve their sentence along with them for re-offending. So you have to stay here, or come back here, if they re-offend." Are there in fact ten people you're confident enough would never re-offend that you'd be willing to submit that list?*

Nope. Nope.

*If they said you could pick from anybody in the whole institution?*

No. Not if they let me pick from all the institutions.

At different points, in a lot of different guys' lives, if I knew what they had by way of plans, there are some guys that I'd bet some money on, but I would have to really know what their plans were.

See, like, I know what a lot of guys say their plans are, but they're showing me other things in what they do. You see what I'm saying? If your plans are to get out and stay clean and sober, you'd be clean and sober in here all the time.

That's the first step. You can't, like, get high once in awhile. You can't buy in, even a little bit. It's, like, "Well, I just smoke sometimes." Well then, you smoke. You know, that's all. You don't smoke two packs of Camels a day, but you smoke. You know, and that's the way it is. It's like being a little bit pregnant. You know, there's just no way to it.

There's guys, though, that, at times in their life, are real with it. Now, life events change those things. I got ten guys in this joint that at the right time in their life I can bet on them. You know, if I can pick the time, if I was allowed to say, "OK, this one goes free now. Not tomorrow, but today." Because it's now that it's all out there for him. It's laid out for him. I'd be willing to bet on some people then.

Like, as far along that road as I am today, there's no guarantee where I'll be next year, or two years, three years from now. I hope and dream that I'm even farther along the road of self-improvement then, but you never know. Enough disappointments, enough bad things happen, the right set of circumstances where I'm confronted with a life and death situation, and I'm confronted where my manhood, my being is at stake, then things'll change.

And once that's crossed, well then, all that other doesn't even really matter; you're going in another direction. You know, does that make sense?

*Oh yeah.*

Yeah. That's probably the biggest flaw in the parole system, is that generally when a guy is ready to go, the opportunity isn't there.

*So it's only a rare coincidence that they get out when they should get out.*

Yeah, when they need to get out.

*It's either too soon or too late.*

Yeah. Yeah.

# JEFF—October 1998

*"You know, when it first happens, you try and rationalize and explain, and say, 'Well, this happened, this happened, this happened,' but the bottom line is you can't explain it. No matter what I can say to anybody, it could never make sense, and it would never be a satisfactory explanation. After three or four years of trying, I realized that it was hopeless."*

M y second taped conversation with Jeff took place in the usual office across the hall from the PAP meeting on a Wednesday evening.

*Last time, we mostly just did a chronology of events, of the crime and what led up to it, of the arrest, and all that. Let's try to pick up that general thread of events. If I remember correctly, you had never done any prison time before you were arrested for this crime.*

No, no. Went to jail once, for shoplifting.

*How long were you in jail?*

Just got booked and released. Never actually went to jail.

*So you never had to stay overnight or anything?*

No.

*Were you just a kid when that happened?*

I was, like, nineteen. You know, I was out of money, and needed something out of the drug store, so. Got caught.

*So this is your first real taste of being incarcerated.*

Yeah, yeah. I hadn't had a history of going to jail, and all that stuff.

*So, you're taken into custody in Everett after the murder. Let's pick it up there. I assume you're in some vehicle. Are you handcuffed, or in some restraints?*

Yeah, they handcuff you, and take you down to the nearest cop car, handcuffed. Have you ever been arrested?

*No, I've been lucky so far.*

Well, they handcuff you, and then they stick the seatbelt through the handcuffs. You know, they put you in the backseat, and then put the seatbelt through the handcuffs, and then lock it, so you're really stuck. Your hands are behind you, and you're not going anywhere. And, of course, the doors have no handles. I always like it when you see these cop shows on TV, how the guys are always getting out of the backseat, or they're kicking the windows out. Cop cars aren't like that. You know, unless they're, like, undercover or something.

*So, the back doors can only be opened from the outside?*

Right, and they all have grating or something. I mean, you can't kick them out or anything like that either. And the seats are hard plastic, because guys are barfing in there and everything else, and they just take the hose to it. They're very uncomfortable. I mean, you're sitting in a hard plastic seat with your handcuffs behind you.

But they do have seatbelts. [Laughs.] They're very considerate. Of course, if you got in a wreck with your hands like that, in the seatbelt behind you,—

*That's what I was thinking, yeah—*

—that would not be pleasant.

*Right. [Laughs.] So where did they take you from there?*

I went right to Snohomish County Jail.

*How far was that?*

Three blocks.

*Oh, OK, so it's very close to the—*

Yeah, it's right down in Everett.

*—motel where you were arrested.*

Right. It was maybe five blocks. It's in the relative vicinity.

Because I was suicidal at the time, they put me up on the psych ward—they call it the "Observation Ward"—where you're not with the general population. They put me in there, where they have closer observation on the cells.

*Slow it down a little bit for me.*

OK.

*When you arrived, they open up the vehicle, since you can't open it yourself from inside,—*

Right.

*—and then what happens? Did they take the cuffs off? How many people are around you? What else are they doing?*

Yeah, there's, like, two or three cops. And they always hold you by the handcuffs. And, then they take you in through—well, they had, like, a little enclosure where they drive in, and then the door closes, so the cop car's in this enclosure with big walls.

*OK.*

It's like a mini-holding cell for the cop car. So, then when you get out, there's nowhere to go. You can't run, because you're in this enclosure inside the jail now, even though the top's open, but, you know, there's, like, big walls, so you couldn't go anywhere. You couldn't run anywhere. My feet weren't shackled at the time, but there's nowhere to go.

Once you're inside the jail, they take your handcuffs off, and you've got to get fingerprints, and they take your picture, and—

*The traditional front and side—?*

Yeah, yeah, you know, your basic mug shots. They take your fingerprints, and your picture, and then they stuck me up on the psych floor.

*What were you feeling from the time you got into the car and through what you've been describing, being processed and everything? Were you just numb, or what was going through your head?*

Well, you don't really know what's going on, 'cause, I mean, at that point, you know, they can drive you off a cliff and it would be, like, "So what?" I mean, it's sort of anti-climactic. I mean, it's, like, clean up work, where the cops got to come in and take care of the situation.

So, yeah, I wasn't really thinking anything. It's, like, "Well, here I'm going to jail, which is not surprising. I mean, it's sort of the natural result of what I did."

*So you were just kind of resigned to your fate? No fear, or anger, or—?*

Well, you know, it takes a couple days to set in, as far as what I really did and, you know, how I got there, and the "What am I going to do now?" kind of thing. Because, whenever you go to jail, for whatever it is, there's sort of an unbelief, a denial thing, where, "Well, this isn't happening," or, you know, "I'll get bail," or, "I'll find a lawyer," or whatever. You're sort of trying to rationalize, to convince yourself that, "Well, it's only going to be for a couple nights."

*Even in your situation, were you thinking that way?*

Oh sure. You know, it's, like, "Well, I'll get out on bail," like you see on the TV shows. But they don't let anybody out on bail. I mean, you got to be like Bill Clinton. You know, the average schmuck, they're not getting out. I mean, if you got a million dollars, sure.

So they book you in there, and then a couple days later they take you to what's called arraignment, where they take you inside the jail to this little room with a TV screen, which is connected to the courthouse next door where there's a judge. So instead of hauling you over there physically, they just do it electronically.

It saves everybody a lot of time. There's somebody from the DA's office there. They say, "This is Mr. so-and-so, number such-and-such, and he's charged with first degree murder," and everybody always pleads not guilty. Even if you got up right then and said, "I'm guilty as hell. Kill me," they wouldn't accept it. You know, you're always not guilty, just by definition.

*OK.*

So everybody pleads not guilty, no matter what, even if you don't want to plead not guilty. And then the judge sets your bail right there. And actually, mine was only two hundred and fifty thousand.

*Was that more than you had on you at the time?*

Yeah. Yeah. But it's within the realm of possibility that, you know, your family can put their home up as collateral, and then they have to put ten percent of that amount down—which is twenty-five thousand—and that's what the bail bondsman ends up getting as his commission. But we didn't do that. So, I got to stay in jail. [Laughs.]

But, one of the first things you want to do is figure out who your lawyer's going to be, because you're assigned a public defender. This is, like, a week later. I mean, it doesn't happen right away.

*So you don't have to request a public defender? They assign you one?*

And also, before I was taken into custody, when the cops were questioning me a little bit in the car, you know, I told them, "Well, I want a lawyer," and so they didn't question me any more. They had already read me my rights.

But, unfortunately, I had said too much on the nine-one-one conversation, which was voluntary, which can be admitted. So, it didn't really matter at that point.

But, ironically, one of the guys I went to high school with ended up being a public defender in King County, and he somehow saw my name pop up on the computer. And he had a buddy that was a hot shot lawyer for murder one cases. So, he came to see me, like, the next week. And he was trying to get me to hire this guy for, at that time, a thirty-five thousand dollar retainer.

*This is a private attorney, not a public defender?*

Right. My friend was a public defender, but his friend was a private attorney. And, so just for a retainer, in Eighty-nine, was thirty-five thousand. It's probably more like fifty now. But, you know, I didn't have that kind of money. And that's just to get him going, to start. It can run you up to a hundred grand for a murder trial, if you go all the way to trial. If you end up pleading out, which I probably would have—because, if I had a good attorney, they would have realized the hopelessness of my situation—you know, it probably would have cost me fifty thousand. But, I would have got ten less years, so, hey, that's a bargain.

But all those things are easy to see in hindsight, whereas when you're mulling them over at the time, you know, they don't seem as clear cut.

*Tell me about the psych floor.*

There was, like, fifteen guys in there. It's pretty small compared to the general population in the Snohomish County Jail, which, nowadays, is over a hundred and some per floor. When I was there, it was probably only seventy-some. But it's much more overcrowded now, I hear.

*Fifteen guys in separate cells, or in one big cell, or—?*

They're all separate cells. Snohomish County was a newer jail, which are all modularized. That's where you got one officer at a desk, and all the cells are controlled by that one officer, and he can monitor the whole thing.

It's kind of a little tier thing. You got a lower section and an upper section. There's probably twenty guys in there. On the big floors, there's probably fifty guys on the bottom, maybe forty guys on the top. And now I understand that they've doubled that up, so, it's, like, a hundred and eighty guys in there on that one floor, which is madness.

But, fortunately, I kind of eased in, because the psych ward was smaller, and half the guys are on medication and they don't know what's going on. They had an ax murderer up there that would just sit there and talk to himself. He was, like, out there. And they had some other guys that were on different sorts of medications. What's the big one now? Depression medicine? Lithium, and Ritalin, or whatever else they got now.

They had a full time counselor person there—you know, counselor or psychiatrist, whatever—that tried to do what he could to help people.

Basically I was there for a suicide watch. I was probably in there for a month or so.

*How did you feel about the environment, and your fellow inmates?*

Well, actually, it wasn't bad. I got booked in right around dinner time, even though I started this thing in the morning. It took me that long to actually get to where I was going, because you've got to wait different places for an hour here and there, you know.

And when I came in, they had the TV going, and they were showing me on TV. They were showing the SWAT team and everything, and saying, "Hostage in a hotel!" So everybody's watching that, and here I come in, and they're all, like, "Damn," you know. [Laughs.]

I'd never seen myself on TV. It was, like, "Oh wow!" you know. Like Andy Warhol says, "Everybody gets their fifteen minutes of fame." And I'm saying, "Well, there I am. Front page news." I was on the front page of the *Everett Herald* for a day or two.

But it's not much to be proud of. I mean, it's not the sort of thing that one looks for.

There was a couple fights in there, but it was pretty mellow. I mean, most of the guys were just not very well mentally balanced.

*You didn't feel in any danger?*

Not really, no. It wasn't like if I had just got thrown into, like, King County. That place is a nightmare. I mean, I haven't been there, but, you know, the stories I hear. You all go into one big tank, and there's, like, forty guys in there, and three-fourths of them are black. And, you know, if you want to eat, you pretty much have to box with people just to keep your food.

Whereas where I was, they just bring a meal cart by. You get your tray, and they just kind of scoot around. You don't get fat on it, but, you know, it's all right.

*How did you spend your time?*

By reading. Yeah, they had a lot of books. Mostly reading.

Trying to figure out what I'm going to do. A lot of people were giving me advice, but everybody's got a bias of course.

As I say, after about a month on the psych floor, I was moved to a different floor, and had my own cell there also—which now they've gotten rid of all that. And the guys that have been in prison, you know, they're advising me to go to trial, to not take any deals. None of them say plead guilty, because they all want you to go to trial and make them spend their money. "Make the bastards spend their money," you know.

Because if everybody goes to trial, then they'd pretty much shut the court system down. But, of course, they're not doing that, because the guys up front are the ones getting fucked. The guys that go to trial and get convicted are getting screwed. So everybody wants everybody else to clog up the system by taking everything to trial, even if they'd make a deal themselves.

My family came to see me and all, but none of them had any legal experience, and, you know, unfortunately, they didn't have any good advice.

*Were you close with your family before this incident?*

Yeah, yeah. Actually, my mom had visited just a couple weeks before I went to jail.

*How did they respond to what happened?*

Well, they weren't terribly happy about the situation. But they've been supportive. My dad's since passed away. My mom has remarried, and she's real supportive. And my brother is too.

Yeah, that means a lot, helps a lot, 'cause a lot of guys in here, they don't have a family, or their families aren't supportive. You know, it makes a lot of difference.

*Tell me more about how they reacted, beyond just that they weren't pleased about it.*

Well, nobody understood why. Nobody knew anything was going on, which there really wasn't to speak of. I mean, we didn't have any, you know, boxing matches or anything like that. And we hadn't really been considering divorce or anything.

So, it was mostly shock. You know, as I say, my mom had just been visiting a week or two before. We went out salmon fishing and everything.

*How did they find out?*

I guess the cops called them. Yeah, the cops called somebody, and—

*So you didn't have to inform them yourself, directly.*

No. No. Yeah, the cops called somebody. I think they called my wife's family, and then, my wife's family called everybody else.

*Tell me about the first conversation you had with your parents after it happened.*

Well, my mom's crying. I mean, she's, you know, she's not—Your first reaction is disbelief, like, "That couldn't happen," you know, "What are you saying here?"

*Did they call you long distance at the jail, or how did you talk to them?*

They have pay phones in the jail you can call collect on.

*So you made the call to them?*

Yeah. Yeah, as soon as I got there. By that time, they had heard from—

*Did you know that they had already heard?*

I wasn't sure. I kind of figured they had by then, because I actually gave the cops my wife's family's phone number to call. So, I knew the cops had called her family. So I figured my family probably already knew it by now too.

This was, like, that evening I think. Yeah, it was probably that evening I called.

*What were you feeling as you anticipated the call, before you actually heard your mother's voice?*

Well, I mean, I didn't know. I mean, you can't explain something like that. You know, it's just one of those things that no matter how many times you try, you can't explain it.

You know, when it first happens, you try and rationalize and explain, and say, "Well, this happened, this happened, this happened," but the bottom line is you can't explain it. No matter what I can say to anybody, it could never make sense, and it would never be a satisfactory explanation. After three or four years of trying, I realized that it was hopeless.

*So you hadn't reached that realization at that early stage.*

Oh no, no. Yeah, it took years.

*So at the time, you were still in the mode of, "I'm going to have to explain this to them."*

Well, yeah, it's, like, denial. You know, not accepting it. Like, "Well, this didn't really happen, but now I've got to—." I was in denial. I wasn't accepting it.

I contacted my wife's family, and, you know, tried to explain what happened. And that was a miserable failure. 'Cause as I say, there's just nothing you can say. There's nothing I can say that'll ever make them feel any better. Now I know that, but at the time, I didn't.

*So when you were calling your family, what kind of emotion or expectation did you have?*

Well, I certainly wanted to talk to them, you know, because here I'm in jail. And, I mean, a very traumatic experience has just happened, so, yeah, I wanted some support, sure. But also, I was real worried about what they were going through.

*How did the call go?*

I can't remember a lot of it. But, I'd say that, you know, my mom asked me, "The cops called and said this happened. Is there some mistake?" You know, because she wanted to hear it from me of course.

And I said, "Well, yeah, it did happen." And, you know, she started screaming and crying and all that. She hadn't heard from me yet, so she didn't know what was going on.

*So she still had some small hope that maybe they'd falsely arrested you, or whatever?*

Well, yeah, sure. Yeah, like it was somebody else, or, you know, it was the Boogie Man, or whatever.

*And, like you said, there was no pattern leading up to this, so it wasn't like they thought, "Well, we kind of saw this coming," or "We were worried something that this might happen."*

Yeah.

*To them it must have been just a bolt from the blue.*

Right. There was no indication.

*Were they as supportive as you had hoped? Or were they accusatory? How did they come across?*

Well, if I had been—I don't really want to say "smart"—but if I had been trying to conceal it all along and never say anything to anybody, then I couldn't really even have these conversations with them, because I couldn't say, "Well, yeah, I did it," because, you know, they could be subpoenaed to testify against me.

But of course, at the time I wasn't even thinking that way. You know, I'd already confessed on nine-one-one that I did it, so, it's kind of hard to take that back.

But, yeah, I told them I did it. I mean, I didn't lie. I wasn't evasive.

My mom and father, they'd been divorced since I was, like, seventeen, and—

*Were they both on the phone with you at this time?*

No. They lived in different states.

*So you called them separately?*

Right. But my father, he never really dealt with it. He was an alcoholic, and he could never deal with his own demons, let alone, you know, his son's. He had had his share of problems with the Mormon Church, and with drinking, and, you know, marital problems. I mean, as I say, my folks got divorced. But, fortunately, he chose the more rational route than I did.

But he'd gone through a lot of similar things himself, and I don't think he ever successfully dealt with them. And then now for something like this to happen, you know, he was never the same after that.

He died, like, five years later from drinking and smoking. It really wasn't a surprise, because he did it his whole life. His dad died at fifty-five from drinking, and he made it till sixty.

*So your mother was better able to deal with it?*

Well, she's a much stronger person. You know, much more optimistic. My dad, he had enough of his own problems that he couldn't deal with, let alone someone else's.

*So what was her initial response in this phone call?*

Disbelief. Crying. Screaming. I mean, shock. "How could you do this?"
I told her, "I don't know"

*Was she thinking in practical terms at all—what kind of attorney should we get, or anything like that?*

Not at that time, no. No.

*So, she was just overwhelmed by emotion?*

Yeah. She came up to visit me in jail the next week.
You get to talk through glass, which is real exciting [sarcastic].

*Where did she come from?*

Utah. Yeah, she was living in Salt Lake at that time. Salt Lake City.

*You mentioned that you also called your wife's family, or tried to contact them. What happened there?*

I never tried calling them. I wrote them a letter. That actually ended up getting used against me in sentencing, because they said this letter showed that I lacked remorse, which the judge himself didn't agree with. They said it was insensitive, you know, which it was, but they also said it indicated I lacked remorse, which wasn't true.

*What was insensitive about it? What did you write?*

Well, it's just that I was trying to explain what happened and rationalize it, but there's nothing you can say. I mean, it was a poor attempt.

But the prosecution actually tried to use that against me in the sentencing.

*How were you attempting to justify your act at that early stage?*

Stress. You know, lost my job, had a new house, had a new baby. You know, all that kind of stuff. Mormon Church, and blah, blah, blah, blah. And this counselor that we were seeing, you know, she kind of set me off.

But, I mean, bottom line is that none of that matters. I mean, it's all irrelevant.

*So her family just turned that letter over to the authorities, or did they respond directly to you?*

No, they sent it to the cops, yeah. I mean, the DA had contacted them, so they were in touch with each other.

*Was that the only time you ever attempted contact with your wife's family?*

No. That was a few months after it happened. But, my mom still sees them. You know, I've tried to use her as an intermediary, but she kind of refuses to do that, 'cause that puts her in a bad spot. But, I sent them a letter two or three years ago, you know, asking them if they were interested in establishing some sort of correspondence. I mean, there was no content to it other than, basically, to ask if enough time had passed to where we can establish some sort of correspondence.

And their answer was no, it hadn't.

*So they did respond to you.*

Oh yeah, my wife's mother did. I was actually real close to her before this happened. We had had a really good relationship.

*Was it a polite kind of, "No, unfortunately we're not quite ready to do that yet," or was it more of a "Hell no, stop bothering us"?*

It was mostly matter-of-fact. You know, "Not at this time," and, "Don't contact us again." But my daughter's still living there. She's nine years old now.

*She's being raised by your wife's family?*

Right. Basically I just have to wait until they decide—if they ever do—that they want to have contact. I think they will, but it's still too soon now. It's been nine years, but the time's not right yet.

*So from talking to your mother and such, your impression is that your wife's family really hasn't softened that much yet.*

Right.

My daughter asks my mom questions about me. She knows where I'm at, what I'm here for, and what happened to her mother. She pretty much knows all that. I think when she gets to be, you know, fourteen, fifteen, maybe at that time we'll get some sort of correspondence going. She's still too young yet. But I'm hoping that we can work out something like that.

But, I just have to wait until they initiate it, because, as I say, there's nothing I can do.

What I do, I keep a journal for my daughter right now, where I write to her, like, once or twice a month. Been doing it for about a year and a half. Actually it was Jimi's suggestion. It was an excellent idea. I'm hoping when she's eighteen I can give it to her.

*So right now you're not even allowed to write to her.*

Right. So I keep this journal for her, and when she's eighteen, then she can decide for herself whether she wants it or not. I mean, there's no telling what sort of animosity might be there, but there's also a lot of questions, I'm sure. There's no way of telling right now.

*So your mother came up to see you shortly after you arrived in jail.*

Yeah. Yeah. She came up. My stepdad didn't come up. It kind of freaked him out too bad. He's never forgiven me, because he was close to my wife. You know, I think he's had a real problem with it.

Yeah, then my brother came up. He had just got married, and they came up.

He's been pretty supportive. I've been trying to get him to go see my daughter, but he's still kind of freaked out by it. He's really anti-Mormon, living in Utah, and my wife's family is really Mormon. That's the reason he uses that he's not comfortable, but I don't think that's the real reason. You know, by meeting my daughter, he has to acknowledge the whole situation.

He's kind of like my dad, where it's easier to ignore it, or, you know, just pretend the situation's not there than to deal with it.

*Is your mother the only one who can bring you news of your daughter?*

Right. She gets pictures and stuff, so, you know, I get pictures. I see how she's doing.

# 9—October 1998

*"When I walk around this place, I try to have the ability to think like a free, independent person, not a prisoner. I mean, for one thing, fuck the convict code! To me, as long as I represent myself as a man, the way I feel is appropriate, then that's my code. If it falls in line with the convict code, so be it. If not, fuck the world. That's the way I believe."*

T he next Wednesday evening, I spent the entire PAP session taping a conversation with 9. Before I turned the recorder on, he asked me if I trusted that my interview subjects for this book were being straight with me. I inferred that he had one or more specific people in mind that he believed were not being honest, and he wanted to feel me out to see if I was picking up on that. I was disinclined to come right out and say that I suspected so-and-so was lying to me, but on the other hand I didn't want to say that I took everything I was told by the prisoners at face value, because I don't.

In any case, I felt it was an interesting place to start.

*Why don't we talk a little bit about what we were just discussing before the tape started. What are your feelings about whether or not prisoners will be honest in a format like this? Do you think I can trust people to be straight with me in these interviews?*

Well, I believe that they're capable of being honest, depending on what question you ask. But, you know, there are certain questions you can ask them, and they could be more worried about maintaining a certain image, rather than being honest about the way they feel, about how afraid they were, if they were scared. To them, it's somewhat of a manly thing to not admit to being weak or being scared.

And I don't think a lot of them would pull those skeletons out of their closet to confess to you some of the things that we've seen or heard or known about them, because they'd be embarrassed. But I feel like it takes away from the whole idea of the project, if you're not able to be honest. Rather than just cover something up or lie about it, just refuse to talk about it, or leave it vague.

You know, because if people were all like they want to present themselves to you, we'd have nothing but solid, honest people in prison, which we know we don't.

*Do you think people are more inclined to lie about the things they've done, or about the things that have been done to them? I mean, if somebody's victimized people, if he's guilty as sin of the crimes he's been convicted of, and he's just been a bad guy, is he more likely to lie about himself? Or is it the guy who has maybe been turned into a punk, or he's maybe been a rat, or he's shown some kind of fear, shown he's a coward? Which guy is more likely to lie to me?*

[Laughs.] Oh, that's easy: the guy that's been a victim. I mean, it's a strange thing, because the guy that has taken advantage of people in the past, you know, he's more likely to kind of brag about it, because he wants everybody to know that he has the ability to be strong or tough. He's looking to impress people. That's just the prison mentality.

But then the guy that's been the victim of such things would refuse to confess or discuss those things, because it makes him look weak, or like a punk. And they're afraid of that getting out, because that can come back to haunt a person. If the rumor gets out, and this person is viewed like that, then of course they'd be a victim again. The prison mentality is, once you're a victim, you're always a victim.

So it's the guy that has been a victim before that's the one that's going to lie.

*One of the most common thing guys claim that one is naturally suspicious of is how even if they admit they committed the crime, there's always some extenuating circumstances—some excuse or justification.*

Yeah.

*Like, in your case, I mean, you claim you didn't even know what was going on. You're just holding a guy down, and you didn't even kill him, and your partner comes along and does it. But what makes me hesitate to say, "Oh, that's just a case of a guy lying or filling in the details to make himself look better," is that there are so many other things you've done, that you admitted to, which don't put you in such a good light, where you weren't just in the wrong place at the wrong time.*

Yeah.

*Like you admitted that you had fired shots at random at some total stranger, just because you were trying to impress an older kid. So, you know, you've admitted to me doing things that were stupid or just plain wrong. That makes me a little more inclined to believe you about your crime, because if you were going to lie about that, it seems like you'd lie about all of it. But, in any case, whether we're talking about you or the other folks, I'm not in a position to know who's telling me the truth about their crime or not.*

Right.

*I have to just let people tell their own story, and kind of reserve judgment. I don't pretend to know, "Yeah I can believe this guy, but I have to disbelieve that guy." You know, I just let people have their say, and let the readers sort out whom they want to believe.*

Right. I mean, like, in my case in point, I got life without. Being honest or lying is not going to benefit me in no way possible, because it's not going to get this life without up off of me. I got nothing to gain.

Yeah, there's a lot of things I've done in my life that I'm not proud to have done, now that I look back on it. Now that I'm an adult. I'm not proud of a lot of it. And, of course, there's some things I've done in my life that could have got me in prison if I would have got caught.

And, of course, I ain't got no problem accepting my own responsibility for the things I've done. But in this case, we're talking about being overwhelmed with a huge amount of time for something that shouldn't have constituted that much time.

My problem, my bitterness comes from one thing. I told you exactly what I did. I was placed in a corner, I was put in a position where I could have testified against the guy that did it, that he and I both know did it, and get twenty years instead of this life without. I could be going home next year, after thirteen/four. But, standing my position as a man, and denying everything but refusing to testify against him, I wind up getting life without. To tell the truth or lie about that point now, where is it going to get me?

So, it wouldn't matter what anybody would think or believe. I was honest with you about the incidents that I've done in my past that I'm not proud of, and I'm being honest with you about this situation here.

Now, as far as everybody else in general, I've seen both sides. I've seen some that have done some horrendous things, like rape, or multiple rapes, and the first thing they want to do is sit up and discuss about how the prosecutor fucked them, or how the judge just violated their rights. And, on the one hand, I'm a skeptic, because I feel, you know, even if your rights were violated, what about all the lives that you violated in the process? But now, of course, being a victim of injustice myself, you know, I can pretty much understand their side too.

But see, I got one murder beef, and for that I got life without. Some people got two murder beefs, and got ten, fifteen years. That is my problem. That is the only thing I'm concerned about. I didn't feel like what I was convicted of justified life without. There's nothing horrendous about my crime compared to some of us that's here, that's going home tomorrow or next week or next year, that been down an equivalent amount of time as I have.

There's some guys that I've known that, like me, they was associated with people at the time that a crime was committed, but they didn't do it themselves. And in this state, if you're with the person that commit the crime, you're treated as an accessory, an accomplice, and you get the equivalent amount of time as the actual perpetrator does.

But a line needs to be drawn as far as a person who has knowledge of what is intended to be done, and is a part of it, or is just with a guy that snaps and do some stupid shit, and just gets caught in the middle. That's the part that they don't differentiate.

It's easy for someone to say, "Hey man, I didn't know what he was doing," but in order for that to carry any weight, you damn near have to say who did it and what exactly he did, and then you're snitching. Then, you're testifying against the guy. But if you play it straight and just deny everything, just say you don't know anything, but you don't snitch, then of course you're in a position like I am.

But, yeah, everybody always got an excuse or a reason for doing something that they've done, and they always blame the system as the reason why they're sitting in the position that they are.

This is my first time in prison as an adult. I never had the kind of second chances I see other people get, including murderers. That's what bothers me.

But you got so many people that ruin it. You got so many people that actually make the system look like it's not working, and they're not getting enough time. Like all these guys getting out and just re-offend, and the media blasts it all over. You know, and that spoils it for everybody.

And the guys that do deserve a chance aren't always getting it. I see guys that have been here nineteen years that have totally, totally changed their lives. These are people that I've seen, that I've known, my friends, that's totally devoted to God, raised a family, created a family while right here, haven't had a write-up in eleven years, and aren't being let out.

But then they got some guys that have been here for the same amount of time or less, they got twenty write-ups, I don't think they're devoted to anything, and they're the ones getting out of prison.

Those are the things I wonder about. OK, do they actually look into the profile of this person to see who deserve to get out, or are they just, like, "OK, we've got a certain amount of people to let out, and this is who we're going to keep and this is who we're going to let go"? It makes you wonder when you're looking from the inside. I can't see it from your perspective, because I'm not from the outside looking in. But being as damaged as I have been for the past twenty years, I see things that's inconsistent that makes me wonder about the system.

*What are the tendencies, or correlations, when you see people being treated unequally like that? Does it seem to be primarily a matter of who's got enough money for good lawyers, and that kind of thing? Is it a racial element? Is it a language element, that people who aren't good with English tend to get screwed over? Age? I mean, do young people get screwed over more? What consistencies do you see there, as far as people being treated unequally like that?*

You know, that's a good question, Craig, and in my experience—and I've thought about this a lot, being a young black man and growing up in prison, you know, since I was eighteen—I've seen an example of every one of those things you just described.

It's complex. It's all those factors. I mean, the same people that is being accused of racism in some situations, I've also seen let some blacks off that I didn't think stood a chance. So that showed me there's more than just the element of racism. Now, I don't know if it's a strategy on their part, but I've witnessed that.

But, also, you know, you got different personalities of people that represent you and that are against you in a courtroom. You got some striving for a career. You got some striving for certain numbers of how many they can convict.

It's a negotiation process. I mean, hell, my lawyer was going out to lunch with my prosecutor. That I thought was totally out of control, but little did I know that he was trying to work a system out with her to represent me appropriately. Who was to say what they were doing; who was to say not? Now that I lost, I thought they was fucking me. If I would have won, I'd think he did a great job. So it actually would depend on the outcome for the person who was involved.

But, what it boils down to, of all those factors, it's actually the money more than anything. I mean, overall, I don't care even if you can't speak English, if you got the money, you're going to have somebody that represent you that can.

You're battling against the entire state, as you see on that piece of paper. It says, "The State of Washington vs. [9]." They use all their resources to come at you with evidence that really incriminates you. And the only thing you have is a lawyer that—if you're able to pay him enough—might be able to hire the necessary resources to conflict whatever they've said.

Now, they come in with medical examiners and everybody else that you never even seen or heard of, but that sit up there and describe the science and the reason why you done what you did. Unless you're able to combat that with somebody—a reference of your own—then everything the jury hears those people say is going to be assumed true.

So, if you can't afford those kind of people to defend or represent you accordingly, then you're in trouble, because it makes it look like the state's put on an overwhelming showcase about why you're guilty, and all you had is an inexpensive lawyer that is probably a rookie, and no money to spend for your own experts and to build a case.

So, it's like you fighting against the entire state. And that's the way it actually feels when you're standing up in the courtroom. It's you and this guy you just met several months ago when you hired him, that's going up against the entire state of people, and you don't stand a chance, unless there's something that the state screw up, or there's something that's so overwhelming that you can actually catch the jury's attention to really consider this.

And in most cases, people have the tendency to listen to the majority, rather than the minority. I have been guilty of that too. I listen to the crowd rather than listen to the person that's standing next to me. And as it turned out, the sole person standing next to me could be the one that's right, but I'm influenced by numbers. And that's just the way human nature is. You got witnesses and experts one after the other telling about how guilty you are, and then it's just you and your lawyer claiming you're innocent. Who do you think people are going to be impressed by?

That is the problem. It's all about the money, the finances to afford the resources that you need to actually defend your rights.

*I want you to help me to understand mentally and emotionally what it's like to exist in this place. I'm not thinking so much in terms of specifics. I'm just thinking about what it does to a person emotionally. Imagine for me that you're back in your cell—late at night, you're in bed—what sort of thing do you think about? When you let your mind wander, and you're trying to fall asleep, and you're in this environment that you've been stuck in for so many years, what thoughts go through your head?*

[Laughs.] Ooh, that's a deep one. There are so many. There's some thoughts I have that I don't think I would have ever had outside of prison.

But the thing that I really think about most commonly over the years, of course, is always going to be freedom, imagining myself on the street. What I would be doing out there right now. The things that I value the most. The things that make me happy—would make me happy—if I were on the street.

I think about the disappointment in myself, that, OK, next year I'll be thirty years old, and I haven't had the chance to actually live a life, to be productive with my life.

The friends that I've known that stood beside me all these years. Not being able to stand there for them, to show them how much I love and appreciate them.

The general things that you usually take for granted. Things I've experienced in my life, but I never have the chance to do now. Even if it's nothing but going to the park, or just going to the movies, and out to dinner.

Wondering, what would it be like the first time I get a chance to walk into a restaurant again? Would I still know my manners?

I mean, all those things. Being in a room with my female friend, or whoever, and sitting up watching a movie in the dark. Wondering how that would feel, just to be in the confidence of somebody that you care about, that you really appreciate.

I think about, if I did get out, how would I be affected by being in prison and all the things that have tormented me over these years, how will I be able to adjust to our society's expectations?

I mean, those are the thoughts that really invade my mind.

And I've challenged myself over the past many years to try to think as I would if I were on the streets, rather than taking the prisoner's attitude in prison. I don't really know if you can understand that. I don't know if a lot of people can understand that. And that's why I think I'm—I can't say unique—but, I'm the only person that I ever heard that from.

When I walk around this place, I try to have the ability to think like a free, independent person, not a prisoner. I mean, for one thing, fuck the convict code! To me, as long as I represent myself as a man, the way I feel is appropriate, then that's my code. If it falls in line with the convict code, so be it. If not, fuck the world. That's the way I believe.

But I try to maintain the compassion, the mentality, the emotions, and everything as a human being, same as if I was on the other side of that wall. And that is the only way that I think is appropriate to condition myself, if I'm to avoid being hung up or caught up on things that I've ignored or neglected in my life should I get placed on the other side of that wall.

If I was to walk out of this place tomorrow, the first thing that I would probably do—after I first thank God—would be to go see the people that stood beside me the longest, and showed me the love and support that I relied on. That was my leverage. That was what enabled me to be alive today, otherwise, I really believe I'd be dead. It's that presence in my life that helps me to strive each day just to survive in this place.

I mean, Craig, I've thought about some of the craziest thoughts, and got so mad, as if I could take on the entire prison, knowing that I can't win, but hell, who cares? If I die, I didn't lose nothing anyway, because technically I'm a walking dead man. But I try to keep my brain and my heart alive to keep me striving, because the day they take away that, or corrupt that, I'll be no more use, not even to me.

I mean, the loss of not having any kids, not being able to have a child to raise up—the fathering thing—those are the things that really haunt me, that bother me.

I look at TV and I see young guys, as young as me, millionaires, or just having a productive life, whether they're NBA, NFL stars, whatever, and living the good life, and being surrounded by the people that they care about. And me in here. I think about that.

And Christmas. Christmas is the most difficult time. That and summer. It's the most difficult time emotionally for me. And it really wears me down. On Thanksgiving Day or any holiday, but really Christmas the most. Because you really think about the people, your family and the loved ones, sitting around the table, and enjoying the festivities and the love in the room, and your not being a part of it. And you wonder, are they really thinking about you? Do they really care?

I mean, these are the things that really bug the hell out of me, that makes me know that I'm still alive, still emotionally alive. These are the thoughts that I go through.

*It seems like it's a difficult balance that you have to strike when you're in prison. On the one hand, maybe it's healthy—like you say—not to let yourself be too caught up in what goes on inside these walls, but to think of yourself instead as like a visitor here whose real self and real life is as a free person, same as anybody else, and to focus on the past and the future and when you were an outside person. But, isn't there a risk there, a danger there, that then your whole life is spent in preparation for something else instead of making the most of what you have in the present? I mean, you may never get out, or maybe you'll get out in five years, or fifteen years, or whatever. Is it right to just treat your life in here as a preparation for that?*

That's a good question. I've thought of that too. But, I think it would be more damaging to not be prepared than it would be to be prepared and not get it. I mean, there's a sacrifice, because you're right: I can feel that way, or believe that way, and not never get out of here. I could die in this place, and I would still have had my heart and my mind on the streets.

As opposed to, I could take advantage of the things I'm surrounded by here and focus on them, and then get out and be unprepared. To me, that would be more devastating. It would actually destroy me worse to not prepare myself to get out.

But, you know, one of the first things I learned when I first got locked up—it was told to me by my mother actually—"They can lock up your body, but they can't lock up your heart and your mind. Don't ever let them take that. The one thing that you should do is to read the newspaper and watch the news. That way, it keeps you in tune with society and keeps you updated."

And, of course, throughout my travels in the state prison system, I've met quite a few guys who have been locked up for a long time, and some of the things I see in them make me think that mentally they're still caught up in the Sixties or the Seventies. The way they dress. The things they do. The things they like doing.

But the part that really bugs me, that really gets to the core of me, of my emotions, is when I see some guy that's been locked up that thinks the way you've just suggested, that he needs to take advantage of the things around him in prison. To me, that means he's institutionalized. And that is my worst fear, besides dying in prison.

I mean, to be institutionalized where you can't think past prison, where this is your whole life surrounding you, you give up on every hope you've ever had, there's nobody that means anything to you out on the streets, and you don't have a life. You're actually dead. Literally, you're dead.

*But just to play devil's advocate, couldn't somebody say that by focusing so much on the outside, and keeping up with the newspapers and the television, and psychologically putting yourself with that world instead of the inside prison world, isn't it almost like a fellow who maybe has a dream of traveling overseas someday, even though he knows it's very unlikely he'll ever be able to do it? Maybe he doesn't have the money or whatever, but there's only the smallest chance he'll ever get to whatever his dream destination is—say, Australia. Now, if that person spent all of his time keeping up with Australian newspapers and television, and learning all about their culture, and their way of doing things, and, you know, their popular books and movies, and all that, and preparing himself to fit in in Australia was the main focus of his life, we would say there's something kind of odd about this guy. He's just too focused on something that's probably not even going to happen. His heart is in a different culture, a different location, a different geography. You know, he needs to get back to focusing on the United States where he lives, and where he really can live a life and make an impact on other lives, or really can make good or bad decisions with his life. Now for me, I'm probably more on your side on this issue, but if somebody—just as devil's advocate—*

I understand.

*—made that point, what would you say to that?*

Well, number one, there's only one thing that nobody can ever take away from you, and that's your dreams. You can take anything away from me, anything from any human being in life, but the one thing they'll always hold—they'll die with it—is their dreams. And as long as you have dreams, you'll always have an opportunity. You can always focus or be prepared emotionally to look toward your ultimate goal. I mean, from some aspect, that's what a goal is: a dream. And whatever you do to achieve that goal or that dream is pretty much up to you.

Now, I think more optimistic than I think pessimistic, simply because I don't know what tomorrow holds. I mean, if I die tonight, I know that yesterday I thought about tomorrow. I mean, that's just the way I try to focus on it, be prepared for it, because that way, I have something to reach for, to strive for.

Now, for the people that will encourage someone to come back to reality, to come back to where they're at, they're probably just describing themselves and their own lack of hope. They're pretty much stuck in a mold, and they want you to be stuck there with them. Or maybe they don't have any focus or can't see past today.

That actually totally goes against my logic, because there's always possibilities, there's always hope, no matter what. As long as you're alive, you got hope. And if I just stay stagnant in my life, or just focus on the things that's in me today, tomorrow will destroy me, because I wouldn't be prepared for it.

When I go to bed at night, I think about tomorrow. I think of what I have to do tomorrow, same as most people do. Well, if we went with that focus you just described, I mean, you don't think about that till tomorrow comes. Which is understandable, which is a realistic thing to do for some people. But, to me, those people, they're stagnant. They're stuck. They can't get past their fears, or their concerns.

I don't have any reason to be fearful, because the worst that can happen to me I've already had, except losing my life. As long as I can stay focused on that dream, on my goals or my hopes, that'll keep me inclined, like I say, to prepare for it, and to keep striving. Because if I ever lose that fire, there's no telling what I will do; there's no telling what would happen to me.

My fear is dying in prison. And that is what that ultimately would lead to.

In here, you're surrounded by so many people that are so negative, that sometimes it's extremely difficult to even think positive. And their attitude wears off on you at points. When you try to get away from it, it actually takes its toll on you and wears you down. Emotionally, mentally, and you can get to the point where you snap, you totally lose it.

I've seen it. I've seen it happen. I've seen some of the strongest that has the reputation of being the strongest just break weak.

I don't deny my emotions. I don't deny my feelings. If I want to cry, I cry. And that's the only way that I feel like I can be true to me, because this is the most difficult situation that any human being can actually live. I mean, being locked up, in this environment, in a cage, under the control of another human being's decisions, told what to do and when to do it.

It's almost like being a child all over again, but without the ability to grow. That is what I see it as. But I'm still growing, and I want to keep growing. And who knows, one day I might get my chance, and I'll be ready for it.

*Do you think that there are some people—and tell me if you think perhaps Henry is an example of this—who have been able to strike a balance, where they have been able to focus on the present and on their own situation and do good with it, but without becoming institutionalized in the negative way you're describing? You know, institutionalized in the sense that they give up hope, they give up their dreams, they wouldn't even want to get out, or they wouldn't be able to handle it if they did get out. Is it possible to do both, to make the most of your life in here, while also being prepared for freedom if it comes? Or do you have to focus on one or the other?*

Yeah, it's possible to do both. Like Henry for example. Here's a guy that's been locked up twenty-one years, but, you know, due to having EFVs,* he created children, who he still have the ability to continue being a father to. He has kids from elementary school age to my age. And sometimes I wonder what would have happened if he hadn't had that. Without that, I mean, his whole life would be prison. I think those are the kinds of things that help him keep being realistic and keep his life alive on the streets, keep his whole image alive.

He don't lose focus a lot, because he read a lot. I mean, he'll read the newspaper, watch the news, and stay in tune. Even some of the things he'll discuss, he don't sit and discuss just things that happen in prison. He will talk about something he's seen on the news, to maintain, you know, whatever sense of value that he may have that correlates to what's going on on the streets.

Yeah, you can do both. I mean, on occasion, I do it too.

Sometimes there will be an issue that arises in prison that I will have to focus on and forget everybody on the streets, and I'll give you an example of that.

You know that there's somebody that I try to stay out of trouble for, because she's dying of cancer, and I know her coming up to see me and the time we're able to spend together, you know, means a lot to her, as well as to me. And I am afraid that if I put myself in a position to be taken to the hole, or to get infracted, it could mean that if we're able to see each other at all, it'll be behind glass, you know, behind a glass window, and that takes away from that moment that I feel that she deserves. But at the same time, if I get caught in a confrontation that I have no choice but, you know, to get physical, then I'll have to take my chances at that confrontation first.

Because, what I got to focus on most importantly is my life, and my survival, and if someone put me in jeopardy, I would just have to put her second, and think about me as a priority, because my safety is at stake. And that's when you have to juggle both. You want to do what you need to do for your people on the outside, but you also have to safeguard your life on the inside. And, you know, when the time is at hand, when there's friction in prison, when tension arises, you have to put everything else aside and focus on that. You have to not look at your family, or consider anything about the outside world, because you never know, it can uproar, and the next thing you know, your life could be at stake, so you're pretty much focused on prison and what you have to do in your present situation.

But, yes, it's done. It's possible to do both. But, there's so many that's either one way or another, and there's so many that's actually focused on prison, that, to me, are merely institutionalized.

*Do you think it's even more common among people who have a sentence of life without, or—?*

Oh yeah.

---

*The aforementioned Extended Family Visits—"trailers." Conjugal visits.

*—a very long sentence, that they're more likely to fall into that?*

Yeah, there's quite a few of those, more than of anything. That's why I feel like I have kind of a unique attitude about it. You know, I've met quite a few people in my travels, and I'm talking about from counselors to people from the outside, and even to this very day, [laughs], when I tell them that I've got life without, they think I'm lying. You know, I've heard it many a time, "Man, for a person with life without, you sure look like you're having too much damn fun! You sure smile too much!"

And, you know, a couple of counselors have told me, said, "Man, you know what? I have to give you praise, because you got a hell of a lot of spirit." I didn't know what they meant by that, simply because some of them I didn't hardly know, and I'm not around them enough for them to get that judgment of me. But, apparently I carry myself—in their opinion—as if I'm a short timer.

And you're right, that could be dangerous, because it could be harmful or painful to yourself internally. But, I don't care, because none of it's more painful to me than being in this prison without being able to get out. Everything else is irrelevant to me. To hell with that pain. The huge pain is the idea of being in this environment for the rest of my life, and dealing with it from day to day. And that's the part that damages me the most.

But as a whole, the life withouters, yeah, they've given up. I mean, a lot of them. Not all of them. There's some I can speak highly of that really keep striving, and have been striving for the whole time, a long time, like Henry. But, there's quite a number of them that have actually given up on life, on themselves, everything. Morally, logically, every way. And it really disgusts me.

*Is it harder having uncertainty, or would it be harder just knowing you're going to be here for a long time? I mean, let me put it this way: In your present situation where you've got a life without sentence, you know there's always a small chance that something could happen, maybe in the near future, more likely in the midterm or long future, that you'd get out, but you don't know when that would be. You don't know if it's ten years from now, or twenty years from now, or what, but you know there's always a chance. There's always a hope. What if you could trade that for a situation where it was absolutely locked in stone, definite, you absolutely would not walk out of this place until, say, twenty-five years from today, but at that point, it's definite you would leave?*

That's a hell of a question. Now, sometimes there's a benefit in the unknown, even though I hate contingencies. I mean, I've always despised contingencies, where one thing is dependent on the other. Yeah, I mean, I hate not knowing. I hate being curious. I hate wondering, having an idea, but not being able to have definite knowledge about it.

But, you know, as far as they're concerned, if the court tell you, it is pretty much locked in stone. Life without is life without. They don't anticipate no law changes or no rule changes, or something that can benefit some life withouters to overturn it.

Well, I'm in a cell with a guy—Henry—that after twenty-one years, with five life withouts, he just got his sentence overturned. And up until they changed that, they thought that was pretty much set in stone. So, it's not as certain as they think.

*And you'd rather have that uncertainty where there's some hope, but you don't know when or if it's going to happen?*

Yeah. Now, there might be a possibility you have that uncertainty, and it'll be thirty years before you get a chance to get out. But, you know, compared to the twenty-five years locked in stone, or thirty years uncertainty, I'd still rather have that uncertainty. Because the uncertainty is what help me to continue, to make it to that twenty-fifth year.

I mean, sometimes it gets to the point where you don't think you can make it to next year. You certainly don't think you can make it through twelve years like I have. And now, to think that same amount of time into the future, ain't no way in hell I believe I can survive twelve more years in prison. If I think about the twelve years that I've done so far, and how far I've traveled, I mean, there's no way. I don't think I can realistically do twelve more years in prison without doing some real bad damage to me, mentally and psychologically. And that's what I'm striving to prevent.

You know, sometimes, Craig, it's almost like there's something that you aim for, that you're going to chase, but then there's times that that chase is actually something that you're striving to prevent. And, I don't know if you understand that, but—

*Clarify that for me.*

OK. Sometimes you see something ahead of you that you really want, and you run for it, and you want to put your hand on it. But then other times, you put forth that same amount of energy and that same effort to prevent something from destroying you.

I don't know how to break that down to simple terms, but I spend more of my energy—or a lot of my energy—trying to prevent myself from thinking a certain way than I do to benefit myself and to think a certain way.

I'm more worried about the things that are coming into my life, rather than the things that I'm walking into, because I can control where I'm headed, but I can't control what's headed to me. That's the things I'm more concerned about.

*Earlier I asked you the question about what kind of things do you think about when you're just alone with your thoughts, maybe late at night in your cell. What if I had asked you that same question ten or twelve years ago, when you were still a newcomer to prison life, when you had been here for six months or a year or less? How do you think your answer would have differed? What did you think about back then?*

Oh, [laughs], well, you know, I mean, the things you thought about back then when you first started prison would revolve around trying to figure out how to do time. What's in store for me? How am I going to do this? I mean, what am I going to do if I'm confronted in a situation I'm uncomfortable with?

I'm scared to death. I mean, literally scared. Nervous. And, where's my family? What's going to happen with them? What about my friends? How long are they going to stay beside me? How am I going to support myself? Who's going to support me?

And then you start looking at God, like, you know, questioning God, like, "Where were you? I thought that you were real," or, "If you really was real…." I mean, it's almost like naïve thoughts that you have that—it's not really naïve, but it's just, you know, premature thoughts you have, wondering before you actually step off into that pit. You have no idea what to expect. You have no idea what to look forward to. You have no idea what your approach should be.

When you first walk into prison, the things that go through your mind are like, where has my life gone? What kind of a life am I going to live? What kind of life am I going to have? What's going to happen to me? What's somebody going to do to me? What am I going to do to somebody? How am I going to deal with this? How am I going to feel when I'm approached by this? I mean, those are the thoughts that you have.

How am I going to convince someone to stay with me, stick with me, give me the support that I need? How are they going to feel towards me now? How are they going to view me?

I mean, if you had a girlfriend, now she's going to be one of your biggest thoughts. She's going to be probably your first thought. There goes that whole comfort zone. There goes that emotional thing. There goes that idea that if you really cared about her—that is what hammers you the hardest. You know, the love in your life, or the emotional feeling that you have for this particular person.

Then your kids come second, if you have any, that's what I'm told. But speaking from personal experience, then is your family, automatically. You wonder about them. Your mom. Did you disappoint her? How does she feel? Why did you do this to disappoint her?

I disappointed myself, you know, because I should have known better than this. These are the things that I thought.

But somewhere—and I really don't know at what point—somewhere along the line, I graduated in my mind. And if you was to ask me at what point did I do that, I think it's from doing that two year stint in IMU for all the violence that I got into. I think that's where I grew up, and I accepted my situation as, "OK, this is obviously real. This is something I'm going to have to deal with. I mean, I'm just going to have to put everything beside me, and act like it don't exist, in order for me to adjust and to accept this and deal with it."

And that's the only way that you can actually mature. Because otherwise, if you don't, you're going to still be going through those same pains and trouble, that same old turmoil road, and you'll be nothing but an emotional wreck.

And some of the people that you come across in this place, whether you realize it or not, that's a transition they were never able to make. That's why some are still weak, some are still vulnerable, because they're still guessing at it. They haven't made that transition to accept it, to deal with it, and say, "Fuck it! Come on with it!" and deal with it. Because, as it turn out, it turn out easier for me when I made that point, when I said, "Fuck it! I don't care," and started dealing with it, that helped me to graduate from that point.

Something was said to me a long time ago, Craig, before I even came to prison. Sometimes it takes going all the way to the bottom in order to plant your feet to go back up again. And getting trapped halfway, you're stuck. I think that's actually the truest statement I've heard in my life.

I had to finally hit rock bottom in order for me to plant my feet and to know how to take off again. I had to get a foundation. That's when I really think I made that transition in my thinking, comparing then to now.

*You mentioned that if you were to get out one day, one of your first thoughts would be to go to the people who stood by you and supported you and enabled you to survive, and to express your appreciation and to be with them. Tell me a little bit about what you had in mind there. Who has been that kind of positive force for you, and why do you say that without them you wouldn't have been able to survive and to come as far as you've come?*

Well, it actually started out with several people, but ended up with being mainly three. Started off, you know, of course, there was my mom. We had developed a relationship after I came to prison.

And then I had a friend, you know, a female friend that I was involved with before I came to prison. We stuck together for about five of my first years. Then that fell apart, even though we're still in communication once in awhile.

And then, you know, I have an uncle that I must have done like my first six, seven years before I could communicate with him again, and we write and talk to each other.

But then I got an aunt. She's not really an aunt, but she was the best friend of my mom before my mom died. I knew her as I was growing up. To this very day, my entire twelve years in prison, I mean, I can pick up the phone and call her and say, "Look, this is what's the problem." It's dealt with. Immediately.

I mean, she actually calls me her son. She has one daughter, you know, that's older than me, but then she had a son before that died at birth. But she calls me her son. And she has literally been that motherly figure to me, for my entire life. I call her my aunt, simply because her and my mom called each other sisters. But she's technically no relationship to me whatsoever, but, I mean, she is—I can't say my best friend—but she's one of my two best friends. I mean, she has been there all this time, all these years, and she has made sacrifices, you know, to help support me in times of my needs.

*What kind of sacrifices?*

Well, you know, like, for instance, when I need money for things I need to buy, she will postpone paying her bills or something in order to send me something that I may need, that to her might be trivial, like buying a TV. She will send me, like, four hundred bucks to buy me one at a time she could have paid her phone bill—the expensive phone bills that mostly I create by having to call her collect. But she refuses to not accept the calls.

I could be hurt or bothered by something, and she will take off from work to come up here to see me. Things like that is what I call sacrificing, that you wouldn't otherwise expect people to do, or you wouldn't want nobody to do, but they choose to do this, simply because they're concerned about you. To make adjustments in their life to make it better for you. Those are the things that I most appreciate.

And, I got a female friend in Port Angeles* who, you know, is basically my fiancée, and she's my heart. I mean, now, she's made some grave sacrifices.

*Give me a little history of your involvement with this woman. Like, how did you meet? How did you become a part of each other's lives? What does she mean to you now? And so on.*

Oh OK. Well, you know, I got out of IMU after doing my second term there—a year in there—and I was at Clallam Bay, and she worked there.

*What's her name?*

Maggie Brunson.† She worked at Clallam Bay. She lived locally, in Port Angeles. She first used to work in the kitchen there. And I got a job in the kitchen. It was a part of my getting out of IMU. I had to work, and I couldn't work on the outside perimeter, so I had to work on the inside, which happened to be the kitchen. So I ended up being up under her—you know, one of her workers.

So she and I used to talk a lot, and really the whole bunch of different assistant cooks got along well and we all used to talk in there. You know, it was almost a friendly atmosphere working there, not just with her, but with everybody in general.

But me and her used to sit down, and we'd talk in depth. And we used to talk about similar things about my life as to what I'm doing right now with you.

Around that time is when I lost my father, you know, and my mom was really sick. It felt like I was losing everybody I cared about most. And she was really supportive of me, you know, as far as sitting down talking to me about it, and discussing it with me. Even though she wasn't supposed to do that, because you couldn't fraternize with an inmate. But, she was concerned, and I seen that genuine concern in her. We used to really talk deep like that

---

*Port Angeles is on the Olympic Peninsula, northwest of Seattle.

†I have changed the name.

for about a year. Just really communicate with each other, every time we seen each other. It developed into a unique friendship.

Well, she quit the kitchen and decided to go work in the law library to utilize the degree that she had.

*She was how old when you met her?*

Forty-eight, I think. It was in Ninety-two.

*And you were what age?*

When I got out of IMU in Ninety-two—I was born in Sixty-nine—I was twenty-three, I think. Yeah, just can't remember that far back. [Laughs.]

*[Laughs.]*

But, you know, she transferred to the law library, and I missed her. I mean, I missed the times when we used to sit down and talk. I missed the conversations we used to have. And, after a month, I quit the kitchen and started spending time in the law library. It developed, like I said, into a unique friendship. It was strange, but we trusted each other.

We had a trust that was actually outside of what it should have been, you know, as far as, like, prison rules. But, she knew where I stood about certain issues, certain things, and I knew where she stood.

It was kind of difficult for her at the beginning, simply because you're worried about, "Hey, you know, if I trust you, if I discuss certain things with you, you could damage me, because all it would take is for you to mention it to somebody on the outside and I'm fired," so her job is in jeopardy there, but she trusted me.

And I swore to her, and I told her, "It's my logic and my belief—I mean, friendship is something I value at its highest level. I don't do nothing to hurt a friend. If I hurt someone, he wasn't never my friend. I will never do nothing to jeopardize you. I mean, they can shoot me, gun me down, before I actually put you in a position to be sacrificed, simply because I value our friendship." But at first, she didn't believe that.

Then, of course, we got caught up in several investigations where we were questioned about our conversations or communication, and I went to bat. I mean, locked up in the hole, I did time in the hole, with them saying, "Well, look, it's easy for you. If you tell us what you and her got going, we'll let you out," and all this and all that.

And I stood my ground. "Fuck you! I mean, are you crazy? I don't have nothing going with the lady. What do you want, for me to tell you that we do have something going, and then I'll be lying just to get out of the hole? Fuck you!" And they believed it. And they respected it.

So, I got out of the hole. We was friends for about six more months. Then she quit.

*Were you violating the rules by being friends and having that contact with her?*

Well, yeah, being as the kind of conversation we was having was discussing in depth about our personal life, like you and I are doing right now. Like I said, it developed into a friendship where we talked about each other's personal lives. That was—

*And that's in violation of prison rules to do that?*

That's in violation, because it's called fraternizing with an inmate. They feel it's a breach of security. We had feelings for each other, emotionally, and we expressed that. That was a violation in its most blatant form.

Well, she quit, and told me what she was going to do, that in about three months, she was going to write me a letter to let me know where she was at, and we was going to correspond.

But when she quit, I really thought that was the goodbye, the final goodbye. But three months later, I get a letter from her with a phone number.

*Is that a prison rule that there must be a minimum of three months after you quit your prison job before you can contact an inmate?*

Well, no, there are no rules about that. You can contact the same day you quit. You can't come to visit that person till six months after you quit, but, you know—

*So why did she set the three months—?*

Well, she was actually concerned about, like, her retirement check that she wanted to get. And she felt like if she would have quit over me, they would have found a way to screw her out of it. So she wanted to make it look like there was nothing going on. That way, once she get her money, after she get her retirement check, then, hey, she was free then. She was no longer connected, or had no obligations to DOC. They didn't have no guillotine they can hang up over her head, to threaten her.

*Did you find it hard in the beginning to trust her, and to let her into your life?*

Oh my God, yes!

*I mean, she's a civilian, you know, a free person. A vast age difference. She's white. She's female. I mean, she couldn't be much more different, in superficial ways, from you. Was she the kind of person you just naturally trusted, or—?*

Hell no! [Laughs.]

*[Laughs.]*

No way possible! I mean, I think she's probably the hardest person I think I've ever had to trust in a long time. I can't remember no one that actually took a longer time for me to trust. I mean, I even questioned her. You know, "Tell me the truth," I'd say, "Don't infringe on my friendship. Are you really a cop? You know, are you, like, working for these people?" And it insulted her. But she understood.

I told her, "There's no way you're going to jeopardize your job over me. You don't really know me. You just met me. You know I'm a menace to this place. The administration hates me, because they think I have a behavior problem. And yet you walk in, meet me, and all of a sudden you just trust me and sit and discuss these things? I mean, what are you trying to find out about me? Is this a set up?"

I mean, that's what I continuously did for a long time, until finally there was some things that we discussed, about her, that was so personal, that I knew at that point, you know, no way is she trying to hurt me. Because if she was out to set me up, she wouldn't give me no evidence that I can defend myself or screw her with, if she was trying to set me up.

And that's actually what did it, is having some type of evidence against her, something, just in case she stabbed me in the back. I could say, "See!" and she knew that. I think she actually gave me that intentionally so I could feel secure or whatever. [Laughs.]

But, you know, it developed into a beautiful, beautiful relationship. We're each other's backbone now. I mean, the things we've known of each other throughout the years—the devotion, the loyalty. I mean, everything in general. The knowledge, the wisdom that she has. You know, we're opposites in so many ways that what I don't have, she has to offer; what she don't have, I have. I mean, it fits.

And, it's strange. I know we look odd. It's totally opposite. People don't understand it. We look strange. But it just feels good.

*How often do you get to see her in person?*

Oh, maybe two or three times a month. I'll see her this weekend as a matter of fact.

*Oh, that's not bad.*

Most months, twice. Three times if I've been good. [Laughs.] But she drive from so far away, so it actually depends on the weather, coming from Port Angeles.

*She's still in Port Angeles?*

Yeah, she's still up there.

*How long a drive is that?*

A three hour drive.

*And do you talk to her on the phone a lot, in addition—?*

Oh yeah.

*—to seeing her in person?*

Yeah. I call her, like, once a week, sometimes twice. Sometimes I go two weeks without calling her. But, you know, when she does come up, I spend a lot of time in the visiting room with her, I mean, like, for the whole day. And I might not call her the next, following, week, and then she'll be up the next week after that.

I don't spend a lot of time on the phone. I'm not really much of a phone person, because it takes away from the time you actually spend together. I don't know, it's kind of a strange feeling to sit there, to talk on the phone. Plus, I'm considerate of the expense.

*Yeah, tell me how that works with the phone. It sounds like it's a total ripoff.*

Oh yeah, my God, yeah. I mean, it's an increased price on the phone. You know, like, our conversations—me and her can talk for fifteen minutes; it cost her twenty-eight bucks. For a collect call. Or maybe I have it backwards. Maybe it's fifteen bucks for twenty-eight minutes. Maybe I got it backwards. But it's double what it would be on the streets.[*]

AT&T have it set up to where the collect call for a certain amount of time costs so much money, and they charge it off to your family. And they make so much money off the prisons that they actually give the prisons a kickback for, like, maybe five thousand dollars a month. I think it's five thousand, or fifty-five hundred, a month.

Of course, none of the money goes to us, even though DOC says it goes to the Inmate Betterment Fund for the prisons overall. But it's a huge bucket that they put the money in every time, and that's what they use, like, for whatever reason, I don't know.

*So you can't pay it from off your own books from inside. It has to be a collect call paid for from out there.*

---

[*]I have received several calls from prison. They run about $1 per minute.

Yeah, it can only be a collect call paid for from out there, with almost double the amount of what it would be for a normal call.

*It sounds like the visits can be fairly long. Can you really spend the whole day with somebody?*

Well yeah, you know, you can go up to the visiting room on Monday, Thursday, and Friday from one o'clock to three forty-five, and then come back at five-thirty till eight-thirty. On weekends and holidays, you can go only for one of those sessions—from one o'clock to three forty-five, or from five-thirty to eight-thirty, one of the two. Tuesday and Wednesday the visiting room's closed.

But, yeah, it's pretty considerate, you know, as opposed to Clallam Bay or Walla Walla. You know, they got their set rules. I mean, you got to sit at a table that they give you, that is numbered, for the visitor. And you got to sit kitty-corner at the table from your wife. You got to stay separate. You can kiss when you walk in, and kiss when you leave, but you can't touch each other for the remainder of the visit. I mean, you can't get up and walk around. You're, like, sitting in the seat, with your feet on the floor—you got to be facing a certain way. It's really, really strict. It's really discouraging too, for a family to come up there and feel the whole tension of that place.

As opposed to here at WSR, where it's very liberal. You know, you can sit, arm-in-arm, hand-in-hand, you know, sit and talk, kiss as much as you want, show the affection that you want, spend time with your kid in the play area. You can get up, sit at any table you want, in any direction that you want, 'cause they got a camera in there. And they got some pretty decent staff that works up there that don't really go out of their way to fuck with you.

*Are you pretty much limited to your own visitor, or is it like a social environment where you can talk to each other's people and—?*

You're not supposed to. I mean, that's against the rules. No cross-visiting. That's a rule. But, here, they're pretty liberal about that, you know, because there's so many people that have been coming up for so long that they've actually developed some type of friendship. They've gotten to the point where some might drive up together. You might sit at this table, and they might sit at the table over across to you, you might say, "Hi," or "How're you doing?" or play with their kids, you know. And then they got some guys that have been here so long that their kids have literally grown up together, since being here.

And they know they can't stop that. They can't stop the kids [laughs], 'cause kids going to be kids anyway. But, they're pretty lenient about that. I'm sure if there's ever a problem that erupts by it that they'll really enforce it, but the rule is you can't.

*Can you have visits all those days? Is there a limit on how many days—?*

No. Yeah, you can have a visit on all those days.

*So, in principle, if you had friends and family who wanted to spend a lot of time in prison with you, you could be in the visiting room for several hours a day, five days a week.*

Five days a week, several hours a day. Or you could come, like, a weekday, stay all day, from one o'clock to eight-thirty, with the exception of going back for count and coming back, and anything following that. But on the weekends, you only get three hours, you know, either morning or afternoon. But, yeah, you could spend all those days in the visiting room.

*Let's jump the tracks again to another issue, another question. When you remember back to how you felt when you came here, and the fear and the uncertainty, and so on—the intimidation—does that better enable you to sympathize when you see newcomers who are scared, and maybe—?*

Yeah.

*—don't handle it as well as they should? I know in this environment, you can't allow yourself to be too sympathetic, but what do you feel when you see somebody who maybe doesn't handle it as well as you did? If you see somebody who comes in here scared, and he is taken advantage of, or he does something cowardly, or something like that, do you have any sympathy for that kind of person?*

I have sympathy for the person that feel that way and admit to it, rather than the one that feel that way and act otherwise. I mean, because I can relate and I can understand, even though I might not say anything, because it's no different than what anybody else feels.

Craig, if they came in here and told you that they don't feel that way, that's a damn lie. I mean, some are even still scared today. It's only human nature to be scared when you walk into an environment such as this place, or Walla Walla especially. Immediately you're afraid, you're worried, because you don't know what to expect from all the things you've heard. The rumors, the books.

But, yeah, when I see the newcomer walking into prison, you can see it all over their face. You can see it in their eyes. And I'm sympathetic. I'm sympathetic even to the point where, you know, they can be inquisitive about, "Man, what do I do—? How do I do—?" and I will help them.

There's quite a few old timers that really would. And if they seen somebody else that they know was either a predator or a vulture that try to take advantage of this guy, they'll stop it. I'll stop it. "Wait a minute. Come on, man. You know, go somewhere else with that."

But you know, it's kind of strange, because, and this is the truth, even though it might not be right, the blacks will do it for the blacks, the whites will do it for the whites, the Indians do it for the Indians, the Mexicans do it for the Mexicans.

Now, if there's any time that there's a crossover, where the blacks do it for a white, or the whites do it for a black, then that white guy that goes with the blacks to be educated or schooled, automatically he's ousted by the whites. And the black guy that is being schooled or being around the whites, automatically is ousted by the blacks. Automatically.

Because, the first thoughts you actually have when you come to prison—it's something I've never seen them actually talk about in the Prison Awareness classes that they do—when you first walk in, the first thing you do is you look for someone to identify with. You're looking for a familiar face. You're looking for somebody you just left the county jail with. Or you're looking for somebody you might know, that you can relax, let your guard down with. You're looking for something to soften your arrival. And that could be it. And then they can carry you around, because now you got some type of bond there, even if it's nothing or just something small.

But, yeah, I can sympathize with that, I mean, with those people that's like that. But then you got them little idiots that come up and, the first thing they feel—and I was one of them, you know—"I got to make a name for myself. I got to make it quick." But that's only an act of being scared. And I understand that too.

Except when now you're coming to try to pick me, because I may be the smallest of the crowd, but I'm going to smash your ass if you're going to try to smash me.

*Is the racial separation that you're describing as extreme at WSR as at the other institutions?*

I'll put it to you this way, and this is my honest opinion. And like I said, I've been honest with you for this entire time, and I'm going to continue to be honest. I think it's equal. Everywhere. But at WSR, it's covered up more. That's what I think. Walla Walla, it's blatant. Clallam Bay, it's blatant as well. Overall, including staff. I mean, blatant. To the extreme.

But WSR, there's the same feeling. You've got to remember, all of these people that's here come from up there.

*Right.*

They come here looking for a chance, trying to mellow out, but they still have those same feelings they've had when they were there. So, they do their best, and cover it up, or hide it, to prevent altercations. I mean, I know quite a few people, Craig, quite a few. I know them all; they all know me. If I don't know them, they know of me, or I know of them. A lot of them you know too. And some of the biggest racists are ones that you would never think. But, at other places, like Walla Walla, they get there, take their shirt off, expose all their tattoos, hang around the Aryan Brothers, and the N-word will be every other word come out of their mouth.

Now, some of these same people, they get to a more mellow joint like WSR, they start hanging around blacks, or they start associating with them, and we're cool with them. But then they get around some of the same friends that they knew at those other joints that have also come here, and all of a sudden, they'll turn back off into that same little group, and you see the attitude all over again.

That pisses me off. I mean, if you can't be the same person all the time, then I really have a problem appreciating you. Period. I mean, you'll be my first enemy.

*Once you rise up in the ranks of convicts, and you establish your name and your reputation, become one of the "Fellahs," or whatever you want to call it, is there less racial separation at that point?*

Yeah, the higher you are, your rank, yeah, because from what—

*So, you can interact with Jerry and people like that as an equal, even at other institutions that are more blatantly racist? There is more of a camaraderie, because you're all convicts?*

Well, you know, once you've made a name for yourself, once you get recognized or respected, no matter who you are—they say, "A convict don't have no color." And that's absolutely true in its truest form. I mean, they're not seen with a color. If you're a true convict, you don't see color. The only color you see is actually the Man, or the enemy—whatever race, whatever color, whatever he represents. And that is the way they think.

The higher you are ranked, or the higher you are respected, the more you can associate with every ethnic group there is.

But, now, the strange part of it, you know, the unfortunate part, is that when it comes down to some tensions, even they still have to identify with whoever they are. I mean, someone can be the most well-respected black guy in the prison, respected by all the whites, respected by all the Indians, but as soon as some tension rises, he got to go back where he belongs, simply because he knows where his back is at.

But, the higher you go in the ranks, yeah, you're respected by every group. I mean, it even comes to the point that if there's some blacks having some problems with some whites, the leader of the whites—or whoever is the most respected there—will come to you and say, "Look, man, we're having some problems between such-and-such and such-and-such. You need to deal with him, and we'll deal with ours."

That is just the prison rule that actually prevents things from getting out of hand. "Either you handle your business, or we handle it. Because if we handle it, it's going to look racial."

And that's one of the bad things about prison, because all it takes is a black and a white to get in a fight, and all of a sudden it's assumed to be a racial thing, when all the time it could actually be a personal thing.

*Just to follow up on what we were talking about a few moments ago, let's say you get a young kid, inexperienced kid, and he's scared, and he hasn't been hardened, he hasn't got the strength, if you want to call it that, that enables one to survive and live by the convict code, and he's thrown into an environment like this. And he screws up. He does something he shouldn't have done. He violates the code. You know, he rats on somebody, or he panics and doesn't handle it well, doesn't handle it the way a convict would say a man should handle it. What's your attitude toward somebody like that? Can you have any sympathy for him? Or do you have to be cold and just hate him as much as all the other convicts do, and shun him, you know, treat him as an enemy?*

No, it actually depends. You have to treat every case on an individual basis. And it's a real serious issue, because it happens a lot.

But, for one, you have to think, did he know better? Do you think he should have known better? If he was eighteen, seventeen, sixteen, and done something stupid, I will give him the benefit of the doubt, because he was scared and that was his first reaction. But if I know he done lived this kind of life before, he done been out there living a life of crime, then he know the rules. So, he knew what he was doing. That's the first consideration.

The second consideration is, what would be his loss? What would he have to gain by doing it? If he did something in exchange for that to get some leniency on himself, oh yeah, he's in trouble. But if he done something without realizing what he's doing, and actually did some damage to himself, then I say he made a mistake.

These are the points that you actually have to evaluate, because you'd want others to give you the same consideration.

# JIMI—November 1998

*"Just like all human beings, you stick me in a
cell, with a tin can and a comb, twenty-four
hours a day, or twenty-three hours a day and
then a shower, and I'm going to learn to adapt
to it. I did something comparable to that in
IMU. I did eighteen months of it. I learned to
adapt.*

*"Human beings learn to adapt to whatever their
environment is, or else they break down, in
which case they're of no use to anyone. What
society has done is as we've become used to the
punishment we're getting, they've insisted on
tougher and tougher sentences. And they still
want more. They always want more."*

With Jimi's release date fast approaching, I taped one final conversation with him on the inside.

*So, we're here to talk about—*

Going home. [Big smile.]

*—getting out of prison, which you're planning on doing soon. How long is it before you get out?*

Sixty days, today. Fifty-nine days, actually. Right around the corner.

*Summarize how a person feels sixty days before leaving this place.*

Well, on the surface, very excited. But, inside, scared. Scared of the details. I mean, you try and conceptualize the details of being free, and staying free. Afraid. Afraid of myself. You know, the opportunities are there. I've grown enough to do it. I believe I've finally gotten it right, but, you know, I believed that before. Now, I've done the work to say that. Before, I hadn't.

The other day, Rico asked me what was different this time, as opposed to last time. And without hesitation, I went through a whole laundry list of things that are different, as far as understanding who I am, and where I came from, which is the work that I did this time I was down, which I had never done before.

Certainly, there's the whole thing about what some call "post-incarceration adaptation syndrome," or whatever the acronym is that they have for it. But, I've done the work and, you know, I feel good about my chances. But it doesn't mean that I'm not afraid, like we all are, of change and the unknown.

And, something else came up today earlier. I was talking to somebody in the office here about the fact that in prison, I'm somebody. Out there I'm not going to be somebody. I'm just going to be the average Joe. I'm not going to automatically have somebody's respect. I'm going to have to earn it. I have to start all over, and carve a niche out there, like I have in here.

But, you know, that can be exciting too. It's shit or get off the pot for me. I'm thirty-six years old. I've got to do it. I owe it to my father. My mom just got out of the hospital again. I owe it to myself, you know, and to the community. They've spent a lot of money on me. [Laughs.] I should at least give them what they've paid for.

*I was listening to the tape of one of our earlier conversations this week, where we were talking about how, in the past, you've been prone to kind of a snowball effect. If you stray in some small way, then it tends to get out of control, and you experience kind of an exhilarating rush as you lose all constraints and all self-discipline. You know, a small indiscretion becomes a lifestyle of crime and breaking rules. Do you feel confident that you can prevent that snowball effect, that you'll be able to make small errors or small indiscretions or have small losses of discipline without then having it take over your life?*

Yeah. I do. I think that actually—I mean, of course it has a lot to do with me—but I think it has just as much to do with the network of people around me.

You know, whenever that happens, I take off alone. My crimes have always been alone. Being out on the run has always been a very lonely experience for me. It's going to be very important for me to have a network of people similar to what you might have in AA, or whatever. A sponsor to call. People that you can be honest with, without being judged, without them panicking and thinking you're losing it.

I have a relationship with my dad that's developed to that point, where I can be honest with him. I've got a couple of friends out on the street that are doing well, and they understand. You know, there's certainly you and some of the PAP people. There's just a large group of people that I feel would be my network. And my network will grow the longer I'm out there.

So, it's going to have a lot to do with the people I choose to be around, the fact that I'm not hiding it this time, that one of my affirmations is "no secrets." That's one of the nice things about my job. In the past, as I've told you before, I've always kept my prison record or my criminal history secret from my job. Well, at the job I have lined up, these people know. They know I'm from here. They're going to know all about me by the time I've been working there awhile. I have no intentions of keeping this secret.

Now another door just opened up to me, which I think is also something that's going to be very important in keeping me close to where I came from. The other day, I was in a reunion for the "Restorative Justice" program, which is a group of victims, citizens, and offenders who get together for ten week seminars. Well, one of the ladies representing the community came up to me—she's a teacher and a chemical dependency counselor—and asked me if I'd be interested in speaking to her kids.

Oh, hell yeah, I would! You know, absolutely, I'd love to! The more I ponder that whole idea, God, I'd love that opportunity! I can't think of a better way to hone my message, to stay close to where I've been, not to forget where I've been, develop more contacts, you know, make it a platform almost for what I believe works and doesn't work in prison.

*You mentioned that in here you're kind of a big shot and you've got respect, and out there you'll have to start from scratch. It seems to me like it's going to be a very different kind of respect that you're going to need to strive for. It'll be different from if you were, say, plucked from here and dropped into prison in Georgia or New York or something, where you're a stranger and you have to start from scratch in that sense, but you're still playing by those same rules, you're still trying to get prison-type respect. Because that you could probably pull off quite easily, just by being the person you are—*

That's a—

*—and having the—*

—very good point.

*—habits and values you have and all that. But, yeah, it seems like on the outside, you won't just be with new people and all, but it's a very different kind of respect that—*

Yeah.

*—you're striving for.*

That's a very good point.

*Can you talk about that a little bit?*

Well, that's a real good point. The respect we get in here is based on our ability to hustle, our ability to manipulate, our heart, what we're willing to do to protect our respect, or to gain our respect. So that's where its genesis is.

But out there, it has more to do with—and whether this is right or wrong, this is just how I see it out there—it has more to do with your ability to make a living, to be consistent and stable in where you live, and paying your bills, and being responsible. And, you know, you can even go further and say that it's based, in some sense, on what you contribute, though you can define that in any number of ways, I suppose.

But, yeah, it's a very different type of respect. But, I'm hoping that it all begins with work. I'm lucky in that I have a good opportunity, work-wise. So, it's not going to be as difficult on me as it might be for somebody that hasn't got the job opportunity and the money that I have.

We're talking a year from now, I'll be making journeyman's pay, which is twenty-three bucks an hour. I'm fortunate that money will probably make it much easier for me to develop stability, and build a network of friends and acquaintances. Whereas, people might not even consider wanting to be around me, based on social standing or economic standing, if I was working at Burger King.

So whether it's right or wrong, that's the system that they have out there.

But heck, I don't know what the system is out there. It's been eight years since I've been out there, as far as that goes, you know.

*I think you're correct that one of the main factors in winning approval and respect out there is the amount of one's income, and one's material possessions, unfortunately. Certainly I hope you don't go overboard striving for that type of respect. I think that would be just as misguided as seeking what's called respect in prison, which to me seems kind of a misnomer. You know, people talk about respect in prison, but when it's explicated, it sounds more like, to respect somebody means to acknowledge that they're willing to use violence to achieve their ends, that they're willing to use violence in their own self-interest to defend themselves and to achieve their goals.*

Almost an oxymoron, isn't it? [Laughs.]

*It always kind of bugs me when people talk about, you know, "I'm respected," or "I respect so-and-so," and I have to interpret it in my mind: OK, all he's saying, really, is that—*

Sure.

*—he's a bully, and he respects that this other person's a bully too. That's all.*

Right.

*I mean, I'm exaggerating. There are other elements to it too, some of which are a lot more admirable than a mere willingness to use violence.*

Well, I mean, that in itself is certainly one factor that we would look at in understanding why prison doesn't work. It's a sick place.

*Yeah, you're given positive reinforcement for the very types of behavior that you're supposedly being punished for.*

Reinforcement from our peers. Right.
I don't think people out there understand that this is a subculture in here. This is a community in here. You know, you just don't see the relationships, prison relationships, on TV.

*I've been thinking about that. I'm not sure exactly how people perceive this, or how I should articulate this point, but I think people from the outside focus almost exclusively on the relationship between the state and the prisoners, or between the staff and the prisoners, and they talk a lot about that. You know, what do we need to do to be harder, or softer on prisoners, or to change the incentives for their future behavior? Will we achieve more deterrence by doing this or by doing that? You know, do prisons treat prisoners too well, or too harshly? I think, like you're saying, that they totally lose sight of the peer pressure, or the influence that prisoners have on each other, in their own little culture in here. And it seems to me, from talking to you guys and spending time in here, that that's a much bigger factor than anything the state does.*

That's a good observation. I think that relevant factors in our behavior, relevant factors in our development during the course of our incarceration, would lie almost twice as much on inmate-to-inmate relationships. Inmate-to-officer relationships are almost minute as far as importance. All they do is open our doors, close our doors, and write us up when we do something wrong. We let them have very little influence on what we do day to day. We are actually very independent.

I think that a lot of times, new officers could probably learn more about how this prison runs by watching us go about our daily routine, and seeing how things normally go, and going along with it, than they ever could from their schooling and their orientation. They'd have a much easier transition. Because, that's where it eventually gets to anyway. I've seen the toughest, shittiest, shit-eaters* come in here to work, drawing the strictest lines, and then those lines get curvy. They change. I mean, they have to. Otherwise, their lives are miserable in here.

But, the loss of liberty is the punishment. Whether it's to separate us from society, or whether it's to punish us, or whether it's to rehabilitate us, whatever the reason, that all comes from the loss of liberty. Everything beyond that—whipping us, beating us, starving us, whatever they add to the loss of liberty—is above and beyond the purpose of incarceration.

And where that comes from, in my opinion, is society. Just like all human beings, you stick me in a cell, with a tin can and a comb, twenty-four hours a day, or twenty-three hours a day and then a shower, and I'm going to learn to adapt to it. I did something comparable to that in IMU. I did eighteen months of it. I learned to adapt.

Human beings learn to adapt to whatever their environment is, or else they break down, in which case they're of no use to anyone. What society has done is as we've become used to the punishment we're getting, they've insisted on tougher and tougher sentences. And they still want more. They always want more.

Well, maybe the fact is that what the system does to the offenders has less to do with the victims getting through their grieving than them working on it themselves. They've got their own process they've got to work with. Sure, it may feel good to the survivor of a victim to see the perpetrator executed, or given life without parole. That may feel good. But that doesn't help them get through the process any better.

It gives them "closure," people say. What the fuck is "closure"? You know what I'm saying? What in the hell is "closure"? You've got to do your own closure. You've got to go through the whole grieving process. You don't get to skip any. You've got to do it all. And once it's over with, then you reach a point where you can accept it, and move on, after what's happened.

There are people in victims' advocate groups—I saw this in the Restorative Justice program—that are twenty-five years since their crime, and they're still angry. And then there are people like this one lady who lost her daughter three years ago, and even though it hurt, she was moving on relatively well. She wasn't, you know, blaming the system.

---

*Prison slang for a correctional officer.

So, what is different between her and this woman who's an advocate of twenty-five years and still angry? There is something that she gets that the angry woman doesn't.

But, back to my point, society's obviously going to keep wanting more, and keep wanting more, and keep wanting more.

*Yeah, and like I was saying, there's a limit to how much the state and its prison staff can really do anyway, because people underestimate how much you all influence each other.*

Yeah.

*People on the outside are concerned about do you have a TV or not? Or do you get one hour versus three hours in the yard? Or do you have a ten year versus an eight year versus a five year sentence? And all of those are things that the state controls. But, it seems to me a far bigger influence is the culture you all have created amongst yourselves collectively that, say, respects this kind of person and not that kind of person, or commits violence against this kind of person and not that kind.*

Right.

*It's a whole system of values and a whole lifestyle that you learn pretty quick you better conform to if you want to survive. Granted, there are parts of it that I think are admirable, that do probably help people to grow, and are good influences on people, but there are also parts of it that are very objectionable. It's no wonder that people get even more screwed up by being in prison, and come out even more rotten and violent and apt to victimize people.*

Right. That would speak more than anything to the process of classifying inmates, from where they go to what kind of time they do to what kind of programming they get.

The way it is now, they classify you by points. There's a basic grid that they go by for points. If you have this many points then you go here, and if you have this many points then you go there. It doesn't have anything to do with you as an individual or your program needs; it has to do with your criminal record and what custody level that fits on the grid.

*Yeah, this is an environment where violence is glorified, and you're required to scapegoat rats and rapists and victimize them at every opportunity, and where the law of the streets rules. There's no reason to throw people into a world like that unless they're already trapped in that lifestyle and it's all they know.*

Right. Recalcitrant. They don't want to change.

*But somebody who's, say, a first-time offender, who doesn't know that lifestyle, doesn't know those rules, there's no reason to throw him in this environment, because then you really do take a person who so far, for all we know has made one significant mistake in his life, and you're going to turn him into a probable career criminal by putting him in a world—*

Right.

*—where those are the values, and he better adapt to those values if he wants to survive. You've created a criminal from somebody who only might have been a criminal if you hadn't put him there.*

Right. Unfortunately, the system has gotten so big, with so many people, that I don't understand how they could possibly get to a place now where they can accurately identify the problems of each individual inmate, and treat them as individuals.

In fact, they lose that even in the court system. It's gotten so big to where you're no longer sentenced on an individual basis. You're sentenced by a grid, based on your crime and based on your criminal history, and that's all there is to it. There's no departing from the grid.

*When you were talking about the kind of respect you get in here, compared to what you would need to do on the outside, where respect is more based on how much money you make and so on, that brought another point to my mind. One thing that has struck me about prison is it's one of those artificial environments where conformity is absolutely essential. If you're not going to play by the rules—that is, the rules that are largely created by the prisoners themselves and only to a lesser extent the state's rules—there are major consequences. It can be a life and death thing if you're trying to be different, if you want to stand on principle and you happen to disagree with some of the conventional convict values and such.*

*In a free society, such as we partly have on the outside, hopefully that kind of conformity is less essential, and the cost of not being a conformist is not quite as great. So I think, when I listen to you, I'm hearing you say that you'll need to, in effect, learn to conform to a different set of rules and requirements and such. But I would say that, if you open yourself up to it, one of the things you might find to be a pleasant surprise on the outside is that you don't need to conform to any set of rules or expectations to the degree that you do in here. I mean, out there, you can disappoint people. You can be something they don't want you to be, or they don't respect, and you're not going to get a knife in your back because of it.*

Right. Right.

*So, I think you're right that a lot of the values out there are based on things like money, but thankfully you don't have to play that game completely, and I've spent most of my life trying not to play it.*

Yeah, I don't have to have people's respect. You're right. That's another good observation. I don't have to have everybody's respect.

*Whereas in here you sort of do.*

Sure. Or it's your ass.

*Right.*

I mean, potentially it's your ass. OK, that's played up a little sometimes. It may not be. And, you know, it certainly wouldn't be for me any more. I've moved past that.

*Well, it would be, though. If you—*

But, well—

*—broke the rules in a big way, like if you became a rat or something, if you—*

Oh yeah, that, sure—

*—went beyond the bounds—*

—certainly, certainly.

*—of what's accepted in that sense, you'd give up your accumulated political capital pretty quick. [Laughs.]*

[Laughs.] Yes. I would. I absolutely would.

But, right, out there, it's not my ass. Out there, I don't have to have everybody's respect.

A good example is with Jeannie. I told her my first big ticket item that I'm buying is a Harley, and she thought I was nuts. Well, just because she doesn't see why I'd want one, or she doesn't approve, so what?

This from someone who just spent four thousand dollars on a god damn couch that she doesn't like, by the way. [Laughs.]

*[Laughs.]*

You know what I'm saying? A leather fucking couch, and she doesn't like it. "So, you're not going to talk to me. I've been locked up sixteen years. I want a Harley!" [Laughs.]

*[Laughs.]*

Now, you know, that's not to say I'm departing from our goals together or whatever, but, there are things that I want that aren't what she'd want. And that's why she's a part of my network, because she's not freaking out about that. You know, she understands, and she's cool.

My dad understands that, too. Even though he doesn't want a Harley, or he wouldn't ride a Harley, he understands why it would be important to me.

*Yeah.*

But for people who don't, fuck them! You know, don't have one then. [Laughs.]
So you're right. That's true. I don't have to have everybody's acceptance and respect.

*Yeah, to some extent you always have to play the game and conform, but there are some environments, and I think prison is one of them, where that's intensified greatly, where conformity is even more essential than in other situations. That's one of the things that's good about living in a free society. There's a little bit of room for non-conformists. We might not prosper, but at least we don't all die young. [Laughs.]*

I think maybe one of my biggest concerns is going to be my work environment. You know, a welding shop, metal fab shop, it tends to be these macho guys that are cussing all day, and drinking beer when the clock goes off. And that's not me either. You know, they're going to be asking me to go to a bar after work—"Well, I don't drink. Go to the bar by yourself. I'm not going to sit at a bar." [Laughs.]

*[Laughs.]*

What do I want to go into a bar and watch those people get drunk for?

*How do you think they'll perceive you, as an ex-con?*

Fortunately, I think that I speak well enough to win them over. That's why I said I felt that I could be a pretty good ambassador, because I've had enough opportunities to speak about what's important to me, and to speak about prison in general. With PAP, Toastmasters, I've had a lot of opportunities to speak about prison. You know, I'm certainly not going to tell them I shouldn't have been locked up. I'm pretty modest, I think, about my experiences. All in all, you know, I think I got a lot out of this experience. I'll try to tell them about that.

*We've talked about the financial end. We've talked about employment. And we've talked about some of the negatives to avoid, that you don't want to fall back into crime, or drugs or alcohol, and so on. What else do you want to do out there? What are your goals? What direction do you want your life to take besides avoiding the bad stuff, and besides having a stable, good-paying job?*

Speaking. That's why I spoke about the opportunity that lady offered. That's why I took Toastmasters, to learn how to speak in front of people, in case the opportunity arose.

My long term goal is, I want to work for about ten or fifteen more years welding, and then I want to buy a shop, a salon. That's been my goal for years. It's just gotten sidetracked 'cause they took my license for a couple years.

I want to buy a home. I want to do some traveling.

*You've mentioned that you might want to have children. Do you think about having children?*

Yeah. I don't know where that lies though. I don't know. I'm thirty-six. I know everybody says, "Oh, it's not too late." Well, realistically speaking, I'll be thirty-eight before I really start considering it. You know, I'm not going to be in a position to start raising kids at least for another year after I get out. At least. I mean, bare minimum. I'm thinking, you know, two years is probably even better. So, it depends on what the dynamics of my life are in two years.

But I'd like to have a kid. I really would. There's something inside me that is going to feel unsatisfied if I'm not able to raise some children.

And that's a big issue between my girlfriend and I.

*Because at her age, she isn't wanting to have any more kids?*

Right. She doesn't even want to consider adoption. I mean, it just isn't going to happen.

*Do you have any goals or any intentions as far as further education? Is there anything you'd like to study, or learn more about?*

Well, I love to study. But I don't have any specific goals, no. One thing I don't want to do—and I learned this from my girlfriend's experience—is I don't want to go in debt to go to college. Fortunately, I think I'll be making enough money to where I may not need to.

I don't know whether I really want to go back to school or not. I like school, now that I'm older. I always feel a lot of energy when I'm taking classes, and I love the experience of learning, and I get a lot out of school. Like, I'm studying math now. I'm studying formulas with metal shop. I'm basically still in school now in a sense. I've always had some kind of schooling going on at any given time. That may be something that I have to do, just to continue to grow.

*What would you like to learn more about? If you could take any kind of class, if you could pick anything from a college catalogue, what would you like to know more about?*

Math and history. Yeah, I'd like math and world history. Definitely. I'd like to know my history better. I really would. I think I'm probably average—well, maybe even below average—as far as knowing history. The history of this country and the history of the world has eluded me. You know, I ran from school, and I ran from learning, when I was a kid.

And the same with math. I'm learning math now, and I'm comprehending it. It's far out, man. It is cool. I'm picking up all these formulas, and I'm remembering them. It's really nice. I'd like to become a numbers kind of guy, which I never have been before.

So, math and history. Definitely.

*Anything else you have your mind set on doing on the outside, that you've been dreaming about doing when you finally get out?*

Oh yeah.

A ferry ride. Taking a ferry to Bremerton.[*]

In August, I'm flying back east to see my mom, and to see my niece's graduation. We're going to probably do that on a surprise thing. We don't want them to know I'm coming.

*Are they in Ohio, or where are they?*

Yeah, Ohio. Yeah. My niece just signed the papers for Ohio State last week. She's going to be a Buckeye.

*Oh.*

Yeah. Pretty proud of her. [Big grin.]

*[Laughs.]*

She's going to be the first doctor in the family. She's wanted to be a doctor for about five years now, and she's just now graduating from high school. She's been really focused. It's unbelievable. I think she's a savant. [Laughs.] Straight A's. Never had a B.

*Wow.*

Driving. Looking forward to driving.

*When's the last time you drove a car?*

Eight years. And I was driving fast. [Laughs.]

---

[*]A ferry system in western Washington connects Seattle and the mainland to numerous Puget Sound Islands.

*[Laughs.]*

I was driving real fast. Forty-five minute high speed chase. Yeah. That was the last time I drove.

*Is driving one of those things that you never lose, you never forget?*

I think so.

*Do you think you could get behind the wheel of a car today and drive?*

I think so. I was going through the driver's manual, so that I could get freshened up for the written test. And none of it seems much different. I mean, given that it's multiple choice, I don't think I'll have a problem passing it at all.

But the driving part, that's a hard call. You know, eight years is a long time.

But I think it's like riding a bike. Just got to get used to the pedals again. [Laughs.]

*[Laughs.]*

I don't know what else I want to do.

I want to go camping, but I'm going to have to probably wait until spring at least.

*Wait until it warms up a bit?*

Yeah. I really want to go camping though. Can't wait to be out in the woods, fire crackling, next to a creek or a river or something. Yeah. Yeah, I've thought of that. Maybe doing a hike. Nothing major, you know, just a day hike, maybe in and out. Or a day in, a day out.

I wouldn't mind going up and down the coast. When I get my Harley, I want to do 101, Highway 101, down to about northern California. That's far enough. I don't need to get any further than that.

That'd be nice. I'd like to do that.

# JIMI—February 1999

*"What we think from inside will be the case is far from the case. We can learn a great deal of information and tools inside, like being responsible, working hard, being dependable, etc., but out here, where the world is in my hands, it's not easy to avoid falling back into the habit of being the armed robber that I am, or was."*

The author and Jimi, outside the WSR front gate in the early morning, seconds after Jimi is released from prison in January 1999.

O n January 11, 1999, Jimi was freed from prison.

A few other members were released during my tenure at PAP, but none that I was very close to. Jimi was different. Jimi was special. He was my friend. I had to be a part of his freedom. I had to see him walk out of that prison.

We were given only an approximate time that he would be released, so I showed up first thing in the morning to be sure not to miss the big moment. The only other person waiting there in the lobby of the administration building to welcome Jimi back into the free world was his father, who still lived in the state of Washington, though a considerable distance away. (Jimi's girlfriend Jeannie was working.) The plan was for the three of us to meet up with some other PAP volunteers at a nearby restaurant for a celebratory breakfast.

I'd met Jimi's father on one occasion before this, and had taken an immediate liking to him. He is a small man, hard of hearing, with a gentle way about him. One senses in him the basic decency and dignity of a long, honest, hard working life. I enjoyed the unapologetically political, pro-worker edge that he displayed even in casual conversation.

He treated me, and later the other PAP outside members, with respect. From talking to Jimi, he knew that the people who volunteered their time to come into the prison wanted only to offer friendship and support to his son.

I asked him how optimistic he was about Jimi's future. His response was little different from how I would have answered the question. He was cautiously optimistic, but did not regard it a sure thing that Jimi would never backslide. Jimi has made the most sincere, sustained effort he ever had to change his ways, he told me, and he is certainly saying all the right things. Now it's just a matter of following through.

A half hour later, we watched Jimi enter the building from the prison side, accompanied by a correctional officer. He walked briskly to us and embraced his father, and then me. His grin was even wider and more expressive than usual. We exchanged a few words, then he went back to take care of some paperwork and to claim his personal property. Moments later, he walked out the door and re-entered the free world for the first time in close to a decade. Was he finally leaving prison forever?

All through breakfast, Jimi's usual exuberance was tempered by a palpable awkwardness. His movements and conversation were slow and deliberate, like a man emerging from a long period underground, feeling his way around cautiously until his eyes adjust to the light.

At one point I watched him grinning to himself, his happily dazed eyes wandering about the restaurant. I wondered what must be going through his mind. I caught his eye, and in response to my unspoken question, he said in a tone of hushed excitement, "There are so many people! I mean, *regular* people!"

Our intent was to get together for frequent interviews to chronicle his adjustment period in considerable detail. At one time I even pictured this as a possible concluding section of the book—one prisoner's life on the outside.

But that plan broke down from the beginning. He stated on numerous occasions that he too was eager to record this part of his life for the book, but it proved impossible to pin him down.

Not unexpectedly, life on the outside was a mixed bag from the start for Jimi. Some things went as well or better than he had anticipated, but he also had his share of unpleasant surprises.

He immediately moved in with Jeannie in some pretty fancy digs south of Seattle. Judging from what he told me and what I observed at a dinner I had with them shortly after his release, in the beginning things were going well. Jimi was settling into a domestic, middle class life. When he told me about his having accompanied Jeannie to some kind of home show in downtown Seattle, he presented it not as some drudgery he had let her drag him along to, but as something he took a genuine interest in.

Though he had arranged a lucrative welding job in Everett through the supervisor of his prison job, he had a noticeable anxiety until it was official. One of the biggest things he had going for him was that he could walk right into a good job and make excellent money. Losing that and having to scramble for an income was something he strongly wanted to avoid.

To his relief, he was accepted into the union and started work almost immediately. From the beginning he was working all the overtime available, keeping busy and making as much money as he could.

The worst thing about the job was its location. Everett is well north of Seattle. With no traffic, it is a good hour from the home he shared with Jeannie. During rush hour it can be double that. Plus, in the beginning he didn't even have a car, so he would have had to rely on Jeannie and others to drive him to and from work.

So he chose to rent a small, ratty, minimally furnished apartment within walking distance of his job. Jeannie would drive him there at the beginning of the work week, he would work four shifts of ten hours plus overtime in four days, and then she or someone else (I did it myself twice) would drive him back at the end of the work week to spend the next three days at home.

It was not an ideal arrangement by a long shot, but it certainly beat the hell out of prison, and it was something he was more than willing to put up with unless and until he found an equally good job closer to home.

Jimi had spoken of finding an AA group on the outside. Interestingly, the state had something of the same idea. He had been under the impression that he would be free of any form of custody or supervision this time, but because he had not completed his parole last time before re-offending, the state re-instituted a form of supervision. A part of this was mandatory AA attendance.

He resented this. In his mind, there was a big difference between using AA voluntarily when and if he felt he needed it, and being forced to go by the paternalistic state. He was willing to do it, but only to get his ticket punched. With all the hours he was putting in at work, and with the long weekly commutes back and forth between his residences, he had precious little time for himself and for Jeannie. He didn't appreciate having to relinquish blocs of this time to mandatory AA meetings.

To make matters worse, the state also refused to allow him to take the test to reclaim his driver's license until he completed a program of regular meetings with a drug and alcohol counselor and AA. So that significantly extended the time he'd have to rely on others for transportation.

Jimi had told me prior to his release that he intended to stay away from drugs completely and permanently. He was resolved to avoid alcohol until his life had stabilized, but would not swear off permanently. He believed he might eventually be able to drink socially and safely.

That's one resolve that didn't last very long. One week after our group breakfast, I picked Jimi up out by his work place so we could go to dinner. He was staying in a motel; he had not yet gotten his little apartment out that way. He let me in to his room, and then excused himself to finish getting dressed so we could go out. There was a beer bottle in plain sight on the counter.

When he came back, he noticed the beer and realized I must have seen it. Whether it had been an oversight to leave it out, I do not know. In any case, he casually (perhaps too casually) acknowledged it before I could say anything. He picked up the bottle and motioned with it to me. "I wouldn't have believed it," he said, "I can't even finish a beer any more. Can't drink one." He took a sip, then took another one, with a look on his face like he was forcing it. "Ah, I'm not going to finish it," he said as he proceeded to pour the remaining half of the bottle down the drain.

"I'm kind of surprised to see you drinking already," I commented.

"Oh, that's because of my dad," he said. "Our first dinner after I got out, he wanted me to have a beer with him. I told him I had decided not to drink for awhile, but he said it should be OK just to have one beer with him. So I did.

"I think I've lost my taste for it, though. I mean, maybe that's a good thing, but drinking just doesn't do anything for me now."

I had a lot less contact with Jimi than I had anticipated. More than once he flaked out when we had plans to get together. Only a small percentage of my calls to him were returned, and only rarely did he initiate contact with me.

He was different on the outside, and our interaction was different. Definitely.

But how he didn't change is as worthy of note as how he did. People had warned me when they found out I had befriended a prisoner that our friendship on the inside might have been a sham on Jimi's part. Not so. Jimi's release did not mean he could now show his "true colors" and go back to being a dangerous, violent character. In no way did he victimize me, display belligerence, exploit me for money, try to entice me into criminal activity, or engage in whatever other nefarious behavior might fit the stereotype of the ex-con.

No, in many ways he remained the same old Jimi. He was always happy to see me. He was friendly and respectful toward me. We still laughed together. In most respects he still displayed the same childlike eagerness toward life that had drawn me to him from the beginning.

But whereas things had always flowed so effortlessly between us in prison, now—on the rare occasions when I got to see him at all—our styles no longer seemed to mesh so well. Instead of conversation occurring freely and naturally between us, our time together was filled with awkward silence and small talk.

In prison, we had spoken often of deepening our friendship on the outside. The things we could share in prison were so artificially limited that we were both excited by the prospect of becoming a bigger part of each other's lives. It wasn't happening. We were like high school acquaintances at a reunion who have used up all their stories of the old days and can't think of anything else to do with each other.

During this time, Jimi was more excitable and impulsive than he had been in prison. Even when he was physically fatigued from work, there was a subtle edginess to him, something unsettled. He seemed simultaneously to crave the constant opportunities for stimulation and gratification that life on the outside provided him, and to be burdened by it all.

Jimi had always loved to analyze himself. He wanted to examine every issue, think through every challenge. It's what made me think he'd be a perfect interview subject to follow on the outside. Of all the prisoners, he seemed the one most likely to want to chronicle all that happened with him, to dig deeply into himself, to articulate what he felt was going right and what he felt was going wrong, and what he had to do to succeed in the free world.

But with fleeting exceptions, once he was out, he shied away from looking too closely at his life and challenging himself. It was as if there was too much going on, and he couldn't expend the time and effort to continue the hard work of self-examination and self-improvement. Let things settle down for me first, his manner seemed to say, let me get my legs back under me, and then I'll resume working on my issues, my relationships, and all the rest. For now, it's all happening too fast. I have to shut down certain parts of me and just hang on for the time being.

For the Jimi I knew, resuming drinking, even on a small scale, would have been an occasion for considerable reflection. Instead, he downplayed it and quickly moved on. Similarly, where he had eagerly thrown himself into every available program in prison, he now saw AA as an unwelcome infringement on his time.

On one occasion he told me he intended to challenge the victims' compensation part of his judgment, to get it reduced if he couldn't get it eliminated entirely.

I reminded him how eloquently he had spoken to me in prison of his newfound appreciation for the suffering of his victims. He defended himself in a perfunctory manner, and then just shrugged the whole matter off with a laugh and changed the subject. You may well be right, he seemed to say, but I can't challenge myself in too many areas at once. For now, in a lot of ways I just have to do what's in my self-interest, to follow the path of least resistance, and not feel guilty about it.

And then there were the admitted brushes with temptation. According to Jimi, he and his friend Nick—who had been out for some time and was doing a good job avoiding resuming his former bad habits—had dropped in on a mutual friend, another ex-con. By the looks of it, their host did not share their resolve to stick to the straight and narrow. Though he didn't do any drugs in their presence or offer any to them, he was, according to Jimi, obviously stoned. Further, it wasn't hard to figure out he was back to pursuing a criminal lifestyle.

"It scared us," Jimi told me, "It really did. We looked at each other, and we just knew we wanted to get out of there. I'm not saying I'm going to start committing crimes because I'm around this guy, but it just felt really unhealthy to be there. We left as soon as we could. We both felt relieved just to get out of there."

Around this same time, Jimi admitted to having unexpected fantasies of going on a crime spree. He had been a little down, he said, "And the thought came to me to just get a gun and go back to doing robberies. You know, it's not something I have any intention of doing, but there I was daydreaming about it. I was really thinking through how I could get a gun, how I'd do the robberies and all that. Then I just said to myself, 'What the fuck, man?' I thought I was past all that. Why would I even think something like that? I was really disappointed in myself that my mind would still even go there."

In late February, for the first and only time after his release, I was able to do an interview of sorts with Jimi. I asked him if he would compose something that could serve a threefold purpose: update the PAP members about his life on the outside so far, contribute to the current Prison Awareness class, and provide material for this book. He agreed.

He wrote up a statement that I could read to the class. We then exchanged some questions and answers via E-mail for me to append to his statement.

Jimi told me he was very conscious to avoid gloating about being on the outside when so many of his friends were still stuck in prison. He wanted to share his happiness with them, but not in a way that was disrespectful of them and their predicament. He especially didn't want to make things worse for those who had sentences of life without parole. (The prospect of being in prison with no hope of ever getting out still scared the hell out of him.)

He also told me that while he wanted to be honest and include his thoughts of getting a gun and going on a robbery spree, when the time came he found himself downplaying it so as not to alarm anyone that he was on the verge of returning to a life of crime.

Dear PAP Members and Students,

I am writing this letter to share with you my most recent experience of being released from prison after 8 years down, and the experience of re-entering society in my shoes. It is not my intention at all to rub this in to my brothers who are still inside, especially those who are never getting out. You know who you are and I apologize to all of you who might be offended by this letter. You are all very much a part of my day to day out here and I walk with you out here as I hope you all do me in there.

I suppose the best place to start would be THE SHOCK! Not the shock of being able to walk out the front door of the joint. Not the shock of ordering breakfast with friends and having it served. Not the shock of how much the area surrounding the joint has changed, grown since I went in. No, I'm talking about the shock of realizing that as strong and as secure as I felt about my chances out here of succeeding I really had no idea that when I got out I'd be the same ol' Jimi with the same ol' temptations and fears.

A lot of time has passed inside those walls and I've done a great deal of work on myself in there. Genuine growth. And perhaps that's why I haven't picked up my old partners Smith and Wesson as a reaction to some of the problems I've faced. But I haven't and I'm actually thriving quite well.

I was very fortunate to have the opportunity to learn a second trade in my last few years of incarceration. As a result I'm making real good money and able to afford the hoops they're putting me through.

For those of you taking the drug treatment up there in hopes that it will satisfy the DMV for your driving privilege think again. The treatment up there isn't STATE CERTIFIED and the DMV won't accept it. That in and of itself is costing me a fortune.

I had to go have an assessment done and even though I hadn't had a drink in almost nine years they said I needed treatment. So now I have to go see a guy once a week and pay him $50 each time. The problem is that I live in Burien and work in Everett so I've had to get a second place to live during the week until I can drive again.

I've found myself starving to see partners I've known in the joint. I have several friends out here whom I knew in the joint and fortunately they're doing very well so we see each other as often as possible.

Things have changed out here in many ways. It seems like everyone has a cell phone, including myself. Nobody answers their voice mail which everyone also has. I can't seem to figure out where all my money keeps going but at $500+ a week you'd think I could save some—haven't saved a dime. I suppose that's to be expected though.

I often feel like a complete idiot because I can't get my way around the Internet, I can't seem to do anything right for the first time. I'm often asking for help. And I'm talking about stupid stuff like writing a check. I'm always forgetting to put the date or the amount on it. I finally got the ATM down. Hell I just had to ask for help while I was writing this. It sometimes feels like I'm a little kid learning to do everything all over again.

But aside from that I feel very comfortable out here after just one month of freedom, and I'm getting more and more sure footed each day. It's wonderful to be free. Seattle has grown into a huge beautiful city. My ol' lady drives like Mario Andretti (FAST) and that's fun. Lots of beautiful new vehicles out here and they're easier than ever to buy. The malls are packed. Food is great out here as all of you can probably imagine. I think I've finally kicked the ramen jones for good.[*]

I think I'll do something different this time around. I think I'll actually try and stay as close to where I came from as I can just as a reminder. I think my total of 16 years in the joint has been at times positive as well as very negative, but regardless of what it's been it's who I am and as long as I stay who I was in there I'll keep myself in check out here. Strangely enough it's in there where I've found the most honor and respect and I'll carry that honor and respect with me every day out here.

I hope all of my brothers in there are well and safe. Again, you're all in my thoughts every day and I carry you with me always.

Much Love and Respect,

Jimi

*What are some of the most important factors that will determine whether or not a person will re-offend after their release from prison?*

The main factors that will determine whether I re-offend would have to fall in the category of addiction. This is based on what I'm seeing out here with some of those I was locked up with.

I have to continue to work and pay my bills as well.

---

[*]In prison, one of the most common store items bought by prisoners who want to cook for themselves and avoid the chow hall food is ramen noodles. They're cheap, and you can cook them on a hot plate in your cell.

I also find it imperative that I have others who will hold me accountable to talk to about what's in my head at any given time. I am still the same person I was when I fell the first time over sixteen years ago. I still have a desire to run from my problems, and rob for my money. But it's unbelievable how insane that sounds when I share that with someone. Saying it makes it seem much more ridiculous and unacceptable.

*Are there any values, attitudes, habits, etc. that are beneficial and perhaps even justified to have in prison, but that must be re-thought and perhaps relinquished if one is to make it on the outside?*

I have to ignore people out here who talk about calling the cops or telling the boss. The free world is full of rats, I'm remembering, and I have to ignore it. I also have to be patient with some of those people who lightly toss around terms like "punk" like they're kidding around. I'm in a new world out here and I am the one who has to change.

*How have you, not your circumstances, changed the most since your release? If a person observed you closely for a typical month in prison, and then for a month since your release, what differences do you think they'd see?*

I'm not quite as much a creature of habit out here as I was inside. An interesting thing about that is that time seems to go by slower when I'm being more spontaneous like this, which works out well for me now that I'm free.

I'm not able to work out like I'd like to, but that may have more to do with my age. I'd cut way down on working out while I was inside these past several years.

*What do you miss most about being in prison? What, if anything, tempts you to return?*

I miss my partners the most. I really miss the relationships with guys I can trust with my life, literally. I suppose that's why I've gravitated to a couple of my partners out here that I did time with. They know what it feels like to lose your freedom and what it feels like to then be free again, and I trust them.

*Given that you were not able to join us for this class, what final message may I pass on from you to our students (not necessarily just about re-entry, but for the course as a whole)? What is the single most important thing you'd like to impress upon them?*

I would pass on to the class what a struggle it is getting out after being confined for so long. It is an eye opener, to say the least. What we think from inside will be the case is far from the case. We can learn a great deal of information and tools inside, like being responsible, working hard, being dependable, etc., but out here, where the world is in my hands, it's not easy to avoid falling back into the habit of being the armed robber that I am, or was. It's very important to go slow and to have someone to talk to every day if necessary.

I read Jimi's statement and our questions and answers to the PAP members and the Prison Awareness class as planned. In my presentation, I noted that even for someone who seemingly had so much in his favor to avoid recidivism—a stable job, money, health, a partner, supportive family, supportive friends, whatever knowledge and skills one could pick up from several years of rehabilitative prison programs, etc.—it was still a considerable struggle to avoid falling back into crime. Ultimate success was far from a sure thing. Imagine, I said, how much worse it is for those who don't have all these advantages.

Jerry concurred: "Yeah, important as those things are, they don't guarantee nothing. I've seen a lot of guys with some or all of that get out and not make it. Jimi himself had a lot of that going for him last time he got out, but he still didn't make it."

Bill's take? "Eight to five says he's back by Christmas."

"Come on, Bill," I said half-facetiously, "At least make him even money!"

"Eight to five," he repeated, in dead-panned response.

Eventually Jimi got his driver's license renewed, and shortly thereafter bought a black pick-up truck. It wasn't a Harley, but he was exceedingly pleased with it. (His father put up the bulk of the money for it.) Not too long after that, he gave up his apartment near work and started making the long daily commute instead.

My contact with him diminished even further. I saw him twice in March, and spoke to him by phone on one or two other occasions. In April, I got him on the phone once, and didn't see him in person at all. The overwhelming majority of my calls were not returned, though when I finally did talk to him, he was invariably friendly and open, and apologetic for not having gotten back to me. I often brought up getting together for an interview, but it never happened.

We weren't upset with each other, there was no great tension between us, but it was clear that this wasn't a time in his life when he was willing and able to build on our friendship. I was torn, because on the one hand I wanted to offer support and monitor his progress, but on the other hand, I didn't want to force my way into his life.

I gradually pulled back. I remained available, but I made fewer attempts to initiate contact. We spoke only rarely.

I continued to speak with others who had contact with him, though. A small number of PAP volunteers saw him once or twice, and a few of the guys on the inside called him once in awhile. So indirectly at least, I was privy to the highlights and lowlights of Jimi's ongoing transition to life in the free world. What I heard was more discouraging than encouraging.

He was drinking regularly; he had used drugs at least once. He had had some small scale verbal confrontations on his job. And things were not so rosy at home either. He had started to bicker with Jeannie, and had lost his temper with her adult daughter at least once.

This latter incident was alarming in what it told me about his faltering self-awareness. As he recounted it, the daughter had made some offhand remark about Jimi overpaying for something and thereby letting the salesman make a sucker out of him. This was simply not to be tolerated. He berated her to take back what she had said, and warned her to never speak to him with disrespect like that again. "I had to put her in check," he told me by way of justification.

To him, it was no big deal, just the kind of thing decades of incarceration had taught him you have to do occasionally to keep people from walking all over you. He had no appreciation for how even a brief flash of temper and a vague threat like "Don't talk to me that way or else!" can be perceived as having magnified menacing implications coming from a career criminal who has just been released from prison. He dismissed such concerns with a laugh, as if his harmlessness and good nature were so well-established that no one who knew him at all well would overreact.

In late May, about a month after I had last spoken with Jimi, I got the most disturbing news yet, through an even more circuitous grapevine. (Apparently Jeannie told someone, who told one of my fellow PAP volunteers, who told me.)

Allegedly, Jimi had been spending more and more time partying, routinely coming home in the middle of the night or the next morning totally wasted. This had led to increased fighting and ultimata between him and Jeannie. Finally, after two of the checks he wrote her to pay his share of the household expenses bounced, she had had enough and threw him out. Where he was staying now was not passed on to me, though it was believed he was still working at his same job and could presumably be reached there.

This was ridiculous. I didn't like hearing such things third and fourth hand. I decided to make an exception to my self-imposed rule of waiting for him to be the one to make contact. I had to make absolutely sure that he knew I was still available and still cared. I hated to think he might hesitate to call me because he thought I was mad at him or was no longer interested in being his friend.

I wasn't going to be satisfied with calling him; I had to speak with him face to face. I knew where he worked and approximately what time his shift typically ended. So I made the long drive up to Everett.

When he saw me waiting for him in the parking lot, he waved happily and gave me a warm greeting. As usual, he apologized for not staying in touch. There was nothing in his manner to suggest he preferred to avoid me.

He asked me to join him at a bar and grill across the street where he was going to get a quick bite to eat. "I can't stay long, because I have to go back to work for a training session in the evening," he said, "But at least this'll give us a chance to talk."

I was interested not only in hearing the substance of what he had to say, but also in observing his general demeanor. As to the latter, he came across better than expected. He was his usual friendly, engaging self. He didn't appear depressed, angry, or panicky. There was nothing unnatural or unusual in his manner. Though he appeared to be in relatively good spirits, his cheerfulness was not so exaggerated as to seem phony or to indicate he was in denial about his difficulties. Even his recent hyperactivity was less in evidence on this occasion.

I asked him to give me his version of recent events.

He mostly confirmed the little I had already been told. He and Jeannie had been at odds more and more lately, and she had finally gotten fed up and kicked him out.

He made a couple of superficial disparaging references to her as "that bitch," but with a half smile and in a perfunctory manner. Out of pride he felt obligated to say what is expected from a jilted male, but aside from that, he freely accepted the blame for the situation, telling me he understood why she had shown him the door. "I didn't handle it well. I've been living under other people's rules for too long. I just didn't want that any more."

Jimi affirmed that he had given her checks he knew would bounce. It hadn't been a miscalculation. He did it to gratify his immediate need to get her off his back, he said. He was disinclined to think about its longer term consequences.

He acknowledged he owed her the money, but I didn't sense that it was any great priority for him. The feeling I got was that he was sorry things didn't work out, and he knew most of the fault was his, but he had done the best he could, and now it was time to put it behind him.

The good news was that he was making excellent money due to all the overtime he was working. He told me he was up to clearing $900 – $1,000 a week.

The bad news was that he still had zero ability to budget his money or discipline his spending. "I just can't get the hang of that," he said. He told me he went through his paychecks so fast he was always broke again before he got the next one. Whatever he saw that he wanted, he bought, until he had nothing left. "Like the other day, I saw a tool set that I really wanted, so I bought it. Didn't worry about the price; just bought it."

I asked him where he was living. He told me he was staying with his ex-con friend Nick in Tacoma temporarily.

As bad as the commute from the south end of Seattle to Everett is, the commute from Tacoma—which is a considerable distance even further south—is ridiculous. He must have been spending four hours commuting each work day.

In a few days he was leaving for Ohio for the two-week trip he had planned to see his family.

He admitted he'd been using drugs. He told me he'd overdone it and gotten totally stoned and stayed out all night twice, and that he had used more moderately a handful of other times. He didn't give me any more detail than that. I knew that what he admitted to might well be an understatement of what he was actually doing.

As far as the alcohol, he told me that almost every day when his work shift ended, he stopped in this bar and grill for a couple of beers before heading home. Beyond that, he sometimes went out drinking on the weekends, but he felt it was mostly under control and had not, for instance, interfered with his job.

"Thought you had lost your taste for it," I noted.

"Yeah," he smiled, "In the beginning. Not any more, I guess."

I offered him my assessment of what he was telling me: "You're taking apart your support system piece by piece. You spent years planning it all and putting everything together the best you could to give yourself the best shot, and now that you're out, it's as if you're testing to see what you can do without. And maybe taken individually, each move you're making isn't totally self-destructive. But by throwing away more and more of what you could be leaning on, you're just taking bigger and bigger chances.

"You had a supportive partner, and you threw that away. Maybe you weren't destined to be together forever, and maybe in the long run it's even justified that you go your separate ways, but having a stable partner and a stable place to live was one of the things you were counting on when you got out, and now that's gone.

"You were going to stay away from the drugs, but you decided you could handle at least some level of use. And maybe it'll turn out you can. Not everyone who uses ends up going on crime sprees or otherwise destroying his life. But abstinence from drugs is just another thing you had going for you that now you've relinquished. Same with the alcohol.

"You had a supportive network of friends, including me and the people from PAP, who were willing and eager to help you. But for the most part you've decided to go it alone without leaning on us. Again, maybe you can get away with that OK, but maybe not.

"You've tossed aside many of the things that you were going to use on the outside to maximize your chances of staying out of prison. And so far, here you are still surviving. But what about tomorrow? What about next week? What about after you throw away your next item of support?

"It just seems to me you're taking greater and greater risks by deciding you can do without so much that you so carefully put together before you got out here."

He listened to me with a more serious demeanor. "You're right," he responded with a slow nod, "Everything you say is absolutely right."

He cocked his head toward the beer bottle in front of him. "And that's a risk right there. Every time I order another one of those is a risk."

But it was time for him to go. I reminded him that I cared, that I was available to him. I made sure to tell him that while I was disappointed about some of his choices, he should not hesitate to call me if there was trouble or he needed my support.

Jimi told me that he appreciated that. "I understand your concern, and I'd be concerned too, looking at things from where you are," he said, "But I'm OK. I really think it's going to be OK."

One of the few positives I took from his present behavior and circumstances was his attitude toward his job. He was being irresponsible and undisciplined about many things in his life, but not his work.

In spite of the monster commute, in spite of the drug use and the drinking, in spite of the personal distractions of clashing with Jeannie and getting kicked out of his house, and in spite of his reacting against prison with a generalized craving to live spontaneously, he was still showing up at work every day.

And there was something else. At least twice already he had been rushed from work to the emergency room when tiny pieces of very hot metal had struck him in the eye while welding. He assured me it was every bit as painful as it sounded.

Yes, they were required to wear protection for their eyes, but the system was not foolproof. These kinds of eye irritants and injuries were a hazard that many beginners had to endure as they learned the welding trade.

Jimi presented this information to me matter-of-factly, not accompanied by any kind of "God, I have to get out of this job, the sooner the better." He seemed to regard it as a tolerable price to pay for having a job that he otherwise valued highly.

At the next PAP meeting, I felt a need to discuss Jimi's situation with some of the guys. Specifically I sought out Jerry and Rico. Unfortunately, Rico was not there, and indeed only rarely attended during this period. (Jeff let me know that Rico was going through one of his periodic phases where he is disgusted with PAP and feeling that it is not worth his time.)

However, Jerry was there, and he immediately agreed to talk to me about Jimi. We crossed the hall to the office where we could speak in private.

I brought him up to date and then detailed for him the last face-to-face conversation I'd had with Jimi. I told him that presumably Jimi was now in Ohio, but would be back shortly.

He listened patiently and attentively to all that I had to say.

Jerry's position was that drug use was behind much of what was going on with Jimi. He has a lot more freedom to use if he's not living with a disapproving girlfriend and having to hide it from her, and look at how he let that relationship fall apart. When he's doing drugs, he's a lot more comfortable being around other ex-cons than being around PAP members or other straights, and look at how he's gravitated to his old prison buddies on the outside and mostly avoided us. Compared to Seattle, Tacoma is reportedly "wide open" for drugs, so even though it's a terribly inconvenient place to live for his job, look where he's ended up living.

All the evidence pointed to Jimi's life again coming to be dominated by drugs.

Jerry thought this visit with his mother might be the best thing for Jimi. Anything to get him away from his present environment, his present patterns.

I asked Jerry if Jimi's friend Nick might be responsible for leading him back into drugs. He responded that the opposite was more likely, that Jimi was the stronger, dominant partner in that friendship, and that Jimi could drag Nick down with him a lot more easily than Nick could influence Jimi.

This was the most treacherous time, Jerry told me. The first six months to a year after release is the time that a prisoner will feel the most overwhelmed, the most tempted to satisfy all the impulses he couldn't satisfy in prison, the most panicky. Living a straight life is not habitual yet; regardless of how you tried to prepare yourself for it in prison, it's still going to feel unnatural, and it's still going to take some time before you can do it without a struggle.

If he could step back from the precipice before it was too late, things should get better for him. The longer he was out, the better he'd get at handling it, and the more likely he could stay out. But here in these early months, missteps were hard to avoid, and he was making plenty of them.

Jimi still had certain advantages of youth, Jerry added, advantages he'd likely have to learn to do without in the future.

In a lot of ways, Jimi is a big, good-natured kid. He's a young, strong, healthy, good-looking guy, with an extroverted personality and a zest for life that draws people to him. He makes friends and charms the ladies with little effort. At this stage of his life, his boyish grin and his general likability result in people giving him assistance and opportunities that may not be available to the next guy.

To Jimi, that's just the way life is, Jerry noted. He may not even be conscious that he has these advantages. But he'll likely notice the contrast when he discovers that at 45 and 55 and 65, somehow people aren't reaching out to him, aren't as friendly, aren't as indulgent of his transgressions, and aren't as easily charmed by him as they were when he was 25 and 35.

I explained to Jerry my frustration with the situation, how I had gone from calling several times a week—with rare responses—to only occasional efforts. I wondered aloud if my behavior was inconsistent with my desire to help Jimi. Had I pulled back because I was hurt and disappointed that he didn't seem to be interested in being friends on the outside?

Jerry felt I neither was being pushy with Jimi nor was abandoning him. He said it was on Jimi to use my support or ignore it.

"And if and when he does call you," Jerry continued, "You'll have to decide just what you are and aren't willing to do. For instance, he may be in trouble and need you to come and pick him up some place in the middle of the night. He may be drunk and desperate and about to get in a serious altercation or commit a crime if you don't come down and get him. It may be the kind of place you would normally not frequent, especially at that time of night. But he needs you to get him out of there. And you'll have to decide what you are and aren't comfortable doing when he needs your help."

As a result of our conversation, I felt closer to Jerry than perhaps at any time in the past. He hadn't been optimistic about Jimi, but I was grateful for his caring, and for his advice. He manifested nothing but respect for my friendship with Jimi, and my desire to help. He too was quite fond of Jimi and hoped he'd make it, but he was realistic about the prospects for failure.

The next news I heard about Jimi was very bad. His downward spiral was seemingly out of control.

Jeff informed me that Jimi had been fired from his welding job. He'd heard this from the supervisor of the welding company that operated inside the prison, the person who had set Jimi up with his job on the outside.

Reportedly, Jimi had worked for much of the day with a key part of his welding equipment turned off (or reversed or something). Never having done that kind of work, I lacked the background to understand the magnitude of the error, but Jeff noted that it was the kind of simplistic blunder that someone trained in welding would likely have to be very drunk or stoned to commit.

In any case, Jimi's negligence had caused a great deal of damage, and as soon as his employer realized what had happened, he fired him.

Jerry added to the grim news, telling me that Jimi had been involved in a one-car accident. He'd even been booked into jail in connection with it—presumably for drunk driving—though for only one night.

I asked Jerry if he agreed with the theory that Jimi must have been high to screw up as badly as he had at his job. "It's not a theory," Jerry responded, "He was fucked up. Without a doubt. He was fucked up. It's the only way to do what he did."

The next day, for the first time since I had last seen him in person, I called Jimi over at Nick's. Jimi wasn't there, but I was able to talk with Nick briefly.

Nick tried to put as positive a spin on things as he could, but the concern in his voice was palpable. He confirmed that Jimi had gotten into an accident in his truck, and said that the vehicle had been totaled in the process. Jimi had left Nick's and was now staying temporarily with a couple. They were people from the straight world, not ex-cons, Nick told me. "These are real good people," he assured me.

Nick gave me their number. He reiterated that this was a good environment for Jimi, and that I shouldn't worry. "He's doing real good," Nick said, with more hope than conviction.

I called the number Nick gave me several times over the next few days, leaving three messages for Jimi on their answering machine, none of which were returned.

I did not hear from Jimi after that.

It came as no surprise in July when Rico gave me the sad news that Jimi reportedly had re-offended and was currently on the run from what would be a third strike conviction that would put him in prison for the rest of his life without the possibility of parole. His precise crime was not yet known. There were rumors that he had already been apprehended, but there was as yet no confirmation of that.

Rico told me this in a tone to indicate he'd known all along this is how it would play out, but that it was pretty much a matter of indifference to him anyway. The façade was every bit as unconvincing as usual. Despite his protests to the contrary, Rico has never come close to shutting off his compassion. He is not a cold person. And I'm convinced he'll always have some degree of fondness for Jimi.

Roughly a month later, word came through that Jimi had been arrested. He was already at Shelton, meaning he was back in the prison system rather than the jail system, so he must have already been sentenced. People inferred from this that he had probably worked out a plea bargain for something short of a third strike. Had the state insisted on the third strike, Jimi would have had nothing to lose by contesting it and forcing a trial, regardless of how unlikely he was to prevail. Thus his presence at Shelton so soon indicated that he had pled guilty to some lesser charge that would not carry with it a life without parole sentence. At least that was the theory.

More information about his crime had come to light. Apparently he had thrown a rock through a jewelry store window and hurriedly taken what he could—a "smash and grab."

"A junkie move," Rico said dismissively.

The assessment of Jerry and others was that Jimi had never really hit rock bottom. On an intellectual level he knew that it was better to give up a criminal lifestyle than not, and he knew at least in broad terms the means to that end, but it was as if he were trying to talk himself into something rather than fully understanding in his gut the urgency to change his life. He had the self-help lingo down pat, but he never made the deep changes in himself to go with it.

One key piece of evidence for this—which some of the prisoners were more willing to talk openly about now—was that Jimi had been lying to us about his drug use on the inside. He had been using fairly frequently all along, I was told, and any breaks in his usage were simply a result of the inconsistent supply in prison, not any will power on his part.

One of the most regrettable aspects of Jimi's failure is that not only did he severely damage his own life by blundering his way back to prison, but he conducted himself in a way that has detrimental ripple effects on his fellow prisoners.

He harmed them in a way that only a few of them would even recognize or resent him for. Had he ratted on one of them—which ultimately would have generated far less total adverse consequences for them than what he in fact did—they would have despised and ostracized him for life. But he didn't. He merely added one little tiny piece more to the general societal attitude that prisoners are incorrigibly evil people who will never be anything other than criminals, and that only the most naïve bleeding hearted fool could favor releasing any of them.

The volunteers in the prison programs, his employer in prison who used his contacts to get him a job in the free world, his employer and co-workers on the outside, Jeannie and her family, his own family, and numerous others believed in him and got burned. That has to have at least some effect on how they perceive prisoners in general and how willing they will be to put themselves out to help them in the future. Certainly a small part of my zeal for PAP died when Jimi failed to free himself from drugs and crime.

It was months before I heard any more news about Jimi. Finally one of the PAP volunteers reported that she had received a letter from him, in which he confessed he had re-offended and was back in prison. He asked her to be sure not to tell anyone else. Of course, there was no secret to protect; we had all known all along. It's amazing to me that someone with Jimi's experience in the system can delude himself into thinking that news like that can stay hidden for longer than five minutes.

I never saw the letter, but the volunteer gave us the gist of it. She said that Jimi came across as thoroughly depressed and hopeless, blaming himself completely, and sounding especially distraught over his having—in his eyes—destroyed any possibility of ever regaining the respect of his father after letting him down yet again.

I could only feel sadness, not anger, toward Jimi. I didn't doubt his sincerity any more after he failed than I had before he was released. I have no inclination to hate someone who is doing the best he can.

# JERRY—March 1999

*"I'm just saying that whereas I was a thief and a crook that wore the hat of a thief and a crook, there's a whole lot of thieves and crooks and predators out there that wear the hat of respectability."*

L ate in 1998, I met with the new acting superintendent of the prison to make sure he knew about my book project and approved my continued work with the prisoners. His only objection was that he was not comfortable with my using PAP meeting time for a personal project like this, and thus he asked me to cease doing interviews on Wednesday nights. He did, however, tell me that I could arrange a one-time-only series of interviews during the day.

It took me until March to set it up, but ultimately I was able to come to the prison with my tape recorder for several days over the course of two weeks. My goal was to meet with each of the prisoners (other than Jimi, who was already on the outside by this time) twice, for about an hour each time.

Predictably, it did not work out as planned. In some cases the prisoners had schedule conflicts with their work or other commitments, and in some cases they just had differing degrees of commitment to the project or reliability about things like this in general, but the upshot was that I was able to secure about half of the planned interviews.

This was to be my last set of in-person taped interviews I had permission to conduct. After this, I would be limited to whatever letters or cassettes the prisoners sent me in response to my questions.

My first interview during this two-week period of afternoon sessions was with Jerry. Jerry, in fact, proved willing to make an extra effort by filling in when others didn't show up, moving his scheduled time up or back as needed, making sure I never made the long trek to the prison for nothing.

*Jerry, I'm going to start off by skimming through some of the notes and questions I had written concerning the very first tape you ever sent me. You mentioned in your chronology of events concerning your crime that you had had some conflicts with Frank, and that that's what led up to him retaliating by raping your wife, which in turn led you to retaliate by killing him. What had been the nature of these conflicts that could be so severe that somebody would think the appropriate retaliation is to rape somebody's wife? What had been going on between you?*

OK, number one, he had also, like, raped a couple other girls that none of us ever knew about. And one of them was just the week prior to him raping Laura.

But anyway, you know, a lot of times when I say we were having little conflicts, I'm actually kind of giving him an excuse. You know what I'm saying? But he never really had no legitimate excuse. He never really had a legitimate bitch. I'd hurt his pride is all. One time he had made, like, a verbal threat about my brother. My brother was bringing the car back, and the car had broke down, and he'd made a threat about what he was going to do to my brother when he got there, or something, you know. And, I called him on it. There was other people there, you know. And, he peed.

You know, I gave him the opportunity—at one point, I had a gun on him, and I said, "You're always talking about how fast you can get into business," and I stuck it in my back pocket and said, "Well, let's get busy then," you know.

What it was is we sold drugs. In our world, there's a pecking order, sort of. And at some point in time, if you're tipped up, clicked up, or you're doing something to somebody, everybody has to know where they are in that thing. It's like a colonel, a general—you know what I mean? You have to know where you're at and what you're really capable of, and what your friends are really capable of, and who's at the top of that food chain.

He kind of rode on his brother's reputation, you know, and his size—he was a great big guy—like, he should automatically be high up in the pecking order. But, number one, he was too dumb to call any shots. And especially with his little funny beefs, once anybody found out about those, they weren't going to follow him anywhere anyway. Because of his size and his looks, he had the potential to be a good lieutenant or torpedo, but that's it.

OK, so at the time, things were kind of deteriorating, as far as our friendship, already, and then he'd lost a lot of face right then, you know.

But here I'm making an excuse for him again. Number one, you sell a woof ticket and then you don't back it up, well that's on you. He shouldn't have held it against me, just because I wasn't faking and he was. You know, your mouth can't sell woof tickets your ass can't pay. And he wasn't willing to pay. That was really the nature of it.

And there was some other things. Like, he had put up some money for a guy's bail, a friend of ours. The guy's in the joint; it's an appeal bond. I'd put up my house. I owned a house at the time, and I put up my house. Frank put up five hundred dollars to a lawyer, under the condition that when the guy gets out, he was going to get paid back. At the same time, the guy's mom put up two thousand dollars at the bonding company out of her income tax refund.

But they ended up raising his bail to where we couldn't come up with enough to get him out. Well, Frank wanted to get his five hundred dollars back out of the money the bonding company was returning to the guy's mother, but I wouldn't let him do it. I called the bonding company and said, "Hey, only two people can pick that up: Laura or his mom." So he couldn't get his five hundred dollars back, and we had an argument over that.

It was just little shit like that.

*So it was mostly little stuff.*

Yeah, but you can see how chicken shit and self-serving the prick was in the first place, you know.

*But even if he had had a legitimate grievance with you—which it sounds like he didn't—it's not part of the code to harm third parties, is it?*

No.

*I mean, shouldn't he take it up with you, rather than hurt your family or your wife?*

Exactly.

What had happened is he'd gone out drinking that night, and he'd been drinking some turpin hydrate.

*What is that?*

It's cough syrup, with a pain killer in it. It's—

*Like codeine?*

Yeah. It's got codeine, yeah. Turpin hydrate elixir. It's one of them that you can buy over the counter. Plus he was out drinking booze at a bar. So, you know, just to give him another excuse, he's fucked up.

You know, and he had made a statement when he had raped her, he said, "You're Jerry's most precious 'property,'" or some fucking thing, "And if I can't get him, I'll get you." It was something like that.

But really I don't think it was even about that. That was just him doing the sociopathic thing, you know, where you give yourself permission to do shit. In his mind, he had to invent a grievance, a reason, for what he did. But what it probably was is he'd always wanted my wife. To be honest, I think that's what it really was.

*And you didn't even know before this that he had committed sex crimes in the past?*

No. Nobody did. I didn't hear about it until after he raped my wife. After they caught me, the two guys that were extraditing me, that were flying me back, said something about how it wasn't his first time.

Then, in the police investigation, it came out that he had even raped the old lady of the guy he was with at the shootout. He had raped the guy's old lady that prior week, or earlier that week. You know, like, I killed him on a Wednesday or a Thursday or something, but that previous Saturday at a party, he had raped this guy's old lady.

And here the guy's riding with him. His excuse was that he was so intimidated by Frank and me—and I didn't even know the guy—that when Frank called and told him he needed a ride, you know, that he was scared not to.

*And this is the fellow who was with Frank the day you killed Frank.*

Yeah. Yeah. He actually got shot too, but he lived.

*Was it your brother or Laura that told you what happened?*

It was my brother. She had called my brother. And then her and my brother—

*Why did she call your brother instead of you?*

Because she didn't know what to do. They know I got a real strict rule. You know, we don't involve the police. We just don't do that. And—

*And she was of that value system also?*

Well, not so much that she was, but she knew that I was. You know, I mean, it wasn't her choice. She didn't have a choice.

Her choice was when she married me in the first place. You know, she had a choice then. And for that matter, she always had the choice to leave me. I'm not one of them guys that's, like, "OK, you're my old lady. You got to stay." You can leave me any time you want. Any time you want, you can leave. I'll never chase you down, make you be my old lady. I don't care if I have an old lady or I don't have one.

But if you do come into my family, if you do come into my world, if you do become a part of that, well there's certain rules that I live by, and you have to embrace those or you have to go. There's no other option. It ain't open for debate, you know.

*So it's not just that you won't call the police; anybody you're connected with, like your wife, is not allowed to call the police.*

Right. Nobody. Yeah. You know, I don't even understand in-laws calling the police, if I'm free, if I'm on the streets.

*So why did Laura tell your brother rather than you? I mean, I understand why she didn't call the police—*

They didn't want to tell me, because they didn't want me to kill this guy.

*But they did eventually tell you.*

Because they knew that they had to. You know, they conferred and they knew.

*So at first they were inclined to keep it from you because they knew what your reaction would be, but then they said, "Well, sooner or later we're going to have to tell him."*

Right. "We're going to have to tell him." And say they waited to tell me until after they told the police. It's not going to make any difference to me doing what I got to do. You know what I mean? But now the police know ahead of time that I have a motive.

*Right.*

But it's not going to make any difference. You know, you do something to my family, I'll go get you in court. I'll go to prison to get you. I'll go wherever I have to go to get you. You cannot do anything to anybody in my family that I don't get you for it.

And that is still part of my life, that you cannot, in any way, shape, or form, pose a threat to my family. You can't, like, verbalize it even. You know what I'm saying? I won't tolerate that. I won't live under a threat, and I won't allow my family to live under a threat. And I don't care what anybody thinks about it.

Except the parole board. I keep that shit from them. [Laughs.]

*[Laughs.] So what did Laura think of your taking revenge? What was her reaction?*

It was very rough on her. She was a Catholic girl. Catholic schools, the whole nine yards. And she had to actually, like, go to therapy and stuff for a long time after this to kind of help her get back on her feet, and recover.

At the time, she had hurt her back on the job, getting a box down that was supposed to be empty, but ended up having a large, antique, adding machine-type thing, which was really heavy. It crushed a couple discs in her spine, and she was on medication. So probably her reaction wasn't as guilt-ridden at first, because of the pain-killers and stuff. But, later, you know, it took its toll.

It's one of the reasons we're not together.

*Now in a situation like that, does the person's opinion matter to you? The person in your family that you're protecting, that you're taking vengeance for—?*

No.

*Is it up to them what the revenge will be, or—?*

Not really.

*—is that up to you?*

Not really. No, you know, in my narrow view of the world, I never acknowledge anybody else's right to determine the ultimate outcome of what happens in our world. I always thought of myself as that person. I keep my own counsel. I don't go to somebody and say, "Man, what do you think we ought to do?" That's just not something I ever ask, you know. I usually do something. [Laughs.]

I'm the same way in here. I don't ask a lot. I do what needs to be done.

*Does it matter that it was a woman rather than a man?*

Well, see, like, if a man was wronged in my family, and he wasn't taking any steps to extract some revenge, it would bother me. I'd probably have a problem with him, and with whoever wronged him.

Number one, when you make that intrusion, you intruded in my family. That's mine. I have a vested interest. That is mine. It's our family name, and that's enough for me. You understand? So, in other words, like, if you wronged James,* you've wronged me. Now, if James ain't doing nothing about it, well I'm going to deal with him in a minute. I'll deal with you now. And then I'll deal with my problem with James. You know what I'm saying?

*You don't think it's more James's responsibility to deal with it in his own way?*

Not in the criminal world. Not in the way we did things.

*So if your brother came to you, and he had been wronged, he had been beaten up or something, and he said, "Jerry, I got my own ways of handling this. Maybe I'll take my revenge, maybe I won't. But I'll do it in my own way. Let me handle this. It's my thing," you wouldn't respect that? You'd say, "No, step aside, I'm going to—"?*

Oh, I would let him do it, as long as he did it, as long as he didn't just let it slide. He can handle it however he wants to, as long as he handles it.

*So he can't choose to not take revenge at all.*

No, see, 'cause then somebody else will think, "Well, fuck, them people ain't about nothing. We'll just go do this to them, and take this—" You know what I mean? Whatever they want to do. You can't allow that.

I mean, now I might react a little bit different. But, you know, at the time, that was how I viewed the world. Like we've talked about, I started out to be a criminal. I wasn't some guy

*Jerry's brother. I have changed the name.

that, you know, one time I lost my temper, lost control, and went and did something wrong. No. I've been involved in criminal endeavors since I was a child. That was my life. That's what I did. And what I'm describing is the way I looked at the whole world.

And bear in mind, we're talking about people that are also in that world. I'm not talking about if some square sideswiped my brother's car; does he have the right to go over and whack this guy. No. Those are non-combatants, and they're in another part of the world. They exist on another level. I'm only talking about if somebody in my world makes a transgression against my family. Because people in the life know the rules. They understand the consequences.

It might be getting a little blurred now, with all these gangs that they have now where they don't take care of each other or nothing. It might be getting blurred now, those lines. Even, like, the Mob, they tell on each other and shit. You know, things have changed a lot. But, in my narrow view of the right and the wrong and the way the world should be running, you can't allow shit to happen that goes unanswered, and if somebody in your family doesn't have the heart or the sack to answer it, well then you got to handle it yourself.

*Tell me about—*

If this ever falls into the parole board's hands, I'll never get out of the joint. I'm going to let you know that right now.

*[Laughs.]*

I'm being honest and candid with you. These fuckers will nail me under a jail. [Laughs.] Go ahead.

*What should we do? Do you still want to move forward with the project? Do you still want to use your real name?*

I'm not worried about it.

*You're willing to take your chances.*

[Laughs.] I'll just say you lied.

*OK. [Laughs.]*

[Laughs.]

*Tell me more about the crime itself, and how you tricked Frank.*

I didn't want him to know it was me until it was too late, so I shaved my head and shit. I shaved my head bald, shaved my beard and everything. You know, I had had a little Rembrandt goatee, and I shaved it off. 'Cause when you drive up on somebody at night, the profile is what gives you away. Boom! So, I had to change my profile, 'cause when I stepped out of the dark, I didn't want him to realize right away who it was.

So when they pulled up—boom!—as soon as he doused the headlights, you know, and their eyes are still focusing down from the light, as soon as I heard the car door being opened—bam!—I said, "DEA! You're under arrest!" See, and now I'm just this hazy outline.

Actually, I should have known better, though, 'cause my voice would give it away anyway.

*Right. He must have known who it was when he heard your voice.*

Well, you know, he acted like he didn't. And alls I needed was a second, and I had the drop on him, see.

*Why did you not want to kill him at that time? On the tape you sent me, you said that after you injured him, "I don't want to kill him yet."*

'Cause the other guy got away. That other guy that I was telling you about. See, we shot him in the chin. Right? Well, he goes down, but then when I was scuffling with Frank—'cause see, Frank had started to fight as soon as he realized how much trouble he was going to be in—well, he jumps up and runs out.

*The other guy.*

Right, the other guy jumps up and runs out. So I can't kill Frank, not knowing where this other guy went. You know what I'm saying?

*I don't get it. How long does it take to finish off Frank on the way out to get the other guy?*

Well, there was no need. He was shot once and he went down.

*But I thought you were saying that you didn't have the time to finish off Frank because you had to hurry and catch the other guy.*

No, no, no, it wasn't a matter of time.

*Oh.*

It wasn't a matter of time. It was a matter of, you don't want to kill somebody, knowing that there's a witness to it, already out in the bush.

*OK.*

Right?

*I got you.*

OK, so he's shot in the chin, so I know he's got to go to a hospital, and I'm trying to find out what hospital. But since he's shot, and they don't have the suspect, all the hospitals are keeping it quiet. You know, I was trying to find out where he was at, but I couldn't. You understand why?

*You wanted to catch him and kill him, but you couldn't.*

Yeah, I couldn't find out where he was.

*And you didn't want to kill Frank without first eliminating the witness. But you weren't able to, and yet in the end you did kill Frank after all. Why?*

Well, 'cause I figured by then I was already looking at two counts of first degree assault and two counts of kidnapping. It's not a big reach after that. You know, the shit's already started by then, it's out of the bag. If they catch me, they're not going to do much more to me if I kill the guy than if I don't.

But, you know, when the time came for me to give them my side of the story, I told them my original intention was to take him out there and just leave him and hope he died. As I look back on it, though, I don't think that's accurate.

Sometimes over time and distance and the telling of it so often, the truth and stuff kind of gets lost in there. You're not really sure which was fact, and which was your logic after the fact when you're trying to explain away shit.

*Right.*

So, I'm not really sure. But knowing me, and being totally honest, I probably was fixing to kill him all along when I took him out there.

*Yeah.*

Just knowing me, I mean, and the way I looked at the world back then.

But the actual chain of events I told them, that was all true. I said I took him out there, and as I'm walking him, he turns and elbows me, and—

*Is this after he's already been shot and wounded?*

Oh yeah, he'd been shot. And he elbowed me right in the temple. And I stabbed him. And I just kept on stabbing him. So, those things took place just the way I told them.

And actually when you're dressing something up, the more facts you can use, the better.

In fact, my brother thought that that's what I was going to do all along, just take him out there and tie him up.

*And just leave him and hope he dies.*

Just leave him. He's on his own. Give us time to get away. Give us time to flee or whatever. But, you know, if you take the next logical step, well, I'll have a lot more time if he ain't getting untied. [Laughs.] You know what I'm saying?

So, I have to think my intent was to kill him all along. When he elbowed me and fought me, that forced my hand, but even if he hadn't, I probably meant to finish him off out there anyway. Like I said, that all gets lost in all the time that passes, and all the ways I have to spin the story a certain way for my own purposes, where pretty soon I'm not really sure myself what happened. But knowing me, even though the events I told them were totally accurate, my intention was to kill him and not to just leave him out there like I told them.

*Did his wounded partner tell the police what had happened?*

Actually, he couldn't really identify us, because by the time I stepped into the light where they could see me and said, "DEA! You're under arrest!," I had pulled a mask down over my face. But, yeah, he still made statements and stuff, and said it was us.

He even testified that the girl we used to trick them into coming there was Laura, which it wasn't. It was somebody else, see. But he was being coached by Frank's mom, you know, which he even admitted later in the investigation.

Given a trial, I would have had second degree murder. You know, given a trial, I'd have had second degree murder.

*So just out of vindictiveness they were trying to drag down Laura too?*

That family was, sure. And that gave the police leverage that they used so they didn't have to take it to trial. Yeah. Laura wasn't even there.

*How did you get caught in Florida?*

I'd left a quantity of drugs with a guy that I thought was a friend of mine, and he was supposed to sell it and then wire me the money. I had some fake ID and stuff. He sent the police instead. [Laughs.]

But they wired money, so when I called they'd tell me there's money there for me to pick up. And I had a lousy feeling about it. I'll always remember that. Man, I just knew better than to go down there. I was on my way to the beach, and I should have gone to the beach, and just let that money go, 'cause I started to have a lousy feeling.

I told Laura, I said, "You know, if you want it, you can go down." She said, "Well, I don't want to go down there." You know, it was awful "dark" out—population-wise—in that neighborhood, in the South, you know, and it was kind of a strange setting for her that she wasn't comfortable with. She said, "Don't make me go down there by myself." "Well," I said, "I'll go down with you, but I'm not going to go in."

So, she went in and I waited in the car. When she came out, she was shaking her head, you know, to give me a hint, to tell me to go the other way. She didn't walk directly at me.

*Right.*

So I knew that something was up. Well, I turned—I'm fixing to break—and everybody on the whole street throws down on me.

There was a bum drinking wine out of a bag. There was a couple talking to a preacher on the steps of the chapel across the street. Everybody in the cars that stopped were all cops.

*So everybody's an undercover cop on that street?*

Oh everybody. Everybody. And they had been told that I would attempt a shoot-out under any circumstances.

*By whom?*

A cop in Seattle that's hated me since I was a kid. He was one of my nemeses forever. He used to make obscene calls to my mom, telling her that they were going to kill me.

*Really?*

Oh yeah, yeah. He was so bad that the Florida police refused to turn me over to him. They said, "You got to send somebody else."

He ended up a sheriff. He was the first Republican sheriff ever in his county. Oh yeah, he hated my guts. Hated my guts.

*What happened to your brother in connection with these incidents? Did he serve time for this?*

Yeah. He—

*Was he caught the same time as you?*

Well, he was actually caught a month before me.

Yeah, I thought he had left. You know, that was the instructions I gave him. He was supposed to leave, but he didn't. He stayed up in the Seattle area, and then that was that.

*What was he convicted of?*

Same as me. Originally, he actually went in and tried to kind of ride the beef. He—

*What does that mean?*

In other words, to claim that he did it.

*That he was acting alone?*

Yeah, that he'd done it. That he was the guy, you know.

So when they get me, I can't make a deal to clear him. I'm trying. I'm trying. I'm trying everything I can, but they don't need to deal for him.

Plus they got my kid and my old lady. So the best deal I could make was one first degree murder, and for the charges against my wife to be dropped, with custody of my kid returned to her, and it would be dismissed with prejudice, so they can't bring them up or ever bother them again about it, you know. And, for that I'd plead guilty. That was the best I could do to protect my old lady and my kid. It was too late to deal for my brother.

See, they kept on trying to hedge after I thought we had a deal, and I'd stop them court proceedings in their tracks when they'd start playing games with me. They'd have to, like, cart me out sometimes. If I didn't like the way it was going, you know, what the hell you going to do to me? You know what I mean? You can't get me in no more trouble. The judge's authority doesn't really scare you in that kind of situation.

*Now why did they need to make any concessions at all? Didn't they have a pretty solid case for first degree?*

No. They had no case for first degree.

*It seems like a very premeditated act.*

Well, the thing is, there's mitigating circumstances. You got to understand, with first degree murder, there have to be other factors, like I have to have done it for money. It isn't just a matter of being premeditated. Every crime is premeditated.

*So a revenge killing is not technically a first degree murder?*

No, technically, it's not if I was moved by—See, I started out as the victim, you understand. You have to put yourself in my mental state. And, there's no jury in the world that would have found me guilty of first degree murder. They would have gave me mitigating circumstances, second degree murder.

No way. Nobody in the history of Man has ever been convicted of first degree murder for killing somebody who raped his wife.

*So you had to go along with first degree rather than second degree because of your son and your wife, just to protect them.*

Well, yeah. That, and the fact that the deal wasn't that bad at the time. When I made the deal, a life sentence meant thirteen years and four months. So, I had every reason to expect that, like, in sixteen years or something, I'd be out.

So when I made the deal, it was a pretty good deal. The deal got worse as time went on, as they changed the system. They changed the deal, which is the point of issue that kind of pisses me off, like we've talked about. I don't really trip on it too much, but if I did, it would give me cause to be angry. You know, me and you enter into a deal, I keep my end of the bargain, and you don't keep yours, it would piss me off.

And basically that's what they do. They trick you into a deal, and they don't keep their end of it. There's, like, no check or balance for them, and if I was in a worse place spiritually and mentally, I'd probably have a grudge about that, you know. I think I'd still feel like society owed me something. It's not a hard reach, for me.

*It sounds like there's no closure with the criminal code of behavior, I mean when it comes to taking revenge on each other. You mentioned that because of what was done to your wife, that entitles you to go after him, but then that gives his brother a legitimate grievance, so he's going to come after you, which in turn means you'll go after him. I mean, you even mentioned on one of the tapes that you expect Jake\* to try and kill you if he ever has the chance, and you intend to kill him if you ever have the chance. So does this just cycle on forever, or—?*

Yeah.

---

\*Frank's brother. I have changed the name.

*It sounds like you're trapped in this, where this revenge will go back and forth forever.*

Sure.

*Any way to break the cycle, or are you just always going to—?*

Something like genocide, you know.

*You mean wipe out one side entirely?*

Yeah. Genocide.

*So it can never end without wiping out one side entirely?*

Well, actually, you wipe out the combatants on one side, you know, and then it's over.

But, I mean, in my case it's probably over anyway, because the one that poses the most threat is doing federal time right now, and it's a bunch of time. And just knowing that he's kind of a shitty dude, there's a chance that somebody'll whack him before I would ever encounter him again. But he's got enough time to do that we're all going to be really old soon. You know what I mean?

*So one of you will die of old age before you kill each other.*

Yeah. Yeah. Chances are, he might never see the street again, you know. I'm the only one that's got a chance to hit the streets again. And that kind of brings things to an end.

You know, the mother is the one who generated a lot of the anger, and she's close to crossing over herself. So, I've pretty much outlived all my enemies, except one.

*Technically, though, what's Jake's grievance against you? I understand that you killed his brother, but you didn't wrongfully kill his brother, according to the code. You killed his brother in a justified retaliation for raping your wife. Doesn't that matter?*

You know what? Like, it's because we'd have to. It's just part of the thing, you know. And, he doesn't disrespect me, and I don't disrespect him.

*So you're like warriors in opposing armies. You can have a mutual respect for each other, but still kill each other when the time comes.*

Yeah, I guess. Yeah.

Yeah, like, his road dog is a hell of a guy, and I respect him a bunch, but I'd whack him [laughs], because I respect him that much. I know that—

*Well, I hope you never respect me that much.*

No, see now, this is the thing: like, he's a guy that I believe his word is his bond. And he's given his word to these people. And even though he's actually sent me word of, you know, a peace thing, that he no longer is obligated to whack me, I'd have a hard time believing it.

You got to understand, these people we're talking about, I don't never want to see these people, and I probably never will.

*Right.*

I don't never want to kill anybody. That's not something that I want to do. But given the opportunity, I'd have to lean towards doing him, because I'd always be wondering, is he going to do me? And like I said, I'm not going to live under a threat. You know what I mean? The stress level's way too high.

People like us, we live in an environment where, you know, like, maybe he means it when he says it, but, bam, a couple months down the road, we have a falling out over something else, well, it pushes him back the other way. That'd be a volatile situation to be in, with a dangerous man. He's a dangerous guy.

So that's what I mean when I say I'd kill him out of respect. I'd have to say that's why I'd be whacking him, you know.

*You've compared prison life to the Land of Oz, with its upside down values and such, and—*

Upside down, yeah.

*—I guess we can extend that not just to prison, but to the world you're describing now, the type of criminal lifestyle on the outside that you're speaking of. Any regret or remorse for entering and remaining in that world? I mean, it seems like such a fucked up way to live. How do you feel about it now?*

Well, never having known the other side, I can't regret it. I didn't never know anything else. You'd have to have actually viewed the other side, the other choice. I had never viewed it.

I mean, [laughs], I know that sounds crazy. I know people just don't understand that. But, to me, I never saw the other side, the other point of view.

I'm ten years old, I go to the Luther Burbank School for boys, and my whole education is in crime. My whole peer group are criminals. Every single one of them, including the staff. You know, everybody is fucked up in this world that I live in. Even the people that you would have thought were responsible adults. I mean, I can tell you horror stories of torture and shit.

So, I didn't go through life and see this middle class world. Ward Cleaver didn't live in my neighborhood. You know what I'm saying? I had guys that would make you stand on the wall from, oh, nine o'clock at night until six o'clock in the morning. "Holding up the wall," they called it, with your fingertips. Nail you with a tennis shoe if you moved.

*This is at the reform school?*

Luther Burbank School for boys. I'm there for, you know, running away from home when I'm ten years old. I'm there for two years and three months. By the time I get out, I'm a hard core little thief.

I grew up in projects. We were kind of transient. My dad was in the Navy and we moved around a lot. We thought everybody that didn't live in a project was rich. It was them and us, and that was my whole life. I mean, I remember we used to tell lies about being a normal family, you know, rather than what life was really like. I remember lying to pretend like I had a normal life. And it didn't exist.

And then, you know, to say, well, do you have any regrets? Let's see, I regret I wasn't a little bit more successful. I regret that I'm not capo di tutti capo. You know, those are the things I regret. I never really rose to the pinnacle of my chosen profession as I had planned, because of this little sidetrack, you know. [Laughs.] That's what I regret.

*But now you are old enough to recognize other alternatives. So can't you now compare your path with what it could have been, and wish that you'd been on a different path?*

You always can wish you were on a different path. I wish that Ward Cleaver did live in my neighborhood. You know what I'm saying?

How can I say this, so it makes sense. I don't—I'm not ashamed. I'm not uncomfortable with Jerry and all that he's been.

The time and opportunity to be a successful crook kind of slipped me by, in all reality. Is it time for me to retire, and try and find a civilized life that'll allow me a minimum of luxuries, and liberty? It's certainly that time. Have I crossed some moral threshold where crime is just, like, repulsive to me? That hasn't really happened.

I don't use drugs any more. I don't just mean I'm not getting high now, that I'm being clean; I don't use them any more. I don't use them to sell, I don't use them to get ahead, I don't use them to get high. But I don't have a moral problem with people that do. It's just that it has no place in my life. There's no real future for me in it.

Crime, pretty much, the same thing. I don't do it any more. I told you once before that at some point in IMU, certain crimes I could no longer give myself permission to commit. I can't see sticking a pistol on somebody and taking some money from him, and putting their life at risk. It just isn't a fair deal.

I'm kind of a fair guy. Fair and real and honest are important things to me. And to go in and put some twenty-one year old girl, pregnant mother of two's life at risk, so that I can get some drug money or whatever, ain't right. It ain't fair. It just ain't right.

Do I got a problem with other people being robbers? No, I don't have a problem with robbers, as long as they ain't robbing me.

Say I was in business, and you know, like, how a banker might foreclose on somebody because they didn't see this clause, or they just trick you in some sort of fashion? I'm not the guy to do that to. See, because there's still enough of the old Jerry present at all times.

In other words, like, I don't see coming back to prison as much of a risk any more for me, 'cause I'm not going to rob anybody, and I ain't going to sell or use drugs. So, there's not many reasons for me to come back to the joint, other than somebody making a transgression into my world.

There I might have a problem, if somebody, like, took my home from me. You know, say I get out and I work the next ten, twenty years, and I get something. And somebody, because of a law or zoning or whatever, thinks they can take something from me. Or a business partner does to me like one time when my dad owned a tavern, and he ended up getting ousted, you know. That shit can't happen to me. That person would just come up missing.

I wouldn't do it to them; I don't expect them to do it to me.

*Actually, several questions come to mind,—*

[Laughs.]

*—[Laughs.] I'm not sure which direction to go in first. But, if there were a child you cared about, a relative, or a friend, just a small child that you could somehow influence, would you prefer that that individual grow up to be a good person in the Jerry Mac sense, or in the Ward Cleaver sense?*

Oh, Ward Cleaver, for sure.

*Why is that?*

I mean, 'cause it ensures a future, and a life.

My kid's never been in trouble. I've always kept my family out of my criminal life, other than the rule that you can't call the cops. I mean, my wife was always kept out of it. And actually, until this beef, my brother had never been involved. I'd never had no fall partners, certainly not from my family. That just isn't what you do.

No. They're not even supposed to know. You know, you should try and ensure their future, not put them at risk. Most guys—I'm talking about most criminals that are real criminals,

I'm not talking about some junkie—their families and stuff very seldom know. The real guys. The families don't know until something like this stuff happens, and then they find out.

But nobody ever tries to raise their kids to be solid convicts, 'cause alls that'll make them is convicts. It gives them no tools to survive out there. I don't want my kid in the joint.

*Well at some level, then, you must recognize that your lifestyle is not what it should be. I mean, if you don't—*

I recognize it at all levels, Craig.

*—want other people you care about to follow you down that path—*

No, no, I recognize it at all levels. I'm not here saying that what I do is right. A lot of guys will come in here and try and convince you that "Society did this, and society—," you know. No, it's not that. What I did was for gain and profit. That's why I was a crook.

*So, is your position, then, that once you realized there were alternatives, it was too late for you?*

Oh yeah. Yeah. I was in prison, doing life.

*So once you're as deep into the lifestyle as you are, you can't just make a decision to be a Ward Cleaver, or to be a whatever.*

No.

*You're stuck for life.*

Hell, I owned a home once, and didn't even know about equity. I needed some money for my bond, so I could stay out of jail, you know, and I went out and committed a robbery to get it. Now that I look back, hell, I could have gone to the bank and they'd have gave me the money. I owned a house! They'd have gave me more money than I got in the robbery.

But I just didn't think in those terms, didn't think about legitimate ways to get what I needed. [Laughs.]

*Well, how do you respond to the argument that there are people who come from similarly deprived backgrounds that don't end up in crime? How do they survive?*

I don't know. I don't know. You know what? I don't care what anybody says, there's a lot to do with luck. I know some guys that I would have swore were going to be in the joint, and something happened along that route—'cause we were all on it—something intervened. Chance and opportunity, and they took advantage of it.

I enlisted in the Marines in 1966. Vietnam was jumping off. In the meantime, I go to sentencing for stealing a seventy-five dollar set of tools. I got the Marine recruiter to come into my sentencing and say, "Hey," you know, "His dad was a war hero," blah, blah, blah. "I've known the kid for the last three years, and he's always been interested in the Marines," 'cause he recruited downtown; I seen him all the time. And he had been working on me for years.

Judge said, "I've seen his juvenile record. I couldn't do that to the armed forces of the United States," and sent me to prison. Fifteen year sentence. Who knows what would have happened if he'd let me go in the Marines instead?

A friend of mine that we just buried, same neighborhood, same everything, went to Vietnam. Came back and actually ended up working here. He was a "blue tag"* —worked here. He was a good, close friend of mine from the neighborhood.

Another guy that I had robbed with and stuff, I remember waking up one time, and I thought we were escaping, because I seen him go by in a cop's uniform. And I'm thinking, "Well shit. It's on!" He's looking for me too. He says, "Jerry Mac! Jerry Mac!" "Here!" I say, "Here I am! Let's go!" You know, I'm thinking, "Shit. This is on!" Right? He works there! [Laughs.] He works there! I remember being in a restaurant one time, and he killed a guy. I mean, he killed a guy that was shooting at him, so it actually was legitimately in self-defense, but we didn't have a self-defense law then. But anyway, after all that, he ends up working here rather than incarcerated here.

I mean, chance and opportunity. A lot of it.

You know, I had an opportunity. I went to the Seattle School of Mixology when I got out of here. I'm supposed to be a troubleshooter for the food and beverage manager over at Inglewood Country Club. He loved me. Thought I'd be excellent at it. My area of expertise was the bar, his was overall food and beverage management, and we had a lady that was going to be in charge of hotel management, and Westin Hotels was going to send us around the country. Around the world actually.

Well, at the same time, two friends of mine call up, and they'd been in a shootout with the cops, and needed a ride. This is the night I graduated from the Seattle School of Mixology. I went and picked them up to take them to Mexico, and ended up getting a beef.

Chance and opportunity. Given all the time that there's choices, you know. Had I gone to work for Westin Hotels, would I be here now? Maybe not. Probably not. Would my life have been different, and would I have a different point of view about some of these things we're discussing? Probably.

*You know, people have a natural tendency to be biased in their own favor, and to interpret things as to where—*

---

*Correctional officer.

Sure.

*—they're being treated unjustly. I guess that's what concerns me about living in a world of Jerry Macs. I mean, how could we conduct business or anything if any time somebody was disadvantaged by something in their personal life or their business life or their professional life, they felt they had the right to take vengeance for that? I'm afraid everybody's going to be shooting everybody in that kind of world. That's what concerns me about everybody having this right to individual justice like that, where I get to decide when I've been wronged and what I'm going to do about it, where it's up to me and not the courts or anybody else.*

Sure, but if Jerry Mac didn't exist, there's still a gazillion of them out there that have that belief system. Everybody ought to treat people the way they want to be treated, and you wouldn't have to worry about me or people with my belief system retaliating against you.

It's, like, you know, people think that because the letter of the law gives them an advantage over somebody else that they can take that advantage. You know, maybe because the other person wasn't smart enough to see the trap. You know what I'm saying? OK, those people are predators without the heart to be predators. They're feeding on weak fish.

So I'm just saying that when they try to feed off of somebody like me that way, well, they actually get their comeuppance. You know, let's say the Lord works in mysterious ways.

You have this tendency that, well, people always think that they've been wronged. I don't think like that. Unless I have compelling belief, truth, whatever, that I'm in the right, I don't take action. I'm not looking for excuses to take vengeance on people.

In other words, like, if I stumble on "Man, I've got this advantage," I wouldn't take that advantage, 'cause it wasn't right. If the next guy takes that advantage, well it still ain't right.

I don't know. It's oversimplifying. Maybe it never even comes to pass. You know, maybe nothing in my whole life will ever bring up this particular situation. I'm just saying that whereas I was a thief and a crook that wore the hat of a thief and a crook, there's a whole lot of thieves and crooks and predators out there that wear the hat of respectability.

The average person out there has absolutely nothing to fear from Jerry. But people like that might. If you wrong me, I don't know until you do that exactly what's going to happen.

*You know, in a way, I'm tempted, I guess, by the notion of having a Jerry out there punishing the white collar criminals [laughs] who are screwing the little guy in business and everything, but—*

[Laughs.] Yeah.

*—in the end, of course, I can't—*

You couldn't justify it.

*—endorse it.*

Yeah.

*I can't say it's completely unappealing to—*

The thought ain't that bad to you. Yeah. [Laughs.]

*Do people in prison always know each other's crimes? Could somebody be here, like, on a sex beef and nobody knows it?*

Actually, it's a lot more now that we don't know. A lot of guys come in, and they pled to first degree assault and shit, and we don't know. Or even murder, for that matter. A guy committed a murder where he also raped the victim, but murder's what he pled to. We don't have the guys in position to get us that information as easily as we used to.

But they're putting everybody's crime up on the Internet here pretty soon, and it'll be pretty easy again. Because that's what society wants. They want to know what these guys have done. Is it crimes against women and children? You know, and what's their history and their make-up? If prisoners are going to be on the Internet getting dates and stuff, people are going to insist on knowing all that stuff.

*From what you've told me, a person's place in the pecking order is determined by a combination of two factors: their crime, and how they conduct themselves in prison. Would it be accurate to say that their crime puts a ceiling on how high they can go? No matter how well they conduct themselves in prison, certain crimes will keep them fairly low in the pecking order?*

Yeah. Probably. But I'd say that their being the kind of people that are capable of committing those crimes in and of itself limits them and separates them from us. Those people tend not to fit the mold. They're not criminals in the criminal sense. They're not even criminals in the druggie, or addict sense. They do things out of a motive that we can only, like, guess at.

It's like somebody who's insane. You know, I've sat with nuts, I mean, guys that are stark raving fucking mad. I've had some pretty good friends that are stark raving fucking mad. And you don't really understand what it is they see when they look around. You have no idea what it is that they see. Well, we don't have any idea what these people see either.

One thing you can tell by their behavior, though, is that they tend to think they're better than us. A lot of them tend to think that they're better than us, because they're not common criminals, they're not thieves. You know, they think that they're regular Joe Citizens, except that they have this illness. They think, "Well, I've got this one problem, you know. I've been seeing a shrink for it, and I'm trying to work through it." That type of shit. You know, like what they do isn't every bit as violent or worse than what they look down on us for.

There's a majority of, like, sex offenders that think in those terms. But then there's also the other kind of sex offender that's a criminal as well as a sex offender. You see what I'm saying? And they can slide in here and we don't know, because their style and mannerisms and the way they carry themselves is that of the criminal. That other stuff they do, that other side of them, they hide.

So there's these squares, with this "social disorder," and then there's criminals, with this same disorder. Well, the guys that are criminal, they grew up in the system, they know the shit that they're supposed to be talking, they can kind of fade in, especially now, you know, when you don't really have as much access to the information of what crimes guys have done.

That guy that killed that little girl—Klaas—down in California, he had a solid reputation in the prison population down there. He kept his history hid. They thought he was one of the Fellahs. They had no idea, you know, that this guy was such a sick puppy.

*Nobody knew his crime when he was in prison?*

No.

*Also I'm asking, though, about cases where people do know the crime. Let's say somebody did commit rape or was a child molester, and came to prison, and you knew that. But in his time in prison, he never rats on anybody, he never betrays or cheats any of his fellow convicts, he's willing to fight for himself—whatever makes a good convict. Once he gets within the prison walls, he does all the things you're supposed to do to be a good convict. Can he ever rise from the bottom of the food chain?*

Yeah. He might never be able to call the shots, but he can gain a certain amount of respect, you know.

*Maybe he can go from the bottom to somewhere around the middle or something?*

Yeah. Yeah. He can gain a certain amount of respect. There's guys around here like that.

There's one—can't remember the guy's name, man, but, you know—when he met you, he'd say, "Hey, listen. I picked up one of them fucked up beefs. I don't know what I was doing when I did it. It's the only time it ever happened," and blam. But he was a Fellah, you know. And so people gave him the benefit of the doubt.

But he's still not somebody you go on a crime with. He ain't somebody that you introduce to your family. You just don't—I would never, like, run with him, you know.

But, see, there's a lot of ways to have smut on you. Protective custody—PC—comes with a lot of stigma.

They had me in PC.

*How come?*

Because of the guy I killed. When I got to the Walls, there were some guys there that had promised Jake that if I hit the yard, they'll kill me.

But they ain't going to. They can't. As a matter of fact, if I hit the yard, I'm going to whack one of them right away, because I already know what they're planning. See, because I got spies that have told me. I got a knife waiting for me that's sitting just outside admissions, up under this window thing, for me to grab when I come out, so that I can get busy and kill the guy as soon as I get out there, and then I can get my hole time over.

And that would be just to serve notice on the rest of them, you know, telling them that if you sign into this battle here, if you want a part of this war, understand the consequences. You know, that way, people just don't sign on.

But they never intended to really follow through. I knew that. They went to the Man and said, "Hey, listen. We feel obligated to move on him as soon as he hits the yard." That way the Man would take action to keep us apart, and they'd be off the hook of having to move on me.

So they did what they call this Involuntary Protective Custody, or IPC. See, but the guys out on the yard, they don't know the difference. Some of them don't make that distinction with "involuntary." They don't know.

So I'm stuck in Big Red, refusing to go over to this Protective Custody unit. I'm stuck living in the hole for the next two years. I'm stuck living down there, and then, like, all these peripheral guys, they don't know the whole story. I mean, I have to deal with that all the time. That little jacket? I have to deal with that all the time.[*]

---

[*]One night well into my tenure in PAP, I was conversing with one of the newer members on the subject of the convict code. He was clearly a firm believer in it. When I mentioned in passing that I had learned a lot about the code from Jerry and others, he quickly stopped me and told me that Jerry was not such a solid adherent to the code as I might think. "Jerry was PC," he told me. He was staring in my face, seemingly searching for clues as to what I would do with this information. There was an intensity and a wariness about him, like he felt an obligation to tell me this utterly crucial negative fact about someone that I was getting mixed up with, but was also cautious about saying too much to someone who apparently was Jerry's friend and might repeat it to him. Jerry, after all, was the big wheel in this club, and one did not lightly speak against him. I said, "Well, it was my understanding that that was some kind of involuntary thing—" "Doesn't matter," he shook his head. "But," I said, "If they put him some place against his will, how can that be held against him?" "Doesn't matter," he insisted, "PC is PC. I don't care if you have to stick a knife in a guard, you don't go PC. There are hard core guys who will never accept him because of that. You can never go PC. Never." I didn't tell Jerry. Given what he says later here, he may well have drummed the guy out of PAP if I had.

*So even now people remember that you were in PC?*

Yeah, it's something—

*Technically, though, were you ever actually in PC? Just as far as the semantics, were you involuntarily placed in PC, or were you placed in the hole as punishment for refusing to go into PC at all?*

Nah, I was never in PC. "Protective Custody" means I went and said, "Hey," you know, "You got to protect me." I ain't never asked for no protection.

*So you refused to go when they tried to put you in PC.*

Yeah.

*And that's why you went to the hole.*

Yeah. But, you know, it doesn't matter. Not everybody knows that. My friends know that. My enemies know that. But the peripheral little dickheads don't know it and still will talk about me like I was in PC. Every once in awhile, one of them will raise his ugly head, and I have to do something about it.

*How are the peripheral people under the impression that you were in PC, since technically you never were?*

Because not everybody loves Jerry, and it's an easy thing to say. This isn't a loving environment, you know. You make enemies, and any way they can, they cast aspersions on your character.

*So they just lie or make up rumors based on the half-truth that they once tried to put you in PC.*

Yeah. See, not all my enemies are men. You know, I got a couple enemies that are men. The rest of them are punks. They grin to my face, and talk behind my back.

Now, the fact that I know that they don't really care for me means I don't seek out their company. You won't see none of them at PAP. You won't see none of them there at the PAP Christmas party, or the annual banquet. You might run into them in one of the other clubs, or in some of them other things, but you won't run into them at ours. I have a certain sphere of influence, and I use it. That way, they know that we ain't cool, and I know that we ain't cool.

Right now, that's the most I can do, you know. But if the Board was to tell me, "Well, Jerry, you're never getting out," well, then that would change the whole thing. 'Cause there's a couple of them I'd like to assault, you know.

*I take it one of the things that puts one at the bottom of the pecking order—though it's not as bad, I guess, as crimes against children—is crimes against women, or killing a woman, unless it's, say, a female crime partner who betrayed you.*

Yeah.

*But if it's an innocent woman, then—*

Women. Old people. Yeah.

*Yet we have people who are among the best convicts, the best PAP members, who are guilty of precisely that. How did they overcome that?*

No, not really. See now, you got to get that straight. Not everybody in PAP is actually dynamite convicts. They're people that most of us have decided that, either because they're never getting out or because they've got a huge amount of time left, that they're not a threat to our volunteers, and they bring another point of view. Some of them are guys that have never been in trouble before. Some of them are guys that have displayed all the other attributes that a convict's supposed to have. So, they carry themselves well, they're not a threat to our members, and they bring something to the group, so we let them participate.

You know, as long as they conduct themselves properly now, we try not to judge them too harshly based on their past. Like, who would I be to do that? You know, I killed somebody.

Hopefully, they're past that. I ain't never killed no old lady, no old couple, or just killed somebody because I wanted to get a car or some fucking thing. But them guys that have done that, man, you know, maybe they were young, whatever, but they've carried themselves well for a long enough period of time since then to give us a sense of what they're really all about.

Now, we're not always right, but so far we haven't lost any volunteers from being stalked or anything like that.

So, I don't know how to explain it. They aren't as respected as the dynamite convicts. You know, like, sometimes when we're sitting in the meetings and we're talking, there's actually a lot of guys in that room that I don't have much respect for at all. But they don't pose any threat to you guys, and they bring something to the group, so we allow them a place there.

*Well, I thought, though, that, in addition to people like that, who are just kind of tolerated for the reasons you're describing, I thought one or more of the people who's here for killing a woman rank among the inner circle of the convicts.*

Oh sure. But, I mean, there's a whole lot to a guy and a whole lot, you know, to his whole history. Things he's done, been there for, been there when the chips are down.

Mostly if a guy kills a woman, let's say, breaks into her home and kills her, most of them guys are persona non grata. But it depends. If a guy was committing a burglary and a woman walked in and he whacked her, you know, for whatever reason, but he don't rape her, abuse her in any way, we kind of figure, OK, hey, whatever reason he was using, man, let's say he was fucked up, but he's got a history of good criminal conduct in the joint, before and after that, so you kind of give him the benefit of the doubt.

You got to remember, most guys that are in the joint right now that do those crimes were on drugs and alcohol. And in a lot of cases, we only have their story, their explanation of what happened. So, based on their explanation, and the way they carry themselves, we might give them the benefit of the doubt.

There's some pretty good guys like that. There's a few of them, you know.

*You mean guys who've killed a woman, but are still highly regarded as convicts?*

Yeah.

*Well, Rico's an obvious example. I mean, there's a really good guy. And he's—*

Yeah.

*—well-respected as a convict.*

To a degree.

*Or Jeff. He's not an elite convict certainly, but by the same token he's not ostracized like rats and rapos.*

Yeah, but the difference with that kind of case is, like, Rico was in a relationship. Now, we pretty much stay out of that. What happens in a guy's relationship, you know, we don't judge that.

*Really?*

'Cause, you know, it's that love thing, and—

*So, like, an O.J. type crime wouldn't be looked down upon? He wouldn't be near the bottom of the pecking order?*

O.J. killing his ex-wife? No, he wouldn't have been looked down on. No.

You know, I hate to say this. [Smiles.] I mean, it makes me sound like a male chauvinist, and if you ever tell anybody—

*[Laughs.]*

—I will fucking kill you. But, the bottom line is—

*[Laughs.] Jerry says this into a tape recorder for a book.*

Yeah. [Laughs.] Yeah, don't ever let nobody hear this one.

But now me, I never beat up my wife or nothing. But sometimes, you can understand it. I mean, see, women have this thing about this last word. They want to talk, even when a guy says, "That's enough!"

Plus, you don't know, over a period of time, how much grief she caused him over his children—them making them fuck flicks when his kids were upstairs. We can't say how much that affected him. So, if he says that was enough to make him want to kill her, well then that would have been enough.

*This is O.J.?*

O.J. and them. Yeah, she made a fuck movie with somebody in the house, and took some lewd pictures and stuff. Remember? 'Cause he stumbled onto one of those pictures in his living room, and that's what sent him into the tirade where he broke the door and the cops came out there that time.

But we don't get into that. That's family business. You know what I'm saying? No, he wouldn't have been looked down on. I mean, like, to tell you the truth, if you kill a woman because she's leaving you or something, that's kind of weak. It's kind of weak. But it's not nothing that we look down on you about either. That's family business. That's your own affair.

*Well, obviously the whole idea underlying that is indefensibly sexist, but—*

Oh yeah. No doubt. That's why I said I'll fucking kill you if you tell anybody I said that. [Laughs.]

No, but what I'm saying is, I mean, what a guy does in his family and in his relationship, we don't try and judge that. You know, we kind of stay out of that area.

*We're solidly in the Land of Oz with a lot of this stuff. Can't endorse a lot of this stuff.*

I seen this comedian one time [laughs], he says, "In New York City alone last year, spousal abuse was up by fifteen thousand cases. I just couldn't get the bitch to shut up!" [Laughs.]

*This is some really classy material for the book, Jerry. [Laughs.]*

This is a comedian on TV! [Laughs.]

*All of your friends will be so proud when they read this.*

# JEFF—March 1999

*"But I've come to know what real friendship is in here. On the streets, I was a wannabe yuppie. You know, you drive around, and "We'll do lunch," or you socialize with the people from your church or whatever, but people are so superficial out there."*

T he following day, I was able to secure an interview with Jeff. For these daytime sessions, I reviewed all of the prisoner's letters and tapes ahead of time, and wrote up a few questions or topic areas I hoped to cover. Invariably we'd hit only a fraction of them, as I let the conversation take its natural course.

*First of all, describe how you're a different person today than when you entered prison.*

In three words or less… [Laughs.]

*That's right.*

Let's see. How am I different today than ten years ago? Well, I'm certainly much more aware of my shortcomings. I mean, perhaps the best thing that could have happened to me ten years ago was to go to prison for a couple years, just to, you know, like, be separated and have somebody beat me over the head and say, "You're fucking up," and "What's wrong with you?"

But, of course, I never would have agreed to that ten years ago. I would have thought they were crazy. But I needed a wake-up call, and unfortunately I got one a lot more severe than I would have anticipated.

I had an easy life out there. I was working good jobs, and before that I had it easy in college. I never was really challenged. So I'd go to work, and I'd fuck off. Or I'd go to the movies, and go mountain biking, and mountain climbing. As far as my marriage, my wife was pretty forgiving. I wasn't the most responsible husband.

Overall, I had it pretty easy. You know, I was spoiled, but I never would have admitted it then. It's one of those things where you just figure you've got it coming.

But then when things did turn down, when things started getting a little more difficult, and my marriage started having problems, and I started having problems at work and everything else, then I wasn't equipped to deal with it. I hadn't really had any prior experience in hardship, which, you know, is nothing you ever want to wish on yourself, but actually, that's the only way you grow, is through hardship.

We were watching *Schindler's List* Sunday night, saying, "Boy, we don't have it so bad in here." Have you seen that?

*I have.*

Yeah. So, I would say I've grown up. I mean, I'm thirty-eight now; I was twenty-eight then. So, those ten years, of course, added a lot of wisdom, and I've worked hard. I'd say mostly I'm just more aware of who I am, and why I do the things that I do.

You know, I had a lot of issues dealing with my father being an alcoholic and things like that that I never dealt with, and I didn't know that it was a problem, and maybe I could have went through my whole life not even realizing it was a problem. But then I happened to get into therapy there a little bit, and this woman just, like, dredged up all this stuff, and it's, like, "Well, now what are you going to do about it?"

*This is the therapist, the marriage counselor, from the church?*

Right.

*This is the therapist that you were not real impressed with.*

Yeah, she just sort of dredged up all this stuff, and it's, like, "Well, there you go," you know, "You're fucked up." [Laughs.] Not the best form of therapy. You know, not real productive.

But certainly I could have benefited from the right therapist. I mean, someone who explained, "Well," you know, "Some of these things, they don't seem to be bothering you, so don't worry about them. And if something is bothering you, then that's when you deal with it. But if something's not bothering you, then why dig it up?"

So, I guess that's the answer to that question.

*So on the whole, are you a better person as a result of your changes in the last ten years?*

Certainly. I would think so. I would hope so. I'd say I'm much more aware of myself and how my actions affect others. I try to conduct myself—somewhat successfully, not always—where my actions don't adversely affect others. Of course, it still happens, but at least I'm much more aware of that, whereas before, out there, I did what I wanted, and if somebody didn't like it, then, you know, that was too bad.

*Has prison adversely affected you as a human being in any ways? Because we hear about prison having the reputation of brutalizing people and making them worse than when they came in the door. Has that happened at all in your case, do you think?*

Oh, somewhat. I'm probably more racist than I ever used to be.

*Because of prison experiences?*

Right.

*Tell me about that.*

It's not justified, you know, in the real world, but in here, it's a fact of life. So obviously that's one negative change.

In other ways, I'm more tolerant. I mean, out there, these weren't the sort of people that I would be hanging out with, you know, as friends.

*Right.*

In here, my best friends are robbers and murderers. You know, the truth be known, the murderers are the best people in here. That doesn't justify their crimes, but generally the killers weren't leading a criminal lifestyle. For the most part, they had a job, or at least they were growing dope or something, but they weren't out robbing and burglarizing people's houses, and they weren't going out and robbing 7-Elevens so they can get another fix. You know, the dope fiends.

The dope fiends are the least trustworthy people, because they'll do anything to get a high. They'll sell their mom out to get another fix. And they take that mentality in here the same way. I've had bad experiences with that.

Whereas, say, with the murderers, it was an incident where, you know, something happened, either out of anger or out of business dealings or whatever, that necessitated, in their mind, killing someone. But, other than that, they were fairly trustworthy people I suppose.

*I was talking to one of the prisoners about the pecking order and the hierarchy and such within prison, and I asked him if it's possible to just not play the game at all. Because in a lot of social situations, you have the in-crowd and you have the people who are kind of ostracized and looked down upon, but then you usually have people who aren't even aware or don't care that that's going on. Like in high school or college or whatever, sure you have the beautiful people at the top, the ones that have all the social advantages and all that, and you have the people who would like to be that, but are ostracized and looked down on, but you also have a huge segment of people who don't even care about those social games, because they're off studying or living their life, or, you know, they don't care about that. And I asked him, is that the case in the prison hierarchy? Are there people who are independent of it and don't really play the game, don't really win or lose at the game? And he said to some extent that goes on. He said, "You know, Jeff's sort of independent of it all. He's sort of outside of the game; he's somebody who doesn't really win or lose at the game." What's your response to that?*

Personally, or for prison as a whole?

*Is that true of you?*

Well, I don't, like, hang out with the PAP guys. They sit over here in the office all morning long, and, you know, I'll go in there once in awhile, but, frankly, I've got better things to do than sit in there and talk crime stories. I don't have any good crime stories. I mean, it's fun to go in there and bullshit once in awhile, but I'd rather do other stuff.

And sometimes, I guess, that's viewed as, well, maybe I think I'm better than other guys in here. But it's not true. It's just that I'd rather spend my time doing other things. I paint. I play keyboard music. I've got a keyboard in my house. And I write and I read a lot. So that doesn't leave a lot of time for other stuff. And I exercise; I go out to the yard.

There's a story my cellee and a buddy wrote, and they've got a line in there that says if you're a loner in prison, you're an outcast among outcasts. Which, you know, is not a real great place to be. But there are men in here like that who could care less about who's doing what.

In the old days—though I wasn't really around then—but, when there was riots and things, you know, if you were a loner, you were one of the first that was getting taken down, because nobody was protecting you. So, it's like, you're just nobody, if nobody's going to stand up for you. I mean, you didn't piss anybody off, but, well, if you've got a TV or something, then they'll just take it. And if you're in the way, then they'll just take you out, because they know there's no force behind you.

Nowadays, there's not that going on, so it's much easier to be separate, because you don't have that fear of retribution.

You know, I probably have more friends in here than I have on the streets. I mean, I had a lot of acquaintances on the streets, but as far as true friends, like Jimi or Rico, I have more in here. I consider Rico a true friend, even though I don't think he'll cop to it. [Laughs.]

*[Laughs.]*

He's looked out for me quite a bit.

*Sure.*

But I've come to know what real friendship is in here. On the streets, I was a wannabe yuppie. You know, you drive around, and "We'll do lunch," or you socialize with the people from your church or whatever, but people are so superficial out there. At least the people I was with.

I think the upper middle class tends to be more that way, whereas, you know, blue collar people are more honest, hard-working. And I never was around those kind of people, and in fact I looked down on them, "[Grumble] blue collar...!" you know, when actually they're the most genuine people around. I mean, really, when it comes down to it. You know, hard-working, honest people. They're much more honorable.

Does that answer your question? [Laughs.]

*Well, mostly. Directly or indirectly. But let me ask it this way: Where do you fit in the prison hierarchy, in the pecking order?*

I'm not at the top. I'm not at the bottom. So, I'm somewhere floating in the middle. As I say, I've got some good friends, but I'm not a leader or anything like that. But I'm not looked down on, you know. I'm just somewhere in the middle.

*OK. I want to talk also about how you adjusted, originally, because obviously you're coming from a very different world, a very different lifestyle. As you say, you have less in common with the people in prison than most incoming prisoners would. As a "square," which all the prisoners are going to think somebody like you is,—*

Oh yeah.

*—as a square entering prison,—*

That's what Rico calls me.

*—were you at risk? Were you victimized? Did you have problems? What was life like for you in your early days in prison?*

I came into Walla Walla in Nineteen ninety, and that had just sort of passed over into the new era where anybody can do whatever they want, with no fear of retribution. In the old days, like, all the rats and snitches, if they told on somebody, then somebody came after them and did nasty things to them.

I guess I didn't know any better in Nineteen ninety. Say it had been ten years earlier, I'm sure I would have got rode up on, and guys'd be pressuring me for money and everything, you know. And I don't know how I would have reacted, 'cause I didn't have to go through that.

But by Nineteen ninety, there wasn't much of that going on. I mean, just because there was such control in the prisons, and they had all their snitches out, and the snitches all had protection, and there's cameras everywhere. All the predators were much more reluctant to do anything, because the system had changed so much.

I had the fortunate experience of moving in with an old convict in Walla Walla. He was an "old school" convict, and he sort of took me under his wing and tried to point me in the right direction. So, I was fortunate to have that.

And Rico, you know, he looked out for me. I mean, he'll tell you some stories about how he heard guys talking about me, and he's, like, "Lay off that guy. He's just a square."

And I'm sure there have been a lot of things that I don't even know about. Like the other night, Bill was talking about his cellee[*] that was hearing things.

Have you heard this story?

---

[*]Not Jerry. Evidently at the time of the story, Bill was celled up with some other prisoner.

*No, I don't think so.*

Well, I was playing my tape recorder one night, and whenever you run your tape at fast forward, you get that real high pitched sound. Anyway, at that time, my cell was right next to Bill's. And his cellee was a little unbalanced. He was an old guy, a murderer, and he was real unbalanced. And he kept hearing this tape noise, and he's going, "Ohhh, they're talking about my son!" and he's wigging out. And, "In the morning, I'm going over there and kill him!" You know, like, serious shit.

But Bill tells him, "Calm down," you know, "That's nothing. That's nobody." And he talked him out of coming after me.

I never even heard that story till a few weeks ago. Never knew I was in any danger.

*[Laughs.] Yeah.*

Just little things like that that you never even know about.

*So, to some extent, it sounds like you just had good luck with timing, that a person like yourself would have been a lot worse off in prison, say, in the Seventies or Eighties than the Nineties.*

Well, you know, back then, guys roll up on you the first week, and, they'll try and take your shit, and either you're going to fight for it or not. If you don't fight for it, you're a punk, and if you do fight for it, you get the shit beat out of you, but at least you're fighting for it.

You know, I never was much of a fighter, so I'm glad I didn't have to go through that.

*Yeah.*

Let's put it this way: there's a lot of guys in here now that wouldn't have made it back then. It was a different world in prison back then, and you had to be a certain kind of person to survive. I mean, you look at someone like Jerry. You know Jerry's done a lot of fighting in his time. I mean, you just know that. And it's real unfortunate, 'cause he's got stories back from juvenile, when they used to beat the shit out of him. And, you know, it's like a dog. You keep kicking your dog, and pretty soon he's pretty ornery.

*Right.*

It's no wonder guys get out of prison and kill people. I mean, it's real unfortunate.

So anyways, I wouldn't say I'm a loner. But there are guys in here that are. There's a guy that I work with, as a matter of fact, that, in all the time I've been here, over three years, I've never seen him anywhere except at work. Never in the yard. Never in the chow hall. Doesn't eat in the chow hall. Lives off what he buys from the store.

I mean, there's guys that that's all they do. They just sit in their house and do whatever they do, and they work and that's it.

He never comes out here to the Prison Activities Building. Not PAP, not the library, nothing. I mean, it's weird, because he used to be quite active. He actually was in PAP, and a lot of the other programs. And he was married. But his wife ended up leaving him, and that was it, and now he's just a recluse. Real intelligent. He's a very intelligent person. But he never leaves his house except to go to work.

*You mentioned that when you first entered prison, from fairly early on you had sort of a mentor. You were rooming with somebody who could teach you the ropes. That relates to one of the questions I intended to ask you, which was how does a person learn the ropes coming in? Especially a so-called "square." I mean, I guess I know some small amount of that stuff just from being in PAP and spending time with you guys, but if I had been arrested and sent to prison before having gone through this experience, I would have broken all kinds of rules without realizing I was doing it. I would have had no idea that if you say this or do that, then it means you're a rat, or you're weak, or you're a despicable person in one way or another. How did you not fall prey to that?*

There were a few times where, in other situations, I would have gotten my ass beat. And rightly so. I'd be being a smart ass, or just disrespecting somebody, and not really even realizing it. But I was lucky enough to get away with it, because as I say, by the time I entered the system, there's nowhere to beat somebody up and not get caught any more. You know, had there been, I would have been.

*So you never had to go into protective custody or anything like that?*

No, no.

I mean, there's guys that come in and get threatened, and they go right into PC. And, you know, a lot of them'll be child molesters or rapists, and somebody knows that they are, and harasses them, and they're, like, "Well I'll check into PC."

But also a lot of guys will run up gambling debts, drug debts, and then they check in.

You know, I used to work in the carpenter crew at Walla Walla—I'd go in and fix stuff— and we'd go over into PC, and fix shelves and tables and whatever. And sometimes there'd be guys that you always wondered where they went, you know, and it's like, "Oh, here you are!"

*Oh.*

You see guys over there in PC that you never knew where they went, and it's like, "Oh wow, imagine that!"

*So is PC typically a separate wing of the prison?*

It's a separate prison of the prison.

*Does every prison have a separate PC section?*

There's not one here.

*What happens if a guy here is in danger? Is he transferred to another institution?*

They send him somewhere else.

*OK.*

There's the hole here. You know, you can, like, check into the hole. You can tell them, "Somebody's going to stab me and murder me." They'll take you to the hole, and then they'll decide. They might just send you to another institution, just to the normal population in another institution.

Anyway, what was your question? PC? You know,—

*Well, there have been many, we were talking about how you adjusted to prison initially, since I would think you'd be something like me in not knowing the rules ahead of time, not knowing what counts as disrespect and such.*

Well, it really helps to be observant. And certainly a lot of times, I've done things where I was oblivious to what I was saying or doing. And, as I say, I had a few people, you know, tell me, "Don't do that; do this," or, "Watch out for this guy," or, "If a cop talks to you this way, do this" or, "Don't talk to that guy."

Interestingly enough, they used to have clerks for the sergeants. Well, actually it used to be they had clerks everywhere, and the inmates ran all kinds of stuff, and they slowly did away with those. But I was the last clerk for the sergeant in the wing I was in in Walla Walla.

And at the time, it was like, "Oh, cool, I got a job," you know. Now, I would never take a job like that, just because of the implications. You know, you're in the sergeant's office, and anybody that hangs out in the sergeant's office is just construed a certain way. It's not where you want to be, you know.

*Oh, so it's assumed that you're a rat.*

Well, I mean, the implication's there. But at the time, it never even crossed my mind that there was even any wrong associated with that. At that time, you know, there was always guys who did that kind of job, so I didn't think of it as something that was looked down on.

*Yeah.*

But there's that implication, like, "Well, why is he in the sergeant's office?"

*How perceptive, and observant, and mentally sharp can you be entering prison, given what else is going on in your life, and what you're dealing with, when you're coming off having murdered somebody and almost committing suicide? Are you in any state of mind to be in a new situation, and to be real perceptive and sharp about it?*

No. Plus, when you're in jail, they're telling you stories about "Prison's like this," and "Prison's like that," trying to make you even more scared and confused.

I was actually expecting prison to be much worse than it was, because, of course, they tell you all the bad stories. But I got there, and I saw an ice machine. I thought, "You know, a prison with an ice machine can't be that bad." [Laughs.]

*[Laughs.]*

I mean, after all the things they told me, and after all the things you see on TV, they got an ice machine. I was, like, "Wow!" you know. That, and they had cable; I figured they'd have, like, three channels.

*Right.*

But they got cable with ESPN and everything. It's like, "Oh, this can't be that bad."

So, I was expecting worse. I don't remember being real scared; I just remember being apprehensive. Fortunately, it wasn't as bad as, like, ten years earlier, when they just throw you in and tell you, "See you later." You know, where you got to go find your own house and everything. Now they just assign you to a house.

As I say, I had the good fortune of being in with guys that were pretty decent. But other people, especially earlier, had very different experiences arriving at Walla Walla. It's four to a cell, and so there's three guys already there, and then you. And they grill you, try to intimidate you. "Who are you?!" "What are you in for?!" "What are you doing?!"

Rico had to go through that. Luckily, I didn't have that experience. Of course, he was much more prepared to deal with something like that than me, 'cause he had had a lot more street experience.

*Have you ever exploited or victimized someone weaker than you in prison?*

Not that I know of. I haven't had any, like, little blond boys in my cell. [Laughs.]

*[Laughs.] Nothing that you've been ashamed of in retrospect, where you wish you hadn't taken advantage of a situation or anything?*

No. Not that I remember. I mean, I'm sure someone might think differently, but no.

*So it sounds like you've kind of avoided being at either end of the nasty stuff we hear about in prison. You've never really been a victimizer or a victim.*

No. Well, I've never been in a fight in prison.

*Never been in a single physical fight your whole time in prison? In Walla Walla, or—?*

No.

*How common is that, that people can exist this long in this system and not have to fight?*

I would say three-fourths of the guys here have never been in a fight. Well, except for the old timers. The old timers, most of them, of course, have, but I would say, of the people that have been in less than ten years, three-quarters of them have never been in a fight.

I mean, I have yet to see a fight here in WSR in three years. At Walla Walla, they're about once a week, at least when I've been there.

You know, it's not like when there were the gangs. I mean, there are still some gang things, but in the old days, it was all about gangs. I mean, you know, the whites and the blacks and the Indians, and the Aryan Brothers, and the motorcycle gangs, and all the rest. I mean, they were always fighting over their territory, their turf, or somebody got in some kind of debt to somebody, and so they have to come after the guy.

Now most of the fights are just, you know, somebody elbowed somebody on the basket-ball court and talked bad to him, and that kind of stuff. It's just little things.

*It sounds like things are a lot tamer than the reputation of prison. It's interesting, I talk to guys, and it seems like half of you say that a lot is being hidden from us in PAP and the class, that "Boy, things are so much worse than that! But, there's a lot of women in the class, and everyone's hesitant to really go into it. You don't want to scare people away," and all that. And the other half of you are telling me, "Oh, the class and such is kind of sensationalized. They make it sound real dramatic and dangerous and evil and violent. But especially nowadays, it's not anywhere near that big a deal. It's mostly not that bad." So I'm getting both sides. It sounds you come down on the side of things being not nearly as horrendous in prison as we might have been led to believe by the media and such. Is that accurate?*

Well, there's certainly a lot of things that have gone on that I don't know about, because I'm not involved in dope deals and all that kind of thing. I know there are some things that go on here that you hear about, but, you know, nobody's been stabbed since I've been here, at least that I know of.

Walla Walla, there was one guy got beat in the head with a rock. That happened right in front of me. It happened so fast that I didn't even know it happened. There was a guy walking along, and all of a sudden, he's laying there on the ground, and there's, like, blood coming out of his head. You know, of course you just keep walking. You just—

*Did you see someone actually strike him, or—?*

No. As I say, it happened so fast, but somebody else told me that somebody had had a big sock—a big rock in a sock, you know—but it was so fast, I was just, like, "Whew!"

*Oh.*

That's the only thing I've ever actually seen. You see a few fist fights, but that's about it.

*So you think if a person kind of minds his own business and does his own time, and he's not involved in drug deals, and he's not trying to play his way up the prison hierarchy, and he's not a rat, and, you know, he's not going out of his way to cross people and disrespect people, but just kind of keeps to himself, does his own time, does his own thing, is he mostly safe, nowadays?*

Yeah, and I would say even back in the old days, if a guy minded his own business, and, you know, wasn't a rat or rapo, for the most part they were pretty much left alone, except in a riot or something. Then it's just a free-for-all.

But, you know, there are a lot of stories from Walla Walla. Certainly there was a lot more stabbings back then. Guys I know well tell me that it happened plenty. And, guys getting raped, and stuff like that. For that matter, there were more escape attempts, guys digging tunnels and all. There was certainly a lot more of that going on back then.

There was just so much less control in general. They didn't have UAs. They didn't have cameras. They didn't have all the fences. So, there was all kind of places you could go, and nobody's going to see you. You could go shoot up all day long.

And the cops, even if they saw you smoking dope, they don't care. They just wanted to do their eight hours and go home. Now all the cops are trying to control everybody. You know, back then, as long as you weren't, like, overtly killing somebody or threatening the cops, I mean, even if you're boxing or something, they're, like, "Well," you know, "Just don't hurt him."

*[Laughs.] A lot of the old timers seem to miss the old days, at least the ones who were on top. They liked having that extra freedom of being able to run things, and exploit people, and so on. But I*

*would think that for most people, most prisoners, it would have been much more difficult back then than today.*

Well, the only benefit from the old system is that there was more integrity, because, you know, a guy had to stand up for himself. Now, it's more like general society, where a person can say one thing and do another, and people don't necessarily figure out as quickly who's real and who's not.

But, back then, it was whatever you are, you are. I guess there was more integrity, as far as, you know, a guy gives you his word or says he's going to do something, then you know he's going to do it. And if he doesn't do it, then he's ostracized or there's retribution. You know, now a guy says he's going to do something and doesn't do it, it's, like, well, what are you going to do if you don't like it?

And so there was much more accountability for your actions. So that part of it, it forced you to be a stronger person, or a better person. But on the other hand, that system led to far more abuse, where there was so much more opportunity for victimizing people, and taking advantage of them. You know, it's one thing to have power, but then to use it inappropriately—

*Yeah.*

It's like the Nazis, they—once you get that much power, like in *Schindler's List*, you know, "Well, let's just start shooting people. What the hell? I get a rush off it."

*So the violence and the homosexual rape and such that people might associate with prison is not so prevalent any more, at least in this state.*

Yeah, there's much less of that. But it happens. There are, like, known predators that go after the little boys and get them to move in, and then it's no big surprise what happens.

*Is it coercive? 'Cause, I've had people tell me stories where it was more like these people enticed the kids in, and they—it's more of an exchange, where—*

Right, they buy them—

*—they give them this and that—*

—store, and they, you know, treat them good and protect them, and—

*So, it's kind of pseudo-rape, or sort of semi-coercive, or—?*

Well, it's prostitution, you know, whatever you want to call it. Coercion. Prostitution.

*How about just out-and-out, unambiguously coercive, rape? Does that still happen in prison?*

Not much. Very rarely, you know. I mean, at Walla Walla, I imagine it happens more so than here. But, you know, it's real rare, very rare. Compared to what you hear, where people make it sound like it happens all the time, no. You know, it's rare.

*When are you likely to be released?*

Twenty Sixteen.

*No realistic chance of earlier release?*

No, my appeals are all pretty much done. There's always a chance, but—

*So, that would be your earliest possible parole? That's when you first—?*

Well, it wouldn't be for parole. I'm under the SRA's sentencing guidelines.

*So it wouldn't just be that you'd be eligible to get out then, but you would get out then.*

All things,—

*Unless you get into more trouble between now and then.*

All things being equal, yeah.

*I know it's a long time in the future, but do you think you'd keep your past secret in your dealings with people in the outside world? How open would you be with people in your life about where you've spent the last twenty or thirty years?*

Well, certainly whoever I was close to would know. But it's not the kind of thing that you advertise, because people will never accept that kind of thing, just on the outset. You know, if a guy walks up to you and says, "Hi!" you know, "I'm a murderer! But I'm a nice guy!" I mean, there's always going to be a prejudice against ex-cons. I'm not going to volunteer any information. I mean, if somebody asks, you know, I might go into it.

*How will that affect your life on the outside, having that in your past, and some people know about it and some people don't. How do you think you're going to deal with deciding whom to tell and when, and all that?*

I can't say. I mean, it's too far away. It's not really worth talking about.

*Do you ever focus on things far in the future? Do you think about getting out?*

Well, sure, yeah. But it's not something that I dwell on.

*You don't think in terms of specifics?*

Well, like, you know, my daughter'll be twenty-six years old—those kind of things.

*At present, your daughter lives with your wife's family, and you're prevented from having direct contact with her, right?*

Right.

*Now, will that change when she's of legal age? Will she be able to decide for herself when and whether she wants to be in contact with you?*

Well, certainly when she's eighteen, she can do whatever she wants. That's another ten years. I'm hoping when she's eighteen that we can establish some sort of correspondence.

*Do you think that there's any potential you'll have significant contact with her before eighteen? Do you think that your wife's family will relent, or anything will change?*

I hope so. It's hard to say.

A friend of mine from work just went to his parole hearing. He's in on second degree murder; he's done twenty years now. He first was up for parole after thirteen years. So he's been up two or three times now. And, through conversations with the parole board and his lawyer and everything, things looked real positive. They were going to give him a release date. And then, the victim's family comes in, and they go on and on and on, crying and bawling, and all that. And they give him three more years.

So, it all depends on how long they can hold onto that hate. I mean, you know, sooner or later, you got to let it go. They're still that upset after twenty years. That's not healthy.

I mean, you know, it's not for me to say, but I would hope, sooner or later, they'd learn to let go of that.

*Knowing what you do about recidivism, and which people seem to come back and which people don't, do you expect that you'll ever be back in prison after you serve your time for this crime?*

No.

*You're confident?*

Yeah.

*Why?*

Well, actually, I would like to be living elsewhere. So, I wouldn't be in the United States, so I couldn't come to prison.

*Are you considering leaving the country?*

Well, I don't know. It depends on what my daughter's doing.
I would rather live somewhere else.

*Other countries have prisons of course.*

OK, I won't be in an American prison. If I go to prison, it's going to be somewhere else.

*But do you think you'd re-offend? Do you think you'd end up in prison, wherever you were living?*

No, I wouldn't think so. No, I have no plans for that. Of course, no one ever does. But no, no. There's no point.

*No point?*

I mean, if I'm going to lead a criminal lifestyle, then I would hope I'd at least be smart enough to, you know, be good at it, and get away with it.
But, I don't have any plans yet to lead a criminal lifestyle.

*So, do you think it's mostly the nature of your crime, that it was the kind of emotional, one-time only thing that usually people who commit that kind of crime don't repeat? I mean, why is it you feel you'll be one of the few people who doesn't come back to prison?*

Well, like you say, it was a one-time thing. I wasn't alcoholic or—you know, a lot of guys have so much problems with drugs and alcohol that they're sober in here, but then once they get out, they go back to it. Or they don't have any money, or they have control problems, where, like, you know, their life's not going the way they want it, and it's, like, "Boy, if I could just rob that bank and get me twenty grand," you know, "I'll be set."

You know, you can never say absolute not. The people who say absolutely not are deluding themselves. It's a whole lot easier to get back to prison than to stay out. But, I don't anticipate leading any sort of lifestyle that would lead me to that.

*Now, it sounds like you've dealt with some of the issues from your past that led up to your crime. Do you think that the part of you, the side of you that was capable of that kind of unpredictable rage, and that kind of violence that exploded once in your life so far, is that gone? Or is there any chance of an eruption like that five years, ten years, twenty years from now?*

It's absolutely not gone. Guys who say, "Oh, that side of me's gone," or "It doesn't exist" are full of shit. It's still there. I mean, it's part of me. But the thing was, at that time, I never knew it was there.

There's so many people out there that don't know that that exists inside them. They say, "Well I could never hurt anybody," you know, "I don't have any kind of violent side." But everybody does. It just depends on how much control a person has, or what sort of situation they're in. You know, most people never get to that kind of situation, where those sorts of emotions become so intense. And a lot of people, even if they do, they have the control to get out of the situation. If you get those kind of emotions to come up, and you don't have the control to contain them, that's when you're in trouble.

And, I didn't know I had those kind of emotions, and I didn't have the control to do anything about them. You know, now I know they're there. They're always there.

But it's like a big dog in your yard. I mean, if you come up to the house and you don't know it's there, it comes out and bites you. But, now that you know this big dog's in the yard, you know, you throw him a steak now and then, just to keep him happy.

You got to know that that rage, that potential, is there, and to anticipate it and control it. You can actually even use it to your advantage, where you use that energy for positive things.

It's, like, Jerry Mac. I don't know if you've ever seen him get mad, but he can get mad. But, you know, he uses it as a protective device. It's like [snaps fingers], you know, like that. And he uses it for, like, his armament.

Most people aren't able to turn it on and off like that. But, you know, his lifestyle has led him to have that option. I mean, it's a survival instinct.

You know, when I was growing up, I never expressed anger. I was always repressing it. I never got mad. My father was a very non-expressive person. He just, like, wouldn't get mad or sad or happy or anything. He just didn't do anything. And I was sort of like that. I never knew how to express it. Instead of getting mad, I was holding it inside. And that's very unhealthy.

I think it's a disservice to kids when, you know, a kid gets mad or they're crying, we tell little boys not to cry. Or we tell them, "Don't get mad at your sister." I mean, it's a natural thing, assuming that it comes out at the appropriate times.

*Right.*

But, it should never be repressed, because those are things that are just part of the person. And you start trying to repress them and stuff them back in, and then it just backfires.

So, to answer your question, yeah, it is there. But I know it's there. You know, so it's like this big dog I have, and I feed him a steak now and then.

*Are people in your life at risk? I mean, let's say you get remarried. Should a woman in your life like that be any more concerned—you know, justifiably concerned—about your potential violence than of just any average person off the street who's never committed murder?*

Well, certainly any woman who wasn't would be suspect. I mean, you know, naturally you don't marry someone who's killed their wife and then think, "Well, gee, I wonder if this guy's got a problem?"

*Well, it's to be expected they'd be concerned, but would it be justified? I mean, are they, in fact, at greater risk being with you? Are they vulnerable to violence in a way that they wouldn't be with the average person?*

I would say no.

Since I've been in prison, there's been a couple instances, you know, where I've been in situations where I wanted to do bad things to someone. And I didn't. I mean, it's, like, when I get to that point, I know what's going on, and I'll leave, or I'll avoid the situation. So, I can recognize it. As I say, the most dangerous thing is not knowing about it. 'Cause then when it shows up, it's overwhelming.

But there have been a couple instances in the past ten years where I've been tempted.

*You were able to control it?*

You know, I recognize it. And I realize that I'm in that situation where I'd better leave, or do something about it.

*Here's a question that the answer is probably insultingly obvious, but it's worth stating explicitly anyway, just to hear how you will articulate your answer: Are you remorseful for your crime?*

Well, if I could trade places with my wife, and I'd be dead, and she'd be—not in prison—but living a normal life, then I'd do it.

During my trial, I was viewed as having no remorse, because I wasn't crying, and—Did you ever see *Shawshank Redemption?*

*Yes I did.*

At the beginning—excellent movie—but in the beginning, where Andy's going to trial, and the judge is telling him he's a cold evil bastard who murdered his wife,—

*But in his case, he's innocent anyway, so there's a reason not to show remorse.*

Right, but I mean, that's just sort of his persona,—

*OK.*

—that he just didn't show a lot of remorse. Plus, you know, he was thinking about whacking her, but it turns out some other guy did it.

In my case, I'm certainly not innocent, that's not what I'm saying. But during this Restorative Justice class I took in here recently, we had to tell our stories, and that was very emotional. I hadn't told this story to anyone besides you except this class. Well, I had told bits and pieces, but not the whole story. And that was a year and a half ago. So, it was, like, eight years after the fact. And there was so much, during the telling of the story, there were so many things that came out that I had forgotten or—you know, I started crying.

I mean, it was a terrible, awful thing that I did. I can never change that. My wife's family's destroyed. My daughter's an orphan. You know, it's the most horrible thing that anybody could do to anybody else. And, you know, there's nothing I could ever say to anyone that's ever going to make them better. I mean, I've tried, and it's totally ineffective to say, "Well, I'm sorry, and da-da-da." I'm hoping one day that I can attempt to tell my daughter that. And, you know, maybe she'll be at a point where she can understand that.

But, you know, I am sorry. I mean, just saying "I'm sorry," doesn't sound like that much, but it's taken me this long to understand the pain of my wife's family. I mean, especially going through the Restorative Justice class, there were stories about families whose children had been murdered. I'm listening to their stories, and, you know, this one lady, she was, like, sixty-something, and her daughter had been murdered when she was in her twenties. Her little girl. And forty years later, you know, she's still very upset about it.

I mean, nobody ever forgets, no matter what, or how many years. You never forget, and you never get over that loss, no matter what. And I know my wife's family never will.

*If there turns out to be some kind of afterlife, and your wife is still existent and conscious, and can hear what you're saying today,—?*

You're a Mormon! You're an undercover Mormon! [Laughs.] You're,—

*That's right. [Laughs.]*

—you're from the church! Officer!

*[Laughs.]*

You're an impostor!

*Do you think you could express your feelings to her? If you ever saw your wife again in another form, or she's somehow listening to this interview, do you think you'd know what to say to her?*

I could hope for the chance. If you follow the Mormon doctrine, then, you know, she's over there, and I'm going to be over here, and that's that.

*Never mind the Mormons; it's just a hypothetical.*

[Laughs.] I don't know. I mean, that question's beyond the scope of this. I mean, it's unanswerable.

*I'm not asking you if that's going to happen. I'm saying, hypothetically, what would you do if it did? What would you say to your wife?*

Well, I'm saying that what would I say is unanswerable, 'cause it's not something you can just make up, just say something and sound trite. It's sort of trivializing it.

*Trivializing?*

Yeah, so I don't have an answer for that.

*What do you miss most about the outside world?*

I've got a calendar on my wall from southern Utah. You ever been there?

*No. I've passed through the northern half of the state. I spent a few days there, but mostly in the northern half of the state.*

Well, stop down in the southern side. Arches, or Bryce Canyon, or Zion Canyon.
I've got a picture of an area in Canyonlands, and there's a big rock here, and there's some little rocks in the background, and there's a big juniper tree growing out like this—sort of a scrubby little tree. And this rock's over here, and a little boulder down here.

And it's, like, this rock is so perfect. I've been in places exactly like that. You can smell it. I mean, just the way the picture is, you know what it smells like. And there's just sort of a storm in the background. It's this time of the year, in March.

You know, it's the smells. I mean, the smells of rocks, and dirt, and trees, and scrubby old juniper trees, and sagebrush. I mean, those kind of things.

*From what you've told me, you went on a lot of camping trips. You spent a lot of time outdoors.*

Yeah, so I miss the outdoors mostly. I mean, other than my family. As far as just everyday stuff that you miss, rocks and dirt and, you know, going out and digging in the garden.

Trees. We don't have trees. You can see the trees, but we don't have any trees.

*You touched briefly on racial issues in prison earlier. What are race relations like in here, compared to the streets?*

Well, as I say, nowadays they're much better. Back in the old days, they had race riots. I wasn't here then, but I've heard all the stories.

When I worked in Texas, I worked with a lot of well-educated blacks. And, you know, I really enjoyed it. I had good friends, and we'd go out to dinner and stuff. And, you know, I really got along with them. But before that when I was in Utah, there were no blacks hardly, so I never really grew up with any other races, except, you know, a few Mexicans and Indians.

But here in prison, of course, you get the worst crimes. You get the gang bangers, and the drive-by shooters, and the rap stars, and that kind of thing. And they're always much louder than white people. You know, it's just their nature. They get on the phone and talk loud, and they're playing loud rap music, and they do a lot of disrespectful things. You know, they'll stand around in the middle of the area where you're trying to get somewhere, and you have to go around them.

You know, guys like Henry, of course, they're older and they were around before all the gang bangers and all that kind of stuff. It's mostly the youngsters I'm talking about. The youngsters come in, and, you know, they don't care about anything. That's the way they were out there, and in here they're the same way. You know, they'll see you've got a bar of soap there and they'll take it, just 'cause it's there. There's no respect for anything.

So, it's mostly the respect issue. And that's what I was saying, back in the old days, the respect issue was much more important. You know, a guy took a bar of soap, he might get stabbed for it.

Just because it's not the soap, it's the respect thing, that he thinks he can just take anything he wants. That kind of retaliation doesn't happen nowadays, so there's much more disrespect, where guys will do things, and they know there's no retribution. Because, yeah, you can go beat him up, but then you're going to the hole, and you lose your job, and there's much more consequences.

# HENRY—March 1999

"When guys leave out of here, or any place else I've ever been, you know, they say, 'Hey man, I'm leaving tomorrow. What can I do for you?' you know, 'Hey, give me a call when I get out there.'

"I tell 'em, 'Hey, look buddy. Look. I don't want your phone number. I don't want to call you. The only thing that I want you to do for me, and I'm serious about this, is just do one thing.' 'What's that?' 'Just go out and be a good ambassador. That's all I ask you to do. I don't want you to send me nothing. I don't want you to try to contact no one for me. I don't need any of that. Just be a good ambassador. And if you do that, not only are you doing it for me, but you're doing it for thousands and thousands more other people.'"

I wrapped things up with Jeff, and conversed on tape that same day with Henry.

*Henry, why don't you update me on the prospects of your getting out?*

Well, at the moment, I was supposed to have gone back to court three weeks ago—yeah, three or four weeks ago. Anyway, I found out that the court date was set back, simply because the prosecuting attorney failed to give the court some information, some notes. And the following week after that, my attorney went on vacation. So, I should have called him last week, but I have to call him this week some time, and find out where we are now.

But, it's the same old daily grind, you know. It's the same as my mom always said: "It's easy to get in trouble, but it's hard to get out." [Laughs.]

*[Laughs.] Given all of the available evidence of what's going on with the situation, what's your best estimate, your best guess, as to when you'll be in the free world again?*

I would really hate to even entertain that thought, because of the prospects of disappointment to myself or to someone else. So, I just play it by ear, day by day.

*Yeah.*

And, once I get into the courts, back into the court system, then I can have more of a vision of where things stand. But, just from this point here, I can't say.

*Once you're out, will you ever re-offend? Do you expect to ever be back in prison?*

Not only do I not expect to be back in prison, I can say for a certainty that I know I won't be back in prison. Unless someone harms my family, or something of that nature. But just for committing a crime? No. No. I'm [laughs], I'm too old for that.

*[Laughs.]*

I'm about crimed out, man.

*So, if you are released, you pose no threat to society.*

No. I could be an asset to society.

You know what I'd like to do? I would really like to get out of here tomorrow—and I was just discussing it with my wife on our trailer visit—I'd like to open up a tamale stand. Just a little tamale stand. And in the summertime, sell, you know, cold beverages and stuff. And in wintertime, sell spiced wine. Spiced wines, yeah. That's what I'd like to do. I don't want nothing elaborate. Just a little tamale stand.

*Yeah.*

Yeah. That's what I told her, that if I got out of here any time in the near future, that that's what I was going to do. That's what I plan to do.

*Do you see your future here in Washington doing something like that, or where would you be?*

Well, no, because I don't plan to live here in Washington. I'm going home. Going back to Louisiana. Going home.

*Where in Louisiana?*

I'm from northwestern Louisiana, right up from Texas.

Yeah, I can't see myself getting rich doing it, but I could see myself making a modest living. It'd be an income.

*Do you still have people back in Louisiana?*

Oh yes. Yeah. In fact, the only people I have out here is my wife and kids. My mom and step-dad was out here, but they both passed away. Yeah, I'm the only one here, other than my wife and kids.

*Let's talk about recidivism in general, not so much in your case, because, as you say, you're not intending to go out and resume a life of crime—*

No.

*You're a little past that point.*

Yeah.

*But, what do you think are the most important factors in determining if somebody will re-offend, or whether they'll be an asset to society once they leave a place like this?*

Well, actually, I honestly believe that the recidivism rate is so high simply because when a person comes to prison—Take these young kids, say, you know, these young guys, like we just got a load of them in the other day, yesterday in fact. They come in. They do their time, whatever the amount they have. I mean, if you're doing a day in prison, it's too much, you know. But if it's a day, or a year, or fifteen, they come in. They do that. And they have nothing in between, from the time they left the streets until it's time for them to go back. There's nothing in between. It's a void. It's just like they step into a web of cotton candy, you know, and they're steady moving, but they're not going any place. You know, they're just living off imagination.

And once they get out, then the reality hits them, as, "Hey!" you know, "This is where I came from. OK, now, what I got to do is I got to move from this block here where I was selling crack, and I got to go two blocks down." You know, not realizing that the same people that enforced the law on you on that one block, they're doing the same thing on the next two.

So, as long as there's people going to prison, and not having anything to do, as far as rehabilitation, there's always going to be a high recidivism rate.

I mean, I don't understand why the lawmakers don't see it. From the Forties, Fifties, and Sixties and Seventies, the recidivism rate wasn't as high as it is now. But, you know, you had crime, and guys would do their time and get out, and a lot of them would stay out. I know a lot of guys that came in in the Sixties and Seventies and, hey, that was enough. They're out there; you know, they never came back.

But now, in the last, say, five years especially, I have seen and heard of so many guys that have been released and are already back in the system. If they're not here, maybe they're at Walla Walla, McNeil, or some place else, or they're in the county jail waiting to come back.

I mean, why leave, then? Shit, you know, why leave? I mean, at least here, you don't have to pay no rent. If you don't have a job, you don't have to do nothing. Why go back out there at all if you're just going to turn around and come back? I don't know.

I don't have an answer for it. But I know that the system is going to have to do something, in order to curb the recidivism rate. Because, either they're going to do that, or they're just going to imprison half the United States, and the other half watch them. It's that simple. That's the only thing, you know, that's the only way I can see it.

*How good are you at predicting who's going to come back and who's not? If you know a guy in here fairly well, do you usually know what he's going to do?*

Well, there's very few people that I know fairly well, I mean, what I would consider as a friend. Now, out of seven hundred people in here, I would say I know five hundred and seventy-five of them, but most of those only as associates. I mean, we know each other to where we can say, "What's up?" but not much more than that.

To know a guy as a friend, I mean, I can count them on one hand. You know, I can just put up a few fingers.

But, yeah, the people that I know as friends, yeah, I know where their heads are, you know. I know where their heads are at.

But in a sense, that's good, because it gives me the opportunity to say to them, like, "OK, look man," you know, "What is the consequences of this move that you're thinking about, that you're contemplating on taking here? What's the consequences of it?" 'Cause whatever idea they have as far as crime go, there's always that example person they bring up. "Well, you remember such-and-such-and-such? He did the same thing." "Yeah? And now where is he?" "Well, he's in Clallam Bay or some place." "OK, so, what makes you any different?" you know.

Or, if a guy's speaking on something that's positive, hey, that's great. You know, "OK, yeah, now, there you go! That's the thing. That's what you got to do."

[Pause.] You know, Craig, there's an old prison thing. Everybody does it. When guys leave out of here, or any place else I've ever been, you know, they say, "Hey man, I'm leaving tomorrow. What can I do for you?" you know, "Hey, give me a call when I get out there."

I tell 'em, "Hey, look buddy. Look. I don't want your phone number. I don't want to call you. The only thing that I want you to do for me, and I'm serious about this, is just do one thing." "What's that?" "Just go out and be a good ambassador. That's all I ask you to do. I don't want you to send me nothing. I don't want you to try to contact no one for me. I don't need any of that. Just be a good ambassador. And if you do that, not only are you doing it for me, but you're doing it for thousands and thousands more other people. But if you don't be a good ambassador, and you come back, I don't owe you nothing, and you don't owe me nothing."

You know, [laughs], my wife tells me that I have a cruel mentality sometimes, to the point of being so blunt with things. But,—

*But that's a good point. I mean, their behavior on the outside will—*

Yeah, yeah.

*—have some effect on the public perception of cons and ex-cons, and that's going to do you a lot more good than if they make a phone call for you, or send you something through the mail, or—*

Yeah, yeah. I say, "You don't have to tell me you're doing all right. I'm watching the TV every day and reading the newspaper, and getting word from different sources, so, hey, if you don't get caught up in that net, I'll know. If I don't hear different, I'll just feel that you're doing all right. You don't have to write to me. I don't need no correspondence from you. Just be a good ambassador. That's what you can do for all of us."

*You know, I've wondered, like in PAP, when we have a member released, I've always thought, I'll bet the other PAP members, people who know this guy well on the inside, I'll bet they'd have a pretty good idea of whether he's going to re-offend, or what his life's going to be like.*

Sure.

*If you actually live in the same institution, and you hear what he's saying, where he's coming from, I'll bet you know a hell of a lot better than a parole board, or a volunteer,—*

Oh God yes.

*—or even, in some cases, the guy's family who he's been able to snow. But, is that accurate? I mean, do you guys have a pretty good feel for that?*

Sure. Yeah, we do. I mean, a lot of times, you know, you see guys that have these macho attitudes and stuff, and you say, "Well, Joe's getting out in a couple of weeks, man. I wonder how long is he going to live?" 'Cause somebody's going to kill him.

It's kind of a cruel thing to say, but it happens quite frequently. I mean, a guy will say something like, "Hey man, I'm going to get out, and I'm going to get me a BMW, and I'm going to get me—," you know, "I'm going to do this and I'm going to do that," you know. "Well, how you going to do all this, man?" "Well, hey man, I got a hook-up. I'm going to have a connection." Well, hey, already I know his chances of making it is very slim. Very slim.

So you say, "Well, OK, I'll hold your cell for you." At Walla Walla, we used to tell them, "Well, I'll hold your bunk."

But, you know, in a way, this is the life of a millionaire, but with his life being sucked through a vacuum, through a hole. I mean, just think about it; there's all type of resources here. I mean, not as much as there is on the streets, but there's so much resources here for a man to gather, and better himself with, you know. Not only here at WSR, but any place that you're locked up.

I mean, it took me a long time to really grasp this, but, once you start spending time, not for yourself, but with yourself, that's time well spent. That's time that nothing can compare to, really. If you're doing something constructive, even if it's just reading, you will find that the growth that you get from that over a period of time is invaluable. I mean, that's why I say it's kind of like the life of a millionaire, just being sucked through the eye of a needle, you know.

Because, you have all of this here, but then I've noticed that so many guys that get released, they just forget about it. They just totally forget about it. I mean, I've had guys that come back, and I say, "Man, what the hell happened?" you know. "Man, I forgot where I was." "How in the hell did you forget where you were? You were free! You were out there in the world! How did you forget that?" "Well, I wasn't prepared, even though all I thought about when I was in the joint was what I was going to do when I got on the streets."

Which makes sense. You can't just think about doing something, and say you're going to do it; you have to prepare. You can't just say, "Well, I'm going to fly an airplane," and go jump in a jet and take off. I mean, [laughs], you have to have some type of instructions, or prepare yourself in some type of way, you know.

So, I don't know, Craig.

*And what can you do to prepare yourself for that? You've mentioned the importance of having rehabilitative programs again. So, talk to me a little bit more about that. What can the individual do, and what can the prison or the society do to affect the recidivism rate, and facilitate people actually turning their life around?*

Well, as an individual, first of all, I think it all starts at the county jail, the city jail—whichever one you go to first. I think it all starts there. You have to stop lying to yourself. You have to just break away and be honest. Face reality for what it is. OK? Now that's the first thing that you got to do. You've got to be honest. I mean, you just have to open yourself up. You've got to be honest with people. I'm not speaking of prosecuting attorneys [laughs]—I mean, with your family, you know. You've got to be honest with people. You've got to be honest with them.

The average guy, when he goes to jail, on the average, it's not a person that just walked from his house one day and walked across the street to get busted for something. It's a pattern that he has set, that he has been doing for a length of time.

And in the length of time that he's doing this, he is upsetting or hurting someone that he knows—a family member, friend, or relative, or whatever. It's upsetting them, you know.

There are things that a person, I think, has to do, once he's brought to a standstill. He's got to say, "OK, I've got to be honest with myself. I've got to be honest with these people." And you have to mend bridges. You have to mend things that you've broken, because you have broken a lot of things. You've broken trust. You've broken friendships.

That don't mean that you have to get down on your knees every day, and, "I'm sorry I did—," but, you know, you have to let people know that, "Hey, I made a mistake," you know, "I'm sorry for that. I made a mistake. It's my mistake. I'm not blaming you."

I have a friend. She has two sons that's in the system. And every time I call her, she's damn near crying, and I'm saying, "What's wrong?" "Well, they're saying that I was supposed to send this one this package, and I was supposed to—" "Hey, they're grown men, aren't they?" "Yeah." "Well, and you've looked out for them all their lives. Made sure they had the things that you could possibly give them and everything, you know." I mean, she was a single mother, but she'd made it the best she could, you know. "And now, they're grown, and you still feel this guilt? Why?"

Because, it's not so much she's feeling the guilt. It's that they're putting the guilt trip on her, from prison. Why? Because they still haven't learned to take responsibility, and to be honest with themselves and with her.

So, you know, what are they going to do when they get out? What are they going to do? Go straight to her, and the first time she says, "Well, I don't have this," or "I don't have that," well, then they'll go back to their same old ways.

Craig, you know, I don't profess to have the answers to all of this now. [Laughs.] I really don't. But, it's really sad. It's really sad and it's getting worse. It's really getting worse.

*What if the head of the DOC brought you in as an unofficial advisor and said, "Henry, we have to do something about this damn recidivism thing. What do you want me to do with this prison system now?" What suggestions do you have?*

Well, first of all, I would make it mandatory that if a person doesn't have a GED or a high school diploma, I would make it mandatory, you got to go to school.

You know, we had an organization in Walla Walla—the DOC didn't, but we did—where we would just grab a guy, you know, "Hey man, you don't have your GED. You don't have your high school diploma. You got to go to school." "Man, I'm—" "Yeah, you're going to school, now! You're going to school one way or the other!" you know, "So, now, either you can go up there and enroll and go to school, or you can deal with us." I mean, some guys would just totally revolt, but then some guys would, you know, "OK man." And they would go.

You know, but I think that should be mandatory.

And not only that. The second thing is, I think that it should be mandatory that a person has a job, doing something. If it's nothing no more than going out in the big yard, picking up rocks, picking up paper.

I remember when I first went to the joint. When you got out of your bed in the morning and went to breakfast, that was it. You didn't get back into your bed. You didn't get back into your bed along until maybe they called noon meal, you know, and if you didn't have a job, you'd go lay down and nap, and when they called chow, you'd come out of there, and you're out until four o'clock, you know. And that's the way it was. I mean, you didn't just lay around all day and watch TV.

TV is one of the most damaging things they have in prison. It really is. Because all it is is just a one-eyed babysitter. And guys just sit there, lay there and vegetate watching their damn soap operas and all that. I mean, there's no value to it.

I could see that there's value as far as, like, news, or sports, or Discovery Channel. I mean, you know, I won't down it too deep, because there's good in it and there's bad. But then, it's mostly bad, because, guys'll just watch anything. Nothing educational. They don't care. Just show us some pictures, you know.

*What do you think the guys who don't have jobs would do with their time if they didn't have TVs in prison? Would they use their time constructively, do you think?*

Well, I think a percentage of them would, simply because they'd get a book and read. They would. Or they would sit there and twiddle their thumbs until they come up with something that they could do that's pacifying, you know.

*Yeah.*

Yeah. But that would be one of the last things they'd ever take from prison, is the TV. Man, but actually, they should.

You know, when I first came to prison in Fifty-nine, Craig, they had jobs like carpentry, pipe-fitting. Jobs that you could learn in here and go out on the streets and have a trade. And they had qualified instructors that was doing it in here. I don't know what happened. I don't know what happened.

We had the farm. We used to make all our own clothing. We did shoe repair. We even made clothes for the women's prison, you know. Now how could you possibly buy Levi's and shirts and socks and shit like that cheaper than you can make it when you're paying a guy what they were paying us?

You know what? I was one of the highest paid guys in the sewing room. And you know how much I made an hour?

*What?*

Eighteen cents.

*This was when?*

This was in Sixty-two. Yeah. It was about equivalent then to the same as a guy making a dollar ten an hour now, you know. About the same thing.

So, I mean, what the hell? There's a lot of things to be done, to help a guy stay out of prison. But that's not what they want.

*You don't think they want to cut the recidivism rate?*

No.

*How come?*

Cuts down on their money. Yeah. It slows the generation of their profits.

*It seems like if anything, that's even more of a problem with privatized prisons. I was reading an article about a convention recently of the people who run the private industry prisons, and they were lamenting the fact that the incarceration rate isn't going up as fast as in the recent past. And they were talking about how are they going to deal with this crisis situation, where we aren't imprisoning quite as many new people as a few years ago. You know, treating it as an obvious negative.*

A million point eight people's not enough?

*Yeah, because the more people in prison, the better for their bottom line. Actually, let's also relate this to the whole job issue, and prison industries issue. I've talked to guys who are very much pro-outside industries, and pro-prison jobs, and there's a lot of good reasons for it. It teaches guys job skills, many of which will help them on the outside. It teaches them, you know, a work ethic, and so on. But the other side of it that you also hear that also has some merit, is do we really want prisoners to be available for low wage slave labor? You know, I'm not comfortable with the idea that anybody's benefiting financially from having people in prison. That's not a good situation.*

You don't think so?

*I don't want people to be advantaged by having more prisoners in prison, whether we're talking about the government, or private industry, or whomever. But what do you think? Is it—in general, for society as a whole—is it a good or a bad thing to have employers being able to employ prisoners at low wages to do their work?*

Well, I would say that it's good. I would say it's good, because actually what that does, if a guy has a job, at least he's making minimum wages. I mean, at least that's enough to carry him over and give him an opportunity to advance, you know. I mean, other than just getting out with forty dollars in his pocket, and seeing no way out. I mean, shit, a hamburger and a shake damn near costs forty dollars now, you know.

So, I mean, yeah, I could see it, if a guy came into prison and he went through some learning process and got some marketable skills, and he gets out and goes to work for an employer and starts at the bottom. Because, I know a lot of people that have started out at minimum wages, and they're making top wages now.

I mean, it depends a lot upon the person. You know, if you want to advance yourself, you're going to do that, either at that company or some place else. But that minimum wage, it helped you maintain yourself, you know, until you could either advance on the ladder of where you are, or go to some other place.

Yeah, even minimum wage would be a good thing. I mean, now that wouldn't support, say myself if I'd have got out twenty years ago, you know, before all of my kids were grown. A minimum wage job wouldn't have been too much of an asset for me, you know. But the average guy that's in prison is unmarried. I mean, he might have a couple stray babies out there some place, but, you know, he has nothing that he's feeling as being an obligation or a responsibility.

You know, so, yeah. A minimum wage job? Sure, he can get a minimum wage job and work forty hours a week, you know, and at least he'll have some money coming in.

*Well, I think we're straying a bit from prison jobs to jobs a guy might get after being released. But anyway, clearly it's better for the individual in prison to have a job, even at minimum wage, than not, but I'm asking more about the long term or big picture implications of it for society. Here's the kind of thing I'm getting at: A documentary was out recently by Michael Moore. I don't know if you're familiar with his work; he does documentary movies. But, he addresses this issue in kind of a half-joking way, saying that, you know, the way things are set up now, an employer can lay off all of his workers or a good chunk of his workers at the factory, knowing that when you lay off people and they're unemployed and they're desperate, a certain number of them will turn to crime. And they get arrested, they go to prison, and he can go set up shop there and hire those same guys for lower wages. I mean, that's kind of a joke the way he presents it, but—*

No, that's no joke.

*—in a more complex way, that's sort of what's going on.*

No, that's true.

*And so, from that angle, moving jobs into prisons seems a lot less desirable. So, I'm kind of split on the issue myself. I'm not decided if I like the idea on balance or not.*

Well, shit, look at Boeing. Look at companies like Boeing. What do they do? All the people that's been working for them for the last fourteen, fifteen, sixteen years, like, twenty, twenty-some years, they lay them off. They lay them off, simply because it's cheaper to lay them off than to have them retire and get full benefits. It's easier to lay them off, give them early retirement, and then go hire a guy at the lowest possible wage scale to replace him.

Now that's economics. It makes sense. I mean, we both have to really, you know, accept the fact that America runs off economics.

I mean, I was looking at the news last night. And they were trying to make it such a big deal for the Dow Jones to reach whatever point, like, if it reached another thousand points, money is just going to jump out of the tops of buildings or something.

*[Laughs.]*

You know, what the hell? I mean, shit, it's not going to change anything. But, it's just, hey, just the thought of that money. I mean, America is just frantic for the money. No morals. No values. All you have to have is money.

*Now, we've talked a little bit about the programs. Tell me more about that? What kind of programs do you think do the most good? What would you like to see more of in prison?*

You know, my experience, Craig, always has been that the programs that are the most helpful in prison are self-help programs. Programs that are, more or less, ran and operated and organized by the convicts themselves.

I mean, not saying that a convict is any smarter than anyone in DOC, but—and I don't know why they don't really grasp this—it seems as when a convict sets up a program of any sort, they don't do it so much for their own benefit. Because you can't look for no benefits here. See, there's no guarantee of no benefits here. None whatsoever. I mean, we're not even guaranteed to have dinner at night, you know. There's no guarantees here.

So, when a convict sits down and comes up with a plan of some type for a program, or something to run or to function, even though they might, in a small way, look for gratification for that, really their whole thing is to try—and I think a lot of people do things unconsciously, you know—but they do it to alleviate misery. And if you can take a guy away from his moments of misery, and maybe replace that with a good, healthy thought, or a smile, or whatever, hey, you've accomplished a hell of a lot.

And I don't think that DOC sees that. I think when they try to implement a program, they try to implement it to the point where it's a fail-safe program, on paper. I mean, "Hey, OK, this will work. This is what you do, and then you do this, and then you'll be OK." But there's no benefits from it for the people its supposed to be for. None. Not one.

You know, a lot of guys that have done a lot of time, they'll tell you, any time we hear they're starting another program that's sponsored by DOC, "Well, I wonder how many people they're going to hire to do that?" Because that's all it is.

*So you mean prisoners trust their own more? They don't trust the motives of the DOC?*

Sure. Oh yeah. Yeah.

*What about private parties that aren't hired by DOC and aren't prisoners? Just private citizens who arrange to start some kind of program inside the prison. How are people like that perceived?*

Well, there's a process that goes with that. [Laughs.] First of all, we have a tendency to look at, "Well, what's the motive?" OK? Then, there has to be benefits. Where are we going? What are the benefits? What are we supposed to get out of this?

Then there's always that thing of trust, you know.

But over the years, we've been fortunate enough to have people from the outside that come in that, you know, are genuine. I mean, they do things from their heart. They're not looking for no pat on the back. All they want is just to see that they're doing some kind of good for the people that they're dealing with, you know. And these are the programs that last. These are the ones that last.

*Is it harder to get that trust if you're being paid? I mean, when I come in for PAP, we're just volunteers, so I don't usually feel that pressure. I don't feel that we're being judged, or people are cynically wondering, "What's your real motive?" or, "How are you benefiting from being here?" But if I came in with a government grant to start a program, or this was something I was doing full time, and drawing a salary or making a living off of, would it be harder for me to gain people's trust in that situation?*

Yeah. I would say so. Yeah.

You know, actually, you'd be surprised, but this is a place where a person learns to trust a person. Or even if maybe not so much to trust a person, at least to really judge a person quickly and to know if they can be trusted or not. I think we judge like that a little more clearly here than people do out in society.

And I think it's real simple to see why. It has to do with the kind of life we have inside these walls, where you can never get away from the little vacuum you're in. You can never get away from it, no matter what you do. You're in a little vacuum, and you can't get away from it. You're just like a dog spinning at his tail. You do the same thing routinely over and over and over and over.

And when I catch myself doing it, I say, "OK, hold it. I'm going to start something new. The next time this cell door opens, I'm not going to just get in that little rut and just follow it around the maze." I do something different on those days. Where I started yesterday, I'll finish there today, you know. Whatever. Just to keep it real.

Because, it's so easy to get caught up in this little vacuum here to where you stop thinking for yourself. The only thing that you do is just automatic things, like breathing and walking, but you stop thinking for yourself. You stop feeling. All your emotions get caught up in a web. You know, you get tangled up, man, and it's kind of hard sometimes.

That's why a lot of guys, you know, flip out in these places. They get lost within themselves. Nobody's doing anything to them. They just get lost.

*So have you developed a pretty good ability to read non-prisoners as well as prisoners? When outside people come in, like the volunteers for PAP or these other programs, do you have a better read on them than most people on the outside would? Do you generally know pretty quick what they're up to, what their motives are for being here, etc.?*

Sure.

*Are you ever surprised after the fact?*

No.

*[Laughs.]*

No, not really. No, I have a pretty good read on people. Not only the outside people, I can read people in here, you know. I mean, see, you develop a sense of observance.

I don't just sit and watch people, but I might see two or three guys sitting some place, just talking, or playing cards, or in the gymnasium, or just walking the yard. And I'll see one guy, and I'll say, "The last time I saw him, he was with those same two guys," and then, you know, I get an observation on him, and I usually be right. Whatever I come up with.

Sometimes I get the wrong impression, but, usually not. I don't have no problem, really, with evaluating people in here or that come in from the outside.

*[At this point, I noticed one of the officers looking in the window and I realized we were nearing the time of day when this building is shut down and the prisoners return to their cells to be counted.] Are we up against the deadline here? Do you have to be back by four o'clock?*

Oh yeah.

*Oh, OK, I've got three fifty-three. Maybe we better go. They're going to lock us in here.*

Oh, I've been locked up all my life, man.

This was my last taped conversation with Henry. Some time later, he responded in writing to a set of questions I had mailed to him, but he skipped many of the questions and answered the rest with only a few words each. His response was completely superficial, and frankly unusable. Clearly he didn't want to make much of an effort in writing, didn't want to dig deep, didn't want to reveal much.

He was no longer giving me material for this book, but we continued to get along fine, if anything becoming better friends as time passed. I saw him at maybe half of the PAP meetings, and he was one of the prisoners I spent significant time with.

Periodically he would let me know how things were going with his case. I lost track of the details, but some of the murder counts had been overturned, and the others had been reopened for re-consideration.

It was all supposed to come to a head with a hearing in early 2000, but as I was learning, these things are always delayed multiple times before they happen, if they ever do. (Henry himself referred to such a series of delays related to an earlier hearing at the beginning of this last interview.)

On one occasion they got so close that they actually transported Henry all the way from the prison to the county jail in downtown Seattle, so that the following morning they could take him from there to the court house. But the hearing was postponed at the last minute yet again.

Through it all, Henry remained guardedly optimistic. He wouldn't come right out and say he expected to win, and he was careful to reiterate that he would accept whatever happened, but you could tell that he felt each development in the case made it more likely he'd shortly be regaining his freedom.

The people around him were less guarded in their optimism. 9 was certainly convinced Henry would prevail. I spoke with Henry's attorney on two occasions, and while he prefaced his remarks by noting that these matters are never sure things, he made it clear that he believed the probabilities were strongly in Henry's favor.

The long-awaited hearing finally occurred on September 29, 2000. This one was open to the public, so I was able to attend.

Henry and his people had told me shortly before the hearing that their side had received one final big break that made victory even more likely. The prosecutor from the original murder trial—from way back in the '70s—had written a letter for Henry's file that they had submitted to the court acknowledging his own wrongdoing and failure to follow proper procedures in the trial (which, I was told, he attributed to the excessive zeal of youth; apparently this was one of the first cases he had ever prosecuted) and stating that he believed that at the very least, Henry's sentence should be reduced to time served.

So the consensus seemed to be that this hearing was now a slam dunk. Henry and his attorney already were looking forward to the few remaining stages before he would be released, trying to anticipate every possible problem and delay to make sure that no small thing unexpectedly tripped them up after this one big thing was behind them.

Gathered in the courtroom to watch the proceedings were, in addition to myself, several other prison volunteers—though no one else from PAP—a small number of outside friends of Henry's, and some members of Henry's family.

During the hearing, Henry had an opportunity to stand up and speak on his own behalf. He was noticeably, and understandably, less relaxed and in control than I was used to seeing him one on one or in a small group within the familiar confines of the prison. But in the end I felt that he gave a pretty good account of himself. I observed the judge, and she appeared to be listening intently and sympathetically.

Next, those of us in the audience were permitted to approach the bench one at a time to speak up for Henry. I had not known that this was going to happen, and it really was not necessary for me to say anything, since I had written out my thoughts in a letter that was a part of Henry's file that the judge had already received, but I decided to participate just to show my support.

I got up in order to change to a seat on the end of the row so as to more easily be able to approach the bench when a turn opened up. A large and particularly brutish guard took several quick steps to me, glared at me, and harshly commanded me to remain where I was.

This reminded me that Henry was not the wise and gentle gnome to these people that he was to me. To them, he was a convicted multiple murderer serving a life sentence in a maximum security prison. He and anyone associated with him was to be dealt with through the usual force and intimidation. They weren't taking any chances.

After the guard had made it clear that it wasn't up to us when or if we'd be allowed to speak or even to move in our seats, in the end all of us who wanted to were permitted to speak on Henry's behalf. I glanced over at Henry. His head was bowed, and he seemed touched almost to the point of tears by the testimonials.

Finally it was time for the judge to render her decision.

She began by summarizing the points of law for and against her having jurisdiction in this case, concluding that the matter of Henry's fate was indeed open to her consideration, that she did have the legal authority to overturn his remaining convictions or reduce his sentence.

She next praised Henry for the remarkable job of self-improvement he had managed in prison. No one, she noted, could fail to be impressed and moved reading the many letters in his file and hearing the many statements in court from those who knew him best and were solidly in his corner. She was convinced, she said, that he was sincere and that he had turned his life around in a way that very few people do in prison.

However, she continued, that by itself was not enough for her to decide the case before her in his favor. In order to render a decision that would ultimately free him, she had to determine that he was not in fact guilty of the crimes of which he had been convicted, or that the sentence he had been given had not fit those crimes.

And that, she said, she did not feel justified in doing. Though she was not legally bound by the decision of the original judge and jury, she believed that to override it would be to say that her assessment of the evidence more than twenty years after the fact would somehow be more reliable than that of those who were in court at the time, those who had seen the evidence when it was fresh, those who had watched the witnesses in person whose testimony she could only read in a transcript.

Thus she felt her duty was to defer to the judgment of the original judge and jury, and to affirm the original convictions and sentences. Henry had lost this battle.

Henry's attorney looked positively stunned. He sought clarification, probed for any indication from the judge that the door was anything other than completely shut, to no avail.

From a teenage girl whom I took to be Henry's daughter or step-daughter came grumblings that gradually increased in volume and bitterness into a full-fledged denunciation of the judge and her ruling. This was much to the visible discomfort of the guards, whose glares were not succeeding in the slightest in quieting her.

The rest of us looked around at each other to see if everyone shared our surprise and disapproval of what we had just witnessed. Before we were permitted to leave the courtroom, Henry was led out past us by the guards. True to his nature, he looked the least upset of anyone.

Moments later, when a few of us gathered in the hall to try to make sense of what had just happened, I noticed that Henry's attorney still had the confused and shocked look in his eyes of a man who had just lost the largest wager of his life when the opposing team scored two touchdowns in the final minute of play.

As was usually the case when things went against Henry, he consoled us rather than vice versa. He called me that very evening from jail, before they transported him back to the prison. He thanked me for believing in him and for being there to stand up for him. He assured me that his fight would continue, that there were several other avenues they were pursuing. (He always seemed to have multiple irons in the fire.) His struggle had gone on for many, many years, and this setback simply meant that it would continue for more. There was no thought of giving up.

Even if everything they were currently working on failed, he reminded me, he would be up for a parole hearing in a few short years.

And off in the distance, another door to freedom was opened just enough to render the light of hope visible through the crack.

# 9—March 1999

"But so often in here, you got to just look at it in the practical way and do what's necessary. You got too many different personalities you're surrounded by. You got to remember that everyone you see on the news or in the newspaper, where you think, like, 'How can somebody do some crazy shit like this?' they're all in here. And they ain't too much changed from the time when you saw them on the news to the time when they walked through these front doors. And the kind of person that you all were so eager to clean up off the street and get them away from you is the same kind of people that I got to deal with every day, and they're in that same frame of mind. So I have to be always watching them, because I don't know what they're capable of doing next."

The day after taping conversations with Jeff and Henry, I drove back out to the prison for more interviews.

In our last conversation, 9 had mentioned in passing that his friend Maggie had been diagnosed with cancer. In fact, it was inoperable cancer, and she was not expected to survive much longer. But in the meantime, she and 9 were to be married. (And, no, it had nothing to do with conjugal visits. Conjugal visits were now only possible for couples who had already been married before the one spouse was incarcerated, and even then were only doled out on a discretionary basis to those who had stayed out of trouble.) We talked of this, and many things.

*Speaking now of the crime for which you are serving a life sentence, why did your buddy kill the person?*

I honestly don't know. I mean, at the time when it happened, I didn't know if it was a robbery, or what it was. I mean, I was across the street from him, and all of a sudden I see he's chasing a guy. I'm assuming that either this guy snatched some drugs from him, or took some money from him, whatever, but he was in hot pursuit. And, it was just my natural instincts to grab the guy, the same as if someone calls out, "Hey, stop that person!" even if you don't know what they've done, you still react to it.

And I honestly didn't know the guy was dead when it was all over. I mean, I knew he got beat up, but I didn't know he had been brutalized to death, till the cops arrived and the ambulance started working on him. Then I realized how far the damage had been done. But I didn't inflict any of the wounds, so I didn't have no idea before that.

We separated after that. In fact, that was part of the reason why I ended up getting aggravated murder, because they said we did it and then fled the scene.

Then they kept us separate all the way through court, through trial and everything, to where I really never could find out why he did it.

*So, when you tackled the guy, and then your buddy came up and inflicted the actual injuries, the actual damage, how did you not know how much damage there was? Weren't you still there watching him stabbing him and everything?*

Well, actually, I'm thinking he hitting him. It's eleven-thirty at night in a dark area; you got one streetlight down on the corner. I'm thinking he's just beating him up and fighting him. I didn't know if he had a weapon even in his hand.

Then when the cops finally showed up, which is, like, fifteen minutes later, and started resuscitating the guy and they ripped his shirt off, then I see the wounds.

From the initial point where he really attacked the guy, I had backed off. I mean, I'm gone, and then he left after he finished doing what he did to the guy. I only realized later exactly what extent it was when the cops actually opened him up.

*So you had grabbed the guy, but once your partner arrived, you didn't stay there.*

No, no, no.

*You weren't, like, holding the guy down—*

No, hell, fuck no—

*—while your partner was beating him up?*

No, no.

I mean, my initial response was to grab this guy and hold him till he catch up with him and take whatever back he stole from him—his money, drugs, whatever. 'Cause he was a drug dealer. And my first thought was, he was selling him drugs and the guy snatched it and ran.

*Yeah.*

I knew the guy. I mean, I had known him maybe thirty, forty days, not even quite two months. And, same as you see somebody snatch a lady's purse and take off and she yells "Stop!" and you just automatically grab the person. If she come up and kill him, you don't realize exactly what's going on until after the fact. But I still don't know why he killed the guy.

*So when he had him down, hitting him, you backed off? You left?*

I backed off. I left. But, you know, I just went back to where I'd just been, which was only maybe a block away. We'd been bootlegging alcohol, you know, too young to buy, had somebody go in the store to purchase it for us, so I went back to get that. Because the person was still in the store. And there was a bunch of people around that I knew that knew me, and knew all of us. I was with them while it was going on. We all thought it was simply a fight.

*And you never did find out why your partner killed this guy?*

No, they got us separated. We can't even communicate, from the day that we went to trial. And I have never seen him since that day. I can't write him. I can't communicate with him. Somewhere they got it where we're separated from everything. I mean, he cannot come to no institution where I'm in; I can't go to where he is. They're thinking that if we ever come across each other, one of us kill the other, specifically they think I would do something to him, because I got the "accessory" charge.

I was hoping that he'd take his own beef. He realized that they had him as the defendant and I was the accomplice. If he would have took his own beef and said, "Hey, I'm the one that committed this. I did this. He was just there," then I wouldn't be in this position now.

*Now, given that he did not abide by the code, in that he didn't take his own beef—he refused to take responsibility for it and clear you—why are you still obligated to him? Why wouldn't that release you from your obligation to conceal the truth about what really happened and pin it all on him now, since he didn't do the right thing?*

Well, because even if I was to say that this is what he'd done, you know, or even if he came forth to say, "Hey, I did this," now, after the fact, they won't believe him, because they'll think that I pressured him into doing it, or he's doing it now because he sees he don't have nothing to lose and might as well save me. But the Court won't trust him. That's my struggle there.

What could I say? Who could I go to? Even if I went to the nearest judge and told him, "Hey, I didn't do anything; he did everything and he's willing to tell you this," that is not enough for the Court. The Court's not going to believe me or him.

*What's the rule in general though, not just in this case, but in general, in a partner situation like that? If one partner betrays the other, as he did to you, are you then allowed to rat on him? Are you released from your usual obligations? Or is it still just as wrong to rat on him?*

No, it's still just as wrong to rat on him.

But, you know, there's really no rule there, as far as, like, from a moral standpoint. It all becomes up to that individual. And if I was to do it, it'd probably be justified and people would see it as that, probably wouldn't even view it so much as snitching.

It's the same thing as when you get called to the witness stand and deny everything. I guess, in a roundabout way, by proxy, it still is snitching, because if I deny everything, that obviously means that he did everything. But I wouldn't be literally pointing in his direction. Indirectly you're snitching, but not literally.

It's like a gray area there. But that's neither here nor there, because what's most important—all I require and request—is the truth to come out about it. All he would have to do is confess what he'd done, and that I had no part in killing this guy.

If I had known, Craig, that this is what was going to transpire, by no way on God's earth would I have stopped the guy he was chasing. In fact, I would have held *him* up, if I knew that his intent was actually to kill the guy, especially on a robbery.

But, you know, when you're standing before a judge, and all these jurors and people just all of a sudden putting these motives together, saying why you did something, there ain't no explaining it to them. They don't hear. All they know is they got a motive, they can convince this jury, they can go for a guilty verdict. So, no matter what you say, they don't care. "You shouldn't have been there." "You should have called the authorities." "You should have stopped it." Like I should have been the Good Samaritan, and put myself at risk.

*In some ways, it seems similar to Henry's case, where he is not really permitted to tell the truth, according to the code. He can't say who did what, and who fired the shots, because that would be finking, in effect. But, I was just curious, if the partner did the betrayal first, does that change the rules? Or is it still an absolute? Is it still just as wrong for you or Henry or somebody like that to come forward and say, "Wait a minute! This guy who betrayed me, he's the one who did it," you know.*

You got to remember too that that's what their tactic is. Even when the partner don't admit it, they'll take you in one room, him in another, then they'll tell you, "Your partner just blamed everything on you," just to try to encourage you to say, "No, I didn't do that! He did it!"

*Right.*

You really don't know who's betrayed who yet, because that's the game they play. But, "Hear no evil, speak no evil, see no evil," is the role that most people take. Solid people, with their rules intact. And, even when it comes down to repercussions that's fallen upon you, you still have to take that role, deny everything.

You've got to weigh your options there. And the rules really don't change much. It's a moral issue. I mean, you got a choice: To either put your life in danger by telling what you know and blaming the other person, or just to totally deny everything and not tell them nothing. That's what, you know, politicians do: Deny it all.

*[Laughs.] So you have the morals of a politician?*

[Laughs.] Well, I wouldn't say that, quite exactly, but close enough. I know their strategy. I know the reason for their strategy.

*[Laughs.] Yeah.*

But, you know, I mean, what would I say, right now, if they put me in a position, like, "Well, who actually did the crime? We'll let you go if you tell us"? My moral thing would actually be—probably, more than likely—to say, "Hey, I didn't do it! All I can say is I didn't do it. I can't tell you who did it, because I don't know. But I didn't do it. I'm only here to represent me. I'm not here to convict someone else." And that's as much as I could tell them.

*Now, you mentioned that if you had known what was going on, you would not have cooperated, you would not have tackled the guy, and so on. Yet, back at that time of your life, when you were a juvenile like that, it's not as if you had some absolute respect for human life. I mean, you were shooting people,—*

Yeah.

*—you were putting people's lives in danger on an almost routine basis, so, how would it have been contrary to your character back then, or your lifestyle, to have done just what they accused you of?*

Yeah, that's a good question. And that question has been asked to me several times before. Similar question like that. My answer still remains the same. I never inflicted no harm on someone that didn't deserve it, or didn't do anything to me. It was always more so as a reaction, a defense tactic, rather than me being offensive.

As far as growing up with the gang mentality and the gang violence and things like this, it wasn't for recreational purposes, to go out to try to make you bigger than what the rest of the people are, simply by the amount of casualties, or whatever harm that you can do. That was never my intent. That was never none of my friends' intent. It was always where either someone was offended by something someone done, or someone in the area was hurt or harmed, or even killed by someone else. And by our grace and respect, you know, it's almost like someone do something to your kids, someone do something to your family, you react to it. You know, you kill my dog, I kill your cat. An eye for an eye, and a tooth for a tooth.

And that's the way you felt. I believed it was more for discouraging it from happening again, not so much as retaliating for what had been done. It was like sending a message—"This is what will happen to you if you ever try this again."

*Deterrence.*

Deterrence, basically.

But, like I said, I never committed any crime or did anything to someone that didn't deserve it, especially inflicting no harm, because my compassion wouldn't allow me to do that. I still think it'd take a sick individual to actually take someone else's life, and I do have a value for life.

This incident that I'm incarcerated for, I mean, this was a situation where the person didn't deserve to die, especially about no robbery. It was almost like a senseless killing. For what? That's not what I was about even back then.

*What kind of a motive did they think you had? Did they allege that he was a rival gang member, or that—?*

No, no, no. He was no way even in that classification. In fact, it was not even considered a gang related crime. The motive was simply to kill the guy to prevent him from testifying—pointing out who actually robbed him.

*OK.*

This was the motive that they said in court. Now, I didn't believe that, simply because the guy didn't know me, and I assume he didn't know my co-defendant either. And he was foreign, so how can he actually point him out? Especially in a neighborhood where it consisted of all blacks.

But that is the motive that was presented in court, and that's why I ended up getting aggravated murder. They said we committed the crime of murder in order to cover up another crime, which was robbery, and that makes it aggravated, and that's why they can give life without. That's why I have life without.

*Is there any chance that that was the true motive of your co-defendant?*

Ain't no way. That's impossible. I refuse to believe that. But then, I can't say. I've never had a lengthy conversation, where I can sit down and talk to him about it, other than being in trial together, and the questions being asked there. And you can't go by those answers, because those are, like, diplomatic answers to pacify the jury.

But as far as the truth goes, I wish I had that opportunity to sit down and actually ask him, not so much to tell me why he did it, but to ask him, "Do you realize what you've done? What you've done to both of us?"

And it kills me, Craig. It really kills me, not knowing. But then again, it doesn't make a difference, because it happened, and this is where we are. But, I refuse to think that was his motive. That's pretty much impossible, in my opinion.

*Well, what is your best guess, then, as to why he did it?*

My best guess is he did it because he wanted to get—I mean, he was from another city—like, Louisiana somewhere—and he hadn't been up here that long, and a lot of people was intimidated by him. And I felt that he was trying to send a message to the people that he tried to intimidate, to let them know he's the big guy, or he's, you know, not so much God, but he's the one to be reckoned with. I mean, he was looking for that image, and I know that by the way he dressed and the things he done, by all the earrings, the flashy clothes, you know, flashing everything. I mean, he was the tough guy. He wanted that tough image.

*So he picked a stranger to prove this point on?*

Better that than a friend.

But, I can't say that I anticipated that he was planning on killing the guy, because this guy was one of the same people that I knew went out with some other people I know that committed other robberies from different, like, jewelry stores and different things like this, and nobody got hurt. He went to different concerts and got into fights, and nobody got hurt. There was fighting, but he didn't use a weapon on nobody.

But then, it's so strange to me, because I'd really like to know why. I don't know if he even intended to kill the guy. Or if the guy really did something to him more than I know. I mean, maybe the guy did something to him in advance. All I do know is that he tried to chase the guy down behind some drugs or some negotiations that went bad and tried to catch him, and the guy took off running.

But this is not the story that the prosecutors wanted to reveal, because it looked more like self-defense, if the other guy was doing something to him first. And that will pacify the jury, get them to soften their opinion. So they made it look like we robbed him.

But I can't believe it was even a robbery, because this guy couldn't have had much money, and my partner sold drugs, so why is he going to rob someone with less money than what he had? I find that odd.

*What kind of foreigner was he?*

Laotian. Whatever the hell that is. I think it's Cambodian or something like that.

*From Laos.*

Laos. Yeah.

*Their neighbor is Cambodia.*

OK.

*Are you in fact still angry with your co-defendant? Would he be at risk if he was in the same institution as you?*

[Laughs.] I would like to say I plead the Fifth on that, but—

*[Laughs.]*

—yes. I just can't swallow the fact that I've spent twelve years of my life in prison, and for what? I mean, I've done twelve years for not stopping my partner killing this guy.

I spent my wonder years right here in prison. At what point is "enough is enough"? I almost want to say I'd feel better if I would have actually killed the guy and did all they said, to justify doing this amount of time.

It's almost as if you steal a car, but I drive it, not knowing you stole it. If that is against the law, then, hey, I accept my responsibility for that, but that was not in my intent, and I shouldn't be punished like it was. If there's anywhere I've crossed that line, then, hey, I've paid for that.

That's how I feel at this point, simply because I see no relief, and this guy hasn't even made an effort to get me some relief, knowing that he's the one who created this whole situation, and didn't do anything to prevent it from coming down on me too. That's a responsibility he has to take upon himself, and I don't have no problem inflicting it upon him.

*But like you say, he needed to take that responsibility originally. If he did it now, it's a little late; it probably wouldn't have any effect anyway.*

It wouldn't have an immediate effect. But it could benefit me in a certain way, because it would elevate some of the issues that I'm already raising. And, who knows? I mean, there's been cases where people come forward after the fact and say, you know, they were forced into testifying against someone and now they want to tell the truth.

He was in a position where he couldn't tell the truth, because he didn't want to hang himself. So I understand that point. In order for him to clear me, he'd have had to pretty much confess. And that was something he wasn't willing to do. He wanted to take a chance on winning on the grounds of a technicality, or a lack of evidence—stuff like this.

But, he had to know by the evidence that they had on him that he wasn't going to win. But that's the road that he took. He wanted to have at least some chance of getting off. So, I understood that, to a point. I mean, if I put myself in his position—which I've done a million times—what would I have done? Quite frankly, I probably wouldn't have done too much too differently from what he done. I would have pled my innocence all the way to the end.

But then there's also the other side to the coin, where there's someone that's being affected by my selfishness, and I won't do anything to stop his bleeding, because I can't stop my own.

But at some later time, he still could have made an effort to try to clear my name. Even if it was nothing but an effort, then I probably would have been a little more understanding of him. I probably would have tolerated what he'd done earlier.

*Did he get the same sentence as you?*

Yeah, the same sentence as me.

*Life without?*

Life without.

*Where is he now?*

Walla Walla, last I heard.

*You mentioned that your gang connections, your friendships from that period of your life, were the tightest friendships, the most significant friendships you've had, that it's an important part of your past, and emotionally powerful to you, and you made some very important connections with people. Yet you also said that you're not any longer in contact with anyone from your pre-prison days,—*

No.

*What happened with those people, with those friendships? If they were that good, if you were so loyal to each other and had good friendships, why are they not part of your life now?*

Yeah, that's another good question. I mean, people have asked me that many times in these last twelve years. "If you're loyal to someone, how come they can't be loyal to you?"

And that happens all the time, even with family. I mean, you expect family to have that type of bond, but when you get caught up in a situation like this, you can lose even them.

People become individuals after awhile. You know, after you've grown and you've matured throughout that lifestyle, you start thinking about yourself, especially when they're living on the edge just like I was. Between prison, death, and moving away and getting the hell away from all of that type of lifestyle, you lose track of people, you drift apart. There's so many of us that's actually in prison that it's hard for someone to keep up with it.

But as far as that commitment or loyalty, those are your friends you depended on when it counted. I mean, your life was on the line with these guys.

It's almost like in prison, where you're in a situation where a riot breaks out. And, the people that turn out to be your best friends are the people that have your back, that stand back-to-back with you to fight off whatever you're confronted with. And, who knows, ten years from that day, you might not never see him again, but these are the values that you have with that person, because when you look back after the fact, and you see who stood by me at the time of my direst needs, and the time when my life was on the line, it was this individual. And this, to me, is the highest honor that you can receive. It's pretty much like someone saved your life, and you feel like you're in debt to them for life.

We'd been through too many situations where it took a collective effort, all of us together, to survive the life that we were living. And those were the values that I had on those friendships. But on the individual standpoint, from a personal level, everyone went their own way, decided to do their own thing. Half of them are in prison. Some are dead. Some I don't know where they are. Some think I'm dead, I mean, have no idea where the hell I'm at. And I'm sure if I came across someone from my earlier life, we'd probably resume the same friendship we had before, but probably on a different level, because a lot of that you grow out of. You learn that, how can you raise a family, how can you be a father, how can you be an individual man without detaching yourself from the things that you grew up with as a child?

So, it's more the survival skills that you were forced to do back then, as you are in prison. But if you're no longer put in that predicament to need to band together to survive, then those connections fade away. Now you got a life, and some stability that you want to maintain.

*When you were young, and involved in the gang activities, did it feel more permanent to you? Did you assume "these are people who will be in my life until I'm dead, and—"?*

I felt that way then. I mean, because I was young and dumb and naïve. The emotions I had at the time for my friends that really stood by my side—friends to me back then were the most precious people to me in life, especially if they prove to be a true friend.

And actually I still feel that way about friendship now. I mean, it's almost as if it's a relative, you know, a brother, or a sister, someone you truly love that you know you can always count on, as you would with a wife or a husband.

So, yeah, I believed that I would probably go to my grave beside some of these guys, or girls, because, I mean, I valued them so much, and I knew they could always depend on me. I wasn't quite as convinced or secure with the fact that I could depend on them, because I can easily be disappointed. And I know it's kind of rare to find someone to put forth the same effort that I know I could put forth. So, I try not to put too high expectations on someone else.

But I felt that. And I was very disappointed when some that I really expected to be there for me wasn't. But I wasn't surprised.

*Congratulations, by the way. You have an impending wedding, I understand.*

Yes.

*Is there a date yet?*

Not yet. We're going to discuss that on Friday. I have to see the chaplain today about it. It'll take three weeks from yesterday for it to be official. Then we'll set a date. But, I'm pretty sure it's going to be somewhere during April.

*In our last conversation that we taped, we talked a bit about your fiancée and how you two first got together. Let's follow up on that.*

Yeah. [Laughs.] I feel like I'm going through marriage counseling again. I had to tell them this whole story yesterday.

*So, as I recall, you ended up at Clallam Bay after a lengthy stint in IMU, and she was an employee at Clallam Bay, and that's how you met her. You became more and more deeply involved emotionally, much to the consternation of the prison administration, until she finally quit. She waited until it was clear they couldn't fool with her retirement benefits, and then she contacted you, and eventually started visiting you regularly. Is that correct?*

Yes, except that actually, they blocked her from visiting me at Clallam Bay.

*How were they able to do that? I mean, I know there's a mandatory six month waiting period, but after the six months, how were they able to keep you apart?*

Well, she had a brother and nephew that work there, so they said it was a security risk, for the relative of an employee to be coming up there to visit an inmate.

It's the same rule as they have here; if someone comes to work here that happens to know someone that's in this institution, they would have to relocate that officer- –which they never do—or transfer the inmate to another institution. It's a conflict of security, breach of security, and that's how they were able to keep me away from her.

But I pursued it—because they rejected the visit, denied it—and I know that you can't deny me my visiting privileges. You can't deny me something that I had coming. I mean, she was able to come up in there and work, so there should be no security risk for her to come in to visit me.

*And that's why they transferred you?*

That's why they transferred me, to accommodate my visiting privileges with a former staff member. That's how I ended up here.

*Is she still coming up pretty regularly to see you?*

At a maximum, I'd say three times a month. A minimum of once a month.

You know, her health problems right now restrict her an awful lot more than what it used to be. For her to come up, it's a long drive. It's over a five hour trip, almost three hours each way. Of course with her health problems—she has cancer—it makes it very difficult. But if she decides she wants to come up, she'll be here.

*Back in the early stages, how did she know to trust you? Wasn't she suspicious, given what everybody tells the employees about prisoners, and how they're all going to try to manipulate them?*

Well, you know, I don't know if she completely trust me even now. [Laughs.]

According to what we talked about in the marriage counseling yesterday, I mean, you know, she trusts me up until a certain point. Because there's some things she's still not sure of.

And I know why. And I told her why. I told her from the very beginning. I mean, I was a very well-known person around the institution, getting into all kinds of problems, involved in so many administrative behavior problems. And she knew that. I mean, she knew the kind of person I was back then and what I was capable of.

I had a life without sentence. That colored everything about me and my attitude and my behavior. There were things I just wasn't conscious of the way I should have been, because of it. And she knew all that, and had to be wary.

But, you know, it got to the point that she was the one person—and I knew we were in trouble when they were doing this—that when certain staff had a problem with me, they'd go to her and say, "Will you talk to him?" And I'm wondering, like, why would one staff go tell another staff to talk to me? They knew already that I'm going to listen to her rather than anyone else, that me and her had some type of rapport. [Laughs.]

But, yeah, in the end she mostly trusted me, because I was honest with her. I didn't try to hide from her what I was. I mean, once you've lived your life a certain way, that's just what your life has been, and there's no denying it.

And there were some things that she knew I could never admit without making myself vulnerable, some things that I was involved in that, like, related to drug activities, or fighting, or gang-related activities, and things like this. But when she asked me about them, I told her. I trusted her, and she came to trust me.

Oh, I was scared at first. I went "Uh oh!" because, if she was actually an administration turncoat, well then I'm fucked. But—and this happened so much, and so frequently, in our conversations—she then told me a lot of personal things about her that no one else, not even her kids, knew, things that could get her in trouble if I spoke about them.

We developed that kind of understanding, that anything we discussed would stay between us, and it would never be exposed.

*So for a time there, you thought that she might be the one manipulating you, that maybe she's just working for the administration trying to get information from you.*

Oh yeah, I mean, she'll tell you that. She'll swear to God that I've always accused her of being Secret Service, or worked for the Feds and everyone else. DEA agent. I mean, she even told the chaplain yesterday, "You know, at first, 9 was hesitant with me, simply because he thought I worked for the administration."

Really I felt this way for a whole year that I first knew her. I mean, we were becoming friends, but at the same time I was holding back. I was pushing her away, because I was scared, thinking that there's no way that someone that don't know me can like me as much as she claim to. And I'd ask her why, and she'd say, "You're someone I see some potential in," and all that. Give me a break. I couldn't see the potential in me, so how could she?

*Come on, you're a likable fellow, 9. [Laughs.]*

[Laughs.] Well, I didn't know that. I didn't know that until I started liking myself.

*OK. [Laughs.]*

But she helped me grow, Craig, she helped me reach from adolescence to manhood. She helped me understand my values, by showing me what values really are. I mean, what I thought was values was minute compared to what I now see as my values. I had no care for life in general, and then I had the most profoundest ideas that make you motivated and inspire you. It's total opposites. One, you're headed down a dark road; the other, you see the light.

And it's nothing spiritual as far as, like, God or religion, but it's more like being in tune with yourself, understanding yourself. I used to reject, like, self-help groups and books and all this other stuff. Then I read all of those, but none of them turned out to be as meaningful to me as the understanding of myself that I got from understanding her interpretation of me.

It's almost like, not just looking in the mirror and seeing you, but seeing what someone else sees when they see you. It's getting a different opinion other than the biased opinion that you would have of yourself. And that's where I think I crossed over.

*What are some of the specific changes that you feel in yourself as a result of what you're describing, you know, your interaction with her? How did you go from adolescence to manhood? And how is this path better than the darker path that you were on?*

Well, my biggest one, that I've always known but she reminded me of it, is compassion. I have the ability now to have compassion. The things that I used to do that was totally unnecessary, I now see as disgusting. And it wasn't something I forced myself to see; it was something I found, like, looking back on something, I realized, boy, was that stupid.

Some of the things I did, back then, I thought was the right thing to do. I took advantage of people, manipulated people. People that I knew can't think too much for themselves, I would take advantage of them.

But now, I won't do it, and I hate to see someone else do it. I mean, I developed compassion. I see someone, even if he's my friend, taking advantage of someone that I see as vulnerable, and I will despise that, simply because I know it's not right.

Determination. I mean, having a focus and concentrating on something I really want, and being determined enough to go for it, or to put forth my best effort. Not caring about the difficulties or any repercussions or whatever. If you want it bad enough, go for it. You know, think positive, and things like this. Think better of yourself. Like yourself.

And education. I mean, she's extremely articulate. She challenges me, simply because of the way we communicate. I mean, sometimes her letters challenge me, the way she write me.

The intellectual way she speaks. That allows me to elevate my vocabulary and my verbal skills and my whole spiel. It gives me that type of inspiration. I view it as so beautiful, so eloquent, the way she represent herself. That allows me to want people to view me that same way.

These are some of the things that she's shown me, helped me see, that I've overlooked elsewhere. I probably could have found it from anyone else, but she just happened to be the person that came into my life that I noticed it first.

*It sounds like you've been very fortunate to come across at least two really quality people to influence you during this part of your life the last few years: Henry—*

Henry, yeah.

*—and her.*

Well, you know, they remind me of each other. I keep telling them I think it has to do with their age.

But yeah, I did get lucky.

They team up on me all the time, though, those two. They think alike. [Laughs.]

*[Laughs.] Is she your best friend?*

She is most definitely my best friend. By far. And I don't care if she die tomorrow and I live to be a hundred, I will never have a best friend more so than her. I don't think I ever could. I don't want a best friend more than her.

*Does it scare you that you're not going to have much more time with her?*

Shitless. I mean, it is absolutely terrifying. And I done had conversations with God, thinking, like, "How come you allow me to feel like this, to leave me at this level on my own? I mean, she's someone that's so deserving of so much. Why do you do this to her?" And I told her I would probably rather it happen to me than to happen to her, because overall she's a beautiful person, not just because I love her so much, but simply because of the initiative and the sacrifices she's taken because of me.

Like we were saying, you know, there's a lot of difference between us two, and her whole family despised our being together because of that fact. But she stood her ground, and she made her choices. She stuck with me when it would have been a lot easier to go our own separate ways, and cater to her family, even including her mom, who's still alive. But they all respect it now, and they all know that it's real. It's been seven years we've been together, and we never, you know, deviated from that.

But, to see her in this misery like this, you know, it make me want to cry even when I think about it. To know that tomorrow or the day after, before she even have the chance to do the things that she really want to do—her goals were to have a grandbaby and see me out of prison, and she finally had her grandbaby.

It hurts me the most not being able to be there for her at a time she really need me. That is what hurts me the hardest. That is what's devastating.

*Is her condition terminal?*

Yeah, it's terminal. "Systemic" is what they call it. It's in the bone, and in the bloodstream. But, you know, she's still more concerned about me than her. Ain't that strange? I say, "You're crazy!" [Laughs.] But she's still more concerned about me; she doesn't even want to talk about her cancer.

But, I refuse to let her give up, because I know, as long as you've got hope, there's always a chance. As long as you're alive, you got hope. And, that's my life, that's what I maintain in the position I am. And I know there's always miracles. I know there is a God. So I'm just keeping my fingers crossed and hoping that maybe a miracle can happen. But from a realistic standpoint, yes, I'm scared to death.

I honestly don't know how I'll react. I probably won't be a safe person to be around. Or they'll probably want to lock me up in segregation and keep me there, until they've determined that I'd be a safe person, because I might lose it. I don't know. I can't prepare myself for that.

*Why the decision after seven years to get married?*

Well, that's a hell of a question, Craig. We have actually been talking about getting married for quite some time. And, there was some differences that we had to get over, because we were worried about how we'd be viewed. She didn't want to see herself as a pedophile, and these things like this.

*[Laughs.]*

[Laughs.] So, I was kind of concerned about that, but we accepted that. We accepted the age difference. And we knew that we were eventually going to get married. Then, the revelation of her illness, you know, set in, and she knew this was something that she wanted to do while we still could.

But a friend recently asked me, like, "Are you marrying her because of her illness, or are you really marrying her because you love her?" And I wanted to say because I love her, because that is true. But I kind of think it's both, in all honesty. And then I keep going through my mind, well, at least it makes me eligible to attend the funeral when she dies. Otherwise, I couldn't go, because she's not immediate family.

*In our earlier correspondence, I asked you about your contact with people from the outside, and whether you can be totally honest with them, or do you have to put a certain face toward them that's different from the person you are inside.*

Yeah.

*And you said that if you're totally honest about who you really are, including your bitter and angry side, and the kinds of things you have to do in here to survive—if you're honest about that part of you, with your outside people, then that takes away from the integrity of your relationships with those people. I thought that was an interesting, kind of peculiar, way of putting it, because normally we would think integrity means just the opposite, that honesty, and openness and communication and all that is a part of integrity. You even said, "I need to manipulate and deceive people in order to maintain the integrity of those relationships." That sounds awfully close to a contradiction, to manipulate people in order to maintain integrity. Could you elaborate on that? And also, what does it do to you, to not have people you can reveal those things to, to have to put on a face even with your friends and your family who care about you the most? What does it do to you to bottle that stuff inside and not be able to be yourself?*

Yeah, I remember that question. Actually I thought of it just now when you were asking me how does she trust me. That reminded me of that.

But I think about it like this, Craig. You know, the vision I have in my head when I gave that answer is the same as someone that's dying of AIDS, or someone on death row. You don't want no one to see your weakness. You don't want nobody to see your fear. And you put on this certain face that you know that it only takes someone to look at you closely and they can see this whole big frown, this fear all through you, but you smile because you try to hide those feelings, simply because you don't want them to know that you're really hurting inside.

The kind of relationships that I have with people I associate with that I like the most, when I say I want to maintain the integrity, I mean that I try to keep my prison life, or the way I'm suffering in here, separated from the life that they're living. Because I don't want my best friend or my wife or my family or my mother—I don't want someone that I care about to do time with me. I got to do this. I want to keep that out of our relationship, because I don't want to turn them into my roommate in here.

And when I say manipulate or deceive, it's, like, asking, "How was your day today?" I could have had a fucked up day, but I don't want to ruin your day by telling you how mine was. Mine is going to be the same way every day. I know that's something I can't change. There's going to be some better than others, but I know my day's going to be fucked up regardless, because I'm still blocked by these four walls. But I don't want that wall to be the picture that you see that prevents you from ever getting an understanding of me, or having the kind of relationship with me that I want to have.

I got a thing that I practice with myself all the time I been locked up. It's something I was told from the very beginning of doing time: Don't let this prison, or this place, dictate to you mentally. It can control you physically, but don't let it dictate to you mentally, because then you become institutionalized.

But it gets harder to manipulate, to deceive, because when people know you, after awhile, they get to know you for who you are. They know you better. Like, she can tell when I'm deceiving her or I'm hiding something from her. And she will try her best to drag it out of me: "What is it? What is it?" And I say, "It's nothing." "What is it? What is it?" "It's nothing."

But instead of actually telling her what it is, I will say, "Look, I told you before that I will never expose my bitterness and anger, anger that I suffer in prison, because it may seem trivial to you: 'Oh, I got upset because the officer did this, this, this…,'" and she could think that it's totally trivial. But what she don't know is what this guy had been doing to me for the past year, and I don't want to sit there and waste time explaining all the background for something that to her may seem trivial. To me, it's huge, but I don't want to drag her into that.

You see it happen so many times. You see people from the outside worried about you losing your mind simply because of the way you react to these things they think are trivial. So that's where the manipulation come in. That's where no matter what—I could have gotten into a confrontation with a cop, or somebody had done something fucked up to me, and be mad as hell, and be on my way to the visiting room, but I got to try to go up there, to manipulate my feelings, and not look like I've been hurt, or not look like I've been damaged by it.

That's only my opinion, now. I can't speak for everybody in general, because some people have prison relationships. Prison is their life, and their family's life. Their wives are up here every day. Their wives are calling the administration every day because of something so small. "Why did he got to stay in his room for three days?" and stuff like this.

I don't want my family involved with shit like that. Let me fight this battle. You just do whatever you're doing out there that benefits you, because whatever you do that's best for you, you're also doing it for us. I will handle this end here. I will take all the pain from this end. I don't never want you to be inflicted by the pain that comes to me; I'd rather take it myself.

That's why I gave that answer like I did.

And, what it does to me? It hurts, but sometimes it makes me feel proud, because I feel like I'll find the strength on my own to envelop all the different things that she would otherwise feel being a part of my life. It's almost like a sponge. Whatever the pain you suffer, whatever the pain you're feeling, let me have it. Let me help you. Like, with her illness, with the cancer, I told her before, several times, "I would rather it be me than you, 'cause you don't deserve it."

Why not inflict all the pain on someone that's already in pain? Let me take it all. I don't want to share it with you. Why can't just one of us die, and spare the other? Spare the one that deserves better.

And that has always been my view. It goes back even to the situation with my co-defendant. Why should we both be in prison with the same offense? Why should both of us suffer when only one of us has to? Take your beef.

*What if the shoe was on the other foot? What if it turned out that Maggie downplays the negativity in her life, and misleads you about it or manipulates you about it? Like, maybe she's in more physical pain than she lets on. Or maybe her friends or family treat her differently now because she's ill, in a way that hurts her. Or maybe a former co-worker insulted her about her relationship with you. But she doesn't tell you any of this. She doesn't tell you that she's scared to die. I mean, if she withheld all that from you, and just said, "Oh, I'm having a good day, and everything's fine. It's cool," wouldn't you feel there's something missing there? Wouldn't you feel, like, "She doesn't care enough about me to bring me into her pain"?*

[Laughs.] Yeah, yeah. You know, I actually feel the opposite when it's her, and that's something that we recently—I won't say a fight—but we had a strong discussion about. And it was almost as if I contradicted what I just explained to you, because it was her instead of me.

You know, she's worried about telling me certain things, because she's worried about the way I feel. And that's something I don't want. I won't accept that. I mean, don't worry about how I feel about it.

But then that would be her same answer if she heard exactly what I just told you. But I honestly believe it's two different things, in my opinion, simply because hers is coming from, not just the illness, but being worried about my feelings. Feelings is one thing—feeling of my emotions is one thing—but feeling my pain is different. It's kind of hard to explain.

I do know she downplay a lot of it. I do know she try to avoid telling me certain things, because, like she says, my plate is already full; she don't want to pile more shit on my plate.

I mean, like, one thing that hurt her that she won't talk about with me any more—something her sister told her when she first revealed that she had cancer—"Well, that's what you get for fucking with that little black dude that was up in prison." That devastated her, Craig. This is her only blood sister, and she had to say something devastating to her like that.

I asked her, "Are you responding to this simply because you're hurt about what she said about your cancer, or the way she felt about me, what she stated about me?" But she said, "Neither one of those two. Simply because the way she did it, and why she did it." She said, "That is so insensitive, so inconsiderate. If you have something like that to say, it'd probably be best for you to not say anything at all."

That made me so furious that her sister is one person on this Earth at that time that I knew I couldn't have been around, because that would have justified me doing something to her, or her doing something to me. And this is the bitterness that her family had because of her involvement with me. They all felt this way, except her daughter and her son, and her mom. The rest hate it. Hate her for it.

She don't tell me a lot, because she's worried about my feelings, she's worried about my reaction. She's worried about piling more shit on my plate. She's worried about how I would react. I say, "You'll never know how I'll react until you tell me."

*I wasn't clear on the distinction you were drawing. You were saying there was actually a disanalogy between your withholding things from her versus her withholding things from you, because she's doing it based on the feelings it will engender in you. I didn't get that. Can you explain that?*

Yeah, yeah, it kind of sounds stupid the way I explained it. I didn't get that either when I said it. [Laughs.] Let me try again.

There's a lot of things I don't tell her, from my position, simply because I don't want her doing time with me. And then, she don't tell me a lot of things on her end, simply because she don't want me to feel the pain that she feels.

Now if you asked her, those are the same thing. But in my opinion, they're two different things, simply because I want her to tell me whatever it is that's bothering her, whatever it is that's affecting her. The whole details, her tests, what level her test is at; I want to know everything. And, she won't tell me a lot of these things, because, "You got enough on your plate. I don't want to tell you this, because I know it ain't going to do nothing but make matters worse." Then I'll pry it out of her, and I'll explain it to her, that hey, I deserve to know. And then she'll tell me.

But she'll reverse the same thing onto me, and say, "Hey, then I deserve to know what's going on in your time, what's going on in your days."

But there's just a difference there with me, simply because I don't want you doing the time with me. I don't want you to feel this prison. I don't want you to know exactly what goes on behind these walls. I don't want you to have to take on a prison lifestyle, prison marriage, prison relationship. I don't want prison nothing to be a part of this. Even though it got me in here, I want our spirits to be together, I mean, outside of these walls, universal.

It's kind of hard to explain, because—

*Yeah, I still don't see the disanalogy, because she could say, "Well, I don't want you to share my cancer. I don't want our relationship to be a cancer relationship. I don't want you to have to go through what I'm going through, imagining yourself in my situation," and all that. So, it seems like cancer and prison are—*

They're the same, but, now, there's a better chance of me helping her than in her helping me. Because, she could never tell me how to do time. And though I could never tell her how to do cancer, I could give her, like, advice, as far as what she should ask when she goes to the doctors, things like this. Or even just as far as trying to help get her emotionally stable, to give her support in those areas, and helping her through this.

But she cannot help me do this time, you know, what I go through every day here.

*But she sort of can, though. She's already helped you indirectly just by making you a better person and giving you a different focus. I mean, maybe she can't help you with, you know, "Here's what you should say to this guy about this dope deal,—"*

Right, right, right.

*—but then that's analogous to her situation after all. You're not a doctor. You're not going to be able to tell her, "Take this pill rather than that pill." I mean, you can cheer her spirits and you can help her through this, and make her a better person through it. But, you can't really give her specifics about treating her cancer; your help and your advice can only be very general. And similarly, she can be supportive and help you with your life in prison in a general way, but not with the specifics of it. So, it still sounds like it's an analogous situation to me.*

You know, you're right. I want to say it's different, but you're absolutely correct.

*I wonder if it's partly just sort of a macho thing, like—*

No.

*—you're a man, and so you should deal with your own pain yourself, and you can help others with their pain, but you can't seek help—*

No.

*—or whine about your own.*

No, no, no way. That's not even a part of it. Whether it was a male or a female on the outside, it's almost like you're taking away from their life by bringing them into a part of yours. When I got arrested, when I got convicted, I got convicted, not them. I don't want any of them exposed to what DOC is doing to me.

*So you don't think it's a matter of it being somehow weak and effeminate to complain about your situation here, and to open up about it to other people?*

Sure, but—

*It's not weak to whine to them about it? It's not, like, you're a man, so you're not allowed to suggest, "I can't handle prison; I can't do this"?*

Oh no. Hell no. I mean, shit, I can't do this. I'm a man, and I admit that to everybody. [Laughs.] I got no problem admitting I can't do this.

*[Laughs.]*

I mean, shit, I don't care how macho you are, if you can do this, then, there's something wrong with you. [Laughs.] I mean, ain't no part of this about being a man, 'cause I've seen a lot of them turned into women. So, it ain't got nothing to do with that.

It's just—the whole idea is, you know, like you get your judgment, and this is what you got to do. This is what God has in store for me. And I'm the one's got to deal with it.

Now, if it's something joyous, I tell her, then I want you to be a part of that. I want to share it with you, because you are so valuable to me that I want you to feel what I feel. And this is something good that I know would benefit you, as well as it benefits me, and would bring us happiness.

But there's also that pain. And if I'm inflicted with pain, I don't want you to feel it. I try to keep that pain far separate from you, simply because I know right now that you can't afford it, that you don't deserve it, that you don't need it, and it will probably take away from your life, take away whatever things you do. I don't want your days spent walking around all day long worrying about, "Man, what is they doing to my friend? What are they doing to my baby? How's he doing? Is he losing his mind?"

That is the worst thing to me, because she'll be so concerned about how I'm living up in here. And I cannot let her opinion affect how I live.

I know this guy over here is threatening me, but if I fight this guy, or do something to him, then if she find out, she going to be mad at me. I can't never let them two intertwine, because that can be the difference between whether I live or whether I die. If I'm so caught up in her being concerned, and how she might react to the things I do, then this guy could sneak up on me and do something to me. But if I can keep these things separate, then I'd probably be able to defend myself and do what I need to do to him.

I mean, it's almost putting me in a predicament where I have to choose between my outside life and my inside life. And I got to do this time first and foremost. I got to do what I feel is best for me in here. And the only way I feel it can work is to try to keep my outside world and inside world totally separate.

*But, can't you ever get any valuable insight from outsiders on the situations—?*

Oh my God, yes.

*—you face in here? I mean, you're stuck in this world, and you're only interacting with people that have the same values and handle problems the same ways and so on. What if it turns out that there were other ways of handling this guy threatening you, but you'd never know it, because you're stuck in a convict mentality? But somebody like her or me or somebody from the outside world with a totally different perspective might be able to say, "Wait a minute. Even though I'm not a prisoner, maybe I spot things in this situation that you're too close to the situation to see."*

Right.

*But see, you could never benefit from that kind of exchange of ideas, or question your own values, or your own way of handling problems, if you always said, "Well, outsiders by definition can't know about prison. They can't understand what I'm going through, how I have to deal with my problems. I won't even tell them about it. I'll do what I got to do in here, and keep it to myself."*

Yeah, but there's a difference, though. I mean, you're right, and that applies in certain cases. It's the outsiders that actually help me better my life on the inside the most, by far. I mean, just meeting with you, and talking the way we do, for instance.

I process information differently than most people. I've always felt that way. When I process information, my values and the way I think pretty much causes me to focus on how it can make me a better person. I think about how it can benefit me, how it can help me be a better individual. You know, like when you and I can sit down together, and you tell me, "OK, 9, this is how I see you. This is some of the things that I've been confronted with in my past. This is what my thoughts was," and issues like that. This helps me become a better person. Not so much a better prisoner, but a better person.

I mean, come on, the outsiders is essentially the key that help most of us survive on the inside, especially me. Because it helps me understand what a quality person should be. I mean, I can easily find me a role model in prison, and it'll probably be somebody trying to be nothing, just like some of these. [Motions dismissively to some prisoners walking down the hall past the window.] But then when I see someone on the outside that's living in that world out there that have the same quality in life that I'm trying to build, then I know that I'm somewhat on the right track. It's almost like I use it as my gauge.

But, see, you couldn't come in and tell me how to be a better prisoner. You can always tell me how to be a better person, but not a better prisoner. And I'd rather be told how to be a better person than a better prisoner.

That's why I value, like, when someone from the outside reminds me, "Whatever the things you suffer in here, they're minute. You should think about more important things in your life," because that's telling me how to be a different person.

But then that's different than if you start telling me, you know, "Ignore that guy that's threatening you, because he's a piece of shit. You need to do this," or, "You need to do that." I need you to help me grow as an individual, and to let me handle being a prisoner. And that's why I try to separate the two.

I hope that makes sense where you can understand that.

*I think so.*

But so often in here, you got to just look at it in the practical way and do what's necessary. You got too many different personalities you're surrounded by. You got to remember that everyone you see on the news or in the newspaper, where you think, like, "How can somebody do some crazy shit like this?" they're all in here. And they ain't too much changed from the time when you saw them on the news to the time when they walked through these front doors. And the kind of person that you all were so eager to clean up off the street and get them away from you is the same kind of people that I got to deal with every day, and they're in that same frame of mind. So I have to be always watching them, because I don't know what they're capable of doing next.

And that ain't something that a shrink or nobody else can tell me how to deal with. All I've got to rely on is my experience as a prisoner, and my observing this person, or people like him, and getting a feel for how to deal with what I see. And what I see you'll never be able to see, unless you know that person, unless you sit down and have a conversation with that person, like you are with me. It's too many different personalities that's clashing in here. I couldn't expect you to give me advice on it, because I know that's something you could never understand unless you've been here.

And for practical purposes, I can't always react the same way, because every situation is different. I can apply something at this end that I can't apply over here, because it's two different situations.

But you carry it one day at a time. You carry it situation by situation, and you can only do what you feel is best for you. You try to avoid whatever possible instances that you see are going to get yourself in trouble, and sometimes you can't.

And I don't know what level it will escalate to. I might only have to fight with fists over here; with this guy, I might have to use a weapon. I never know. I can't treat everybody the same, or react the same to every situation. Sometimes it's hard. And I can't expect some advice from an outsider on that, simply because you don't understand.

But it still comes back to when I'm just frustrated throughout the day, and I'm just continuously having, you know, problems in different areas throughout the day from different people, whether it be a cop yelling at me or talking shit to me or calling me a name, and things like this, these are things that I've suffered that I probably don't want to dwell on with her. I mean, she can know what she needs to know, like if a package got sent to me but the color was too dark so I couldn't have it, because then she can go back and get a brighter color. But not just all the stuff that piles up in here.

I don't want to know that the only reason she loves me or cares about me is because she's concerned about me being in prison. Sympathy, you know, "I hate to see him there," you know, "I can't turn my back on him because look where he is." I want her to like me for me, whether I'm in prison or on the streets. That's the kind of understanding I want. It feels more rigid that way, more solid that way. Our relationship can't be about prison, where I drag her in here mentally to do this time with me. I refuse to let that happen.

*One other thing I wanted to ask you about, 9. Two people that you're close to in here, two people that you respect amongst your fellow prisoners, have had opposite kinds of parole news, or release* *news, recently. You had Henry on the one hand getting unexpected good news, where it looks like there's some realistic chance he can actually leave here, in spite of his life sentence.\* And you had Jerry come up for parole last year—I know you were rooting for him—and they turned him down. He's going to be here at least a few more years, maybe a lot longer. Talk to me a little about what you felt being with those guys, going through those experiences that had such opposite results.*

Well, these are two people that I totally respect, two people that's totally respected throughout the system. And, yes, I did root for both of them, because having known them and been incarcerated with them for a number of years, I know they've done enough time, that they've earned their chance to go back to society.

With Jerry, you know, in my mind, I feel like he deserve to go, because he's a totally different human being than he was when he first started doing time. And, he proved that he's not only been rehabilitated, but he's become a more rational human being. To see him get denied is extremely discouraging, because I know it takes away all the hope. I mean, it takes away your whole dream of one day getting out of here, taking advantage of whatever life has left.

Seeing him go through that, it's almost like the equivalent to something I see in myself, my hatred for being in prison during the best years of my life. And I can understand why he's so hurt, because it's not like he's a young guy. His clock is ticking, and it's ticking more with him in here. That decreases how much length of time he have out there. And, he got family, and different responsibilities he would like to take care of. So, it really does concern me to see him still stuck in here, with the element of not knowing when he'll get out, if ever.

With Henry, it almost is, like, reverse with him. He never seen himself ever getting out of here, because he's almost sixty years old. He done twenty-one years out of five life sentences. So, I can't say he's accepted it, but he's realized the possibility of him dying in this place.

But he don't focus on that. He don't cater his life around the fact that he will die here. He's still a father. He's still a husband. And he maintain that status. I mean, he's still actively involved in his family's life. And he's still making decisions for them, you know, the best ones he can. And those are the things that I really respect the most about these guys, because doing time doesn't change them, doesn't make them institutionalized.

And, yes, I'm really happy for him. And, yes, I've really got my fingers crossed for him, because I see too many undeserving people get out of here, as opposed to people that I think deserve it. Who am I to say? But I know these guys have been infraction-free for quite a number of years, have stayed out of trouble.

But the one thing that I see most about both of these guys is they educated me. They've helped me to understand about prison life. They teach me different things about where they come from to the way they are now, throughout doing time. How to do time. How to be—I'm not saying just a convict—but a man. How to be a humanitarian.

---

\*This interview was prior to Henry's defeat in the hearing I attended.

And Jerry, unlike his image, bends over backwards to help a guy that he really like, or someone he think deserve that chance. And he'll educate him. When he'll see him do something wrong, he'll pull him up on it.

I seen the Jerry before, where he'd have laughed at the idea of somebody screwing up, or enjoyed it. Used to be he wanted to see a fight, whereas now he'll stop one.

You know, you value that, because you see the difference that they make, not only in you, in educating you, but in improving themselves. The same with Henry.

I look around me here, and there are plenty of the older people that have given up, that I never want to be like. I'm concerned about that, about how it'll be for me if I have to be locked up for the number of years some of these guys have. But, when I get to be, say, fifty years old, I wouldn't mind—I would enjoy, I would feel like I was successful—if I would have the same values and act like Jerry and Henry. Totally respected and respectable. And that's why I root so much for them guys.

*Part of what I want to do with a book like this is to enable readers to have some kind of a feel for what it's like to live in prison. And I think I get bits and pieces of that from various interviews I've done with guys, but it seems like a lot of it's still left very mysterious. I'll ask them about their life in here, and they'll talk about it in very general terms—"Well, it's not as bad as you think," or "Well, it's a lot worse than you think." But I'm just not confident yet that the reader is going to be a lot more knowledgeable than before about what prison's like on a day-to-day basis—what kinds of things you do, what kinds of things scare you, what kinds of things you're proud of, how people interact, how they spend their time, etc. I mean, what can you tell me as far as descriptions or stories that would enable a reader to have some sense of what it's like to exist in prison?*

OK, well, I could tell you this: the reason why there's probably differences in people's opinion is because everyone lives differently in prison. Some people have families; some people don't. Some people get trailer visits; some people don't. Some people have responsibilities to their kids; some people don't. And the people that have the luxurious part of doing time, as far as going out to trailers, having frequent visits because their families live nearby, having a nice job, being able to afford some of the things that they're able to have in prison, these are people who say it's not that bad. But you'll probably generally get that response from mostly people here at WSR.

But I could never forget the times up at Clallam Bay and at Walla Walla, not as much here, when you walk down the tier and you see some guy jacked up in his cell by four or five guys, bullied, getting raped, or beat down.

You're seeing this, and knowing that, not only is it happening to him, but it's also possible that it'll happen to you. You start imagining, what if that person was you? What would you do? How would you react? And, it's easy to say what you would do if you were in that position, but then when you get placed in that position, I mean, you can't think any more; now it's all about your actions. I mean, I just—

*Have you seen things like that with your own eyes?*

With my own eyes. Oh my God, I've seen some things that I still have nightmares about to an extent. I mean, I've seen people get smashed in the head with weight bars, their whole skull cracked in, you know. And, you wonder, like, what did this person do? I mean, then you find out the reason why it happened, it was so small. It was real easy for this person, or anybody, to get caught in that position, 'cause he really hardly did anything.

And then you can always feel this tension, you know, especially when there's something racial. All it takes is a fight between a black and a white guy, and all of a sudden, you've got that tension in the prison. You're watching your back everywhere you move now. You're being tense every time you get around people of another color, because you don't know if these people are trying to get revenge or trying to start something. They got a bunch of ignorant people here, where all it take is one incident to make an uproar.

I was involved in an incident with the Lifers organization shortly after I got here two years ago, when I seen it was nothing but a militia group. Lifers is supposed to be a non-racial club for everyone. But the volunteers would come up, and the only thing they seen was the skull and bones, the lightning bolts, which signifies Aryan Nation. Very limited blacks was involved with Lifers—maybe three out of two hundred and fifty. And, of course, all these years that they'd been existing like this, no one ever went up to them and asked them, you know, what's going on, what would it take for someone non-white to get involved?

Well, I happened to be the first idiot that did. And, it spun downhill from there. It got so bad, even the associate superintendent met me out here in one of these offices, asking me what the hell is going on. And I said, "The only thing I want to do is be a member of the Lifers." And then he questioned me, "Who qualifies you to judge who should or shouldn't be in Lifers? I mean, who are you?" And, it just turned into a whole dispute, a whole racial conflict.

The attitude a lot of prisoners had was that it was quiet around this prison, and you don't want to do anything to put that at risk. Even blacks were pulling up on me, like, "What are you doing? You're new here. You just come into the prison, and you're making an uproar?!" And my response was, like, "You been a convict for all these years, fifteen years, and you've never done anything about it? And then you're going to get up in my face about what the hell I do?!"

But ultimately, by my doing the right thing—and I'm giving this as an example of the point I was making a little earlier—people, even whites, seen it was the right thing. I mean, they were wrong for trying to use this hatred to prevent people from getting involved. And I ended up getting more support from people I didn't know, even than people I did know.

The people in these clubs can be a lot like gang members. You have conflicts within the clubs and between different clubs. You have people that have different enough opinions, so they separate into a new club.

It's almost like a power struggle, where you want to get into the position to be top dog, or you want to run something your way and you're not going to accept somebody else doing it, or "I don't trust your view, because you're black." I mean, this is how far the ignorance has spread throughout the system.

And, it's easy for someone to sit around and preach all day long about, why are we fighting each other when the real enemy is the people that's keeping us locked up here? But then all that it would take is an isolated incident to bring out the racial hatred again, and you forget all about everything except what this person or this group is capable of doing to you. I mean, there's a lot of things that go on in prison every day, where you've got to be careful—it's almost like walking on eggshells. That respect thing is so rigid, and so sensitive, that even what you don't think is disrespect, someone might classify that it is.

You could be in the visiting room and someone could be up there with their daughter or their wife or a friend of their wife or whoever, and you just look up at her, and you think, "Oh, she's cute." No big deal. But to that guy, maybe he sees that as disrespectful.

So now, he's confronting you, like, "Why are you looking at her like that?" "Hey, I can look at what the fuck I want to look at!" There's a problem.

And even if it was something that you didn't intend to do, well simply by the way he approached you, you can't back down. "Yeah I did it! What are you going to do about it?" You'll be backing down if you tell the truth and say, "I wasn't looking at that person like that." Then he will think that he got the better of you.

Well, before I allow someone to feel that way, I will probably tell him, "So what? I did that. Now what?" just to let him know that you're not going to punk me or push me around.

And, these are the things that you have to do in prison, even if you know it might not be something that you would otherwise do. But you have to do this to get the message clear, that I'm not a person that's going to be easy for you to take advantage of. That usually is a deterrence.

But, I mean, the stabbings and all these things—I've seen that happen up at Clallam Bay. I mean,—

*Now, I can see how something like you were describing can happen, where a guy's in the gym and somebody clubs him with a weight bar, because that's so quick. The attacker could easily get in a swing, or a few swings, before staff could intervene. But I have more trouble with the sustained, time-consuming attacks, like you were talking about the person getting ganged up in the cell, getting raped. How can that happen? How can the staff be that far out of control of the institution that they have no idea that there's a big group of people in a cell doing something like that over a significant period of time?*

Well, for instance, right here in this institution, you have as many as three hundred and some people in one building, with three staff. There's no way possible they can watch all that. While they're focusing on their right, something could be happening on their left. "You go keep his attention this way, and I'll get up in the cell." I mean, it's the same way as on the street when someone's casing a joint. "Turn him, distract him over here, and I'll be over there." There's all kind of different ways.

You know, staff got their job to do. They got mail to pass out, they got—

*So you only have three staff for over three hundred people?*

Over three hundred and some guys in each unit. That's right now, because it's double bunked, but when it goes back to these single bunks, you'll have three staff to maybe a hundred and sixty people in one unit. But it's still too many. A hundred and sixty cells. There's no way possible. And that's even assuming they're trying. But of course, you've got those that don't like doing their job.

Bottom line is you can never depend on staff to protect you. In fact, I'm probably more afraid of them than I am other prisoners.

They're here to maintain the security of the prison, and to make sure no one's getting hurt, that they can see. But, there's been too many times when I walk by a cell, seen a guy totally hurt, go up in there and find out he's been knocked out for a whole day.

*Really?*

Yeah. That happens. It's easy. Now they got all the cameras, but even so, they can't watch all of us at the same time. It's impossible.

*I assume there's no realistic way you can intervene when you see something going on like that, if you see somebody getting beaten up, somebody being raped, whatever. You have to kind of walk by and not get involved. Is that accurate? I mean, even if you know it's an innocent guy, and you totally sympathize with his position,—?*

Yeah.

*—you can't really do anything, can you?*

Didn't see nothing; didn't hear nothing; don't know nothing.

*How do you feel about that? To me, that would maybe be the hardest part of all, to be confronted with evil going on like that, and to know that you're so helpless in the face of it, that if you even open your mouth about it, even speak the truth about it, all it's going to do is you're going to put yourself in—*

Some trouble.

*—danger.*

Exactly. And, yeah, it is, you know, it's disgusting, especially knowing that you can't do anything about it.

You start viewing the people that you see inflicting it as people you could probably never have any mutual understanding with, never have a one-on-one conversation with about anything from that point on, because you would probably always be looking at them with a wicked eye.

They'll come up all proud and say, "Did you see the way I did that guy?" and all this, you know. I tell them, "Yeah, man, y'all are crazy," and leave it at that.

You can't say no more. You can't show ever that you're offended by it, because then, of course, they're going to take offense to your taking offense. You got to ignore it. You got to say, "Hey, to each his own." I mean, you know, each person that comes into this prison has got to learn to stand his own ground.

But, then again, there's a rule in prison, and as far as I know this has always been this way: As long as you stand up, even if it's against five to one odds, as long as you stand up to it and fight it off, whether you get beat down or whatever, you're going to get respected for that, and you more than likely will get some help. But when you accept it, and don't put up a fight, then I'm not going to fight for you. I'll fight with you, but I won't fight for you. That's the rule in prison.

I don't care how big of a coward you are. I don't care whether you deserved it or not. But if you stand up against it, you'll probably get some people that will back you.

It also depends on the individual. I mean, there's certain people in prison that have a certain status to where if something happens to them, all hell's going to break loose, and the administration knows who these people are.

That's the way the administration views me. If I get in a fight with a white, and I go to the hole, tomorrow it's going to be some chaos between some people that's in prison that respect me, because the people that know me, they will say, "I know 9, and I know that's not him. So for this to happen, it meant that somebody had to have inflicted this on him."

All it would take is for me to say, "Hey, man, this guy jumped me," and there it is.

But like I said, a lot depends on who you are. If you're just a nobody, someone that's not respected or recognized, it can easily be ignored. Very easily.

*I have had one or more prisoners tell me that the violence is not as unavoidable as they thought it was going to be, that it's kind of overblown. I was talking with somebody this week who's been in prison for a pretty long time—mostly at Walla Walla and here—and he said that if you want to talk about Walla Walla in the Seventies or something, back in the bloodiest days, then, yeah, it's like the movies or worse. It's like the horror stories people tell you. But then he said that for his era, in the last decade or whatever, it's very different. He told me that he had never been in a prison fight in his life. Never had to fight. Never got into any trouble for refusing to fight. And he said he'd estimate that seventy-five percent of the people that live within these walls at WSR have not been in a fight in at least the last ten years, that conflicts like that are just not common any more. Now, is he being misleading, or—?*

Very misleading.

*From what you're telling me, it sounds like guys have to fight all the time to maintain their reputation, and to avoid being victimized, but he's claiming, "Oh, most people don't have to fight."*

You know, it's possible that you can actually go a long way without ever getting into a fight. I mean, it depend on who you associate yourself with, or the way you choose to live in prison. You might just be a "cell warrior," meaning someone that stays in his cell all the time, that rarely come out. I mean, it's probably somebody that keeps himself occupied going to school, or work, or stuff like this. Yes, it's possible.

But it's not possible that seventy-five percent of the people here have never been in a fight. I'd say it's more like the opposite, that seventy-five out of a hundred have at somewhere or other got in a fight in the system. And some have gotten in some extra, doing other people that haven't fought's share.

In here, at WSR, yes, it's a smaller percentage than at other institutions. I mean, you don't see very many fights here, that get caught. There's still a lot of them that happen, but not that get caught in the act. I mean, a cop might see a guy with a black eye tomorrow and know he been in a fight, but he don't know who did it to him. Things like that. But, yes, you can mostly avoid it here at WSR, because there's, like, a certain group of people here that have been staying out of trouble to get here that have prevented that. We'll kind of police ourselves so the ones who want to do the fighting don't ruin this whole thing for all of us.

But as a whole, as far as fighting, I mean, yeah, sure, back in the Seventies at Walla Walla there was fighting every day, killings, stabbings. All this happened frequently. At Walla Walla right now, ain't none of them killings and that stuff going on, but there's still stabbings going on up there. There's fights almost every day. Clallam Bay, there's fights almost every day, sometimes two or three of them.

But the person who would tell you that, I mean, I got an idea what kind of person he'd have to be. He stays away from a certain kind of people. He's a loner. He just works all the time, or keeps to himself. I mean, I don't know who it is, but I know the type of person whose prison experiences would lead him to tell you something like that.

So, yes, it's possible to avoid the fights. But you can never be sure. Somewhere down the line—I mean, all it takes, Craig, is you'll be in the chow hall and waiting in line, and some guy is, like, "Man, can you move it on? I mean, I'm trying to get up here!" And you're, like, "Fuck you!" you know, and he says, "Wait. Wait till I get there!" And then there's no backing down.

# JERRY—March 1999

*"I had a guy beat me twenty-one days in a row, when I was a kid. He beat me twenty-one days in a row.*

*"He was a security guard in the juvenile joint. They had me in an old military cell, with the corner of a mattress cut out. The cell was exactly the size of a mattress. You know how small a military mattress is? They're really small. The corner of it had to be cut out to put in a pound coffee can that I shit and pissed in throughout the day. And I never got out of that cell for six months."*

T he next week, with the administration's permission, I returned during the afternoons for a final set of taped interviews. On the first day, two of the three prisoners with whom I was supposed to meet were no-shows, and the other—Bill—was working. I was told he might or might not be able to get away. Luckily, Jerry was in the building, so we had an impromptu session while I waited for Bill.

Yeah, I think we need to talk about last week's thing being off the record. [Laughs.]

*[Laughs.]*

Jesus, I said some terrible things.

*You said more than you should have? [Laughs.]*

Yeah. [Laughs.] That's all right.

*Well,—*

As long as the book comes out after my release.

*[Laughs.]*

[Laughs.] And we won't send, like, no copies to the warden.

*We won't send any autographed copies to the parole board?*

The fucking board. Yeah, yeah. [Laughs.]

*Actually, speaking of the parole situation, there was one more thing I wanted to ask you about that. When the parole decision first came down—last summer I guess it was—and they informed you that you had been denied, I remember I was having a conversation with one of the other PAP guys. He made a comment—and I wanted to get your reaction to this—he said, "Jerry really didn't expect to get out, and Jerry doesn't think he deserves to get out. If they did let him out, he wouldn't respect them as much. He'd think they're weak. 'Cause if the roles were reversed, he would never let anybody get away with the things he's done. If the shoe was on the other foot, not only would they not be free, they wouldn't even be alive. And if the State or anybody else doesn't respond the same way to his transgressions as he would, then to him that's a sign of weakness, a sign that they're easily conned, that they don't have the strength of their convictions, and so on. So, yeah, if they let him out, he'll take it and he'll be happy with it. He'll be laughing all the way to the bank, in effect, that he put something over on them and got something he didn't deserve." Now, is that an accurate reflection of your position?*

Well, you know, that's, like, the kind of thing we say in prison, not just about my parole situation. See, let's be realistic: they do treat us better than we'd treat them. You know, guys sit around and snivel, "Oh the guards, they can't do this and they can't do that!" Well, to tell you the truth, they treat me way better than I would have treated them. OK?

Now, having said that, let's qualify what we're really talking about here. Jerry McLaughlin at his worst, when he was at the worst, most violent stage of his life, had I had the opportunity to treat them in a fashion, would I have treated them as nicely as they treat us around here? I'd probably treat them a little harder, to be honest, than they treat me.

But that's just something we say to express how it's really not as hard on us here as some want to make it out to be. It isn't really saying literally what I would do to them if the tables were turned; it's saying that, hell, if we were the guys in charge, we'd be running it worse than they're running it, so quit sniveling. You understand what I'm saying? It's directed at prisoners whining or feeling sorry for themselves.

OK, so, like, somebody may misinterpret my attitude if I say, "Yeah, fuck it! I'd have thought they was weak if they did let me go!" It's just an expression. It's a way of blowing it off. You know what I mean? It's my way of not ever allowing what they do to me to hurt me to a degree that I would feel compelled to express it to someone. So you dismiss it: "Yeah, I'd have done worse to them if I were in their shoes. Just shows you how weak they are."

And a lot of guys do let themselves whine about this shit. You'll hear them all the time, talking about how bad they've been treated, how the courts fucked them over. Well, I don't bemoan fate. So what I do, rather than moan, is I blow it off, you know. "Hell, I didn't expect to go. They'd be weak if they did let me go."

But that's not to say that there isn't a grain of truth in it. Did I expect to go this time? I don't believe my behavior over the past twenty years warranted me being released. I don't think I tried hard enough to get out until recently. And I don't think you can wait until the last minute and then start trying, and really expect to get out.

I knew when I was a kid and doing a lot of the things that I was doing that at some point in time, it was going to cause me some additional grief. But at the time, I was willing to risk that. The unfortunate part of that is that when it comes time to pay the fiddler, you're kind of sorry that you wasted all that time. But, who would I blame? I can't sit here and blame the parole board because I wasted that time.

Hell, if they'd let me go the first time, well then maybe it would have been kind of weak, if you think about it. Come on, they can't be that stupid. It can't be that easy. I get to party for twenty-something years, and be cool for a couple, and they let me go? You know, come on.

So, part of the statement holds a certain amount of truth. Would I have "laughed all the way to the bank"? Well, whenever they let me go, I'm going to be ecstatic. But, to what bank I don't know. If they were to let me go in the future, would I feel like, "Well, then they're weak punks; I deserve to just continue in this life in here"? No. That ain't even in the part of the statement that's true.

So, you take a bit of truth, and an actual statement, and you can stretch it into anything. You can dress up a pig anyway you want, but it's still just a pig. You know, and somebody dressed up my statement to be a lot more than it really was.

Sometimes people actually, like, believe everything that comes out of my mouth. You've heard me talk. I talk in—I want to say a grandiose way—but in extremes. I say things in extremes, to make a point.

The Bible does that. You know what I'm saying? There's different parts of the Bible, when they use these—you know, "The mountains moved, and the Earth moved." Well, maybe they didn't actually move. But they add that for the significance.

Well, I do that when I talk sometimes. Now, most of the things I say, you can count on it, like if I say, "Hey, I want to kick your ass!" What I say is really what you get. But sometimes I'm just making an overstatement, or blowing something off, so they don't notice that the thing bothered me, and people will take it literal, and blow it all out of proportion.

But these are people that probably don't really know me, even if they think they do.

*Speaking of your tendency to speak in extremes, that reminds me of another question that I was going to ask you. There are times you talk about how the treatment of the prisoners or of you personally has been very unjust, for instance some of the things that happen in IMU. But many other times, I've heard you make statements in PAP or in the classes saying things like, "I've never gotten an ass-kicking I didn't deserve," or "Anything that's ever happened to me, I deserved it. I probably deserved worse," or, "I'm as bad as anybody in here." One gets kind of conflicting pictures there. Is Jerry being treated unjustly and inhumanely, or is he being treated by the state the way he deserves?*

No, see, you're misinterpreting some things I've said.

Most of the times I've done major time in the hole, it's been for things that I had not done. So in that sense, I didn't deserve it. And there's things that happen during those stretches that I might tell about in the class, not to whine about it, but to use it to emphasize the mistreatment of us as a group. They'll push your food tray in till it falls on the floor, and then blame it on you—that kind of thing.

But given some of the things I've done, life hasn't dealt me no real bad shit. And most of the ass-whippings that you take in the jails and stuff, you invite a lot of those. I'd say it's, like, fifty-fifty, to really be honest with you. Half the time I deserved the ass-whippings, and the other half of the time I didn't.

I told you about that time when they were beating me to a degree where I believed they were going to kill me. The only thing saved me was another cop who wasn't in on it came into the room, and witnessed it. So, I'll let you be the judge. You judge that for the type of treatment you think it is. You know what I'm saying?

I'm a participant here. I'm not just a victim. Never claimed to be just a victim. I know that some of the time, I'm putting myself in harm's way, even risking my life. There's other times that I haven't put myself in harm's way, but it happened anyway. But when it happens, I'm not really surprised. I'm not, like, shocked that they would take the opportunity to get me when they can.

My sentence. I killed the guy that raped my wife. They gave me a life sentence, not for the crime, but because they could give it to me. For my life. For all the things I'd done in my life. For who I was and the lifestyle I'd lived. That's why they gave me that sentence. And, you know, it had something to do with the murder, but had you committed it, you wouldn't have got what I got. OK? Well, then, for the crime, I didn't deserve it, but for the life I'd led up to and including the crime, I kind of earned what I got.

I don't blame anybody but me for the overall direction of my life. But, I hold certain people personally accountable for shit that they did to me along that road. You dig what I'm saying? In other words, like, when some shit-eater takes the opportunity to do something specifically bad to me that I don't have coming, well, that's on another level, you know.

But did I put myself in a position to be treated like that? Yeah. I don't blame society for that jerk. It's on me for putting myself here, and it's on him for doing what he's doing, but it's not society's fault.

There was a time, now, when I was a younger man, when the picture wasn't as clear, when my view of the world, of a sense of community inside and out, wasn't as clear as it is now, when I would have held society responsible for what those individuals did. And, a lot of times, you'll hear guys in here speak from that point of view.

In other words, like, I take a certain amount of responsibility for being here in the first place to have been abused. But I'm not alleviating that guy from his responsibility of the abuse. And I'm also not holding some illusionary group of people—Joe Citizen, faceless Joe Citizen—responsible for siccing that guy on me. See? But a lot of guys are, especially younger guys. They can't draw that line yet.

What I try and do is accept my share of that responsibility. So I can't blame anybody for any of the things that's happened to me. I can blame a guy for taking advantage of my situation, though, and maybe putting some personal shit on that wheel. You know what I mean? Now, I hold those guys responsible.

Don't ever mistake what I'm saying. [Laughs.] There's some people that I'll never forget. You know, given an opportunity, I'm going to put that shit back on the wheel for them.

*So what you're saying is that there are specific guards or wardens or politicians or whatever who've made your life worse than it should be, but that's different from blaming society as a whole, or the world as a whole.*

Yeah, you know.

And fifteen years ago, I would have said I would actively pursue those people, given an opportunity. Now, you grow a little bit further as a human, and you say, well, God willing, I just hope I will never come face-to-face with having to make that choice, you know. I don't know what decision I'd make, given an opportunity to extract revenge.

I had a guy beat me twenty-one days in a row, when I was a kid. He beat me twenty-one days in a row.

He was a security guard in the juvenile joint. They had me in an old military cell, with the corner of a mattress cut out. The cell was exactly the size of a mattress. You know how small a military mattress is? They're really small. The corner of it had to be cut out to put in a pound coffee can that I shit and pissed in throughout the day. And I never got out of that cell for six months.

They told my people that I wanted to go to a foster home, that I never wanted to come home again, which was a lie. I mean, I ain't never told nobody that in my whole life. The reason they told them that is because this guy had gone so far, had come so close to killing me, that they were afraid to let me get back to my people. They was actually kind of stuck in a little limbo situation, where the administration and some of the staff weren't going to let him kill me, but they didn't know what else to do with me. So they kept me in a military brig with absolutely no contact with anybody else, ever, for over six months, till my mom come up there and demanded to see me.

And when she saw me, and I had big sores all over me and shit, she went off. They put me on a bus that night. This is how far out of line they were.

They put me on a bus that night and sent me to Seattle. No parole, no nothing.

And I didn't even know where my people lived when I got to Seattle. You know, 'cause I had been out of touch, and they had moved. They had got a divorce, and they were separated, and everybody had gone different directions, and so I had nowhere to go. And actually since then, I've always been on my own, on the streets, hustling to survive.

*Why didn't you go with your mother when she saw you?*

Because they wouldn't let her have me. The staff that was on duty, they didn't know what to do. They were in a jam. They didn't know if they were supposed to let me go with her, so they didn't. She was yelling and screaming. Her and her brother were fighting over a gun. You know, she was trying to get a gun she was so upset. Oh, yeah, it was quite a scene.

Then later that night, after she left, they decided they better just get rid of me on a bus to Seattle.

*How old were you at this time?*

About thirteen.

Yeah. And, so, like, could I hold them responsible? The guy who beat me like that for twenty-one days straight? Yeah, I could.

There was a time when I thought I saw him walking down the street. I jumped out of my car, and my car just kept going down 4th Avenue in Seattle. I chased this guy down. It wasn't him. My car had crashed into a parked car. I had to run and jump in it and get away.

*You didn't have time to put it in park before you jumped out?*

Well, I thought I had.

*[Laughs.]*

I thought I had, but I hadn't, and I didn't have time to stop it when I realized, because I was more worried about catching this guy.

That's how intent I was on extracting some revenge back then. Would I look for him now? No.

What if I saw him again? That's a question. That's a question. You know what I'm saying? But would I go looking for that guy? No.

The guys that digital probed me in IMU, was there a time when I would have hunted them down? Yeah. Did I want to hunt them for years? Yeah. Would I now? No. What would I do when I was confronted with them? Don't know. Does that make sense?

*Yeah.*

But, I put myself in prison, you know. That's really the main thing, isn't it? That's the main part of your question.

*I understand.*

Yeah.

*There is an almost universally negative perception that the prisoners have of the notion of protective custody and the people who are in protective custody. And I can understand some of it. For instance, if a person's there because they wronged one of the other prisoners by making up some story and ratting on him, or, you know, doing something like that phrase you use—"they're feathering their bed with the misery of another man." But what about, like, a scared kid? Somebody seventeen years old, he comes in, he's just scared to death of prison,—*

Well—

*—doesn't know what to expect, and maybe the guards even trick him into doing something, like you guys have described in some of the Prison Awareness classes. Is there any sympathy for a guy like that?*

We're aware of that. The thing is, at one point, the only way into PC was off the misery of another man. It was the only way you could get there and they'd protect you is if you sold out another prisoner. It was that way for several years.

OK, then, they set up IPC—Involuntary Protective Custody. Administrative Protective Custody. See. That's where they'll put you in protective custody if they believe you to be unsafe in the general prison population, even if you haven't gone over to their side and become their rat. But, the guys on the compound aren't aware of this transition of policy. Guys are saying it, but there ain't nobody believing it. They're still thinking that if you're in protective custody, then you must have betrayed your fellows.

You got to remember, we're in a criminal society, where, you know, betrayal is of the highest cost. Trust is something that is hard fought. It's something that, you know, once gained, you don't ever want to lose.

I've been in PC. Told you that.

*Well, they tried to put you in it, but you refused, and so went to the hole, as I recall.*

But in the perception of a lot of people, that still means I was in PC.

*That still counts as PC? Even though you went to the hole to avoid it?*

Yeah, you know. To those who want to use it against me.

One of the things that I had the benefit of—and a lot of guys in that position don't—is I had a history long before that. There were people who knew my situation at the time, and knew that I actually got a raw deal, you know.

There's a lot of guys, actually, that are kind of ashamed that they didn't take a more active role in making sure that that didn't destroy my reputation, 'cause they were on the yard when I showed up, and they could have spoken up on my behalf. I mean, I got friends that apologize to me constantly.

But then there's other guys who don't like me. I'm an easy guy not to like. There's a bunch of people don't like me. And they dress shit up different. It raises its ugly head all the time.

But there's a reason I've survived and earned a reputation, and that is that I'll get up. You know, I'll get down a little quicker than a lot of people will. And that ain't changed. You can't just disrespect me.

And the fact that people are willing to disrespect me behind my back is actually OK. See? The point is, they'll smile in my face. Think about it. If I sat here and told you, "Fuck, this guy's a jerk, man. I won't have nothing to do with this fucking guy. He's a creep, rat, punk, mother fucker," but then when he comes around, it's, "Hey, how you doing man? Yeah? All right, man!" Well, what are you going to think of me? You know what I'm saying? What are you going to think of me when you see how two-faced I am like that?

That's always been my get back. I can make them grin when I come. As long as I see them smiling, they won't have to worry about me kicking their ass. But the minute they put their mouth on me, I'll fuck them up. That ain't changed.

I killed a guy raped my wife. I ain't in here for molesting somebody's little boy, and I will not be disrespected like someone who is. You know what I mean? I'm not here to be singled out, picked on, or anything else. You do your time, I do mine, but you're not going to get over on me. Not like that.

*So you don't have an automatically negative impression of everybody in PC. I mean, if you found out somebody—?*

Only because I was in—

*—had been in PC,—?*

—the hole in Big Red, and had the opportunity to be victimized by the system also. I know that there's a good number of people that are all right that have been put in that situation.

But at the same time, if they're not willing to redeem themselves, step up to the plate, bring their paperwork, explain themselves, then I don't have too much to say for them. Like I said, I'm not going to let nobody put their mouth on me. If you're going to allow people to call you something, well, you're only that far from being that. If you don't mind somebody putting that label on you, then how hard is it to be that? You know, you've already accepted the label.

That's another reason that you don't want to trust somebody that's got a reputation as a rat, even if maybe the guy didn't tell, or even if I know the guy didn't tell. If they're calling him a rat and he ain't doing nothing about it, then the next time something happens, and me and him do something, and then they get him to where he's got to give me up or take the fall himself, how hard would it be for him to say, "Well, you know, they think I'm a rat anyway"?

*Right. "What have I got to lose? I'm already at the bottom of the food chain."*

"What have I got to lose?" Yeah. "I might as well be a rat."

*Yeah.*

You know, I actually knew a good solid dude, that because he was labeled a rat, ended up being a rat. And when it happened, he admitted to me, he said, "Man," he said, "I never thought...."

But once he did it, he realized he had sold out. It was too late. He had sold himself out. He let everybody else think a certain thing about him, and it ended up being true. This guy lost so much self-respect over that, he was never right again.

*What about guys who just spend their whole sentence in PC? You're talking more about guys who get a certain reputation and then have to deal with that in general population, but what about guys who don't have to sell out other prisoners, or don't have to confront people who think they sold out other prisoners, because they just bypassed the whole thing by going straight to PC?*

Those guys like that, they're out of the pecking order. They're not something to be concerned with, really. I don't worry about them. You know, they're not in my life. I don't have a thought one way or another.

What do I think of them? Oh, I think they're probably miserable. And certainly if they don't deserve to be there, they're doubly miserable, you know.

But you can do something about that. All's you got to do is decide what's most important to you, you know.

Sometimes guys say, "Well, I don't want to lose any good time." Well, hell, you can take all my good time. You don't never have to let me out of prison. Better that then to let people label me a rat.

You know, people that tell me that they don't care what people think about them are people I don't really trust much. I care what people think about me. You don't have to like me. You don't have to agree with me. But you have to view me the way I want to be viewed. There's a lot of people that don't like me, or wouldn't never respect anything that I do. But there's no, like, gray area about what I am.

*Well, one of the things that's been eye opening to me is to learn about precisely this pecking order and values you guys have in here. This was a totally foreign world to me when I entered this program. So, if I had for some reason gone to prison before I ever got to know you guys and your worldview, I wouldn't have even thought that there was a negative stigma to being in protective custody. I would have thought, well, of course that's where you'd be if you're going to be in any kind of danger. I wouldn't have thought of it as being that kind of a compromise, that kind of a trade-off, like, "Well, since I lack self-respect, I'll go into PC," or, you know, "Since I'm not good enough to be a real convict, I'll go into PC." I wouldn't have thought of it in a negative way like that. It's only now that I'm getting to know you that I can at all put myself in your frame of mind, in the convict mode, and begin to understand why it would be such a source of shame to be under protective custody.*

*I mean, put it this way: Isn't it the state's obligation to provide a safe—?*

Environment?

*—environment for the people it imprisons? And—?*

Sure, but let's not fool ourselves what they use PC for. They also use it as a tool to divide groups, cliques, to smut some guy up who they don't like. In my case, they used it in a negative way like that.

But, yes, they are obligated to protect those people.

What I started to say before you asked the question was actually in this vein. See, you're assuming that you came to prison, like, by accident, like you just rolled up here. Well, that's not what jails are really full of. You know, people don't accidentally wind up in prison very often. There's the acts of passion where they kill their wives or something, but they're a real small, teensy percent of our population.

Now, there's a lot of guys that don't have a real extensive criminal record that have a lifestyle that can still land them here. They were using drugs, they were stealing, they were boozing, they were fencing, you know. There's a lot of small time criminals like that that when confronted with the realities of convict life, just can't hang.

They're not really criminals, in their mind. "Well, this isn't such a bad crime. I'm just fencing stolen stuff," or, "I'm just doing pornography," you know. "I'm not really a criminal, I'm just taking money from welfare." You know what I'm saying? There's a lot of ways to get into prison, but these are all lifestyle ways.

Now, those people, just as much as the people with the more serious criminal records, if you carry yourself right when you get to prison, you're OK. This is the society and the world that we live in. You know, this is our just desserts.

That's why I say, like, we wound up here because we probably deserved to wind up here. Very few people just accidentally wind up in prison.

*So if I understand your point, you're saying that most of the people in prison are already part of an outlaw underworld culture, so, in effect, they knew the rules. Even if they're not totally hard core criminals, they've already internalized the prevailing convict attitudes about PC and everything.*

Sure.

*They know what they're supposed to do and not supposed to do in the criminal world.*

Sure. And they at least pay lip service to it, even them that don't pay heart service to it, that don't really believe it in their heart. Then when they get to prison, it's "Oh, Jesus, where's a safe place to live?"

And PC is good for them. Let them get out of here.

*So, let's talk about one of the minority of people who is not of the criminal underworld at all, some-body like me or the people that I would mostly socialize with on the outside, and he gets convicted of vehicular homicide or something when he runs somebody over by mistake, and he has to do time in prison. If he doesn't really want to be in a world of kill or be killed, you know, to be in the typical convict world where you have to constantly prove yourself the ways you guys have described to me, and he finds out that there is such a thing as protective custody, and he spends his whole sentence there, would you look down on someone like that? Would you think he should have a negative self-image, or is less of a man?*

No, no. Nobody would even know them. They just come from a different world. They're non-combatants. We understand that. Most of us understand that. They're people that we wouldn't have known or associated with much anyway.

But not all those people end up in PC. You take Jeff, or—oh, there's a half a dozen of them in our club. These are guys, much like yourself, who are in that small minority that accidentally wound up in prison. But they've carried themselves in a sufficient manner to co-exist.

Now, there's no way you can ever put Jeff, or half them guys, into a category of kill or be killed, you know. And nobody expects that of them.

We got little guys in here that can't whip anybody, but they have the respect of everybody, because they ride their own beefs, and they're not trying to feather their bed with the misery of somebody else.

Don't get into debt. Don't get out there in traffic. Don't get into the middle of the road, and then say, "Oh, time out! Shit's going too fast! I can't hang!"

*Right.*

Nobody comes up to you, "Hey, hey man, what do you want? You want to get into this?" That isn't the way it works. Most times you have to go looking for shit to get into shit.

You know, there's guys that come through the joint constantly who are the most mild-mannered peace-loving guys in the world, and they never have a bit of trouble. The fact that I don't know their names doesn't mean anything. They're not part of our world.

I see them, you know. Most of them I have no feelings one way or the other about.

*So there are people sort of independent of the pecking order? They're not really at the top or the bottom, they just don't play the game?*

Yeah.

*They don't have the advantages or the disadvantages of being in the pecking order?*

Yeah. Yeah, they don't buy in.
But at the same time, they don't violate certain rules.

*Right.*

As long as you don't violate those certain rules, you can be there, in the crowd. That's no problem. You start spending too much time with the Man, then you got to watch yourself.

See, the problem with guys like yourself is that you don't think there'd be any problem with sharing a story or having an ordinary conversation with the cops, especially if you went to WSR first, before you went to a real prison. Because here, we talk to the cops.

It happens all the time. Guys leave from here and then get there, and, boy, they can't make it, you know. You get into the bowels of the beast, and it's rough.

But there's a lot of squares that started out at the other places and didn't pick up any bad habits from how casual we are here, and never had a lick of problems. Served a lot of time. I've known guys like that that served ten, fifteen, twenty, thirty years. Never had any problems with anybody.

After awhile, there's some you actually learn to like and respect. You can actually respect their ability to live like that in here. Got the utmost respect for them.

*Yeah.*

Yeah. So, don't let our version of the pecking order convince you that it's just that way and no other. 'Cause it really isn't. There's a co-existence with those people.

*So if I come to prison, not particularly wanting to be a tough guy, and establish my manhood and all that, but at the same time, I don't want to be a victim, I don't want to be a punk, it's not as if PC is my only alternative.*

No.

*I might be able to live that way without ever going to PC.*

Yeah. Yeah, like Jeff—well, I don't want to use Jeff every time I talk about a square—

*[Laughs.] Right.*

You know what I mean? But there's squares that have existed for a long time in prison, with no problems.

*But does that also depend on the era and the prison? I mean, what if somebody tried that in Walla Walla in the Seventies?*

Well, Walla Walla in the Seventies would have been a little tougher.

*Yeah.*

Would have been a little tougher.

But it happened. They were there doing it. They were real quiet, at a distance. They kept to their own selves. They did their own little things. You never had reason to know what they were about, and they never had reason to know what you were about.

See, it's the ones that come around and say, "Hey, what are you about?" you know. And then they fade. Those are the ones that you're a little uncomfortable with, the ones that don't keep to themselves but want to get part ways in our world, in our business.

The ones that just do their time, and mind their own business and stuff, and live their own lifestyle, they're usually fine. That's just what they do.

You know, there'll be somebody to test them, now, if they're not careful especially. You know, somebody will want to know, "Has this guy got money, man?"

But if a guy come to you like that, then you say, "Hey, I ain't got no money," whether you got money or not. Problem is, a lot of people have a tendency to want to brag. Well, you start bragging, and then pretty soon somebody expects you to be able to put up, you know. That just happens.

That's probably a square's biggest trouble.

*Letting on that he's got money?*

Letting on that he's got money, influence, something. Bragging in some fashion. Wanting to be one of the Fellahs. You know, 'cause everybody wants to belong.

# BILL—March 1999

*"The guys kind of accept I'm a curmudgeon, you know. I've got to where I stopped being an obnoxious son of a bitch, and I'm a colorful old guy now."*

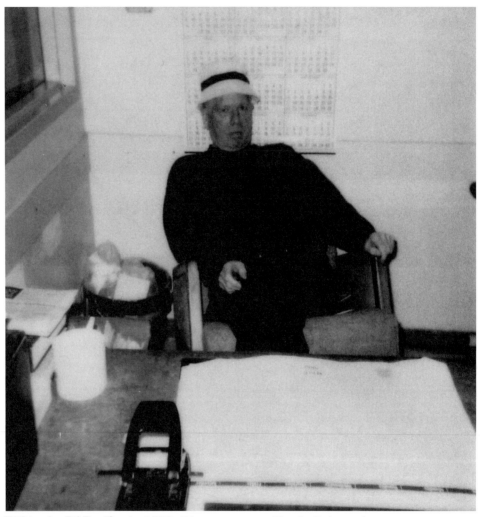

Bill in the PAP office in 2000. (Photo courtesy of Linda Coleman.)

Bill caught the tail end of my conversation with Jerry. He wasn't pleased to hear us talking about the convict code and related matters again. "Seems like you've covered that plenty," he said to me disapprovingly. I don't know that he had any specific suspicions of me, but like any devout believer in a fundamentalist religion he just sensed that no good could come from rational discussion of first principles with an outsider.

*Some of the questions I have are based on things we've already done, just follow-ups and clarifications and such. On one of the tapes, you said that having female correctional officers is "a mixed blessing." Can you elaborate on that?*

Well, it curtails a lot of things that should go on in a prison. You know, you shouldn't be that concerned about your privacy.

One guy, a friend of mine, he had to get ready for a visit. And a lot of these women aren't tens, you know, that work here—or eights even—but, one of them's talking to one of them big husky kids in the cell, and this guy comes in. They called him for a visit, he's coming off the yard and wants to change his clothes. And apparently he don't wear shorts. So he just finally said, you know, "Hell, it's just a guard." He pulls his shit down, just for a split second, then pulls his visiting pants on. So she wrote the guy up for sexual harassment. You know, he's in his own cell, back by his toilet there.

So, there's that aspect, where if they go by the cell and you're taking a piss or something, it's kind of embarrassing to a guy. And in some way, it offends them.

Of course, when I was in Texas and Georgia joints, you didn't see a woman. It's good to talk to a woman, even if she's a hateful bitch, you know. [Laughs.]

*Better than nothing.*

Better than no woman at all. So, yeah, it's good to have a woman to talk to. You can't talk to them like a real woman, because they're the god damn enemy, and what their opinion is of you and the way they act like it is might be different.

You sure as hell can't tell an off-color joke or anything with one of them.

*What if tomorrow they legalized most or all recreational drugs? What effect would that have on the criminal justice system? And overall, do you think it would be a good or bad move for society?*

For crime statistics and for people getting knocked in the head and robbed, it'd be excellent, you know. The great majority of these people in here are drug-related. To get drugs, they commit atrocities and bogus felonies that they wouldn't commit otherwise. Those guys are real peaceful guys, except they're going to do whatever they have to do to get their narcotics.

Kenny,* when he was here said, "It's all about medicine." You remember him saying that? "It's all about medicine," he said. And that's what it is. Probably seventy-five percent of the people in prison wouldn't be in prison if they could go down and get welfare and their weekly or daily maintenance drug shot, whatever it took.

*So do you think overall it would be a good idea?*

Yeah. I can't even imagine it happening, though. It's on a similar vein as, like, sex education in schools. They say, "Well, if you tell the little bastards about sex, they'll want to do it. So, keep them ignorant." All the girls'll be pregnant, but that's a small price to pay for not discussing rubbers in front of them, you know.

*[Laughs.] Sure.*

It's the same shit with drugs. If a guy could get them without resorting, well, he won't resort. These guys don't have any ambition about anything, except maybe on a real superficial basis; they know everything they get is going to go to the bag man. They'll sell their mother, whatever.

*You've mentioned that, in your own time in prison, you've exploited other prisoners. You actually used the word "exploit," talking about loan sharking, and gambling, and running card games and such. Why is that not a violation of the code? Because other ways of harming your fellow prisoners would be. If you rat on a guy, then that's denigrated as "feathering your bed with the misery of another man," as Jerry says. Why isn't exploiting them in the ways that you've done regarded similarly?*

Because, one way you're helping the Man to put these guys down. The other way—see, you don't have some kind of an exemption, they don't give you a yellow card when you come to prison to keep you from getting robbed or swindled or anything. These same bastards if they were out on the streets, you'd still be taking their money. It's no different in here.

---

*One of the oldest and most popular of PAP members, Kenny (I have changed the name) spent the bulk of his adult life in prison, all for drug-related offenses. He often played the role of the clown prince of PAP, dropping in some oddball pro-drug or pro-crime witticism when he sensed the proceedings were getting too solemn or someone was getting too preachy for his tastes. His long time partner, who also was in PAP for a time, wrote the book *Drugstore Cowboy* based on some of their real life misadventures. Utterly not in keeping with the image he so carefully constructed, Kenny ultimately swore off drugs, got out of prison, and is reportedly living a contented, drug-free retirement with his family.

But, there's no reason ever to bring the Man in on anything. The Man's the enemy, and if you cross that line, well, you'll cross it in other ways, so, anybody that's ever done that can't sit at my table or circle the track with me, or anything like that.

*So you don't look as negatively on prisoners victimizing each other. It's only if they victimize each other with the assistance of the administration.*

Yeah, if you sell out to the cops, that's what the difference is.

*You've also mentioned that you pride yourself on your loyalty to your fellow prisoners. On one occasion, you wrote that your fellow prisoners that you respect can count on you "to back any play they might initiate, up to and including," and then you just put "dot, dot, dot," without getting more specific. Talk to me a little bit about that. Isn't there a difference between loyalty to people and loyalty to their choices, and the things they get themselves into? I can be loyal to a person, but does that imply that I need also be loyal to everything they choose to involve themselves in? Why can't I say, "I love this person," or "I'm loyal to this person, but I'm not going to support them when they do 'dot, dot, dot'"?*

Well, I'm talking about half a dozen guys in the whole system. I'm not talking about, you know, two hundred people, but maybe six guys in four, five joints that, if they get in a knife fight or whatever, you don't even need to know who's right and who's wrong. You know which side you're on.

You know, that guy's your partner. Like, outside, what we say is, somebody you can cut up money with. You know, you've been on the road, and you're guarding each other's back and assets. And your wife should be safe to stay at that guy's house without her getting hit on or none of that. You could leave your money with him and go to prison, and come out and your money'd still be there.

And it's those kind of people, not just some guy who's a good convict or something. Some of the guys that are in PAP are my friends, but not on this level. From one to ten, I'd rate them a six and a half or something, you know, and if they kill each other, that's up to them.

But, there are three or four other guys in there—even when I know the guy's wrong—I'll back his play.

*Even when you know he's wrong.*

I know he'd do the same for me.

*Now you've stated, or at least implied, that it's too late for you to turn your life around and be a law-abiding citizen, and go out there and have a straight job and be square, and all that. Based on the choices you made from a young age on, even if you now recognized certain things as being flawed, it's a little late to all of a sudden have a different life.*

Yeah.

*But, do you feel any responsibility toward other people to steer them away from the same path, to help them to not develop in the direction you did, and not get trapped in your lifestyle?*

No. No. I was in Father Flanagan's boys home and all, you know, and I read sociologists and different bullshit. People talk to me about when I was young. And I say, "Jesus, when's this bastard going to pause for breath so I can get out of here!" you know.

What am I supposed to say? "Yeah, I'm an old outlaw, and I've been through this. You don't have to make the same mistakes I made, kid." And they'll say, "Uh huh. Now how do you go about getting in one of those safes?" "Well, I'll tell you that…"

Someone in your position, you might help them get a job, or something like that, if you knew a guy who was looking for a good hand, and you knew this kid's headed in that direction but he's not there yet. You can tell him, "Man, look here. Why don't you take this job? Make some good money," you know. "You can buy yourself a car, and you won't have to steal." You might do it, it might work, for a certain few, at a certain point when they're still young, because they see a reward in doing it.

But they're not going to respond to advice from me just because I have experience or I'm a solid convict. "Fuck man," you know, "What time's supper?"

*[Laughs.] You're very cynical about these things.*

Yeah. You know, a prime example is Jimi. He eats every program in here. And Jimi's just a half stumble from the bag, and shit, you know. Like I told you, if I don't see Jimi by Christmas I'll be surprised. And he eats and drinks and sleeps these god damn programs.[*]

It's different when they're out there. They don't have the incentive to, you know, get out by doing this shit, to save six months in prison.

The same with what we used to call "riding the Bible to the gate." Shit like that. Them guys that go to that church—which is the best spot I've seen for a hand grenade in the god damn history of the world[†]—the main thing in their life is the Bible. Some guys have, you know, a dozen copies of assorted Bibles and shit.

---

[*] Again, this was before Jimi got back into trouble and back to prison.

[†] Because the chapel provides sanctuary for all prisoners, including those at the bottom of the pecking order, it is not uncommon for some of the stricter adherents to the convict code to refer to it in derisive terms as if it were little more than a clubhouse for rats and sex offenders.

And they won't be out five minutes before they'll be looking for a bush to hide behind to leap out on some unsuspecting youngster.

*[Laughs.] Well, you're cynical that people are going to change. Can I at least get you to admit that it would be a good thing if they did? I mean, do you root for guys to go on the straight and narrow? Would you be happier if you found out Jimi didn't re-offend than if you see him in here a few months from now? Would you care?*

No. I'm indifferent.

*Kind of neutral?*

Yeah.
You know, Jimi's just a guy. He's all right, but he's not, you know, in the top ten.
He's all right. In fact, when he left here, Jimi left me a pair of Levi's that he got from somebody else. We're on good terms, and I do step up for him to a point. But past a certain level, you know, guys like Jimi, they're on their own.

*I guess what's frustrating me a little bit, Bill, is at some level, I know you recognize that the world would be a better place if there were fewer people victimizing each other, and robbing and killing and stealing and all the things that you and your peers do that land you in a place like this. But it's almost like you can't bring yourself to say that, or you can't acknowledge any obligation to help that happen, either by changing yourself, or by influencing other people. I can't even get you to admit that it would be a good thing for someone like Jimi to stay away from crime. But why is that? Why is it you sometimes speak as if you don't recognize that people shouldn't be victimizing each other?*

Well, you say "victimizing," but I've been a thief all my life, and I put property crime on a way different level than I do crimes against people. I even count stick-ups as property crimes. If you're using the gun as a prop, if you're not going to beat some old lady in the head, or shoot some guy that doesn't need shot, I count that as a property crime instead of a crime against a person.

Yeah, I feel bad about crime against people, especially against helpless people—women, kids, and such. You know, especially if you're excessive with it. Like, there's guys in here that you talk to every day, and you and me both know that they've done shit way beyond anything they had to do to, to accomplish the task they had set out to do.

One of them, in fact, he robbed this joint in Spokane, and went back and shot the guy. He had the guy tied up and thrown behind the counter, and he was half a block away and he doubled back and shot him. This was a guy trying to work his way through college, and he went back and shot him.

Those kind of people are never my friends, because I don't trust them. But if they've got a good reputation in the joint, they can get, you know, maybe thirty dollars from me, or something like that. But they couldn't get a hundred and seventy-five.[*]

*OK. [Laughs.]*

No matter how much I had.

*Bill, are you really going to sit there and tell me that armed robbery is not wrong?*

Well, sure it's wrong. A good percent of the stuff we do is wrong, you know. I bet you do wrong every day.

The only difference between you and me is that I'll drive two thousand miles to do it. [Laughs.]

*[Laughs.]*

But you do things you shouldn't, or you offend people, and—

*Sure.*

—you've got a conscience and maybe you'll say, "Well, God, I shouldn't have said that; I shouldn't have did that."

But me, I never have said, "God, I shouldn't have robbed that guy." The only thing I ever have said is, "I wonder if I missed something? If I had only looked in...."

In fact, I did that one time. Nineteen sixty-three. I went in an old farm house, a hundred miles out in the country. I knew the woman who lived there had gone to the State Fair and taken the kids. Two old coots were in there; I went in and stuck them up. Tied them up and went down the basement. I had word that the woman had gone down the basement with five hundred dollars and hidden it. I didn't know how much total she had stashed down there.

So, I went down there and, you know, I stood and looked. There's cobwebs, and I'm looking for a clean spot. And I see there's a stove over there, and I looked and there's a rafter with a big old tobacco can, and there's twenty thousand in this tin can, so I take that and go.

Forty miles down the god damn road, I say, "You know what? That son of a bitch had that stove turned with the oven against the wall. I should have turned that stove over." I still

---

think that's probably where the main money was. I will always believe that there was serious money in that oven.[*]

But I didn't feel bad about sticking those people up and taking their money.

*I think you have a lot more respect for property rights when it's your property.*

Well, not really. I've been robbed a couple times. You know, not stuck up, but burgled and stuff. I said, "Ah, there's more where that came from."

But a lot of these guys that are the worst robbers, they'll say, "If there's anything I hate, it's a jailhouse thief." I say let the guy do his thing. What'd he steal, some fucking cigarettes? Probably needed it more than I did to do that, you know. Guys'll want to beat guys up for stealing something out of a cell. I'm not in on that.

*You know, there's a lot I admire about you and your values. I think you're an honest person, in the right circumstances. I mean, you're not going to be honest with a guard or something, but ordinarily you're an honest person. You're a loyal person. I think you care more about people than you sometimes let on. Maybe that's why so much about you troubles me more than it otherwise would. I like you and respect you, yet at the same time I think a lot of what you believe in is just bullshit, and I want as few people as possible to emulate you and go down the same path you're on. I don't know. Those are just my feelings, but—*

It's really almost a concept that escapes me, when people say, "You don't feel any remorse." I say, "You know, what the hell. It was an either/or situation: Either I get away with the money or I go to jail. I'm in jail, so what the hell am I going to feel sorry about the money for?"

I haven't killed anybody. I haven't raped anybody. I haven't beat anybody in the face with a pistol. If I go to rob some place, and there's big money there, but the situation comes up where I have to confront somebody, I'll leave without the money rather than hurt them. So, it's not totally about the money.

*Yeah.*

I say, "Well, I'll get somebody else," you know, "This didn't work good." What are you going to do, tie somebody up and torture them, make them tell you where the god damn money is? You know, there's money everywhere.

I think that same thing about, like, if you and I go in on a burglary, and you're standing watch, and I go in and I see this big pile of money that you don't know about, and I put it

---

[*]I would have thought that $20,000, especially in 1963, would count as "serious money," but I later asked Bill if he had misspoke when he told me this story, and he confirmed the amount. He just believes there was considerably more than $20,000 down there that he missed.

in my pocket, and I just take the rest of the stuff, and we divide that up, and I don't tell you about the money—that's a hell of a flaw.

Mainly why I despise a guy who'd do it is because that shows me he's a weak son of a bitch that don't think he can ever make another score in his life.

*Are most criminals honorable about that kind of thing like you, or would most of them keep all the money in that situation?*

It's a very few people who are honest with their partner. In fact, guys brag about it, you know, "Yeah, I clipped him."

I file all that shit away.

*Sure.*

Twenty-eight years later, the guy couldn't get thirty cents from me.

*As you've pointed out, we all have our flaws, our imperfections. We all do wrong things, including me. It sounds like you've just settled into a certain level of imperfection and become comfortable with it. It's as if you've said, "Look, I don't go beyond this point. Ethically I won't allow myself to do x, y, and z." But aside from that, you don't have any urgency about improving yourself; you don't acknowledge any obligation to even try. You're just kind of comfortable with the certain set of "wrong" things that you're used to.*

Yeah, that's the thing. If I got out tomorrow, I'd say, "Let's see, where's the money? Where's the safe?" So.

*Well, it's better than being phony, and telling everybody, "Oh, I've changed! I'll never rob again!"*

Yeah, "I've seen the light!"

*"I've found Jesus!"*

"I've seen the light!" Yes, indeed.

Are you a religious man?

*No.*

I had a philosophical talk with the little chaplain out here, the little Irish woman, I said, "You know, this doesn't make sense, all this shit. That guy turned water into wine. If he did that today, he couldn't get on Johnny Carson doing that shit." So.

*[Laughs.] Actually, one of the things I was going to ask you, you touched on a few moments ago. One of the most common questions people ask about prisoners is whether you have any remorse for what you've done. So, Bill, do you have any remorse for the crimes you've committed?*

No, not a damn bit.

You know, like I said, it's an either/or situation. This is the risk you take, and if you gamble, and if you lose, you go to jail; if you win, you get the money. I don't see anything to feel sorry about.

I mean, like I think I said before, if I can individualize it, it's a little different. If I'd say, you know, "God damn, you robbed Craig, and he lost his furniture, man, all his god damn furniture," then I'd feel bad, you know.

But, it's not Craig and Bob and Jim; it's just people. I might know their name 'cause I researched them. I looked them up in the city directory, and got their house number, and where they worked, and all that shit. But I've never drank coffee with them or anything like that.

*Yeah.*

Like, you and I; I won't rob you. And if I knew where your money was, and anybody wanted to go get it, I'd tell them no, you know, we're not going to do that. We can work on another one; we're not going to get that guy.

*Interesting comment you made one time, and I think I know what you meant, but let me ask this anyway. In talking about why you don't intend to be rehabilitated, and give up a life of crime, you said, "I won't live low class." And my immediate thought was, "What do you call this?" I mean, you've followed a lifestyle which has meant that you've spent the bulk of your adult life in this environment, which I would think is very low class in most respects. How do you respond to that?*

You must have missed what I said at the end; I meant I won't live that way without a gun tower over me.

As long as it's within my ability to improve my situation, you know, I'm going to do it, in here or out there, whatever.

So, yeah, you're gambling a high degree of comfort against something very, very low, instead of staying in the middle all the time, you know. Your highs are higher and your lows are lower. You know, you might be laying on a god damn concrete floor without a blanket, eating oatmeal, with nothing, or you might be at the top.

*Leaving aside the ethical issues that I've been pushing so far today, if you look at it just on the level of your own self-interest, has it been worth it? Have their been enough highs to offset the amount of time you've done in prison?*

Yeah.

When I was on an escape, I went back to my home town and seen the guys I went to sixth, seventh, and eighth grade with. Most of them were railroad men. You know, they're sitting around this tavern playing pitch. And I come in, and, you know, "How you guys doing?" I'm just passing through town. "God damn," I thought, "Boy, those poor bastards!" [Laughs.]

They worked their ass off their whole life and this is all they got. Sitting in a god damn tavern playing pitch for pennies and dimes and shit. Fuck, they never breathe any oxygen in this town. They breathe the smoke off that god damn railroad, they got a frumpy wife, and, you know, lousy furniture. What the hell did they do, you know?

I wouldn't trade places with them, no.

*On another subject, how do the mentally ill fare in prison?*

Oh, not very many people will bother them here. We call them "dings." If a guy's a ding, he's not able to cope with the shit going on around him. Down south they're real hard on them, for some reason. In the county jails and shit, the guys beat them up, make them wash underwear, and shit like that, you know. Just misuse them, take their stuff if they have any, which is seldom. You know, make them do all the menial work.

I think it's bad karma to fucking exploit people that are helpless, whether through mental condition, or whether they're just little, or whatever.

*Now, a "ding" and "mentally ill," those aren't synonymous, right? Mentally ill's just one kind of ding?*

Well, he don't have to be mentally ill, he can just be ineffective. But, if he can't cope with the situation around him, he's a ding, in prison parlance.

A lot of dings come up to me because, you know, I look directly at them and listen to them sometimes. Eventually, I'll run them off. Tell them, "I got to go, so," you know, "I'll give you fifteen minutes. That's all I can spare." Something like that.

*[Laughs.] So you're not openly hostile or violent toward them; you just don't want them around.*

I don't mind talking to them for ten minutes. If they have a problem or something that I can help them solve, just with conversation, with a small favor, sometimes I'll do it.

*Yeah.*

They need a letter typed to their mother or something, I'll do that. You know, I'm not going to beat them up, not going to take anything away from them, or not going to spurn them or anything. But they don't talk on a level I want to talk on, or about anything I want to talk about.

But even some guys that have intelligence, like Jeff, I won't talk to him two minutes.

*Because he's too much of a square? He's not really a part of your world?*

Yeah, what he wants to talk about is shit that, you know, if I wanted to hear it at all, I'd hear it from Oprah.

*[Laughs.] I'm flattered you're willing to talk to me. I'm probably ten times more square than Jeff.*

You're an interesting guy, but you're a little weird. [Laughs.]

*[Laughs.] I'll accept that.*

You're not a ding, but you're weird.

*[Laughs.] You mentioned that riots can be intentionally provoked by the administration, just to stir up trouble and have an excuse for a lockdown. In general, are prisoners easily duped into turning on each other and doing what the administration wants them to do?*

Oh yeah, it's easy. By other convicts, or by cops, you know.

I was in San Quentin when I was a youngster, and I'd tell them guys, "That boy over there, he told me he was going to tear your fucking head off. Now, Craig, I better go and ask him about that. I want to make sure; I don't want to get no bad information." And then I'll go over to the other fellow, and I'll point back at you and say, "Hey, that guy said you're from Omaha, right?" And the guy'll nod and look over at you. And I'll come back and I'll say, "Yeah, man, it's your ass."

But then I'd usually square it up before the guy went and got something to stab him with.

*"Usually." Good.*

[Laughs.] Usually would. Yeah.
But that was funny to me at the time. I wouldn't do it today.

*Because you were a sick individual then? [Laughs.]*

Oh it's just that humor was hard to find in there. Almost all humor is about doing something disgusting or mean to somebody. Any joke you tell, somebody catches it in the shorts, and it's not us, so we can laugh, you know. So, it's just a little harsher maybe, living under the gun tower.

*Have you done any time in IMU?*

Yeah, two sessions in IMU.

*How long?*

Six months, both times. Once was for starting a food riot, which was total bullshit. You know, I had several hundred dollars in store tickets, and I hardly ever went to the mess hall unless I wanted to talk to somebody down there. I don't know, for some reason they thought I was the ringleader of that fucking thing. I think somebody probably, you know, whispered in their ear. So, I was totally innocent that time.

The other time, they found a hundred dollars in loose scrip in my cell, which somebody that owed me no doubt had told them that I had, you know, since I'd been loan sharking and stuff. I went to IMU over that.

*What's it like in IMU?*

Oh, it's just a god damn cell with what they call a solid door, with a little window so they can look in and count you, and a hole with a flap that bends down so they can put a food tray through. You got a mattress, and some of them have outside windows in them, but some of them don't. And they're painted atrocious; they're orange in color.

There's six cells on top and six cells on the bottom in each pod. Twelve prisoners, they're all single celled, and a lot of them are maniacs. And guys are on protective custody in there, and they scream a lot, you know, beat on metal shit with shower shoes and stuff, constantly. They're miserable; they don't want anybody else to not be miserable.

So, the noise is the only bad part. Otherwise, you can get library books and shit in there sometimes. You can just tune that shit out and read. Run your little pictures across your forehead. So, you know, it's nothing I can't cope with. It's just the fucking noise that's bad.

*How do the guards treat you, compared to regular prison?*

Oh, they treat you like shit, you know.

*Are they worse in there than in regular prison?*

Yeah, they're all goon squad guards, and, like, any time they take you out of the cell for any reason, they'll back you up and put your hands through that slot, and they'll handcuff you up. They're standing there with sticks and stuff, when they open the door. Some guys that they've had trouble with, they put, like, a dog collar on them with a choke chain, and hold it, you know.

If you've got to take a shower, the shower's got a big barred cell door across that they slam, and you got just the one showerhead in there. And they might come back in two minutes, "Get up! Time's up! Get out of there!" Or you might get done showering and they leave you in there for an hour and forty minutes, just standing on that cement floor, waiting to get out and go back to the bathroom, you know.

Anybody in the wing who does anything, you know, they're coming after all of us. There's twelve guys in the pod, and if one of them throws shit on the guard or something, they just come in there and gas the guy, and then, you know, that gas just gets everybody. It doesn't just get on that guy that they're after.

So, there's that. And then they come in there with fire hoses sometimes and shit. Not a real pleasant situation.

And you only get one hour of yard a day, you know. They try to keep you separate.

One time they had, for some reason, three people out walking the yard at one time, and then two of them jumped on the other one and beat him down, because he had told on somebody. So, usually they try to kind of keep you separate.

*In one of my written questions, I asked you about friendships in prison, and we talked about that a little today also, about being loyal to a certain core number of people. Do you have any stories that can kind of humanize the prison experience? Can you talk about friendships in prison, just from your own personal experience, that might be effective to a reader that doesn't know what it's like and why you connect so closely in prison with certain people?*

Well, naturally, like any place you gravitate to people that have similar interests. These guys, they're all out of Seattle, or these other guys are all safe burglars, and so you have some commonality there to discuss together. You just run into people, like you would in the free world, where you're just attracted to the way each of them thinks or something. Like, Jerry Mac and myself. I knew him years ago. We were both card players, both thieves, and both robbers. And, so, you know, we had a lot to talk about.

I don't remember if I ever told you this or not, but one time I went and asked Jimmy,[*] I said, "Jimmy, do you know this guy?" I think the guy wanted to borrow some money or something, and Jimmy said, "Hell yeah!" he said, "That guy's been in half the penitentiaries in the country. He's a good son of a bitch." [Laughs.]

*[Laughs.]*

---

[*]Former PAP member, and the author of *Drugstore Cowboy*. Kenny's crime partner.

"OK, man," I said.

*Tell me about race relations, and racial tensions in prison. How would you compare it to the outside world?*

Well, except in, you know, in certain situations where there are some kind of real hateful ringleaders and shit—black or white, and sometimes Hispanic—generally the guys get along. It's the same thing I was saying, like, some of these guys are, you know, professional thieves and shit, and, so, I'd rather have a black friend that was a professional thief than a white guy that was an asshole, by a long way.

In the free world, I've never had a black person in my house, or eat at my table or anything. I just never did go around that kind of area where it was predominantly black, except in prison. But in here, though, you know, there are certain guys, like Henry or 9-0 or some of them, that are welcome to come over and get coffee from me, or sit at my table, where there's a lot of white guys that aren't.

So, except for, you know, a few fringe lunatics, it's not real bad.*

*From what I understand, there's been a lot of tension on that issue, even with some of the programs in the past, and I guess still to a lesser extent in the present, with Lifers and PAP and some of the ones that aren't specifically racial.*

The Lifers, the blacks took that over. That's a black club now. 9-0 and Henry and those guys are kind of running it now.

This club, we like a little bit of a mixture in here, but we're not going to let anybody dominate, you know. It started off as an all-white club. It used to be a kind of a white power club. That's how it started out. 'Cause, you know, they had a Mexican club, a black club, an Indian club, a Chinese club, but they didn't have any white clubs, so they started this.

---

*9 tells me that one of the reasons it's hard to be simplistically racist in prison and hate all whites is that certain individual whites have surprised and impressed him with their consistent and principled stands against white supremacists and all hate-mongers. He's mentioned Jerry and Buck in particular, but the one he emphasized the most, interestingly enough, was Bill. I hadn't seen anything from Bill at PAP that would have led me to think he was particularly out front on this issue, and race is not something he and I had ever discussed much. I'm sure he read me well enough to know that I would regard this behavior of his in a very positive light, but ironically that might have made him less rather than more apt to bring it up with me. With his self-effacing style, and his carefully cultivated image of cynical amorality, the last thing he wanted was to come off as some kind of liberal hero. But in an important way, it does fit the Platonic ideal of the Convict, as the convict code is indeed colorblind.

But, you know, circumstances and times change. We want this to be the one non-racial club. If we have six black guys and a black guy gets out, we won't put a white guy in that slot. You know, we want to keep that mix.

*Is it fairly stable? Do you think it can retain its quality of being multicultural, multi-racial?*

Yeah. As long as these same guys are in power.

This is really Jerry's club. Jerry started this son of a bitch twenty-five years ago. He's real volatile. Jerry's the bull dog, and I'm the pacifier. He rides them; I chill them out. I mean, I've only been here at WSR a short while, so this is Jerry's club. No doubt about that. Whoever is the president or the vice-president at any given time, Jerry pretty well sets the agenda.

*How come Lifers hasn't been able to have that same characteristic, as multi-ethnic like that? I mean, it sounds like it went from being a white group to being a black group.*

A lot of the white guys in there had a little power trip going, and they are kind of racist, and they didn't want to be ruled by a bunch of "jungle bunnies," or something. So they got out of there. A lot of them quit. They didn't want to work with a partially black leadership, so now the leadership is all black.

You know, I don't have much use for that club anyway. Somebody put my name on their roster, 'cause they thought I might want to go to their annual banquet or something, but there's only half a dozen guys in there that I'd talk to on the yard.

They have no standards for who gets in and who doesn't. There's a bunch of rapos and child molesters in that son of a bitch. I wouldn't want to be associated in any way with them.

I'm an honorary member of the Indians.[*] They keep a pretty steady roster in there. Guys that can pass the acid test, you know.[†]

*Do you ever go to the sweat lodge with them?*

No, I never have. I'm not interested in that shit. I told them, "If I want to be miserable, I'll just go stick my fucking finger in a light socket." [Laughs.]

*[Laughs.]*

Only it don't take four hours.

---

[*]Indians of All Tribes.

[†]I.e., like PAP, they do not let in any known rats or sex offenders.

*[Laughs.] But there's no religious significance to that, Bill.*

[Laughs.] No. Or to me in any of that shit, you know. Free worship and whatever, man, but it's not me.

The guys kind of accept I'm a curmudgeon, you know. I've got to where I stopped being an obnoxious son of a bitch, and I'm a colorful old guy now.

*I know from one of the earlier interviews that, like me I suppose, you have some cynicism about the so-called "victims' rights" movement. A lot of that is surely just right wing political rhetoric, but, beyond the rhetoric, what should be done for victims? Do you think that crime victims get a decent break from the state right now? Do you think there's enough attention—legitimate attention, not just political bullshit, but legitimate attention—paid to the rights and interests of crime victims?*

Well, with a few exceptions, like, people who have been raped or mutilated or something, you know, what the fuck is a victim? You lose your money, you just soak it up and you go on, you know. And you say, "Well, I was going to buy that fucking boat. Now, god damn it, I have to wait another four months to get it!"

But, you know, the guy that did it's getting punished. Or he might have gotten away with it, whatever. I don't know what the hell they could do for him except pat him on the head and say, "There, there, son. That's all right," when we know it isn't.

But, as far as the political part of "victims' rights," it's total bullshit. You know, they take ten percent of our money, whether we earn it or get it mailed in, to set aside for victims. I'd like to see one of them bastards that ever got a dime of it. They use that shit for bullets for the rifle range, and shit like that. The victims aren't getting any of it.

There ought to be some way you can make those bastards give an account of what they did with that money. And it's millions.

But, no, I don't really think anybody's got anything special coming from being a victim. Fuck, we're all victims of something—the political system or whatever. Not that I wouldn't take it if somebody wanted to call me a victim and offered it, but it's nothing we deserve, I don't think.

*What's your position on private employers coming in and hiring prison labor? I know there's a lot of controversy about whether it does more harm or more good in the long run to let the outside employers come in here and pay minimum wage to prisoners. What do you think about it?*

But there really isn't controversy in here about it. There's only, you know, a half dozen guys here that think it's a bad idea.

I mean, fuck, you're in prison. That means you got nowhere to go, and you're going to be in here using newspaper for toilet paper and shit if you don't have some kind of a payroll.

You know, these guys are doing life, and outside connections fall off, so you don't have any money coming in from out there.

Like, down south, they don't have any paid jobs. None. Zero. You don't get any money. And it's tough. You know, I've been down there.

So, if a son of a bitch can do something constructive and make five dollars an hour, I think it's a damn good idea. If they're being exploited, well, you know, exploit me a little.

Of course, I went up and worked in that fucking phone room for awhile before you were up there, and I got sick of it. They got a little tired of me too, at the end. [Laughs.]

*[Laughs.] Well, clearly it can be in the self-interest of the prisoners who happen to have the jobs, but do you think it's a good idea for society overall to allow employers to pay those low wages and use prison labor? What gives me misgivings about it is that it seems like we're making it very much in the self-interest of employers to favor keeping the prison population as high as possible, and that can't be healthy.*

Well, you know, your means are minimal. Minimum wage is a good wage in prison. Jesus Christ, people are so much better off with it than without it.

But, you know, everybody's going to get theirs. That's the capitalistic system. There's no way there could be such a thing as a millionaire that hasn't exploited people and has always given them what they had fairly coming. I don't think it's humanly possible to get a system where the guy that can do it won't take more than what would be considered fair with a computer rule or something.

But overall, yeah, I think it's a hell of a good thing. It puts money on the yard. It's like what they used to call the "trickle down," theory, which Reagan meant to piss off the building on me, I think. But it puts a lot of money on the yard, and guys that can make greeting cards and sell them to these guys, or do other little things like that, everybody gets a little taste of it, you know. They make wallets, or steal food out of the kitchen, and now there's someone to sell it to. [Laughs.] Whatever.

But everybody can live a little bit better. Living conditions is up a pretty good percentage because of these jobs. Go through one of those prisons in the south where there's no god damn paid job in the whole state, and people are living like rats.

*One thing you mentioned in one of the interviews is that the prisoners have a tendency to try to guess people's motives and figure out why they're here. I'm thinking now of outside people, volunteers and such. Is there going to be a significant difference in perception if a person is paid, versus an unpaid volunteer? I mean, compare the way I might be perceived in, say, PAP or a volunteer program like that, versus if I come in next week with a government grant to run some self-help program, and I'm drawing a salary and actually able to live off doing that. Are prisoners going to view me differently in those two cases?*

Yeah, I think in a way, because, you know, you're kind of coming from the Man's perspective. You're not with us; you're with them. If a guy acts up in that room, you're going to go tell on him, and get him locked in the hole and shit. So, yeah, there's a little difference.

A majority in here think these programs are total bullshit anyway, especially the ones that are compulsory, you know.

Yeah, like I said, if a guy comes in and donates his time, that's OK. He's just weird. But if he comes in and gets paid for it, he's got an ax to grind.

# JEFF—March 1999

*"But, nobody wants to look at the big picture of what's best for society when a guy gets out. They don't care about that. They say, 'Well, this guy's an asshole. He robbed a bank and killed somebody. He's got nothing coming.'*

*"Well, if that's the case, then kill us all. I mean, you know, if you're going to be tough on crime, then go in the prisons and shoot every person in there, and then you'll be happy. But if you're not going to do that, then you got to do something with them. 'Cause they're getting out, you know."*

T he next day, I sat down for a conversation with Jeff. He was the only one of three scheduled interviewees to show up.

*OK, let's just jump into a few topic areas here, Jeff, and we'll see if you have anything brilliant and profound to say on them.*

All rightee, then.

*[Laughs.]*

That's me: brilliant and profound.

*How much contact with the outside world do you have, and how important is that to you, and to prisoners in general to have those connections with people on the outside?*

My mom and my brother live in Colorado and Utah, respectively. So, they come up about once a year. Every year or two, we'll have a family visit out in one of the trailers here. So, if they were closer, I'd get more visits.

But I don't have any family local here. It'd be nice. My daughter's in Utah, but I don't see her. I don't get that many visits. I have a few friends locally, and I get a visit, like, a couple times a year. Nothing regular.

*Are these friends from before you were in prison, or since then?*

Since then. Met through correspondence.

*Oh.*

Friends. Friends of friends. Hopefully after a year, Jimi will be able to come up. I think that takes a year to get to where they let him come back in as a visitor.*

*I think so, yeah.*

---

*Again, this final series of taped interviews was while Jimi was on the outside, before he re-offended.

I think it's very important to have contact with the local community. But if you don't have anybody here already before you fall, it's hard to establish that. That's one thing that PAP does, is it allows a lot of interaction, and it's unfortunate there's not more programs like that.

But, especially for a guy who's getting out real soon, I'd say that's the number one factor in determining whether or not he's going to have problems. If you take someone like Jimi, he's got a girlfriend, he's got a house, he's got plenty of money, he's got a job, he's got a lot of support from sponsors and his dad and family, and so he's got a really good foundation to start with.

Take somebody else who their family doesn't care about them, or they don't want him staying with them. They might go to a halfway house, and the only people they know are guys they met in prison.

Especially if a guy's got a girlfriend or a wife or kids, I would say that's the number one factor of whether or not they're going to come back to prison. 'Cause the guys I see come back, they got out and didn't have anything. They didn't have anywhere to go, and they just went to a halfway house or work release, and the only people they hung out with were their friends that weren't doing anything either.

And I would think if the public really understood that, and if DOC really understood that, they would foster more programs like the family trailer visitation, which is an excellent program to have. Unfortunately, it doesn't apply right now to people who get married while they're in prison. Anybody who's been married before Ninety-five gets visits, but after that, they don't.

*Can you still have trailer visits with a non-spouse? Like, with your parents?*

Sure. Yeah, I get them about once a year with my mom and my brother. Yeah, anybody can have them with their family, which is real important. It's really an excellent program. I would think the prisons know that. They know that's one of the number one reasons guys don't want to get in any trouble here. They don't want to do drugs and 'cause trouble, because, like, "Well, you know, I got a trailer next week."

I mean, you hear that all the time. Guys don't want to make waves, because they've got the trailers. That's the number one stabilizing influence. A guy that doesn't have any of that, you know, he don't care. So what he goes to the hole? He doesn't have anything to lose.

This prison knows that, but the DOC as a whole doesn't encourage it. They've grudgingly allowed the program to stay, so far, but they don't encourage it. Ever since that incident at Clallam Bay, you can't get married right now and have trailers. You have to have already been married.

*What was the incident at Clallam Bay that affected that?*

A guy had a trailer visit with his wife. She was coming up to tell him that she was divorcing him, and he stabbed her. Fortunately, she didn't die. They went running out of the trailer and a cop shot him. Unfortunately they didn't kill him; they shot him in the shoulder or something.

*You say "unfortunately"? [Laughs.]*

Well, you know, he had that coming.

*Let's be careful here: Guys who stab their wives have it coming?*

Well, I mean, you know, if a guy—well, that one guy there screwed the program up for the whole prison. There's hundreds of guys in the system that would be married and getting trailers right now if it wasn't for that incident.

*So, is the Extended Family Visit policy, is that statewide, or does it differ from prison to prison?*

Well, originally, as soon as that incident happened, they stopped the whole program. Stopped everybody's. And then, within a month or so, they continued it with the families—moms and dads and brothers—but not the wives. And then, in a couple more months, they made everybody go under a review. They had to go before a committee, and they had to review their case, and da-da-da-da. And most of the guys that were married before, got their trailers back.

But then they kept it stopped for close custody prisoners. So basically Walla Walla shut the program down, except for the few medium guys that were still inside for holds. And that happened right when I was leaving there, and there was like five guys getting trailers there, out of two thousand. And, I'm not sure if they've reinstated it for close custody now or not. I'm not sure. I think it is now, but it's on a case-by-case basis.

And someone like me, I would not be approved. You know, even if they brought it back for new marriages on a case-by-case basis and I were to get married tomorrow, they wouldn't approve me.

*What kind of factors do they look at?*

Oh, domestic violence. You know, if you're a child molester, and the woman's got kids. That kind of thing.

Yeah, I think it's mostly sex crimes, or domestic violence.

*So you wouldn't be approved, because of the nature of your crime?*

I sincerely doubt it, just 'cause that's the way it works. And, you know, frankly I can understand that.

*Interesting that it's not left up to the visitor. I mean, it's rather paternalistic to say, "We don't think your new husband can be trusted with you in a trailer, so we won't let you be with him." I mean, isn't that kind of up to her?*

Yeah, but she doesn't count.

Well, it's like the women who marry Ted Bundy and, you know, all these freaks that these women want to marry. And that serial killer down in California, the—

*Sure.*

—Hillside Strangler. You know, they're getting married, and, what these women see in them, I don't know. But there's women out there that want to do that kind of thing.

*It's an interesting phenomenon.*

Yeah. And if they got the trailers with them, you know, then maybe the women know they might get killed. And, it's, like, kind of a turn-on.

*Right. Add a little excitement to the relationship.*

"Yeah, I'm up there screwing a serial killer."

*Well, your case, I assume, got a decent amount of press. You mentioned you were front page news for at least one day. Did you get any nut cases writing to you, any strange correspondence or anything?*

No. No. I mean, I wasn't, like, you know—

*As much of a celebrity?*

Yeah, I mean, you got to kill a lot of people.

Unfortunately, wife-killing is more mundane than—you know, it's sad but true, but, it's something that happens more than it should.

But to get back to your question about the outside world, there was a local TV show on the Prison Pen Pals program awhile back. That's a program on the Internet where they match up prisoners with people from the outside who want to correspond with them. Did you happen to catch that?

*I heard about it, but I didn't see it.*

Well, you know, they had the host, who's an asshole, and they had this prosecutor lady from King County, and they're really against it. "Well, we shouldn't have these prisoners on the Internet," da-da-da-da-da. And the other side says, like, "Well, it says they're prisoners. Nobody's being misled here." They say, "Yeah, but it doesn't say what they're in for." So the other side says, "But you can find out if they don't tell you. You know, look it up at the county courthouse, or just look it up online. It's all on the Internet."

Anybody's crime's on the Internet nowadays. If you want to go look it up, it tells everything on there.

In that sense, it's actually a lot more open and aboveboard to correspond with a prisoner. If you're writing to just some person you meet in a chat room, and he says he's a twenty year old guy, or girl, well, he could really be a fifty year old freak.

*Right.*

At least with the prisoners, you know where they're at and what they're in for, you know. I mean, they're actually safer.

*In that sense.*

That concept is hard to get across. But it's true.

*Well, do you think that when prisoners are able to make contact with strangers that way, whether through that program or any other program, that there is a lot of exploitation? Because I've heard some stories even from guys in here of things that have happened that make me wonder.*

Certainly. But I would say the rate of exploitation is really no higher than on the outside, because certainly there's plenty of women who get in with the wrong guy, whether in prison or out, and he ends up, you know, screwing them over.

I saw on "Sixty Minutes" where there's this guy in a Texas prison—he's a black guy—and he put an ad in the paper or something, and this lady starts writing him. He sends a picture of this handsome white guy, and tells her, you know, "I'm in for cocaine," when really he's in for murder and stuff. And, she didn't check on him. I mean, she never investigated, and she was gullible.

But he had a scam where he would buy a money order in prison for a dollar, and they were able to alter it so it says a hundred dollars—or I think they bought it for seven dollars and they were able to make it into seven hundred dollars. And he would send the money orders to her, telling her that it's his pay from his prison job, and asking her to cash them and put the money in some account that he or his people had on the outside. You know, and she's, like, "Well, he's not asking me for money or anything. He just wants me to deposit his own money for him." But as soon as they find out all the money orders were fake, this money's already moved, and it's traced back to her and she's the one who gets in trouble for it.

*But what you're saying is that that kind of thing could have happened on the outside too. There are people who play games like that out there too.*

Right. There's plenty of people in here and out there that want to scam somebody.

If you're writing a prisoner, you should automatically be on your guard. I mean, people are at risk anywhere, you know, no matter who you talk to. But, if you're talking to a prisoner, you should automatically know this guy's maybe less moral than the next guy, you know.

*What would be your advice in general to somebody who's considering being that kind of pen pal or contacting a prisoner? Maybe somebody has a singles ad somewhere, and they get some responses, and one of them—one of the more intriguing ones—has a return address from a prison. And the guy seems pretty normal in his letter; he seems like a nice guy. What would be your advice?*

I can't remember where the phrase came from, but "Trust, but verify." I mean, trust the person, but check him out. Write the prison, say, "What's this guy in for?" Or get on the Internet and you can find anybody's crime, history, everything.

*Now, it sounds like you don't get a whole lot of visits. Do you have much contact with the outside world by phone or mail?*

Yeah, I have a lot of people I write a lot of letters to. I used to write a lot more. In Walla Walla, I was writing twenty-five people. You know, I had one of those foreign pen pal things. I was writing girls in Ecuador, and Colombia, and—what's that island off in the Indian Ocean?—Mauritius.

Yeah. I still write a girl in Holland. I write a few girls in Seattle. And they come up now and then, but they don't have cars or anything, so they don't come up often.

It's actually kind of a better relationship through the mail than it is in person, because we're more literary type people, where we communicate better in writing, really. As I say, we have some visits, but it's not as much fun as writing.

*Oh.*

I mean, nobody writes any more. "Snail mail," they call it, you know.

*Right.*

Everybody uses E-mail now. So very few people write letters.

But there are people out there who like to write letters, and they don't have anybody to write to. All except prisoners.

*[Laughs.]*

It's kind of ironic, 'cause prisoners are really the only people that write regular. I mean, there's guys in here that, on the outside, they wouldn't write a letter in twenty years. You know, but in here, you're sort of forced to.

*Is that the kind of people who mostly end up corresponding with prisoners, people who just have kind of a literary itch, they like to write letters, and they don't have anyone on the outside to write to?*

That's been my experience. A lot of them are older, divorced. Divorcees with kids. And a lot of them like to write. They read a lot of books, and they like to write, and that's something they're looking for.

*How many people are you currently corresponding with?*

About four. You get burnt out after awhile. You know, it takes a lot of energy to write that much. So now I got three or four I write to. A little less time consuming.

*How much phone contact do you have with people?*

Oh, my family. I call them every couple weeks. I talk to Jimi now and then since he's been out. A couple other people in Seattle.

*Is there anybody from your pre-incarceration days, other than your family that you mentioned, that you're in contact with by phone or mail?*

Not right now. I have been off and on, but they've sort of faded away.
You find out who your friends are when you go to prison.

*Were you surprised that people faded away? Were there people you thought would be part of your life beyond that?*

No, I wasn't really surprised. I mean, it's kind of human nature. You know, unless you're, like, really close to the person.
I guess that's why they invented families.

*They're stuck with you.*

Yeah, you know, they'll generally stick by you no matter what. I mean, otherwise, everybody'd be in trouble.

*When you have contact with people on the outside, whether through visits, or with your letters and such, how honest and open are you able to be? Or do you have to put up a certain front?*

Well, they all know what I'm in for, so.

*How about just your day-to-day life, and your emotions and such in here? Can you be pretty straight with people?*

Oh yeah. I mean, actually you can be more honest with them than you can be with people in here, just because, they're in a separate sort of world.

*So you can show some vulnerability or weakness or something?*

Right, I mean, you can talk about things that you don't share with someone else in here. It's nice to have that outlet.

*Is it easier to open up about stuff like that with your family, or with the people who were strangers before, who don't have any preconceived notions about you or anything?*

Well, probably the people I write. Yeah.

And it's sort of the same way from their end, where they know you're not getting out and talking to anybody any time soon, so maybe they can tell you things that they wouldn't feel comfortable telling someone on the outside. You know, their friends don't have to know. It's all very discreet.

It's kind of funny. It's kind of like a chat line, but through the mail.

*How'd you hook up with most of these people?*

Through the ads in newspapers.

*Singles ads and such?*

Yeah.

*Do you answer ads, or do you put an ad in yourself?*

Both. I've answered ads and put ads in.

Any more, though, it's all through the phone now. They want their six ninety-nine a minute.

*Right.*

People can put the ads in free, and then anybody who wants to call them up, they have to pay so much a minute to listen and respond to the ads, which of course we can't do from in here. It used to just be you had your address in there and all that. But now everything's through the phone.

Plus, a lot of places don't even want prisoner ads any more. In about the last six years, there's been a real difference in public attitudes toward prisoners, at least in what I've viewed. Say, in Ninety-two, when I was in Walla Walla, I put an ad in the Seattle paper, and I got twenty responses. I mean, a lot. And I put the same exact ad in in Ninety-eight, and I got, like, two responses, even though I was much closer. Other people have said the same thing, a lot of people I talk to.

I don't know if it's public opinion, that they're really down on prisoners. That's a lot of it. And another part of it is the phone thing, that people don't want to write. They want to get on the phone. They want the instant gratification.

*It's probably both. It's probably more of the latter.*

I've really noticed that switch just in the last five, six years.

*I think it's more of the phone versus mail thing. That would be my guess. Because people hated prisoners before too. I don't think you're that much more unpopular now than six years ago. [Laughs.]*

[Laughs.] I don't know. I was sort of curious if that was part of it.

As I say, a lot of those places, they don't want ads from prisoners, and they tell you that. And in a lot of magazines, you see the ads for, you know, the mail order brides, like, from Russia, and The Philippines, and all these countries, and if you write to them, they tell you, "We don't want to mess with prisoners." They're looking for a rich businessman to marry.

*Have you ever had to do time in IMU?*

No.

*Have you had much in the way of infractions during your time incarcerated?*

Three or four majors.

*What did you do that was so major?*

I had a good one, this last one here out at work: "Honking the forklift horn."

*That's a major infraction?*

Well, it depends on the interpretation by the officer.

*OK.*

I got, let's see, I got an "Inciting a riot," a "Hunger strike," a "Gang activity," an "Unauthorized activity," a "Reckless behavior"—

*Give me the story behind some of these. What did you do that fits into those categories?*

Well, this is all from—

*Oh, this is all from the one incident.*

Right.

*From the honking the horn.*

Right. Because, out at work, at night time, they're supposed to bring us a sack lunch. And the cop's, like, way down the hall. It was, like, five o'clock, and he hadn't brought it down yet. So, I was yelling down the hall, "Hey, bring the lunch down!" and he didn't hear us because the machines are going. The forklift was there, so I started honking the forklift horn, trying to get his attention. Because if my machine is going, I can't leave it to go down there and get him.

So he hears the horn and he thinks something's going on. He comes running down the hall, you know, freaking out, and calls in and says, "Something's going on down here."

So, he gets down there, and they're trying to call him back on the radio, but he can't hear the radio because there's so much noise down there. So they think something's happened to him, and they send the whole squad out.

*Oh.*

You know, so, if they send the squad out, somebody's going to the hole. And we had a real prick lieutenant was on at that time. He didn't care what the story was; we're going to the hole. So, we went to the hole, and we got written up for all this stupid shit. And, the next day, it got all dropped and we got out of the hole. They reduced it to a minor. You know, it was just one of those ridiculous situations.

*What other major infractions have you had?*

Refusing a UA. You know, I didn't want to pee in a bottle.

*Why did you refuse?*

I mean, they're going to find something, so it's, like, well, why bother?

*So you had been doing drugs in here and you knew it would show up?*

Oh, well, actually, refusing is better than testing positive. If you get a dirty UA, then they've got proof. Whereas if you refuse, then you get the same infraction, but there's no proof. You lose ninety days good time, but if you go, like, two years without an infraction then you get it back.

Ultimately, I got it all back.

*How many times did that happen, that you refused a UA?*

Oh, just the one.

Yeah, like, in Walla Walla, if they've got you on call for hospital, for a UA, and you miss it, they give you a major. Even if you just didn't see it. Here, they're nice enough to give you a little notice that you're supposed to be there.

Also back at that time—I think they stopped doing this, but that was, like, Ninety, Ninety-one—they were making every prisoner give blood for DNA samples. I haven't seen them do that any more; I think the courts have since blocked it, but, you know, they were trying to get a DNA data base of every criminal. I know a lot of states do that.

But I missed one of those too. I didn't refuse on purpose; I just didn't see it. But they treat that like you refused, so they gave me a major. It's stupid shit like that.

But I never got any majors for, you know, beating anybody up, or running amuck.

*Was this just bad timing on the drug test?*

Yeah, yeah. It's, like, well, I knew it—

*You knew they caught you? [Laughs.]*

Yeah. They give you randoms about every six months.

*Is it truly random, or do you have some idea when it's coming?*

Well, they kind of go alphabetically, but, you know, they go forwards and backwards. So, if your name begins with an S, and you hear the Ps and the Qs, or you hear the Ts, you know you're kind of close. They call them out every day. You hear them call them out.

If you go to a trailer, they give you one before and after the trailer. They used to just give them after, to make sure you weren't doing anything out in the trailer, but then, you know, some guy got busted, and they were going to deny his trailers, and he said, "Well, I was doing that before the trailer." You know, and he beat it. I mean, he got the infraction, but he kept his trailers. So now they make you do it before also, so you can't use that argument.

*Did you use drugs before you ever came to prison?*

Yeah, I smoked pot.

*Smoked a bit recreationally, or were you very seriously into it?*

In college I smoked a lot. I inhaled.

*[Laughs.]*

But, you know, then I became a good Mormon, and they don't approve of such activities. Ever since I got married, I really didn't do it all that much.

*Was pot the only drug you were into?*

Yeah, pretty much. You know, a few hallucinogenics. Mushrooms. College, you know. Go to Grateful Dead concerts. People tripping.

*What about in here? Have you tried anything in here that you didn't do on the outside, or just a little pot, or what?*

No, in here it's, like, there's heroin and stuff around, but, you know, the rigs the guys use are so nasty. I mean, I'd probably like heroin. I've never done it, but I'm sure I'd like it. But in here, I just would never do it, because it's so unsanitary. You're just asking for trouble. I mean, I know guys in here that got hepatitis and stuff from sharing needles, and that's not cool.

*How readily available are drugs in prison?*

They're around. If you want them, they're there. But you can go years without ever seeing them. If you look for them, you can find them.

*Oh.*

But it's not like they're out smoking in the big yard. I mean, it's pretty low-key. I've never seen anybody smoking anywhere unless I was doing it. But, I mean, you just don't, like, walk around the big yard and see guys lighting up their doobies or anything. They watch. You know, they've got the towers up there.

*Are they pricier, because of the risks of bringing them in and such?*

Oh, hell yeah. It's at least five to ten times the price.

*How do guys afford it with, at best, minimum wage jobs? How do they afford drug money?*

The same way they do it on the streets. They wheel and deal, you know, whatever they got to do. I mean, there's dope fiends in here that run up big old debts.

*But at least on the outside, you can rob, or borrow or whatever. I mean, there's more money around to get, in honest or dishonest ways. It seems like in here, there wouldn't be as much disposable income floating around.*

Well, you know, there's money on the streets that some of them are able to get.

*You mean money that people mail to them from the outside?*

Right, that kind of stuff. So, you know, if a guy's got money out there, he'll have someone send it to him. If he doesn't got nothing, then he's going to have to go without.

But it's there if you want it. It's just not really readily apparent. I mean, you never see it if you're not looking for it.

*Are there different amounts, different availability, at different prisons? I mean, are some prisons run in ways that are actually effective in controlling drug use, and others aren't? Or is it pretty much the same all over?*

Well, any more, it's pretty tight, because of the UAs. They only started doing those in about Nineteen ninety. Before that, prisoners were doing much more drugs,

The UAs is the way they stop it. Because it's not that you can't get it in; it's that if you keep doing it, then sooner or later they're going to catch you, 'cause of the UAs. Usually after two dirty UAs, or especially three, they'll send you out of this place back to Walla Walla or wher-ever. I mean, if you get caught three times in a couple years, you've got to be doing a lot.

But, yeah, in the old days, you could walk around the yard, smoke joints, and, you know, do whatever you want. And they didn't care. But not any more.

*Speaking of the drug issue, in your opinion, would it be a good or a bad thing to legalize most or all recreational drugs across the board? What effect do you think that would have on crime and punishment, prison issues and such?*

You mean outside? As a whole?

*Yeah.*

I think marijuana certainly should be legal. I mean, the huge amount of money they're spending trying to make it illegal is ludicrous. All the people in prison for marijuana, and all the DEA agents, and all the stupid shit they got out there trying to bust pot smokers, you know, if they spent some of that money on something more worthwhile, like more education and treatment, then you'd still have a huge amount left over to do something good with.

You know, schools instead of prisons. I mean, thousands and thousands of guys are in prison for pot possession. It's beyond stupid.

*I'm surprised at how few drug crimes we run into at PAP. Maybe it's mostly just because we have people with much longer sentences, but it seems like it's all murder and some major thefts like bank robbery. I'm sure some of those are drug-related, but I never hear people say they're in just for selling drugs.*

Well, most of those guys are minimum custody, and they're all at the camps, the minimum facilities. A lot of them never make it to a close custody institution like this one, or even medium. A lot of them only got two or three years to do. They're out planting trees; a lot of them are on work crews.

So in a way, it's, like, subsidized public works projects. You know, you get these guys for smoking pot and you maybe make them go to work for a couple years.

*Yeah, that leads to another issue I wanted to bring up. Interesting that you kind of tied the two together. What's your position on prison jobs and prison industries? I know some people are very much in favor of it, just on the grounds that at least prisoners have some opportunity to get some money, to get some job skills, and such. And then the flip side of it is, do we really want the state or corporate employers to benefit from having people in prison? Do we want them to have labor available to them that they can hire cheaper than hiring people on the street to do the same thing? Where do you come down on that issue?*

Well, I'm very much for the prison industries. Every prison should be run like this one. I suspect that very few institutions in the country have as many good jobs as this institution does right here.

According to law, we're supposed to make sixty percent of prevailing wages, local. We've done some investigation, and it seems to be more like forty percent. Like, I make almost eight dollars an hour, and the going wages for a water jet operator with a couple years experience is about twenty dollars an hour. And so in theory, I should be making twelve dollars an hour.

And even beyond the pay, the boss is still getting a bargain, 'cause we don't have vacations, we don't have sick leave, we don't have benefits. He doesn't have to pay any of that, so he's getting a bargain. He's paying less than half of what it would cost on the streets, and plus he gets a deal on the rent here, on the building. I think he has to pay the power bill and everything, but I think the building itself is basically free rent.

So they're getting a tremendous reduction in costs. So, you know, if I owned a similar company on the street, I would take offense that here's a company in here that can afford to underbid me because he's got so much less costs. And supposedly that's been worked out through the state legislature. I mean, those concerns have been brought up, and supposedly there's only certain industries that can be eligible for prisons, and I don't know what their criteria are.

*Right.*

But as far as prisoners go, it's hugely beneficial, because if a guy's got some money when he gets out, and a skill, he's far less likely to go back to his old lifestyle.

Like Jimi. He learned a skill here. He went through the trade school, and now he's got a good welding job. You know, if he worked in the laundry, and he didn't have his girlfriend, he'd be in a whole different boat right now, much more susceptible to doing something stupid. Having job skills and education, and a place to go when you get out are really the key factors in staying out.

*Well, on the other hand, just to play devil's advocate, do we really want the state benefiting from having this source of cheap labor? Do we want it to be in the state's self-interest to keep as many people in prison as long as possible?*

Well, like, say you got minimum guys in for drugs, and you're having them plant trees and clean up the roadside. But even though you're not paying them much, the cost of the corrections and the prisons and everything far outweighs any benefits you're gaining from these crews. If these guys weren't in prison, and you were just to pay them, you could pay them a real nice wage to go out and plant trees and clean up the roadsides, and you wouldn't be paying prison guards to watch them. You'd just be paying wages to the people doing the work.

Once you add in all the other administration, and bed space and everything else, the state's not coming out ahead economically, except for how many tax dollars they get. You know, and of course they get more tax dollars for prisoners, and they can spend it hiring guards, and, you know, creating this gigantic prison industry.

*So maybe it's not in the state's economic interest. That's a good point. But how about the employers? Are we giving employers incentive to favor higher incarceration rates and such? And is that healthy?*

That's a good question. I don't know. Overall, with the existing prison system, it's certainly beneficial to prisoners. It's very beneficial to the employers that are here, because they're making a lot more money than they would be on the outside. I mean, our boss, our company's tripled in like two years.

You know, usually for a new business, if you're even making money after three years, you're doing good. He started making money in the first year. And he was able to buy new machines, and, you know, we're even talking about going to a third shift now. So he's really on the accelerated track, and he wouldn't have been able to do that out there at all.

*Yeah.*

But the other thing is, out there, let alone you have to pay employees more, but even finding them. You know, when the economy was real crazy here a year or two ago, you couldn't find people, because everybody's going to a better job, because the economy's booming. You can't find anybody, especially skilled workers. Whereas in here, you've got seven hundred guys all fighting each other to get out there. And many of them are skilled.

*Right. Let me hit a few other things quickly, because we're almost out of time. On the whole, are prisons too soft? Are criminals "coddled," as we're constantly being told by politicians and such?*

What I feel is that a man should not be able to leave prison without, at minimum, a GED. If you don't want to get a GED, then you're not getting out of prison.

*Literally? So even if a person has, like, a one year sentence, and they're just obstinate about this, they should spend the rest of their life in prison if they refuse to get a GED?*

Well, if they've got a one year sentence, and they don't spend that year at least taking classes, then maybe you give them, like, an extra year. Or, you definitely penalize them in some way.

*OK. You don't literally refuse to let them out ever.*

Well, no, but, say if a guy's got a ten year sentence, they should tell him, "Well, you can do ten years, or you can do seven years if you'll get an education."

*Right.*

You know, so that's three years you're saving of what it's going to cost to lock this guy up. That's thirty thousand a year, or ninety thousand dollars. Ninety thousand dollars, you ought to be able to give that guy a hell of an education. And about thirty other guys.

So, you know, you tell a guy that's his choice. "See," you know, "You got a choice: You can do your ten years, do whatever you want, fuck off, do drugs, and do every day of that ten years. Or, if you want to get an education, job skills, blah, blah, blah, you do seven years."

*Yeah.*

And, you know, the big thing the public has with this is, like, "My kid's got to pay to go to school. He doesn't get a free ride. Why are they giving these fucking convicts a free ride?" And it's a valid argument.

But, nobody wants to look at the big picture of what's best for society when a guy gets out. They don't care about that. They say, "Well, this guy's an asshole. He robbed a bank and killed somebody. He's got nothing coming."

Well, if that's the case, then kill us all. I mean, you know, if you're going to be tough on crime, then go in the prisons and shoot every person in there, and then you'll be happy. But if you're not going to do that, then you got to do something with them. 'Cause they're getting out, you know. They're, like, "Well, everybody wants to shoot them, but we can't do that. So we'll just ignore them until they get out." And that's what they're doing.

But I'm a firm believer in the merit system, which is basically what parole used to be. It never really worked, because they didn't do it right, but I believe in it in theory. So, you know, if a guy's getting a degree and da-da-da, he gets out earlier than if he isn't making that effort. You might be doing ten to twenty, and you can get out in ten years if you take your programs, stick in school, and so on.

So, it's been tried before, but unfortunately with limited success. Some of the guys get out and they still become serial killers or whatever. And, it's those sensational cases that screw it up for everybody.

*Right.*

You know, ninety-nine guys get out and do good, and the one guy gets out and hacks somebody up, and they decide, well, then we screwed up on all of them. That kind of thing.

But, you know, now they're going in the opposite direction, where they're taking education away from here. There's less classes now available than there used to be. You used to be able to get an AA degree; you could even get a Bachelor's at one time. Now you can only get the GED.

But I'm a firm believer in making a guy, you know, do something to better himself. I mean, you can't force anybody to do anything, but you can certainly give them incentives. I believe there should be that kind of system.

*What about other factors that lead people to think that we're too soft on prisoners? Do you think that's a myth, or do you think there's something to that?*

Well, you know, on TV, people see, oh, we got weights in here, and they think it's a big health spa. Or we got cable TV, and ice machines.

I knew a guy in Walla Walla who came from Tennessee. And in Tennessee, when they sentence you to hard labor, you go out to a rock pile, and you break big rocks into little rocks. That's what you do all day. I don't know if they still do that, but in the early Nineties, you go out and break big rocks into little rocks. And I could see maybe, you know, a couple months of that, just for a little wake up call.

But, after that, it becomes very counterproductive, where it's just going to piss a guy off. I mean, he's out there breaking rocks for ten years, he's going to be pissed off when he gets out. I don't care who he is. He's either going to be pissed off, or he's going to be so broke down that he don't give a fuck. And either way, it's not a kind of person you want out in society. It makes no sense.

So are they "coddling" prisoners? No. Are they being too harsh? Well, they're treated in a way that I don't think people will like the consequences. I mean, if you put a dog in a cage and poke sticks at it, you know, after awhile you get a pretty pissed off dog. And everybody knows that. And there's people out there who know it. But, they don't care. It's, like, "Well the guy's a criminal, a piece of shit; he's got it coming!" But, you know, one day the guy's getting out and living next door to you.

*Let's relate this to deterrence. Do you think it deters crime if a potential criminal—somebody who's considering committing a crime or pursuing crime as a career—knows that the worst that's going to happen to him is he'll be going some place where the prisoners get three square meals a day, they only have to work if they choose to, they get cable TV, and they get weights and all the things you described? Do you think that creates enough of a disincentive to commit crimes?*

Well, again, it's back to the choice thing. And, you know, even the shittiest prison, where you can't do anything, and you only get an hour a day out of your cell, there's going to be some people that would rather do that. You know, there are hard cases. They don't give a fuck, and there's nothing you can do with them. They'd rather go do their time, five years in a real hole, then do anything these people want them to do. But that's a very small minority. You know, ten percent.

But the other guys, you say, "You got a choice. You can go to this nice prison where you can get a job, we'll give you some education, give you a break on your time. But you got to bust ass. Every day, we're checking up. You're getting good grades, you know, you're not getting infractions. You fuck up, you're going back to this place."

Life's about choices. And I think that that should be the way it is. But there are certainly some people that, like I say, there's nothing you can do with.

*But that doesn't really address my question. I'm asking about the deterrence issue. If prison isn't some horribly scary place with, you know, pointless dehumanizing labor like breaking rocks and all that, then maybe people won't bust their ass to avoid it. If it's not something horrible, then maybe it won't be that big a deal to risk ending up here.*

I can see your point, but, in a way, why should we make it so someone is afraid of prison?

Well, 'cause it keeps them from doing crime, OK.

But, I don't think, even if prison was, like, the most horrible place, it's still not a deterrent, because when you're out doing crimes, you're not thinking about getting caught. When a guy's out there holding that bank up, he's not thinking about getting caught. When he's killing that guy, he's not thinking about getting caught. Nobody thinks about getting caught.

*I always hear that. I'm skeptical that that applies across the board. That—*

I'm not denying it's in the back of your mind, but—

*—implies that if somehow we abolished punishment entirely that the crime rate wouldn't go up or down at all, because nobody is concerned about the punishment to begin with. That suddenly if there was no punishment for robbing banks, then the number of bank robberies would stay constant. But I don't think so. I think that there are people who would be robbing banks but aren't because they don't want to go to prison.*

Well, I would also couple this with, if it's your first time in prison, you're treated more leniently, where you're given these programs and da-da-da.

You know, if you come back, though, then I believe your options should shrink. They say, "OK, this is your second time, you can still take these programs, but we're really going to be on your ass. If you fuck up once, you know, you're going to this place." And then if you come back, like, a third time, then you're done.

I mean, if a guy's given a decent chance the first two times, then it's much more of a deterrent when a guy's out there and he knows that if he goes back to prison, he's done.

But for a first time guy, I guess there wouldn't be much of a deterrent. It's, like, "Well, if I rob this bank, even if I get caught, you know, I can go to prison, and I can go to school or get a job and make some money in there, and stay drug free for a couple years, and get back out. You know, it doesn't sound so bad." [Laughs.]

*I see your point that maybe the window of opportunity gets smaller and smaller each time a guy comes back, but I wouldn't want to take it to the extreme where after x number of chances, you literally have no opportunity at all, that at that point we just throw away the key, and don't let you in any programs or give you any chance at all. I always have hope even for the guy who's been a repeat offender for thirty years of his life or whatever, that sooner or later, something might click. And just in case it does, I want to be ready for that.*

Yeah.

*I mean, there are some really good guys in PAP who took a lot more than one or two or three trips to prison in order to turn their life around and change their thinking.*

Right, you just make it a little more demanding each time and really make them prove themselves. If you're going to work your way back from the third or fourth time, you've really got to do an outstanding job.

*How do you respond to pro-death penalty advocates, who would say that a person who commits murder should be executed to balance out their crime? You know, "an eye for an eye." Do you deserve to die for what you did?*

I used to think that the victim's family should be able to make that choice. And if they didn't want the person to die, then the state had no business killing the guy.

Now I'm not so sure about that, because most victims' families would kill the guy, I'm pretty sure.

And, really I don't agree with it, but in a way, I can't have a problem with it, because, you know, in a way, that's their right, the victim's family.

The problem comes down to all these cases where the degree of guilt is so questionable. My God, you know, they've got all these guys on death row and it turns out through DNA analysis and stuff that they weren't even the right guy.

*There's no doubt about whether you committed your crime. Do you deserve to die?*

What the fuck with all these questions? [Laughs.]

No, I don't deserve to die. But, if it was in the family's power to make that decision, then I wouldn't disagree with their killing me.

But I would disagree with the state trying to kill me. The state has no business killing anybody.

*Why?*

'Cause it's not their prerogative.

*But don't we turn that function over to the state? If the family has the right to kill you, why can't they delegate the actual carrying out of the killing to the state. I mean, you could just as easily say the state has no business imprisoning you, that only the family can imprison you. I mean, as a society, we turn these functions over to the state. Why shouldn't the state run the electric chairs if they can run the prisons?*

Well, because I don't think the state has any business doing that. I think that's beyond their scope. You know, the state can lock people up, they can run the prisons, and do all that, but killing somebody's a whole new area that they shouldn't be involved in.

*Why is it OK for individuals to cross that line into that new area, but not the state? Why wouldn't you say that individuals should be allowed to imprison you, but not to cross into that new area by taking your life? Why should the family be allowed to kill you if the state's not allowed to kill you?*

Well, because they're the victims. I mean—

*They're the victims in both cases. Why can they say, "OK, we want the state to be the ones to do the imprisonment," but they can't similarly say, "OK, we want the state to be the ones to do the execution"? I mean, I think you're drawing two distinctions. First, that the state can decide on all punishments except for death, as only the family has the right to decide that. Second, that the state carries out all the punishments except for death, which again only the family may implement. But I don't see your grounds for your position.*

I don't know. [Laughs.] It's just one of those weird things.

I don't believe in the death penalty. But, like I say, if the victim's family feels strongly enough that this person deserves to die, then I think that's their right.

I can't really justify it, but—

*Yeah, it still sounds to me like a contradiction. On the one hand, you say you don't deserve to die for what you did, and on the other you say that the victim's family has the right to kill you.*

Because there's a lot of cases where the state has gone ahead and killed somebody even when the victim's family has fought against the death penalty for that person. They've actually lobbied for the person that they're trying to kill. And the state goes ahead and kills them anyway. You know, they say, "Well, you don't matter. We don't care what you think. We're going to kill him."

And, you know, that's really wrong, because the state has somehow superseded morality and ignored the victims.

You see, the victims are left out of the criminal justice system. What they care about or think doesn't seem to matter any more. But, a lot of times, they should have a voice, even though usually they're just going to say to kill the guy or lock him up for a million years.

I mean, I've read some of the letters that people wrote about me, you know, that my wife's friends wrote to the court about me. And, you know, they're not nice.

*OK, but what I'm still missing is why the family has a right to treat you in a way that you say you don't deserve.*

Oh, back to that point.

Well, I guess I would say their rights supersede my rights. Because of what I've done, they have the right to, you know, impose their will on me, to kill me if that's what they want.

*Is there a maximum that they may do to a person? Are you arguing for some kind of "eye for an eye" type thing, that they have the prerogative to go up to the level of what the criminal himself did to the victim, but no farther?*

Well, I'd say whatever makes them happy.

*What if what would make them happy is to torture you before they kill you?*

[Laughs.]

*Or what if the only thing that would satisfy them is to massacre you and your entire family? I mean, there must be some line beyond which they're not allowed to go to get their revenge. How far can they go, do you think?*

That's a good question. I don't know. I don't know. I'll have to think about that one. I'll get back to you on that one.

That's an excellent question. Leave it to you.

# BUCK—March 1999

*"You know, most guys who've been down awhile realize that there's no call to terrorize even the people at the bottom of the pecking order. Do we like sex offenders? No. But it ain't right, you know, to brutalize anybody, as far as I'm concerned. Not in my house. It's not my way, you know."*

Buck in 1997.

T he next day marked the end of this final two-week stretch of daytime interviews. We could still perhaps risk making a tape surreptitiously in the office across the hall from a PAP meeting, but really this was supposed to finish the taped interviews.

Buck was someone with whom it was very important I meet. He had the potential to be an excellent subject for the book, but I had precious little material from him thus far. He was reluctant to communicate in writing, and I had missed him the previous week, so it was now or never.

When I arrived, I found Buck with a couple of friends in the PAP office. He looked up at me, and his face registered surprise, and then the "Oh God, was that today?" realization. It was purely a coincidence that he was even in the building. He sought to beg off doing the interview.

Turns out he had a rather weighty reason. Unbeknownst to me, and I think to most of the volunteers in PAP (because of his work schedule, he could no longer regularly attend the meetings, and in any case, he was not nearly as apt as many of the prisoners to talk about himself and his situation), Buck had had his first parole hearing recently. And earlier this same day, he had been informed that he had been turned down. He was not in the frame of mind to do an interview.

I explained to him why it was important we not miss this opportunity, but I fully expected him to turn me down anyway.

With a sigh, and a half smile, and an "Ohhh man, Craig" or two, he got up, crossed the hall with me to the meeting room, and proceeded to give me the longest interview I had yet had with any of the prisoners. He responded to all my questions with patience and thoughtfulness, and other than jokingly he never belied any preoccupation with other matters or any desire to terminate the proceedings. My respect for him reached a new high.

(I must say, Buck's soft spoken nature made it torturous to transcribe this tape. Through repeated listenings, I was able to reconstruct a decent amount of the conversation, but much was lost.)

*Well, Buck, before I turn to my notes and questions for this session, why don't we get your reaction to the news you've just received. You had a parole board hearing recently, and the ruling has just come down. What can you tell me about that?*

Was I expecting better? Yeah. But, can I live with it? Yes. Am I mad? Angry? A little bit.

*So, they turned you down?*

Yeah.

*And they gave you how much more time?*

Well, they gave me three years, but I see them in two years, 'cause I get a third off for good time. So, it's not forever, but it just puts your life on hold for two more years.

*Was this your first time before the board?*

Yeah.
I'm a little bit disappointed. I thought I was doing pretty good for the last five, six years or so. You know, I thought I was ready. They thought different.

*And you don't know yet what their reasons were?*

No.

*Maybe we'll find that out in the future.*

Difference of opinion. [Smiles.]

*[Laughs.] How did the hearing itself go? What kind of questions did they ask you?*

Actually, they don't ask too many questions. You know, they ask you about some of your criminal past. They ask you about the things that you've done in the last eighteen, nineteen years in prison. They ask you, what does your future hold? What do you want for your future? You know, what are you going to do upon release?
It's mostly those kind of questions. And then, I have a drug history while incarcerated, and they asked me what I've done for that. You know, that might be one of the hang-ups that I have with the parole board, why they turned me down.

*Has it been a number of years since you had any drug problems in here? Any infractions?*

Yeah, actually, it's been three and a half years. I quit drugs over three years ago.

*So it's not just that they haven't caught you; you quit.*

I actually quit.

*Yeah.*

October Fourth, Nineteen ninety-five.

*That's good.*

Yeah, so, I mean, you know, it's kind of hard, because now I got to tell Mom, tell the family; that's the hard part. Me, I take my lumps as it comes, but it's hard on them.

*Did your people have a lot of confidence, a lot of optimism?*

Well, a lot of my people, it's, like, "You've done enough time." They have their own understanding about how much is too much and how much is too little, which may not match what the Board thinks. They just know me, and then they're, like, "It's been too long. Now it's your time."

And then they see the discrepancies in the sentences people get and how long they're in prison compared to me. Well, but I realize that even though some people that murdered get out sooner than me, there's also people that get life without.

But if you mention someone like that to my mom, she's, like, "That ain't my son," you know. [Laughs.]

*Yeah.*

So, that's going to be the hard part. There's going to be a bunch of crying. It'll be hard.

*So no one knows yet. None of your people know yet.*

No. No, you know, let's deal with Buck first. [Laughs.]

*Yeah.*

I'll call her tomorrow. Yeah, or later this week. If it was good news, I'd have called her already. [Laughs.]

*How do you feel when you go before the board? Are you nervous? Is it like auditioning, like you're "on," and everybody's judging everything you do and say?*

Oh, most definitely.

I mean, they basically hold your immediate future in their hands. "You can go home. No, you can't go home. All right, next!" You know.

*How do you prepare for something like that? I mean, do you have to rehearse how to bullshit them, or can you actually come in there and be spontaneous and honest?*

Actually, I didn't really rehearse. Some guys do. But I really didn't.

I thought it went pretty well. I think it's just, you know, maybe next time. They're going to deny you your first time, I guess.

You know, it's a lot of stress.

*Sure.*

Especially for me, because most of the guys who had hearings around the same time as me got their decision last month. They denied them right away. They held mine an extra month.

*Tougher decision. Closer call.*

Yeah.

*They had to think about it more, it sounds like.*

Well, maybe next time.

*Do you think they have a general practice of turning people down the first time?*

Most people I know got turned down the first time.

You know, maybe it's just an attitude adjustment, to see how you react to it for the next two years. Which is their call, you know.

I couldn't do that. I couldn't make decisions like that. Especially, 'cause they're not really looking closely at your crime and at how much rehabilitation you've done since.

*That's so hard to judge.*

They're supposed to look at all that, and at what the likelihood is of your committing further offenses if they let you go.

*I would think the pressures they're under just makes it easier to err on the side of keeping people in than letting them out, because if they keep somebody in a couple years longer than they needed to, it maybe pisses off him and his family, but who else cares? Whereas, if they let somebody out too* early and he re-offends, well, then everybody comes down on them. So, I guess the safe choice is to keep people in prison.

Yeah. If they could, they wouldn't let nobody out. That way they're liable for nobody.

*Since you're under the board, and not the new guidelines, can they just keep you here indefinitely?*

Oh, yeah.

*So, if they wanted to, they could turn you down every time, and you'd be here the rest of your life?*

Yeah. Yeah. They got to give you cause, but, I mean, their causes are so wide-ranging. There's always enough to justify keeping any of us in here, in society's mind.

*So, technically your sentence is a life sentence, and that's why they can do that.*

Yeah. I got life top. It's twenty to life.

*And you've been in how many years so far?*

Nineteen years.

*Well, let's perhaps turn away from that depressing topic, to other depressing topics. Tell me a little bit about your initial incarceration, after you were arrested and you first hit jail—I guess you went to the county jail—and then, what? Shelton?*

Never been to county jail.

*Oh, you didn't have to go to county jail?*

Well, I was in juvenile. I wasn't old enough.

*And then you went straight to prison from juvenile?*

Actually, I was in juvenile during my trial. Since I was not sixteen years of age, they couldn't keep me in a county jail, so they had to transfer me from juvenile each time I went to court. Detectives picked me up. The courthouse was, like, across the road. So it wasn't very far.
And then I went from the juvenile institution to Shelton. But, they wouldn't let me in Shelton, 'cause I wasn't sixteen years of age. So, I sat in the parking lot for, like, about four

hours, till the Attorney General made a decision where I was going to go. So, when he made a decision, I went to Green Hill instead.

*Now, what is Green Hill?*

Another juvenile institution. They put me in the maximum security part of Green Hill.

*So where was this other institution where they had you first, during your trial?*

In Vancouver, Washington.

*OK. So first you go to a Vancouver juvenile facility, and then after the trial, they take you up to Shelton, won't let you in, and send you to Green Hill.*

Yeah. Green Hill's, like, where all the juveniles go. It's the state-ran juvenile detention center. Juveniles, most of the hard ones, go there. They have a maximum security unit.

*So, what's the one in Vancouver? Is that, like, the equivalent of a county jail for juveniles? It's analogous to that? And Green Hill's more like a prison?*

Yeah, exactly.
Then, after the day I turned sixteen, they transferred me from Green Hill to Shelton.

*And where did they assign you from Shelton first?*

Actually, originally they assigned me to go to Walla Walla, but then they said, "Well, maybe not." Then they sent me across the street, which is, you know, the correctional center.

*Where is this? In Shelton?*

Yeah. See, they have a prison in Shelton.

*Oh, so it's not just a transfer point.*

No, they have, like, eleven hundred prisoners in the correctional center, across the street from the reception center that serves as the transfer point for all the prisons in the state. It's in the same complex.

*Is it the usual policy that as soon as someone turns sixteen, they have to leave the juvenile institution and go to a real prison?*

No, but me, since I had so much time to do, they transferred me right away. And, actually, Green Hill didn't really want to keep me there, for whatever reason they had, you know. They said, "Oh, you're out of here."

*You're somebody else's problem? [Laughs.]*

Yeah, going to be somebody else's headache.

*Had you ever done any kind of time in a juvenile facility before you fell?*

Just in and out of the county juvenile facility, not at the long term facility at Green Hill.

*For what length of time? Was this just overnight, or—?*

Thirty days. Thirty, sixty days.

*So, you had had some taste of it.*

Yeah, you know.

*How'd you learn the ropes of jail, and juvenile facilities and such? That's one of the things I'm kind of curious about, when somebody enters the system, how do you know not to violate what turns out to be the convict code?*

As far as juveniles, or adults?

*First time you're incarcerated anywhere. How would you have known, unless you grew up in that kind of culture. See, I'm thinking, like, in my own case, if, either as a child or as an adult, if I was arrested and sent to a facility like that, I wouldn't know what counts as snitching and what doesn't, or what counts as breaking the convict code and what doesn't. I mean, I would just innocently do stuff without realizing I was doing something I'm not supposed to do. How do you not fall prey to that? Why didn't you get into trouble?*

Well, actually a convict taught me a lot. He said, "If you think it's telling, it's telling." You know what I'm saying? So, if there's any doubt there, it's telling.

*So even a close call,—*

Yeah, it's telling.

But I was fortunate—well, fortunate or unfortunate—because when I came in, I had a bunch of time. I was the youngest one, and all the guys knew I was going to be there awhile. So, it's kind of, like, "All right, kid, this is what you're going to do," you know, "This is what you're going to do and what you're not going to do."

*So they actually took you aside, and kind of clued you in to all this.*

Yeah. And then they put out the word, "This kid ain't the one to," you know, "have homosexual tendencies toward," and shit. [Laughs.]

*[Laughs.]*

You know, but there's, like, other kids that have got incarcerated, only a little bit older than I was that I feel sorry for, that have had lots of problems. But was it my business?

It's hard. It's hard to see that and just mind your own business. You know what I'm saying? But when someone's new to a facility, and new to being incarcerated, they haven't developed no friends that'll back their play, because no one knows them that well yet. So even if I were to say, like, "Well hey, man, let's go get this kid out of trouble," people would just say, "Oh shoot. You go get him out of trouble." So, it can be hard.

I mean, there's a few though, that you know, hey, leave this one alone.

*How did they know to leave you alone? How did they know you're not the type to be victimized?*

I fought a lot. Yeah. I mean, I would fight.

And then I wasn't trying to get caught in the middle of a bunch of things that weren't my business. You know, drugs and stuff like that. 'Cause that's what most people fall prey to. They're, like, "Hey, where's—?" No. Adjust first, then you do all that.

*How did the fighting come about? Were you attacked, or did you have to pre-emptively get into fights so they'd know that you're not to be messed with?*

Well, I mean, they'll test you, as far as, like, the respect thing. And if they disrespect you, then you got to fight.

I ain't fought in years, you know, and don't hope to be fighting in the future. But when you're young and first incarcerated, most people will fight. I mean, first of all, you come from the streets with a chip on your shoulder. It's all the world's fault that you're locked up. I mean, when you're first locked up, it's "Hey, that judge! That cop! That prosecuting attorney!" That's what's going on.

*Yeah.*

It's never Buck's fault.

*Right.*

You know, it isn't. It's Mom, Dad, and everybody else, but never you. It's society's fault. I mean, it takes years to realize, hey, you're the one that hurt yourself.

So you got this chip on your shoulder already, and then somebody brushes by you, and you're, like, "Hey!" you know, "Watch yourself!" "You watch yourself!" Well, hey, it's on. You know, "Kid, you ain't nothing but a punk!" "Oh yeah? Well, here! Punk this!" You know, stuff like that. Somebody takes your seat in the chow hall, you know, that's all it takes.

*Is what you're describing very similar in a juvenile facility as in a prison?*

Well, see, one thing is, in the county ones, you don't interact too much. And in Green Hill, they wouldn't let you interact none. The idea is, "Oh no. We ain't letting these guys riot."

So I was mostly isolated in juvenile.

*So most of what you're describing is when you entered prison, not when you entered Green Hill.*

Right.

Actually, from my first day at Green Hill, there were guys who treated me like their idol. They were in awe that I was going to prison. They were throwing things underneath my door, you know, sneaking drugs to me.

*Really?*

Yeah.

*How did that make you feel?*

Huh? I smoked it. [Laughs.]

*[Laughs.]*

"Bring more when you're done," you know. [Laughs.] Yeah.

No, actually, I wasn't the idol type. I was just a stupid kid.

*Did you think of yourself as a stupid kid then, though, or did you like the attention?*

I was one of them kids that didn't really care about anything. Live day by day and, you know, whatever Buck wants that day, that's all that matters. And respect? Didn't respect nothing. You know, and would say anything that I felt like saying.

*Do you think the prison authorities take into account the need to be more aggressive and to fight more early in your incarceration? If they look at a guy's record, and they see, "Jeez, he's got twenty fighting-related infractions his first five years in prison, then two the next five years, and zero after that," do they understand that that's because everybody has to do that?*

I think it depends whether you're talking about people close to the situation like a line bull or someone farther up. Wardens, superintendents, associate superintendents, they don't see all that. Especially, like, the parole board. They don't see that. All they see is violence. They don't have an understanding of the situation, because they're not actually part of the system.

The people in Olympia don't understand that. And it's hard to teach them, you know, what a guy'll go through coming up here. I mean, it's, like, you can be dead or you can eat. [Laughs.] That's just the way it is.

*It sounds more circumstantial than anything. If a guy has on his record that he was fighting a lot in the early years and not very much after that, it doesn't mean necessarily that he's a different person, or a less violent person than before. I mean, he may have been very violent all along, or not violent at all all along. It's just that the circumstances differ. The first few years, he was confronted with more situations where fighting is called for than he was in later years. I don't know, but I would think they'd want to take that into account when interpreting somebody's record.*

Yeah.

*Otherwise it can be pretty misleading.*

Plus, you learn to be more manipulative the longer you're in the system.

*You mean to figure out how to survive without fighting all the time?*

Yeah, you know, or, "I can get that without fighting. I'll just have to go about it this other way." [Laughs.]

*You mentioned something that fits in with one of the things I was going to ask you about, that a lot of the conflicts, a lot of the fighting, a lot of the trouble people get in is because they're messing in areas they're not ready for, like getting in over their head with drugs and such. Actually, I'm getting kind of differing pictures from different people I've talked to. Some people present prison as if, especially early on, you're fighting all the time, and you really can't avoid it. You know, if you're going to survive here at all, you've got to fight. And I talk to other guys, and they say, "Ahh, that's a lot of bullshit. If you don't stick your nose in where it doesn't belong, if you don't want to be one of the leaders, don't want to get involved with the drug dealing, don't want to make a lot of money in prison and do things you shouldn't be doing—if you just want to mind your own business and do your own time—you very rarely have to fight, even early on. Just keep to yourself, and nobody bothers you." What's your comment on that?*

Well, that's true. But you have to realize most guys care about where they stand in the pecking order. So, I mean, it's not that we all want to be kingpins or whatever, but we want our voice heard.

Now, you got guys around here that probably ain't never been in a fight their whole time incarcerated. Ten, twelve years, and never been in a fight. But then again, you know, some of that's 'cause they will let people walk over them. They're not standing up for themselves; they're hiding who they are.

You know, you got to remember, the people you're meeting in PAP and interviewing for your book are mostly the kind of guys that want to be the ones to say, "Hey," you know, "This is the way it's going to be done!" [Laughs.] I mean, not necessarily talking about the drug trade or anything like that, but just guys who demand respect and who expect to call the shots.

But you go to the chapel, and it'd be a totally different interview. "No, I've never been in a fight. No, I've never gotten an infraction. And, yes, they did this to me, they did that to me." Not necessarily a sexual thing, but, "Yes, they disrespect me." But, you know, the way they feel is, "Well, I have God, so it's all right. They can't do nothing to me that'll change that." They're happy.

But you talk to me, it's, like, "You're not going to disrespect me. I am still a human being," you know.

A lot of the violence in prison now is racially motivated. It might not be because one guy's a white supremacist, and one guy's of another race; it's just that we all come from different, you know, social backgrounds. I don't understand his background; he doesn't understand mine. Maybe he's talking loud because that's just what's normal for where he comes from, but to me, it's, like, "Hey, quit yakking!" you know, "Quit loud talking!" "Oh, shut up!" And then it starts. We're different races, different backgrounds, so it ends up in a conflict because we don't understand each other.

You got to understand, like, here comes Craig, into prison. There are five black guys, five white guys. Where are you going to go? You know, you're going to be with the five white guys. Now, they might or might not be Nazi-types, but that's where you'll likely go. People just tend to separate into races like that.

You know, I can understand those guys that have swastikas and stuff. It's funny, because I know a bunch of them, and actually they're not that racist. It's just that when they got incarcerated, it was like, "OK, I'm going to go hang with them white guys, because I know they're going to protect me. And, you know, what I've been hearing about them black guys, they're just going to try to bugger me." You know, especially young kids think that way. And they adopt all the symbols and such to try to fit in with the group of whites they perceive as the most powerful.

Me, I've never done that. Even when I first got to prison, I was, like, "I don't care about either one of them. Where's the drugs?" [Laughs.]

*[Laughs.]*

No, no, just kidding. [Laughs.]

*How do you steer around the different gangs, the different groups? Because when I've spoken with people, any time your name has come up in connection with the racial stuff, it's been in a favorable way. Your influence on PAP has seemingly always been to keep it a club open to all races and all cultures. I remember you made a statement, at least a year ago when you were president, you said, "We actually bend over backwards to make sure everybody's represented. If anything, it's almost like an affirmative action thing where we want to have everybody." And even the few people who are dissatisfied with the level of diversity always make it a point to tell me that you're definitely not the problem. I assume you realize you have that kind of a reputation, of being able to work well with all the groups, and to never fall prey to racism yourself. How do you do that? How do you deal with the different conflicts between the blacks and the Nazis and all that?*

Well, because, first of all, I understand where they're all coming from. My mom's full-blooded Italian, so she don't really consider herself white. She considers herself Italian. I was never raised with the idea that I'm white and that makes me superior. So I can kind of see things from the perspective of the non-whites.

It's a matter of respect for people, for who they are, and treating them as individuals. And that's how I do. I might not like you, but it's not 'cause you're black. You might be black, but it's because you're an ass. And the same way with white guys.

I mean, there's guys I associate with who are racists, yeah, but not openly around me. They know how I feel, and out of respect they're not going to go there around me. They know this ain't the place for that. You aren't going to come in our office with that kind of talk.

*Do they respect you for your stand against racism, or do they think you're disloyal to the white race?*

Well, they understand it.

Actually, I'd say we have a real mutual respect. They know that my attitude is, like, I'm going to back your play when you're right, not because you're a white supremacist, but because you're in the right.

And if you're wrong, I'm going to tell you you're in the wrong.

You know, Buck'll decide what's right is what's right; what's wrong is what's wrong. And I'm not going to decide it on a racial issue. I'm going to decide based on what's best for all of us around here, which is not always best for a certain race, or even necessarily best for me. But it's what's right.

And, they know I will play mediator. "Now check this out. What's the problem? OK. Now, this is the way we're going to do it." You know, and you have their respect.

They understand when I tell them, "Hey, I wasn't raised like that. I ain't like that. You know, I understand where you're coming from, but black people don't bother me. I'm not afraid of them."

And a lot of it is fear. I believe it is.

*Fear of something different. Fear of the unknown.*

Yeah. You know, and then it's ignorance, 'cause you don't want to understand them. It's the same on both sides.

And in prison you always want a group that's like you.

But me, if I need back-up, it'll be, like, multi-racial. You know, 'cause I go down to Lifers, I go to BPC,* I go into IOAT.† You know, I go to UAC.‡ [Laughs.] I don't care. I go to them all.

*Now, you've established a reputation and such, and you've got a lot of connections and people who will support you. But is it harder for somebody maybe not as well established to not fall prey to the racial game? I mean, I'm thinking, for instance, if there's a riot over racial issues, what's going to happen to a white guy who hasn't identified totally with the white supremacists? Is he going to be kind of out in the cold, like, they're not going to support him or trust him as much, because he's been too much on the fence?*

Well, you got to understand, it's, like, there's white supremacists, and white. Not all the whites agree with the white supremacists. But they are all white. And they'll come together in a riot like that.

But if there's a riot, what's funny is, it seems like the Indians will side with the whites, the Mexicans will side with the whites. Against the blacks. It's always been like that.

*So, when there's racial fighting, racial tensions, all the non-black groups tend to get together, and the blacks are by themselves?*

---

*Black Prisoner's Caucus.

†Indians of All Tribes.

‡United Asian Coalition.

Yeah, for some reason. That's been my experience in the past.

*Interesting. Why do you think that is?*

I have no idea, you know.

*Is it just the numbers? In most prisons, are the majority black, so everybody else has to band together?*

I don't know.

It's usually the whites that stand up first, if they feel threatened by the blacks. Then the other groups will follow.

See, a lot of us white guys will riot, you know, we'll fight. But, I've been fortunate never to really be put in that position, because, I mean, if they're right, they're right; if they're wrong, they're wrong. Either side. I'll riot with the whites if they're right, but not because they're white. You know, I'm not going to riot over some drugs or something like that. You got to go settle that somewhere else.

You know, but most things are over just that issue. You'd be surprised. It's ridiculous. But it's, like, the biggest moneymaker there is, in here.

*So, if there was a riot, or something erupted, and, let's say, in your opinion, it was kind of an ambiguous situation—nobody's obviously right or obviously wrong—but, from what you understand of it, it sounds like the blacks are somewhat more in the right, it seems like you'd be under conflicting pressures, because people would expect everyone to base their allegiance on the color of their skin, but you're not inclined to do that. What would you do in a situation like that?*

I'd try to stay in the middle, be a kind of mediator if I could. My butt would be in the middle.

I mean, I've been there before. Some guys had a problem with this one black guy recently. This is a guy who I don't like myself, but still, you know, I knew that if they did something, it would turn into a whole racial thing. So, I went right into the BPC and told them, "This is what's going to happen if you don't do something here. And I ain't going to have nothing to do with it. I'm just telling you the way it is." And they're, like, "You know what, Buck? Don't worry about it. We will take care of the guy."

Because, I mean, right is right. That's the way I look at things. Right is right. What he did was totally out of line, but rather than start a race riot out of it, they needed to let him know, "Don't do it again."

*We were talking earlier about the people who are able to avoid fighting and conflict. And you mentioned that they're still vulnerable to being disrespected. What form does that take? What is their life like? I don't mean somebody who is a rat or committed a crime that puts him at the bottom of the pecking order, just a guy who's minding his own business and not fighting for himself and trying to climb up the pecking order. What kind of existence does that type of person have in prison?*

Well, it all depends how many confrontations about not fighting he has. You know, if he's been here awhile, then, like, he has his little group of friends, and that's it. He don't belong to nothing, you know.

And then you got the guys at the chapel. Not all the guys who go to church, 'cause I go to church myself. I'm a Christian. But a lot of them, they've been around this place a lot, and they still get disrespected, more verbally than anything else. Usually no more comes of it, 'cause you can't get no reputation off of fighting them. You might as well leave them be.

You know, most guys who've been down awhile realize that there's no call to terrorize even the people at the bottom of the pecking order. Do we like sex offenders? No. But it ain't right, you know, to brutalize anybody, as far as I'm concerned. Not in my house. It's not my way, you know.

I was talking to a friend of mine the other day. Good friend. An Indian. And, you know, he surprised me. A lot of Indians have a tendency—well, first of all, they weed out their own.

*What do you mean "weed out their own"?*

If you're a sex offender, you can't go in the circle. That's sacred ground. You can't go out in the circle. So they've always weeded out their own.

But my friend said, "You know what, Buck? I've been trying to tell them brothers, they ain't always right, some of the things they do. Dude's in prison; he's got a right to Native American ways." He says, "I'm not necessarily going to invite him home for dinner, but he's got a right to take part in his own culture." And actually, he's, like, at the top of the hierarchy of the Indians. And I enjoyed hearing him say that, 'cause he's got a good point. They have a right to their own culture, you know. They have a right to be happy.

Now, when I was younger, no, I didn't think that way. They had a right to get this foot in their butt.

*[Laughs.] Yeah, I've kind of observed that too. It seems like the youngest guys are the most dogmatic about the convict code and such, because they want to prove to the world how pure they are. They always seem to be the loudest about making sure everyone knows how solid they are about the code and about how no exceptions are allowed.*

Yeah. Well, you always have more anger when you're a kid. You know what I'm saying? Things mean more to you.

But you realize when you get a little older, the convict code, yeah, you live by it, but, it's not, like, 'cause he don't, then he's got to be stomped.

Plus, kids always feel like they need to prove something to the older convicts.

*Right. Yeah, they still have to prove themselves.*

Yeah. But I'm, like, "Hey kid, you ain't got nothing to prove to me." But they're thinking they have to impress me, like, "Well, you were here in the gladiator years!" So what? You know what I mean? I was here with a bunch of fools.

*Yeah.*

You know, basically that's what they were. And most of them are still incarcerated. The ones who got out mostly came back. These aren't people to be glorified.

*The hierarchy based on a person's crime doesn't make a whole lot of sense to me, at least not without a lot of exceptions to it. I can't imagine that everyone who's committed something that would qualify as a sex-related crime is always going to be a worse person than everyone who's committed a robbery or a murder or some other crime. I mean, am I that much more horrible a person if I grope a thirteen year old at the theater, than someone who goes out and shoots somebody? Or than someone who commits the kind of crime you did, holding someone up and killing her? How do you feel about the way people are ranked?*

It's always been there. You got a sexual beef, you'll never be one of the "Fellahs." If they find out, that is. There's some that are undercover.

You know, and I'm not going to blow anybody's cover. I might know some things about somebody from years ago, but if somebody asks me, "I don't remember." It ain't my place.

But, I mean, everything comes to light. Everything comes to light. We used to have one who used to scream it all the time. He'd say, "I'll just whip all of them!" Come to find out, he's one. You know, and he checked in that day, as soon as his paperwork came to light.

*"Checked in" meaning went into PC?*

Went into PC. He had to. Because, like, "As much as you screamed,…."

But, it's always been that way. "Oh, he's a rapo. That's all you need to know." That's just the way it is, you know. It don't make a difference if we're talking about thirty years ago or today.

*So a person like that could never prove himself, could never overcome his crime and win respect.*

No. And I've done it myself. "Oh, he's a pretty good dude. He ain't never snitched on anybody. But he's a rapo." I mean, that's all we ever need to know. I've said that kind of thing myself.

Then once in awhile, it hits me what I'm saying. I mean, but what are you going to do? Things are ingrained into me. Probably for life, but who knows?

*Yeah.*

You can't change overnight.

*But objectively, you recognize that there's something a little bit odd about classifying every sex-related crime as automatically worse than every other crime?*

Yeah.

*Certainly there are murderers whose crime was worse than what some of the sex offenders did, I would think.*

Yeah. But you got to understand that most of us don't understand them and the things they do. "What made you do that?" None of us understands that.

*So, do you get more of the sense that there's just something insane or something off about them, more than evil? That there's something crazy about them?*

Well, not so much crazy. But most of us feel like, well, if we want it, then we can get it. We don't understand why somebody thinks they have to take it against the woman's will. And most of them are not bad-looking guys. Our attitude is, "What the heck were you thinking about taking some? I mean, come on! They give it away!"

Most of us, you know, we're egomaniacs. It's, like, "Well shoot, if I was out there, I'd get it like this." [Snaps fingers.] "You had to go out and take some?!"

We all like to think we're Casanova. I mean, we got a couple who really do think they're Casanova, but.

*[Laughs.]*

There's some in here that are bad. I mean, you got some possessive people in here. See, I don't like possessive people.

*How do you mean "possessive"?*

You know, women tell them no, and, like, they ain't going to rape them, but they'll burn their house down, they'll stalk them, and everything else. Come on, man. That's just as bad to me. You know, let them be.

The ones that get me is the guys that have to have a woman, or they're fucked up. I mean, come on.

Well, they need to know that they're still all right, you know, that they're a man.

But all them guys that put their names in the paper, getting on the Internet, like, come on, fellahs! [Laughs.] I mean, I understand you're lonely, but come on!

It's funny. I laugh at them.

*[Laughs.] You can do that, though, because you have a fiancée.*[*]

Actually I don't. Me and her are kind of, ah,—

*Oh, OK. Things have cooled a bit there?*

Yeah, well, see, I'm the kind of guy, you know, I understand where she's coming from. It's hard having a relationship in prison. And if she ain't happy, well, go find what makes you happy. And if you decide it's me, I'm here. You know, and if it's not me, then go find what makes you happy.

*But before her, you actually had a marriage while you were in prison, didn't you?*

Yes.

*Tell me about that.*

Two of them.

*Two of them? How did this come about?*

Actually, one of them was someone I knew before I got incarcerated. She was older than I was. Then the other one was my mom's secretary. Her executive assistant.

*Are prison marriages typically sham marriages in a sense? People who are getting married because you have to be married to be allowed to have conjugal visits and have sex?*

Some. Some. I'd say most are not, though. Most of them have very good intentions in the beginning. But DOC does not make it easy. I mean, they're not supposed to. But after awhile, you know, you come up every week to visit your husband, you go through all that bull up there,

---

[*]Two years earlier, I had briefly met Buck's girlfriend and her children at the annual PAP banquet. I had heard later that they had plans to marry upon his release.

and you get tired of it. You're, like, "Hey, I don't need this." You know, and I understand. But most have great intentions in the beginning.

But I think the divorce rate ain't no different in here than it is out there. I mean, both mine lasted six years.

*Six years combined, or each?*

Each. So, I mean, out there, that's a good run. [Laughs.]

*[Laughs.]*

You know, and we're still great friends. We're still friends. I still get letters. I write them at holidays, you know, call once in a great while. I'm friends with one of them's husband. We're all still friends.

But then again, I'm not one of them that will take advantage of them. I don't use people; I'm not, like, after money. But some guys are. I mean, so that's always going to go on.

*Of course, that goes on on the outside, too. People enter into relationships with bad motives, and they use people and such.*

Yeah.

*Would you have any advice for people on the outside who respond to singles ads from prisoners? I mean, would you tell them to not do so? Should they be wary of getting involved with a prisoner?*

Be very careful. And know what he's in there for. I'm not saying just sex crimes, because there's guys in here for stabbing their wife that had never had a sexual beef. You know, in here for killing their wives. And then there's guys that will lie about themselves and their crime and everything. I mean, you got to understand, these guys are lonely, they've got all the time in the world to write and think up all the things that you want to hear. You know, just be very careful.

But, I mean, there is some good guys in prison too. I got a buddy who's been married for years, and he don't get trailer visits, so it's not about that. But he goes to the visiting room to be with his wife every visiting day. I mean, you look at them, and they're great together, you know. So, there are good guys in prison.

And then there's, you know...[Laughs.]

*[Laughs.]*

Yeah.

*I think you mentioned to me once that you'd never get married again while you are in prison.*

No, I won't. No. You know, I've been there twice.

*So, you would get married on the outside, but just not while you're in prison.*

Yeah, not while I'm incarcerated.

I want to be married for the right reasons. I don't trust myself to do it for the right reasons in here. You know, like we were talking about, guys do get married for trailers. I mean, yeah, we want sex.

*That's assuming they change the trailers rules back to where they include new marriages. But anyway, I don't know that that's so horrible that prisoners would be motivated by sex. I mean, I guess people from the outside would look down their nose at it, but I can't be too judgmental about that, as long as it's consensual and the woman shares that motive. I'd be more concerned if prisoners are manipulating people to break the law and put themselves at risk, by smuggling drugs in or stuff like that.*

Right.

But speaking of the trailers, guys don't want to lose their trailers. They don't want to get any kind of infraction that'll cost them their trailers. First of all, you don't want the woman nagging you, "What'd you do? What do you mean they cancelled our trailer?!" Then, you don't want the fellahs, like, "You gave up your trailers for that?!"

*[Laughs.] Well, since you're not married now, do you get trailers with your family instead? Can your mom or your family stay with you in a trailer?*

Oh, once a year. Once a year, my mom flies in and I have a trailer. I mean, she lives in Connecticut now.

See, that's one of the concerns the parole board's got. They say I have no immediate family in the state of Washington, so it's, like, "Well, who are we going to let this guy out to?" You know what I'm saying?

*Yeah.*

Yeah, but I do get trailers with my mom. My brother can come up too, you know. If you weren't married before the cutoff date, you can't have your spouse, but you can still have anybody else in your family. You can even have your spouse's kids come out. They might not be your kids; they can be her kids. They can come out. She can't.

You know what, though? I look at it this way: If a guy wants sex so bad that he'll get married just for sex, then he's going to have some young guy—or some old guy—in here. If he wants sex that bad.

I mean, it happens in here. And it's not that big a flaw, in my opinion. I know guys that do it. Do I agree with it? No. But do I understand it? Yeah.

*Is most of the sex, most of the homosexuality in prison, consensual these days, or is there a lot of rape, a lot of coercion?*

Most is consensual. Most is, at least in here. But you get up in them four man tanks at the Walls, it's not all consensual. I mean, come on, you got three guys in a room with each other, and here comes, you know, not necessarily a kid, just a guy, you know. Things happen.

I mean, especially if the guy's gay. You know, even if the guy comes in gay, it doesn't mean he wants to be with these guys, but they figure his being gay makes it consensual. You know, he's gay, so even though he don't want it, "Come on now, dude!" [Laughs.] Which, in my world, that ain't consensual.

*Yeah.*

I look at it this way, you know, rape is rape.

*That's interesting that people can look down their nose on it so much when it happens on the outside when you rape a woman, but all of a sudden if you rape somebody in prison, it's OK.*

Well, for most guys who've been around awhile, and actually, you know, live by the code, we realize rape is rape. That's what it is. If you'll rape somebody in here, then you'll rape somebody out there, you know.

*So, does it tend to hurt people in their position in the pecking order?*

Oh yeah. Some. I mean, I consider him to be a rapo.

But then a lot of times, he's not being forced. And then, I mean, do you try to talk him out of going along with it—you know, a kid? I don't agree with what's happening, because the kid is being used. But, it's not like the guy had to beat him up or anything to do it.

So, you know, it's not so much like a rape, it's more like if you had a woman friend on the street, and you knew she was choosing to be with a guy that was bad for her, I mean, do you talk to her about it or do you mind your own business?

*So there are different degrees of coercion and pressuring.*

Yeah. I mean, it's, like, she's your friend, so you want to be able to tell her, "You ain't supposed to mess with a dude that all he wants to do is get in your pants," you know. [Laughs.] But then again, it's her own decision.

*Now you mentioned earlier that one of the things that you had to learn, or one of the things that was troublesome when you first came into prison, was the necessity to look the other way and tolerate the victimizing and such that was going on around you. You had to accept the fact that you couldn't intervene in other people's problems, fight their battles for them, and so on. Does that change at all, over the years, as you rise in the pecking order and you get more respect, and people care more about what you say? Do you develop any power at all to intervene in situations? Can you say, "Don't mess with that kid," or—?*

Yeah. Oh yeah. Actually, your reputation precedes you. And you can tell somebody something like that, and he knows, "Well, now if I mess with this kid, I got to mess with Buck, and all his friends too."

And see, especially me, because my friends are a wide range of, you know, cultures and nationalities. I mean, I can go to pretty much any group and say, "Check this out. Leave this kid alone. Tell your partner to leave him alone." And they'll take care of it.

I don't do it often. You can't do it too often. But people will respect what you're saying, because they realize what's right.

And the thing is, there ain't a whole lot of violence behind it. There's really no violence behind it. It's not, like, "Hey, if you don't leave the kid alone, we'll whip your ass," you know, "We're protecting this kid." It's kind of, "Leave the kid alone; let him grow."

*But isn't it the threat of violence that makes them stop?*

No, I don't think so. See, I'm asking for a favor. They realize some day they might ask me for a favor, so they go along with it. Me, they know I look after the kids. If I see one that's in trouble, and he's a good kid, you know, I'll tell them, "Why don't you leave the kid alone?" They respect that my motive is trying to save a kid.

*So you don't have as helpless a feeling any more as you used to in that situation, it sounds like.*

No.

*I guess it doesn't happen as much here as at some prisons.*

See, but even when I'm at the Walls, I do the same way.

*So now, if you are in your cell, and you hear in the cell next to you that some new guy who just got transferred in is being pressured, is potentially being raped or something, you don't have to just sit there helplessly any more and keep your mouth shut; you can actually do something.*

Yeah. Right.

But it wouldn't be with a threat of violence. It'd be more like I'm asking a favor. Now, if it was a black guy, and I went to the blacks and asked them, they might threaten the guy.

*You mean if it was a black rapist, and you told the blacks about it, they might threaten him?*

Yeah, they might say, "Hey, leave him alone! Leave this kid alone!" But I wouldn't have to do it in a direct way myself. I wouldn't tell him I'd whip his ass.

No, I'd tell him, "Hey, these guys will whip your ass!" [Laughs.] No, just kidding.

*[Laughs.] Do you think your early prison experience was different than the typical prisoner because of your age? Was it a factor that you came in when you were sixteen, or was it pretty much the same as if you had come in when you were thirty?*

Well, actually, it is different. Because, well, a lot of people realize you're going to grow up in here, so they're going to teach you. But if you come at thirty, you come in with all of the baggage of thirty years. See, at sixteen, you got a mind to work with. You know, "We can make this guy, like, King Convict." [Laughs.]

*[Laughs.]*

You're more impressionable at sixteen than you are at thirty. Your morals and things are still growing at sixteen. You know, at thirty, you're kind of set in your ways. At sixteen, you think you're set in your ways, but they're not always, you know, the right ways, and you can still change. So, there's definitely a difference.

*If and when you are released from prison, will you re-offend?*

No. I will not re-offend. I don't see it happening. I know most guys will re-offend, but most guys in here use drugs, or they're career criminals. See, I was a kid with an anger problem, and I'm learning to deal with my anger.

Now, I do feel I'm more comfortable with life in here than life out there. So, will I need help out there? Yes. Can I make it work? Yes. When it gets hard, will I just raise my hand and say, "Hey, I give up"? I don't see it happening. I'm too strong-willed. Do I see me taking my ways with me out there? Of course. Do I have to change to fit in society? Yes. But, I mean, I've lived this for eighteen years, and of course I'm going to take some of it with me, you know.

*But taking it with you won't mean committing crimes?*

No. No. Because, I'm not really like that in here. I'm into helping people in here. You know, and I don't really get in a lot of trouble.

I just want to get on with life, you know. Just want to work, be happy. I don't see myself getting in trouble out there.

*So you think you'll make it on the outside?*

Oh, most definitely.

*And what does that even mean to you? What does "making it" mean?*

It don't mean I got to be a millionaire or nothing. Just be happy. I mean, I know guys that are out there, and they're not happy. You don't need a lot of money. You know, you just need whatever makes you comfortable. If it's a wife, with a couple kids, well, if that makes you happy, that's what you need.

*What are some of the things that you expect that you would do with your life on the outside that you can't do in here?*

That I can't do in here? Well, I'd like to help kids, talk to kids more. You know, and I do that in here, but, it's not really where I want to accomplish it. You can't really get through to them the way I'd like. You know, I want to help kids.

But then again, I'll be thinking, you know, the stereotypical—anybody who comes out of prison who wants to help kids, "Oh, he must be a child molester." And, I couldn't handle anybody calling me that. [Laughs.] "Let me tell you something, dude, you know, do I got to bring my paperwork with me here too?" [Laughs.]

*[Laughs.]*

You know, do I want to be comfortable with a lady? Yes. But it's not, like, the first priority on the list. That'll come. I always look at it like, hey, one will come when it's meant to be. I'm not one of them guys who, you know, just needs to have it.

*What else do you see yourself doing in the future that's not possible here? Any other educational or career plans, or travel plans?*

Well, your travel is limited to the United States, 'cause you can't really travel outside the United States.

*You mean while you're on parole?*

No. See, they aren't going to let you have a passport if you're an ex-convict.

*Oh, OK. So, for the rest of your life, even after your parole ends, you pretty much have to stay in this country.*

Yeah. Being an ex-felon, I mean, there's a bunch of paperwork you got to go through, and there's certain countries that will not accept you at all.

But do I want to travel the United States? Yes. I want to go back east. I want to visit my family. Do I want to live back there? No.

*Do you see yourself staying out here?*

Yes. Not just for the period I'm on parole, but beyond that, 'cause it's not a bad place to live. Actually though, I've spent very little time in the state of Washington. Well, a lot of time in the state of Washington. [Laughs.] But I mean not incarcerated.

I'll have a job, you know. Most guys don't want to work. I know some lazy people in here. They don't want to work.

*So they're almost guaranteed to come back.*

Yeah. I know guys who spend more energy avoiding work than they ever would working. I tell them, "If you just put that much energy into working,..." [Laughs.]

You know, but they don't see it that way.

*In our earlier taped conversation, you made a comment, "I have a convict mentality. But then again, I don't." I have a general idea what you're getting at there, but why don't you explain what you meant by that?*

Well, see, if you go through the convict code, the convict mentality, certain people take certain parts of it and highlight them, then forget the other ones. For instance, if you're a true convict, you're always supposed to look out for your fellow man. You know, you're supposed to respect each other. I mean, that's part of the convict way too.

But most people are hung up on, like, "You can't do this. You can't do that." To them, the convict code is about not having anything to do with the wrong kinds of people. And it's, like, do I believe in all that? No. But, see, I have friends that know that I know and talk to rapos and such, and so I have to kind of keep those things separate. I know I can't talk to them and the others at the same time.

So, it's, like, do I agree with the convict ways? Yes. But do I go over there and attack everyone at the bottom of the pecking order? No. I mean, 'cause anybody has a right to grow.

And I still say our problem is we do not understand them. If we did, we probably wouldn't fear or hate them so much. But, even the shrinks don't understand them.

*Aren't there some criminals of other kinds that you could also say that about? Aren't there some murderers that you have the same difficulty in understanding why they did what they did?*

Well, like, I don't understand the people who let drugs dominate their life. You know, what makes you want to do that more than anything in life?

*So even though you've had pretty much experience with drugs, you still can't understand where they're coming from?*

No. You know, I'm just a bud smoker. I mean, I ain't never stuck a needle in these arms. But I see the effect it has on people. I see their morals go so far down, you know.

*When people that you're close to get released, like Mitch or Jimi, how much does their success or failure on the outside impact you?* Does it affect your confidence of whether you'll be able to make it on the outside? How much do you have riding on what they do?*

---

*Jimi of course you know. At the time of this interview, he was still on the outside. Mitch (I have changed the name) was a very close friend of Buck's whose time in PAP just barely overlapped with mine. He was released very shortly after I joined the program. Mitch had been a very popular member of the club, a favorite of the volunteers due to his youthful exuberance and upbeat style. I thought he was a likable guy. But after he left, the more I gradually learned about him from the guys, the more I realized he was not such a good person after all. One of the prisoners, for instance, shared with me that Mitch's favorite hustle was to put personal ads in gay publications, and to pretend to be interested in guys to get them to send him money. When one would become suspicious and gradually reduce the flow of money, he would feign some kind of a fight and break-up with him, and move on to the next. It was the kind of thing the other prisoners would just laugh off, or they would roll their eyes at the memory of him, as if he were just some incorrigible mischief-maker. In general, Mitch was clearly a person with a cruel side, who had no compunction about using people and hurting people. Since his release, he had already been incarcerated again at least once. I didn't keep up with his situation closely, but what little I heard through the grapevine indicated that he was likely to be in and out of trouble for the foreseeable future.

It all depends if they come back, and what they come back for, you know. So, if they come back from drugs, no. It has no impact on my life. Because I've stayed away from drugs for a lot of years. It don't even faze me if they come back from drugs, because that don't apply to me.

You know, and most that come back, like Mitch, they come back from drugs.

But I also know Mitch has a streak in him. You know, I might not let Mitch out. [Laughs.] No, he just has a streak in him.

*Yeah.*

He still needs some growing, you know. Some people outgrow certain things, and some people just take a little longer. Eventually, you just find a reason to say, "I'm through. I am through with this way of life." But until they reach that point, some people still run around like knuckleheads. If you knew Mitch, he was a knucklehead.

*[Laughs.]*

But he was still my friend, you know.

I've had times with Mitch where I tell him, 'We're going to go walk this yard. You ain't going to talk no shit to nobody around this track. We're just going to walk this yard." I says, "If you do, I'm leaving."*

And a minute later, there goes Mitch, running his mouth at somebody, "Rowr-rowr-rowr-rowr-rowr-rowr!" [Laughs.]

*[Laughs.]*

You know, but that's my boy! [Laughs.] Yeah, that's my boy!

But Jimi, I wish him the best of luck. And Mitch. And all the guys who get out.

But most of them—I mean, you got problems, you need to realize, first of all, what your problem is. OK? But most of them don't want to face what their problem is.

I talked to Jimi awhile ago, I said, "Jimi," you know, "If things don't go right, you could go to the bag. And things out there ain't always going to go right."

*Are you feeling more confident about his situation than if he'd been released sooner? Do you think he's overcome that problem at all?*

---

*In other words, Buck wants to just take a walk around the yard with Mitch, but he knows Mitch is one of the fiercest proponents of the convict code who will never miss an opportunity to torment a rat or rapo that he happens to come across in a public space. So he knows what to expect, even if he'd rather Mitch would give it a rest for once.

I think he has. But you never know until he's tested, you know.

I even told him, you know, about his lady friend, I said, "Hey, if it don't work, it's OK." He has a lot of baggage about her. But things with her aren't always going to be what he expects. They both have a lot of adjusting to do with him just getting out from being incarcerated. So, I said, "You still need to look out for Jimi. That don't mean you don't try as hard as you can to make the relationship work, but, you know, those things, sometimes it just ain't right, and you can't be too dependent on it. You got to do what you need to do for you, whether things work out with her or not."

*I think that's a good point, 'cause a lot depends on how people deal with adversity out there, how they deal with what happens when things don't go the way they were expecting. I mean, I think a lot of people that I've talked to seem to be pretty good at setting things up ahead of time to make sure to give themselves the best chance, but there's still that issue of what happens when that breaks down.*

Yeah.

*You know, when that job that you had the foresight to set up in advance ends six months from now, and you get laid off or something, then what? Or what happens when you clash with the people you thought were going to be your support network on the outside? So, I agree that you need to set things up as best you can, so you can have the people, have the job, but you need more than that.*

Right.

*You also have to be able to deal with the situation when those things you set up fall apart, as they inevitably will sooner or later.*

Yeah, I mean, you have to think about, "All right, if these things happen, how am I going to deal with it? Am I just going to fly off, go back to the bag, what?"

*And how do you deal even with the personal interactions with people on the streets? I mean, it seems like coming from here, you're in such a habit of interpreting everything as disrespectful, and as something you have to stand up against, that it must be hard to break that habit. Well, when a prisoner gets out—especially someone like yourself, who's been here forever, literally since you were a child—when a prisoner gets out, and all of a sudden somebody cuts him off in traffic and gives him the finger, or some obnoxious drunk gay guy at the bar makes a pass at him, or he's hanging out with some friends and somebody casually insults him, "Ah, you're a punk!" or something, how is he going to react to those things, you know? Do you just—?*

[Laughs.] Why do you have to bring up "punk"? We were—

*[Laughs.]*

—fine till you said "punk." [Laughs.] I was listening to you, thinking I'd be able to handle everything you mentioned, then you had to throw that in.

*[Laughs.]*

You know, somebody cuts you off, well, the first thing you want to do is get out of the car and say, "Who the hell are you, and where are you in the pecking order?" [Laughs.] No, I'm only kidding.

I don't know that yet. That is something I have to work on.

Especially, like, at work. There's things, like, where I work out here that we just don't accept, but would probably be standard procedure on the streets. I mean, as far as, you know, telling the boss. I mean, that's probably standard procedure.

Well, in here, telling is telling. You don't tell a boss anything about another worker. You know, I can go up and tell a guy, "Hey, check this out," you know, "What you're doing ain't right. You doing nothing is creating too much work for me. So, get busy." And it'd be understood. You take it up with the guy himself if you have a problem with him; you're never supposed to go to the boss with that.

When that goes on in here, it just ain't right. I've seen people do it, and I have no understanding about that. I've seen some people, and I'm thinking, "OK, he's a good dude. What the hell he doing telling the boss that?"

But, I got to understand that on the streets, yeah, that's just how people do.

But I'd still tell them, "Hey, check this out. If you got something to say to me, or about me, just say it to me. I mean, you ain't got to go tell the boss. If you think I'm lazy, tell me I'm lazy. Maybe I'll work a little harder.

"Maybe I'll work a little harder putting my boot in your ass." [Laughs.] No.

*[Laughs.]*

You know, but I understand there are differences like that.

*Do you think a lot of people fall prey to that, though, that they can't deal with those common provocations on the street, because they're so ready to interpret everything as disrespectful toward them, and they're so ready to retaliate for everything?*

Yes and no. I don't think they fall prey to that too much. Unless people are too disrespectful to them. But then again, if somebody's being too disrespectful, you're going to let him know before it reaches that point.

I know guys who fall prey to refusing to take too much shit over being an ex-con. You know, they're not going to let people constantly abuse them and discriminate against them because they're an ex-con.

I don't think I could handle too much of that myself. "Yes, that's what I am, but I'm still a good person." You know what I mean? "And you ain't going to tell me I'm not."

*Do you have any contact with your victim's family?*

No.

*Are you allowed to?*

No, I'm not.

*You mentioned that you had heard something through the press about the—*

Well, I heard, you know, that I was forgiven and such. It was in a newspaper article.

*If you could talk to the family, or if somehow your victim could hear you now, what would you say about what happened? What would you want to tell them, if you could?*

Well, I think the littler you say, the better. 'Cause basically, you're sorry. I mean, but how do you go about explaining that to people you've hurt like that? You just don't. Whatever you do, it ain't going to make them feel any better. I mean, you can't tell them, "All right, this is where I was then; this is where I am now," when their significant other, son, daughter, is dead, because that sounds like you're trying to justify it. You just can't. I mean, "That's great, you were there, and you're here now. But where's my wife or my mother at?"

You know, that's a complicated one there.

*No, I know what you're saying, and I don't know that there really is a good answer, a good thing you could say.*

It all depends on how far they've come. Not so much how far I've come, but how far they have. And I don't mean come towards my side, or understanding or forgiving me. Because, I never expected, "Well, you're forgiven."

Basically, I'm sorry. Just, I'm sorry.

I mean, it's not something you forget. It's something you live with every day, if you've got a conscience. Some guys maybe it doesn't bother so much. But me, it's, like, "Well, you took a life," you know.

*Do you think most people in prison are able to face it when they've taken a life like that, or do they find a way to rationalize it, to convince themselves that they didn't do anything wrong after all?*

A lot of people rationalize it. "She had it coming," you know, or, "I killed him 'cause he raped my wife," or "He did this and he did that. He would have killed me if I didn't kill him first."
Not saying those things didn't happen. I don't know.

*[Laughs.] We're not talking about anybody specific here, are we?*

Oh no. No, we are not. [Smiles.]

*Have you ever had to do time in IMU?*

Yeah.

*How long?*

A year.

*What for? Drug-related?*

Partly. Under investigation for homicide.

*Guilty or innocent?*

Innocent. Totally innocent. Actually, [laughs], it's funny, the guy I got locked up with over it is up in the hospital. I mean, I ain't seen him in years. Actually, he'd been out for quite awhile, about three, four years.

*Out on the streets?*

Yeah. And he just got brought back recently for a minor violation for drinking, but while he was in the county jail, he got something wrong—a disease or something, or the flu—and he can't walk. So they had to bring him here. He's in the hospital here. And they won't let him go until he can walk.
But anyway, me and Floyd,* we caught a guy stealing on the tier.

*Stealing?*

---

*I have changed the name.

Yeah, actually from this other guy that was in the hole. Stealing drugs, you know. And, I go to him, 'cause I know he got them, and—

*So he stole them from the guy's hiding place somewhere?*

Yeah, he had them stashed by his house.*

I says, "Give me the drugs! I ain't got all day!" And, I beat him up. Floyd's watching for the guard while I'm beating on this guy. Then Floyd gets into it. "Give him the drugs!" he says, and the guy's still saying he doesn't have them. Well, Floyd's, like, six foot three, just huge. So this guy sees Floyd coming, you know, and figures we're both going to beat him up. So he slips away from us, runs out of there, you know, just runs right by Floyd—whoosh! [Laughs.]. I said, "Ooh, look at him go!"

And he's banging on the door, "Hey, help me! They're going to kill me up here!" I'm, like, "No we ain't." [Smiles and rolls his eyes at the memory of the victim's overreaction.]

*He's yelling for the guards?*

Yeah.

So, what happened is, they got him off of that tier. They took me and Floyd to the hole for ten days, and they moved this guy from our tier to another tier.

Now, when he was on the other tier, somebody got the bright idea, you know, "This guy told on them guys, and we need to kill him." So, they killed him.

But me and Floyd were in the hole. We didn't know none of this was going on. You know, actually, I didn't even hardly know the guys who did it.

But after our ten days were up, they were, like, "Ah, you two ain't going nowhere. You're under investigation for homicide." That's how that works.

Actually, the guy that did the killing is here in this prison now, and he's as stupid now as he was then.

*Did the other people involved—the ones who did the actual murder—did they also have to go to IMU, or just you and Floyd?*

Oh no, they were in IMU.

*So the authorities ultimately found out who actually committed the murder?*

Well, some guys told on them.

---

*Cell.

*Do you have any remorse about what happened? Do you feel at all responsible for the death of that guy?*

No. No, because, I never was going to kill him, and I never wanted him dead. I mean, if I had been there instead of in the hole, I'd have told them, "No, no, no, no, no, no, no, no. No."

I didn't even beat him up that good, but I admit I did beat him up. You know, I just wanted him to understand, "Hey," you know, "You can't do this. You can't be stealing up here on this tier. Especially when the guy ain't here to even defend his property."

*Was this at Walla Walla?*

No, this was at Shelton.

Floyd wasn't going to kill him either. You know, it was a couple guys who needed to make a rep. Well, they made it. When they got caught, they panicked. One told, then the other one told. I was, like, "Yeah, you got a rep." [Laughs.]

*What was it like in IMU for a year?*

Peaceful.

*Peaceful?*

It actually was. I mean, I did a lot of growing up in IMU. You realize, hey, this might not be the way to do the rest of this time.

*No one's described it as "peaceful" to me so far. It sounds like it's a chaotic, noisy hellhole.*

It can be. But see, I slept most of the day, and stayed up nights. That way, everybody else was sleeping.

You know, you hear guys getting beat. But, come on, sometimes there's a reason. If I'm a guard and you throw shit on me, I'm going to whip your ass. That's my view.

Something like that happened to me one time. Not in IMU, but when I was seventeen, some guards threw me out of the back of a truck when they were taking me to the hole. Thing is, though, I was spitting on them, I was trying to kick them and stuff. I would have threw my ass off the back of the truck too.

But, you know, back then, I would have loved to get back at them for doing that. But now, I wouldn't ever do anything, 'cause they only did what I would have done in their shoes. I was the one who was out of control, spitting on them and carrying on.

*What exactly did they do?*

Well, I was drunk and mouthing off, and got sent to the hole. It was a ways to the hole, so they got a little truck come to pick you up, you know, with a canopy. And I should have known—usually they put you in the front, you know, closest to the cab, but they stuck me on the back end. And they hit a pothole, and the dude hit me in the ribs, and out I go. Handcuffed, you know, no way to break my fall. I went, "Oh, is that how things work!" [Laughs.]

So I come in all bloody, all scraped up. And the sergeant asks, "What happened to you?" They're, like, "He fell outside the truck, you know, stepping into the truck," and they looked at me like they expected me to tell. I kept my mouth shut. I ain't telling.

*So, according to the convict code, you're not supposed to tell even against staff and non-prisoners, right?*

Right.

*So, it's not just your fellows that you don't fink on; you're not supposed to tell even on the enemy.*

Yeah, telling is telling, you know. Telling is telling.

It's the same thing with, you know, filing grievances. I mean, we have a grievance system, and I've filed one grievance in all the years I've been incarcerated. Telling is telling.

*So grievances are looked upon as telling?*

Yeah, though it all depends what's your grievance.

See, like, some guys even out in these offices, that's sometimes how they go about getting what they want. They'll see one group has something that they don't have, and they'll file a grievance. They're, like, "It ain't right that they got it and we don't." But that's telling.

Plus, most of the time it don't work. They complain, "Well, why do they get it and we don't?" and guess what? They decide, "Then nobody needs it." You know what I mean? And that's how a lot of things get messed up.

I mean, is it right all the time, how they handle things? No, but if I think we're entitled to something, I'm not going to draw you into it and talk about you got it and we don't. I'm just going to say, "Why don't we have it?" And if they say, "You can't have it," I'm, like, "OK, maybe next time." [Laughs.]

*[Laughs.] Could you articulate for potential readers the importance of having the kind of programs you have at WSR? Why should it matter to society that these kinds of programs exist in prison?*

Most programs here are volunteer programs, and there are a lot more than the Prison Awareness Project and the clubs like that. Most of the other programs, like Breaking Barriers,

Leonard Shaw, Stress-Anger Management, are all self-help programs. They're goal-oriented programs, and that's where they're most valuable. Guys need goals. None of us know how to do goals. We all know how to live day-to-day, but we don't always look at the big picture.

With programs like PAP, it's more of an interaction, and a teaching. Actually our volunteers teach us a lot. Take me, for instance. Been living eighteen years in prison. Somewhere along the line, I'm going to have to realize how to deal with people from society. And it ain't the same way I deal with the Fellahs. So, if I have no contact with society, how am I supposed to know how to deal with them?

In order to make a guy a better person, you need to teach him right from wrong, and you need to teach him something other than the values he'll pick up in prison. There ain't a whole lot of Craigs in our world, in prison. The programs let us interact with people we'd otherwise never encounter, people who can give us a different perspective and show us a different way of looking at right and wrong.

Also, if a guy's gotten to know the volunteers, then he's not going to want to harm them. And I don't mean just them; I'm talking about their kind of people, you know, people in society in general outside of prison.

*So, it personalizes potential victims.*

Yeah. And actually, the thing I think helps most is that it helps me to realize it ain't all of you. You know, a lot of us come out with a chip on our shoulder, that it's us against society, that I'm going to go do battle with society. From interacting with the volunteers of the programs, you realize, well, not all society is your enemy.

I mean, 'cause if you go by the newspapers, TV, you think, "Well, these people hate me." You know what I mean? 'Cause you never hear too much good about prisoners.

*True.*

Then as prisoners, you start thinking the best thing for us is to cocoon ourselves, "Well, I'll hate them too." I mean, that's real easy to fall into that. "If they hate me, then I hate them." And once you come out with that shit, it's, like, whoa!

I've seen guys do it. "Screw them people. They ain't got nothing coming." I know guys like that that are getting out soon. Oh my goodness, wait until they hit the streets!

But, I mean, programs are very important. Education is very important. We have very little education any more.

*Now, that's changed quite a lot in recent years. Hasn't it been cut back dramatically?*

Yeah. You can get a GED. That's all.

*How was it before?*

Well, you could get a two year degree. But it's not so much that; it's more the training programs that we used to have. The vocational programs. Cut back drastically. We need to train while we're incarcerated.

And, yes, it costs money. But it's such a small part of the budget, for one. More importantly, you can't tell a guy, you know, "Do ten years. Learn nothing. And then get back out and be a productive member of society." You'll be ten years behind everybody else, especially your peer group. "Oh yeah, I know how to catch up. Be right with you." You know what I'm saying?

We all want to look good compared with our peers, or at least adequate. You know, you don't want to look like you're ten years behind.

*Right. Let me ask you one final question, and I'll let you go, because you've been very patient, and stuck around for a long time for this interview on what I know is a difficult day for you. How are you a different person from, let's say, the day you committed your crime? And, why? What's enabled you to develop the way you have?*

Oh, [laughs]. That's kind of a long question, Craig. Hit me with that one last, huh?

*[Laughs.]*

Well, for one, I respect other people. I respect me. I love people. I love me. See, you know, Buck had to deal with Buck before he had to deal with people.

You know, there's a progression from being sixteen to thirty-three, first of all. I mean, things that are appropriate at sixteen are no longer appropriate at thirty-three.

I've learned that I don't need to be rich, that I like to work.

I like people. I respect people's differences. I don't think any more that everybody has to be what I consider to be in line with, you know, my way of thinking.

People are going to be people, you know, and you have to understand them for what they are.

As time went on, Buck drifted in and out of PAP. He was generally working the evenings of the meetings, but he dropped by when he could. And when he did, he was always warmly received, as he remained one of the favorites of the volunteers.

I sent Buck transcripts of our interviews, along with many new questions, but he did not respond. It had been clear from early on that I would have to be content with whatever we did on tape, as he was not going to work on the project in writing.

# RICO—March 1999

*"If a guy hasn't worked on the issues that have gotten him here in the first place—whether they be mental, whether they be psychological, social, whatever the issues—then you got a walking time bomb when he walks out of here. Because, all you've done is just stirred that up in his mind."*

Of all the prisoners, Rico managed somehow to be both the most and least eager to do these interviews. He craved the opportunity to talk about himself, to open up to a sympathetic friend, and he felt an obligation to be straight about himself and prison in a way he believed few of his fellow prisoners were willing to do. However, doing that, especially with the tape recorder running, seemed to require a certain intensity that he found draining.

He was the only interviewee to be self-critical after the interviews. "I should have said this," "I shouldn't have said that," and even, "I shouldn't be doing these interviews."

The others took the interviews more in stride. They opened up when they wanted to, they left out or carefully spun what they preferred to conceal, and they didn't betray a lot of self-doubt about it. With Rico, it was as if he could only give himself permission to either do this right or not at all, and you never knew which of those two to expect. In the space of a week, I got both.

I had scheduled an interview with Rico for each of the two weeks that I came into the prison in the afternoons for this final extended set of interviews. The first week, he was to follow 9.

After I wrapped things up with 9, Rico still hadn't shown up, so I went to check with the guard at the entrance to the building. He hadn't seen him, and said he was probably still at work. He offered to page him for me.

I went back to the room where I was conducting the interviews, and 9 and I chatted to kill the time waiting for Rico. A little while later, I was fairly sure I caught Rico's face peering briefly through the door, but he didn't come in. I assumed he had just gone to the office across the hall to get a cup of coffee, or had stopped to talk with someone, so I didn't think much of it. I figured he'd join me shortly.

When there was no sign of him for several minutes, I went to look for him, but he wasn't in the office or anywhere in the building that I could see. I asked the guard at the door if he knew where Rico was, and he looked a little surprised. "He was just here. Didn't you talk to him? He said you were busy with somebody else, and he went back out to work."

Oh, great, I thought. He's slipped away from me, and in a way that, for all I know, he's going to be angry at me, or feign anger at me, on the grounds that I took him away from work when I already had an interview with someone else scheduled.

At least the next week I was able to secure an interview with him. He made a perfunctory effort to explain his behavior of the previous week—he didn't want to interrupt my interview with someone else, so he hung around a few minutes, saw that 9 and I were still talking, and decided to go back to work rather than intrude—but he knew the explanation was as lame as I did, so he didn't really push it. Clearly he had not been in the right frame of mind to converse for the tape recorder, and he had grabbed the first opportunity to get out of it without blatantly standing me up.

But at least he was here now, though we only had time for a comparatively brief session before the prisoners would have to vacate the building to return to their cells for the afternoon count.

*Rico, I wanted to start off by going back and discussing some of our earlier taped interviews. You and I have spoken since then—off tape—and I know you had some interesting reactions to the interviews. You shared with me that reading the transcripts had had a significant emotional impact on you, and that there were things that you felt you wanted to correct or elaborate on, so as not to give the reader any wrong impressions of you. So, I wanted to give you the opportunity to do that now.*

Well, it wasn't so much, you know, as far as adding or deleting from. When I read those transcripts, you just gave me a new awareness that I've done something I didn't want to do. I've always said I don't want to get caught up in a certain mentality. And I pride myself in trying to be my own man, and trying to do my own time. But when I read the transcripts, I saw that I had, without fully recognizing it, bit into the convict mentality. And even though I'm a man who believes in doing my time in my way, and there are some ethics and values that I stand firm on, on how I do my time, I still don't view myself as a quote-unquote "super, hard-core, convict." OK?

I believe a person makes a mistake, does his time, learns from his mistake, and moves on. This shit about having to come back and forth into the system, and hugging each other once you get back into the joint, and claiming to be one of the good old boys and a solid convict, that's not what I'm about. And when I read the transcripts, and I saw that I fell right into that group, I didn't like it. It was a time for me to reflect on just how far I'd fallen, and it woke me up.

And as far as my crime, I was adamant about what had happened and how it happened, and in expressing it, I may have come off kind of arrogant, or sounding as if I didn't care. And that's not the case. I hate what I did. However, I have to move on, you know.

I'll have a second chance, though I'm sure many in society would say, well, my victim didn't have a second chance. I fully understand that. I don't have an argument with that.

But the law is written as such that I have to do this time. I will do this time. I will pay the restitution. I will do what I have to do, you know. And in the process, I will try to be a totally different man, and not put myself in the position that I put myself in back then to commit that crime.

*Perhaps you could also talk a little bit about what's happened since the last interview in terms of your family. When we spoke back then, you sounded almost totally estranged from your family, but from what I understand, there have been some significant changes there.*

Well, it was amazing. My mother visited me for the first time in fifteen years. After your interviews and reading the transcripts, you know, and reflecting on all the bitterness, I knew I needed to deal with my emotions toward her and toward my family.

She came to see me. We spent four days together, and she really put a lot of things in perspective for me. I needed that. I needed to hear what she told me. I needed to hear what my family was all about—their position, my position. It helped me out a lot.

I have an excellent rapport now with my mom. And with my father, whom I've held a lot of baggage for. And I realized that all this grudge and hate and resentment, and all this other crap that I've been carrying all along, was for nothing. I mean, it was just something that I chose to carry, because I guess it was my comfort zone to carry it, and it was justifiable emotion.

When it was all said and done, all this garbage, and all this bullshit that I carried, didn't matter. Didn't even matter. I felt real small. I felt real small. I felt like such an idiot. I felt so stupid, you know. Because, it really didn't matter.

You know, when you really look at the inside of a person, and you start using the eyes of the heart instead of the eyes of judgment, then you can really get the whole picture. And a lot of things had to happen, you know.

But you'll never hear me say thank you for bringing this to light. [Laughs.]

*[Laughs.] If you've established a good rapport with your parents, especially with your father, that's a dramatic change from the last time we spoke.*

Very much so. Very much so.

A major, significant, emotional event happened in his life. And I had the opportunity to help him through it. And, you know, we never discussed our past. We never discussed how we felt about each other. We never discussed, "You wasn't there for me! You was a piece of garbage! You were never in my—!" We never discussed all of that.

We came together at a point of crisis—and it's amazing how that works—where things needed to be done. All that other stuff needed to be put aside.

He was diagnosed with cancer, and I started doing my research. I started getting a support group. I got information, and put it all together. We spoke on the phone, and none of this other stuff ever came up. I never told him, "Hey Dad, I didn't—" None of that ever came up.

We just came together and clicked, like two people who hadn't seen each other in twenty-odd years, but somehow didn't skip a beat. I got the father I wanted. He has the son he wants. But of course, he would have liked me to be at home, and not have to go through all these changes, but, you know, that's understandable.

*It sounds almost too good to be true. Have you just temporarily set those other things aside, and they're going to re-emerge, or are you really into a new era with your relationship with your father?*

I've gone to a new era, because I'm not into the blaming mode. I was into the blaming mode before. It's so easy to blame. It's so easy to get caught up into, you know, "Well, I'm this because of that. I was a Puerto Rican in the Lower East Side, in the projects. And I was a victim of my own environment. And my father did this."

That's crap. When you really look at it, the bottom line is, what was my responsibility in the role that I played all throughout this? And when I looked at that, you know, I got slapped about fifty million times, and in the process I woke up.

And I was able to accept that, hey, none us are perfect. He did the best he could, as the man he was in the situation that he was in. And, looking at the role that I played, I wasn't no altar boy. So, you know, he had his hands full. So, leaving it at that, I'm not going to accomplish anything by throwing mud in his face.

So, life goes on, and I like the relationship that we have now. He understands that I'm not looking to blame. He understands that what he has here is a man that wants to grow. You know, I still got a lot of growing to do. But I like the direction that I'm going. I don't like what I have to go through to get there, I'm going to be honest with you. Because, there's a lot of prior conditioning that has to be worked out. But, slowly but surely it's happening. So.

*When your mother came for a visit, was it just her, or were your brother or father or other family members with her?*

No, my father, being the man that he was, he sent my mom on a recon mission. You know what I'm saying? "You tell me what the boy's all about," you know, "See where his head is at. Report to me, and then I'll see about going the second shot." He's supposed to be coming up here this summer.

So, she came up here, and I chose not to dwell on the negative stuff. When I first found out that she was coming, it was, like, "OK, where do we go from here? You either deal with this, bring it up, blame, or you accept Mom for her role in your life, and receive her as she is." And that's what I did. That's what I did.

I can't say enough about the fact that I had a choice to make when I knew Mom was coming out here. Do I get into the blaming mode, or do I receive Mom as Mom?

I dealt with a lot of issues prior to her visit. I was forced to deal with them, because when you don't see them, "out of sight, out of mind." You know, I can understand the mentality. But when you hear after fifteen years, "Hey, your mom wants to see you." "OK, when is she coming?" "She's coming next month." "Oh really?" Well, a lot of emotions start to resurface.

*Did she tell you she was coming? Or did she ask you if you wanted her to come?*

No, no. She was coming. She was coming, period. From what I understand, she had told my father and my brother that she didn't want nothing for Mother's Day. All she wanted was to see her son. That was me. When I heard that she had said that, then I was more than willing to meet her all the way. You know, but I was anxious. I was very anxious. Anybody who knows me will tell you—administration, staff, guys included—that I was very, very anxious, looking forward to seeing my mom.

*When was she here?*

She came for my birthday. She came in October.

*Were you able to get a trailer?*

No. No. I didn't want her first experience to be in the joint. It was bad enough that I was going to bring her in the visiting room, and have to go through those changes; I didn't want her coming all the way into the prison and spending several days here in a trailer.

You got to understand, she has a son who's a judge in Florida, and she's got another one who's in the joint. So I would imagine it's very difficult for her emotionally, but she came, and we had an excellent visit.

*So she came four consecutive days to the visiting room?*

Yeah. She made a statement, she says, "You know, you and I have never shared this much quality time when you was out." And it hurt, but it was true.

But we established a friendship and a relationship. I'm very much in love, and respectful, and appreciative of what I have. I really am. I really am.

She's an angel. She's an angel. Dealing with me, dealing with Pop; she's got a straight ticket to Heaven.

*Now, you say that you were able to set aside the issues that had caused conflict, but are those things you're going to have to deal with eventually, or do you feel like you're past those anyway? Do you think you'll have to one day sit down with your father and talk these things out?*

You know, I'll let Pop decide that. If Pop wants to some day say, "Hey, there's something I want to get off my chest," or he asks me if there's something that I want to get off my chest, then, if that situation presents itself, then we'll sit down, you know.

But I still won't get into the blaming thing. See, 'cause I did a lot of work, and as soon as I was able to accept the role that I played in all of this, and took on the responsibility, then I was able to release and just let it go. Since then, none of those past issues have come up.

You know, my brother's still walking around with that baggage. And he's up on this pedestal. I'm in the joint, and I'm not walking around with baggage. OK?

So I consider myself free, as far as that's concerned, and at the same time, I have the family that I've been longing for, and respect, with no strings attached. As soon as I accepted responsibility, and I looked real close at my world, and I saw what they had to go through, come on. We all have our flaws. And I was not going to gain anything by slinging mud.

I wanted to be free. I wanted to release myself from that, and, you know, I'm thankful that I was able to do that on my own.

*Where does Rico fit in the pecking order in prison? Are you at the top, in the middle, on the bottom, independent of it?*

I guess it all depends on who you talk to, you know. If you ask me where do I want to be, I could care less.

I'm a person that demands respect, because I give it. I'm respected, or would like to think I am, by the blacks, as well as the neo-Nazis, as well as the haters. OK?

And the reason why is because there's a mutual respect there. With the haters, I know I'm not going to dinner with them, the same way they know they're not going to dinner with me. But there's a mutual respect level there that's due to the fact that they know that whatever they do is their business, and whatever I do is my business. And I'm never going to infringe on what they're doing, the same way I don't want them to infringe on what I'm doing.

So, that's how I do my time. I do my time. I work. I like to play. I like people. You see how I am at the meetings. I like to bust chops. I don't care who it is. I'm a guy who loves people, you know. I hate only those who hate me for no reason. I wasn't brought up that way, to hate for no reason. I liked everybody.

As far as the pecking order, I could care less. As long as I'm doing what I need to do, and I'm allowed to do what I need to do, and I'm respected, or at least left alone to do those things, then I'm fine. And as long as the administration is not on my back, and as long as these guys are not on my back, and I'm not chasing the bag, or doing any of that other stuff, then I don't have to worry about any of that, you know. If you're doing it right, then you don't have to sweat the load.

I don't know if I've answered your question, but that's how I do my time.

*When is your release date? Do you have a definite date?*

My release date is December, Two Thousand and Four.

*Is there any kind of gradual transition, or are you going to go straight from prison to the streets on that date?*

I'm not under the old guidelines, so I don't have to transition out. If I have my own choice, I would stay where I'm at, continue to work, sharpen up my skills, continue paying my restitution, my legal financial obligations, so that way, by the time I get out, that'll be off me, and I can leave here and put this behind me, you know. I look forward to that.

*Rico, have you conquered your drug and alcohol problems?*

You know what? I believe I have, because I can find either one here in the joint, and I've chosen not to. The last time I used was in Nineteen eighty-eight.

Have I had the urge? Hell yeah. Hell yeah. But, you know, I've chosen not to. I don't know if it's because of all the consequences that'll happen while you're in the joint, the different things that you'll lose, but there will be consequences like that on the outside too.

I know that the urges will always surface. Now I also know, and I practice it to some extent, that it's what I do with those urges that makes the difference.

I've chosen not to mess with it. I can handle life sober. I can be a smart aleck, or, you know, have fun and not have to worry about being the life of the party. My self-esteem is fine now. I think I have to bring my self-esteem down a couple of notches. [Laughs.]

*[Laughs.] We'll work on that. That's what I'm here for; I'll help you not to get too swelled a head.*

Yeah. Thanks. [Laughs.]

*[Laughs.] Will you re-offend, when you're released? Do you think you'll ever be a criminal?*

You know, I wasn't a criminal when I fell. Yeah, I got high. Yeah, I got drunk. You know, I was just a pathetic human being.

*Well, you committed the crimes of drug possession and the sale of drugs, and you committed murder obviously.*

Right.

*So, in that sense—I mean, you committed crimes. So in that sense—*

You know what—

*—you were—*

Listen, listen,—

*—a criminal.*

—listen, listen—

*I mean, I understand that—*

—listen, listen, let's not yank each other's chain.

*OK.*

You know what a criminal is. OK? You know what a re-offender is. OK?

*Tell me what a criminal is.*

A criminal is a guy who chooses to go out there and continue robbing, continue stealing, whether they're property crimes, whether they're sexual crimes, whether they're assaults. You know, it's a person who continues putting themselves in that position. OK?

*Yeah.*

I'm going to do everything possible not to put myself in that position. I'm never going to say never. I never thought I'd be in the joint in the first place. However, I know what my focus is. If I do drugs, if I do alcohol, if I get to the same frame of mind, and I let my focus, you know, diminish the way I did the last time, then I might as well not even leave the joint. Because I know what's going to happen.

But, I like to think that in my time here, I've developed a better sense of consciousness and awareness. You know, I don't want to be part of this any more. Never did in the beginning. Never thought I would be put in the joint. Seventeen-plus years is enough for me.

*Do you think that people in society, people reading this interview in the future, should have confidence on this issue? Should they be optimistic about your future? I mean, I'm sure people are going to wonder, "Why are we letting a murderer out of prison?" and, "What's he going to do next?"*

Oh, very much so. But the first thing they need to look at is the statistics. A first time offender who commits murder has less than a one percent chance of re-offending. That's across the United States. That's number one.

Number two, I definitely understand where they're coming from. I do not expect society to receive me with open arms. That is their prerogative. I will tell them that—I won't even tell them; I will ask them, 'cause they've got that coming—that I will come out there, and I'm not going to fool you with words. Don't listen to what I say. But listen to what I do. You know what I'm saying? Let my actions speak. OK?

I've always told people, I don't care if I have to go out in the middle of I-Five, during rush hour, stark naked, to mop I-Five, to blend back into society. I will do that. I will do that. I have no problem with that. A lot of guys when they leave the joint, they want to start off on the top. I know I blew it. I know I dug a big hole for myself. And I don't have no problem, you know, digging my way back.

*You've touched on some of this already, but, what are some of the main factors that determine if a person will re-offend or not, in your opinion?*

In my opinion, it's how they do their time. If a person's chasing the bag in here, what are the chances of him stopping when he walks out? OK? If a person hasn't educated himself, or gotten himself a skillful trade, or anything that'll make him marketable when he walks out of here, what are the chances of him getting a job? What are the chances of him, you know, picking up a gun and just stealing what he wants?

If a guy hasn't worked on the issues that have gotten him here in the first place—whether they be mental, whether they be psychological, social, whatever the issues—then you got a walking time bomb when he walks out of here. Because, all you've done is just stirred that up in his mind.

So, if a person comes into the joint and does not deal with the issues that got him here in the first place, and all he's doing is the same thing that he was doing out in the streets, but only to a higher degree, then all you've got is a more skillful criminal when you release him. Because he spent his time in the yard, walking with his buddies, kicking rocks, and sharpening up their skills. And you can see it time and time again.

There was only one guy that disappointed me, that I saw leave the joint with the potential.[*] Great potential. Had a lot of things going for himself. Had a scholarship to art school waiting for him. But the dope bag got him. He knew darn well that he wasn't supposed to touch that dope bag. And he didn't weigh out his options, went to the dope bag, and came back over here.

He's out there again right now. He's doing real well from what I understand. Has a lot of support. The minute he touches that dope bag, I'll see him again. Same with me, and same with ninety percent of these guys that are in here.

*Just judging from the outside, as a layman who hasn't done time, one of the things that strikes me about the transition back to the free world—one of the things I would think would be a real problem for people—is adjusting to no longer having to have a hair-trigger temper, and having to interpret everything as an insult to one's dignity, and an insult to one's respect. In here, you can't let anything go. You can't let insults go; it'll just get worse. Well, what's going to happen on the outside? Say you've been in prison for months or years, or in some cases decades, a guy like yourself gets out, having lived the way you have for so many years, you're back out on the streets, a guy cuts you off in traffic for no reason and gives you the finger. Your employer shorts your check two or three weeks in a row, and you know he did it on purpose, because you know he knows what he's doing. The*

---

[*]Jimi. Jimi was on the outside when this interview was conducted; Rico is referring to his re-offending the time before that.

*math doesn't add up there; you know he cheated you out of some money. You're down at the bar, and some obnoxious gay guy makes a pass at you. Or you get into an argument somewhere, and someone says, "Ah, you're just a punk!" you know. What are you going to do when stuff like that happens on the outside?*

Well, see, as a convicted felon, in my opinion, you go to bars, you're asking for trouble. My opinion.

But you have to learn when to walk away. You have to learn when to walk away. Otherwise, you're going to wind up shooting half of the population.

*It just seems to me that's a skill you don't pick up in prison. How in prison do you get experience at knowing how to walk away from a fight?*

In here, you're always walking around with that edge. And that edge is coming back. It hasn't been as bad here as at most prisons, but it's coming back, because of the transition to a higher custody level. I just spoke to a lot of the guys that came over here with me from Walla Walla. It took us almost a year to lose that edge, because this was a nice, comfortable, relaxed atmosphere compared to Walla Walla.

And in the course of this changing into a higher custody level, the guys that found themselves relaxed are now seeing that it's time for us to revert to that other mentality where we build that edge around us, where that perimeter that we built was always a skeptical one. You were always conscious and aware of your surroundings at all times for your own safety.

And we don't like it. A lot of us are talking it out, and we don't like it.

We're getting to a point where these young guys that are coming in here, they're very disrespectful of us, because they have no idea of the potential of what us guys who have been in the system for quite some time are capable of doing, because they've seen us very peaceful, very calm, very respectful at times. But we've only been that way because the population and the environment called for that.

Now, they're taking it to this higher custody level, and bringing in a lot of prisoners from other joints who don't appreciate what this place has been about, and don't have any respect. They're bringing in cops that don't know their ass from their elbow, and have got that John Wayne mentality. Now they're beginning to poke a stick at a fellow. OK? So that dignity and respect that we were used to receiving when we first got here is lessening.

So now that we're not getting that, and we're being going back to the old days of being treated like the "pieces of garbage" that we've been labeled as, or tagged as, we're responding.

So, to get back to your question, yes, it is something that a person leaving here has to think about, even myself, because I saw how quick I got to that position in here recently. I saw what the changed environment in here was provoking in me, and I said, "Whoa!" These are issues that I'm definitely going to have to deal with. I'm going to have to think about them prior to getting out, and I'm going to have to be conscious of them once I get out, you know.

I don't know right now exactly how to deal with that mentality you're describing. I know I can't just go swinging at everybody. I know I can't, you know, put myself in those positions. Bars are the last thing I want to see. OK? And road rage? I may not drive.

But right now, I couldn't answer that question.

*I don't think you can avoid every possible situation that could provoke you or lead to a conflict out there.*

No, you can't.

You know, those mountains up there look pretty good. I was just on the yard looking at the top of those mountains and thinking maybe that would be a nice place, where I wouldn't have to come back down and deal with anybody.

But we know that's not a reality.

*You'll probably run into some bear that disrespects you up there.*

A talking bear that'll call me a punk.

*Yeah. [Laughs.]*

You never know. [Laughs.] Just my luck.

You know, but I think, honestly, that that is something that definitely I have to look at. Because it's so easy to get triggered. You go to different spots, and this person disrespects you, and this person disrespects you, and this person disrespects you, and this one disrespects you, and you hold all that in, and then that final person that disrespects you in some sort of way gets the brunt of all of that, you know. So, I have to find a way I can release that, and be bigger than that, and not allow that to affect me.

I'm not just going to take an ass-whipping. But then again, the Good Lord only gave us two cheeks. So, this thing about "turn the other cheek," we only have two, you know.

I will definitely need some help, and I need to look into that area, yes. But, I haven't been in a fight in quite some time. I think I'm growing in that area. OK? If I have to defend myself, I will, but I'm just hoping that I never have to be in that position where I do, you know.

But I would like to think that I am doing the work right now necessary not to respond like that to provocation. There's a lot of things that a person has to put up with inside here that hopefully you don't have to put up with out there. But I like to think that I've held my mud, so to speak, in here to such an extent that it can carry over as common practice out there also. I recognize idiocy for what it is, you know. So.

*How do you respond to the common perception in the public that we're too soft on crime, or that, in that phrase politicians love, we "coddle criminals"?*

I would say that they should get more for their tax dollars. Instead of hiring all these creeps that they're hiring—these blue suits that instead of giving them welfare, they're giving them a job up here—what they need to do is make us accountable. Make us accountable for getting that education. Make us accountable for getting that job skill. Make us accountable for being marketable. Make us accountable for getting those social skills.

If you don't have none of that, if you're not walking the talk, then don't let a fellow out, is what I'm saying. If they have that, if they've proven that, then give a fellow the opportunity to prove himself.

I don't believe in three strikes. I believe in two. If a guy kills twice, fuck him. He don't deserve to be back out there. Some people say once. OK. But if you're out there killing, robbing, and all that other stuff, you don't deserve three strikes. No.

*But do you simply say that because you've killed once, so two becomes the borderline? If you had killed zero times, then it would be once; if you had killed three times, then it would be four?*

Good point. Good point. But I don't think I would say twice, you know, now make it three; three, make it four. I'm quite fortunate, even though it's not guaranteed, that I have a release date. And I'm going to make the most I can of this opportunity, not hold out for another one later.

But what I'm saying is, to answer your question, you know, if you want to beat us over our head, and keep poking sticks at us, you're going to make a dumb angry convict dumber and angrier. Is that what you want? Knowing that most of us will eventually be getting out? Is that what you want to do?

If your tax dollars are going towards education—which is less than one percent of the tax dollars—then hold that man accountable to get that education, especially these young guys coming in here. If a guy comes in here and he doesn't have a marketable skill, make him accountable to get that marketable skill. "Wait a minute. You came in here like this. You had a drug problem." OK? Now, if he's getting dirty UAs, "Sorry, partner, you ain't dealt with your drug problem."

There are programs. There are ways of seeing whether a guy is walking the talk. And if he's not, then he's not ready to come out. OK? Hold us accountable. But, this poking a stick at us, lock us up, mentality is not productive for anyone. Only for the cops that are getting paid.

*Do you think the public has an accurate picture of how easy or how difficult it is in prison?*

They do not have a clue. They do not have a clue. All they're hearing is what the newspapers are telling them, and what the news is broadcasting. But they do not have a clue of how their tax dollars are actually working inside the system.

*What are the inaccuracies that a person would get from relying on the media?*

Well, for the first thing, they need to take that "Department of Corrections" title off, and maybe write "Department of Collections," and that'll be a more accurate picture. OK? They need to come in here and see where their tax dollars is going.

We're paying for damn near everything right now. The profits are unbelievable that are being made out of inmate funds, out of the vending machines, out of the store, out of taxable items that people out there don't even pay taxes for when they buy them.

We pay for our weights. We pay for our TV. We pay for our radio. We pay for cable. I don't care if you have a cell, you just walked in here, and all you have is a pillow and a mattress, you're going to pay for cable for a TV you're not watching. OK? If you have a minimum wage job, you're paying rent. Where's all this money going?

*But we pay all that too. I don't think the public's going to feel sorry for you that you have to pay for—*

But you know what? You know what? And this is going to sound crazy to you, but it's accurate. I'm a taxpayer also. I work a minimum wage job. I was a taxpayer before I came in here. And I'm a taxpayer now. So, they can't get that argument from me, you know. And I'm a proud taxpayer. I don't mind paying my own way. Just let me pay my own way.

Let me get my own education. I'll pay for that too. Allow me to do that. But don't tell me, "We don't want to pay for it," and then when I say, "Well, OK, I'll pay for it," tell me I can't.

So, all I'm saying is, to answer your question, no, they have a very gross, inaccurate picture of what's going down in the Department of Corrections. A very gross, inaccurate picture.

*I don't know, though, that they're going to be very sympathetic about—*

I don't want them to be sympathetic.

*But, if that's really the only, or the main, inaccuracy, is that you guys pay for more of the things you have than people realize, I think they're just going to shrug and say, "So what? So do we." Because everybody pays for those things.*

No, but wait a minute. Wait a minute. They're out there thinking that we're getting Master's and BA degrees. They're thinking we're getting degrees. They're out there thinking we're stealing jobs.

*But even if you're paying for things rather than being given them, whether it's weights or TV or whatever, a lot of people are still going to be resentful that you have them, period. I don't think they care as much as you think about who paid for them; they care that you're allowed to have them in the first place, instead of having to suffer as much as they believe you deserve to.*

OK, but we go back to: what is it that you want? What is it that you want? You want a dumber, more pissed off convict? Or do you want somebody that you hold accountable to sharpen up their skills, get marketable, get themselves an education, so that when they do come out, they become a productive citizen?

Accountability. That's the fancy word that they've come up with—"Accountability, accountability, accountability." Well, let's put it to work then. OK?

But I challenge people to really look at what's going on within the system, inside a prison. Don't just take a tour. Really find out.

*What's the best way for people to find out?*

Taking that Prison Awareness class. [Smiles.]

*What about the ninety-nine point nine percent of the population that doesn't live near a prison that has that class? [Laughs.]*

Write to it. [Laughs.]
No, but on the serious side, they need to really look at the overall picture.

*Yeah.*

You know, now they're just looking at one side of the coin, that we deserve to be in here. And that's right; we very much deserve to be here. No doubt about it.

But now that we're here, and we are going back out to society some day, what do you want us to do while we're here? You know, what kind of a job am I going to get busting rocks?

This turned out to be the last material I was able to get from Rico for this book. At one point I thought I had him talked into making a tape on his own of his responses to some follow-up questions I mailed in, but he never got around to it.

Like Buck, Rico had only an intermittent presence at PAP during and after the period of this last interview. In his case, it wasn't just his work schedule, but his hot and cold attitude toward PAP itself. He was disgusted with the imperfections in it, and the ulterior motives he discerned in so many of the prisoners, but he never seemed able to make the final break. Just when you thought he was gone for good, he'd show up again, putting a lot of energy into the group, trying to help it live up to its potential. Then he'd get disillusioned a week or a month later, and he'd be gone again.

The most extreme instance of this came about four months after this last interview. As was his wont, Jerry had carefully set up the annual elections to come out the way he wanted—some old blood, some new blood, maybe some racial or cultural diversity, people he knew he could work with and influence, people who had the right kind of respect from the other prisoners, etc. Rico was the choice to be president.

It was a risky choice, because Rico was so all or nothing about PAP that they didn't know if they could rely on him. Jerry talked to him at length about it. "Now, you're sure you're serious about this Rico? You're definitely committed this time Rico? We can count on you Rico?" Jerry was reassured, and he enlisted Buck and 9 and others to circulate among the members the week prior to the election to allay any concerns about whether Rico would really go through with it, and to make sure the vote would go as intended.

Election day came, on cue Rico was nominated to be the next president of PAP, and Rico promptly declined the nomination, with little or no explanation.

In the end, Jerry scrambled and pushed somebody else through as president—a newcomer—but Rico lost credibility with a lot of the guys that day.

When I eventually had a chance to speak to him about it, Rico was vague as to why he had changed his mind. Basically, he was Rico being Rico. The day the election was held was a day he couldn't bring himself to commit to something he didn't fully believe in. PAP included people he respected and could work with, but it also held racists and liars and hustlers who were doing nothing to improve themselves or the people around them. PAP was too impure for him to save.

Had the election been held a week earlier or a week later, he may well have made the opposite decision and thrown himself into the task of bringing PAP's integrity up to the level he demanded of it.

Rico wasn't gone from PAP entirely after that, by any means. In fact, he continued to have an active role in some of the periodic Prison Awareness classes. But there was certainly no more talk of making him president.

# 9—April 1999

*"Crips in general are independent, hating all outsiders, with only a few allies, which of course is certain other Crips."*

Right around the time of my last taped conversation with 9, I mailed him a set of questions. The bulk of these were tying up loose ends from the tapes we had previously made. There were spots where the tapes were unclear, and I asked him to help me piece together what he had said, and the point he was making. I do not reproduce that material here, as it would be largely repetitive. Where appropriate, I have corrected the earlier transcripts in light of this further correspondence.

Two questions, though, were more substantive, and I present them here, along with 9's responses.

*I'd like a little more information about your gang. At times it sounds like it was very small, just a few friends who grew up in the same area. How big was the membership, how fluid was the membership, and how clearly demarcated was the membership? You spoke of being involved with the gang as early as age 6 or 7, being "officially" and "actively" involved by about age 11, and being an actual "member" by age 13. Can you explain the differences among these different levels for me a little more?*

The membership of the 90s was very fluid, and the membership is very large. It's difficult to determine the size now because so many things have changed since I've been home, and considering so many is in prison that I hadn't even met, but on the streets there were approximately 300-400 members, including all "sets."

My involvement at an early age of 6 or 7 stems from living in the neighborhood, surrounded by members much older than me, and looking up to those individuals. My young friends were their relatives whom I went to school with, "claiming" to be a member and pretending to be a part of the 90 family that I knew. My "active" involvement was my association on a daily basis, hanging out, and hating anybody that was not from the neighborhood. Being an actual member was through initiation as a part of the gang, accepting a pledge to remain loyal and dedicated to those that represent the 90s.

*What is the relationship between, say, the Crips in general, and your small individual Crip gang from your neighborhood? Are the Crips and their member gangs tightly organized with a clear hierarchy and such? Or do the various Crip gangs have little connection with each other beyond the fact that they choose to go by the same name?*

The relationship between the Crips is different for all sets. All Crips do not get along. Some of our biggest enemies are Crips. That's where turfs and areas come into play.

Crips in general are independent, hating all outsiders, with only a few allies, which of course is certain other Crips. A flex of muscle showing others that they're not needed, and power struggles is the reason for a lot of differences.

The hierarchy is the O.G.s,* the elders who have been a part of the gang a lot longer than most. The O.G.s get the most respect and recognition, they're the most well listened to.

It's similar to families in the Mob, all aiming to be the best respected and the most feared.

---

*"Old Gangsters."

# LARRY—December 1999

*"I don't think anyone feels worse than I do about what took place. It's really hard to get up in the morning and not think about it day after day."*

D ue to his work schedule, Larry was the one prisoner with whom I had not been able to secure a taped interview in my final go-round in March 1999. Indeed, we almost never saw him any more at PAP.

As I had not been able to interview him in person, I sent an extensive list of questions to him, hoping to get some material that way. They went unanswered for many, many months, until I assumed I was not going to hear from him again.

Finally, I did receive a long letter, containing the answers to my questions. And the next time I saw him, I received an explanation for the delay.

First, he acknowledged that the bulk of the delay was attributable to his own procrastination. But it turns out that he'd had another problem: my questions had been confiscated.

Periodically, correctional officers ransack a prisoner's cell, looking for any form of contraband. Sometimes it's random, and sometimes it's based on some specific suspicion, often something they are told by a prisoner informant. It was the kind of indignity that was less common at WSR than at most prisons, but perhaps that was among the things that was changing with the switch to a higher custody level.

Larry was subjected to such a cell search, and they found little to interest them, except my letter. "Who's this from?" "Why would he be asking you all these questions?" "Why does he want to know all this?"

They weren't satisfied with his answers, so they confiscated the letter for the time being. Larry thought I might get stuck in an investigation at some level, but no one ever contacted me about this matter.

They did not return my letter to him for over a month. "What in the world would take them so long to decide that it was OK for you to have my questions?" I asked him. "Oh, I think they were sending me a little message, letting me know who was calling the shots." "Why did they feel a need to do that?" "I mouthed off to them pretty good when they turned over my house," he smiled, "Really went off on them. Pissed them off good."

*How old are you? Summarize your background for me, before your crime.*

I am now 36 years old. (5-16-63). I have no previous criminal history other than a speeding ticket. (35 in a 25 zone. Extreme, huh?)

My crime was committed because of my involvement with a drug running ring. I was a runner, a name given to those who picked up and delivered packages, either money or drugs. The people I worked for dealt mainly in heroin (China white), a very good top grade imported from Pakistan with a top dollar value. I did not use, one of the reasons I got the job.

I owned my own business. I was the owner and instructor of Snohomish Taekwando. I had over 350 students at the time of my arrest.

I obtained a rank of 2nd degree and was a certified instructor. I had won (1st place) the 1986 Nationals. 1st in Kumatae (Fighting), 3rd in Kata (Forms). Ranked #1 in '86, #4 in '87.

I placed 4th in the 1987 world championships.

In 1988 I was to compete in Reno at the Nationals. However I was arrested before that event.

*It sounds like you just went home after your crime and were there when the police arrived. Why did you not flee or take any action to avoid capture?*

I did go home. I was really upset and confused. I had just shot two of my best friends. I didn't try to flee capture mainly because I felt if I told my side of the story people would understand the situation I was in.

*When you got home after your crime, did you tell your wife everything? How were you feeling about confiding in her? How did she respond to the situation?*

When I got home I didn't say anything to my wife about it, nor did I say anything to anyone. I was trying to figure out what I was going to do. When the police called me on the phone she answered the phone. She was shocked and I assured her I would be OK. She had a hard time coping with all the pressure of friends and work. But she stood by me. We later divorced after I was imprisoned at Washington State Penitentiary (Walla Walla). It was better for both of us so we made a mutual agreement and separated on good terms.

*When we were talking about retribution, and how much a person deserves to suffer for their crime, etc., you made some interesting remarks. You said that sometimes "things [just] happen," that there is "no reason for" some crimes.*

*This reminded me of an HBO show I saw many years ago about a prison program that allowed a man who had been severely beaten and permanently damaged to be brought together with the perpetrator of the crime. The victim had been thinking about this encounter for years, and when they finally met, he calmly summarized for the criminal how he had suffered, how his life had been permanently altered, what extreme emotions he had gone through, etc. When he finished, you could see that he was now starving for a certain kind of response from the criminal. I don't think it was just remorse he was hoping for; it appeared that he genuinely wanted to understand why it had all happened, why a person would feel justified in damaging another person in these ways.*

*But nothing like that was forthcoming. The criminal seemed sympathetic, but he had nothing like that to communicate to the victim. He had just been a kid strung out on drugs. There had been no premeditation to the crime, no deep thought about it, no attempts to justify it to himself, no personal involvement or even acquaintance with the victim before the crime, no political implications, nothing like that at all. Whatever motives there were had been totally mundane and superficial, and there had been large elements of chance involved.*

*It was very much like you said. Sometimes "things happen" and there is "no reason for it." The victim was, perhaps, committing the fallacy of assuming an effect must resemble its cause in certain ways. He seemingly wanted the cause of what he had gone through to match the effect in its significance, enormity, intensity, etc. He needed this crime to have been as big a deal to the perpetrator at the time as its aftermath had been to the victim. His efforts to understand the perpetrator and the crime, to discover some great plan or purpose in response to his question of "Why did this all happen to me?" called for something more than "You were unlucky." But if there's nothing more to it, there's nothing more to it.*

*I don't know that I have a specific question here for you. I just wanted to share with you what thoughts your remarks provoked in me. Is there anything you'd like to add to elaborate on your comments in this area?*

Your HBO show summary is exactly what I mean. Another example I know of: As we know people sometimes get into fights at events such as parties, concerts, a tavern (could be anywhere depending on circumstances). Most of the time they are spur of the moment. Now imagine two people fighting for whatever reasons, small or big. One person gets hit and falls to the ground hits their head and dies. Did the person who hit them intend to purposely kill them? I think not. I would say it was a bad chain of events. But someone is now going to be charged with at least 2nd degree murder, manslaughter at the least.

There was "no reason" for the death. It just happened. It wasn't intentional or planned.

*The circumstantial evidence in your case must have been quite damning. Even hearing only your side of it, I can see why people would think the worst. At first glance, it does sound like a drug dealer gets into a dispute with his partner, or perhaps just wants to eliminate his cut, goes over to the guy's house, shoots the place up in an effort to kill the partner and any potential witnesses (his innocent wife and child), and then burns the house down in a futile effort to destroy as much of the evidence as possible.*

*If it all happened like that, then anyone other than a complete psychopath would presumably go through hell having to live with the knowledge that he had done something like that. However, assuming it happened instead like you said, I would think a person would still go through a different hell.*

*Assuming all that you have told me is true, you killed one person in a way that was at least partially justified by self-defense, since he too was armed and you likely would have died if you had not shot him. The other shootings and damage you did were entirely accidental. But the state through its criminal justice system, and presumably the victims' people and a lot of third parties who are familiar with your case, have decided that you are guilty of something massively worse than that and are treating you accordingly.*

*I won't say that even in your version, you're an "innocent" man being treated unjustly. But tell me what it's like to have such a huge discrepancy between how you're perceived versus who you really are and what you really did.*

No matter what the circumstances were in my case I still committed a crime. To me there is no justification. I ask myself nearly on a daily basis "why?" and to this day I still don't have an answer.

I try not to let the whole picture bother me. My family and friends who knew the victims understand more about who I am than those who don't know me and the victims.

Personally if I didn't know myself or the victims I would think just like everyone else and I'm sure my family and friends would also. At this point in my life I am extremely sorry for my actions. Not only did I hurt the victims' family and friends but my own also. So there was never one person to benefit from my crime on either side. As far as the state goes they can say what they want to. It may hurt to hear it but everyone must come to grips with their crime in their own way. I choose to not let it bother me and go on with my life the best I can from where I am.

On my way back to the jail from the court house the police sergeant escorting me said to me, "Larry if you ever want to tell me what really happened you know where to find me." This was after I had been found guilty by the jury, the same jury that obviously completely believed what they were told by the prosecutor. So maybe by what the sergeant said to me not everyone believed things had happened the way the state said they did.

*You mentioned that you have "personal reasons" for being strongly "anti-rat," and that you would share these with me if I wanted. Tell me this story.*

My reasons are very simple. The FBI came to ask me questions about who I worked for. If I would of told them, they said they would work a deal with the DA I gave them nothing! I went to trial and now I'm doing 2 life without parole sentences. Even the DA offered me 54 years total and said they would lower the time for exchange of information. I don't play the telling game.

If you do the crime do your time and don't run and tell your mama.

*What would you do to a rat if you knew you wouldn't be found out? Do you have the same animosity toward rapists and child molesters as you do toward rats? Do you have anything like this sort of animosity toward any staff or members of the public or whatever that you feel have perpetrated injustices against you (e.g., guards that have physically mistreated you, written you up on a "bum beef" to get you punished, etc.)?*

I dislike rapists and molesters more than rats, for personal reasons.

As far as what I would do to one of them, the same thing I would do to anyone else who were to call me out or disrespect me in a way to make me want to do something. Other than that, if they don't provoke me and stay out of my business, I'm not going to be in theirs.

As far as animosity goes I really don't have any towards staff or the public. Everyone has an opinion. I may not agree but that's part of life here and out there.

*Are all the people in prison that are believed to be rats or rapists really so? Are there people who are one or both of these things that successfully conceal this? How big a problem are such misidentifications?*

Most sex offenders are really guilty. With today's technology, DNA, etc., there's not going to be a lot of mistakes. But as we know to err is human.

Most rats and rapists try to conceal what they're doing or in for. But it always comes out sooner or later. The good ol' paperwork check never fails.

*Do you believe that you will ever be released from prison? Tell me what feelings this issue stirs up in you, how you deal with it now compared to earlier in your incarceration, etc.*

I don't have a real answer here. I hope I get a chance to be released. I really believe I can go about my life and never see the inside of a jail again. Having life without sentences is hard to deal with. It's a personal battle every day. I can't let myself give up, you know, say why do this or that I'm not getting out. I don't believe it would be healthy for me to give in and say I'm never getting out.

In my early years I felt I've still got a chance to get out. I still feel that way.

*Tell me about acts of kindness or friendship in prison that stand out to you—either that you've done, that someone has done toward you, or that you've observed—that might surprise people on the outside who think of prison and prisoners in a totally negative light.*

Acts of kindness are few and far between for the most part. However there are a lot of fellahs who will go out of their way to help guys out. A good example is when someone comes in from another institution. The guys will get together and put a care package together to help them out until they get their property.

The fund raisers are a good act of kindness.* No one makes us raise money for charities.

Me personally, I helped to start a youth football league in Walla Walla. I painted the sponsorship signs to raise most of the money for new uniforms and to help build the facility.

---

*The Lifers and many of the other programs raise substantial amounts of money for charity.

I think in general most prisoners would help if they could, like in a disaster situation. I think you could take the guys from a camp and do flood clean up or sand bag dikes. This is just an example. But I'm sure inmates would be willing to jump on the opportunity to do it. I would, just to get some sightseeing in.

*Part of what seems to have been lost on our tape was the section where I had asked you what you would say to your victims or their survivors if you were face-to-face with them, or if they were to one day read this book. Please address this again.*

I'm sure facing my victims and their families would be very emotional. There's a lot of bad memories I've tucked away. I don't like to bring them to the surface. I'm personally embarrassed by my actions. I'm not sure what I would say. I'd like to just be able to communicate what all the circumstances were and what happened from all sides. I would hope I could answer their questions. I'm sure there are a lot of unanswered questions. Maybe I could help them to get some closure. Sorry just doesn't say enough for how I feel. I don't think anyone feels worse than I do about what took place. It's really hard to get up in the morning and not think about it day after day.

*Tell me the story of the most fear you have ever experienced in prison.*

My worst fear is getting called in by the chaplain. When my grandmother passed I found out 3 days later, one of the worst feelings I've ever experienced. So my fear is getting news that my mother or father or another family member has passed away. Being in here you feel so helpless and it's hard to let go.

*From what you've said, clearly you think the restitution you are expected to pay is out of proportion with that of others convicted of similar crimes. Are you being overcharged, or are they being undercharged? What in general are your thoughts about the state imposing restitution requirements on convicted criminals?*

I hate the restitution deal. With me it's really personal. As you know I've got an ongoing case in the courts.

My restitution was $110,165.50. Now it will be over $200,000.00 with the interest at the beginning of the new year.

The laws of this state clearly say the court cannot give restitution over double the cost of the damages. All fines and fees must be set in accordance with a defendant's ability to pay, which means the court must show proof that a defendant can or will have the funds to pay his or her restitution. The court can only collect restitution for a period up to 10 years *or* 10 years after your release.

My feelings are this: If the court follows the state law and sets fines and fees in accordance with the policy then it's fair.

But like in my case, the court set fines and fees to keep me from profiting from writing a book. There was no inquiring of my ability to make payments or if I had any assets. The court was just spiteful. I have not come across another prisoner with life without parole who has fines or restitution even close to mine.

Without the ability to pay restitution it costs the state more to carry the debt month to month, year to year. The interest makes it impossible to ever catch up on the debt.

Taking a convicted criminal's money will only make him a poor criminal, which can only lead to one conclusion. How can he survive when he or she gets out? They're right back were they started.

*Do you have any religious beliefs that are relevant to your ability to cope with being in prison, your remorse, your interpretations of why things have happened as they have, your intentions for the future, etc.? What are your thoughts about religion in prison in general? (That is, are the religious rights of prisoners respected?, how sincere are prisoners who claim to have found religion?, does religion seem to turn a lot of prisoners' lives around?, to what extent are the programs motivated by religion?, or anything else you want to address.)*

I choose to study Buddhism, mostly for the meditation. I can keep my thoughts in line and live out my day by planning ahead in meditation. It's basically my own escape from the inside.

I really don't want to comment on the religions of prisoners. We all do what we have to, to be able to live with ourselves. There are prisoners who are *very real*, and there are those who are fake and use it to hide from population.

*What is the most violent you have ever been in prison?*

I'm not a very violent person and I believe you could ask anyone from inmates to guards and they would agree.

My only act of violence was a fight with another inmate who provoked me to defend my "mother." Even then it was only a couple of blows and it was over, apology accepted and it was done.

*One of my earlier written questions to you had to do with the "convict code." In your response, you said that "the code is not really enforced," but that one's "partner might put one in check," and then "one might have to deal with the situation." Elaborate on this for me.*

I'll use an example on this one.

My partner's outside walking the big yard. I see him and notice he's walking and talking to someone who I know to be a stool pigeon and a child molester. So I pull my partner up and ask him what's up. Maybe he's heard and is confronting the guy. If not, now I'm clueing him in on the guy's beef. If they had conversation that was maybe what to some was confidential he might have to go to him and say, "Hey, why didn't you tell me you're a f——ing rat?"

Another example: Two partners—crime partners. One gives evidence on the other to get a lesser sentence. They end up in the same joint at different times. Someone says, "Hey, isn't that the guy who ratted on you?" Well, you better go deal with it. Purely the old "peer pressure" get up.

There are many different situations.

*What is your take on prison industries? What are the pros and cons? Is it good or bad for society to have private companies employing prisoners?*

I think prison industries are great. Inmates can make money to support their restitution, their families and *save money for when they get out.* Just think if a guy works for 5 (or 10) years and saves money (10% mandatory by DOC), when he gets out, he can get some transportation to look for a job. I don't think there's anything worse than getting a job and then losing it because you couldn't get to work.

Society should love it. It teaches new skills to survive in a real workplace. More companies should try to use prison labor. The overhead is lower, so more profit for them. Everyone benefits.

I would have to ask myself if I were out there who do I want to move in next door, an ex-con who has no education never worked the whole time of his or her incarceration or an ex-con who has educated themselves and worked in an industry program—AutoCAD engineer, welders, water jet programmer, etc.? Society should talk to the private company owners.

*How valuable are prison programs? What makes the good ones good? What is flawed about the least valuable ones? Do you have any stories about a significant impact any of the programs have had on you or someone you know?*

Prison programs are great. The interaction between volunteers and inmates is very valuable. It's a terrific way to keep both groups informed, what's going on inside, what's up on the outside. Times change so fast, it's hard to keep up without contact. The relation skills inmates have would really go by the wayside if they couldn't talk with someone from the real world from time to time. It's not the same as talking on the phone.

The good programs are the ones that have good relationships with the volunteers. Those volunteers really make it happen. It may be who they know (contacts), their ability to contact media, Congress, important figures, or just good old fashioned leg work. The same goes for the inmates. They have to be willing to make a program work and to put time into the program with new ideas or make the old ideas better.

I'm not going to single out any particular program. I have seen inmates in many different programs get involved and really make a commitment to follow through on the project(s) they were working on.

*Describe the state of race relations in prison. How does it compare with the outside world?*

I don't think the race relations are too much different from the outside. Race tension is just that. People either choose to hate each other or move on. There are always those occasional times when everyone gets along. I don't know about other prisons, but I have heard from out of state inmates that certain inmate groups run some factions of the prison or dominate over other groups of inmates. I think that to be the biggest difference, control. Outside you don't see too many groups controlling what another group does.

*What would you recommend to deal with the problem of recidivism?*

Recidivism? Such a hard question. My belief is that it has to be dealt with on an individual basis. Some people are never going to change their lifestyle. We can't help those who don't want to be helped. The group we can help, the self-help group, are the ones who want to change. Unfortunately these are usually the ones who don't have a chance to get paroled or released. It's a rough system. It keeps the ones who are likely not to re-offend and releases the ones we know will.

I would recommend we find a place to start all over. It will take a lot of work and personally I don't know where to start. I'm speaking in terms of prison population as a whole.

We need to look at the time structures that are given to offenders. If the public doesn't want to build more housing (prisons) for offenders then we must let someone go but who selects who that person will be and what group of prisoners would be targeted?

Craig, you're killing me here. Just tell them to let me go. I would love to be the one person to get out and stay out just so I could say "I told you so." Fat chance of that happening, huh?

I did send Larry some thoughts on his responses here, as well as several new questions, but this was the last material he contributed to the project.

# BILL—February 2000

*"When you get old, it doesn't make any difference where you are; it's a bummer. I expect the majority of people wish they had made better financial preparations for the non-productive phase of their life. High-class thieves, if that is not an oxymoron, have less cause to reflect in sorrow than many other more prosaic citizens. At a certain period in life, one's memories are the only souvenirs of the sweet ride taken on this planet. Hopefully we made the juice fly to a sufficient degree to make us smile, or even chortle, with the penultimate breath before the eternal sleep. Adventures are the only treasures with real shelf-life."*

B y the time 2000 rolled around, what time I could devote to this project was mostly spent transcribing tapes, and trying to piece this whole thing together. I had sent at least one set of new questions each to almost all the participants, but little was trickling in any more.

Bill, however came through for me as always.

*In the "official version" of your crime, it says you "expressed a willingness to shoot it out with police," and you "at all times was obviously willing to use the loaded firearm that he had in his possession. His only reason for surrendering was his belief that he would not survive a gun battle." In dismissing robberies as not morally wrong, you said, "And I even count stick-ups, if you're using the gun as a prop, if you're not going to…shoot some guy that doesn't need shot." (This is something of a disturbing qualification.) On the other hand, on other occasions, you've said that you would not harm someone, even if doing so was necessary to obtain what you were there to steal, or even if doing so was necessary to accomplish an escape from prison. So, let me ask this: You are burglarizing a home and a police officer stumbles onto the scene and discovers you. If you shoot him, you can escape apprehension. If you do not, you will be arrested and, with your record, will not ever get out of prison again. What do you do? Does the police officer "need to be shot" in this situation?*

The "Willing to shoot it out," assertion is pure prosecutorial caca de toro. If I had intended to shoot, it would have happened in the first couple seconds of the encounter. To qualify to "need to be shot," someone would have to ignore and defy every caveat and try to kill me. Which answers the hypothetical about the cop between me and freedom. I'd offer a stalemate. If he made the first move toward a shoot-out, I'd resist with any and all means available.

*Again according to the "official version" of your crime, in addition to "playing games" for several hours (in an effort, you told me later, to stall them so that you could make bail before they could find out you were wanted on an escape), it sounds like you revealed a lot of incriminating information, such as that much of what you had in the car was stolen, and that a lot of other things had been, or were intended in the future to be, used in the commission of various crimes. For that matter, as mentioned above, you allegedly said you had intended to shoot your way out of there if it had been feasible to do so. Why did you admit all this?*

Again, there is much misquoting by police. The reason I had that stuff in the car was to "reluctantly" admit where it came from and get a free ride to a soft county jail. It was a tried and true get-away scheme. That was the first time it didn't work.

*Any thoughts on the general issue of guys getting married while they're doing time?*

The main beef about prisoners getting married is the complaint that it's just for sex. Of course that's part of it. Sex, companionship, working in tandem toward shared goals, etc. Pretty much why people get married in any circumstances. Gives new meaning to the expression, "Wed-lock."

*You mentioned in one of the interviews that most prisoners feel entitled to pursue their self-interest through the legal system in any and every way they can. Do you share this position? If a person is actually guilty of what they're accused of, is he under any ethical obligation to accept punishment for it, or is all fair in love, war, and the criminal justice system?*

Is this a joke? Of course any reasonable person wants out of prison whether they committed a crime or not. The alternative is the idiot position of wanting to stay in a cage. Although most energy spent in the law library is wasted motion. WACing off,* to coin a phrase.

*Is there a single crime you've ever committed that you now regret, that you feel you wronged someone who didn't have it coming? If so, what would you say if you could to the person(s) who was harmed by your crime?*

No regrets on any specific crime. Stealing was my vocation and my avocation. Morality never entered into it. Feasibility, accessibility and degree of potential reward were the criteria. Culpability? It is to larf.

---

*WAC = Washington Administrative Code.

*Like sports or rock music, professional crime strikes me as something of a "young man's game." The adventure, risk, machismo, fast pace, rebelliousness, etc. of it all seem more easily associated with youth than with age and maturity. Aging is hard on everyone. (I despise it; I'd love to turn the clock back ten or twenty years.) But for the criminals who survive to their 60s or beyond—the few who "live fast and don't die young"—is it especially difficult or poignant to experience the years taking their inevitable toll?*

When you get old, it doesn't make any difference where you are; it's a bummer. I expect the majority of people wish they had made better financial preparations for the non-productive phase of their life. High-class thieves, if that is not an oxymoron, have less cause to reflect in sorrow than many other more prosaic citizens. At a certain period in life, one's memories are the only souvenirs of the sweet ride taken on this planet. Hopefully we made the juice fly to a sufficient degree to make us smile, or even chortle, with the penultimate breath before the eternal sleep. Adventures are the only treasures with real shelf-life.

Get with it, Craig. Climb a mountain; seduce Dolly Parton. Steal a huge diamond and blow the proceeds on cheap blondes and fire water. Don't grow old with no treasures in the memory bank. "To live," is an infinitive. An action verb waiting to be unfettered. Stop moralizing and rusticating. Get out there and *do* something.

Bill's final answer epitomizes his approach to life. His closing advice stays with me as much as anything he ever said to me.

He is constitutionally incapable of giving advice in a preachy or judgmental way; advice from Bill is issued in a "take-it-or-leave-it-makes-no-difference-to-me" manner, with just the right wry turn of phrase that never fails to bring a smile to my face. It is, for all that, no less genuine, heartfelt, or wise. Or appreciated.

# 9—April 2000

*"I'm convinced that almost everybody have done something that could've sent them to prison, some of the same things that some of us are here for now. We are you. We should be understood, rather than ostracized."*

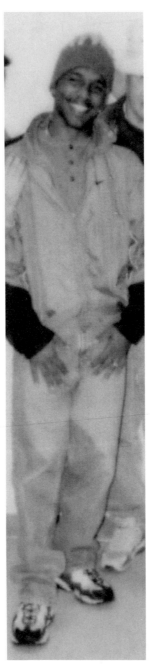

9 in 2001. (Photo courtesy of Linda Coleman.)

For many years, WSR was a place of hope for prisoners, a place they were sent as a reward for good behavior elsewhere, a place where the notion of rehabilitation was on life support rather than already dead.

WSR provided an environment where a man had some chance of improving himself for re-entry into the outside world, or of living with some modicum of dignity if his fate was a life forever behind bars.

The prisoners themselves deserve a good deal of the credit for making WSR what it was. They helped themselves more than anyone helped them. And to some extent they policed themselves. The comparative looseness of the rules at WSR was something that could be used in positive ways or exploited for more nefarious purposes. The veterans made sure that newcomers understood they could only keep this good thing going if the ratio of people doing the former to people doing the latter remained fairly high.

WSR was also blessed with an unusually strong volunteer base. The programs could not have thrived without a great number of people from the community coming in to the prison on a regular basis to participate. And nearly all of these outside people were unpaid volunteers, not employees of the state or third parties drawing a paycheck for working with the prisoners.

Not to be overlooked in this equation is the prison administration itself. Throughout the staff there were people who supported the notion that prison need not be wholly punitive. By all accounts, the most significant such figure on the administration side was the man at the top: Superintendent Ken DuCharme.

For years, DuCharme was a bulwark against the forces in the state government and the DOC who otherwise would have seen to it that WSR lost its special character long ago. He kept WSR an anachronistically liberal institution during a time when rehabilitation was a notion scorned in most circles.

Not coincidentally I'm sure, the end of DuCharme's tenure as superintendent came at roughly the same time WSR changed from a medium security institution to a close custody one. By the time he retired in the summer of 1999, we were many months into the transition phase to close custody, and he had already relinquished most of his authority to an acting superintendent.

As a gesture of gratitude for the respect he had shown them, and for his tireless efforts to keep open certain doors of opportunity, the prisoners decided to give the retiring DuCharme a sort of farewell party.

9 took upon himself the task of organizing the event. He received some guidance and support from Henry and a few others, but this was mostly his baby.

It was held in the chapel, open of course to the prisoners themselves, and also the outside volunteers from all the programs.

I found myself eager to attend, not just to honor DuCharme, but as a show of support for the guys themselves, and especially 9. It was clear that he and they were putting a great deal of effort into this, and I was impressed by their willingness to do so for someone who was, formally, their adversary. (Even hard-core purist convict Bill allowed that DuCharme was "not as bad as most of them," or words to that effect.)

The chapel was packed, but the prisoners pretty well maintained an atmosphere of order and respect. As a few prisoners selected for the role quietly made their way in and out of the folding chairs offering soft drinks and other refreshments, 9, as master of ceremonies, brought people up to a podium with a microphone one by one to offer their tributes to the retiring superintendent.

The prisoners and volunteers alike thanked DuCharme for all he had done for them and for WSR over the years. The prisoners told story after story of how their lives had been touched by DuCharme, how he had believed they were redeemable when others had given up on them.

The speakers included several prisoners I knew from PAP. I particularly enjoyed hearing Jerry speak of the relationship he'd had with DuCharme all the way back to the mid-'60s when he had first encountered him as a teenager. They had always been on opposite sides of the criminal justice system, and yet there had always been a mutual respect between them.

Closing statements by 9 and DuCharme himself brought the affair to an end.

The event had been an inspiring and positive one, though permeated with a depressing quality. Or at least so it seemed to me. After filing out of the chapel, we walked past the recently erected chain link fences blocking off what previously had been open spaces; past the concrete that had replaced all the greenery inside the prison, including the flower garden so carefully and lovingly nurtured by the prisoners themselves. The end of an era indeed.

If there was a downside to the ceremony, it was what I interpreted as a shameful snubbing of DuCharme by the prison administration. Of the highest ranking officials, two were on vacation. (One of those two had allegedly arranged to take his vacation at a different time so that he could be on hand for the event, but had subsequently changed his mind.) Another was called away on a "family emergency" that day. The acting superintendent had committed to attend—indeed he had been slated as one of the leadoff speakers—but he had cancelled at the last minute. If he offered up an excuse, I never heard it. And certainly no DOC bigwigs from outside the institution made the trip to WSR to attend.

In the end, it was the prisoners themselves, and those of us from the outside who've chosen to stand with them, who stepped up to let DuCharme know how appreciated he was.

Certainly 9 did a remarkable job in organizing and running the whole thing. Everyone I spoke with afterward agreed that he had exceeded all expectations.

The next time I saw Henry at PAP, he was beaming over his protege's performance. "See what I've been telling you about him?" his smile said.

In the preceding year, I had sent quite a few questions in to 9, but perhaps some degree of fatigue factor had set in with the project, for he took much longer than usual to respond, and when he did, there was a perfunctory quality to many of his answers. Indeed, several questions he skipped entirely.

At one point, we even decided to make another tape, in spite of the fact that I wasn't supposed to do that on PAP time any more. But he happened to have his Walkman and a blank tape with him, and he had told me several times he would much prefer to talk about the more complex of my questions rather than write about them, so we found a somewhat quiet spot and did an impromptu thirty minute interview.*

We weren't particularly surreptitious about it; I don't know that the guards knew I had been told not to do any more interviews, and I don't know that they would have cared. They were pretty laid back about such things (though perhaps not quite as much now, as the general mood of the institution drifted in an ominous direction).

As fate would have it, the machine malfunctioned or we pushed the wrong buttons, because nothing we said ended up on the tape. The biggest loss is that he had given a fascinating account of his very nearly successful escape attempt early in his incarceration. (He and a confederate had hidden themselves in the back of a delivery truck. At the last minute they had agreed that a third person could come with them, but the third person, in his excitement, forgot that his work duties necessitated him being in a certain place at a certain time, and that he would be missed before the delivery truck left the institution. This is indeed what happened. Minutes, or perhaps even seconds, before the truck would have been out the gate and they would have been on their way, the whole institution was locked down and everything searched because they realized they were missing a prisoner. They all ended up in IMU.)

I was left with what little he gave me in writing.

---

*We could no longer simply cross the hall to the PAP office. There were no more such offices. Among the recent changes in the institution was the removal of those little rooms from the prisoners. The new regime had little interest in prisoner-friendly policies in general, or in facilitating the volunteer programs specifically. Many of us were developing a fatalistic attitude that the programs would be done away with entirely before much longer.

9 remained one of my favorite prisoners to talk with at the PAP sessions. I was conscious, however, not to dominate his time. While gracious and friendly toward me, he was so active that I had the sense that in his mind there were twenty other people he had to touch base with before the meeting was over.

First he was down the hall with Henry and the Lifers officers planning something or other, then he was in our meeting room greeting all the PAP volunteers and working the room. Moments later I'd see him out in the hall huddled with a couple of members of the Black Prisoners Caucus, then he was back in the meeting room off in the corner having an intense exchange with another prisoner. And, highest priority of all, he'd be making time with anyone female that happened to be in the building. (He was married now, but that was a platonic marriage to a best friend; it had no visible effect on his flirting.)

I was reluctant to interfere with his whirlwind of conniving, cajoling, communing, and charming. I'd catch a few words with him when and where I could, and then step back and observe him in action. I never presumed to know what all he was up to, only that he was juggling a huge number of balls, and seemingly keeping them all in the air successfully. Some of it was probably stuff it was best I not know about, though I'm sure there was also much that was admirable or at least harmless.

I found out from one of the other volunteers that 9 had given her an account of the murder that had landed him in prison which was vastly different from the things he had told me in writing and on tape.

He told her that he and his partner had shot the victim, and that they had done so because he was an undercover police officer, or at least some sort of informant working with the police. Of course, he had always maintained to me that 1) his partner and not he had committed the murder, 2) the murder weapon was a knife, 3) the victim was just some stranger, some civilian, and 4) he had no knowledge of what the motive for the murder could have been.

I suggested that we ask 9 to explain himself, but she wasn't comfortable with that. She didn't want him to feel like we were trapping him in a lie. She was content just to let the matter die.

I wasn't particularly upset; I mostly just wanted to give him the business about it. And that was pretty much the approach I took when I eventually asked him about his conflicting stories. We laughed over it, and he told me that he had just embellished the story for her. At the time, she had been doodling some casual sketches, and had invited him to do the same while they talked about his crime. He had attempted to sketch his partner with a knife, then switched it to a gun, on account of "It's a lot easier to draw a gun than a knife." He changed the story accordingly, and then got caught up in making it more interesting, and making himself the lead. So he identified the figure with the gun as himself, and took it from there.

He assured me the version of the crime he'd told me was one hundred percent true. He said he took the book project a lot more seriously than a casual conversation with a woman he'd just met, and that if he were going to lie he wouldn't do it into a tape recorder, knowing that I could research his case and catch him in the lie.

Then he managed to dig himself in deeper by telling her quite the opposite when they spoke later the same evening. As she recounted to me, he assured her that what he had told her was exactly what happened. He explained that he had gotten together with me, and we had discovered that I had simply gotten confused and had run together two different stories—that of the murder, and that of the knife fight at the bus stop in front of the antique store that occurred earlier in his life.

I wasn't able to get any farther with him on it. I brought it up with him once or twice more, but he slid off the subject pretty quickly. And any further written questions I sent him that touched on the murder were ignored.

My take on it is that he's telling people what he thinks they want to hear, or what it will benefit him that they believe about him. I'm guessing he made a snap read on her as some sort of radical chic type who could be intrigued by the macho gang member cop killer (which would be an inaccurate read on her, in my opinion).

On the other hand, maybe he read me as someone who would be more impressed by a humble, sincere person in prison for a crime he didn't commit, diligently improving himself and growing as a person.

I'd like to think he was honest with me for the book, but I don't claim to know that he was or wasn't.

Here follows our final set of written questions and answers, omitting the ones where he offered up little or no response.

*Referring now to the incident in front of the antique store when you stabbed the guy in the neck, was it your intention to kill him? Going for a person's throat with a knife would seem to be extremely life threatening. Could you have defended yourself in a less extreme way? Did you feel that his actions toward you and your partner justified his losing his life? Did you feel that your own life was at stake if you did not respond in the way you did?*

No, it was not my intention to kill him, but to frighten him. After repeated attempts to discourage him from stomping my friend, he ignored the display of my knife and continuously beat him. Due to my size disadvantage, and there being four of them and two of us, I only wanted to damage him enough to stop him long enough for my friend to regain consciousness and we both get away. Plus being called niggers during the onslaught convinced me that there was probably no limit to their attack. Of course I felt like my life was at stake, or at least our health, after witnessing the vicious beating of my downed friend. The stabbing was necessary to stop it from happening, and convince the others to back off.

*Recall our talk about how you believe in keeping your life compartmentalized, where you refrain from being open and honest about your prison experiences with outsiders, even your family, friends, wife, etc. You present it mostly as being for the benefit of others, not wanting to depress them, worry them, etc., and you say that the kinds of things you deceive them about or hide from them are things that they could have no insight into anyway. Is there also, though, an element of self-interest in all this? Are you, in a sense, pretending to be something you're not, because you want the outside people to think well of you? Is it possible, for that matter, that you are not so sure that all of what you do in there is necessary, and you'd rather not have your attention called to that by outside people?*

The reason I don't discuss or reveal my prison lifestyle to family and loved ones is because some things are too difficult to explain, at least where they could understand its reasoning, and I get frustrated trying. It's impossible to explain instincts, other than to say that you develop certain instincts through experience that enable you to survive in prison. Only having the prison experience yourself could answer certain curiosities and questions, and indicate that some things that may not be necessary out there, are warranted in here.

My overall reasoning is that I don't have the energy or answers for a lot of things in here, while the motives are too deep to explain the chain of events that lead to certain reactions. Some things are best unmentioned to avoid confusion and concern.

But you're accurate in all the theories you posed in this question. I'm sure those motives are present.

*You mentioned to me once that drugs finance the gangs, but then we never really followed up on that in our interviews. Tell me about that, your involvement in drugs, the connections in general between drugs and gangs, how—if at all—your take on all this is different now from how it was when you were out there, etc.*

Difficult question to answer briefly. Obviously drugs produce the money necessary to gain resources to get more money, recognition, and guns, and so on. This creates power, and the stability of entire neighborhoods. The toughest gangs are usually the ones with the most guns, and recognition for their elaborate lifestyles of fast cars, money, women, etc. All of those encourage battles through jealousy, which is a fundamental reason behind gang violence.

Now, my take is completely opposite of what it was then. I recognize now that the core of my hatred stemmed from issues that used to seem serious, but were really trivial. I have an understanding of it now, based on maturity and growth, but there is a continuous cycle of new members steadily joining, seeking identity and status.

*How do the mentally ill fare in prison?*

They don't fare well. Spaced out, ridiculed, and uncared for. They are shunned, and behave like zombies, often abused through neglect and ignorance.

*What would you like to tell a general readership about the kinds of prison programs that have been available at WSR?*

The programs provide opportunities for those involved to accept responsibility and perform the essential duties that are taken for granted on the outside. Self-worth, dignity, and pride is afforded to those who take it serious.

I'm talking about the volunteer programs. The DOC operated programs are different. They are too difficult to participate in in a beneficial way. They are structured like something communist ruled, with no deviating and no consideration for individual circumstances.

*How do you feel about the accusation that the outside industry jobs are a bad idea, because it is wrong for prisoners to be exploited as low wage workers by outside employers?*

I agree with that.

Perhaps I might disagree if the outside employers took more responsibility rather than pure profit. Since they pay far less to operate their business in here than they would out there, they should pay higher taxes to offset the unfairness that taxpayers and other competing business owners must pay. Or what they save on wages should reduce the retail cost to consumers, rather than just going in their pocket as profits.

What's the difference between our position, and the child labor overseas where corporations profit through a violation of equality?

*Tell me what it was like for you in IMU.*

It was difficult, but once I adjusted, I spent most of the time reading and writing to ignore the idleness and loneliness. Correspondence and support was vital, which provided my mental strength to handle the oppression.

*Of all the crimes, all the things you've done in your life, what do you feel the most remorse for? What would you like to say to the victim if you could?*

I feel worst about being ignorant and reacting without realizing the consequences. Until I experienced pain myself, I didn't realize the pain I had inflicted, or the damages I caused.

There's nothing I could ever say or do to change anything I've ever done. I'm just fortunate that I've developed an understanding for life and its importance, although I learned at the expense of someone losing their life.

There's no excuse for some of the things I did except that it felt like war, where your life is immediately threatened. Only during war is murder accepted, where murder is necessary to maintain life. I'd rather be a living survivor than a dead hero. That wasn't true in my case, but it sometimes felt that way at the time.

I accept my punishment, but my conviction is stiffer than any other murder conviction. I only disagree with that disparity, not the idea of my being punished.

*What do you think the average person off the street would be most surprised by about prison or about prisoners?*

The average person would be surprised at learning the economics behind prisons. Rather than an institution to salvage lives by rehabilitating, and sanctioning those who broke the law, its corporate operations generate money in unusual ways that could some day be turned against society.

They would also be surprised how many prisoners are no different than others they live around or associate with. We're still rational humans that made a mistake out of ignorance, desperation, or knew no other way. We're often generalized as if we're all the same, but each one of us has a different and unique reason for their actions.

I'm convinced that *almost* everybody have done something that could've sent them to prison, some of the same things that some of us are here for now. We are you. We should be understood, rather than ostracized.

# JEFF—May 2000

*"Men that are really trying to make a difference here receive little or no support from 'the cons.' They are constantly fighting resistance from DOC and the guys in here."*

J eff drifted away from PAP toward the end of the time I was gathering material for this book. Though he cited a change in his work schedule, truth be told, I suspect an unrequited affection for one of the female volunteers was a bigger factor in keeping him away.

I mailed several questions to him after our last taped interview, and he eventually responded in writing.

Reading through the transcripts of our conversations is quite mind-blowing and I am reluctant to read them again as I actually find them quite disturbing. What a Pandora's box you have opened. Such is the lot of all seekers of knowledge and truth.

*You mentioned in our last taped conversation that you had read the letters that your wife's family and friends wrote to the court about you. Tell me about that, and what you thought and felt when you read such things.*

Yes, I had read some of the letters that were written against me during the trial. The one that comes to mind is from someone that I had never met who wanted to have me killed. This woman was a friend of my wife's when she was going out with the boyfriend before me who didn't treat her right. His name was Pete.* This woman had heard bad things about Pete when my wife was going out with him and she had worked with this lady.

Well, when my wife was killed, somehow this woman assumed that Pete did it. She wrote a letter to the judge saying how I had mistreated my wife and that I was a bastard that deserved to die. This was a woman who I had never even seen before.

How quick people are to judge. What if I had been innocent? These are the kind of people that cause the wrong men to go to prison.

*How would you summarize the sorts of programs that have been available at WSR, and the reasons the public should care about them and favor their continuance?*

---

*I have changed the name.

There aren't enough programs that exist in prison that educate men on how to become pro-social citizens. I told you in one of the interviews that I don't think men should be released unless they have gotten their GED and some sort of vocational skill. The public seems to want this, but somehow DOC isn't providing it, and there lies the gap. We need even more programs, and more college level classes, and I would go as far as to give a guy a one-to-one sentence reduction for every full day spent successfully in school.

*How are you affected by Jimi's failure to make it on the outside?*

How am I affected by Jimi's failure? Well, what is most disturbing is the way he treated people that really went out of their way for him. It wasn't so much that he screwed up. That's one malfunction. But to hurt his father, his girlfriend, and his welding teacher here, well that is just plain shitty and hard to forgive. Not that every one of us in here hasn't done the same thing when we came to prison, but to do it AGAIN is really fucked up. That's the best phrase to describe his behavior. I wrote him a Christmas card and he didn't even have the balls to answer it. I just don't understand that level of self-destruction given the substantial level of support that he had.

How am I affected? Actually it has affected me positively because it has caused me to get involved in programs that are trying to teach guys the skills and the attitudes that keep one from coming back to prison. I am currently the president of our Toastmasters club and am involved in several other programs that teach guys how to set goals and how to achieve them, and that give us alternatives to criminal behaviors.

*You mentioned in one of our conversations that the dope fiends in prison will do anything and everything to get a fix. You said that you had learned this through some bad experiences you had had with such people. Tell me more about this. What happened?*

It has been my observation that the people that get themselves in the most trouble in here are the dope fiends. They do whatever they have to to get another fix. They will go heavily into debt, borrow from friends, whatever. Most of them either end up getting hurt real bad or "check in."* I've seen good friendships break up over drug debts. There is no

---

*I.e., voluntarily seek admission into Protective Custody.

stronger pull than the pull of addiction. It makes people crazy, that's how a lot of them get here in the first place.

I have personally been burned twice by "friends" who said they would pay me back, etc. Of course, I'm not as gullible as I used to be either.

Ironically, the person who has taught me the most about getting what you want from dealing with prisoners has been Rico. The man is a master of turning the deal his way in such a way that the other guy doesn't know how it happened. I've seen him in action when we lived together. It was like watching a master at work. He could make a lot of money in sales out there if he wanted to.

*Almost everyone who has never been inside a prison likely assumes that the people are all evil and the experiences are all negative. What stories can you tell that don't fit this stereotype? What can you tell me about friendships, acts of kindness, and generally positive things that you've experienced or witnessed in prison?*

The societal view is that anyone in prison deserves to be there because they did something bad. They view us as the TV stereotype, with tattoos and bad teeth. Not that there aren't plenty of those types in here, but they are in the minority. Most guys in here are just from the wrong side of the tracks and had a lot of problems making it out there. A lot of alcoholics and drug addicts trying to escape their unhappy lives. A lot of them discovered the rush of power that comes from robbing and stealing. It put them in control of their lives again. Until they got here.

I believe that people are basically good. Evil is learned. There are many cruel, violent men in here, but they learned to be this way from their experiences in childhood and later because in order to survive in such environments, you have to be vicious, or be a victim. I can't hold such behavior against someone, but sometimes that is a rather naïve approach. There are certainly men in here that should never get out of prison. They're beyond help and will never change.

On the other hand, there are men in here who have had really shitty lives, but will succeed in spite of that. They have learned from their mistakes. Some of them have done really terrible things, killed people. They have come to an understanding of the magnitude of their crimes. They know there is little they can do to repay the victim or their families, but they do understand that they can help those here around them. There's so many lost men here in need of a little human kindness. Such moments are few and far between, which makes them all the more precious.

Men that are really trying to make a difference here receive little or no support from "the cons." They are constantly fighting resistance from DOC and the guys in here.

*Toward the end of the last tape, we talked about the death penalty. Now that you've had time to reflect on it, and I'm not just hitting you with a bunch of questions on the spot while the tape's rolling, how would you summarize and defend your position? You state on the tape that you "used to think that the victim's family should be able to make that choice." However, for the rest of the interview, it sounded like that's still your opinion, albeit with certain misgivings. Are you anti-death penalty, but are seeking to compromise or qualify that in some way because it might otherwise come across as self-serving or hypocritical, coming from a murderer?*

This is still quite a hard one to answer. I still think that the victim's family should have the ultimate right to execute a murderer. There are of course serious problems trying to institute such a system. The defendant would have to be given all the existing benefits of the legal system. Then after his appeals are exhausted, only the family could choose to execute the person. It would not be an option for the state. Government has no business killing people. If the family decides not to execute or there is no family, then the defendant automatically gets life with parole. Such a person could be eventually released after a long demonstrated pattern of rehabilitation.

# JERRY—July 2000

*"See, I don't believe that I've got the right
to run around and just kill people because
I feel like killing people. But if people
do something that crosses the line of what I
believe is outside the conduct of man, and you
step outside that circle, and you choose to
make me or my family the victims of that, well
then, the consequences are yours. You know what
I mean? That's on your head."*

A
s time went on, I became closer friends with Jerry. We didn't always talk about prison. We probably talked sports as much as anything. We shared the hobby of sportsbetting, and we liked to talk especially about the NFL and the prospects facing each team.

The longer I knew him, the more impressed I was by his mind, and by his continued growth.

One of the little projects I attempted that never fully took off was a sort of Introduction to Philosophy class for the guys. I was granted permission to come in on a different evening from the usual Wednesday PAP meetings, and I put together some lecture notes and handouts, and tried to recreate a college class as best I could.

Unfortunately, the turnout was weak. We met for about two months, and anywhere from two to six people showed up each session. Bill was almost always there, but he made sure to state for the record that it was just to be supportive. (Perish the thought that he'd have anything to learn from reading the great philosophers of history.) Jerry was a regular attendee.

We ended up spending a considerable amount of time on Socrates and Plato, and I even had the guys acting out scenes from "The Apology" and "Crito," with Jerry as Socrates. And he got into it. It was fun watching him in action, jabbing at the prosecutor, explaining himself and his ways to the jury. All he needed was a toga.

He would finish reading the dialogue on his own between classes, and the next week he'd have questions and comments about how Socrates had handled himself.

He liked Socrates, he decided. Liked his style. He did note, though, that if he were Socrates, he'd have found a way to avoid the death sentence without compromising his principles.

We didn't have time to do the death scene, but I did hand out copies of "Phaedo" so the guys could read what ultimately happened to Jerry/Socrates.

The next week, Jerry seemed pleased with how he/Socrates had accepted death. "He didn't break weak," he said with a certain pride, "I think about that a lot myself. Will I have that strength when the time comes? How will I handle it? Will I ever let adversity defeat me? That's real important to me. But Socrates, he was true to himself to the end, the way I want to be. He didn't break weak."

I spent a part of one session presenting Plato's theory of Forms. There was a prisoner there who had just dropped in for the first time to see what we were up to. I was self-conscious, because I knew that not only did he have zero background in philosophy, but he struggled considerably with English as his second language. I was aware he wasn't understanding any of this, but I didn't know what to do about that without slowing down so drastically as to lose everyone else's interest.

But there was Jerry, taking him aside during a break and patiently, enthusiastically, recapitulating my lecture with examples the prisoner could understand. "OK, you know when you're out on the ball field out here, and you're up to bat, and the pitcher grooves one, and you get a hold of it just right and blast it out of the park? You know how that feels? Well, what this fellow Plato is saying is that before you were ever born, you were in this perfect place, this Heaven. Everything was ideal. And now we go through life, and when we see or experience something that we know is just right, that we sense is just the way things should be, then we flash back to what it was like up there before we were born. So, check it out, when you get that feeling where you know your swing was perfect and you know you hit the ball perfect, you're connecting with Heaven, you're connecting with what's perfect inside you and in your memory." Of course, twenty minutes earlier, Jerry had never heard of the theory of Forms or any of this. But after one brief lecture, he was good to go.

I also observed Jerry at a meeting of a secular alternative to AA. He was helping to get this group off the ground, so that non-religious prisoners would have a place to go to deal with alcoholism. I attended one session.

Anybody other than Jerry would likely have just gone through the motions, since as he had told me in one of the interviews, his motive for doing AA and related programs was to have more on his record to show the parole board next time. But it wasn't in his nature just to put his time in and get his ticket punched.

Instead, he was fully focused the entire meeting, listening intently to all that was said. (It was just me, the volunteer who ran this program, and three or four prisoners sitting around a table. The conversation went well beyond alcoholism to deal more generally with life in prison and issues concerning reentry into society.) His mind never stopped working. He would pick up on the nuances of what a prisoner said, of what he neglected to say. And he would comment when something was said that didn't sound right to him, like if a prisoner was deceiving himself, or manifesting an attitude that could get him into trouble later.

He was frank, but not hostile, not judgmental, not showing off. "You mentioned just now that you have a sister who's offered to help you until you get back on your feet out there, but you don't want to impose on her and her family. So you'll make do on your own, but you were vague about how. That's pride talking. That's pride getting in the way of your success. That's pride that's going to send you right back to the joint. If you can get help from your sister, you take that help. This isn't a time to prove you can go it alone. This is a time to accept it when a loved one steps forward to help you. You're not putting her out. Otherwise she wouldn't have offered. You'll be hurting her a lot more if you avoid her help out of pride and end up back here in six months."

Or, to a prisoner lamenting how he had so lost control of his life due to drugs that he had "three strikes" before he knew it and was now destined to spend the rest of his life in prison for crimes that were not that severe: "No, you're shirking responsibility. You knew when you had two strikes you had to change your approach. You have to protect the plate when you're up to bat with two strikes. There's no more room for mistakes. You knew that, but you didn't adjust. You knew the risks you were taking."

When Jerry spoke, the other prisoners knew that he was speaking from the accumulated wisdom of several decades of exposure to this lifestyle

This final interview is a set of written questions I mailed in to him. He tape recorded his responses.

*Do you worry about being judged for killing Frank after you die? Do you think you will ever have to confront him in some form?*

You know, well, I'm not worried about being judged. Me and Frank lived a lifestyle, and he knew the consequences. And to my way of thinking at the time, I didn't have much recourse. And, as far as confronting him in some form, you know, I wouldn't mind doing that. I mean, I've paid for his idiot act for the last twenty-five years. I'd kind of like to haunt him.

I'm not worried about being judged, and I'm not worried about confronting him at some time. In the cockles of my heart, I still think I did what was right.

*In the past, I've heard you make some very articulate statements about the plight of the mentally ill in prison. Please address this.*

You could make a whole tape about the consequences of incarcerating the mentally ill for displaying the symptoms of their disease. I mean, that's a society issue, you know.

Most of us in here, we don't really make life hard for the mentally ill. A lot of us actually kind of look out for them. But, it seems like the so-called civilized society, they have no problem casting them off or ostracizing them or punishing them for displaying their symptoms.

Shit, I just think that there ought to be more attention to that. You know, they shouldn't even be in prison. That's number one. Then when they get to prison, the rules that apply to me certainly shouldn't apply to some guy that doesn't know what he's even doing.

We got a guy right now walking around here—I'll point him out to you—walks around and talks to himself, and throws imaginary stuff all the time. Well, it makes the cops uncomfortable. And every once in awhile, you know, he'll find himself down in the hole. He's got no idea what he's done.

*What's the best case you can make, to a general readership, in favor of prison programs like exist at WSR?*

Man, I think you've heard me say it a million times. You know, if we don't interact with society while we're here, we're certainly not going to be able to interact with them when we get out. You can't live totally isolated in a place that the rules are upside down, and get out, and expect people to be normal. That's ridiculous. It's ludicrous.

The best case I can make is that it doesn't seem to be logical that you would lock me away some place, and deny me any social intercourse, and feed me nothing but a diet of hatred and pain, and expect me to come out healthy and whole. It doesn't make any sense to me.

And the person that it makes sense to has got to be a small, itty-bitty-minded vengeful son of a bitch. And that's all I can say. I don't know.

*Almost all prisoners seem to be in favor of outside industries employing prisoners, yet there are some who make the case that such an arrangement exploits prisoners as slave labor, and in the long run is bad for prisoners and unjust for society. What is your opinion?*

Well, you know, you talk about slave labor, you got to remember that before outside industries came here, we've always had correctional industries, and they're here right now. They've built furniture and all kinds of stuff, and they pay you almost nothing. A buck-ten an hour is as high as you can go, but you start out at, like, thirty-five cents an hour. For office furniture and shit, there are companies out there that make office furniture, and they can't sell to none of the state, federal, county, any of the municipality buildings. We furnish and furbish all those buildings with straight slave labor.

Now, flip it around, and they got an outside industry that pays us enough money that we can support our families, develop a little pride, have a sense of what life's going to be like when you're on the street, and you can see it can be done. It's a learning process.

To change our lifestyle, we got to have confidence in the lifestyle we're going to. And you can't really do that unless you practice it.

So, I don't know. Is it bad in the long run for prisoners and unjust for society? I think it's good for prisoners. And it might be unjust for society. But it doesn't alter the fact that we have slave labor here anyway. And it would still be unjust for society. I think, at least this way, the society gets a little bit back, because we learn that we can support our families with an eight-to-four job, you know, an eight hour job.

You know, come on, man, we've been slaves in prison forever. The only difference with the outside industries is at least we get some money. We're able to do some things for our family. It generates an economy in here where we can actually, like, help each other and do things.

Just recently, me and two, three other guys chipped in and bought a couple of brothers TVs that can't afford it no other way.

So, no, it's made prison better. It might be wrong for society, but it's pretty good for us.

*Given the ways in which you feel you are a significantly different person from, say, ten years ago, how do you think you might be different ten years in the future?*

You always seem to ask, like, a lot of questions in each question, you know. You kind of cheat. [Laughs.] It looks like there's only about fifteen questions here, but there's really about forty-five.

I don't know. I'm significantly less violent than I was ten years ago. To be honest with you, it's what I hope to be even less ten years from now. If I'm out in the community, I think that eventually I'll be able to shed my prison mentality and get further and further away from responding to situations the way I have for the last thirty years.

*Talk about prison riots. What is it like to be in a prison riot?*

I wish I could tell you more about the riot thing, you know, what it's like to be in a riot.

But, you know, I don't know if I told you about when my dad passed away. We were on a fishing boat and we hit a rock, and the boat sank, and we were in the water for—well, I was in the water for eight hours, and he died after five, you know, of hypothermia. Well, there's just no way I can convey to people what was going on with me at the time—the worries, the emotions, the thoughts running through my head—because it's one of those situations where you would have to be there to understand.

And I think the same thing holds true of a prison riot. There's an energy and a chaos that's going on. It's like a releasing. Because, you know how many times a guy wants to say, when the Man's woofing at him or something, and you're sitting there looking at him, thinking, "You know what? It wouldn't be no fun if the rabbit had the gun there, Elmer Fudd." You know what I mean? "If I was kicking your ass, and I had the gun."

And when a riot jumps off, and you've got a hostage situation, well, that's kind of the case, you know. All of a sudden, the look in their face, and "Hey, man, I've always been fair, man! Hey, I never did nothing to you!" And all that shit that they've done to you comes back.

It's kind of a power thing, you know. You finally get to tell the captors exactly what you feel. You've been biting your tongue for ten years, and finally you get a chance to tell them exactly what's on your fucking mind. And you're already in trouble, so you ain't worried about any consequences.

And in some cases, they take it further. I never have, but in some cases that people feel grievous about, they feel that they have a reason, or a justification to, like, kill them or something. Myself, they've never done nothing so bad to me that I felt like I could kill them, except for maybe the guy that gave me that digital probe in IMU. I wouldn't mind catching that son of a bitch.

But, for me, I've never felt like extracting the ultimate. But I can understand if, in somebody's mind, if they had been put upon, had their ass kicked, and been bothered, tortured, or whatever enough that they feel that they have the right to take a life. I don't think I could argue with them, if that's the way they truly felt about it. I might try and reason with them, but I certainly wouldn't argue with them.

If you take all of the things that I just said, and think about it for a minute, and put it in a scenario where chaos is taking place, and there are no controls, then you got kind of an idea of what's going on in a riot.

*You once made a statement about the need to honor the chapel as a place of sanctuary for ostracized prisoners. It sounded like even though you and the prisoners like you cannot and will not accept and befriend and try to help rats and rapos and such, you still do not condemn those who do reach out to such people, and in fact you seem to even have a kind of respect for them. Please elaborate on that.*

Yeah. Basically, you know, like, especially with the sex offenders, we used to just beat them down every chance we got. And as I got older, I started to get a sense that, you know, if I'm stopping somebody from seeking help, and then they get out and re-offend, well, then I might share a certain responsibility in that.

So they got to have a place. It just doesn't have to be with me. And I think a lot of us feel the same way. There's always the sense that those people that come in here, and walk with them, they—I had a lady friend that wrote an article called "Any Neighbor on Any Cross," you know, and when they're called to fellowship with people in prison, they can't pick and choose who they're going to like and who they're not going to like, based on what they've done.

You know, and, like, a lot of us are in for murder and stuff, and it's always nice to know that if you ever need a friend, you can go over to the chapel and find one. I'm not talking about the rats and rapos [laughs]; I'm talking about the outside volunteers. So we always respect them, and give them a lot of consideration when they go through the yard and stuff.

*After years of doing what you have to do to survive in prison, and building up certain habits, how will you be able to adjust to life on the outside? Will you be able to ignore something on the outside that's considered an act of disrespect in the artificial world of prison?*

I kind of addressed that a little bit. You know, it's going to be tough. I'm going to have to exercise a lot of the little lessons I've learned in some of the stress/anger type programs I've taken here. You know, it's going to affect me. I'm going to be angry. The thing is, as long as I don't put my hands on anybody, as long as I don't act it out, I'll be all right. It's all right to be angry, you know.

I'll let people know they're pissing me off. If they don't like it, they can get the fuck away from me. And that'd be better.

It's easy to stay at a verbal level. It's not necessary for me to take it past that.

I think that comes from being older, and a little bit more confident in a guy's self, you know. I can just let people know when they've crossed that line, and apprise them of the precarious situation they might be in. If they want to take it further, I think that might be on them.

Hell, I got to work on it, you know. Will I be able to ignore something on the outside that's considered an act of disrespect? I won't be able to ignore it. I think I'll react to it. The key is that I just can't take it to the level that I would have took it in the past.

But, hell, I haven't taken it to the level that I normally take something for years. I mean, I don't even do it here any more. So, I don't really see any problem of not assaulting somebody. I'm not out of control, so. But now, would I draw a line in the sand? Yeah. Would I give a fellah an ultimatum if he disrespected me? Yeah, you know. [Laughs.] I think I'll always make a guy stop and think before he treads on me. And I hope it never comes to that, you know. I'm a serious guy, and I don't see anything wrong in that.

So, I don't know. I just have to keep my hands off the sons of bitches. [Laughs.]

*What would be the impact on the criminal justice system and the prisons if most or all recreational drug use was de-criminalized? Overall, do you think this would be good or bad for society?*

Well, come on, you'd keep all them kids out, that the worst thing they did is smoke some weed, take some acid. They come up here and listen to all the war stories, and look up to old convicts that have wasted their whole fucking life, and they think that's something to do.

Society and the whole world would be a lot better off if they'd do that. You know, get the criminal justice system out of substance abuse, 'cause they don't do anything to alter the substance abuse.

*Was your decision to intentionally take a human life a rational application of principles you've chosen to live by, or was it a response of emotion and anger? How would you describe your emotional state at the time you committed the murder? Before, during, or after, did you have any misgivings, any hesitancy, any indecisiveness, any remorse, any guilt, etc.?*

See there's, like, ten questions there, and you keep cheating on this shit, Craig. [Laughs.]

Well, you know what? It was a fairly rational application of principles, but that's not to say I wasn't angry. I mean, I started out that evening as a victim. I don't know if you've ever been a victim, but it pisses you off. My choice to handle it myself, to deal with it by myself, was a rational application of my principles. You got to remember, at the time, the option of calling the cops, it just didn't even exist for me. So, I mean, I had a choice. I could, like, leave my old lady out on the porch, or I could deal with it.

And, as far as, you know, my emotional state at the time, it was kind of fucked up. But I was in control. I made the decision, and I'll live with that.

I had misgivings only in the sense of getting away with something, you know. I came to the conclusion I probably wasn't going to get away with it. But I felt I had to do it anyway.

*About how many years of your life total have you spent incarcerated?*

I've spent about thirty years in prison.

I don't know what that means, except that for twenty-three, almost twenty-four of them, I've been in here for killing a guy that raped my wife, but I probably would have spent a good deal of that time in prison anyway. You know, they might have caught me for something eventually. I got away with most of the things I did, but, you know, I lived that lifestyle that was always fraught with opportunity to lose.

*Your brother was apprehended about a month before you, and attempted to take the rap for the murder by himself. Apparently you didn't intervene and try to deal to lessen his punishment until you were apprehended. According to the code of conduct you accept, what is the appropriate thing to do in this kind of situation? Were you in the right to remain on the lam, even if it resulted in your brother taking all the burden of punishment on himself? Once he had been apprehended, should you have come forward voluntarily to take responsibility for the murder and to, in effect, try to trade places with him and get him off?*

For some reason, you think I should have turned myself in, and helped take the burden of punishment off of him. Well, let's just point out the fact that when I was caught, and I did take full responsibility for the murder, and I did tell them that he didn't do anything, he still received a life sentence. So, me turning myself in and shit, you know, you live in a fantasy world when you think that there's something fair about our criminal justice system. I don't live with any false pretense about what our criminal justice system is really about.

And, no, James knew what he was doing. He's an intelligent guy. He thought, "Well, there's no sense in us both taking the beef," if he can get it off of me. And I respect him for it.

He should have kept his mouth shut, though, and just pled not guilty all along, and then I might even have been able to help him when I got caught, but I couldn't once he did that. And for that, he's got to take a certain amount of responsibility.

He knows how you're supposed to conduct yourself when you go to jail. He knows that you don't make any statements. He knows that you got to take it all the way to trial before you make a decision one way or another. And, for whatever reason, he didn't do that.

I think it was mainly because he had been using drugs, and he was coming off the drugs, and he just wasn't thinking clearly. And, I mean, that's that.

I did try and get him off once I was caught, and as you can tell by him being out right now, everybody in the Department of Corrections understood what role he played. But that wasn't sufficient for the criminal justice system. They just wanted to remove us from the streets. And, they didn't see any reason that they couldn't get us both.

So, you know, so that's how I felt about that.

James knew what he was doing. He's a grown man. He'd been to jail, he'd been to the joint, and he knew what to do. And he didn't do it. I had no idea that he wasn't doing it. You know, so that's another thing. As a matter of fact, I didn't even have any idea that he was in jail, for sure. He was supposed to leave town, just like I was leaving. And he didn't do that. So, you know, I kicked him in the butt for years over that.

But, it's all in the way you look at shit, you know, when you go back and think about stuff. I don't know. Bad situation. Got worse, is all.

*Prison seems, perhaps surprisingly, to offer some opportunities for positive multicultural experiences and understanding. I'm thinking of, for example, the way that you and some of the non-Indian prisoners have participated in the Native American sweats and other rituals. Do you see this happen much, where prisoners who on the outside might have remained strictly in their own little world, are able in prison to make positive connections with people from other groups and to learn about and experience other cultures?*

Yeah, that happens a lot in prison. You know, we live in here on top of each other, and sometimes you're living so close to somebody, begrudgingly you start to like them, and respect some of the things that they do, and then you become interested in what it is that they're doing. And sometimes for guys that don't have much faith, it's like a curiosity thing to see what gives them the faith or whatever, and so you might go to a Muslim thing, or a Native American thing or something, just to see what's going on, see where these people are getting it.

You're always curious about what somebody else is doing. How do they get their faith, you know? From where does it spring? And so you go to see. You never know when you're going to stumble on a right answer, or something that's a good answer for you. So, we're all looking.

It is unique, but, I mean, we have, like, unique friendships in here. It's like in the armed forces and stuff, where you're drawn closer to people that come from different walks of life than you do, and you're drawn together by necessity or whatever—just maybe the close confines. And you find you have things in common.

It makes it easier to bond, and once you find out about people and their faith and stuff, it opens your eyes and lets you know that we all share a common mission. We're just trying to get through life. Everybody's got the same ups and downs.

But it is unique, because of our close proximity to each other all the time, twenty-four seven. I mean, right now, probably Bill and maybe even the guy on the other side of me can hear me talking. What are our houses? Six feet wide, or whatever they are? Well, hell, that means that every six feet, there's a body. And that's up and down, too. So we're on top of each other all the time in real close confines, see. You know, it's better to find some things you like about somebody that's that close to you than to dwell on all the shit you don't like about them.

*On the one hand, you have a persona and a reputation as being blustery, tactless, abrasive, quick to violence, etc., etc. But aren't you, in a deeper sense, almost the opposite of these things? I mean, you've played a major role in holding together the disparate personalities in PAP, you have maintained the standing to be able to negotiate in certain ways with the administration, you've said that you've had some good friends who are "stark, raving mad," you can co-exist with people like our mutual acquaintance who used bald-faced lies about us to get me fired, etc. It seems to me that to live every day of your life surrounded by unpredictably violent people, lunatics, abusive authority figures, people you've crossed, people who've crossed you, people you don't respect, and so on and so forth, a person would need to be extremely tactful, patient, aware, diplomatic, tolerant, etc. Any comments?*

Oh Jesus. No, I think I'm all of those things. And holding together PAP, it was necessary to be "blustery, tactless, and abrasive" at times. [Laughs.]

But as far as the guy who told lies on you to get you fired and shit, you know what? If I was in a different prison, I wouldn't co-exist with someone who had did that. If I wasn't afraid of their ability to manipulate the Man and cause me some serious grief, they'd know exactly what I thought about them.

To be honest with you, that's something that actually bothers me. When you ask in your next question here what bothers a guy's conscience, that shit bothers me. You know, having to act like they're all right.

But the part about having friends who are "stark, raving mad," I mean, shit, some of my best friends are crazy.

Then you say, "A person would need to be extremely tactful, patient, aware, diplomatic, tolerant, etc." Well, I think I'm some of those things, too. [Laughs.] You have to be.

I've become rather adept at hiding what I truly feel.

*During all your criminal career, does anything you've done stand out to you as particularly calling for remorse? What, if any, crime do you regret the most, where you feel you were clearly in the wrong in how you victimized some person or persons? What would you say to the victim(s) today if you could?*

You know, I always think about when I was a kid. Shit, I was only, like, thirteen or something. And I would pick out an old couple, maybe snatch a purse, or just roll the guy, or whatever. That's actually the thing that sticks out most in my mind as just the wrongest thing I've ever done. That's probably the thing that's haunted me the most.

I mean, the murder was no great thing, but victimizing the elderly bothers me. You know, it only happened a couple times, but I've never forgot it.

Mostly I never felt I was victimizing other people, though I was. I'm talking about, like, the cashiers and stuff if I committed a robbery or something. Now, I've grown to realize just how bad I victimized those people.

But you ask me what one stuck out the most, and I got to admit, that was it.

And that's not to say I don't also now feel uncomfortable thinking about some of the robberies and stuff I've committed where the people weren't elderly, when they were just at work and shit, you know. I mean, that's something I'll think about, but I don't think it's as bad as what I did when I was, like, rolling an old man for his wallet and shit.

I just can't believe I did that, because even at the time, I think I knew in my own mind that I was out of line. Or at least I hope I did.

You know, like, if feeling bad about something atones for anything in any way, well, then I've atoned for that, 'cause I've felt bad about that the whole time.

Not that I'm saying that feeling bad about something really pays a price. I don't think it really does, you know. I should probably do something specifically for that, but I don't know who they are, or where they are, and they'd be dead by now anyway. And I wouldn't know how to make it up.

But, I guess, to think about it, never doing it again might be a way of making it up.

*In the Prison Awareness classes, you and some of the other prisoners have told about how in the past at other prisons, you were humiliated with digital probes and such, and apparently they were videotaping it at Walla Walla and eventually got in trouble for it. Can you tell me about that?*

Well, they'd come in, and you knew what was going to happen, and they'd goon you, tie your coveralls around your waist, and take you up and have a guy—he wasn't even a doctor—cram a finger up your ass looking for contraband. And all the time they were video-taping it, you know. And, some of the officers were caught with the videos. You know, there'd be, like, one after another on each videotape, like a whole day's work, and then they'd take the tapes to their parties, and be laughing and drinking beer watching it.

But just knowing that these people had viewed that, and that, you know, the people that work in our prison system are the type of people that would not only do that, but then groups of them would sit around watching it on tape and enjoying it is enough to fucking drive you to distraction, when you think about it.

I don't even like going there.

*Would it be accurate to say that your decision to avenge your wife's rape by murdering Frank did significant damage to both her and your brother (as well as other third parties for that matter)? Were their lives substantially harmed by your choosing the course of action that you did?*

Yeah. Yeah. But I refuse to take sole responsibility. Let's say this: Would it be accurate to say that my decision to avenge my wife's rape by murdering Frank after *he* made a decision to rape my wife had those consequences? I mean, the damage was collateral damage from his initial act.

I'll just quote what the judge said: "No right thinking adult could have expected any other response from Mr. McLaughlin, having known Mr. McLaughlin and his nature."

So when Frank went out and raped my wife, he knew in the back of his mind that I wasn't going to take that laying down. And so the collateral damage he shared a responsibility in. "He died as a direct result of a crime he perpetrated, to wit, the rape of Laura McLaughlin." That's what the state said when his family sought damages, and I believe that.

I'll take my share of the responsibility, but I won't ride that beef alone. Frank has got to ride it with me.

You know, like, sometimes I get a little aggravated with the average person who thinks that just because I won, the other guy was the victim. He knew when he did it what the consequences were. He should have been on his feet. He should have been ready. There's no way that if I harm somebody, I'm going to let him catch me unawares.

He started the war; I just finished it.

Everybody wants to find some reason that I got to ride the whole beef by myself. I don't think that's the case, you know, and if that's not accepting responsibility, well then, hell, I just ain't going to accept it.

I'll accept the punishment. I've accepted the time. I've never whined, like, hey, I don't deserve to be here. I've always thought that I did.

Now, I'm responsible for introducing Frank to my family. I'm responsible for bringing him into the circle of my friends and family and loved ones, where he could perpetrate this crime. So, yeah, I'm responsible for that.

You know, the damage to my wife, and to my brother, because I killed him, I mean, I'm not sure that the damage wouldn't have been worse if I don't do anything. The loss of respect amongst our family members. It's just hard to say.

It all depends on the way you read what happened. My family was attacked first, man, and I did what I thought was necessary. And, you know, like, third parties, people that stand outside my family, you know, that don't know me and my brother seem to think that maybe my brother or my wife or somebody would be mad at me about what I did. But they're not. We're all kind of in agreement.

So, you have to know our family, and you have to walk a mile in our shoes before you can judge us.

You know, I've noticed a lot of the times when you ask a question like "Do I think I'll be judged for what I did to Frank?" or all that, you base it on your assumption that there is no reason for violence. Yet the state takes people's lives like it's second nature. The police force, the goon squad around here, have no problem applying whatever physical force is necessary to impose their will on us.

And the same thing with the police departments out there. I mean, look at all the police that are under indictment in Los Angeles alone. Every day you're seeing something. Right down in Tacoma, there's a case where they've been persecuting a family. It was just on the news here the last couple of weeks.

So, to say that only the state or only these officials have the right to impose their will by force may be your assumption, but it's not mine. You've given over that authority to the

Man. I myself have not. I believe that I have a God-given right to do whatever's necessary to protect my family.

If she had called the cops, and if she had pressed charges, the son of a bitch would have done a couple of years and been out and been in a position to reap revenge. He is *not* in a position to reap revenge right now.

See, I don't believe that I've got the right to run around and just kill people because I feel like killing people. But if people do something that crosses the line of what I believe is outside the conduct of man, and you step outside that circle, and you choose to make me or my family the victims of that, well then, the consequences are yours. You know what I mean? That's on your head.

And whether they let me out or never let me out, nothing will ever change about that. You can't do something to my family with impunity. And I'm not going to the Man to get justice. I don't know how many times you've seen where somebody stalked somebody, and gets back out of prison and whacks them. I won't let that happen.

Mine's an ultimate decision, and maybe you don't believe, or society doesn't believe I have that right. But when somebody comes into my life, and tries to do something to us, well then that's between me and my Maker. And so be it. I feel real strongly about this.

Like I said before, you know, me and my family, we're not of an opinion that I did anything that was so bad. And, like, with the amount of time that they've made me do, it's swinging back over onto the state. I mean, come on. They been kicking my ass for twenty-four years now for killing a guy that raped my wife, victimized us in the first place, perpetrated the crime, and started the whole thing. You know, just when is the pound of flesh paid?

I never really complained about it, but I'm getting to the point where I don't think I really owe anybody anything more for this.

And if there was a reckoning at some point in the hereafter or whatever, I'd welcome it. You know, I'd tell God or anybody else exactly how I feel right now. You know what I mean? There wasn't nobody looking out for Laura but me.

And that's all there was to that. So, we won't go there no more. [Laughs.]

It's just that sometimes when you ask me questions, here and in the past—and it's probably the right thing that you do so—but it's like you believe I've done something wrong, and you believe that *I* should think that I've done something wrong.

Well, I don't necessarily believe that I've done anything wrong. So, what can I tell you? I've done something severe. I've done something extreme. But not necessarily wrong, you know.

And the people that matter to me haven't really led me to believe that they feel I've did anything really wrong. They all wish that—well, you know, they would rather have suffered whatever other consequences would have been available than to have me locked up for this period of time, or to have our family torn apart, but they don't feel that I was wrong, you know. And that's just where we come from.

It's kind of like that riot question; unless you walk with us, it's really hard for you to understand where I've been.

# EPILOGUE

I left PAP in September 2000, and in fact moved out of state less than a year later. As a result, I mostly lost contact with the prisoners.

Whenever I could get the time, I continued to work on this book, transcribing interview tapes, editing transcripts, writing the connective material, etc. By early 2002, I had finished the first draft.

I wrote to all nine prisoner participants, enclosing copies of the edited transcripts and asking them to check them to make sure I had not misrepresented something they had said. I also asked them to update me on what had been happening with them and the institution since the last interview, and I told them if they had any final "message to the reader" type thing to offer, I'd be glad to include it in the conclusion of the book.

Of those that responded, none found fault with the transcripts beyond some very minor corrections.

Larry, with whom I had had the least contact of any of the prisoners involved in the project, did not respond.

There was no response from Buck, which is unfortunate, because I very much wanted to know what happened with his attempts to get parole. (You'll recall at the time of our last interview, he had just been turned down on his first opportunity.) According to Jeff, "Buck got paroled, but then they screwed him and paroled him onto another beef, so he has to fight them in court over that." The DOC lists Buck as having an earliest possible release date of January 2008.

9 did not respond initially, but after I sent a follow-up letter he did eventually write back. He was struggling emotionally as he attempted to adjust to the deteriorating post-DuCharme prison environment.

He apologized for taking so long to get back to me, and explained the delay: "The real reason has been my attitude and mood over the past few months. It's been a combination of heavy court involvement, constant changes, lockdowns, violence, and trying to maintain my sanity through it all." He expressed uncertainty that the programs would last much longer, at least in any useful form.

9 tried to close his letter on a more optimistic note: "Despite the circumstances, I'm doing fine. Besides a lot of frustrations and irritations, eventually I'll pull out of this slump and get my spirits back up. I pray every day."

During a visit to Washington in May 2004, I asked some of the prison volunteers for updates about the prisoners. Among the things they told me was that 9 and the majority of the prisoners we knew had been transferred out of WSR. Reportedly the new regime wanted to rid itself of any prisoner it perceived as a potential leader who could generate opposition to their destruction of all that had made the prison unconventionally tolerable. The programs had been cut back, with PAP eliminated entirely for a time. Later it was allowed to resume after the volunteers inclined at all toward prisoner advocacy had been purged, and the remaining volunteers had pledged henceforth to be suitably docile.

9 had been shipped to Walla Walla. I was told he had spent most of his time since in the hole or in IMU. He was described to me as depressed.

The one piece of good news was that his wife Maggie was somehow still surviving the inoperable cancer that should have killed her years ago.

Henry's hearing (recounted earlier) happened right about the time I left PAP. The last time I heard from him was a few months later when he called just to see how I was doing and to ask if I would be coming back to PAP. He sounded in reasonably good spirits, and it was certainly good to hear his voice.

He did not respond in 2002 when I mailed the edited transcripts. 9 mentioned in his letter that "Henry...hasn't wrote for the same reason I hadn't," implying that Henry was letting the changes at WSR get to him, which surprises me since I am so used to taking his emotional strength and forbearance for granted.

He too was subsequently shipped out to Walla Walla. Reportedly he is not with 9 there, as he is in the medium security wing, while 9—when he is not in the hole or IMU—is in the maximum security wing.

According to the DOC, Henry is still saddled with a life sentence (well, technically he has an earliest release date of September 2182), so one can infer that his further attempts to have his conviction overturned or to gain parole have not been successful, at least not yet.

Jeff wrote back to me when he received the edited transcripts. He has an earliest release date of July 2016.

Jeff's letter made me sad. About WSR itself, he reports, "I've seen more fights here in the last year than I'd seen in the previous ten. Ever since DuCharme left here, this place is going downhill quick.…At least the jobs will always be here because the state makes so much money off us. The education department keeps getting smaller and smaller." He says he has given up on PAP and the programs, due to the volunteers and prisoners in them being "retarded."

He has grown more bitter and cynical since the time I was seeing him regularly. This is not just my assessment; he says it himself: "Yes, perhaps I have grown bitter. Prisoners are their own worst enemy and always will be. Rehabilitation is a dubious prospect at best."

I can't just dismiss him or condemn him for his attitude, because I would likely be at least as embittered and depressed if our roles were reversed. That's what makes me feel sad for him.

I asked Jerry if the read I had on Jeff from his letter was accurate. He believes it is. Jeff's alone a lot now, he said, or you'll see him with maybe one friend walking the yard.

Why? I speculated that it was the changes in the environment, that a square like Jeff was a lot less suited to what WSR was becoming (the typical dangerous, brutal prison) than what it had been (a more open institution where prisoners are given some opportunities to better themselves and are treated with a certain amount of respect). Jerry said that could be part of it, but it also could simply be the passage of time. Some prisoners just get worn down by doing too much time. They hate where they are for so long that it gradually generates in them a more generalized bitterness and hatred toward anyone and anything around them, even toward themselves.

Most of the older prisoners I knew at PAP seemed to have mellowed with age, to have outgrown their anger. They typically had healthier attitudes than their younger counterparts. But Jerry maintains that in the general prison population, you will at least as often see age have the opposite effect. There's a common and often accurate stereotype, he says, of the old con as the angry, negative, lonely fellow always grumbling about something. Not that Jeff is particularly old, but he has done a lot of time.

Bill, always a willing correspondent, replied to the transcripts immediately, enclosing some of his poems and excerpts from the autobiography he was working on (a very good read—likely to be published in late 2004 or 2005).

Of WSR, Bill reported, "The joint is much more restrictive than when you were here. Every time we exhale, the python tightens another inch." He had resigned from what was left of PAP. "I turned it over to the nerds."

His letter included a marvelous anecdote that is quintessential Bill:

```
Friday I was summoned to the hospital. They
have several uniforms in attendance. They say
they want a blood draw and a picture of me. Fat
fuckin' chance, I reply. What's this about?
Paternity suit, they say. Ha Ha. Seriously!
They say they want the hemo and a pic of me
from the waist up. You guys are reading that
wrong, I tell them. If it's a paternity suit,
you'll need a pic from the waist down. Etc.
Etc. Turns out they wanted a guy with a similar
last name. I thanked them for the compliment
and the chuckle and exited stage left.
```

Bill had been eligible for parole for several years, but had turned down the opportunity. Has he been so severely institutionalized that he prefers life behind bars to the free world?

Well, not really. As he explained it to me, if he were to accept parole from Washington, he would then be required to return to Georgia—the scene of his last escape—and serve the time he still owed them. That meant a minimum of two years in Georgia's version of IMU and eight years in one of their regular prisons before he could even see the Georgia parole board. And even a deteriorating WSR is more desirable than a Southern prison, and vastly more desirable than a Southern IMU.

So, he figured at his age, he might as well live out his life under the guardianship of the Washington DOC, rather than subject himself to a decade or more of a more brutal incarceration, even though the latter would give him some shot at eventual freedom.

Some time later, though, that situation changed. With the help of a lawyer, Bill was able to negotiate a better deal with Georgia, good enough that he finally accepted a transfer there in 2003. The agreement was no IMU time, and at least the possibility of parole within about two years. Furthermore, even if they turn him down for parole at that time, he would likely be allowed to transfer back to Washington. Due to an oddity in the rules, he could then serve out those additional Georgia years in Washington. (By contrast, during that time between when his Washington sentence ended and he accepted the transfer to Georgia, no time was ticking off his Georgia sentence. It was completely wasted.)

I spoke with Bill very briefly by phone in May 2004. He remains incarcerated in Georgia, moderately confident he'll be free soon. He is pursuing a serious relationship with one of the former PAP volunteers, and in fact there is a good chance they will marry if and when he is released.

I did not get a response in 2002 from Rico. About a year later, I spoke to him very briefly when Jerry called me and Rico happened to be standing alongside him, but we didn't have a chance to really get into things.

In recent years Rico has been featured in the local newspaper at least twice—once in a story about private employer jobs in prison, and once in a story about prisoners counseling at-risk youth.

I finally spoke at length with Rico in the summer of 2004, just as this book was about to go to the printer. In one of our interviews he had stated that as an SRA era prisoner, he would not transition through progressively lower custody level institutions to the street, but would likely be released straight from prison once his sentence was up in 2004. However, for whatever reason, it didn't happen this way. By 2003 they moved him to a minimum security facility, and in 2004 he was sent to a work release facility in Seattle, which is where he was when I spoke with him.

The work release facility sounds surprisingly unrestrictive. For all intents and purposes, it's as if he's a parolee at a halfway house. He goes to and from work on his own, and he is free to come and go a certain number of hours a week for social or other non-work purposes. He can receive phone calls rather than just make outgoing collect calls.

He noted that despite the fact that the people who make it to this stage have a lot of freedom and have very little time left to do, escaping and being sent back to real prison to serve significant additional time is very common. Why, I wondered, when you're so close to being done with prison do you do something so blatantly contrary to your self-interest? His response was that many prisoners, especially junkies, have no capacity to perform even minimally rational cost-benefit analyses. They do drugs the first opportunity they have, which means they then can't go back to the work release facility without flunking a drug test. That this is moronic even in terms of their future opportunity to do drugs—they'll obviously have easier access in the free world if they behave themselves another few days or weeks than they will back in prison—doesn't enter into it. The drugs are in front of them now.

By October 2004 Rico will be free even of the minimal restrictions of work release. He is in excellent spirits and sounds very confident he'll make it on the outside. He has a well-paying job doing the same kind of work he was doing for a private employer in prison, and he intends to remain in the Seattle area and keep that job when he is released.

Given that he has no long term habitual criminal history to overcome, given that he's been free of drugs for many years, and given just the kind of person he is and how committed he is to improving himself and living a life that is respectful of others and of his community, I'd put his chances of remaining out of prison much higher than those of most released prisoners. I think he'll do it right.

I had no contact with Jimi for years since shortly before he re-entered the system. Even the prisoners at PAP were uncertain where he had ended up, and uncertain whether he had been third struck or would get at least one more chance.

I contacted the DOC in 2002 to make sure my other prisoners were still at WSR, and to find out Jimi's whereabouts so that I could send the transcripts. They informed me that he was at Clallam Bay. He was due to be released in late 2002 or 2003.

I was uncertain whether or how he would respond to me after all this time, but he wrote back almost immediately. I felt an excitement but also a certain trepidation opening his letter. I don't know exactly what I expected or what I wanted.

He sent me several handwritten pages, and followed up by both phone and additional correspondence thereafter. He did not recall how much he had told me at the time about what happened on the outside, so he gave me a quick summary of it in writing. It jibed reasonably well with what I had pieced together at the time, partly from him and partly from others, though it contained some new material as well.

> As you may recall, I found great comfort in
> the company of those I'd been locked up with.
> In the beginning I actually believed they were
> all doing well, especially the one I was clos-
> est with (Nick).
> Well, one night I was at his house in Tacoma
> visiting him and his wife and kids. Come to
> find out, he was not only hooked on heroin but
> smoking crack as well. Making a long story
> short, he had me smoking it that night, and I
> was way too high to go home. I did the same
> thing the next night, and Jeannie asked me to
> leave (which I'd been ready to do since her
> daughter moved in with us).

I moved in with Nick and spent the next two weeks commuting from Tacoma to Everett and smoking crack at night. That ended when I fell asleep at the wheel and ran my truck through the main gate at Submarine Base Bangor. That was an eye opener and ended the crack.

I flew back east for two weeks to visit the family and got back on track from there.

I moved to Port Orchard and took a job doing the ironwork on an Albertsons, met a nice girl with two boys and was renting a room.

What I did do is start drinking more than I should be. Marcia* and I got into an argument one night and I took off to the bar and started slamming rum and cokes. When the bar closed, I went downtown to sulk. There I took a hammer and broke a window of a jewelry store and stole three watches, which I didn't need. That's what I'm here for.

The first two years of this I was *very* depressed and pretty much feeling that I belong here. Dad was so hurt and disappointed he wouldn't talk to me *at all*. That was terrible!

Now I'm here at Clallam Bay, working in the weld shop and making plans for another try at freedom, which comes November 25th this year.

Dad and I are closer than ever. He has retired and we are closer than ever, and that, as you may remember, means everything to me.

My plan is to go do a 90 day contract on a processor in Alaska and come back, get a place, cheap vehicle, computer, and start school at Olympic College in Bremerton. Fine Arts. I've filed my financial aid and am in the process of finalizing things with Olympic.

---

*Evidently the woman he was seeing. I have changed the name.

Something struck me about his tone, both in writing and especially on the phone. There was almost a nonchalance to it. It wasn't that it was completely lacking in emotion, but relative to the subject matter there was an odd lack of intensity. It was like listening to someone talking about some character in a book that had caught his interest to a moderate degree. There was some degree of intellectual engagement, and a lesser degree of emotional engagement, but it wasn't like someone talking about something hugely important in his own life.

Toward me, he was perfectly friendly, but again there was a paucity of strong emotion, a lack of intensity. He did not accuse me of letting him down; he did not apologize for letting me down. He didn't come across as sheepish or reluctant to talk with me in any way, but he also didn't exactly seem thrilled. He spoke to me as if we had been casual buddies for awhile in college, had gone our separate ways after graduation, and now happened to run into each other years later. He was pleased to be in touch with me, and happy to quickly get caught up on each other's lives, but I sensed nothing deeper.

Other than toward his father, he expressed no remorse or any strong emotion concerning anyone else. Jeannie was only mentioned in passing, and nothing was said to indicate if he was even still in touch with her.

Maybe he went through all the emotions and hit his rock bottom during those two years after his most recent arrest, and now he's at a different place emotionally. But even aside from his verbal style, I was undecided if he "got it" substantively. For example, he said nothing about renouncing drugs and alcohol until I specifically brought it up. I told him that regardless of whether AA is correct in claiming that the only viable option for all alcoholics or drug abusers is complete abstinence, the evidence is overwhelming that, for him, that's the answer. He responded that mine was an interesting and very plausible point worthy of his consideration.

To me, that meant he was intellectually persuadable on the matter, but that at a gut level he still doesn't react to those substances with a powerful aversion nor a direct awareness that they are poison to him and to any possible future he could have.

He did not come clean (I didn't ask him, but nor did he volunteer) about his using drugs in prison, nor about losing his welding job due to alcohol or drugs. You'll notice he skipped right over that in his narrative.

I told Jerry these things and asked him if my reaction made sense to him. He chuckled in recognition. "He doesn't have the urgency you'd expect," he said, "That's exactly what I saw in him the last time. We can spot that kind of thing on the inside better than you, because we see it so much. Jimi's a great guy, and he's really doing everything he knows to do. But I knew last time it was going to be real tough for him on the outside, because he just wasn't ready the way he thought he was ready. We see guys like that all the time. They really think they're on the right track, but it just hasn't gotten through to them the way it has to. They're still doing their drugs or whatever on the inside, talking about how they'll give it up as soon as they get out. No, that's not going to happen. You have to go beyond words and make the deep changes while you're still in the joint; you can't wait to change out there."

So would it be different this time? Is he different this time? To me, his intentions, confidence level, general attitude, etc. sounded about the same as last time. He even told me "there aren't a lot of changes necessary." He spoke of the need to budget his money better, and that this time he would make it a point not to gravitate to other ex-cons, but it sounded like he thought he mostly had the right approach last time and just needed to do some tinkering.

I checked back with DOC one last time in May 2004 just before this book went to print. They told me Jimi had been released as scheduled, and had not returned to the system. I breathed a sigh of relief.

A little too soon perhaps. In the summer I had a chance to speak with someone who had seen Jimi, and who subsequently had spoken by phone to his wife. (Evidently he had remarried.)

Bear in mind that this is all third and fourth hand, but here's what I was told: Jimi burned through at least one woman (was unable to live with any kind of self-discipline or responsibility, maxed out her credit cards, then ran or was kicked out), then burned through his father yet again (the same, to the point where his father warned Jimi's eventual wife she was making a huge mistake marrying him), then burned through his wife (she has just kicked him out). He has resumed using drugs.

The patterns started in a childhood marked by dysfunctional family life, petty crime, and juvenile detention. The way of life, the habits that grew out of that, have proven too hard to break, in spite of his putting far more effort into understanding himself and changing than most people ever will. You can't rule out that he'll attain a greater maturity and strength in the future, but if and when that happens he'll almost certainly be sitting in prison with a life without parole sentence for his accumulated convictions, the system having long since tired of his failures and given up on him.

By a wide margin, the prisoner I've had the most contact with in recent years is Jerry.

Shortly after I left PAP, I wrote Jerry a detailed explanation of why I decided to do so. I didn't hear back from him directly until considerably later, but I spoke with his grown son Josh* regularly and got brief messages from Jerry through him.

---

*I have changed the name.

I hadn't formally resigned from PAP as of yet; I simply was no longer attending. But I was considering taking that next step of relinquishing my membership, as that would mean that after a six-month wait I'd be eligible to get on a prisoner's visiting list. (It's one to a customer, by the way—you can only be on one prisoner's list.)

Especially with Jimi no longer at WSR, the obvious choice was Jerry. We had grown closer over time; he was the person whose company I most sought out when I was at the prison.

I hesitated though. What's the protocol when it comes to getting on a prisoner's visiting list? Is the prisoner supposed to ask, or does that put pressure on the outside person? Is the outside person supposed to ask, or does that put the prisoner in the awkward position of seeming ungracious if he does not agree to it?

That's in general. As far as this individual case, I was almost sure I wasn't misreading the relationship I had with Jerry, but the prison environment makes every perception shaky.

Mostly it's a matter of the inability to share life with any of the prisoners in any but the most restrictive ways. On the outside, you see your friends and family at all different times in all different circumstances. The variety of experiences gradually gives you a better and better feel for who they are as people. With PAP, we see these guys for, at most, two hours each week, in the same room, doing the same things, having the same types of conversation. Everything else we gather about them and their lives is inference and hearsay.

It's like your teenage niece that you only see on Sundays at the semi-formal family gatherings after church. Or your boss that you've never spent time with socially outside the job. Even after years of experience with them, a lot of what you infer about their life, their personality, their character, is highly speculative because of the lack of variety in the circumstances of your interactions with them.

How much are they really like what you've seen of them in these extremely limited situations? What do they really think of you?

With the prisoners, there is the added paranoia-inducing factor that the prison administration, and indeed society as a whole, constantly warn us that we are dealing with skilled con men who will mislead and harm us if we let our guard down.

I believed that by now I had established a genuine friendship with Jerry, that he liked and respected me and wanted to maintain ties with me, that he was worthy of my trust. But the unnatural circumstances of our interaction left me with just that tiny bit of doubt. Maybe I was someone who was temporarily useful to him for certain purposes as a volunteer, and from his perspective there was nothing more between us.

I am pleased to say, though, that Jerry and I did remain friends, and I did get on his visiting list. In fact, he was the one to broach the subject. About four months after

I left PAP, he asked me through Josh if I would be interested. I agreed, and contacted the prison to get the process started.

By the time the mandatory six-month waiting period was over, I had left the state for unrelated reasons. I did, however, come back briefly in September 2001, and I took that opportunity to enter WSR for the first time ever as a prisoner's visitor.

The visiting room is a communal area of twenty to thirty small tables where prisoners sit with their visitor(s). Guards keep an eye on things, but they are unobtrusive. There are vending machines, and a little play area for small children.

They'll allow a small amount of physical contact. For instance, Jerry and I embraced when I arrived and when I left, and they aren't going to say anything if you occasionally shake a person's hand, pat him on the back, or touch his arm.

My time with Jerry was a very positive experience. He was in excellent spirits and was happy to see me. We spent some two and a half hours together, before the next count. It passed like twenty minutes.

Unlike my encounters with Jimi outside of PAP when we often had trouble connecting conversationally, Jerry and I fell into an active conversation immediately and were still going strong when time came for us to part. We must have spent two-thirds of that time talking football and other sports. The NFL season was just days away after all.

That didn't leave much time for other news, but Jerry did fill me in on his efforts to gain parole. I continued to follow that developing story from out of state, mostly through occasional updates from his son.

When I left PAP in 2000, Jerry had been just a little overdue for his next opportunity to see the parole board. At the time of my visit a year later, he was still waiting.

I lost track of all the reasons for the delays, but his counselor forgot to submit a certain form, then somebody didn't sign off on something, then a member of the board was unavailable for a time so they couldn't schedule a hearing, and on and on. This was an even more slothlike performance than I had come to expect from the DOC, but Jerry attributed it to incompetence rather than malice.

Finally, in October 2001, I got the word from Josh that the parole hearing had taken place and that Jerry had been notified of their decision.

After twenty plus years in prison for killing the man who raped his wife (thirty plus years total of incarceration), Jerry McLaughlin was to be released from prison.

The procedure was to transition him out gradually, over the course of more than a year, from the close custody of WSR to the streets. Early in 2002, he took the first step in that transition, transferring to the minimum security facility (the "Farm") that is part of the same complex as WSR.

That's where he was when I sent the edited transcripts to all the book participants. He called me in response not longer after that. I had not spoken with him since last seeing him in person, as all my news had come through Josh.

He sounded great, like he had plenty of positive energy and was all set to go. He had things lined up pretty much the way he described in our earlier interview. He has a closer relationship with his son Josh than he's ever had, and Josh lives close to Seattle, so Jerry was looking forward to spending plenty of time with him on the outside.

I remained in regular contact with Jerry as his time grew shorter. The next time I was back in Washington, I visited him at the Farm. It was another very upbeat visit. He was full of optimism and energy.

He was next transferred to a different minimum security facility—the Pine Lodge Pre-Release—across the state in the Spokane area.

For awhile it looked like his release would come in early 2003, then later in 2003, and then it was pushed back into 2004. Again, these delays weren't in response to anything Jerry had done—they weren't disciplinary. They had to do with such things as getting the right paperwork filled out and waiting for a slot to open up at the next facility or halfway house where he was supposed to go.

Jerry finally was paroled from Pine Lodge on May 3, 2004. His son picked him up and drove him across the state to Seattle.

He paroled to group housing for ex-cons run by a non-profit agency called Interaction Transition. It was only after he arrived that he discovered, much to his chagrin, that the residence houses primarily sex offenders, the very people he had spent decades shunning. Furthermore, though one of the stipulations for his going there had been that he'd have his own room (the rooms are like very small dormitory rooms—barely bigger than the cells he was used to), overcrowding has caused them to double up. Also, whereas he had been under the impression he'd only have to be there for 90 days before being allowed to get his own place, there was talk from as soon as his release that they might require him to live in that supervised setting for longer, maybe as much as a year.

The sales job for the moving company that he had tentatively arranged years earlier was no longer available, but he obtained other employment almost immediately with Pioneer Industries, a firm that hires primarily people who've been incarcerated or are coming out of rehab programs. He quickly settled into a full time work schedule of 2:30 PM to 11:00 PM, plus a substantial bus commute, five days a week.

Starting the day of his release he has been videotaping himself, recording his reactions to life on the outside. (The camera was my "getting out of prison" gift to him.) He's hoping to make some kind of documentary out of the footage. It's a project I think has a lot of promise, and I've told him I'll assist him with it however I can.

He's very pleased with the parole officer to whom he was assigned. He says she is sharp, experienced, and understands quite well what someone getting out of prison goes through. He feels he can be very frank with her.

I spoke with him a few times the first two to three weeks after his parole, and then made the drive up to see him later in May. Not only did that enable me to see

Jerry, but there was a party for him that functioned as a sort of reunion for quite a few of the PAP volunteers from my era, people I hadn't seen in many years. It was a pleasant opportunity to touch bases with some old buddies. Plus I was able to meet Jerry's brother up for a visit from Eugene, Oregon (incarcerated for being Jerry's accomplice in the murder, he was released from prison nine years before Jerry and has never gone back), and Jerry's son (whom I had spoken to countless times on the phone, but never met in person). Both made very favorable impressions on all present—the brother through his keen intellect and well-spoken nature, and the son through his quiet, humble, very polite manner.

As always when one of our people is released, the question is: Will he re-offend, and land right back in prison?

As Jerry says, he didn't end up in prison by accident. He always knew exactly what he was doing, exactly what the consequences were.

I believe Jerry's wisdom, self-discipline, and strength of will make him unlikely to stumble back into a life of crime. He is far from being too immature, unprepared, or weak to handle life on the outside.

He has grown as much as one can in prison. He's been a leader and has achieved as much as the limited opportunities on the inside allow. He needs new challenges, new worlds to conquer. He's ready.

I would never say there is no risk, though. There's no getting around the fact that Jerry still believes he is justified in going beyond the law to impose his will violently in situations that warrant it. And while many armchair vigilantes talk the way he does, Jerry has a track record of following through.

I spent a lot of time with him during my trip back to Washington after his release. (I'm sure I spent more total time with him in those few days than I spent with Jimi over the several months he was out in 1999.) He was pretty much the same Jerry I had known for years on the inside. I did sense, though, some of that same frenetic air about him that had been so apparent in Jimi, that feeling that there's an awful lot of new stuff to deal with all at once.

The difference is with Jimi—though maybe this is something I can only really say in hindsight—one got the sense that all the stimulation overwhelmed him, whereas Jerry seems to be taking it more in stride. Maybe it was 25% positive excitement and 75% stress for Jimi, and just the reverse for Jerry.

Jerry is hyper by nature, so being additionally pumped up by this experience is not something to take lightly. I didn't get the impression that he was very close to the edge, but I don't claim to be infallible in reading such things. It really hasn't been that many years since violence was a first resort rather than last resort for him, and surely the natural volatility of his personality has not disappeared entirely.

On the whole, I have faith that he will succeed, because I think he's at a point in his life where he has made a commitment to himself and others. And when he puts his mind to something, he accomplishes it.

Actually he will be displeased to read that I'm speculating at all on this point. He's spending a lot of time with the PAP folks on the outside—not just at the party, but in general—and mostly he's loving it and really appreciates our support, but the one thing he's annoyed with is the sense that we're monitoring him and scrutinizing everything he does or says for clues that he's manifesting some mentality that will return him to prison.

"Have I ever let you down?" he said to me, "Have I ever let any of you down? In all the years you've known me, have I ever told you that you can count on me for something, and then not done it? You know what I mean? Failure is not an option for me. It's not an option."

He feels judged or underestimated at times. During my visit, he manifested a certain amount of frustration that it was taking a little longer than anticipated to get his driver's license so he could get a cheap car and not be stuck on the bus. One of the volunteers mentioned to us that he had said to her that if he was delayed much longer, he could always just get a car and drive unlicensed for the time being, which naturally she didn't like the sound of. She said he said it in an offhand manner and so she didn't expect it was something he was really on the verge of doing, but she took it as a disturbing sign that his mind would even go there.

I mentioned this to him when I saw him next. "OK, see, that's just what I was talking about," he said, "That's the kind of shit that can piss a guy off. That's completely twisting what I said. You know what I mean? I was saying, like, really the opposite of that. I was saying, 'I could easily just get the car before the license, but that's not what I'm doing.' I wasn't saying I was going to do that; I was *contrasting* that with what I'm doing. Like, check it out, instead of doing it the criminal way, here I'm doing it the right way. And instead of getting credit for that, people act like I'm looking to steal a car so I can take my driving test or something."

We were able to laugh about it, and we agreed that time was the key to changing perceptions. People have been burned too often when they've let their expectations get too high about how a released prisoner would fare on the outside. It's understandable that they'd be wary, and that they'd be alert to signs of trouble. But after a month that'll fade a little. After six months it'll fade more. After two or three years it'll seem normal that Jerry is on the outside and not going back.

His release did bring one ominous development however—not an indication that he'd fail out of some weakness or character defect, but the very real possibility that his past would catch up with him in a way that is beyond his control.

As we discussed in the interviews, the family of the man Jerry murdered is just as convinced that they have a right of retribution against him as he was convinced that he was justified in avenging his wife's rape. Apparently it's mostly Frank's elderly mother who retains an insistence that Jerry pay with his life for what he did. The most logical person to do the deed would be Frank's brother, but he's incarcerated and will remain so for quite a few more years. There are other, less likely candidates to do the mother's bidding—former crime partners of Frank or his brother, and such—but what degree of a threat they represent is uncertain.

What has given Jerry renewed cause for concern is that within days after his release, he received a letter from an acquaintance of both him and Frank's family tipping him off that the mother was aware that he was out (as a matter of policy, DOC informs victims and survivors of victims when a perpetrator is paroled), and was trying to find out where he was living. Just idle curiosity, or does she have the wherewithal to send somebody after him? He himself doesn't know. "I didn't sleep much for a couple nights after I got that letter," he told me. He told his parole officer about the letter, though he doesn't expect there's much she can do.

He's also uneasy that one or more other people have similarly sought to contact him on the outside, people he says he was never really all that close to to show this much curiosity about his whereabouts. Could they be passing information about him to Frank's family?

It was unnerving to even hear these things. There were times walking down the street with him that I had the sense of what it must be like to be with a Kennedy. If a car had backfired within earshot I probably would have jumped ten feet.

It's a real problem. His best guess is she doesn't have anyone willing to come after him for her, but it's not at all far-fetched that he could be a target. Plus even if it's uncertain what they can or will do, one need only consult the interviews in this book to see that he has never been reticent about declaring that he will not live under a threat, and that he will act pre-emptively if need be.

Though I don't regard it as likely that he will clash with these people, I can't say it would come as a shock to me to find out that he has been killed, that he is back in prison because he went after one of them first, or that he has violated his parole by disappearing underground to avoid them. I believe that kind of scenario is more likely than his simply failing on the outside and returning to a life of crime.

Jerry, sans hair, with the author days after his release in 2004. (I could have sworn
he was taller in prison.)

In the media, in classrooms, and in casual conversations in everyday life, I am struck by the pervasiveness of the "us" versus "them" dichotomy in discourse about crime and prisoners. We who are out of prison are the good guys, those who are in prison are the bad guys, and it's all about what "we" should do with "them." Conservatives want to kill or lock away forever as many of them as possible, and thereby scare the bejesus out of the rest of them in the name of deterrence. Liberals—to their credit—are more inclined to try to save at least some of them through rehabilitation.

I see it a little differently.

Each of us is a complex bundle of strengths and weaknesses, good and evil. During the course of our lives, we do countless wise things and admirable things, but also countless stupid things and wrong things.

The people in prison are there because their particular combination of traits and behavior intersected with a great number of circumstantial factors—which particular types of ill behavior their society made illegal, whether they got caught, what discretionary decisions the prosecutor and judge and others in their case made, whether they had their own attorney or a public defender, and so on and so forth—to put them there. They aren't there because they're bad and we on the outside are good.

Granted, typically people out of prison are morally better human beings than people in prison, but only as a rule of thumb with numerous individual exceptions.

I abhor most of what prisoners have done to land them in prison, including the prisoners in this book. I think much of the "victims' rights" rhetoric is a lot of malarkey, but I detest most crime, and I detest its consequences for the victims and for society as a whole. The hardest part of my volunteer work and my research for this book was hearing the accounts of crime and violence. I never got used to it. I never got jaded about it. It never stopped bothering me to think about Jeff's wife, or Rico's girlfriend, or any of the others who had their lives stolen from them through the willful, evil and blameworthy actions of other human beings.

Yet as undeniably terrible as these crimes are, countless people who never spend a day of their lives in prison routinely do equally stupid, wrong, and destructive things.

There's no excuse for Buck killing the store owner, no way to downplay how wrong it was. But on any given day, lawyers, advertisers, politicians, bankers, members of the media, priests, generals, and others make choices that will ultimately do vastly more damage to vastly more lives than Buck or any of the prisoners in this book ever have or ever will do. Most of this behavior is legal. It doesn't bring punishment down on their heads, but is more likely to bring money, power, fame, awards, sex, or the approval of others (just as in other societies, throwing virgins into volcanoes, herding political enemies into concentration camps, or crippling women through foot-binding were not illegal and could have favorable consequences for their perpetrators).

As Jerry says, "There's a whole lot of thieves and crooks and predators out there that wear the hat of respectability."

Prisoners constitute the tiny minority of wrongdoers that an extremely imperfect criminal justice system in an extremely imperfect society happens to have singled out for our collective wrath. I choose not to fall into line with such scapegoating.

If I'm going to hate these prisoners, and insist on delivering vengeance on them, then I'm going to feel obligated to respond the same way to the many equally harmful folks outside of prison. Then the next step is to extend that hate and vengeance to anyone who facilitates such destructive behavior, or even to anyone who does not do the maximum they are capable of to oppose it. Since that pretty much covers all of us, I'll soon be nothing but a raging ball of hatred, trying to punish the whole world.

No. That's not for me.

So when I enter the prison, I don't think of the prisoners as defective people who are all inferior to non-prisoners. They tend to be bad (and good) in interestingly different ways from those on the outside, but they are not some lesser form of human.

Still, that's not to deny that the behavior that society has criminalized, and that is most apt to infuriate the public, is usually wrong and something we'd be much better off without. So even if we could set aside the loathing, and the scapegoating, it would not diminish the desirability of reducing crime and recidivism.

The facile response of most politicians—and much of the public—to crime continues to be that we must stop "coddling" criminals and affording them so many dubious "rights," and instead should return to some golden age where the threat of harsh punishment deterred crime. Many of the prisoners I met, on the other hand, regard it as self-evident that deterrence is a myth, insisting that no one ever rationally calculates the costs and benefits of committing a crime, and opts not to commit it due to the fact that the consequences would include harsh punishment.

I regard the prisoners' opinion as too absolute. There are plenty of people who are deterred from committing crimes because of how strongly they disvalue going to prison—the fact that this is rarely part of the conscious thought process of a criminal notwithstanding. It is a mistake to dismiss the notion of deterrence entirely.

But simply ratcheting up the undesirability of prison is bound to be a futile strategy in the end. The prison culture and its convict code explain why.

For the state to threaten an even greater use of brute force in order to dissuade people from criminal behavior may be reasonably effective with me or with other squares who fear having to contend with prison. But for those enmeshed in a criminal lifestyle—because they have made an emotional commitment to a certain way of life, and more importantly to other individuals who share that way of life—it just adds another challenge along the difficult path they're on. Many of them will never succumb to such pressure, for in their mind to do so would entail losing their self-respect and the respect of their peers.

Will a soldier desert and abandon his fellows because he has to march a little farther, or because his rations are a little skimpier, or because his sergeant is a little more verbally abusive? Will a single parent give up her kids because child care is a little more expensive, or because employers are a little less cooperative in giving her the schedule she needs, or because welfare has been further reduced? Will an athlete abruptly walk off the field because he is fatigued and his opponents are putting up more of a fight than he anticipated?

A convict's sense of self-worth is wrapped up with manifesting certain values, engaging in certain criminal or violent behavior. For the state to make it more costly for him to commit crimes won't cause him to abandon what he has embraced. As long as he secs nothing wrong with how he has chosen to live his life, then "tough" treatment will just inspire him to get tougher.

Harsher treatment only creates more challenges, more grounds for being proud of defying authority, more opportunities to bond with one's fellows who similarly refuse to give in. To endure the roughest prisons becomes a proof of manhood.

So if not on deterrence, where ought we focus?

It's always worthwhile to reiterate the liberal truisms—that all else being equal, higher unemployment will result in more crime, crumbling and inadequately staffed schools will result in more crime, closing off certain avenues for advancement to people based on the color of their skin will result in more crime, eliminating whatever's left of the safety net of poverty and welfare programs will result in more crime, etc.

But as helpful as it would be to make society more just, more humane, and less discriminatory, there are also changes necessary on the level of the individual.

Here, though, I'd draw another distinction. Most of the prisoners I talk to want help in improving themselves, but typically only in obvious, economic ways. That is, they want job skills, job experience. They talk about education too, but nine times out of ten, what they have in mind is vocational training. They aren't talking about reading Shakespeare or learning more about the heroes of Greek and Roman mythology; they aren't seeking to learn how to appreciate or create fine art. They want to know enough about using computers or operating certain kinds of machinery to become employable.

And I'm all for that. But it doesn't go far enough. Maybe vocational education and experience are sufficient for the guy who reluctantly stole just enough food to keep his family alive, but the other 99.9% of prisoners have other issues to deal with—issues of values, attitudes, lifestyles, and habits.

People in prison have some fucked up ways of thinking. Raising the minimum wage by a couple of bucks and making sure they have a GED before they leave prison won't change that.

Insulting and patronizing attitudes toward women; greed; judging the worth of oneself and others by materialistic criteria; the "two wrongs make a right" tendency to victimize others in response to one's own past abuse; seeking solace in intoxication; competitiveness; the inability to delay gratification; violent machismo; racism. These are not matters of economics, but of moral philosophy.

In arguing for more job training in prison, one of the prisoners once said, "I won't rob people if you convince me that I can make just as much money with a conventional job." That's true, I suppose, but it's also indicative of a troubling attitude.

Why should we have to "buy off" a person by providing him with an alternative means of achieving what he currently achieves via victimizing others? How about instead he gets a clue that maybe there's something wrong with walking into a store and sticking a gun in someone's face and taking his money?

Prisoners are neither too stupid nor too stubborn to make ethical connections like that. While I don't doubt there are a small number of "criminally insane" types who just don't get it and are wired in such a way that they likely never will, the prisoners I dealt with were not lacking in values by a long shot. If they heard someone say, "I won't rat on my partners or sell kiddie porn on the Internet if you convince me that I can make just as much money with a conventional job," they'd laugh at him—or do a lot worse to him.

Like people in general, the prisoners have learned to rationalize their own moral corner cutting, but that doesn't mean they have lost their ability to judge behavior from a moral perspective. I think the potential for true moral growth is present.

Are people in prison really going to change their lifestyles, change their world-views, ethically improve themselves? Most won't. Most will keep re-offending, a few will be bribed out of the life by the carrot of greater legitimate job opportunities and education, and a few will be driven out of the life by the stick of harsh punishment. Only a comparatively small number will choose to forego crime in the future because they now regard it as wrong.

However, it does not follow from this that prisoners are uniquely evil or irrational by nature, or that it would be futile to try to convince them there are better values to live by. In fact, I contend that those who have achieved success outside prison walls are even less apt to change their ways for the better for moral reasons.

Rico took a hard look at his life and came to a realization—and I think he's being sincere—that it's wrong for him to let his life be dominated by drugs, wrong for him to have macho, double-standard attitudes toward women, certainly wrong for him to murder. If Rush Limbaugh and his ilk ever go through a similar process of self-examination and renounce deception and demagoguery the way Rico has renounced murder, I'll be shocked.

Jerry, as he has matured, says that he no longer can give himself "permission" to act in certain hostile or unfair ways as he did in the past. Plus, I can reason with Jerry. I can challenge him about where he's drawing his new lines, and have some hope of influencing him. I'm not deluded enough to think I could similarly reason with a tobacco industry lobbyist.

Let Larry out of prison tomorrow, and I think the chances he will murder again are very low. I cannot say the same about a successful businessman whose campaign contributions have bought him politicians willing to weaken environmental laws to favor his industry. That businessman is not likely to wake up tomorrow and volunteer to stop killing people with his poison.

So yes, I'm frustrated that it's more the exception than the rule for prisoners to be honest and self-critical, to act from motives of principle rather than selfishness, to be self-directed rather than mimic the stupidity of their peers. I wish we'd more often see genuine moral growth from them. But I feel the same way about people outside of prison. In fact those at the "top" in society are typically the most incorrigible.

When Jerry asks why he should cease to lie, cheat, and steal when those who imprison him do the same or worse to him, I can look him in the eye and say, "Because you're better than them. I expect more from you."

In summary, what "we" should do about crime and prisoners has to include both societal and individual components. Clearly the socioeconomic factors associated with crime need to be addressed. In addition, we need to provide individual prisoners with the means to make their way in the world without having to resort to crime. But we also need to challenge the prisoners—not patronize them as patients or sinners, but challenge them as equal rational beings—to rise above what they have been and what they have done.

And whatever we do must be informed by the realization that the prisoners themselves are part of this "we," not some scary race of devils who have cornered the market on wrongdoing. They are not merely objects for our punishment or our charity, but genuine subjects, as worthy of respect as ends-in-themselves as any other human beings.

For more information about *Prison Conversations*, including ordering additional copies direct from the publisher, please see our website at www.prisonconversations.com.